CALIPHATE REDEFINED

Caliphate Redefined

THE MYSTICAL TURN IN OTTOMAN POLITICAL THOUGHT

Hüseyin Yılmaz

PRINCETON UNIVERSITY PRESS
PRINCETON & OXFORD

Published by Princeton University Press,
41 William Street, Princeton, New Jersey 08540

In the United Kingdom: Princeton University Press,
6 Oxford Street, Woodstock, Oxfordshire OX20 1TR

press.princeton.edu

Cover art: The Sultan Suleyman the Magnificent (1494–1566)
with two dignitaries; Reis Haydar, Nakkep, called Nigari (1494–572).
Topkapi Palace Museum, Istanbul, Turkey, Bridgeman Images

First paperback printing, 2019
Paperback ISBN 978-0-691-19713-5
Cloth ISBN 978-0-691-17480-8

Library of Congress Control Number: 2017936620

British Library Cataloging-in-Publication Data is available

This book has been composed in Miller

To my father and mother,

Yusuf and Melek

CONTENTS

ACKNOWLEDGMENTS

THIS BOOK TOOK ITS FINAL SHAPE through indispensable contributions of scholars, friends, colleagues, institutions, and my family. My special thanks and gratitude are due to scholars who took part in this endeavor from early on in different capacities. Cemal Kafadar, besides his unremitting support and supervision throughout my graduate training and writing, has been a continuous source of inspiration at every level of my research and analysis. My conversations with Cornell Fleischer, as well as his encouragement and support, helped me overcome major challenges of this project while his comments saved this work from many probable pitfalls. My discussions with Roy Mottahedeh on various aspects of political thought throughout the process provided me with exciting questions to explore. During the early stages of my work, the late Şinasi Tekin exerted as much effort as I did in grappling with the idiosyncrasies and complexities of Turkish manuscript texts that helped me to proceed with confidence. Each time I visited Hossein Modarressi to seek help in my quest to make sense of what seemed to be the most ambiguous passages from Arabic and Persian manuscripts, he startled me with his instant grasp of what I had previously despaired of comprehending. Ridwan al-Sayyid helped me acquire a deeper understanding of the major issues and problems of pre-Ottoman Islamic political thought and kept me up-to-date with new publications in Arabic on the subject. The late Halil Inalcik, who pulled me back to Ottoman history from a possible career in political science and directed my attention to some little known but exciting texts on political thought, was a true mentor all along.

I am grateful to a number of institutions and their staff that provided indispensable assistance of various kinds during the research and writing stages of this monograph. Among them, the Center for Middle Eastern Studies at Harvard partly funded my summer researches for several years. The American Research Institute in Turkey provided a generous grant for one of my research trips to Turkey. The Foundation for Arts and Sciences in Istanbul offered me the use of their facilities and access to their resources needed for my research. The Center for Islamic Studies in Istanbul granted me access to its library resources, which saved me much time and labor during the early stages of my research. Nevzat Kaya at the Süleymaniye Library and Filiz Çağman at the Topkapı Sarayı Museum Library turned my research at the library into one of my most memorable experiences. Charles Fineman and the acquisitions department of Widener Library helped me acquire many hard-to-obtain manuscripts from collections abroad. I am truly grateful to Muhittin Macit and Ferruh Özpilavcı of the Turkish Manuscript Association for their professionalism and collegiality; they consistently spared no effort in delivering my never-ending requests, always faster than I could hope. The completion of this monograph owes a great deal to the support and opportunities provided by the Introduction to the Humanities Program at Stanford University, University of South Florida, International University of Sarajevo, the Internationales Forschungszentrum Kulturwissenschaften in Vienna, George Mason University, and the Ali Vural Ak Center for Global Islamic Studies. Needless to say, this monograph required the use of manuscript sources in a long list of libraries throughout the world. Among them my special thanks go to colleagues, curators, and staff of Bibliothèque Nationale de France in Paris; the British Library in London; Dar al-Kutub in Cairo; Gazi Husrev-Begova Biblioteka in Sarajevo; Österreichische Nationalbibliothek in Vienna; Staatsbibliothek zu Berlin; university libraries at Princeton, Harvard, Chicago, Yale, and UCLA; al-Zahiriyah Library in Damascus; and virtually all manuscript libraries in Turkey, most notably the ones in Istanbul, Konya, Bursa, Amasya, Manisa, Kayseri, Ankara, Kütahya, and Izmir.

My heartfelt thanks are due to a number of friends and colleagues who shared the burden with me throughout the research, writing, and the publication process. First and foremost, Himmet Taşkömür generously worked with me in solving a myriad paleological and philological problems posed by sources, shared his insights on Ottoman intellectual history, and commented on my analysis during our numerous lengthy discussions. Hayrettin Yücesoy never grew tired of sharing his unmatched expertise on the history of Islamic political thought and often accompanied me in my contemplative journeys into solving intricate problems of intellectual history. During the early stages of my research, İhsan Fazlıoğlu and Harun Anay offered me their expertise in navigating through manuscript collections in Turkey. Cengiz Şişman's company and our never-ending book-talk made the writing of this monograph more pleasant than it otherwise may have been. Günhan Börekçi, Seyfi Kenan, and Akın Kiren helped me obtain some source material that was beyond my reach. My ever more enlightening conversations through many years with Ali Vural Ak, Cemil Aydın, Süreyya Er, and Erol Çatalbaş must have spilled over the pages of this monograph, albeit without quotation. I am particularly indebted to the late Shahab Ahmed, who initiated my conversation with Princeton University Press, for his continuous stream of encouragement and insightful comments without which this monograph would have been less than what it has become in many respects.

I thank a number of colleagues and editors for their guidance and feedback in preparing the manuscript for publication. When demanded by the exigencies of academic life, Bassam Haddad and Ahmet Selim Tekelioğlu were always ready to help me spare more time for writing. Mack Holt offered his experience and insights in shaping up the manuscript for publication. Mark Farha read and commented on my entire draft in early stages of writing.

K. E. Duffin, Eileen P. Duggan, Mary E. Benson, and Brittany Dawson edited and commented on parts of the manuscript. Sami Erdem proofread the entire text for foreign vocabulary and references. My copyeditor Theresa Kornak diligently worked on the text to improve its style and language. I offer my special thanks to Fred Appel, my editor at Princeton University Press, not only for his unremitting support throughout the publication process but also for his invaluable suggestions in revising the manuscript.

Above all, no words can express my indebtedness and gratitude toward my family, whose role in the completion of this monograph has been much greater than mine. My father Yusuf and mother Melek have always supported me, often beyond their means. My wife Selma has shared with me both the joy and the hardship of research and writing throughout. My brothers Mustafa, Recep, Fahri and Hasan and sister Şerife have done more than I could ask to ease my work and my distance from home. Finally, my precious times with my son, Ahmet, were my most awaited moments of joy and relief during the entire process.

NOTE ON TRANSLATION, TRANSLITERATION, AND PRONUNCIATION

THE GENERAL SYSTEM of transliteration of Turkish, Persian, and Arabic words is that of *The International Journal of Middle East Studies*. For words that appear in *Merriam-Webster's Collegiate Dictionary*, Eleventh Edition, such as Sunni, Sufi, Shii, Hanafi, and ulema, modern Anglicized forms are used. For readability, diacritics are generally avoided except in endnotes and bibliography, and when necessary to avoid misunderstanding or when quoted from the source text. Hamza is not transliterated when appears as the first or the last letter of words. In endnotes and bibliography, some words may have been transliterated differently to reflect varieties in pronunciation per the language of the source text. When used without a reference to a specific text, words are by default transliterated in their Ottoman Turkish readings. Translation of words, phrases, book titles, and quotations reflects intended meanings of a given author or context rather than the literal equivalent or broader cultural connotations.

CALIPHATE REDEFINED

Introduction

The Ottomans and the Caliphate

With the fall of Baghdad in 1258, the historical caliphate, embodied by the Abbasid Empire, formally ended with traumatic consequences that, in response, facilitated the rise of a new wave of self-reflection, exploration, and experimentation in all segments of Islamicate societies.[1] In the absence of the imperial caliphate, along with the rise of independent regional Muslim dynasties from the fourteenth century onwards, the idea of the caliphate, reinterpreted in response to profound changes taking place in the broader Muslim community, regained its prominence in Islamic political discourse, and, with the rise of the Ottoman Empire, became the linchpin of imperial ideology in the sixteenth century. Modern studies on the question of Muslim rulership repeatedly assume that the historical caliphate, as conceived by Muslim jurists during the Abbasid period (c. 750–1258), continued to define both the concept and the institution in subsequent political thought and praxis. This assumption confines the theoretical construction of the caliphate to jurisprudence, overlooks the impact of later historical experiences, and disregards the formative influence of broader intellectual traditions in framing the caliphate as both an institution and an ideal. The post-Abbasid caliphate, or the making of the non-Arab caliph in the Ottoman case, was reconstructed in the language of Sufism infused with indigenous traditions of rulership and shaped by defining historical experiences, rather than through the juristic canon of medieval universalism. In sixteenth-century political discourse, the Ottoman caliph was a mystic, in the sense that he was a friend and deputy of God on Earth, with sway over both temporal and spiritual realms. The House of Osman was God's chosen dynasty commissioned to serve divinely assigned purposes, and the Ottoman rulership was the seal of the caliphate to last until the end of times.

In the sixteenth century, continuous Ottoman expansionism in all directions entailed that the Ottomans counter and appropriate the legitimating apparatus of their opponents, most notably the Habsburgs, the Safavids, and the Mamluks, which helped introduce the belief in the uniqueness of the Ottoman dynasty into the mainstream of political thinking. Through mythologizing the origins of the Ottoman state, esoteric interpretations of religious texts, and prophesies of the great spiritual men, the ruling elite perceived the Ottoman dynasty as the chosen one. Further, the triumphalist mood of the age, invigorated by seemingly incessant victories, made statesmen and intellectuals see achievements in the arts, architecture, literature, and government as further signs of Ottoman exceptionalism. In political geography, early sixteenth century Eurasia witnessed the emergence of confessional empires with claims of universal rulership that engaged in a stiff competition for ideological ascendancy. The Sufi-minded theorists of rulership, unchecked by the limits of authority set in juristic and bureaucratic traditions, provided a useful repository of symbolism and imagery to claim the superiority of the Ottoman caliphate. The discourse on the caliphate included an extensive engagement with theories of government expounded in various disciplines and literary genres in the context of Islamic learned traditions. The full corpus of mainstream political theory was widely available to Ottoman statesmen, who appear to have been staunch collectors of such texts and patrons of scholars on statecraft. The discourse reflects competing visions of rulership, languages, concepts, norms, imageries, and styles articulated in an increasingly Islamic but versatile and vernacularizing Ottoman culture. Jurists, Sufis, and bureaucrats contested rival notions of authority and sought to formulate an imperial image that best represented their own ideological imprints, confessional convictions, group interests, and cultural idioms.

Despite their accommodating approach to rulership, jurists per se in the Ottoman Empire ceased to be the leading exponents of the theory of the caliphate because of both theoretical and practical problems they could never definitively resolve. One was the juristic fixation with the historical caliphate as a successorship to Muhammed through an established lineage from his tribe, the Quraysh, a ruling that manifestly stood at odds with that of the Ottoman dynasty. Second, although a few jurists radically altered the theory of the caliphate, the canonical formulation of the caliphate proved impervious to the demands of coercive power or even captivating esoteric visions, and remained unchanged in all the juristic and theological textbooks taught in Ottoman madrasas, creating an unresolved tension between formal Islamic training and individual opinions. This cognitive dissonance created an irreparable rift between jurists who pursued academic careers in the Ottoman madrasas and remained loyal to the medieval ideal and those who pursued legal careers in the imperial judicial administration and tended to be pragmatic by accommodating divergent political realities. Because of this rift, the leading jurists either abstained from writing on the question of the caliphate in normative juristic language or resorted to the mystical philosophy of prominent Sufi intellectuals, such as Ibn Arabi, to reconfigure the caliphate outside the disciplinary confines of Islamic jurisprudence.

Relatively unbound by juristic doctrines, the Sufis offered a radically new understanding of the caliphate that better suited the legitimation needs of a rising Muslim empire. As Sufi orders and their leaders became increasingly involved in public life, their notions and imageries of authority permeated into dynastic visions of authority. Almost all the books on rulership that were taught to dynastic heirs between 1400 and 1600 as part of their training in statecraft were written by prominent Sufi authors. Tutors for princes were mostly renowned Sufis or Sufi-minded scholars whose teaching centered on esoteric, spiritual, and moral interpretations of rulership. Princes had little training in jurisprudence but were deeply exposed to mystical visions of rulership. The close association between the Ottoman ruling elite and prominent Sufi orders turned Sufism into the principal medium of formulating Ottoman dynastic legitimacy and inculcating a sultanic image as a spiritual leader. The Ottoman court countered the political challenges posed by powerful Sufi orders by adopting mystical visions of authority, and by depicting the Ottoman ruler as a caliph who conforms to Sufistic expectations.

In his study of kingship and sainthood in early modern Iran, Central Asia, and India, Azfar Moin perceptively noted that "the scriptural notions of the messiah (*mahdi*) and the renewer (*mujaddid*), the mystical cencepts of the pole or (*qutb*) and the perfect individual (*insan-i kamil*), and the kingly notions of divine effulgence (*farr-i izadi*) and the lord of conjunction (*Sahib Qiran*) all referred to human agents who could usher in and maintain the just religiopolitical order of a particular historica era."[2] One may easily add to this mosaic of imageries a long list of other notions and concepts that originated from various learned and indigineous traditions including those constructed with *dawla* (fortune), *ḳūt* (fortune), *khātam* (seal), *ghaws* (succor), *maẓhar* (manifestation), *ẓill* (shadow), and *āya* (evidence). Granted that each term retained its peculiar meanings in specific contexts and usages, in various strands of Ottoman political thought, it was the caliphate that served as the anchor concept into which all these otherwise little related notions of human distinction could harmoniously be assimilated as its descriptive markers.

The caliphate, in both concept and practice, could tie the historical with the utopian, the temporal with the spiritual, the individual with the communal, and the object with the subject. It could be equally meaningful in philosophical, juristic, and Sufistic discourses, and utilized for conversation among different disciplines, world views, and social structures. Whether simply considered as "succession" of authority in historical practice or the very act of "creation" of human beings per Sufi cosmology, the term's defining qualities remain to be "representation" and "performation." As one Arabic text in the sixteenth century formulated, *khilāfa* does not materialize unless the *mustakhlaf* (successor) fully reflects the *mustakhlif* (succeeded).[3] Namely, however it was conceived, the caliphate was always contingent on something else, having no significance without the signifier, no status without what it stands for, or no existence without what it manifests. The very etymology, semantics, scriptural sanction, and historical applications of the term made it inherently suitable and infinetly flexible for political speculation and craftmenship.

In Ottoman practice, envisioning the caliphate as a comprehensive cosmological position that encompasses both temporal and spiritual realms was embroidered in discursive narratives constructed by dynastic apologists and enigmatic letterists as well as mainstream scholars through literary articulation, artistic representation, and occultic revelations. This caliphal myth, as part of the central theme of the imperial ideology, entailed that the House of Osman was commissioned to rule as the "Great Caliphate" of the end of times foretold in the Qur'an, prophesied by Prophet Muhammed, envisioned by saints, and proven by discernible manifestations of divine providence. The caliphate as such was closely tied to an eschatology drawn from indigenous traditions and Abrahamic teachings conveyed via Islamic sources. The Ottoman caliphate, turned into a powerful foundational myth that was enhanced by a syncretic amalgamation of popular imageries and formal teachings of Islamic disciplines, then became the defining mantra of Ottoman imperial ideology continuously adapted to new political configurations and confessional manifestations, and reworked until the end of the empire.

The Caliphate in the Age of Süleyman

This study examines the mystification of the caliphate from its post-Abbasid origins to the late sixteenth century by privileging the age of Süleyman the Lawgiver (r. 1520–1566) for a more detailed analysis during which the caliphate turned into a patently Sufistic concept. In explaining the rise of Sufi tariqas in the late medieval Islamicate world, Marshall Hodgson briefly but perceptively hinted at the newly forming mystical notion of the caliphate:

> The *ulama* never ceased to think of the ideal unity of Islam in terms of a *khalifa*, a Caliph ruling a human empire. The Sufis made much of a very different sort of *khalifa*, the human being who as perfected microcosm is the final end of, and holds limitless sway over, the world of nature and men together. He is a Muslim, and exercises his power largely upon and through Muslims (the Abdal); but there is a recognized place under his care for the believers in every faith however crude, not only peoples of the Book as in the historical Caliphate, but outright pagans. The kings who come and go are but the servants of such a saint, as many beloved anecdotes make clear; no Caliph had such power over his governors as the Sufi *shayhks*, and especially the supreme *shaykh*, the Qutb of any given time, had over the earth's rulers.[4]

But Hodgson's signpost was largely overlooked in subsequent studies. The impact of Sufism on political thought, however, has been getting increasingly more attention in Islamic studies in the past few decades. Among others, Cornell Fleischer, Kathryn Babayan, Mercedes García-Arenal, and Azfar Moin masterfully demonstrated how rulers of the post-caliphate Islamicate world from Morocco to India constructed colorful visions of rulership by decorating themselves with mystical imageries and posing themselves as caliphs, lords of conjunction, renewers of religion, Mahdis, and saints. These studies treat the politicization of Sufism or mystification of politics within the larger framework of Islamic eschatology, messianism, millenarianism, and revivalism. While this study complements previous scholarship and furthers the inquiry, it parts ways in several directions. First, it focuses on the idea of the caliphate and treats messianic visions only to the extent they are related to it. Second, while taking the broader cultural and social context into consideration, this study mainly examines the political literature in all its diverse strains. Third, it tells the post-Abbasid story of the caliphate as a process of negotiation between Sufi groups and the Ottoman ruling establishment. Finally, it traces and explains the trajectory and transformation of the core vocabulary of political thought in Ottoman experience, or the rise of the Ottoman vernacular in political discourse.

The caliphate, in its various conceptions and manifestations, became more pronounced during the age of Süleyman as displayed in the extensive political corpus, royal titles, artistic representations, and public displays. More, Süleyman appeared in Ottoman thought as the personification of the supreme universal leader of the Muslim community whose image was made to fit various notions of leadership theorized in different Islamic disciplines and proclivities. The age of Süleyman is by far the most extensively studied period in both academic as well as popular historiography because it is considered a pivotal era of Ottoman history, if not of the entire early modern world. No other period of Ottoman history has attracted such a degree of interest. Süleyman has been the subject of more biographies than all other Ottoman sultans combined to quench the thirst for understanding this archetypical ruler, ranging from the crude Orientalist inquiries into the mystique of oriental rulership to contemporary infatuation with Süleymanic enlightenment. In the sixteenth and seventeenth centuries, more than twenty memorializing epic biographies with the title *Süleymānnāme* (the Book of Süleyman) were composed.[5] At the height of his power, Süleyman was arguably the most commonly recognized universal ruler across Eurasia, from Sumatra to France. It is no surprise that his contemporaries called him with such titles as the second Solomon and Mahdi. As reflected in his more common epithet, "lawgiver" (*ḳānūnī*), Süleyman was commonly perceived to be an epoch-making sultan both in Ottoman memory as well as in modern historiography.[6]

In this study, the Süleymanic age refers to the period that roughly corresponds to the tenth century of the Islamic calendar. It is marked by the ascendance of a new imperial elite that started to take form after the conquest of Constantinople, thrived under his reign, and carried his classicizing legacy after his death. Süleyman's birth coincided with the beginning of the tenth century, which lent an added excitement to the brewing millenarianism of the period. The age of Süleyman thus conveniently corresponds to the millennial century of Islam, which also loosely syncs with the sixteenth century. Süleyman's mark was already evident before his succession and remained afresh long after his death. Neither Süleyman's succession nor his death caused any major disruption in administrative continuity. Although Süleyman was enthroned in 1520, he appeared on the Ottoman dynastic scene before 1512 during the succession struggle of his father, Selim I. By playing a crucial role in his father's takeover of the throne, Süleyman secured his own succession as the crown prince. As the sole heir to the throne, the only such case in all of Ottoman history, he himself was well aware of his uniqueness, and his contemporaries were keen to highlight this exception as a sign of his chosenness. When he succeeded to the throne at the age of twenty-five on the sudden death of his father, he continued to rule along with the statesmen and ulema promoted by Selim I, most notably Grand Vizier Piri Paşa (d. 1532) and Sheikh ul Islam Zenbilli Ali Cemali Efendi (d. 1525). When he died in 1566, Grand Vizier Sokollu Mehmed Paşa (d. 1579) and Sheikh ul Islam Ebussuud (d. 1574), two major figures of his later reign, remained in office until Selim II's death in 1574. Major intellectual figures of his reign such as Ibn Kemal (d. 1534), Taşköprizade Ahmed (d. 1561), Celalzade Mustafa (d. 1567), and Birgivi Mehmed (d. 1573), had a defining impact on later Ottoman thought.

The intellectual landmarks of the political thought of Süleymanic age are Idris-i Bidlisi (d. 1520), who wrote his treatise on political philosophy, *Qānūn-i Shāhanshāhī* in Persian, and Kınalızade Ali (d. 1572), the author of what came to be the Ottoman canon in ethical philosophy, *Aḫlāḳ-ı ʿAlāʾī*. During this time, Ottoman intellectuals displayed a burgeoning interest in writing on various aspects of rulership and government. After a long tradition of political writings in the form of translations and reworkings of previous works, as well as a few original compositions since the rise of the Ottomans, *Qānūn-i Shāhanshāhī* appeared to be the first major attempt at an elaborate theory of rulership following the reconfiguration of the Ottoman polity from an ambitious frontier state into a universal empire under the reigns of Mehmed II and Bayezid II. Perceived by later generations as one of the major legacies of the Süleymanic age, despite the considerable debt it owes to previously formulated theories of ethics, *Aḫlāḳ-ı ʿAlāʾī* was written with a claim to surpass all other works on the same subject and conceived to be an exposition of Ottoman moral, social, and political ideals of the period.[7] The period between Bidlisi and Kınalızade was a flourishing era of intellectual vigor, creativity, and curiosity among Ottoman men and women of learning.

The age of Süleyman is best known in historical memory, modern scholarship, and popular imagination for its classicizing legacy in arts, literature, learning, lawmaking, and institutionalization. Yet, in originality and future effects, political thought was no less spectacular than any other achievement of the era. The most conspicuous development of this period was the emergence of an extensive corpus of political literature across various genres and disciplines with an unprecedented range of dissemination. Juristic, philosophical, ethical, sufistic, and theological views were expressed in the conventions of their respective disciplines or in the synthetic genre of mirrors for princes. The sheer number of political texts in circulation alone attests to the emergence of a broad-based interest among the reading public on questions of rulership. Accompanying this surge of interest was the gradual broadening of the field of political thought. Increased contact of Ottoman men of learning with the non-Ottoman body of political writings led them to deal with issues and questions that had not appeared in pre-sixteenth century Ottoman political literature. *al-Siyāsa al-sharʿiyya*, for example, a field that developed during the Mamluk period, came to the attention of Ottoman scholars only toward the middle of the sixteenth century, after the conquest of Egypt. Similarly, the question of *bayt al-māl* or public treasury, a topic not included in previous Ottoman political writings, became an important issue in this period, largely because of the influence of the Mamluk tradition of political writing. In addition, the Ottoman experience in government posed new questions to address in the political literature. *Ḳānūn*, for example, in the sense of law, had never made its way into political theory before this period, because no pre-Ottoman polity had such a highly developed legal system characterized by *ḳānūn*.

This broadening of the spectrum of political writings did not bring all conventional issues of previous political corpus into the Ottoman context. On the contrary, except for a few issues, most of the common questions that had busied pre-Ottoman authors on rulership did not resonate among the Ottoman audience and were simply ignored. The question of required qualifications for the caliphate or imamate, for example, which preoccupied jurists and theologians for so long, fell from favor in this period, even though the Ottoman sultan always implied his superiority over all other Muslim rulers. The broader field of political thought in this period was exposed more to influences from the Turkic and Persianate east than from the Arab south. For practical reasons, Ottoman authors found political teachings formulated in the East more relevant because of the affinity of the Ottoman political system with its Eastern counterparts. This influence was facilitated by a constant influx to the Ottoman realm of eastern scholars, bureaucrats, and literati, who carried political ideas and conventions along with them. Despite the full incorporation of the Arab south, Ottoman political thought remained to be articulated mainly on the cultural plane of what Shahab Ahmed called the *Balkans-to-Bengal complex*.[8]

Although the Ottoman authors of this period wrote on a variety of subjects in different genres, the Sufistic language dominated the overall discourse on rulership. Besides the mystics who wrote on government, most scholars writing on the subject were either themselves affiliated with a Sufi order or were well versed in mystical teachings. Most works on rulership and ethics are imbued with teachings, imageries, and vocabulary of mostly Turko-Persianate Sufism. Advice literature, in particular, was largely under the spell of, in Dabashi's words, Persianate literary humanism.[9] The ritualistic terminology of Ottoman Sufism was largely Persian because of the popularity of Persian works on the subject as well as the dissemination of Sufi orders that originated in the East. The Sufi world view that captivated Ottoman intellectuals naturally shaped the mode of thinking and the language of writing on rulership. Among others, works of Attar (d. c. 1221), Sa'di (d. c. 1291), and Rumi (d. 1273), as repositories of Sufi wisdom on government, were among the shortlist of classics of which any rank and file Ottoman intellectual was expected to have mastered.

Yet, despite the continued prestige of Arabic in normative thought and of Persian in literature, Turkish established itself as the primary language of political discourse in this period. Although the combined number of works compiled in Arabic and Persian was still much higher than those in Turkish, only Turkish texts reached a wide circulation. A large number of translations produced in this period demonstrate the existence of a growing readership in Turkish that turned this language into the principal medium of political discourse. The availability of a large number of classical works on rulership in Turkish certainly facilitated its rise as a language of choice in writing on rulership. The spread of political texts in Turkish texts and the upsurge of interest in reading on the subject were two developments that fed each other. In terms of terminological richness, conceptual sophistication, and literary and artistic potentialities, Turkish became a more convenient language for expressing political views. While Arabic and Persian stood relatively apart, Ottoman Turkish evolved in full engagement with both languages and their cultural backdrop. For the learned who were typically well versed in three languages, Turkish evolved to become the only venue where diverse traditions represented in Persian and Arabic could be amalgamated into a single medium of expression.

The Caliphate as a Moral Paradigm

In the age of Süleyman, the general tenor of political writing was set by the moralist tendency that had dominated political discourse since the rise of independent rulers in the eleventh century against the overarching rule of the Abbasid caliphate. During the high caliphate of the ninth and tenth centuries, the main quest of juristic political thought was to establish the normative principles of governance, whereas theological writings were limited to the proper definition of imamate in response to alternative claims of authority. Philosophical works, in the main, treated the political as part of their search for the best form of human association that leads to the attainment of a higher form of life. Regardless of disciplinary interests and priorities, the dominating theme of political discourse was defining the best qualified candidate to lead the Muslim community. The holy grail of political theory during the formative age of Islamic thought was to define the most perfect ruler to lead the community in the right direction towards its ideals with less regard to moral technologies of reforming the ruler-in-charge.

With the decline of the central caliphate and the rise of independent rulers, the discrepancy between classical juristic theory and political practice widened. As best illustrated in a burst of mirror for princes literature, moralism replaced idealism as the central theme of political discourse. This fledgling breed of political literature, which ultimately originated from the writings of Ibn al-Muqaffa in the eighth century but was overshadowed by the juristic discourse, shifted the focus from the qualifications of the universal caliph to the moral recuperation of the ruler in office, and from the uncompromising but abstract *sharʿī* principles of governance to specific instructions to turn existing administration into an efficient but just one. Because instating the best qualified candidate to the universal leadership of the Muslim community remained an unrealized utopia, the moralist tendency that aimed to turn the ruler in office into the best possible one found widespread appeal among statesmen, jurists, philosophers, and Sufis alike. Despite this shift of focus toward specific principles of rulership, the medieval fixation that the best governance could only be undertaken by the best of people survived as a noble ideal in political writing.

Guided by the moralist-pietistic tendency, most Ottoman authors pursued to improve the quality of rulership while totally disregarding its form. Ideal rulership was to be achieved not by finding the best form of political authority but by improving the moral quality of ruler and his aides in government. Thus the defining element of rulership was not its institutional sophistication but the human agent at the helm. Those moralists commonly defined rulership, in the generic sense, as the mere acquisition of sufficient executive power to rule. This ordinary rulership transforms into true rulership only when the ruler achieves personal sophistication in morality, spirituality, and piety. False rulership, also dubbed as worldly, material, and temporal, was most commonly labelled as *ṣūrī* (in appearance) and regarded as an imperfect form of rulership that should be turned into a superior one. True rulership, characterized by such designations as *maʿnawī* (in meaning), *raḥmānī* (manifesting God's mercy), and *rabbānī* (manifesting God's lordship), extends its authority over both the material and spiritual realms as a result of the ruler's moral perfection. Morally conscious authors with these convictions did not pay much attention to the institutional features of government or the principles of governance but simply extended the teachings of ethics, piety, and Sufism into the realm of rulership. With their focus on the human agent as the benchmark of true rulership, there was virtually no difference between reforming an individual initiate in a Sufi tract and a ruler in power. For Sufi moralists, the Qur'anic concept of the caliphate, not the historical one, provided the perfect model, a moral paradigm for the perfection of rulership. The historical caliphate, as a legal and social construct, was the political embodiment of the Muslim community's collective responsibility to uphold and execute Islamic law and services. The Qur'anic caliphate, in Sufi idiom, was the fulfillment of the very purpose of creation *par excellence*, the materialization of God's representation on Earth through human being's manifestation of the divine by adopting God's attributes (*aḫlāḳullāh*) as his morality.

The Rumi Character of Political Writing

The scope of this study is limited to Rumi expositions of political thought that include Ottoman authors who either dedicated their works to the sultan or lived in the core provinces of Asia Minor and the Balkans, excluding other parts of the empire. Many authors who wrote on the subject from the Arab provinces, such as al-Hamawi (d. 1529), are excluded from the study.[10] Although the practices of past rulers, as recounted in mirrors for princes, continued to inspire political writings, moralists and *ḳānūn*-conscious bureaucrats alike increasingly idealized the Ottoman precedence in government as a benchmark for good governance and a penultimate objective of perfect rulership. These Ottomanists perceived their own achievements in state building to be on a par with the greatest accomplishments of the past that filled their imaginations from histories, epics, and legends. While still greatly revering such past idols as Alexander the Great (r. 336–323 BCE), Khosrow Anushirvan (r. 531–579), Harun al-Rashid (r. 786–809), and others, they illustrated their teachings more and more with anecdotes and aphorisms attributed to the past Ottoman sultans, statesmen, scholars, and Sufis. For them, government and rulership reached its unsurpassable perfection in the realm of Rum under the Ottoman dynasty, just as the Rumis perfected human potential in character refinement, morality, and creativity.

A flurry of conquests in all directions in the early sixteenth century turned a large number of learned men living in these regions into Ottoman subjects within a generation. But the self-perception and cultural identity of the Ottoman elite did not extend to include every subject of the Ottoman sultan, especially those who fell under Ottoman authority in Arabic-speaking lands. The expansion of the Ottoman Empire was at the same time the extension of the universal authority of the Rumis. Ancient centers of Islamic culture and learning with their distinct institutions and cultural traits preserved their autonomy after the conquest. Numerous madrasas in Iraq, Syria, and Egypt, for example, were not integrated into the central and hierarchical Ottoman system of learning. Although an increasing number of Arabic-speaking scholars and bureaucrats entered into service in various branches of the ruling establishment, only a few of them were included in biographical dictionaries composed by Ottoman scholars. Ottoman authors, intellectuals, scholars, literati, and a variety of other designations that are constructed with the adjective "Ottoman" refer to a cultural identity and perception, not an ethnic, political, or geographical one. The adjective "Ottoman," in a strictly political sense, referred to the entire imperial establishment, territory, and subject population. In a sociocultural sense, however, it referred to *ehl-i Rūm*, namely, the people living in Asia Minor and the Balkans, whose primary medium of communication was Turkish. Biographical dictionaries written in this period, most notably those of Taşköprizade, Sehi, Latifi, and Aşık Çelebi, included in their works, scholars, Sufis, and poets who were deemed to be Ottoman, or *ehl-i Rūm*, excluding their counterparts outside Asia Minor and the Balkans. In an increasingly diverse and cosmopolitan social fabric, the Ottoman elite differentiated themselves from the rest of the sultan's subjects by their Rumi identity.

The age of Süleyman was also the time when the Rumi elite increasingly added their own voice into the broader tradition of political thought. Geographical expansion and increasing contacts with the outside world sparked new curiosities and interests that turned the learned more inquisitive about non-Ottoman cultural repositories. The unification of the central lands of the Islamic world had by itself transformed the Ottoman ruling elite from being distant recipients of the cultural heritage of this region to its inheritors, protectors, and promoters. Increased mobility of scholars and circulation of classical works opened new venues for Ottoman men of learning to become acquainted with political ideas that found expression before their time or outside their former cultural geography. During the age of Süleyman, for the first time in their history, Ottoman men of learning became fully exposed to the vast corpus of political writings produced before them outside the Rum. Ottoman readers and authors on rulership became fully integrated to diverse traditions of political writing in Arabic and Persian. The Ottoman court and institutions of learning were exceptionally resourceful on the subject. A contemporary witness and the author of a political treatise, Taşköprizade, praised the reigning Süleyman for his unmatched investment in library building and book collecting. He observed that these libraries provided all kinds of books, religious or nonreligious (*sharʿī wa ghayr sharʿī*), in Arabic or Persian, to the extent that there was no book one could not find there.[11]

In addition, the expansion of learning institutions and bureaucracy created more appetite for reading and writing on political theory that turned the question of rulership into a staple of Ottoman public discourse. Struggles for succession among princes, factional rivalries in government, voices of dissent in society, competition among social groups to gain the favor of the sultan or to influence his policies, and clashes with neighboring dynasties turned various political questions into public matters. Ottoman political writings before this period were dominated by translations of some of the well-known classics of political works in Arabic and Persian. While the translation activity continued with accelerating speed and diversified interests, during the age of Süleyman, Ottoman men of learning from different walks of life grew more confident and began to compose their own works on the subject. This fast growing political literature was accompanied by a large body of official documents that came to be produced en masse and became increasingly laden with political ideas. Law codes, sultanic decrees, inscriptions, correspondence with other states, legal opinions issued by the leading ulema and official chronicles, in addition to the specific reasons for their compilation, served as media to express political views. Further, histories, poetical works, biographical dictionaries, and hagiographies were charged with contemporary ideals, interests, and sensibilities regarding rulership and government. In the age of Süleyman, writing on rulership and government, once the preserve of a small group of leading men of learning and statesmen, became part of a public discourse where ordinary scribes, obscure mystics, low-ranking provincial commanders, and poets with no training in statecraft could write on political matters. Although most of the political corpus was still dedicated to the sultan or the grand vizier, they ceased to be the sole addressees of political writings. Taşköprizade, in his encyclopedia of sciences, explained why ordinary people needed to learn about governance:

> The science of governance (*ʿilm al-siyāsa*) is the body of knowledge that concerns state (*mulk*) and executive power (*salṭana*), condition of dignitaries and subjects, and the welfare of cities. This is a science which rulers need first, and then other people. Because a human being is by nature social. It is a religious obligation that a person resides in a virtuous city, migrates from an unvirtuous one, knows how the residents of the virtuous city can benefit from him, and how he can benefit from them.[12]

As profusely illustrated in dynastic epics and histories, the imprint of the Rum in political theory was often marked by Ottoman exceptionalism that articulated the Rumi style in government based on laws, wisdom, and principles of perfect rulership. Writing within the confines of conventional genres, scholars such as Kınalızade and Celalzade, despite their unflinching conviction about the greatness of the Ottoman state and society, were still reserved in incorporating the Ottoman experience into political theory. Their works, still reflecting the timeless wisdom of good morality and governance envisioned in non-Ottoman cultural and political contexts, were not suitable to express political views with specific relevance to the realities of the Süleymanic age. In the face of such inherent constrictions, the rising Ottoman consciousness that introduced the Ottoman experience into political theory brought about the genesis of a completely new type of political writing, the epitome of which was Lütfi Paşa's *Āṣafnāme*.[13] Despite its innovative approach to the question of governance, *Āṣafnāme* owed as much to pre-Ottoman traditions of political writing as to the genius of its author and the unique Ottoman experience in government. Writing around the same time, the anonymous author of *Meṣāliḥü'l-Müslimīn* achieved a complete break with traditional forms of political writing and conventional ideas by dissociating political theory from the ruler and his morality and replacing them with state and law as primary objects of political reasoning.[14] This new breed of works that increasingly dominated the crowded scene of Ottoman political discourse from the mid-sixteenth century onward was marked by a focus on contemporary issues of Ottoman rulership and government. Authors who wrote in this vein were mostly statesmen or officials who employed an empirical method of analysis, a critical perspective from their observations, and a terminological framework drawn from the current administrative language.[15]

The prescriptive exaltation of the Ottoman experience brought about an extensive reshuffling of ideals, visions, symbols, and theories pertaining to rulership and governance that had a lasting impact on the way the Ottoman ruling elite viewed their ruler, government, and society. This paradigmatic watershed in the course of Ottoman political thought was no less original than any other spectacular achievements of the Süleymanic age. The pursuit of moralism in government that dominated the political theory gave way to legalism that evaluated rulership by its conformance to the now archetyped Ottoman model of government rather than moral excellence. The observance of customs and sultanic laws became the touchstone of measuring the quality of government that was previously gauged on the basis of ethical norms, piety, and juristic prescriptions. The caliphate in this model was envisioned as a cosmic rank between Man and God, attained in the spiritual sphere, with the implication of a comprehensive authority over both temporal and spiritual planes as conventional conceptions of rulership in mainstream political theories became increasingly infused with esoteric teachings of Sufism. The focus of political analysis shifted from the personality of the ruler to the existing government and its institutions. From this perspective, institutional aspects of government and procedural practices mattered more than the personality of the ruler or his direct control of day-to-day affairs of state.

This development gradually led Ottoman authors to envision the state as the primary object of analysis and an entity separate from the household of the sultan or the dynasty. Unlike previous conceptions that once reigned supreme in political theory, in the new paradigm, the grand vizier replaced the sultan as the center of government. The sultan was then conceived to be a distant but a legitimating figure for the dynasty while the grand vizier was promoted to the position of actual ruler of the Ottoman state. Consequently, in contrast to the moralistic, idealistic, personality oriented, and sultan-centric paradigm of the broader political literature, this realist and empirical approach to the question of rulership promoted such ideas as "government by law" and "institutional continuity of the state" as primary objectives of rulership. While the Ottoman sultan was exalted to have the same comprehensive authority as the prophets, poles *(quṭbs)*, rightly guided caliphs, and the Mahdi, the Rumi ruling elite, in turn, attached themselves to the Ottoman state as much as to the ruler and assumed exclusive authority to rule the government by reconfiguring the state as a rational institution that operates per prescribed laws and procedures under the management of properly trained statesmen. In the post-Süleymanic era, the state increasingly detached from the sultan's household, and such questions as the independence of high bureaucrats within their respective spheres of authority became common problems to deal with in political theory.

Outline of the Book

This book details the post-Abbasid trajectory of the caliphate and its Sufistic reconstruction in five chapters. Chapter 1 examines the Ottoman political discourse from its origins in the early fifteenth century to the third quarter of the sixteenth century. Views on the caliphate were expressed through a diversified corpus of works on government and rulership across various genres and disciplines accompanied by a broad-based interest in engaging with issues related to government among the Ottoman readership. This diverse body of political literature, written in different languages and genres, was produced by an equally diverse group of authors from various backgrounds, including statesmen, jurists, and Sufis. Along with the expansion of the public sphere in sixteenth century social life, not only did ordinary folks come to be more interested in matters of government but new questions and sensibilities were introduced to the sphere of the political as well. The conventional form of political discourse that was largely confined to providing advice for rulership by a select few gave way to presenting views on all aspects of government by people from different walks of life.

In the early fifteenth century, the Timurid invasion of Anatolia created an existential crisis that led the early Ottomans to engage intensively in studying rulership and statecraft as part of the reconstruction of the Ottoman state. The little-educated early Ottomans and their ruling entourage sought to remodel their new state on the example of the Timurids, whose cultural florescence in Central Asia was more luminescent than any other center of classical Islamic civilization. More than a dozen classical texts on Islamic political thought were translated to serve as handbooks for statecraft and envision the Ottoman ruler in a way that suits the expectations of learned Islam. This humanistic enterprise was coupled with extensive translation activity through which almost all the canonical works of Islamic political theory in Arabic and Persian were either rendered into Turkish or reworked to serve new purposes.

By analyzing authors, texts, audiences, and specific issues raised, Chapter 1 lays out the full scope of the Ottoman discourse on rulership and its impact on state and society. A key problem discussed in this chapter is the question of intended media to convey political ideas. In the context of the sixteenth century, proponents of different visions of rulership expressed their ideas via three principal languages that emerged in this period. The administrative language of the bureaucrats was empirically drawn from the very Ottoman experience in statecraft and therefore exclusively belonged to its specific context. The juristic language was part of the standard Islamic law and enabled one to speak for and engage with the universal legal imperative of the broader ulema network. The esoteric and symbolic language of Sufism was an encrypted medium of communication and always purported to have contained hidden messages intelligible only to the properly trained.

Chapter 2 deals with the formative period of Ottoman political thought from the formal end of the Seljuk state at the turn of the fourteenth century to the Egyptian campaign of 1517. It argues that political ideals and imageries inculcated from the Ottomans' own historical experience, appropriation of Arabic, and the Persian corpora on Islamic political theory; and its exposure to indigenous practices of authority constituted an integral part of state formation and ruling ideology that redefined rulership in general, and the caliphate in particular. Having been founded at the western fringes of the Islamicate society in the midst of nominally converted Turkish-speaking nomadic populations, the Ottomans at large were only gradually exposed to learned traditions of High Islam. Popular spiritual orders of autonomous frontier dervishes who imagined rulers in the image of their shaykhs played a crucial role in the process whereby the Ottoman elite acquainted themselves with Islamic notions of rulership. Two foundational epics of the Ottoman Empire, *Ḫalīlnāme* and *İskendernāme*, were composed in this period. These narratives were among the first Turkish texts that defined the Ottoman state in Islamic terms and portrayed the Ottoman ruler as caliph. Translation of political texts and composition of frontier epics gradually transformed Turkish, which was continuously despised by the learned as a profane language of illiterate nomads with no alphabet, into one of the three principal languages of Islamic learning and culture.

A steady influx of émigrés into Ottoman territories, mostly mystics who fled political turmoil in the Persianate east, continuously furnished the Ottoman elite with Sufistic imageries of authority. Transmission of Islamic knowledge was expedited by deliberate policies of fifteenth-century rulers who sought to attract prominent Sufis, jurists, poets, and artists with exceptional favors and privileges. Among them were a number of scholars who specialized in statecraft and played critical roles in the process of empire building. With the conquest of Arabic-speaking lands in 1516–1517, which entailed the acquisition of a vast juristic literature on government, the Ottoman appropriation of the full corpus of Islamic political thought was complete. By inheriting the scholarly establishment and cultural repositories of Syria and Egypt, the Ottomans also fully incorporated the legitimation apparatus, iconography, and ideological manifestations of the Mamluk dynasty, including the title of "the Custodian of the two Noble Sanctuaries." Having unified the central lands of Islamic civilization, the Ottomans appropriated all the symbols and material representations of preceding Muslim empires while commanding the largest and the most versatile contingent of scholars to craft an imperial ideology based on the caliphate.

Chapter 3 examines the innovative panoply of views on the nature of political authority, and visions of the sultanate as its form of embodiment. Virtually every author writing on rulership felt it necessary first to address the question of what political authority really was, its *raison d'être* and status among humanity, how it was acquired or lost, the nature of the ruler and his morality, and historical models of rulership. No author doubted the consensus-confirmed view that the sultanate was the highest rank a human being could attain, but they took divergent paths in defining its nature, scope, and entangled boundaries. A common attitude was to reconcile between various historical and theoretical models of political authority including philosopher-kingship, prophethood, and imamate by defining them in ways compatible with their own visions of rulership. Elaborating on a particular vision of rulership almost always involved an explanation of human nature, human beings' existential status, and the purpose of life. There is a strong correlation between one's perception of human nature and vision of ideal rulership.

The practical application of this ontological consideration was worked out through three principal theories of acquiring rulership. By largely disregarding qualifications formulated in medieval Islamic sources, Sufis, bureaucrats, and jurists argued whether rulership was attained by grace, merit, or executive power. The prevailing view, however, purported that it was a grace from God (*niʿmet*). It was a grace for humankind for which all should be grateful, as without political authority chaos and anarchy would prevail in the world, and people of different dispositions, interests, and talents would be unable to cooperate. It was a grace for the ruler because it placed him at the highest position among humankind, in the line of the prophets and the rightly guided caliphs, and offered him the opportunity to become the governor of both the material and the spiritual realms at once. Undergirding these arguments were different perceptions of human nature, both as individuals and social bodies. For Sufis, for example, a human being is inherently related to and is a reflection of God through his nature and therefore created to be His deputy on Earth. Every individual is considered to be a political being and, by nature, qualified to be His caliph. Such a perception made virtually every Sufi saint a potential claimant for universal caliphate as shown by many high-profile uprisings by rebel mystics who challenged the legitimacy of the Ottoman ruler.

This Sufistic conception of the caliphate was qualitatively different than its medieval construction as it represents an epistemological break with the juristic imperative of High Islam. Sufi-minded authors engaged in a phenomenological undertaking in order to cultivate imageries of rulership drawn from an esoteric interpretation of Islamic ontology that led to the invention of an all-encompassing notion of political authority equated with the caliphate. This notion of the caliphate was illustrated through archetyping based on the Sufi cosmology. The absolute model for the caliph was God Himself, his attributes and relation to His creation. This conception was not simply an imitation of God's government on Earth but referred to a condition of being entrusted with God's very government. Prophets with executive power, including Adam, Moses, Solomon, and Muhammed, were portrayed as perfect role models in practicing the human extension of God's government. Historical figures drawn from past empires whose grandeur and mission the Ottomans were purported to have inherited—such as the Persian Ardashir, the Greek Alexander, and the Abbasid Harun al-Rashid—were cited as ideal models of how prophetic government is exercised by fallible human agents. As such, the Ottoman caliphate came to be spiritually envisioned, theologically sanctioned, and historically established.

Chapter 4 continues to examine the views on the nature of authority in Islam, diverse visions of the caliphate and its relation to sultanate as a political regime, and portrayals of the perfect ruler through archetype-building and reinterpretation of Islamic history. At the core of this discourse was the question of prophethood that came to be widely contested in the post-Abbasid Muslim society, namely, who was Prophet Muhammed, who inherited his position, and in what capacity? The emergence of Turko-Mongolian dynasties whose Islamic credentials were at best questionable, the decline of the power of the jurists, and the spread of Sufi orders in response to spiritual anxieties of fragmented Muslim society enabled the Sufis to resolve this question in their favor. It was consensual among Ottoman Sufis to argue that the Prophet had three distinct natures: spiritual (*wilāya*), political (*salṭana*), and prophecy (*nubuwwa*), where the latter two emanate from the first one. In this configuration, the jurists, as inheritors of Muhammed's prophecy, and rulers, as claimants for his political nature, were obliged to submit to the spiritual authority, namely the perfect human being among the Sufis whose identity was disclosed only to the worthy.

The juristic conception of the caliphate formulated by medieval jurists was, in theory, a contractual relationship between the ruler and the Muslim community, provided that an elaborate set of conditions—including the ruler's descent from the tribe of the Prophet—are met. Being a non-Arab dynasty, the Ottoman authority could hardly be legitimized in the form of a caliphate on the basis of the juristic canon. The fragmentation of the post-Abbasid unity of Muslim polity and society had irreversibly compromised the universality of Muslim rulership. For the medieval caliphate, it was the jurists who formulated the script for the political ecumene, exercising a near monopoly for religious justification by establishing the standard of law across the ecumenic cosmopolitanism of the Abbasid Empire. In the post-Abbasid world, this role was overtaken by the Sufis whose esoteric and syncretic teachings let them profoundly reinterpret the concept of the caliphate by dissociating it from its historicist justifications and juristic normativism. While the Ottoman historians successfully docked their dynastic lineage to the historical caliphate, the juristic conception was confined to the scholarly study of legal texts in Ottoman madrasas. The juristic/historical caliphate was a successorship to Muhammed (*khalīfat Rasūl Allāh*) in his political capacity through a sanctioned physical lineage. The Sufi-minded proponents of the Ottoman dynasty, however, envisioned the caliph to be God's unmediated deputy (*khalīfat Allāh*) and attributed to the Ottoman ruler the same spiritual qualities and powers accorded to the axis mundi (*quṭb*), the invisible perfect human being to whom God entrusts the management of His whole creation in Sufi cosmology.

Chapter 5 analyzes the mystification of the Ottoman caliphate and the apocalyptic-messianic reconstruction of imperial ideology in the context of the long Ottoman–Safavid conflict of the sixteenth century. Current studies in the main treat the Ottoman–Safavid conflict as no more than a sectarian conflict between two expanding Muslim empires. The Ottomans, however, perceived it as an apocalyptic conflict between primordial forces of faith and disbelief, often expressed in manicheistic dichotomies. Being one of the most aggressively fought religious wars in Islamic history, it profoundly altered both Sunni and Shiite conceptions of history and rulership. The Safavids, being at once a Turkoman chieftainship, a Shiite dynasty, and a Sufi order, were better endowed with esoteric image-making skills than the Ottomans, whose juristic and theological arguments against heresy were, simply, by definition nullified. Despite the Ottoman military might that overwhelmed the Safavids in multiple battles, the Safavid–Shiite call resonated much more strongly among the vast Turkoman diaspora from Central Asia to the Balkans, particularly among popular mystical orders of the countryside. In response, the Ottomans renewed their weakened alliances with prominent Sufi orders and rehabilitated discredited Sufi figures with controversial teachings. Ibn Arabi, for example, perhaps the most potent of medieval mystics whose extensive corpus of writings provide an endless repository of possibilities for alternative interpretations, quickly rose to the status of a patron saint for the Ottoman establishment. Endowed with the teachings of Ibn Arabi, or the Greatest Shaykh, as now commonly called, it was Sufis who fought at the forefront of an intensive ideological warfare against the Safavids. The principal goal of this undertaking was to invalidate the Safavid claims for spiritual authority and propagate the Ottoman sultan as a Sufi-caliph, or even the awaited Mahdi of the end of times.

Sufi-minded Ottoman historians reconstructed Islamic history in which both the Ottomans and the Safavids were identified as the parties of the same perennial conflict since the creation of Adam. In the final chapter of this struggle, the Ottomans and the Safavids—both ethnically Turkic dynasties—were identified as the Romans and the Persians in allusion to the well-known Qur'anic prophecy that the former would defeat the latter. Perception of the Safavids as the perfect other for Islam was not mere war propaganda. The conquest of Constantinople, reportedly prophesized by Prophet Muhammed, and the approach of the end of the first millennium of the Islamic calendar had already sparked apocalyptic anxieties. Astrologers, geomancers, divinators, and occult specialists who were long discredited by the Sunni scholarly establishment now became respectable figures of religious and political discourse. Even the mainstream jurists and Sufis openly engaged in the practice of prognostication. Occultic practices, long performed by enigmatic esotericists, now turned into sought after mainstream arts with which the learned began to be increasingly endowed. Believing in their own divine mission, a series of Ottoman rulers provided patronage to a large contingent of such scholars who continuously occupied themselves with revealing prophecies; unearthing God's hidden messages; and deciphering meanings behind names, numbers, heavenly conjunctions, and the like. Through the endeavors of high-profile jurists and mainstream Sufis, this esoteric epistemology was fully reconciled with the formal teachings of Islam and became an important component of political imagery and imperial ideology.

To counter the Safavid propaganda, Sufi-minded scholars first fabricated a noble lineage by infusing Abrahamic, Persian, and Turko-Mongolian traditions of origination that not only tied the Ottoman dynasty to prestigious empires of antiquity but also Islamized its lineage and portrayed it as divinely ordained to rule. Second, they put Islamic sources to a new scrutiny to discover divine revelations regarding the Ottomans, which resulted in constructing an elaborate eschatology in which the Ottomans were specifically foretold to rule. Third, the Ottoman rulership was depicted to be the seal of the caliphate; that is, there would not be any other Muslim authority until the end of times. Süleyman I was often compared to his namesake, King Solomon, and found mightier than the latter, for in fighting the war of the end of times he was endowed with unique qualities by divine providence. One of the most interesting texts of the entire Islamic corpus on political prognostication was written in this period by a prominent Sufi, Ibn Isa Saruhani. This was an elaborate future history of the Ottomans from 1516, the year it was composed, until 2028 CE, the year it was believed the world would end. For generations, the text was continuously updated to refresh the Ottoman myth as God's chosen and final caliphate by validating Ibn Isa's prognostication. This and similar undertakings produced a new genre of political writing that exclusively narrated the unique qualities of the House of Osman and its Islamic credentials. First conceived and drafted by Idris-i Bidlisi in his chronicle, this account was continuously updated and expanded at critical junctures, and served as the basis of imperial ideology with constitutional import until the very end of the empire.

ABBREVIATIONS

ACTA ORIENTALIA	*Acta Orientalia Academiae Scientiarum Hungaricae*
BDK	Beyazıt Devlet Kütüphanesi
BNF	Bibliothèque Nationale de France
BSOAS	*Bulletin of the School of Oriental and African Studies*
D.	died
EI^2	*Encyclopedia of Islam*, second edition
IJMES	*International Journal of Middle East Studies*
İÜK	İstanbul Üniversitesi Kütüphanesi
JOS	*Journal of Ottoman Studies*
JSAI	*Jerusalem Studies in Arabic and Islam*
JTS	*Journal of Turkish Studies*
MS	Manuscript
MÜİFD	*Marmara Üniversitesi İlahiyat Fakültesi Dergisi*
ÖNB	Österreichische Nationalbibliothek
R.	reigned
S.	served
SBB	Staatsbibliothek zu Berlin
SK	Süleymaniye Kütüphanesi
TARİH DERGİSİ	*İstanbul Üniversitesi Edebiyat Fakültesi Tarih Dergisi*
TDAY	*Türk Dili Araştırmaları Yıllığı*
TDVIA	*Türkiye Diyanet Vakfı İslam Ansiklopedisi*
TSMK	Topkapı Sarayı Müzesi Kütüphanesi
TTK	Türk Tarih Kurumu

CHAPTER ONE

The Discourse on Rulership

IF WESTERN ASIA MINOR is taken as the broader cultural context of the early Ottoman state, then it was born into one of the most vibrant and versatile cultural milieus of the Muslim world, albeit being relatively less exposed to the broader learned traditions. The region was marked by high social mobility, indefinite political identities, frequently shifting frontiers, and nascent institutions of learning. Looking for a definitive date or a source for the beginning of Ottoman literature on political thought, much like the endless debate on the formal start date of the Ottoman state, is at best a futile effort and, more likely, a potentially misleading endeavor. It is not because we do not have enough textual knowledge of the period but because the very porousness of political boundaries and cultural affinities among the Turkoman emirates of western Asia Minor renders the characterization of any historical artifact, text, or personality from that era as "Ottoman" an arbitrary assessment, at least in the cultural sense of the word. With that caveat, the adjective "Ottoman" in this study cautiously refers to political affiliation when used in the context of the fourteenth century. In the context of the fifteenth century and afterwards, it is used in reference to both political affiliation and cultural articulation as both traits became more pronounced following the Battle of Ankara, and turned into manifest identities in the sixteenth century, especially after Selim I's military campaigns against the Safavids and the Mamluks from 1514 to 1517.

Translations excluded, there is no known text that can safely be included in Ottoman political literature from the fourteenth century. Because of the special circumstances of their frontier principality, Ottoman statesmen of this period, if they could be so called, seem to have shown no notable interest in sophisticated political theories that had been formulated in well-developed polities. Instead, it was epics that seem to have served as the principal medium of conveying and inculcating princely virtues for good governance. Reading epics was popular both at courts and public audiences of western Asia Minor. These epics were replete with moral lessons and political advice as illustrated in the lives of heroes, therefore functioning as entertaining and dramatic media for education on rulership, well suited to the profiles of chivalrous frontier princes. They functioned to bridge courtly and public ideals of morality and leadership. If there was any interest to read on statecraft per se, the statesmen and the learned must have relied on political texts written elsewhere. What we may more confidently classify as "Ottoman" in political writing started at the turn of the fifteenth century and culminated in a broad-based discourse on rulership by the mid-sixteenth century. This chapter surveys and examines this output in three phases marked by three turning points with far-reaching consequences for all aspects of Ottoman history including visions of rulership: the Battle of Ankara in 1402, the conquest of Constantinople in 1453, and the Egyptian Campaign of 1516–1517, each initiated a new phase in political writing.

The Age of Angst: Turkish Vernacularism and Political Expression

From the beginnings of the Ottoman state until the sixteenth century, when Turkish established itself as the principal language of administration and literary articulation, writing in Turkish had always been a contentious issue. Almost every text in Turkish from the fourteenth and fifteenth centuries included an apology for the use of this language. Among others, two commonly cited reasons to justify writing in Turkish were addressing the Turkoman base in their own language and facilitating learning for students who were yet to master any one of the two conventional languages of learning, literature, and administration.[1] Otherwise, as a medium of Islamic learning Turkish was still considered a profane language and a crude one unfit for artistic expressions, a complaint voiced by even the staunchest advocates of writing in Turkish vernacular. For writing in the language of illiterate nomads one could easily become stigmatized as being unlearned or unrefined. Hoca Mesud, for example, in the mid-fourteenth century, despite writing in Turkish for its instrumental value of speaking to people in their own language, nevertheless ridiculed himself that, for doing so, he lost half of his body weight out of shame.[2] But the sudden change of political conditions in the early fifteenth century made Turkish the language of choice at the Ottoman court, albeit not being fully exonerated.

The utter humiliation of the Ottomans by Timur in the Battle of Ankara and the ensuing civil war not only disassembled the fledgling early Ottoman state and its delicate alliances but also unleashed a fierce competition in a chaotic theater among disempowered princes, ambitious chieftains, prestigious learned men, and charismatic Sufi leaders who emerged as leading figures vying to reestablish order per their distinctive visions of social organization and political leadership. This moment of elevated sentiments of despair and hope as well as astonishment, anxiety, and self-reflection manifested itself on the literary plane as a sudden burst of interest in writing and reading on the art of rulership by reconnecting with Arabic and Persian learned traditions. Princes turned into curious patrons of learning and the learned became advisors with books on rulership at hand. The most visible outcome of this cultural florescence was the translation of texts from all fields of learning, of which mirrors for princes were among the most prized. Political uncertainty and the struggle for consolidation made works on statecraft relevant for those who were content with reading epics as mirrors. Yet, except for a small group of scholars, the ruling elite were not well equipped to read in Arabic or Persian or, at least, they had not yet developed the courtly taste of reading or hearing in a language other than Turkish. That made translation the principal medium of training on government for Ottoman princes and statesmen. As a result, during the first half of the fifteenth century, Ottoman learned men translated and reworked a remarkably diverse list of political works for their patrons.[3]

Among them was Ahmed b. Hüsameddin el-Amasi, whose *Mir'ātü'l-Mülūk* (Mirror for Kings), despite being a translation, can cautiously be considered the first genuine work of political thought by an Ottoman author. Written as a mirror for princes, *Mir'ātü'l-Mülūk* provides an illustrative case for the development of early Ottoman political writing. Amasi dedicated the work in 1406 to Mehmed I (r. 1413–1421), who consolidated his rule after more than a decade of civil war (1402–1411), later dubbed as Interregnum (*Fetret Devri*). As suggested by his toponym, he was from Amasya and was born to a well-established local family, the Gümüşlüzades, who raised scholars, Sufis, and statesmen. The extant two copies of *Mir'ātü'l-Mülūk* suggest that the work did not reach a wide audience.[4]

Mir'ātü'l-Mülūk is an early example of a long-lasting pattern in which some authors opted to express their own views on rulership by extensively quoting from the canons of Islamic political thought in Arabic and Persian. Those who undertook this approach chose well-known texts and limited their discretion to making selections and organizing them in a format suitable for conveying their own convictions. Ebu'l-Fazl Münşi's *Dustūr al-Salṭana*, which was based on Najm al-Din Daye's *Mirṣād al-ʿIbād*, and Kemal b. Hacı Ilyas's *Ādāb al-Mulūk*, a work drawn from Ghazali's *Naṣīḥat al-Mulūk*, were two sixteenth century examples of this pattern. This eclecticism opened a new channel for the spread of political ideas propounded by authoritative figures of learned traditions in Persian and Arabic, thus creating a literary bond between the ideals of rulership of the Ottoman milieu with those of the broader Islamic culture. Through the works of subsequent authors who shared Amasi's approach, political views of non-Ottoman scholars, philosophers, and Sufis, such as Mawardi and Farabi, were introduced to the Ottoman audience anonymously while their works remained untranslated into Turkish.

Mirʾātü'l-Mülūk consists of two parts. The first part derives its material from the thirteenth century philosopher Nasir al-Din Tusi's (d. 1274) celebrated work of practical philosophy, *Akhlāq-i Nāṣirī*.[5] The second part is mostly taken from Ghazali's (d. 1055) *Naṣīhat al-Mulūk*, the most widely circulated work of the mirror for princes genre in the Islamic world.[6] In *Mirʾātü'l-Mülūk*, Amasi does not make any reference to either of these works or their authors, and explicitly presents himself as its author.[7] He combined the content of these two works by selective translations adding only a few modifications of his own. It seems unlikely that he intended to appropriate the content of two well-known works without this being noticed by his contemporaries. Per the authoring conventions of the time, the text may well be considered as a compilation rather than a plagiarism. Many later authors who followed the same pattern clearly stated that they composed their works through compiling and translating from authoritative works on a given topic but often avoided citing them. Authors who composed by compiling often preferred works with entertaining features and simple literary styles to convey in Turkish. The outcome was an abundance of mirrors for princes literature and a scarcity of philosophical and juridical works dealing with politics. Considering the two sources of Amasi, although there is no known translation of *Akhlāq-i Nāṣirī*, there were at least five different translations of *Naṣīhat al-Mulūk* by the end of the sixteenth century. While Amasi followed an exceptional path by partially translating *Akhlāq-i Nāṣirī*, he also put his work into the mainstream by combining it with *Naṣīḥat al-Mulūk*.

The language used in the two parts of the work differs significantly: in the first part, it is more philosophical and the terminology more scholarly; in the second part, the content is more literary whereas the terminology is closer to the Ottoman usage of Amasi's time. Political terms such as *raʿiyyet* (subjects), *pādişāh* (ruler), and *ẓulm* (oppression), which are widely used in the second part, are rarely used in the first part, where more philosophical words such as *abnā-i jins*, *malik*, and *javr* are used instead. Excluding the works that were catered to the consumption of a wider public, the general trend among Ottoman authors was to diligently preserve the terminological framework of works composed in traditional Islamic disciplines, grammar, and philosophy. Through this literary proselytization, the once profane and mundane language of early Ottoman Turkish evolved into a sophisticated language of political discourse by the sixteenth century. The use of such an elevated language by Amasi indicates that he wrote the work for a learned audience. His compilation of a mirror for princes in Turkish by using selections from two classical works offered his audience a new text on the ethics of rulership with a refined language and a sophisticated conceptual framework.

In compiling *Mirʾātü'l-Mülūk*, Amasi included chapters that have more practical relevance for the ruler. He made use of only three of the eight chapters of *Akhlāq-i Nāṣirī*: on the need for civilization, the government of the king and the government of servants, and the manners of following kings. These subjects were commonly dealt with in the mirrors for princes literature and largely linked to the relations between rulers and their subjects. Chapters Amasi did not include were on love, divisions of societies, fidelity, and friendship, topics that are more social than political in nature. While the integrated chapters deal with a vertical relationship between the ruler and the ruled, the omitted chapters basically deal with a horizontal relationship among groups or individuals in society, and are therefore less relevant to governance. By using *Akhlāq-i Nāṣirī* as his source text, Amasi created an exclusive treatise on rulership from a general theory of ethics.

Amasi undertook the same approach in deriving his material from Ghazali's *Naṣīḥat al-Mulūk* as well. He made Ghazali's already practical book of mirrors more relevant to actual situations by excluding its first half, metaphorically entitled "the roots of faith," which explained God's attributes. By contrast, a mid-sixteenth century translator of *Naṣīḥat al-Mulūk*, Alayi, wrote an extensive commentary on the first part of the work while simply translating the second part that used literary devices to educate the ruler on statecraft.[8] Writing during the height of the Ottoman–Safavid feud with its flaring theological disputes, Alayi was more concerned with the creed of the ruler than with the ruler's education on statecraft. Amasi, however, writing at a time when the Ottoman state was just consolidating after a long civil war, was more interested in the principles of good governance. In appropriating the second part of *Naṣīḥat al-Mulūk*, Amasi was content with selecting stories and leaving out the moral lessons and explanations given by Ghazali. He puts the ruler in a more central position than he occupies in the original work by excluding sections that deal only indirectly with rulership. This part of the work exhorts the ruler to do justice and warn him against oppression. By incorporating only the illustrated section of *Naṣīḥat al-Mulūk*, with exciting stories and memorable aphorisms, Amasi turned *Mirʾātü'l-Mülūk* into a performative text with an added value for entertainment.

When molded into *Mirʾātü'l-Mülūk*, the philosophical content of *Akhlāq-i Nāṣirī* and the theological content of *Naṣīḥat al-Mulūk* received less emphasis. Philosophical abstractions and theological formulations regarding government that had little relevance to early fifteenth century Ottoman rulership were left out. A chapter of *Akhlāq-i Nāṣirī*, for example, that discusses characteristics of various types of associations and rulers, is not included. Likewise, from Tusi's lengthy discussion of four different types of government, only government by a king is included in *Mirʾātü'l-Mülūk*.[9] Among the readers of *Akhlāq-i Nāṣirī*, Amasi is not the only one who disregarded these two chapters, which displayed one of the most genuine discussions about alternative forms of political associations in Islamic political thought. More influential later figures such as Davvani (d. 1502–1503), Kashifi (d. 1504–1505), and Kınalızade (d. 1572), who wrote ethical works that also relied heavily on

Akhlāq-i Nāṣirī, likewise omitted these topics. They seem to have shared Amasi's objective of turning the general theory of ethics composed by Tusi into a practical handbook of morality for rulership by focusing only on righteous political association and behavior, leaving out the philosophical discussion of other possible classifications.

While philosophy and religion still served as two main sources for political ideas in the first and second parts of *Mir'ātü'l-Mülūk*, respectively, Amasi opted to exclude abstractions in both cases to make his book more relevant to the current vicissitudes of rulership. In *Mir'ātü'l-Mülūk*, one can still find the ethical philosophy of Tusi, and the religious counsels of Ghazali as well as historical anecdotes and aphorisms from sages; however, they are not molded into a synthesis. Making few modifications, Amasi concisely presented the distinct ethical and religious content of both works. Through such a combination he put philosophy, religion, and history side by side and presented the eclectic narrative as a mirror for princes. In this way, while he introduced philosophical content into this genre, he also made ethical philosophy more comprehensible by relating it to history, and more binding by grounding it in religion.

Considering the sequence of the two parts of *Mir'ātü'l-Mülūk*, the theoretical weight of the work lies in the first part, which is taken from *Akhlāq-i Nāṣirī*. In this format, which is widely used in Islamic wisdom literature and later Ottoman political writings, such as the works of Arifi, Ensari and Hızır Münşi, the first part serves as a philosophical introduction to the empirical second part that consists of illustrative stories and precedents taken from past experience. The first part outlines the governing principles of human nature and social life while the second part presents actual historical events through which these laws can be observed and lessons drawn. With few exceptions, all the themes in the second part of the book have their theoretical counterparts in the first part. Almost all major topics in the political sections of the first part, such as justice, fiscal administration, and punishment of criminals, are illustrated in the second part.

Combining two works with two different perspectives only solidified what Amasi intended to convey. In the first part, he explained rulership as a natural outcome of an inherent human need for association, and justice as maintaining equity in society.[10] In the second part, however, he portrays rulership as a grace (*ni'met*) from God and justice as a return of God's favor.[11] Well-entrenched in diverse strands of Islamic political literature, these two ideas became staples of later Ottoman political thought. The first part explains the relationship between the ruler and his subjects whereas the second elaborates the ruler's relationship to God. Richly supplemented by actual historical cases, the text draws the profile of a just ruler as one who observes justice as a requirement of nature for maintaining order and an obligation stipulated by the divine for the continuity of one's rulership. In this way, political ideas in *Mir'ātü'l-Mülūk* became philosophically defined, religiously sanctioned, and historically proven.

Mir'ātü'l-Mülūk is not a handbook of statecraft that explains administrative structures and practices; it therefore bears little on institutional aspects of government. Instead, it focused more on the cultivation of a just ruler than designing a just government. More, it privileged principles of personal perfection over the rules of government efficiency. The personality of the ruler and his actions rather than administrative structures occupied the central place in the book. Amasi set the conditions for just rulership as moral integrity in the first part with a focus on virtues and piety in the second, which highlighted good deeds. In both parts, however, intellect is given a superior status compared to all other personal traits and disciplines of training. As one anecdote clearly illustrates, one of the main messages of *Mir'ātü'l-Mülūk* was that the attainment of moral perfection, religious salvation, and political justice was dependent on the ruler's intellectual capabilities: "It is narrated that an angel came to a certain prophet and asked him to choose one among intellect (*'aḳıl*), religion (*dīn*), and knowledge (*'ilim*), which the angel brought; the prophet chose intellect; the angel told knowledge and religion to leave; they replied, we cannot be separated from intellect."[12] This emphasis on the primacy of rational faculty in rulership became another commonly held idea in later Ottoman political thought.

Amasi was unique among the fifteenth century authors in producing a novel treatise on rulership by translating from different source texts. Many of his contemporaries opted for a more straightforward approach and rendered various political works selectively or entirely into Turkish but without any amalgamation except for their own editorial discretion to reshuffle, add, omit, or interpret. Both *Akhlāq-i Nāṣirī* and *Naṣīḥat al-Mulūk* continued to serve as source texts throughout later Ottoman history. Yet, whereas the former was never translated again, the latter became the most translated text in the sixteenth century. For this early period, however, a standard mirror for princes was Kaykavus b. Iskandar's *Qābūsnāma*, which offered a comprehensive recipe for the inculcation of a virtuous ruler. Kaykavus was a Ziyarid ruler, whose realm had flourished in western Persian lands between c. 931 and 1090, surrounded by rival dynasties, much like the early Ottomans. He wrote the work in 1082–1083 for his son and intended successor Gilan Shah to educate him in good governance and prepare him for the vicissitudes of rulership. It is composed in the form of a testament in the long line of similar Persian works that were in circulation since the early Abbasid period, such as the ones attributed to Ardashir and Anushirvan. The work served as one of the principal mediums through which Perso-Islamic ideals of government and society passed into Ottoman political culture, first through translations and then through the Persian originals.

The book was translated into Turkish at least six times during the fourteenth and fifteenth centuries, three of which were dedicated to Ottoman rulers or statesmen.[13] There are two anonymous translations from the fourteenth century.[14] As commonly seen in many other translations of this period, both authors edited the original text per their own political views or to make it suit the expectations of their patrons within the broader context of western Asia Minor.[15] Şeyhoğlu translated it for the Germiyanid ruler Süleyman Shah (r. c. 1368–1387), Akkadıoğlu for a certain Hamza Beg from the entourage of the Ottoman Prince Emir Süleyman (d. 1411), and Bedr-i Dilşad for Murad II (r. 1421–1444 and 1446–1451) in 1427.[16] None of these translations seems to have entered the wider stream of Ottoman thought, probably because of the rapid evolution of the Turkish language, which rendered these texts increasingly out of fashion, especially among the courtly readers. Mercimek Ahmed's translation for Murad II, however, became the definitive Turkish rendition and was widely read throughout the Ottoman dominions.[17] Mercimek Ahmed translated it in 1431–1432 at the behest of Murad II, who found an earlier Turkish version distasteful and asked for an open translation that was pleasing to read. As the first canon of mirrors for princes that caught the attention of the Ottomans, *Qābūsnāma* had a long lasting impact on Ottoman rulership.

Another work from the same period with even a more defining impact was Najm al-Din Daye's (d. 1256) *Mirṣād al-ʿIbād*, a comprehensive compendium of Sufism whose fifth part dealt with government.[18] Daye composed the work in 1223 for the Seljuk ruler Alaeddin Keykubad while he was in Asia Minor, seeking safety during the Mongol onslaught.[19] Daye was a disciple of Majd al-Din Baghdadi of the Kubrawiyya order that flourished in Transaxonia and Iran but did not take a firm hold in Ottoman lands.[20] He also studied with Najm al-Din Kubra (d. 1220), the founder of the order.[21] Daye arrived in Asia Minor with a letter from one of the most famous Sufi shaykhs of the time, Shihab-al-Din Umar Suhrawardi, to Alaeddin Keykubad but soon left disappointed. Yet his teachings of the Kubrawiyya influenced all branches of Ottoman Sufism through his *Mirṣād al-ʿIbād* as well as his Qur'anic commentary.[22] As the fame of *Mirṣād al-ʿIbād* quickly spread from Cairo to China, it was widely read by the Ottomans in its original Persian as well as in its Arabic and Turkish translations. Many of these copies consisted of only the fifth part of the work, circulating as a separate treatise on government. Ebu'l-Fazl Münşi, for example, dedicated the fifth part of *Mirṣād al-ʿIbād* to Süleyman as a separate book, with few changes and without mentioning the book that was its source.[23] It was first rendered into Turkish by Şeyhoğlu in 1401 with the title *Kenzü'l-Küberā* and dedicated to an Ottoman statesman Paşa Ağa.[24] Much like Amasi, Şeyhoğlu did not mention the source and presented himself as the author of the work. He included in his translation only the first four chapters of the fifth part, and turned it into more of a mirror for princes by adding lengthy poems of his own.[25] A definitive Turkish translation of the work, however, was achieved by Kasım b. Mahmud el-Karahisari who dedicated the work to Murad II during the early years of his reign.[26] This was a full translation of the work and was widely read throughout Ottoman history. Kasım Çelebi (d. 1518), a scholar and a mystic who succeeded Çelebi Halife in the Halveti order, translated the work for Mehmed II (r. 1451–1481) for which he received the sultan's compliments.[27] He was also Bali Efendi's shaykh, a prominent figure in the mid-sixteenth-century debate on cash foundations, who wrote a separate treatise on rulership and a commentary on Ibn Arabi's *Fuṣūṣ al-Ḥikam* (the Bezels of Wisdom).[28] In addition to *Mirṣād al-ʿIbād,* Daye wrote another work on Sufism called *Manārāt al-Sāʾirīn* in which he explained the stations and experiences of human beings' spiritual wayfaring.[29] This is a text that gives one of the most extensive treatments of the Sufi concept of the caliphate, a concept that deeply affected sixteenth century Ottoman political thought. While the work was well received in the Ottoman world of learning in its Arabic original, a certain Ali Şibli al-Dugehi translated it for Bayezid II (r. 1481–1512) from Arabic into Persian, the prevalent language among the learned strains of Turko-Persian Sufism.[30]

A text similar to *Mirṣād al-ʿIbād*, written from an exclusively Sufi perspective, was *Enīsü'l-Celīs*, translated by one Kasım b. Seydi el-Hafız Ankari and dedicated to Murad II.[31] Apart from Ankari's statement that he translated it from a Persian text that was in turn translated from an Arabic work by Hacı b. Isma'il Tabrizi, there is no information on the original text or its author. The original author as well as the translator appear to have been better versed in mystical philosophy than in statecraft. The text is a rich repertoire of Sufistic admonitions for moral perfection rather than an advice book on statecraft. The translator made the text particularly relevant for Murad II, as he frequently parts ways with the main text and makes references to conditions and peoples of the land of Rum and practices of past Ottoman sultans. In a way, the author turns otherwise abstract Sufi imageries into a concrete set of ideas and principles to define the specific case of Ottoman rulership. Although the author does not reveal his sectarian identity or Sufi affiliation, he makes his Sunni stand purposely clear and warns against heresies such as Rafidis and Kharijites as well as occultists that appear in the guise of learned men with esoteric knowledge. Being from Ankara where the powerful Hacı Bayram had a strong presence, the author may well be a Bayrami initiate as the teachings in the book closely resemble those of the Bayramis. It is not a distant possibility to consider this text as a Bayrami gift to the Ottoman sultan to make amends and perhaps convert the Ottoman sultan to Bayrami spirituality as it conveys exceptionally lofty statements in glorifying the status of the ruler.

The four political tracts above were by no means the only textual exposure of the Ottoman ruling elite to Perso-Islamic ideals of virtuous rulership. The very fact that all these texts were translated from Persian indicates the presence of a group of scholars well-versed in the Persianate culture and close to frontier rulers including the Ottomans. For the first half of the fifteenth century, these and other scholars remained busy translating works from different strains of Islamic thought and disciplines, including many from Arabic, often in response to specific demands from rulers and statesmen. Translations in literature, jurisprudence, theology, Qur'anic commentary, history, and Sufism all conveyed political ideas embedded and refined within these traditions and disciplines. However, because of the very nature of translation, translators played the role of interlocutors not only for the specific texts they conveyed but also for different strains of political thought. Besides choosing what to translate, despite occasional claims of literality, all translators used some degree of discretion in editing these texts per their own convictions and taste as well as the demands of their target audience. *Qābūsnāma*, for example, granted that each translation is different in some respect, reached the Ottomans through the intermediacy of these translators in six different readings. This heyday of vernacular Turkish and translators also coincided with the expansion of Ottoman madrasas as well as convents of learned Sufi denominations that supplied an increasing number of educated men for Ottoman bureaucracy and courtly circles. Further, Ottoman princes now were subjected to a rigorous training in letters supervised by tutors who were considered to be at once both scholars and moral guides. Because Turkish was not yet a literary or scholarly language, education inevitably began with learning Arabic or Persian, or both. As embodied in the personality of the young Mehmed II, the expansion of learning cultivated a new class of ruling elite who were self-reliant in reading in Persian or Arabic, thus marginalizing the role of translators as interlocutors.

The Age of Excitement: From Conquest to Exploration

The period marked by the two most cherished conquests in Ottoman history witnessed an extensive institutionalization in state-building accompanied by forging a new social order through instituting a balance between traditional and emerging social groups. In rulership profile, Mehmed II established himself not only as the first Ottoman ruler with all the regalia, symbolism, and credentials that befit the image of a universal emperor but also as a chosen and an awaited Muslim leader whose conquest of Constantinople confirmed the good tidings attributed to Prophet Muhammed and stirred apocalyptic sentiments far and wide.[32] No less striking was the rise of Selim I as the unifier of the three holiest sites of Islam under a single banner and a champion of Sunni Islam against the Safavid Shiism, thus prompting Ottoman historians to register his name on the noble line of legendary conquerors on par with Alexander and Chingiz. Immediately after his military campaigns to the east and south, poets and historians composed epic stories of his conquests, mostly in verse and Persian, on the model of widely circulating *Shāhnāma* of Ferdowsi (d. c. 1020–1026).[33] Despite being overshadowed in glory by both his father and son, Bayezid II inculcated a unique image of himself as the first saint-ruler of the House of Osman, therefore surpassing in rank all earthly majestic titles in, at least, the Sufistic imageries of rulership. Further, he successfully realigned the Ottoman center with disillusioned traditional allies including the Sufi orders, the *gazi* establishment of frontiers, and Turkoman families while maintaining a delicate balance of power with both the Mamluks in the south and catholic powers of Europe in the west who sought to exploit the rebellion and the subsequent captivity of Prince Djem for their own interests. Reflecting this new policy, a certain dervish penned a letter to Bayezid II, portraying the sultan as a saint and prophesizing that the sultan will soon conquer Egypt.[34]

Having earned their distinguished names as poets writing in both Turkish and Persian, all three sultans were exceptionally well educated in letters and generously invested in arts and learning. They were particularly extolled by their learned clients as wise rulers, as profiled in the Perso-Islamic mirrors literature, many of which were available in their personal libraries. Aside from their political affiliation, the learned of this period started to express their Ottomanness as a cultural identity in more pronounced terms, especially in the rising genre of history writing. The appellative Rumi, a broader term in reference to peoples living in Asia Minor and the Balkans as well as their cultural, social, and political characteristics, became closely associated with the term Ottoman of which the semantic field was consistently expanding from a reference to the House of Osman to state, society, and culture of the realm ruled by the Ottomans.[35] Yet, neither Rumi nor Ottoman was an exclusive term in their ethnic or linguistic references. In fact, the principal language of high culture of this period was Persian, which did not seem to pose any contradiction to one's Rumi or Ottoman identity. The instrumental value of Turkish of the earlier period was somewhat diminished with the marked increase in the degree and extent of learning among the ruling elite whereas Arabic continued to enjoy its unquestionable prestige as the standard language of Islamic sciences.

Political thought of the period continued to be written under the shadow of Murad II. Both Musannifek and Şükrullah, whose works marked Mehmed II's reign as the period of transition from translation to composition in political thought, were recruited to Ottoman service by Murad II. Mehmed II himself was an exceptionally accomplished intellectual, well versed in multiple languages, an ambitious collector of books, and a very determined patron of learning and arts who managed to lure a number of sought-after scholars in a very competitive marketplace of the Persianate world as well as renaissance Italy. Yet, in political thought his reign looks faint in comparison to that of his father, with only a handful of texts written and none known to be translated. This relative disinterest in political thought, however, was overly compensated in a host of other writings ranging from encyclopedic compendiums to mystical works of various stripes. Writing on rulership became fashionable again during the reign of Bayezid II, prompted by a series of succession crises that plagued the Ottoman polity; conflicts with the Mamluks and then with the

Safavids; administrative reforms; and confessional unrest on the part of Sufi orders, the mainstream ulema, and Kizilbash communities. The renewed interest in political thought continued during the short reign of Selim I, who had to grapple with the same problems that pervaded his father's rule.

Translation as the preferred type of political writing during the first half of the fifteenth century gave way to genuine compositions following the conquest of Constantinople. Of those writing on rulership in this period, the most decorated scholar was Musannifek (d. 1470). Also known as Bistami, Shahrudi, or Haravi, he was already a famed and prolific scholar before his move to the Rum in 1436 from Transoxania.[36] Throughout his career, he remained in the close company of Mehmed II and, more so, that of his grand vizier Mahmud Paşa, to whom he dedicated his renowned work on vizierate, *Tuḥfa-i Maḥmūdiyya* in 1456.[37] If Mahmud Paşa can be taken as the first model grand vizier of Mehmed II's new world empire in which this highest position was further bureaucratized and reserved to the *devşirme* statesmen, then *Tuḥfa-i Maḥmūdiyya* is the first handbook of the vizierate of this new government. Candarlı Halil Paşa's execution soon after the conquest of Constantinople symbolized the end of the early Ottoman vizierate, which had little institutional basis but functioned as a venue for the powerful with deep roots in Ottoman state and society to have a say in government. In Mehmed II's new empire, the vizierate was to represent the executive power of the sultan in clearly delineated bounds by people of his own training. The revival of this traditional Perso-Islamic institution in a new form created a long lineage of curious but insecure statesmen ever more eager to learn about the intricacies of the vizierate in an increasingly competitive Ottoman polity. Musannifek's treatise responds to this administrative overhaul by catering a refined synthesis of the rich Perso-Arabic literature on the vizierate to a man who later registered his name in Ottoman memory as a wise vizier.[38] Mahmud Paşa was particularly noted for his intellectual refinement by the learned of the time but more praised for his spirituality to the extent that he was accorded a saintly status soon after his death, and further immortalized by his sixteenth-century hagiography.[39]

An overtly Sufi grand vizier might have been a novelty for the Ottoman state but that was exactly what Musannifek pictured in his *Tuḥfa-i Maḥmūdiyya*. Musannifek profiled a vizier per ideals of his own mystical convictions that he detailed in his commentary on one of Suhrawardi's texts, *Ḥall al-Rumūz wa Kashf al-Kunūz* (Solving Mysteries and Discovering Treasuries), which he dedicated to Mehmed II.[40] *Ḥall al-Rumūz* introduces the ruler to ideals of Sufism including visions of rulership, in particular the caliphate. Despite his troubled relationship with the Abdalan, Mehmed II was an avid student of Sufism as he maintained a close company of leading Sufi scholars of his time whom he commissioned to write on some intricate ontological questions.[41] On the authority of an impressive array of sources ranging from

Ibn Arabi to Qushairi, *Ḥall al-Rumūz* addresses some of the most subtle issues of Sufism. It is a comprehensive survey of Sufi thought, written to appease the juristic anxiety on heretical-appearing ideas while correcting the perceived heresies expressed across increasingly versatile Sufi groupings. Along the lines of Molla Fenari, a Sufi-jurist who set the Ottoman scholarly paradigm of navigating between juristic normativity and Sufistic discursivity with equal ease, Musannifek reconciles Sufism with Sunni theology and jurisprudence by presenting the two as different manifestations of the same truth in faith and praxis.

Musannifek penned two other works on politics, probably as a tribute to his new patrons, though not dedicated to anyone specifically: *Tuḥfat al-Salāṭīn* (Gift for Sultans) and *Tuḥfat al-Wuzarā* (Gift for Viziers).[42] Both are quite unusual in style and structure, albeit familiar in content, organized into forty chapters, with each chapter listing four advices. The total length of each text, however, barely reaches a mere few folios, looking like a table of contents for a larger treatise. Despite the size, the works are crafted with a lofty claim to summarize wisdom literature on rulership. Putting aside some ethical works that were composed in a chart-like abridgement, mostly recounting virtues versus vices, Musannifek introduced a new genre of political writing that did not seem to have gained favor. The texts are written in the formulaic and concise style of juristic and theological textbooks that are produced to be commented upon by instructors or even memorized. A good example of this genre is Omar Nasafi's (d. 1142) short text *Aqā'id,* which was later subjected to numerous lengthy commentaries by a series of famed scholars. Though less common, this approach was extended to other disciplines as well. al-Iji's *Akhlāq al-ʿAḍudiyya,* for example, summarized and theologically filtered teachings of ethical philosophy on which such famed scholars as Davvani and Taşköprizade wrote commentaries.[43] Musannifek was himself a renowned commentator, having written dozens of commentaries on many famed books. Reminiscent of such formulaic textbooks, the entire fourth chapter of *Tuḥfat al-Salāṭīn,* for example, is as follows: "Four things are essential for the good fortune to rule (*davlat*): divine light (*farr-i yazdānī*), confirmation from heavens (*ta'yīd-i āsmānī*), experienced minister (*dustūr-i jihān-dīda*), and commendable laws (*farmān-i pasanddīda*)."

Musannifek was only one of many other scholars with distinctly Sufistic inclinations who served as statesmen and advisers during the reign of Mehmed II. Among them was Şükrullah of Amasya (d. after 1464) who, during his long life as a diplomat, instructor, and judge, closely witnessed and was involved in the reconstruction of the Ottoman state from its dissolution after the Battle of Ankara and later institutionalization following the conquest of Constantinople. Modern historiography duly credits him as one of the founders of history writing in the Ottoman Empire.[44] He composed his world history in Persian, *Bahjat al-Tavārīkh* (Joy of Histories), and dedicated it to the aforementioned

Mahmud Paşa in 1458.[45] The work not only places the Ottoman turn in rulership within the grand scheme of world history but also furnishes the reader with encyclopedic knowledge on a range of subjects that an ambitious ruler of an emerging world empire and his grand vizier might have found helpful including such topics as cosmology, geography, and accounts of philosophers, ulema, and Sufi shaykhs. It is a world history of Islam from Adam down to his day except for a brief history of ancient Persia inserted before the start of Muslim dynasties. The work is written in a didactic tone to inculcate in the reader a strong sense of historical identity by rooting the Ottoman period in a particular political continuum and cultural setting. Şükrullah wrote another work of encyclopedic scope, drawn from some fifty-eight sources he listed, with the same intention Musannifek had in composing his *Ḥall al-Rumūz*.[46] Dedicated to Mehmed II in 1459, the work informs the ruler on a range of topics pertaining to proper execution of rulership, including types of calendars, astrology, prophecies, heretical sects, and articles of faith and praxis. Besides these two well-received oeuvres, Şükrullah also composed a little noticed work on ethics in Turkish.[47] Unlike his other works that reflect the cultural and linguistic taste of the post-conquest period, *Enīsü'l-ʿĀrifīn* (Companion of Knowers) was written in vernacular Turkish, probably during the reign of Murad II when Turkish was more fashionable.[48] It is a comprehensive and lengthy treatise touching on all conventional topics of ethics yet written for statesmen for good governance rather than the moral perfection of individuals. That explains the text's limited reach among Ottoman readership. By comparison, Eşrefoğlu Rumi's (d. c. 1470) *Müzekki'n-Nüfūs*, written in a similar language but for the general public, quickly turned into a staple of rank-and-file readers for centuries.[49] *Enīsü'l-ʿĀrifīn*, however, sharing the fate of many early Turkish books written for the consumption of the ruling elite, soon fell out of favor first by the rise of Persian and then by the transformation of Turkish into a more ornate language.

A like-minded contemporary of Musannifek and Şükrullah was Sinan Paşa (d. 1486), who wrote *Maʿārifnāme* (Book of Intuitive Knowledge), also known as *Naṣīḥatnāme* or *Aḫlāḳnāme*, from a distinctly Sufi perspective. Coming from an established ulema family, he received exceptional training from a very early age starting with his father, Hızır Beg, the first judge of Istanbul after the conquest. Thanks to his erudition, he was appointed as preceptor to Mehmed II and became a confidante of the sultan, a relation that led to his appointment to the rank of vizier, at a time when Mehmed II crushed the influence of the ulema and promoted his palace-trained recruits to high ranks in government. Probably as a result of an intrigue orchestrated by rival ulema and statesmen, he later incurred the wrath of Mehmed II and was dismissed from his position. He narrowly escaped execution through the intercession of many leading scholars of the time on his behalf. After his dismissal, he fully devoted himself to the Sufi path and became an initiate of the head of the

Zeyniyye order of Shaykh Vefa (d. 1491), one of the most revered mystics of his time. His fame and stature were restored with the succession of Bayezid II to the throne, during whose reign he wrote all of his Turkish works, some of which are masterpieces of the fledgling Turkish prose.

Maʿārifnāme reflects Sinan Paşa's vast learning as much as his mystical itinerary: "My aim is to say a few words on moral purification. Some advice would be added and whatever comes to mind would be put down. Although I reiterate what Plato had said, I take it from the Qur'an and prophetic traditions."[50] It is an encyclopedic work in scope following no particular genre, a collection of instructive advice on various topics ranging from philosophy to poetry, aimed at moral purification and spiritual perfection. While his ideas in *Maʿārifnāme* testify that Sinan Paşa was an erudite scholar well versed in traditional learning, the way he composed the work shows that he was an antinomian, uneasy with following established conventions of his time. In addition to his sporadic thoughts and advice regarding rulership that are scattered throughout the work, *Maʿārifnāme* contains a number of topics related to government, the vizierate, the sultanate, and justice. By resorting to strong and personal language in his criticism of the vizier, he implied that he held the vizier responsible for his own demise.[51] The work paints a bleak picture of the moral and scholarly standards of his time with a sense of disappointment and vanity of life to which, as a response, he proposes a spiritual rehabilitation and moral purification. When he discussed issues of government and rulership, he identified the reasons for corruption and provided a brief prescription, consisting of moral recuperations and time-tested principles of government.

Sinan Paşa's younger contemporary historian Tursun Beg (d. after 1490), who worked in various scribal positions before becoming treasurer in the reign of Mehmed II, does not display the explicit Sufistic mindset of other political authors of his generation.[52] He came from a military family and accompanied the restless Mehmed II in his numerous military campaigns. He worked in the service of Grand Vizier Mahmud Paşa, whose love of learning attracted many scholars to his entourage.[53] Tursun Beg prided himself on the training he received from the grand vizier.[54] His only known work is *Tārīḫ-i Ebū'l-Feth̩*, a narrative history of Mehmed II's campaigns, written from an eyewitness perspective.[55] He wrote a long introduction to this history, which stands alone as a separate work on rulership. Among other books of philosophy, as he calls them, he consulted and cited Tusi's *Akhlāq-i Nāṣirī* in composing the section.[56] Although *Tārīḫ-i Ebū'l-Feth̩* was crafted as a theoretical exposition on political philosophy with a sophisticated terminology, bearing in mind that it was written at a time when Prince Djem (d. 1495) was still a contender for the throne, Tursun Beg's main objective surfaces as the elimination of doubts about the legitimacy of Ottoman rule. Addressing a broader audience than the ruler and statesmen, his writing turns markedly panegyric when emphasizing Bayezid II's superior moral qualities. After proving human beings' need for rulership, he emphatically argued that the status of the ruler is second only to that of the prophet. As such, the position of the ruler was the highest in the world and one that required full submission. The work exalted Bayezid II as the ideal ruler, and Mahmud Paşa, the grand vizier of Mehmed II, as an ideal grand vizier. When explaining the moral traits required of the ruler, Tursun Beg proudly stated that he would simply list those of Bayezid II. After profiling the perfect ruler, Tursun Beg reported Mahmud Paşa's responses to questions regarding rulership, government, and ethics. He then illustrated Mahmud Paşa's resolutions with historical cases and anecdotes from the experience of past rulers. *Tārīḫ-i Ebū'l-Feth̤* is not only one of the earliest Turkish texts to genuinely deal with political thought but, by virtue of its being a history book, it appears to be the first one that took Ottoman experience in government into account in developing political theory.

Yet, despite its novelty in introducing the Ottoman experience into political discourse, Tursun Beg's work was still a chronicle, not a well-rounded treatise on political thought. Nevertheless, the text speaks for a new consciousness in political reasoning: the Ottoman elite in the second half of the fifteenth century grew confident enough to present their own achievements as a benchmark of good government. Reflecting this new attitude, one of the first political texts that emphatically portrays Ottoman rulership as a model was composed by a contemporary of Tursun Beg who chose to remain anonymous to the reader. *Mukhtaṣar fī al-Siyāsa wa Umūr al-Salṭana* (Compendium of Governance and Affairs of Rulership) was composed in Arabic and dedicated to Bayezid II with a clear agenda: to promote Mehmed II's style of governance as a response to the dramatic shift in rulership. As hinted by contemporaries, Bayezid II was the least favorite of Mehmed's heirs and certainly much less resembled his father than did Prince Djem in both character and management skills. Both his admirers and adversaries portrayed Bayezid II as a deeply spiritual personality with strong attachment to powerful figures outside the court. The text does not show a trace of Sufism in conceiving rulership or the practice of government and does not aim to cater to the specific expectations of the reigning ruler.

The author seems to be an outsider by origin, in the sense that he is neither of *devşirme* origin or the product of the Ottoman learned establishment, which was still largely dominated by a Muslim-born Turkish-speaking constituency. Nor was he one of many eastern émigrés who flooded the flourishing Ottoman court from different Persianate dynasties of Iran, Caucasia, and Central Asia. Despite concealing his identity, textual evidence points that he arrived from Mamluk domains, most probably from Egypt. The Mamluk origin of the author is more significant in understanding the course of Ottoman political thought than in merely establishing his cultural identity. First of all, the text carries the unmistakable marks of the vast fifteenth-century Mamluk literature on government in the broader tradition of Arabic mirrors for princes. This trait makes the *Mukhtaṣar* the earliest Ottoman text composed in the style of Arabic-Mamluk mirrors. In comparison to their Persian cousins, Arabic-Mamluk mirrors tended to be less abstract, more hierarchical, imbued with juristic rulings, and written for a military elite. The author manifestly finds that the Mamluk ideals in government best represent those of the Ottomans. Mehmed II's policy of replacing the Turkish aristocracy with trained officials of *devşirme* origin brought the Ottoman system closer to the Mamluk model and distanced it from Persianate governments of the east. Yet the author is still keen on pointing to major differences between the two polities.

Mukhtaṣar is an administrative manual for the sultan and his dignitaries. Disregarding the customary panegyric for Bayezid II that defines the sultan as the ruler of the time, there is no glorification or extolment of the Ottoman sultan. The only specific designation used in the text is to portray the sultan as the Prophet's successor (*khalīfat Rasūl Allāh*), which is a strictly juristic term.[57] The text does not promote a particular conception of rulership but rather principles of good governance under five topics that include the sultan's management of the self, the dignitaries, neighboring rulers, and enemies. The extensively illustrated text involves anecdotes and long stories from jurists, philosophers, and statesmen but not from the legendary rulers of antiquity. Besides those of the Ayyubid and Mamluk sultans, the only notable story was narrated from the Roman emperor Constantine, the founder of the newly conquered Constantinople, on dealing with enemies. Two oft-presented key figures of good government are Aristotle and Bozorgmehr, two legendary viziers of the lands of Rum and Persia. Such world rulers as Solomon, Alexander, Ardashir, al-Ma'mun, and the like, who would be granted a new fame as the only comparable rulers during the reigns of Selim I and Süleyman I, are not mentioned at all. But, with a grain of irony, this may well be what is intended by the author, namely, singling out Mehmed II as the sole model of governance.

Mukhtaṣar is also a training manual for the new configuration of the Ottoman state with an expanding bureaucracy and a large contingent of courtiers for which Mehmed II's management is presented as a precedent to be upheld by later rulers. As profiled, Mehmed II's rulership and observation of principles of government rest on good morals and manners, with their effectiveness proven by past models and religious rulings. The text further elaborates a moral regime to govern rather than establishing the laws and structures of an ideal government. A good many stories convey morals pertaining to skillful management of differences, steering through intrigues, pleasing the privileged and the ruled at once, appeasing discontent, and duly eliminating adversaries. As evinced by a series of high-profile executions of high-ranking officials, the imperial period from the very start showed that governing the government became at least as important as governing the subjects. On one occasion, *Mukhtaṣar* recounts, a serious breach of trust that involved conflicting testimonies of high officials was resolved by consulting with the official registers of the state (*defter*).[58] As displayed by *Mukhtaṣar*, the empirical approach to rulership, namely, promoting the Ottoman precedence in government as a benchmark for good governance, received increasingly more attention from later Ottomans, especially from the bureaucrat authors writing on laws and institutions.

Although *Mukhtaṣar* did not seem to have reached a wider audience or have any visible impact on later authors, it nevertheless stands as a clear milestone in Ottoman political writing. Excluding occasional references to praiseworthy deeds of Ottoman sultans in a hagiographical style, as in the case of Ankari's *Enīsü'l-Celīs*, a typical work on rulership, whether a translation or an original composition, would involve plenty of historical stories to illustrate and promote principles of good governance, all taken from pre-Ottoman dynasties. This conspicuous absence of Ottoman rulers in political treatises, however, is not surprising. First of all, there was already a vast literature in circulation, offering an extensive repertoire of maxims, aphorisms, and stories from idealized rulers of the past. For every conventional principle of good governance there was already a set of illustrations that became standard quotes in a large number of kin texts. Second, despite all their achievements and fame, in literary representation, Ottoman rulers were still *gazi* rulers depicted in the fashion of pious and chivalrous heroes of folk epics that were so popular in western Anatolia. The rapid advent of history writing during the reign of Bayezid II started to profile Ottoman sultans with the same imageries as the legendary kings of the past and crowned the Ottoman dynasty as part of the noble lineage of world empires, thus offering a sanctified reservoir of exemplary deeds for later political authors to tap for in-house references for good governance. But instead of anecdotally replacing the past icons of kingship as a display of items of exemplary traits, in the writings of bureaucrat authors, Ottoman rulers made their debut as state-building prophetic figures in the sense that, with divine guidance, they set the precedences of ideal government that should be maintained and protected from corruption.

Despite the novelties it offered, *Mukhtaṣar* was still a moral treatise that considered rulership as an extension of one's government of the self. But it manifested an evolving consciousness among statesmen and their advisors in distancing rulership from morality by giving primacy to institutions and laws of government over the moral qualifications of the ruler. An early endeavor in this pursuit was undertaken by Şemseddin Jahrami, who wrote a short but dense treatise for Selim I in 1513, *Risāla Barāya Sulṭān Selīm* (Treatise for Sultan Selim).[59] Jahrami was not a notable figure, probably from Jahram, a small town south of Shiraz in Iran. His long eulogy, crafted to gain the heart of the ruler, his highlighting of the Sultan's fight against infidels and heretics, and his appeal for his work to be accepted suggest that he was one of many Sunni scholars who fled the Safavid persecution to take refuge in the land of Rum and look for a new patron.

As much as the preface of the book is a fine example of ornate literary Persian, the main body of the book was written in compact but plain Persian in the familiar idiom of mirrors for princes. Regardless of the author's personal aspirations in presenting the book as a gift, *Risāla* proves to be a very sophisticated work of political theory as well as a practical handbook for the sultan in governance. The treatise consists of three sets of admonitions (*tanbīh*): on the government of self (*siyāsat-i nafs*), of the retinue (*siyāsat-i khāssa*), and of the commons (*siyāsat-i 'āmma*). Although well versed in political theory, Jahrami did not quote a particular authority or depend on any classical work on the subject. He displayed little concern with the juristic, theological, or spiritual aspects of rulership but instead focused on the practical rules of statecraft. The treatise makes little use of poetry, Qur'anic verses, or prophetic traditions, and does not illustrate admonitions with exemplary stories, a feature that distinguishes it from a typical advice book of the Persianate tradition. The presentation of political advice through three layers of government owes its origins to medieval canons of ethical philosophy that typically divide ethics into three categories such as government of self (*tadbīr al-nafs*), of household (*manzil*), and of cities (*mudun*).[60]

In *Risāla*, Jahrami's political philosophy rests on three principal convictions about rulership. First, he envisioned the ruler to be in full control of government and then catered his teachings to inculcating a strong ruler who governs his self, retinue, and subjects effectively. Jahrami found the ideal ruler in the personality of Selim I, as he considered him in the same line as the legendary world conquerors. Writing in 1513, before Selim's eastern and southern campaigns, Jahrami ended his preface by praying for the extension of Selim's rule from China to Cairo, a wishful prophecy that partly came true only four years later with the conquest of Egypt.[61] Second, because he envisioned a strong sultan, Jahrami made the question of improving and preserving the sultan's physical potency and moral purity a priority to address in his treatise, a concern that led him to prescribe specific instructions for maintaining complete health. In contrast with the prevailing admonitions, he even privileged the sultan's health over his piety and permitted him to drink wine.[62] Third, he envisaged rulership as governance through the medium of institutionalized functions, in the way it was elaborated in Nizam al-Mulk's *Siyāsatnāma*, and tied good government to the efficiency of its institutions. Unlike a typical advice book that would cater these ideals through the medium of literary devices, Jahrami opted to give a full profile of a well-functioning state. In accordance with Ottoman practice, for example, he divided the ruling elite (*khāssa*) into two categories, inner (*andarūn*) and outer (*bīrūn*).[63] He then elaborated on the organization of the outer section that corresponded to the government around ten major offices and established principles of administering the officials working in these services. Whether intentionally or because Jahrami was an outsider, his portrayal of an ideal state does not perfectly overlap with the status quo of the time but still offers a benchmark for good government.

While Jahrami was hoping to gain access to the ruling circle of the Ottoman sultan by offering a book on statecraft, the towering figure at Selim's court as political philosopher, advisor, and statesman was Idris b. Hüsameddin el-Bidlisi, whose impact on Ottoman self-perception pales that of any other scholar of his generation. Bidlisi was by far the most successful and the best known of the scholar statesmen who emigrated from an eastern court to the Ottoman Empire in this period. On the collapse of the Aqquyunlu dynasty, where he was a court secretary and a tutor for princes, he left his home in search of a new patron and entered Ottoman service.[64] Bayezid II was already aware of his secretarial skills and excellence in prose writing thanks to a series of diplomatic letters he composed on behalf of the Aqquyunlu rulers and sent to the Ottoman court. After joining Bayezid's court in 1502, he quickly established himself as a prolific author depite failing to attain the status he had expected. That rapid rise as an outsider inevitably earned him more foes than friends. Even though he received generous gifts for his service from Bayezid II, he felt underrated and had a strained relationship with a powerful palace faction headed by Grand Vizier Ali Paşa and his former friend Müeyyedzade (d. 1516), a fellow scholar from the same Persianate tradition who was a student of Bidlisi's teacher Jalal al-Din Davvani (d. 1502). After a long battle with his adversaries, he obtained the sultan's permission to go on a pilgrimage in 1511 and moved to Mecca after a brief sojourn in Cairo.[65] During his self-imposed exile, Bidlisi spent time at the Mamluk court of Cairo and later continued to flirt with the Safavids to gauge the possibility of joining their administration.[66]

On Selim I's succession in 1512 he was recalled to service once more, to which he responded with enthusiasm and arrived at the Ottoman court in 1513 after a risky journey slowed down by a plague outbreak. During his second tenure in Ottoman service, his statesmanship prevailed over his scholarship, marked by a series of critical diplomatic missions and administrative positions. In addition to his scholarly and literary credentials, his family connections and inherent knowledge of the buffer zone between the Ottoman and Safavid spheres of influence made him an ideal diplomat to broker a deal with the unruly chieftains of these areas, populated mostly by Kurdish tribes.[67] His success in incorporating eastern Asia Minor under Ottoman authority and securing order in the region at a time when Ottoman rule faced the greatest threat from the east earned him the unquestioned confidence of Selim I, a sultan who found it difficult to trust even the most trustworthy statesmen. In his name, a third office of military judgeship, the highest ulema rank after the sheikh ul Islam, was created for Arabs and Persians (*ʿArab ve ʿAcem ḳāḍīʿaskerliği*), a position that was dissolved only a year after his retirement.[68]

Bidlisi was a versatile scholar and a prolific author who wrote on such diverse subjects as history, music, cosmology, medicine, philosophy, poetry,

Sufism, and jurisprudence.[69] Coming from a learned family, he received a solid training in classical Islamic sciences as well as in literature, philosophy, and Sufism. He was born and raised in Ray, today's Tehran, in a cultural environment where Nurbakhshiyya, a branch of Kubrawiyya with a Shiite and messianic bent, had a strong presence. His father, Husam al-Din Ali, a respected scholar, was a disciple of the founder of this order, Sayyid Muhammed Nurbakhsh (d. 1464), and well connected with the broader Sufi and scholarly community of the Persianate world. Bidlisi's exposure to Sufism at an early age through his father's nexus of mystics had a defining mark on his thought and pursuits in life.[70] Throughout his career, at multiple courts and in between, he lived and traveled extensively in a region spanning from Iran to Egypt. His roster of royal patrons to whom he dedicated works include the Aqquyunlu ruler Yaqub Beg, the Mamluk Sultan Ghansu Ghavri, and the Ottoman sultans Bayezid II and Selim I.[71] His equally impressive network of scholars and mystics included such venerated names of his time as Abd al-Rahman Jami (d. 1492), Davvani, and Ibrahim-i Gülşeni (d. 1534).[72] Bidlisi arrived in Istanbul as a seasoned student of Persianate learning in literature, Sufism, philosophy, and administrative traditions that made him a rare find for the Ottoman court, which was yet to make itself visible in the royal language of the literary high society dominated by masterful poets and prose writers in the service of eastern courts.

Bidlisi, like many other Persianate literati before and after him, was not a devout servant of the Ottoman dynasty and certainly did not share the Rumi identity of the broader ruling establishment. Despite acting as a Sunni, he did not seem to have a strong sectarian affiliation either. Like many in the Persianate nexus of the learned, such as Jami, Davvani, and Kashifi, he smoothly navigated between Sunni and Shiite spirituality mediated by Sufism with little regard to theology. He belittled other Ottoman histories written before him for their simple language, crude style, and misinformation.[73] He did not get along well with statesmen and the learned at the Ottoman court, even with Müeyyedzade, who came from a similar educational background. He glorified and vilified both Bayezid and Shah Isma'il on different occasions but in similar terms. He could offer his services to any of the Turko-Mongolian courts with equal ease and a reserved loyalty. He displayed clear signs that he could write the same work for any ruler or statesman by just revising its dedication. But these qualities do not make him a treacherously opportunistic professional marketing his literary expertise and refined statesmanship for the highest bidder. Not being firmly connected with a particular medrese, Sufi order, or chancery, Bidlisi's primary affiliation was with the Persianate republic of letters whose defining marker was Persian literary humanism in the sense that, in Dabashi's observation, "this humanism belonged to no ethnicity, but to the language and literary imagination in which it was produced."[74] He came to the Ottoman court as a refugee but, at the same time, as a representative of

Persianate learning and finesse that he thought represented a higher level of humanistic and artistic refinement. Whether writing on history or rulership, coated by glamorous literary devices of the Persian language were humanistic ideals he promoted to inculcate the perfect ruler as portrayed in the post-Mongol Persianate tradition. But the structurally different Ottoman court limited Bidlisi's influence and forcefully inserted a distance between him and the sultan. Hence despite all the favors he received from Bayezid II, he remained a chronic malcontent for feeling underrated.

Bidlisi composed four works of note that extensively dealt with the question of rulership, two in history and two in political theory. While still a newly arrived stranger in Istanbul, he composed the first exclusive history of the Ottoman dynasty in Persian at the behest of Bayezid II. *Hasht Behesht* (Eight Gardens), completed in slightly more than two years in 1506, is a work of art in its prose, a comprehensive account of the first two centuries of Ottoman history, and a philosophical interpretation of events that make it a milestone in Ottoman historical writing.[75] Bidlisi was fully cognizant of the propagandistic significance of his history at a time when the integrity of the Ottoman state was seriously threatened for the first time since the Timurid invasion. After leaving Istanbul as a resentful historian in 1511, he courteously blackmailed Bayezid to honor the pledges given to him by telling the sultan that he would not complete the introduction and the conclusion of the work, and that the work had already started to circulate far and wide unfinished.[76] He finalized the work only on his return to the Ottoman court two years later at the new sultan's invitation. *Hasht Behesht*'s impact on Ottoman historiography was immediate, defining, and long lasting.[77] He composed the work on the model of such memorializing histories of the Ilkhanid and the Timurid courts as those by Ata Malik Juvayni (d. 1283), Vassaf (d. 1329–30), Mu'in al-Din Yazdi (d. 1387), and Sharaf al-Din Ali Yazdi (d. 1454).[78] *Hasht Behesht* is the epitome of Ottoman myth-making efforts that started with Yazıcıoğlu's *Tārīḫ-i Āl-i Selçūḳ* (The History of the House of Seljuk) of which the first part, better known as *Oğuznāme* (The Book of the Oghuz), constructed a noble genealogy for the newly structuring Ottoman state in the wake of the Tirmurid catastrophe.[79] What makes this work unique is that, in interpreting history and profiling Ottoman rulers, Bidlisi fully incorporated the canonical teachings of Islamic ethical and political literature, the royal language of Persian chanceries, and the idiom of Sufism. More specifically, Bidlisi offered the House of Osman a grand narrative of dynastic history with the finest exposition of the mystical conceptions of the caliphate that were reverberating forcefully from Cairo to Samarkand in the post-Abbasid world. The unusually elaborate and idealized sultanic profiles of *Hasht Behesht* demonstrated how Bidlisi wished them to be rather than how he perceived them.

Bidlisi's main work on rulership was *Qānūn-i Shāhanshāhī* (The Essence of Kingship), which seems to have been completed before Bayezid's reign ended in 1512. He wrote the work in four parts as a guide for rulers (*dustūrnāma*): the nature of rulership, ethics of government, responsibilities of the ruler, and the attainment of spiritual authority.[80] With few stories of illustration, *Qānūn-i Shāhanshāhī* is primarily a work of political philosophy written from a markedly Sufi perspective. Despite his trenchant synthesis of philosophical, theological, and juristic doctrines of rulership, Bidlisi's terminological framework was drawn mostly from Sufism, with particular debt to the mystical philosophies of Shahab al-Din Yahya al-Suhrawardi and Ibn Arabi through their interlocutors such as Davvani.[81] It is a comprehensive treatise covering all principal aspects of rulership, ranging from the vizierate to law, and from ethics to principles of government. Bidlisi considered rulership an extension of God's divine government and predicated it on moral perfection, which he defined as the ruler's resemblance to God in His attributes. Before elaborating on principles of government, Bidlisi wrote an epistemological introduction to establish the necessity of rulership.[82] Much like the Suhrawardian exposition, his notion of authority is grounded in epistemology.[83] He divided knowledge (*ʿilm*) into two categories: "knowledge appropriate for Godservants" (*ʿilm-i khādim*) and "the knowledge of God" (*ʿilm-i makhdūm*). The ultimate purpose of existence was to attain knowledge of the Served, which was the knowledge of God (*maʿrifat Allāh*). The servant knowledge, which he defined as the conventional disciplines of Islamic learning, was only instrumental in leading to the Served knowledge. This distinction roughly corresponds to the exoteric learning and the esoteric experience. As a reflection of this epistemic duality, Bidlisi divided practice into two categories as "practice appropriate for Godservants" (*ʿamal-i khādim*) versus "practice of God" (*ʿamal-i makhdūm*), and then placed rulership within the second category because he considered it to be a part of higher knowledge and practice.[84]

Bidlisi wrote two other less known works with political import. He composed *Mirʾāt al-Jamāl* in 1503 for Bayezid, soon after he arrived at the Ottoman court, perhaps as an early demonstration of how he could profile the Ottoman ruler.[85] Rather than advising on rulership or proper governance, the work portrays the perfect human being, ergo the perfect ruler, in the tradition of Persianate literary humanism. Bidlisi's discursive language and florid style replete with symbols and metaphors, perhaps deliberately, obscures or even mystifies the message but nonetheless creates majestic imageries. In substance, it is a prelude to his *Hasht Behesht* and *Qānūn-i Shāhanshāhī,* into which it is partly incorporated. While Bidlisi made a splashy debut into the elite literary circle of Istanbul with *Mirʾāt al-Jamāl,* he crowned it with *Selīmshāhnāma* (The Book of Selim Shah), a glorifying account of the reign of Selim I, toward the end of his life in 1520.[86] He composed the work as a sequel to *Hasht Behesht*, with the claim of outshining it, for Selim had surpassed all his predecessors in glory. Yet, despite manifesting his literary virtuosity at its best, *Selīmshāhnāma* is less doctrinal and more empirical. But more than a mere record of events, the work is an interpretive history of the reign of Selim I, whose life served as an illustration of the political ideals Bidlisi advocated. Inspired by Ferdowsi's *Shāhnāma* and imitated by many afterwards, including Celalzade's *Selīmnāme*, Bidlisi crafted this work as an epic narrative to inscribe Selim I in Ottoman memory as a universal ruler and a role model.

The Age of Perfection: From Engagement to Exceptionalism

Outshined by the oft-quoted glittering achievements of the reign of Süleyman was a little noticed but unprecedented upsurge of interest among intellectuals of all proclivities in writing on rulership. No fewer than thirty texts on various aspects of rulership were written during his long reign of almost half a century, more than the total number of political works composed in the preceding two centuries of the Ottomans. The same is true for the number of translations and reworkings of non-Ottoman political texts that reflect changing interests and tastes among the broadening readership. This diverse body of political literature, written in different languages and genres, was produced by an equally diverse group of authors from various backgrounds who belonged to different segments of society and was accompanied by an expanding reading community who developed a new appetite to converse on public issues. A good number of texts that turned into canons of Ottoman political thought in later centuries, such as Kınalızade's *Aḫlāḳ-ı ʿAlāʾī* and Lütfi Paşa's *Āṣafnāme*, were composed during this period. There is no single phenomenon to pinpoint as triggering this rising political consciousness during the reign of Süleyman. But a number of developments proved particularly conducive for the rise of political writings and their spread among the Ottoman readership. The influx of eastern Sunni scholars seeking refuge from the Safavid expansion; the integration of major centers of learning from Baghdad to Cairo into the imperial cultural orbit; the rise of a wealthy but insecure class of ruling elite that valued literary production, with a particular hunger for manuals of statecraft; the triumphant self-perception of the Ottomans as the final heirs to the lineage of world-conquering empires; confessional anxieties sparked by the Kizilbash ordeal and a series of uprisings by defiant Sufi groups; millenarian excitement stirred by the dawning of the first millennium of the Islamic calendar; and rivalries among princes, political factions, social groups, schools of thought, and spiritual proclivities all added to the growing interest in writing and reading on rulership.

The ruling establishment of the sixteenth century Ottoman Empire was not as orderly as both the Ottoman sources and contemporary scholarship lead us to believe. While the steady wave of institutionalization that started with the reign of Mehmed II continued in full bloom, the Empire also incorporated the vastly different local structures and conventions of newly conquered territories, spanning from Iraq to Hungary, into its central governing apparatus that permanently transformed the Ottoman state and the way it was governed. While the empire's territory doubled in the life of one generation in the early sixteenth century, Ottoman educational institutions had no difficulty in meeting the demand for new administrative and judicial positions. On the contrary, a surplus of graduates by the mid-sixteenth century caused serious tensions between the unemployed population of learned men and the government that led to widespread student uprisings.[87]

Because the Ottoman political culture equated philanthropy with good governance and the established conventions of state did not accord the same protection to statesmen's property as that of subjects, the Ottoman ruling elite were eager to convert their accumulated wealth to social prestige by way of investing in public works such as libraries, schools, hospitals, and the like.[88] Ancient Turkic customs of sharing the accumulated wealth appeared still in effect in early Ottoman history, only further enhanced by Islamic and Persian traditions of good governance.[89] Besides their own interest and taste in courtly life and companionship, these statesmen were socially compelled to offer patronage to famed scholars and artists in order to promote and sustain their public images as benefactors.[90] While the explosive growth of Ottoman ruling institutions, from the judiciary to administrative bureaucracy, created an ambitious class of statesmen curious about the craft of governance, an increasing number of Ottoman learned men and literati who mostly congregated around dignitaries were eager to write on the subject to improve their own prospects.[91] With the increasing surplus of manpower trained in palace schools, military facilities, madrasas, Sufi hospices, and courts of dignitaries, Ottoman high society turned into a cruelly competitive stratum and so was the realm of political ideals, imageries, and recipes of rewarding achievement. Both statesmen and their learned clients had to walk a fine line marked by social etiquette, group loyalties, ideological commitments, and imperatives of realpolitik. For statesmen, similar to the education of princes, reading works of statecraft became an indispensable component of training. This demand created a vibrant marketplace for copying, translating, abridging, and compiling treatises on rulership catering to varying literary tastes, linguistic capabilities, and levels of comprehension.

The institutional and territorial growth of the empire spawned a large contingent of statesmen, bureaucrats, men of learning, and affiliate communities who sought to shape Ottoman rulership and the imperial establishment per their interests and ideals as manifested in a series of succession struggles that plagued the latter half of Süleyman's reign. This new political configuration made the education of princes even more important than before. Despite the smooth transition of power to Süleyman and his subsequent long rule of forty-six years during which he faced no serious challenge, his reign witnessed violent clashes among his sons to position themselves for succession. Until

Selim I's rebellion against his father, Bayezid II, struggles of succession among the contenders turned violent only after the death of the ruling sultan.[92] As his father's only son and heir apparent, Süleyman was among the few rulers since the inception of the Ottoman state to succeed without a contender.[93] His grandfather and father, however, despite both being the underdogs in the contest, had succeeded only after exhausting clashes with their brothers. These internecine rivalries divided the empire into spheres of authority and led to the formation of political factions supporting contenders with vested interests. As the three hopeful princes Mustafa, Bayezid, and Selim grew older during Süleyman's long reign, they formed their own political factions within the administration, military, and the palace as well as their clientele among poets, ulema, and shaykhs.[94] Further, rivalries among princes were inherently vulnerable to turn into full-blown proxy wars between interest groups which, at times, may involve outside powers, as in the cases of Djem, Murad, and Bayezid, who ended up as bargaining chips at the hands of Ottoman rivals.[95]

Although Süleyman was fortunate to inherit the rulership of the empire intact with the sealed and enthusiastic support of the ruling establishment, his sons drew an important lesson from the case of Selim about how the throne was attained. Süleyman, a man of exceptional literary talents and a patron of scholars, assigned distinguished tutors to his princes to prepare them for the throne. As governors of their respective provinces, these princes founded their own courts that mocked the one in Istanbul and gathered tutors, advisers, influential ulema, and poets under their patronage.[96] Manisa and Amasya, for example, emerged as two major centers of learning in the sixteenth century thanks to housing the provincial courts of the two most senior contenders for succession.[97] As proven by previous struggles of succession, being the father's favorite was often misleading in calculating one's chances of becoming the next sultan. Instead, a contender needed to show outstanding performance as a governor and garner support from the ruling establishment. This challenge made the education of princes in statecraft an indispensable component of their survival strategies. In response, sixteenth-century intellectuals and tutors looked eager to supply these insecure princes with translations of political works as a practical way of preparing manuals of rulership. Translations had an added value for political writing by enabling the translator to convey his own ideas under the names of more authoritative figures in Islamic learning and Sufism. No political work is known to have been translated and dedicated to Süleyman during his princeship but, only a generation later, offering the canons of Islamic political literature in Turkish translation to the contending princes became commonplace.

If the political arena was torn by dynastic struggles and factional clashes, intellectual life during the Süleymanic era was marked by a series of resounding controversies among scholars, Sufis, poets, and statesmen. The process of institutionalization, canonization, and lawmaking was accompanied by a broad-based public debate on questions concerning religion, government, and social life. The spread of interactive spaces such as grand mosques, madrasas, Sufi lodges, marketplaces, and coffeehouses after the 1550s, in tandem with increased mobility among the ulema, dervishes, statesmen, and merchants, turned otherwise local issues into public discourse, some resonating from Syria to Bosnia. The bureaucratization of the ulema and the general proximity of Ottoman men of learning to the government facilitated the perception of scholarly disputes as political matters. Further, proponents of particular views and interests turned otherwise apolitical social and religious issues into political questions in a quest to gain the support of the Ottoman authority. Heresy (*zandaḳa*), harmful innovations (*bidʿa*), cash foundations (*vaḳf-ı nuḳūd*), slave property, land law, and Sufi rituals were but a few issues that were debated with varying intensity and political ramifications. As in the cases of Prince Korkud (d. 1513) and Grand Vizier Lütfi Paşa, at times members of the dynastic family or high-ranking statesmen participated in controversies in their scholarly and intellectual capacities.[98] Few of these debates directly problematized conceptions of rulership or challenged the legitimacy of the ruler. Yet, because of their relevance to government and social order, they nevertheless resonated across different audiences.

The social and cultural developments of this period were conducive to the rise of a broad-based and diversified public discourse on issues that reflected the social ideals, interests, and sensibilities of the politically attuned. The spread of a diverse body of Sufi orders with creative social ideals, world views, and rituals gained broad appeal across all layers of Ottoman society, including the ruling elite, which created a lingering source of friction and suspicion between them and the conventional structures of authority within the ruling establishment.[99] The fascinatingly diversified Ottoman spiritual space, populated by numerous Sufi orders as well as nondenominational mystics, was often shaken by doctrinal splits as much as convergences with strong political underpinnings.[100] The common ground for Sufism was their esotericism, which was also their main source of differentiation as, by virtue of their distinct epistemology, there cannot be a verifiable source of doctrines, rituals, and social organization. Accusations of heresy were more common among the Sufis than between them as a collectivity and the ulema. The broader Halvetiyye order, for example, always housed widely divergent mystics ranging from those who rebelled against Ottoman rule to those who turned into its staunchest supporters.[101] Bayrami and Melami orders were no different. Bali Efendi (d. 1553) of Halvetiyye and Ibn Isa (d. 1559–60) of Bayramiyye, for example, were writing treatises in praise of the Ottoman dynasty while their fellow shaykhs of the same orders were facing trials.[102] The Ottoman ruling elite, particularly its juristic and bureaucratic core, was particularly sensitive to ideas and movements that were perceived to be a threat to social order, stability, or the political legitimacy of the Ottoman ruler. The long-lasting Ibn Arabi controversy, for example, was not simply a theological dispute among concerned doctors of Islam or pious vigilantes. At a time when Ibn Arabi was fast gaining the status of a patron saint for the Ottomans, rejecting or accepting his ideas had far-reaching repercussions for the legitimacy of the Ottoman dynasty, how rulership was conceived, and the status and privileges of Sufi orders that considered him as the Greatest Shaykh.[103] In this vibrant and electrifying intellectual atmosphere, political discourse served as one of the principal venues where social tensions were mediated and newly conceived social ideals were put into circulation.

The overall confessional awareness of the sixteenth century was long in the making as different sectors of Ottoman society, including Sufi groups, the ulema, and the *gazi* establishment, increasingly expressed their conflicts with one another or the central government by aligning themselves with deeper sectarian and theological divides of Islamic history and the contemporary Muslim community. As the case of Molla Kabız (d. 1527) heresy shows, the Ottoman ruling elite grew more sensitive to divergent theological views with potential political implications. He was charged for claiming the superiority of Jesus over Muhammed, tried, and executed.[104] Yet, conflicts among the ulema were more personal, prompted by patronage networks and to some degree by differences of opinion, and hardly amounted to theological disputes with charges of heresy. Even the spectacular execution of Molla Lütfi (d. 1495) on charges of heresy was, as commonly believed by his contemporaries, a result of a typical ulema jealousy rather than doctrinal sensitivity of the scholarly establishment.[105] An exceptionally accomplished scholar and teacher of many later high-profile Ottoman jurists, Molla Lütfi was instantly memorialized by his colleagues and, soon after his death, unanimously remembered as a martyr in all subsequent Ottoman biographical and historical sources.[106] Among the Sufis, however, conflicts were predicated on more visible doctrinal and social questions. Despite differences of opinion, the ulema still maintained their esprit de corps as a self-disciplining network of learning. Self-criticism, accusation, jealousy, and completion were but the normal state of affairs in ulema life at all times. In retirement, former grand vizier Lütfi Paşa warned his successor: "The ulema, judges, and professors are in constant state of jealousy against one another. So, do not take seriously what they say. Only consult with the head of the ulema."[107] Similarly, Prince Korkud, who ventured into the scheming world of Ottoman learning, felt utterly dismayed by the moral decay of the ulema. While criticizing the ulema for corruption, he accused a number of Sufi groups and high-profile mystics, past and present, of apostasy.[108]

Granted that confessional lines and identities often remained contested, fluid, porous, and blurred, Ottoman society at large went through a process of Sunnitization and non-Sunnitization at once.[109] If Sunnism was better established and defined in the sixteenth century, so were many other groups despite being marginalized. In fact, the increasingly Sunni color of the Ottoman ruling establishment made non-Sunni characteristics of various confessional communities in society more visible. The widely shared Alid-piety of both Sunni and Shiite proclivities, for example, turned into two distinct forms of Alid-loyalism in service to two competing political ideologies. In refence to religious affiliations in early Ottoman society, Cemal Kafadar defined metadoxy as "a state of being beyond doxies, a combination of being doxy-naive and not being doxy-minded." In the context of Ottoman–Safavid conflict, the Sunnitization and Shiitization turned the once meta-doxic character of Alid-piety into politically charged and theologically sanctioned sectarian identities.[110] Sufi orders, such as the Halvetiyye and the Bayramiyye, with strong attachments to Alid-piety at both doctrinal and spiritual levels increasingly, and often apologetically, felt compelled to express their teachings in Sunni vocabulary. At the same time, Ottoman rulers such as Bayezid sought to turn the Alid sensibilities of these orders from a liability to an asset in countering the more powerful Alid call of the Safavids.[111]

While the Ottoman Sunni establishment suppressed or appeased dissent among the ulema and antinomian Sufis with relative ease, the Safavid threat that sparked a widespread sectarian opposition among Turkoman subjects of the sultan posed a more serious challenge. The Ottoman ulema, who were in disagreement on many issues among themselves, were deeply concerned about the appeal of the Safavid propaganda in Asia Minor and the Balkans, and were almost unanimous in their opposition to Shiite confessions. High-profile jurists such as Sarıgörez Nureddin Hamza (d. 1522), Ibn Kemal, and Ebussuud, despite having different opinions on the nature of the Safavid heresy and how to confront them, all strived to show the irreconcilable differences between the Sunnis and Shiites.[112] Not only did the Ottoman men of learning write refutations of Shiite beliefs and issue legal opinions to invalidate them, but they also articulated anti-Shiite views in political treatises.[113] The messianic cast of the Safavid ideology also compelled the apologists of the Ottoman dynasty to devise formulations of rulership to offset challenges to legitimacy, and to profile the Ottoman ruler as superior to all others. The Safavid challenge generated a new interest in Sunni theories of rulership, with particular attention to juristic and theological underpinnings.[114]

At a time when the general Sunni-consciousness reflected itself on matters of faith, the more specific Hanafi views on matters of law became more pronounced in the political literature. A number of high-profile jurists, most notably Ebussuud and Ibn Kemal, managed to reformulate Ottoman law and government in accordance with the precepts of Hanafi jurisprudence.[115] If the Safavid conflict turned Ottomans more cognizant of their Sunnism, the takeover of Kurdish and Arab provinces populated by Shafi'i, Maliki, and Hanbali communities made them more aware of their own Hanafi affiliation. In Egypt and Syria, just before the overthrow of the Mamluk dynasty, there was a fierce competition among the representatives of the four major sects to persuade the ruler and statesmen of the superiority of their own sects.[116] Despite the Hanafi supremacy, however, Ottoman jurists were open to utilizing the corpus pertaining to other schools of law, especially on controversial issues that required a more comprehensive argumentation based on the analysis of views representing a broader spectrum of ordinances from various Islamic legal schools. On the question of *al-siyāsa al-shariʿiyya* (capital punishments), for example, Prince Korkud, Dede Cöngi, and Aşık Çelebi displayed Shafi'i, Maliki, and Hanbali views respectively.[117] Concerning rulership, Ottoman scholars and the ruling elite were more interested in the general Sunni views, embracing both Maturidi and Ash'ari traditions rather than the particularistic views of individual schools of law. Especially in the context of the Ottoman–Safavid conflict, but also before and after, a number of Ottoman scholars either composed or translated cathechistic texts on the description of heretical sects per the Sunni canon.[118] The unifying precepts of the Sunni theology became more defining of Ottoman political thinking than the particular legal injunctions of the Hanafi school.

If one reason for the marked Sunni identity in Ottoman political writings was the unrivaled status of the Hanafi school, another reason was the Safavid ideology, which was imbued with Shiite imageries of governance. While the Ottoman scholars never felt seriously challenged by Shafi'i, Maliki, or Hanbali jurists whose conceptions of rulership were hard to reconcile with those of the Ottoman dynasty, both scholars and the ruling elite felt obliged to respond to the existential threat posed by the Safavid State and its Kizilbash sympathizers in Anatolia and the Balkans. While Shiism was a historical relic for Mamluk scholars, its new manifestations by the Kizilbash were a contemporary issue for the Ottoman ulema to deal with. Besides numerous juristic and theological refutations Ottoman scholars penned against Kizilbash Shiism, some introduced those sectarian polemics into political literature as well. Those anti-Kizilbash authors elaborated on the Sunni principles of creed, criticized Shiite beliefs and views of rulership, and exhorted the ruler to take action to promote correct beliefs and eliminate heresy from society. Sunni authors such as Hızır Münşi and Şirvani, who fled the Safavid persecution and took refuge in the Ottoman Empire, voiced their anti-Shiite views with frantic zealotry in their treatises on rulership. Thus sixteenth-century Ottoman political thought turned more Sunni than before, where inculcation of the true faith and elimination of heresy were promoted to be among the foremost ideals of legitimate rulership and good governance.

Apart from the pietistic temptations of responding to exigencies, whether expressed explicitly or not, a more common motive that led jurists and Sufis to write on government was the self-assumed task of commanding right and forbidding wrong in public life, a collective function of the community and the individual, conventionally perceived to be the domain of learned men in society. Statesmen and bureaucrats, who wrote on rulership in advisory language, lacked any learned authority and had to rely on the power of their own experience, skills, and position. The ulema and the Sufis, however, as self-proclaimed successors to the Prophet's mission to guide society to the right path, acted with the authority of speaking for religion when advising on government. As a self-justifying rule of rightly guided leadership of community reiterated in the works of all Islamic disciplines, the ruler's consultation with learned men was promoted as a universal sign of good government. The collective responsibility felt by the learned to guide the ruler to the right path prompted individual scholars to admonish the ruler about what was right and wrong in government through consultation and writing on the subject of rulership. This advice literature mostly concerned the ruler's piety and morality, with less interest in political philosophy, juristic imperatives, or principles of statecraft. Yet any learned men trained in Ottoman educational institutions were also taught the basic juristic principles and theological premises of rulership. Standard theological and juristic textbooks, such as *Sharh al-Mawāqif*, contained sections on the leadership of community.[119] The Sufis, however, were even better grounded in statecraft mainly through hagiographies and the vast literary corpus on spirituality that served as a hidden repository of political ideas as well.

The literary economy of sixteenth-century political writing turned self-interest into sufficient cause of writing on rulership. The majority of political texts were dedicated to rulers, princes, and statesmen of high status. Gifts presented to men of high stature in the form of written works were handsomely rewarded by the recipient. This was a culture in which histories, poems, and legends praised statesmen's protection and care of literati, with special veneration. Numerous works on subjects as diverse as jurisprudence and Sufism had titles beginning with "gift" (*tuḥfa*) because of their compilation as a present to a man of stature. Even a well-received poem could bring its author a coveted position or promotion. Depending on the taste and needs of a given dedicatee, histories, poetry, and advice books were among the most appreciated gift items. This gift and reward system resulted in the establishment of the mirrors for princes genre as the preferred form of political writing in the Ottoman Empire. Few statesmen had the scholarly background to read and appreciate political works composed in the highly technical language of philosophy, jurisprudence, or theology. For that reason, works written within the strict disciplinary frameworks, such *al-Siyāsa al-Sharʿiyya* of Dede Cöngi, were usually not dedicated to any particular statesman. Instead, regardless of their views, political authors liquidated the philosophical, juristic, or theological content of their teachings and presented them along with proverbs, poetry, aphorisms, and anecdotes, turning their works into literary creations.

The centralization and institutionalization of the educational system forced the ulema to forge good relations with statesmen to ensure a successful career. Although the proximity of the ulema to rulers was almost universally condemned in the judicial tradition, the Ottoman ulema had to position itself besides the political authority because of the integration of madrasas and the judiciary into the same official hierarchy. Further, the accumulation of wealth in the hands of statesmen created a patronage system whereby the livelihood of Ottoman literati became closely tied to the prospects of wealthy viziers, governors, and other dignitaries. The public duty of commanding good and forbidding wrong justified their closeness to the statesmen. As the primary executers of this duty, scholars and Sufis consistently counseled the statesmen that the best way of governing was to ask for guidance from men of learning. Other literati, such as poets, formulated and canonized their own code of conduct that regulated their relationship with statesmen. Their works marketed a universal image of an ideal statesman as one who protected men of learning and kept them within the circle of counseling in government. Thus, whether or not a given statesman had any taste in learning or literature, he invariably felt compelled to cultivate an image of himself as a patron of learning and a friend of learned men. Such a reputation then facilitated the production of political works that were dedicated to men of stature in expectation of a reward.

Besides the noble pursuit of commanding good and forbidding wrong, writing on politics became an effective instrument to advocate a particular view of government or a proposed policy in reflection of personal or communal interests and ideals. Celalzade, for example, portrayed a government in which men of the pen were given priority.[120] As a seasoned bureaucrat, he wrote about the interests and ideals of the social class to which he belonged. By contrast, Lütfi Paşa, who belonged to the men of sword with *ḳūl* origins, was not enthusiastic about learned men having priority in government.[121] Instead, his proposals were more protective of the *ḳūl* class and more critical of the ulema. Şirvani, on the other hand, passionately advocated the sultan's submission to spiritual men in making his rule part of the cosmic government of saints.[122] With a similar objective, Ebu'l-Fazl Münşi, who dedicated his work on the ethics of rulership to Süleyman, informed the sultan in his preface that the science of ethics (*ʿilm-i makārim-i akhlāq*) was the reserve of Sufis.[123]

Besides displaying a given author's views, writing on government and rulership was an act of engagement with the corpus that preceded it. Each text was shaped by its author's learning and grasp of other works on the subject as well as his own experience, objectives, and creativity within the cultural and social confines of the time. The Ottomans inherited a remarkably large body of scholarship on governance in various disciplines and genres that conveyed political theories and concepts produced in Islamic, Turkic, Persian, Indian, and Greek polities. When writing on rulership and government, these authors were usually well acquainted with the different cultural zones of the empire, if not the far corners of the Islamic world. The abundance of political works in Ottoman libraries of Asia Minor and the Balkans suggests that rulership and ethics were among the most appealing subjects to readers.

Thanks to their useful linguistic talents and universally recognized identities, scholars, Sufis, and men of literature were conventionally a highly mobile group, traveling across the cultural and governing centers of the Islamic world for purposes of learning, teaching, propagating, and seeking better prospects for life.[124] The unification of the greater part of the Middle East under a single administration and the turning of diverse populations into subjects of the same political authority opened more channels of interaction among men of learning and the ruling elite. The rotation system, for example, required graduates of Ottoman educational institutions to serve in different corners of the empire, exposing them to local traditions and populations while ensuring the standardization of administrative and judicial practices across territories. Rotational sojourns for government service enabled Ottoman men of learning to discover in the local libraries of Arabic-speaking provinces works that had not yet circulated in Turkish-speaking zones.

The rapid expansion during this period and increasing contacts with the outside world sparked new curiosities among Ottoman scholars and statesmen about the history and culture of other peoples. Among many, histories of the West Indies, France, and China speak for this awareness.[125] It was reported that Selim I, for example, on his way to conquer Egypt, wished to read Ibn Taghribirdi's history of Egypt, *al-Nujūm al-Zāhira*. He commissioned for its translation Ibn Kemal, who translated a section each night for the Sultan to read it the next day.[126] One of the most widely read political translations was a product of this curiosity: the same Selim I, who demanded to learn more about the government of Egypt and to benefit from its past experience, ordered the translation of *Nahj al-Maslūk*, a work compiled by Shayzari for Salah al-Din Ayyubi, the defeater of the Mongols and the founder of the Ayyubid dynasty in Egypt.[127]

While developing new curiosities about the world beyond their boundaries, with territories stretching across the central lands of Islam for the first time since the Abbasids, sixteenth-century Ottomans rediscovered their own past and the broader Islamic heritage at the same time. While in the fifteenth century it was comparable in size to the territory of the Mamluks and other dynasties in the Fertile Crescent in the sixteenth century, the empire at its zenith of territorial expansion was comparable only to the greatest of the past empires, such as the Abbasids. This made the Ottoman Empire worthy of scrutiny in the eyes of Ottoman intellectuals who had previously been more interested in the polities and histories of past glorious empires. For the first time in this century, elaborate world histories began to be written situating the Ottoman Empire among the greatest empires of the past. Perceiving themselves to be living in one of the foremost empires of history, Ottoman intellectuals turned to their own past to find and study the elements of its greatness and continuity. A conspicuous sign of this new self-realization was the institution of the *şehnāmecī*, the office for recording the glories of individual Ottoman rulers.[128]

Imperial Turkish and the Translation Movement

> In our time, the majority of statesmen possess a better command of Turkish. Although readers of Persian and Arabic are in abundance as well, this humble author intended to translate this sweet treatise from Arabic and Persian into Turkish.[129]

In the preface to his translation of Ghazali's *Naṣīḥat al-Mulūk*, a work dedicated to Selim II, Alayi offered an apologetic explanation for translating the text into Turkish. His apology for the use of Turkish in writing on rulership perfectly captures the state of affairs in terms of the Ottoman elite's cultural background and linguistic preference. Despite the obvious expansion of education and linguistic training to broader sections of Ottoman society, Alayi's observation that the statesmen of his time had a better command in Turkish reflects the prevalence of Turkish among the new imperial elite, many of whom came from *devşirme* origins and had received their training in Turkish. It was no accident that a good number of statesmen who commissioned the translation of texts on statecraft were using Turkish as the only language they needed for their services and professions. By this time, unlike in the previous century when Arabic and Persian were still extensively used in state registers, imperial Turkish became the principal language of official records. While scholars and learned Sufis would still have no difficulty in reading Arabic or Persian, the broader Ottoman administrative elite grew more dependent on Turkish. The sheer abundance of translated texts attests to the fact that rendering Arabic and Persian texts into Turkish for the consumption of statesmen who sought to be better informed on statecraft became a handsomely rewarded business. This general demand was even more amplified by the now traditionalized hands-on training of princes for rulership under the mentorship of learned tutors who translated texts for pedagogical purposes. Finally, the development of the Turkish vernacular for two centuries and the expansion of literacy through the medium of madrasas, Sufi convents, and administrative institutions, created more demand for Turkish reading on topics beyond literary entertainment, matters of faith, and scientific inquiry. The end result was a translation boom in political literature that was qualitatively different from the equally impressive translation activity of the first half of the previous century in the sense that this new breed of texts was composed in ornate literary Turkish rather than spoken Turkish.

Until well into the nineteenth century, Ottoman culture was more exposed to the artistic and literary works composed in eastern Muslim states than in any other part of the Islamic world. This cultural kinship, established with the arrival of the Seljuks in Asia Minor, never waned as a steady wave of artists and scholars continued to settle in Ottoman domains for various reasons.[130] Works on ethics and government written in the east of the Ottoman Empire historically enjoyed a wider circulation among Ottoman men of learning. Even the translation movement of the sixteenth century shows that the Ottoman men of learning of this period found more cultural and political affinity with the Turko-Mongol states in the east than the Arab states in the south. Although the Ottomans fully inherited the cultural heritage of the Fertile Crescent and had politically dominated these areas after 1516, the cultural impact of this region in terms of political and ethical teachings was limited. Most Ottoman intellectuals writing on ethics and rulership translated the works of the easterners, took them as models in their own writing, and were greatly inspired by their teachings. Owing to cultural and administrative affinities, the Ottoman men of learning were better conversant in political thought expressed in Iran, Transaxonia, and India.

Kınalızade modeled his work on that of Davvani, who lived under the Aqquyunlus and saw no oddity in applying the same political ideals to the Ottoman case. Similarly, Celalzade based his ethical work on that of Kashifi, who composed his work in Herat. Both Davvani and Kashifi were renowned mystics, which made all of their writings immediately available to an Ottoman readership through the closely knit Sufi networks. Scholars with a mystical bent whose writings on a wide range of topics offered exciting spiritual perspectives were in high demand in fifteenth- and sixteenth-century courts from Herat to Istanbul. This is one reason why the Ottoman rulers tried to lure intellectuals such as Jami and Davvani from the courts of the eastern dynasties.[131] By contrast, the huge number of political and ethical works compiled during Mamluk times found very little reception among Ottoman intellectuals before the conquest of Egypt and even for a while thereafter. Besides the similarities in these polities, a major facilitating factor that led the Ottomans to fully embrace Eastern ethical teachings was their infatuation with Persian literature. The literary renaissance taking place in the East made the Ottomans closely follow the literary and scholarly achievements there while largely remaining indifferent to the culture of the south. In addition to their status as authors of works on ethics, Sufism, and various Islamic disciplines, Davvani and Kashifi were, above all, literary icons for the Ottoman literati.

One of the most influential works on sixteenth-century political and ethical thought was Kashifi's *Akhlāq-i Muḥsinī* (The Muhsinian Ethics). Thanks to the established fame of Kashifi, on its completion in 1494–1495, the work quickly disseminated throughout the Turko-Persianate world, along with many other works by its author. Kashifi wrote *Akhlāq-i Muḥsinī* for Abu'l-Muhsin, the son of Sultan Husayn Bayqara. Ottoman intellectuals, especially those close to the dynasty, found in *Akhlāq-i Muḥsinī* a ready recipe for the ethics of rulership to groom Ottoman princes for their future positions. The work was less philosophical than the works of Tusi and Davvani and more artistic, embellished with anecdotes and poetry, thus making it easier to read and more suitable for Ottoman taste. In addition to numerous copies of the work in Ottoman libraries, which indicates that it was widely read in its Persian original, it was translated four times in the sixteenth century alone. Among these translations, Azmi Efendi's (d. 1582) *Enīsü'l-Ḳulūb* (Companion of Hearts), which he dedicated to Selim II in 1566–1567, became a popular read among Ottoman intellectuals.[132] Azmi Efendi, a famed poet, was a professor at the Süleymaniye Madrasa at the time of his appointment as tutor to Mehmed III in 1580.[133] He was a son of treasurer Pir Ahmed Çelebi (d. 1543) and, thanks to his father's connections, received excellent training from distinguished scholars.[134] During the early stages of his career, he was an assistant to Kınalızade Ali, who wrote the most celebrated work of ethics in all of Ottoman history.[135] Firaki Abdurrahman Çelebi (d. 1575–1576), who translated the work in 1550, was a well-known poet and preacher.[136] Among the attendees at his sermons in Kütahya was Prince Bayezid, for whose succession he preached publicly.[137] He was a close friend of Lami'i Çelebi (d. 1532), a Sufi scholar who compiled, among others, two works on Sufi ethics, *ʿİbretnümā* (The Exemplar) and *Şerefü'l-İnsān* (The Honor of Human Being).[138] His contemporary Ebu'l-Fazl Mehmed (d. 1574–1575) was a son of the famed judge, statesman, and political philosopher Idris-i Bidlisi.[139] Receiving his first education from his father, and also editing his father's works, Ebu'l-Fazl Mehmed was already well versed in political theory. After serving in various judicial and teaching positions he became chief treasurer, gaining him his epithet Defteri (bookkeeper).[140] The last of the sixteenth-century translators of *Akhlāq-i Muḥsinī* was Nevali Efendi (d. 1594), who served as Mehmed III's tutor, replacing Azmi Efendi in 1582.[141]

No less popular than Kashifi's *Akhlāq-i Muḥsinī* was Hamadani's (d. 1385) *Ẕakhīrat al-Mulūk* (Treasure of Kings), which was translated three times over the course of the sixteenth century. Hamadani was affiliated with the Kubrawiyya, and himself founded the Hamadani branch of the order. He was well known to the Ottomans through his works, in which he labored to harmonize Ibn Arabi's teachings with those of the Kubrawiyya.[142] Although the Hamadaniyya order did not flourish in Ottoman lands, with his writings and the order he instituted, he was among the most influential mystics in the history of Indo-Persian Sufism. Hamadani composed *Ẕakhīrat al-Mulūk*'s sections on ethics and piety by heavily depending on Ghazali's two celebrated works *Iḥyā ʿUlūm al-Dīn* (The Revivification of the Religious Sciences) and *Kimyā-i Saʿādat* (The Alchemy of Happiness).[143] On sections regarding rulership, the caliphate, and spiritual perfection, his ideas reflect those of Ibn Arabi, mainly through the works of Davud-i Kayseri.[144] To an Ottoman reader who grew up in a culture that greatly admired Ghazali and Ibn Arabi, the teachings of *Ẕakhīrat al-Mulūk* were already familiar, a factor that contributed to the warm reception of the work by the Ottomans. Among the translators of the work were Zihni, who translated it for Selim II, and Mustafa Katib, who dedicated it to Murad III in 1577.[145] Although Zihni's identity cannot be established with certainty, he probably entered the service of Selim II while he was a prince and later served as treasurer in Diyarbakır and Aleppo.[146] As for Mustafa Katib, he was probably a scribe in the civil service, working during the reign of Murad III. Besides these obscure translators, a high-profile scholar and mystic, Süruri Efendi (d. 1561–1562), a close friend of Aşık Çelebi, translated *Ẕakhīrat al-Mulūk* for Prince Mustafa.[147] Süruri was a famed poet, a polymath scholar, and a prolific author, who attributed his failure to advance in the learning profession to intrigues that led to his devotion to the mystical path. Among the leading ulema he studied with was Taşköprizade, who himself made extensive use of *Ẕakhīrat al-Mulūk* in composing his treatise *Asrār al-Khilāfa*.[148] Süruri tutored Mustafa Âli, who later wrote a comprehensive political treatise, that dealt with the question of decline in the Ottoman Empire.[149] He became affiliated with the Nakşibendiyye order and established himself as a popular voice on Sufi poetry through his sermons, public lectures, and commentaries on such past masters as Sa'di, Rumi, Jami, and Hafiz.[150] He accepted Süleyman's request to become tutor to Prince Mustafa in 1548 against the wishes of his friends and foes, a decision that cost him his career and prestige because of the execution of Mustafa by his father in 1553.[151] As part of his duties, during his sojourn at the court of Mustafa, Süruri produced a number of other works for the education of the prince.[152] Süruri Efendi chose to translate *Ẕakhīrat al-Mulūk* into Turkish to educate the young prince on political ethics and piety from a Sufi perspective.

From the stream of Eastern political wisdom, Ghazali's *Naṣīḥat al-Mulūk* (Counsel for Kings) was probably the most influential text on Ottoman political thinking. From very early times on, the Ottomans were infatuated with this work, translating it numerous times and extensively using it in compiling their own treatises on rulership and ethics.[153] Ghazali wrote the work in Persian toward the end of his life for one of the Seljuk sultans, Muhammed bin Malikshah or Sanjar.[154] *Naṣīḥat al-Mulūk*, in both the Persian and Arabic versions, turned out to be one of the most widely read books in the Islamic world. It was an ingeniously crafted work, a simple and entertaining mirror for princes, embellished with telling aphorisms and anecdotes. It was a book on the morality and piety of the ruler with little specific guidance on government practice, which made its teachings appealing and equally applicable in every setting. Composed in two parts, the first part was on the right creed and the second was on the right morality, with an overarching emphasis on justice as the single most important virtue of rulership.[155] Unlike authors of juristic works that instructed the ruler about government and religion through strict principles, Ghazali aimed to achieve the same end in a more entertaining fashion. For a translator, this characteristic of the work made it an ideal gift for any ruler to guide him in justice and make him observe religious principles.

Among the translators of the work were Muallimzade, Aşık Çelebi, and Alayi, all contemporaries. Muallimzade (d. 1572) translated the work for

Süleyman and presented it to Rüstem Paşa.[156] Muallimzade was the son of a revered shaykh of the Zeyniyye order who chose to advance on the judicial track. Though praised for his command in giving legal opinions, he does not seem to have produced much scholarly work. Thanks to his friendship with Selim II's tutor, Ataullah Efendi, he became chief military judge, the highest position after the sheikh ul Islam.[157] Like Muallimzade, Aşık Çelebi translated the work in 1562 for Süleyman and submitted it to Grand Vizier Rüstem Paşa to convey it to the sultan.[158] Among his teachers were Taşköprizade and Süruri, two mystics who conveyed Hamadani's *Ẕakhīrat al-Mulūk* to the Ottoman audience. Much like his younger friend Mustafa Âli, Aşık Çelebi was a chronic malcontent throughout his career in the judicial track. Although he was better known as the author of his celebrated biographical dictionary of poets, *Meşāʿirü'ş-Şuʿarā* (Stations of Poets), he was a prolific translator. Unlike Aşık Çelebi, Alayi was not a notable figure of his time despite his dozen other works on various subjects. He translated the work for Selim II and it was well received by the wider audience, as its many copies suggest. He wrote an extensive commentary on the first part of *Naṣīḥat al-Mulūk* that deals with the principles of creed.

A work similar in format was Hatibzade's *Rawḍ al-Akhyār* (Garden of the Virtuous), which was translated by Aşık Çelebi.[159] The work was itself an abbreviation of Zamakhshari's massive *Rabīʿ al-Abrār*.[160] Zamakhshari (d. 1143), a Mu'tazili prodigy of Arabic language and literature, was best known to the Ottomans through his *al-Kashshāf*, a Qur'anic commentary that was standard reading for every advanced student of Islamic disciplines in Ottoman madrasas. He wrote *Rabīʿ al-Abrār* (The Spring of the Virtuous) in the same format as Ibn Qutayba's (d. 889) celebrated *ʿUyūn al-Akhbār*, an encyclopedic collection of wisdom literature that contained poetry, anecdotes, prophetic traditions, and aphorisms.[161] Books of the *muḥāḍara* genre, which includes such excellent samples of Arabic literature as Raghib al-Isfahani's (d. early 11th century) *Muḥāḍarāt al-Udabā*, were in high demand among the learned across the Islamic world. Besides having their own literary, entertainment, and didactic values, they served as a major repository of quotations for authors writing on any topic. Hatibzade abbreviated this work and turned the new version into a mirror for princes with chapters regarding rulership in the beginning, making it more readable and relevant for the ruler.[162] Originally from Amasya, Hatibzade was a polyglot scholar who taught in the highest institutions of learning and was appointed tutor to Prince Ahmed by Bayezid II.[163] He completed the work in 1515 and later dedicated it to Süleyman I. Aşık Çelebi, who appreciated the endeavor, decided to make it available for Turkish readers as well and translated this work for Selim II while he was prince, without interfering with its content or form.[164]

While mainly operating within the broader Turko-Persianate cultural zone, sixteenth-century Ottoman scholars grew more attuned to the cultural heritage produced in Arab lands and started to translate works of political import. The most notable among these was Vusuli Mehmed Efendi's (d. 1589) translation of Turtushi's (d. 1126) *Sirāj al-Mulūk*.[165] Vusuli, better known as Hubbi Mollası for marrying the daughter of the female poet Hubbi Hatun, had been a protégé of Selim II since his youth.[166] On Selim II's assignment to governorship, he shifted his appointment to Kütahya and was a regular member of the prince's retinue. Thanks to this connection, he quickly rose in the teaching and judicial track and served as the judge of Istanbul. *Sirāj al-Mulūk*, which he translated in 1584 with the title *Şems-i Hidāyet*, was one of the two works recommended by Taşköprizade in his *Miftāḥ al-Saʿāda* on the science of manners of rulership (*ʿilm ādāb al-mulūk*).[167]

Turtushi, a Maliki and ascetic-natured scholar from Spain, whose older contemporary and role model was Ghazali, wrote the work in Egypt in 1122 for Vizier Ibn al-Bata'ihi. Despite being translated into Turkish only once, *Sirāj al-Mulūk* was one of the most influential works on sixteenth-century Ottoman political writing. It was one of the most comprehensive treatises written on government in medieval Islam that addressed both the ruler and the ruled. With very few specific instructions or principles of government, *Sirāj al-Mulūk* is a work of literature that explains principles of good government through philosophical aphorisms, anecdotes, historical cases, and exemplary stories. This characteristic made it one of the most quoted works in Ottoman political literature, a source book consulted to find appropriate stories and aphorisms to illustrate political views.[168]

Aşık Çelebi also made an abridged translation of Ibn Taymiyya's *al-Siyāsa al-Sharʿiyya* (Governance in Accordance with the Sharia), adding two chapters on war and treasury, respectively, and dedicated the work to Selim II.[169] Ibn Taymiyya, a prolific author, activist, and controversial Hanbali scholar of the fourteenth century, wrote the work between 1309 and 1314 during the third reign of Muhammed b. Qalawun (r. 1310–1341). Unlike many other authors of works on government who intended to persuade the ruler of the supremacy of a given legal school or to provide a sectarian prescription for rulership, Ibn Taymiyya (d. 1328) composed his work to vindicate the Sharia in general, and it contains no particular criticism of other sects.[170] By addressing all office holders, *umarā* and ulema, both of whom he considered legitimate authorities to command (*ulī al-amr*), Ibn Taymiyya advocated an uncompromising application of the Sharia laws and for keeping the believers under close scrutiny with respect to observing duties.

While the Arabic version of the work enjoyed widespread popularity in both the Arabic-speaking and Turkish-speaking halves of the Ottoman Empire, Aşık Çelebi's translation also seems to have attracted a broad interest. There was nothing in the work that would cause unease for the Ottoman elite about legitimacy, for Ibn Taymiyya did not consider the rigid conditions elaborated in the classical theory as necessary for the enactment of the caliphate, particularly the

Qurayshi descent, which Ottoman rulers lacked.[171] Ibn Taymiyya's shift of focus in juristic political theory from the question of the conditions and legitimacy of the universal caliphate to the conformity of government practice with the Sharia was completely in line with the sixteenth-century approaches of leading Ottoman jurists. Despite having conflicting views among themselves, such jurists as Kınalızade, Ibn Kemal, Ebussuud, Birgivi, Çivizade, Dede Cöngi, and many others sought to ensure the conformity of government practices with the prescripts of the Sharia, as was apparent in their writings and major debates of the sixteenth century, such as the cash foundations controversy. More tangibly, Ottoman jurists were an integral part of the *ḳānūn*-making process to make sultanic laws compatible with the Sharia.[172]

Besides these high-profile scholars who ventured to translate works of famed scholars from Arab-speaking lands, two little known scholars opted to convey into Turkish a text by an obscure Mamluk author, Khayrabayti. A certain Abdüsselam b. Şükrullah el-Amasi translated *al-Durra al-Gharrā*, with the title *Tuḥfetü'l-Ümerā ve Minḥatü'l-Vüzerā* (A Gift for Statesment and an Offering for Viziers) during the reign of Süleyman in a surprisingly simple language reminiscent of the fifteenth-century Turkish vernacular.[173] Ibn Firuz (d. 1609), a relatively better known scholar, translated it for Selim II with the title *Gurretü'l-Beyżā* but with an ornate Turkish reflective of the literary trend of the time.[174] The son of Grand Vizier Ahmed Paşa's steward Firuz Bey and a low ranking madrasa professor, Ibn Firuz left no known work other than this translation.[175] Khayrabayti (d. after 1439), a Hanafi jurist, wrote the work for the Mamluk ruler Sayf al-Din Chaqmaq (r. 1438–1453) in 1439 as an instructive manual for the *sharʿī* foundations of rulership, government, and public law.[176] The treatise was written from a strictly Hanafi point of view, in refutation of the views of other major schools of law on rulership, especially the Shiite views. The introduction of this work to the Ottoman audience came at a time when the legitimacy of the Ottoman as caliph seemed to be the subject of renewed doubts among the jurists.[177] A strictly juristic work in its judgments, *al-Durra al-Gharrā* was written in the form of a mirror for princes, where juristic dictums and opinions were supplemented by authoritative and exemplary stories, mostly from the experience of Muslim rulers. Although the original was noticed by only a few, Ibn Firuz's translation seems to have found some readership among Ottoman intellectuals.[178] Qualifications of the caliph, his responsibilities, rules pertaining to the government and the military, and various branches of the Sharia law were among the topics broached. Despite using discretion in reshuffling and interpreting the original text, both Abdüsselam and Ibn Firuz remained silent on the question of the Qurayshi descent and simply conveyed that "the imam should be from the Quraysh or appointed by someone from the Quraysh," a cliché of Mamluk jurists which fits to the Ottomans as well, who by now had firmly established in historical memory that their very founder Osman had received investiture from the last independent Abbasi ruler, albeit indirectly.[179] Elsewhere, both translations offer juristic notions, which only confirms the Ottoman caliphate, as they both equate the imamate with the caliphate, and the caliphate with the position of a prophet (*ḳā'im-i maḳām-ı nübüvvet*).[180] Further, Abdüsselam placed Süleyman in the noble lineage of rightful caliphs that followed the death of the Prophet, after the rightly guided caliphs and the rightly guided imams (*e'imme-i mehdiyyīn*).[181]

Despite offering the Hanafi perspective in legitimizing rulership, Khayrabayti's *al-Durra al-Gharrā* did not provide a viable solution for the genealogical deficiency of Ottoman rulers.[182] It was *Tuḥfat al-Turk*, a work by another Mamluk author, that offered a workable solution for the endemic legitimacy problem of the post-Abbasid Turkic dynasties.[183] It was translated into Turkish before 1559 by an anonymous author under the title *Naṣīḥatü'l-Mülūk*.[184] In plain Turkish, the work is an exact translation of *Tuḥfat al-Turk*, with no mention of the original work. Tarsusi (d. 1357), the chief judge (*qāḍī al-quḍāt*) of the Hanafis in Damascus from 1345 until his death, wrote his polemical treatise during the second reign of Nasir al-Din Hasan (r. 1354–1361) to vindicate the legitimacy of the rule of the Turks and strongly criticize other major schools of law, exhibiting more animosity toward the Shafi'is.[185] By comparing the rulings of Hanafi and Shafi'i jurists on government, Tarsusi demonstrated that the Shafi'i view delegitimated the rule of the Turks and many of their current government practices. He aimed to convince the sultan to promulgate Hanafi jurisprudence as the official law of the state because it fully endorsed the legitimacy of the ruler as well as various government practices.[186] Further, *Tuḥfat al-Turk* is an instructive treatise on how to reconcile government practices with the prescripts of Hanafi law. Written in a format much like a mirror for princes, its content bears the mark of three distinct genres: the law of government (*al-aḥkām al-sulṭāniyya*), disagreement of jurists (*ikhtilāf al-fuqahā*), and reform treatises (*iṣlāḥ al-siyāsī wa al-dīnī*).[187] Despite the sophistication of its arguments, the fame of its author, and the solution it provided for the Mamluk dynasty, *Tuḥfat al-Turk* did not reach a wide readership.[188] Even though the Hanafi school dominated the Ottoman juristic establishment, no legal treatise was written to legitimize rulership on the basis of Hanafi law. This gap seemed to be filled with the appropriation of the works of Mamluk jurists who endeavored to justify and glorify the rule of Mamluk sultans who suffered problems similar to those of the Ottomans. In addition to these two translations, after the conquest of Egypt, the Ottomans appropriated a large number of juristic works on government and rulership written for the Mamluk sultans, many of which were kept in the palace library.[189]

In the sixteenth century, even a Venetian ambassador to Istanbul could hope to gain the sultan's favor by presenting him with a political text that contained the wisdom of one of the sultan's most revered ancestors.[190] Ambassador Marino de Cavalli's gift to the sultan was purported to be a Turkish translation of a long dialogue between Murad II and Prince Mehmed, allegedly recorded by his grandfather, Andrea Coscolo, who had witnessed the conversation.[191] Cavalli stated that he found the manuscript among the papers of his grandfather and decided to present it to the sultan as a goodwill gift. Cavalli had the manuscript translated into Turkish by a Hungarian renegade, Murad Beg, who was working at the time as an interpreter at the Ottoman court, and presented the work to Süleyman in 1559 with the promise that he would also have the work translated into Latin and many other languages so that Murad II's advice would be known by others as well.[192] The work consists of Murad II's responses to Prince Mehmed's questions about old age. The stark message of the text is that a prudent ruler should give privilege to reason over the sword in his government, a point commonly reiterated in other mirrors for princes as well. Since Rossi's 1936 study, the work is commonly mentioned as a loose translation of Cicero's *de Senectute*.[193] There is a similar section on the comparison of old age and youth in *Qābūsnāma*, which was translated and presented to Murad II, and in *İskendernāme*, an epic story of Alexander's life composed by Ahmedi and dedicated to Murad II's father Mehmed I.[194] By presenting it to Süleyman at that particular juncture, Cavalli must have aimed at ameliorating Venetian–Ottoman relations at a time when they were strained. The ambassador attempted to gain the favor of Süleyman by presenting him with an invaluable gift, the wisdom of his ancestors. The ambassador could only hope that the peaceful message of Murad's advice to his son Mehmed could temper Süleyman's expansionist policies in the Mediterranean.

The unprecedented demand and curiosity that led the Ottoman men of learning to translate from the east and the south brought one of the most influential texts of medieval political theory to their attention. It was the aforementioned Nevali, the translator of Kashifi's *Akhlāq-i Muḥsinī*, who undertook the translation of the pseudo-Aristotelian text on rulership, *Sirr al-Asrār*. With meager literary skills, Nevali was a respected professor, known for his excellence in scholarship and piety, who taught at the highest learning institutions including the Süleymaniye.[195] He translated the work for Grand Vizier Sokollu Mehmed Paşa in 1571, during the reign of Selim II.[196] As he believed, *Sirr al-Asrār* (Secret of Secrets) was a book of advice written by Aristotle, the grand vizier of Alexander the Great, regarding the sultanate and the caliphate.[197] Although he did not reveal in the text the original copy he used, the colophon of the book stated that Nevali translated the work from Greek, a point that cannot be substantiated because there was no such complete book in Greek. In fact, even Aristotle's *Politics* was never translated into Arabic while his *Nicomachean Ethics* enjoyed great popularity.

Sirr al-Asrār, also known as *al-Siyāsa fī Tadbīr al-Riyāsa*, took its final form in the tenth century after going through a number of revisions and expansions for two centuries in the hands of various authors.[198] The final version established itself as the definitive translation of Aristotle's treatise on government, and claimed to have been made by Yahya ibn al-Bitriq.[199] Although spurious, the final work was a great success, as it became one of the most popular works on rulership in both the Muslim and the Christian worlds soon after its completion.[200] It had an immense effect on Muslim political theory, particularly on the mirrors for princes literature. Among the later works that fell under the spell of this work were some of the most renowned examples of this genre, such as Ghazali's *Naṣīḥat al-Mulūk*, Nizam al-Mulk's *Siyāsatnāma*, Kaykavus' *Qābūsnāma*, and Ibn Arabi's *al-Tadbīrāt al-Ilāhiyya*.[201] After being translated into Latin as *Secretum Secretorum*, of which some fifty manuscripts survived, the work was rendered into a number of European vernaculars as well. At least fifteen different translations exist in English alone.[202]

Besides the prestige Aristotle enjoyed in Islamic learning and the intrinsic value of its teachings, what made this work popular was the extent of its scope in advising on rulership and government. Unlike many other advice books of its kind, *Sirr al-Asrār* included sections on onomancy, physiognomy, and hygiene, in addition to more conventional topics regarding principles of government, just rule, and ethics. *Sirr al-Asrār* contained one of the earliest, but certainly the most elaborate exposition of the circle of justice, an ancient maxim that pervaded the literature on government and ethics, and reached a paradigmatic status in designing the ideal polity in Ottoman culture.[203] Nevali's work is not an exact translation of *Sirr al-Asrār* when compared to that work's standard edition. As indicated in the preface, it is an abridged and selective (*telḫīs ve intiḫāb*) translation of *Sirr al-Asrār*.[204] Aside from Nevali's aptly made selections to make the work more appealing, three features of the translation turned it into an exposition of the pseudo-Aristotelian ideals of government within the Ottoman context. Nevali wrote a long preface to the work, where he described the lives of Aristotle and Alexander the Great, which he claimed to have gathered from a variety of sources. Nevali's presentation portrays both Alexander and Aristotle as Muslims endowed with excellence in wisdom, judgement, and government. He converted the main text into Islam by inserting aphorisms, prophetic traditions, and Qur'anic verses to support Aristotle's advice to Alexander. In translating the text he used the current political and administrative terminology, equating Aristotle with the grand vizier, and Alexander with the caliph. He eliminated historical distance and made the text a fresh product of Ottoman culture and relevant to current expectations in political thought and government practice. Nevali managed to present the pseudo-Aristotelian teachings as proven by experience, sanctioned by Islam, and fully compatible with the Ottoman vernacular in government.

Four Ways of Writing on Politics

Political texts written during the age of Süleyman roughly correspond to what the modern scholarship commonly refers to as the *siyāsetnāme* literature. This appellation largely originates from the Ottoman experience of political writing itself, for numerous works that are related to some aspect of rulership, regardless of their original titles, are simply dubbed *siyāsetnāmes* by copyists. Dede Cöngi's treatise on criminal law, for example, was better known as *Siyāsetnāme* than as *al-Siyāsa al-Sharʿiyya*, its original title. In most taxonomic depictions, a vastly variegated corpus of Ottoman political literature is commonly classified under a single category of the *siyāsetnāme* genre as a continuation of the chiefly Persian tradition of mirrors for princes.[205] The Seljuk vizier Nizam al-Mulk's *Siyar al-Mulūk* is commonly cited as the archetypical model of this form of political writing.[206] According to mainstream conviction, a standard feature of the works in this genre is that they are mainly manuals of rulership with a focus on administrative practices and just government, consisting of counsels illustrated by exemplary stories, aphorisms, and other literary devices. This consideration led to a widely shared assumption that there is a great deal of continuity in form and content between the Persian mirrors for princes genre and Ottoman treatises on government. Further complicating the issue was the tendency in modern scholarship to categorize works simply by reference to what their titles connote. This modern confusion was largely the result of equating the whole body of works known as *siyāsetnāmes* or bearing titles suggestive of works of advice with the genre of mirrors for princes, or *Fürstenspiegel*, as they came to be known in the European literature.

However, a close examination of the Ottoman political corpus does not confirm any of these established views.[207] First of all, the so called *siyāsetnāme* genre is not uniform in content, format, or message. There is a great deal of variety among such works, which include those written from juristic, administrative, philosophical, Sufistic, and literary perspectives. There is hardly any common feature among these diverse works except for their relevance to rulership. Second, even when the broadest definition of the genre is accepted, that still leaves out the bulk of Ottoman political writings. Works such as Dede Cöngi's *al-Siyāsa al-Sharʿiyya*, for example, a juristic exposition of government, were not written as "advice books" and do not resort to literary devices. This *siyāsetnāme*-centric perspective that tends to bundle together a variety of works with different formats and content veils the genuine features and messages the works might offer.

Parting ways with the aforementioned approach, the vast and diverse political literature of the age of Süleyman may be grouped under four principal headings as ethics, statecraft, jurisprudence, and Sufism. These are by no means neatly definable genres, exclusive thematic categories, or schools of thought. Any taxonomic attempt to classify political texts on the basis of language, genre, or discipline will most likely generate more problems to address than it resolves. Most texts, if not all, freely transgress linguistic, literary, and disciplinary bounds set by earlier canons of political writing. Lütfi Paşa's polemical treatise on the caliphate, for example, written in three different languages, is juristic in its reasoning but still extensively quotes from Sufistic and even occultist works, such as Abdurrahman Bistami's *al-Fawāʾiḥ al-Miskiyya*, in support of its arguments. When compared to others, the text nevertheless stands out as one written in the idiom of jurists with the purpose of proving the legitimacy of the Ottoman caliphate on legal and theological grounds. Even if it looks rhetorically unfit, it is more suitable to place it within the linguistic and methodological conventions of jurisprudence. This fourfold division offered here is therefore for analytical purposes only in reference to the broader linguistic and intellectual conventions in which these texts were produced. These conventions function as paradigmatic frameworks marked by distinguishable objectives, parameters, and sensibilities that may convey but not necessarily dictate certain types and imageries of rulership.

A text written primarily in the convention and idiom of ethics, for example, entails that it treats rulership as a question of ethics with less attention to legal considerations of legitimacy or institutional aspects of governance. By the same token, juristic writings, with all the diversity of opinions they may have, are governed primarily by the idea of legalistic legitimacy of authority on the basis of Islamic law and the organization of government per demands of the Sharia. Writings on statecraft, composed mostly by bureaucrats, promote the primacy of institutions and conventions of the state while according much less significance to the ruler's morality or Islamic legitimacy. Finally, the Sufistic writings, the most diverse of all, still operate within the parameters of Sufi cosmology and, as their trademark, consider rulership as the union of both temporal and spiritual components. We can further note that ethics tends to be philosophical, statecraft empirical, jurisprudence normative, and Sufism speculative. Yet the literary identification of a text may not reveal the purpose of its author. As in the cases of jurists writing in the idiom of Sufism such as Taşköprizade or Sufis writing in the idiom of jurists such as Bali Efendi, it is not always clear whether the author resorts to the literary conventions outside his professional or learned affiliation as a mere rhetorical instrument to promote a particular set of views or because of his synthetic reasoning. But, all these complications aside, one paramount feature of Ottoman political writing in the sixteenth century becomes clear: anyone who writes on rulership has to incorporate and negotiate with the Sufistic idiom in some capacity in order to convey ideas, whether framed primarily within jurisprudence, ethics, or statecraft.

Taşköprizade's *Miftāḥ al-Saʿāda wa Miṣbāḥ al-Siyāda fī Mawḍūʿāt al-ʿUlūm* (The Key of Happiness and Light of Nobility in Objects of Science), a massive compendium on the description of 355 individual sciences, provides us a contemporary perspective as to how the increasingly versatile political literature is categorized by a Sufi-minded jurist.[208] Ahmed b. Mustafa el-Taşköprizade (d. 1561), who served mostly as a madrasa professor during the reigns of Selim I and Süleyman I, was one of the most prolific and versatile authors of his time. All written in Arabic, his works cover such diverse fields as grammar, literature, logic, hadith, theology, biography, medicine, and jurisprudence.[209] He came from a celebrated Turkish ulema family that had produced prominent professors and jurists since the early fifteenth century. Helped by his family name, he quickly rose through the ranks of the learned hierarchy and proved himself a competent professor by teaching in the most prestigious institutions of learning, including the ones in Skopje, Edirne, Bursa, and finally the Sahn in Istanbul. Despite his bright prospects for advancement that might eventually have led him to the office of sheikh ul Islam, he ended his career by retiring at the age of fifty-nine because of failing eyesight, while serving as chief judge of Istanbul, his first judicial appointment.

Unlike many other high-profile ulema of his time, Taşköprizade opted to remain in the learning establishment and did not pursue high-paying judicial posts until late in his life. He was not well connected with prominent statesmen, perhaps because he deliberately avoided being too close to rulers and governors.[210] Testifying in his autobiography to his passion for teaching, he enumerated not the books he compiled but the books he taught in each of his teaching appointments.[211] He was not an active participant in the literary circles of his time, nor was he considered a notable poet or prose writer. In a culture in which literature enjoyed such high esteem and practically every intellectual was a poet with a high degree of poetic knowledge, his name appears rarely in biographical accounts of sixteenth-century poets. He did not take an active stance in the hotly debated controversies of this period such as the cash foundations, religious innovations, Sufi practices, or heretical views. Taşköprizade was better known to his contemporaries and later Ottomans as the author of *al-Shaqāʾiq al-Nuʿmāniyya*, a biographical dictionary of Ottoman ulema written in Arabic. The work, written in his retirement when he was already blind, was translated many times into Turkish, beginning during his own lifetime.[212]

As one of the most outstanding achievements of sixteenth-century Ottoman culture, *Miftāḥ al-Saʿāda* was a product of life-long scholarship, written toward the end of the author's life. Above all, the work demonstrates the extent of scholarly interests and scientific horizons of a madrasa professor, defying the prevailing idea in modern scholarship that portrayed the Ottoman ulema as parochial, with interests and expertise confined to religious sciences, grammar, and logic alone. With a total of about 2000 titles cited, Taşköprizade prepared the compendium as a reference work for the beginners who would like to study these sciences. While the author was content with giving a very brief introduction to many fields of study, for more established disciplines, he described the subject matter in detail, explained key concepts, approaches, and theories, and provided a short bibliography of prominent works in that field. The author also evaluated the uses of each discipline and, in cases of nonreligious sciences, after an objective description of the field, discussed the problematic aspects of that discipline from a religious point view. *Miftāḥ al-Saʿāda* was a jurist's guide to the study of religious and lay sciences.

In addition to the host of different sources he used to compile his compendium, Taşköprizade's principal source in writing the sections on ethics, religious sciences, and Sufism was Ghazali's *Iḥyā*, a work written to revive the religious sciences and deeply affected all strains of Islamic thought afterwards. But Ottoman intellectuals had an added interest in reading Ghazali whom they credited for definitively establishing the compatibility of rational sciences with Islam. In the fifteenth and sixteenth centuries, the compatibility of Islam and philosophy, for example, was revived in Ottoman intellectual circles where the Ghazalian synthesis was overwhelmingly preferred.[213] Thus *Miftāḥ al-Saʿāda* was not only a jurist's view of the sciences but also a Ghazalian restatement, a re-revivification of Islamic sciences.

Besides its portrayal of sixteenth-century Ottoman conceptions of the sciences, *Miftāḥ al-Saʿāda* provided the most extensive treatment of disciplines and teachings pertaining to government. Scattered throughout the book, Taşköprizade's instructions on government fall into three main categories. First, he enumerated individual disciplines that deal with different aspects of government. These included practical wisdom, ethics, government (*siyāsa*), manners of rulership (*ādāb al-Mulūk*), manners of the vizierate (*ādāb al-wizāra*), market inspection (*iḥtiṣāb*), military administration, commanding right and forbidding wrong, divinity (*ʿilm-i ilāhī*), and others. This was one of the most extensive diversifications of disciplines on rulership in the tradition of encyclopedic compendia of sciences.[214] Second, Taşköprizade recommended books in each of these sciences, providing a fairly comprehensive list of works that were known to an Ottoman scholar writing on politics in the sixteenth century, indicative of the author's preferred classification of sciences on government. The books he recommended on rulership also reveal that the author was familiar with major pre-Ottoman writers on government such as Mawardi, Ghazali, Farabi, Razi, Tusi, Davvani, Tarsusi, Ibn Zafar, and others. Third, the author conveyed his own views on government. In this sense, *Miftāḥ al-Saʿāda* was not only an informative introduction to sciences of rulership but also a refined account of reliable teachings on the subject. Although there is no study showing the overall impact of *Miftāḥ al-Saʿāda* on later Ottoman learning, it must have guided later Ottoman authors' writing and reading on government.[215]

Although Taşköprizade's *Miftāḥ al-Saʿāda* provides us with a select list of books within his reach on rulership, it does not convey much information about the circulation of these books or reading preferences of the time. Atufi (d. 1541), however, a royal librarian of Bayezid II, who compiled an inventory of the sultan's palace library in 1502–3, informs us better about reading on politics at the Ottoman court.[216] First to note is that the inventory registers about a hundred different titles on rulership, excluding the works of literature and

Islamic disciplines, representing all strains of political thought from Muslim Spain to India.[217] But what is hidden behind this deceptive display of diversity is the primacy of Persian and Sufism. Most titles were either in Persian or a product of the Persianate culture, showing that readers at the Ottoman court had not yet developed a taste for reading in Arabic on politics. Despite the impressive translation movement of the fifteenth century, none of these works in Turkish was acquired by the Ottoman court of the time. Only two decades after, however, reading in Arabic and Turkish became at least as trendy as reading in Persian at Süleyman's court, judging by the explosive number of books composed in these languages and dedicated to dignitaries. More striking than the linguistic preference of the Ottomans was the prevalence of Sufism in the choice of titles and the way they were described. Most books on rulership were either explicitly written in the Sufi tradition or by Sufi-minded authors in a markedly Sufistic idiom. Further, Atufi classified a number of works on ethics and politics written in different genres and disciplines simply as "*min qibali taṣawwuf*" (pertaining to Sufism). This classification shows that the "subject" of various writings on rulership and ethics, regardless of the genre and discipline to which they belong, was now considered as Sufism. Namely, advising on governance, envisioning one's ideal rulership, or proposing to reform government were now all considered part of the same fundamental pursuit of Sufistic moral perfection. Bayezid II's palace library shows that the mystical turn in political thought which started in the late Abbasid period now turned into the mainstream.

ETHICS

Alayi b. Muhibbi el-Şirazi el-Şerif lived during the reign of Süleyman and wrote his works in the latter part of that reign. Originally from Shiraz and a descendant of the Prophet, he grew up in Konya and was initiated into the Mevlevi order where he became a *Masnavi* reciter, and was capable of writing poems in three languages.[218] In his works he displayed a strong mystical tendency and was particularly pretentious about his authority in such fields as geomancy, onomancy, occultism, and esoteric teachings.[219] Despite his engagement and expertise in these unorthodox practices, he presented himself as a staunch Sunni who demonstrated his proficiency in the mainstream religious sciences and professed his affiliation with the mainstream Sunni confession. He wrote two works on governance: a long treatise on the vizierate and a longer work on rulership. He compiled *Düstūrü'l-Vüzerā* in 1558 and dedicated it to Lala Mustafa Paşa, Prince Selim's tutor.[220] Alayi composed the work in Turkish because he had not come across "a new work or a useful compilation in the Turkish language regarding the vizierate, judgeship, and governorship."[221] The introduction is devoted to an etymological analysis of the term *wazīr* and its hermeneutical interpretations. The rest of the work elaborates on the traits of a good vizier, exemplary stories of past viziers, and protective incantations.[222] Throughout the work, he illustrated his views with stories and embellished the text with Turkish and Persian couplets and quatrains.

Alayi's second work on the subject, *Netīcetü's-Sülūk*, is a Turkish rendering of Ghazali's *Naṣīḥat al-Mulūk*.[223] Of the three parts of Ghazali's treatise, Alayi translated the last two parts as literally as possible while commenting extensively on the first part that dealt with the principal tenets of the creed. In this unusual commentary, Alayi revisited medieval controversies on theological questions and offered his responses with current debates in Ottoman society in mind by highlighting the principles of *ehl-i sünnet* while disproving the views of non-Sunni groups, such as the Shiites and the Mu'tazilites. In support of his views, he drew evidence from such post-Ghazalian ulema as Fakhr al-Din Razi, Baydawi, and Davvani, all belonging to the Asharite school of theology.[224] By recycling Ghazali's recipe for the Seljuk ruler's creed and updating it to purify that of the Ottoman sultan, Alayi seems to have felt the same concern as other prominent Ottoman ulema who busied themselves with issuing juristic opinions, writing defensive treatises, and commenting on the canonical books of kalam in order to face the challenges posed by perceived heresies of the time.

Another émigré from the east who wrote in a fashion similar to Alayi was Muzaffer b. Osman el-Bermeki, with the pen name Hızır Münşi (d. 1556).[225] He fled Azerbaijan, took refuge in the Ottoman Empire, and composed *Akhlāq al-Atqiyā va Ṣifāt al-Aṣfiyā* (Morals of the Devout and Attributes of the Pure), a long treatise on ethics that he dedicated to Süleyman.[226] He devoted a long section to eulogizing Süleyman, whom he called "the lord of conjunction of the end of time" (*ṣāḥib-qirān-i ākhir al-zamān*). *Akhlāq al-Atqiyā* does not easily fit an established genre in ethics. It is an eclectic composition that combines stylistic features of various genres of which the principal sources are Ghazali, Tusi, and Davvani. The three major themes of the work are ethical theory, moral virtues of the ruler, and historical illustrations for exemplary acts. As such Hızır Münşi turned ethical doctrines of Sufi-minded philosophers into a mirror for princes.

He inserted a short résumé of his scholarly background in the preface of the book with a dramatic story of how he fled Safavid oppression for Ottoman justice. His tragic flight story interwoven with tidbits of clashes sparked by confessional identities, political loyalties, and imperial ambitions explains the permeation of anti-Safavid sentiments into Ottoman political thought. As he recounted, he used to serve in the court of the Shirwanshahs, who ruled in the eastern part of Caucasia, in his words, "since the time of the Sassanids."[227] Although he did not display a marked anti-Shii bias, he blamed Safavid aggression as the principal cause of his departure, a move he called a hegira. As a Sunni scholar, he chose flight because of the Safavids who broke down the order of religion and the world (*niẓām-i dīn u dunyā*) in Shirwan. He first fled to Georgia in 1533, where he could only stay for nine months because of being harassed by infidels (*kuffār*) before moving to Trabzon.[228] This was a time of turmoil in eastern Anatolia, Caucasia, Iran, and Iraq over which the Ottomans and the Safavids were engaged in a fierce competition. In 1533 the Ottomans waged a massive military campaign against the Safavids and occupied Tabriz in 1534. Shirwanshahs, for their killing of the founder of the Safavid dynasty, Junayd, were already natural allies of the Ottomans and archenemies of the Safavids. At the time of Hızır Münşi's flight, the reigning Shirwanshah ruler Khalil II (r. 1524–1535), whom he probably had served, had already been reduced to a vassal by the Safavids. The Shirwanshahs were subjugated by the Safavids after Isma'il I's invasion of the country and execution of Farrukh Yasar I in 1501. Shirwanshah rule was finally ended in 1538 by Tahmasb I despite Khalil II's attempt to regain his dynasty with Ottoman help. During this struggle between the local dynasty and the Safavids, Hızır Münşi might well have played a role in forging an alliance between the Sharvanshahs and the Ottomans.

Unlike these obscure men of learning from the east, Celalzade Mustafa, also known as Koca Nişancı, was already at the height of his career when he was composing his works.[229] He was a notable poet and historian who served as the chief of chancery for almost a quarter century during the reigns of Süleyman and Selim II. He came from a Turkish family that produced jurists and scholars, and made an early entrance to the bureaucratic service after his graduation from madrasa. Because of Celalzade's talent in language and excellence in prose writing, Piri Paşa employed him as his secretary and his affiliation with this respected grand vizier enabled him to secure his steady ascent on the bureaucratic career ladder.[230] While enjoying political support from Piri Paşa, he received his professional training from the chief of chancery Seydi Bey, whom he regarded as his mentor. After Piri Paşa's retirement he became a secretary to Ibrahim Paşa (d. 1536), who had been appointed to the vizierate with very little experience in statecraft against the established custom. Ibrahim Paşa's ignorance of governmental affairs made Celalzade his confidante and indispensable assistant. Celalzade was promoted to the position of chief of clerks, which he occupied for a decade, and finally became the chief of chancery from 1534 to 1557.

Contemporary accounts unanimously agree in attesting Celalzade's excellence in chancery and prose writing. He spent his career compiling numerous law books and decrees that came to be known by his name, and he also composed and translated a number of works, mostly in the field of history, during his retirement years after 1557. His best known work of history was *Ṭabaḳātü'l-Memālik* (Degrees of Kingdoms), planned as thirty volumes, of which only the last volume survived—or was written at all.[231] As perhaps the foremost expert on the Ottoman state of his time, he planned to write other volumes on Ottoman institutions, laws, and procedures, a project that probably never materialized. *Ṭabaḳātü'l-Memālik* is a work of belles-lettres as much as a chronicle of contemporary events in which the author, in the words of his contemporary Kınalızade, sacrificed meaning (*maʿnā*) in favor of pompous style.[232] His chronicle of the reign of Selim I, *Selīmnāme*, however, was a political treatise as well as a literary work of art.[233] In *Selīmnāme*, Celalzade not only described major events but also interpreted them to derive lessons, make normative judgments, and infer binding principles and proscriptive precedents. He devised the work as an illustrated manifesto demonstrating a model rulership as personified by Selim I and his grand vizier, Piri Paşa.

Celalzade's only book specifically devoted to the ethics of rulership was *Mevāhibü'l-Ḫallāḳ fī Merātibi'l-Aḫlāḳ* (Gifts of God in Ranks of Morality), a massive work organized into fifty-six chapters.[234] The book addressed statesmen and was better known as *Enīsü's-Selāṭīn ve Celīsü'l-Ḫavāḳīn* (Companion of Sultans and Comrade of Khakans), a handbook of ethical principles to be observed in statecraft. In addition to chapters directly related to political theory such as those dealing with governance (*siyāset*), justice, and consultation, the two longest chapters in *Mevāhibü'l-Ḫallāḳ* are on rulership (*salṭanat*) and the vizierate (*vezāret*). Despite addressing statesmen, the book reached a wider audience. The number of copies in libraries as well as testimonials from contemporaries indicate that the work was well received among Ottoman literati. In composing the book, Celalzade adopted a novel approach to ethics, different from Kınalızade's philosophical *Aḫlāḳ-ı ʿAlāʾī* or Eşrefoğlu Rumi's Sufistic *Müzekki'n-Nüfūs*.[235] Celalzade made a topical arrangement of the book around virtues, paying little attention to vices. He included only positive moral traits, declaring them degrees (*mertebe*) to be attained. Celalzade's principal source of inspiration was *Akhlāq-i Muḥsinī*. For the most part, *Mevāhibü'l-Ḫallāḳ* appears to have been an expanded translation of *Akhlāq-i Muḥsinī*. While fully incorporating Kashifi's book into his work, Celalzade rearranged the topics, added new topics, and significantly expanded each topic by adding his own views and illustrations, some of which were drawn from Ottoman history.

An equally celebrated statesman and scholar of this period was Kınalızade Ali Efendi, who belonged to a family of scholars from Isparta and was one of the most revered figures of the Ottoman learning establishment in the sixteenth century. Despite his complaints of being ignored in the early stages of his learning career, he quickly rose to top positions in both the learning profession and judiciary, including the professorship of Süleymaniye Madrasa and the military judgeship of Anatolia. After graduation from madrasa, he entered the service of Çivizade (d. 1587) and continued to be one of his most favored students. Çivizade, who briefly served as sheikh ul Islam, was a leading figure among the ulema faction critical of certain Sufi practices and government policies. Failing to obtain a teaching appointment through Çivizade, who had fallen from favor, Kınalızade turned to Ebussuud, Çivizade's critic and rival, and managed to impress the sheikh ul Islam with his competence in religious sciences, whereupon he received his first appointment as professor.[236]

Kınalızade, a jurist, poet, and statesman, was a respected name in scholarly, literary, and government circles. Besides writing poems in three languages, he established himself as a truly outstanding prose writer and gained fame through his short treatises on various subjects. All biographical works of his time unanimously describe Kınalızade as a polymathic scholar, an epitome of wisdom, and a virtuoso of literary articulation. In an age of towering literary figures, Beyani, who only gave mediocre descriptions of such figures as Baki and Celalzade, praised Kınalızade as having "no equal in prose and no match in verse."[237] In a punning manner, Mustafa Âli compared his erudition in diverse sciences to that of Ibn Kemal [literally, son of Erudition], perhaps the most revered of all Ottoman scholars, and claimed that had Kınalızade lived longer he would have surpassed Ibn Kemal's fame and could well have become known as Ebu'l-Kemalat, literally, father of erudition.[238] Similarly, Aşık Çelebi compared his mastery in numerous sciences, ranging from geometry to grammar, to that of the greatest figures in these respective sciences.[239]

Regardless of the scholarly and artistic value of his works, Kınalızade seems to have been a very engaging person at scholarly and literary gatherings and had an electrifying effect on anybody he met, mesmerizing them with his character, knowledge, and skills. As all his biographers agreed, Kınalızade was a sage of the time, an ultimate authority on all branches of learning whom his peers would consult on the most intriguing questions of their respective disciplines. Yet, excluding his many short treatises, commentaries, and poetry, Kınalızade left only one sizable work as proof of his vast learning, *Aḫlāḳ-ı ʿAlāʾī*.[240] The work was, by the consensus of his contemporaries as well as later readers, one of the highest achievements of Ottoman learning. Beyani stated that it turned the works of Tusi and Davvani into old garments (*aḫlaḳ-ı siyāb*).[241] Kınalızade completed the work in 1565 and dedicated it to Grand Vizier Ali Paşa, after whose name he titled it: *Aḫlāḳ-ı ʿAlāʾī* (The Book of ʿAlī or, by allusion, The Exalted Book).[242] The young Mustafa Âli, who had the privilege of having met with him, witnessed how Kınalızade wrote his work:

> While he was a magistrate in Damascus he was busy with composing his esteemed work *Aḫlāḳ-ı ʿAlāʾī*. He would show a great affection and friendship toward this poor soul and invite me to join his exhilarating conversations. He would hear a chapter from my book *Enīsü'l-Ḳulūb* (Companion of Hearts), which I was composing. Then he himself would read a chapter from his *Aḫlāḳ-ı ʿAlāʾī* and ask me to say if there is anything that requires intervention. He would say that the purpose of friendship is to look at the work with an enemy's eye and point at human errors. Essentially, the work of a given week would be presented

by both of us. When there is something to oppose, a correction or a rephrasing would be considered an obligation.[243]

The modest and scrupulous Kınalızade composed *Aḫlāḳ-ı ʿAlāʾī* with a lofty claim that reflects the increasing self-esteem and self-confidence among Ottoman intellectuals of the period who sought to compose works comparable to what they once deemed to be the unsurpassable achievements of pre-Ottoman sages. In the preface, he stated that before him three previous authors had written on the same subject.[244] The first was Nasir al-Din Tusi, the author of *Akhlāq-i Nāṣirī*, whom he credited with renewing the foundation of philosophy after its demise. The second was Davvani, whom Kınalızade praised for renewing the religious creed and embellishing the library of philosophy with his *Akhlāq-i Jālālī*. The third was Kashifi, who Kınalızade noted did not follow philosophical inquiry (*taḥḳīḳāt-ı ḥikemiyye*) and scientific scrutiny (*tedḳīḳāt-ı ʿilmiyye*) in writing his work *Akhlāq-i Muḥsinī*. Yet he still valued *Akhlāq-i Muḥsinī* for its style and readability that made this work more popular than the first two. Noting that there was no such work in Turkish (*zebān-ı Türkī-i rūmī*), he decided to write the fourth book and wished that it would be more popular than the previous trio: "It is my hope that this book will be more widely received than the previous ones and become a new robe for the book of beloved wisdom, not a worn cloth."[245] To bring his hope to fruition Kınalızade, despite largely depending on Davvani's *Akhlāq-i Jālālī* for its format, designed the work to reflect the distinguishing features of the previous three works. Namely, he composed *Aḫlāḳ-ı ʿAlāʾī* as a work of practical philosophy that conformed to Sunni theology and embellished it with a literary style. As he praised Tusi for founding the science of ethics, Davvani for disseminating ethical teachings, and Kashifi for adding a literary flavor to ethics, he justified and praised his own work as refreshing the teaching of ethics that had undergone a fallow period since the composition of the three earlier works.[246]

As its numerous copies in Ottoman libraries demonstrate, *Aḫlāḳ-ı ʿAlāʾī* lived up to its promise and became an instant success soon after its completion and remained the definitive work of ethics among the Ottoman literati thereafter.[247] Writing almost a century after Kınalızade, Katib Çelebi recorded that *Aḫlāḳ-ı ʿAlāʾī* was superior to all other works of ethics that had been written before.[248] There were three principal reasons why the work gained a privileged status among many other compilations on ethics and government. First, having the Ottoman audience in mind, Kınalızade adapted the teachings of ethical philosophy to the Ottoman context. He left out issues and questions that he deemed not relevant to Ottoman society and instead elaborated on questions of particular interest for his audience. Second, he introduced the Ottoman experience into ethical philosophy by drawing his examples and illustrations from the deeds of revered Ottoman figures. This made *Aḫlāḳ-ı ʿAlāʾī* an expression of Ottoman ideals in morality, government, and social order. Third, he turned Tusi's and Davvani's cut-and-dry ethical philosophy into a literary masterpiece, embellishing it with poetry and crafting it to suit Ottoman taste. For the Ottoman literati, who were accustomed to reading the major achievements of Islamic culture in philosophy, literature, and religious sciences in their original languages, *Aḫlāḳ-ı ʿAlāʾī* demonstrated in the field of practical philosophy that such sophisticated works could also be written in Turkish.

While Celalzade and Kınalızade followed and even claimed to have surpassed well-known canons of ethics, Abdülkerim b. Mehmed (d. 1574) opted for a relatively new genre for his short treatise on ethical philosophy of rulership. Ottoman sources highlight Abdülkerim as the grandson of Ebussuud, Süleyman's chief of the religious establishment, who remained a towering figure in later historical memory. Thanks to his family dynasty of scholars, Abdülkerim quickly rose in ranks and served as professor in some of the most prestigious madrasas of his time but was little noted for his scholarly achievements besides his teaching skills, probably because of his death in his early thirties.[249] Abdülkerim wrote at least one well-received work, *Neṣāyiḥü'l-Ebrār* (Counsels of the Righteous), which he must have completed in his early twenties, and dedicated it to Süleyman. [250] It is a compilation of aphorismic statements collected from Persian sources on moral principles of good governance. He seems to have composed two other short treatises on political ethics: One is a collection of stories on wise kingship from well-known names from Alexander to Bozorgmehr and the other is a compilation of advices from philosophers, mostly from Aristotle and Plato.[251] In format, *Neṣāyiḥü'l-Ebrār* is an exact replica of Musannifek's two formulaic works on government, each maxim involving four elements. It is also a close kin to those of Musannifek in content as most topics of advice are identical. Unless Abdülkerim used and modified Musannifek's texts to his own liking, both authors must have used similar sources, most possibly *Jāvidān Khirad* of Ibn Miskawayh.[252] Yet Abdülkerim's text differs from those of Musannifek in two respects: First, he composed the text in high Turkish of the sixteenth century and turned it into a literary masterpiece. Thanks to this quality, the text reached a wider audience than Musannifek's similar works. Second, while Musannifek presented the maxims as his own craftsmanship, Abdülkerim quoted each from a respectable name, thus rendering the work more authoritative and quotable. As such, Abdülkerim turned the text into a Turkish digest of political wisdom representing multiple learned traditions, a reference manual for ethics of rulership.

STATECRAFT

A close kin to ethics in political writing and, in some cases, undistinguishably enmeshed with it was the literature on statecraft that became increasingly differentiated in this period with its shifting of focus from elaborating on govenance as part of self-government to governance of others and institutions of the state. Abdülmuin Lütfi Paşa (d. 1562), having no respect for literary expressions of political views, wrote on rulership from a completely different perspective. He was the only grand vizier who wrote on political theory in this period. He came to Ottoman service as a child levy from the Balkans, probably from Albania, and received his education and training in the palace school. He served in various capacities and offices throughout the reigns of Bayezid II, Selim I, and Süleyman, which enabled him to gain a unique experience in statecraft. He was appointed to the grand vizierate in 1539 as an experienced, successful, and respected statesman who also enjoyed the distinction of being a dynastic son-in-law. During his term, he undertook significant institutional, military, and financial reforms that he later bragged about, but failed to forge friendly relations with palace factions that were increasingly becoming powerful in government. Despite his record of excellence in government service, his grand vizierate lasted for only two years, ending with a humiliating dismissal that forced him to choose retirement.

Lütfi Paşa was the first political author who critically analyzed Ottoman politics as the benchmark of good government. Although he served as a grand vizier to Süleyman, his influence on subsequent generations of statesmen and scholars endured not because he was a model of a grand vizier but because he was the first author to formulate the Ottoman canon in government. His long service in a variety of government offices, both at the political center and in the provinces, including appointments on land and sea, gave him a unique experience for developing his thoughts on all aspects rulership. Compared to his contemporaries, he was a self-taught scholar, mostly relying on his own experiences and conclusions in attuning his views on politics. He stood out as a statesman scholar who wrote on contemporary government and politics using his own observations. Lütfi Paşa was one of the first authors who significantly took the Ottoman experience into consideration in political theory. He was a defender of the Ottoman dynasty, a critic of government and a political reformist at the same time. Lütfi Paşa shifted the focus of Ottoman political writing from the sultan and religion, including morality, to government and law. He criticized past and contemporary government practices that were not compatible with the Ottoman law (*ḳānūn*) and reprofiled the sultan as one who makes, observes, and implements laws in accordance with the foundational principles of the Ottoman Empire.

During his retreat after retirement, Lütfi Paşa devoted himself to learning and writing on history, government, jurisprudence, theology, and even medicine. He wrote simple works for the general public, and none of his works appears to have been acclaimed by contemporary scholars, except for those he wrote on government, his field of expertise. Despite his skills as an administrator, reformist, and scholar, he seems to have suffered from an inability to forge productive social relationships. He did not even abstain from criticizing the most distinguished scholars of his time, such as Ebussuud, for being ignorant.[253] He had very little esteem for his colleagues in government and the scholarly community, an attitude that left him with few friends to appreciate his work. For Lütfi Paşa, writing about such diverse fields was a way of proving the validity of his views and opposing the people who failed to appreciate his excellence.

Lütfi Paşa wrote *Tevārīḫ-i Āl-i ʿOs̱mān* as a general history of the Ottoman dynasty from its inception to his own day.[254] *Tevārīḫ* is not a simple chronicle of events but is a public statement of Lütfi Paşa's perception and critique of Ottoman government as well as a record of his own deeds within the general framework of Ottoman history. In the preface, he declared that the Ottoman dynasty was a chosen one, superior to all others that preceded it, a dynasty that produced rulers who were renewers (*müceddid*) of their respective ages. Throughout the work, he compared the statesmen and ulema of his time to those of previous periods and showed the decline in the quality of people that occupied these positions. In recounting the events of his time, Lütfi Paşa focused on his own deeds and demonstrated how he reformed the government and instituted just practices. Through historical evidence, *Tevārīḫ* aimed to display the ineptitude of the statesmen and the ulema of his time while praising the Ottoman dynasty and highlighting his own performance in government as exemplary. Yet it shares the general attitude of Ottoman chronicles in redeeming the dynasty from all blemishes and attributing all the blame for perceived failures to specific individuals or groups from the ruling elite.

Lütfi Paşa made a name for himself in Ottoman history not as a scholar, historian, or a statesman but as the author of *Āṣafnāme*, his manual for the vizierate. The work received such great acclaim that it became the most widely read treatise on political theory among the Ottoman literati. Lütfi Paşa wrote the work after 1553, more than a decade after his retirement, probably during the second term of his successor, Rüstem Paşa. According to his own statement, his purpose in writing this treatise was to guide his successors in the vizierate. But the tone of his language and the content of the treatise show that it was more than a compilation of recommendations on the profession. *Āṣafnāme* is a record of Lütfi Paşa's accomplishments during his short term in office as well as a prescriptive statement of the uncompromising rules of the vizierate in Ottoman state tradition. It was a reform treatise written by a disgruntled former grand vizier who was unhappy about, and critical of, the way the vizierate was run after his forced retirement.

Āṣafnāme was an innovative treatise in both form and content. It does not fit into any of the conventional genres of political writing. Unlike juristic and theological works, it does not take its authority from canonical religious texts, nor does it provide formal statements in its quest to conform government and rulership to religious law and creed. In contrast with works of ethics, it does not offer moral recommendations for the betterment of government. Except for being an advice book, there is no resemblance between *Āṣafnāme* and the popular mirrors for princes genre. The most distinctive features of works in the mirror for princes genre, their literary and entertaining qualities, were absent in *Āṣafnāme,* which contained no poetry. The few brief anecdotes it provided were prescriptive precedents rather than remote stories to draw moral lessons. With *Āṣafnāme,* Lütfi Paşa created a new form of political writing that inspired numerous other authors to write along the same lines.

A text similar to *Āṣafnāme* was *Meṣāliḥü'l-Müslimīn ve Menāfiʿül-Mü'minīn* (The Affairs of Muslims and Benefits of Believers) by an unknown author.[255] Textual evidence suggests that the treatise, long believed to be a seventeenth-century text, was most probably written in the 1550s, shortly after Lütfi Paşa revolutionized Ottoman political writing with his *Āṣafnāme.*[256] Both *Āṣafnāme* and *Meṣāliḥü'l-Müslimīn* addressed the grand vizierate and promoted the idea of law in government. Unlike *Āṣafnāme,* however, which had an immense impact on subsequent authors and of which there were numerous manuscript copies across Ottoman libraries, *Meṣāliḥü'l-Müslimīn* remained relatively unnoticed by a wider audience until modern times.

Meṣāliḥü'l-Müslimīn must have been written by a seasoned civil servant, for the text indicates that its author was among the close circle of people around the sultan. The anonymous author displayed an impressive command of the current state of ruling institutions, market conditions, and social structures in the Ottoman Empire, covering topics ranging from the janissaries to market inspectors, and from taxation to heretics. In each chapter, the author made a brief evaluation of the contemporary situation from a historical perspective, pointed to shortcomings, deficiencies, and problems, and suggested reforms. The treatise provided the most detailed portrait of Ottoman institutions and the political responsibilities expected from Ottoman rulership in the sixteenth century. Along with Lütfi Paşa, by discussing political questions in reference to the actual government, the anonymous author marked the beginning of the transformation of Ottoman political theory in the mid-sixteenth century. This new breed of statesman or bureaucrat-authors abandoned the conventional tendency to elaborate on abstract principles of government, ethics, and jurisprudence, and instead focused on law and institutions in political theory.

Lacking an obvious influence from *Āṣafnāme, Meṣāliḥü'l-Müslimīn* appears to be the second text on government in this period that broke with conventional genres of political writings in both form and content. While *Āṣafnāme* was the first treatise that portrayed the ideal Ottoman government, *Meṣāliḥü'l-Müslimīn* was the earliest of reform manuals for government. In contrast to the *Āṣafnāme,* which urged the grand vizier to comply with the existing laws of state as the ideal way of governing, *Meṣāliḥü'l-Müslimīn* advocated the idea that the best government could be achieved only by enacting laws in response to changing circumstances and abandoning redundant and outmoded laws. Unlike some well-known seventeenth- and eighteenth-century reform treatises, *Meṣāliḥü'l-Müslimīn* never advocated a retrospective reform project or called for a return to an idealized past by eliminating innovative practices. In a more radical voice, it proposed to reorganize government by enacting up-to-date laws in response to changing circumstances.

The composition of *Āṣafnāme* and *Meṣāliḥü'l-Müslimīn* around the mid-sixteenth century was by no means accidental. These so-called reform treatises, often lump-summed as the decline literature, herald a new orientation in political thought that dominated Ottoman perceptions of rulership for the next two centuries.[257] This patently Ottoman genre shifted the focus of political writing from advising to analysis where *ḳānūn*-consciousness and the idea of governing in accordance with the precedence replaced juristic normativism. The pursuit of morality, upheld by Sufis and ethicists as well as idealistic designs, undertaken by philosophers gave way to empiricism that promoted the Ottoman model of government with focus on institutions, customs, and procedures. Yet, it was hardly a reaction to the prevailing paradigm of unified authority that had been in the making since the foundation of the Ottoman state through the works of Sufis and Sufi-minded scholars and bureaucrats. More so than any other sultan, Süleyman epitomized the perfect Ottoman ruler as envisioned through the mystical conceptions of the caliphate and increasingly voiced with a messianic tenor. The Ottoman sultan, as imagined by the ruling elite, having combined the rulership of both temporal and spiritual realms with perfect morality and unmatched executive power, was considered to be detached from the actual government. The mundane government simply turned into the executive arm of the sultan's cosmic rulership under the exclusive authority of his deputy, the grand vizier, who was fully bound by the prescribed Ottoman *ḳānūn*. The Sufistic ideal that envisioned the caliph, pole, or succor (*ghaws*) as God's deputy on Earth, with worldly rulers as his representatives, was materialized in Süleyman's bigger-than-a-sultan persona.

The ruler-centric tradition of political theory faded away in favor of the vizier-centric vision of government. The very Ottoman experience in government made the vizierate the main battlefield of clashing visions of ideal rulership. Such developments as the withdrawal of the sultan from actual government, the rise of *ḳānūn* as the definitive law of government, institutionalization of government functions, the establishment of procedures of conduct, and the emergence of the vizierate as the highest office in the empire with extensive powers, brought the vizierate into the focus of political theory. Bureaucrat authors acquired more freedom in profiling an ideal vizier than the ruler. Further, with few exceptions, anything they could hope from the ruler could be done through the vizier. The personality of the ruler, which had been the focus of pre-Ottoman moralist tendency, lost its importance. The qualifications and capabilities of the grand vizier became more important than those of the ruler for the establishment of good government, a perspective that turned the state and law into principal objects of analysis in political theory.

JURISTIC PERSPECTIVES

Unlike the writings of statecraft, which were largely the preserve of statesmen, authors writing in the juristic convention tended to have different professional backgrounds. One such author was the former grand vizier Lütfi Paşa who composed *Khalāṣ al-Umma fī Maʿrifat al-Aʾimma* (Salvation of the Community in Recognizing the Leaders) in 1554, at a time when Süleyman was leading a major campaign against the Safavids, to defend the legitimacy of the Ottoman caliphate or, more specifically, the Ottoman sultan's right to bear the titles caliph and imam. He wrote the treatise to oppose the twelfth-century theologian Nasafi's (d. 1142) ruling that Qurayshi descent was a condition for a legitimate caliphate. Nasafi's short text and Taftazani's (d. 1390) long commentary were both popular textbooks widely read in Ottoman domains. Although Lütfi Paşa wrote the treatise against the advocates of Nasafi's view, the question of the Ottoman claim for the caliphate did not seem to have caused a visible controversy in this period. As the title caliphate came to be used for every independent ruler during this time, the debate Lütfi Paşa addressed, in terms of its scholarly value, was already an obsolete one. He nevertheless took the issue seriously and, perhaps driven by the desire to teach the ulema a lesson, he wrote the treatise in both Arabic and Persian to prove his linguistic capabilities and juristic erudition. Further, as a former grand vizier, he was still tuned to the polyphonic voices in the global theatre of competition for universal sovereignty for which it was essential that the Ottoman ruler is portrayed as a caliph per the juristic canon and an heir to the historical caliphate. He disproved Nasafi's view by extensively quoting the canonical sources of the Hanafi school of law, thus juxtaposing the juristic views of the Hanafis against the theological view of the Asharites. What makes this text more striking is Lütfi Paşa's use of esoteric texts in support of his argument, most notably Abdurrahman Bistami's *al-Fawāʾiḥ al-Miskiyya fī al-Fawātiḥ al-Makkiyya* (Perfumed Fragrances on the Meccan Openings).[258] This esoteric and prognosticative work on the enumeration of sciences, written in Arabic and dedicated to Murad II in 1440, was rediscovered in the sixteenth century as a master text for occultists and translated into Turkish in 1570.[259] If this is not a sign of his poor juristic credentials, it shows his pragmatism in developing juristic argument by circumventing the discipline's methodological principles and freely using any supporting argument in favor of building his case for the legality of the Ottoman caliphate.[260]

Lütfi Paşa's juristic defense of the Ottoman caliphate was unique in the sixteenth century. A more typical juristic text, *Risāla fīmā Lazima ʿalā al-Mulūk* (A Treatise on What Rulers Need), whose author remains anonymous, was composed for Süleyman, advocating government in accordance with Islamic law.[261] It is written as a true advice book for statesmen, replete with principles of government, ethical norms, and anecdotes of wisdom drawn from a diverse body of sources. The author, who appears to be well versed in both religious sciences and literature, wrote the work in Arabic, a language that addressed a smaller audience but enjoyed a higher authority in relating the intended message. The treatise lacks a systematic structure and all sections start with the phrase "know that" (*iʿlam*) without a title, a literary style that evokes the master-pupil relationship, mostly used by the ulema in various types of advice books. The text is rich in its references as the author quoted from such authors as Avicenna, Ghazali, Abu al-Lays, Baydawi, and many others.

Through the seemingly unorganized collection of political wisdom, the author underlined three main points. First, the author urged the sultan to be diligent in undertaking a fight (jihad, *ghazw*, *muqātala*) against the people of polytheism (*shirk*) and sedition (*faṣād*), eliminating vices (*dafʿ al-sharr*), and cleansing disbelief while warning against innovations (*bidʿa*).[262] Such views were commonly voiced by many leading ulema who wrote treatises and issued fatwas to urge the sultan to continue his expansion policy against the realm of Christians, eliminate the Shiite threat posed by Safavid propaganda, and suppress the frequent heretical movements that could easily turn into rebellions.[263] The general tenor of the vast jihad literature of the time was not so much waging military campaigns against the infidels but cleansing the abode of Islam from impurities in faith. Second, the text elaborated the behavioral aspects of good governance and underlined the significance of proper etiquette in rulership. With special emphasis on the vizier's relationship to the sultan, his advice was directed toward securing the attendees' safety in the face of the sultan's temper as well as showing ways of making one's word effective in the presence of the sultan. He urged visitors to the sultan (*dākhil ʿalā al-sulṭān*), for example, to observe certain rules because he expected them to perform the duty of commanding right and forbidding wrong (*al-amr bi al-maʿrūf wa al-nahy ʿan al-munkar*) and praised it as the most virtuous form of waging jihad, according to the authority of a prophetic tradition.[264] Third, the author devoted a long section to the personal life of statesmen and admonished them against the harmful effects of wine drinking. The subject was commonly dealt with in most advice books that regarded the moral and physical health of statesmen essential for good government. In contrast with the prevailing view in the advice literature that displayed a degree of complacence in allowing the ruler to breach certain religious prohibitions, the author put forth strict warnings against drinking.[265] While the anonymous author enumerated formal juristic views on the subject as well as moral teachings from respected figures, he displayed more concern about preserving the health of government than about keeping the sultan from committing sins. On rational and empirical evidence, the treatise instructed the sultan that drinking would impair one's judgment in decision making, lead to negligence in rulership, and cause failure to protect the realm, which might result in losing one's auspicious turn in rulership (*zavāl al-dawla*). Among pious authors with strong convictions, admonishing against drinking was a crafty way of socially distancing the sultan from the company of drinking courtiers whose lax moral standards could affect the sultan's governance in abominable ways. Jurists and Sufis, instead, invited the sultan to have their company to ensure that his decisions were in line with their world views and group interests.

Writing from a similar perspective but in a completely different format, Hüseyin b. Hasan dedicated his work on the vizierate, *Laṭāʾif al-Afkār wa Kāshif al-Asrār* (Fine Thoughts and Revealer of Secrets), to Grand Vizier Ibrahim Paşa.[266] Besides his self-identification as a qadi, there is no information available in contemporary sources.[267] He wrote the work in 1529, the year in which Ibrahim Paşa was appointed commander in chief (*serʿasker*) and governor of Rumelia in addition to grand vizierate, just before Süleyman's fourth military campaign headed towards Vienna.[268] Hüseyin's extolling of Ibrahim Paşa in his succinct eulogy in the preface portrays a truly exceptional grand vizier with extraordinary powers.[269] Hüseyin compiled *Laṭāʾif al-Afkār* as a concise encyclopedia of government, ethics, history, literature, and religious traditions, an instructive handbook for the education of a grand vizier who had risen to that position at the age of twenty-nine. *Laṭāʾif al-Afkār* consists of three parts: government (*siyāsa*); history of caliphs; and miscellaneous topics including ethical virtues, manners, literature, and wonders of nature.

In *Laṭāʾif al-Afkār*, Hüseyin gives the first juristic exposition of Ottoman government by outlining the legal requirements for government offices by explaining principal government functions, *salṭana* and *wilāya*, and two principles of government, consultation and justice. *Laṭāʾif al-Afkār* is among the few texts in this period that used juristic terminology in explaining the structure of government. Similar to the aforementioned anonymous author, Hüseyin instructed the reader with an authoritative language, introducing juristic rulings, ethical admonitions, and useful information with the word "know that" (*iʿlam*). He then distinguished between what was required in government and what was recommended through juristic terminology as "required" (*wājib*) and "recommended" (*ḥasuna*). The first part of the text established the sultan's responsibilities and obligations toward God and his subjects followed by layers of government, including different forms of the vizierate and principal offices of government: the office of legal rulings (*iftā*), judicial system (*qaḍā*), inspection (*ḥiṣba*), chancery (*inshā*), bookkeeping (*dafātīr*), and treasury (*amvāl*). The qualifications Hüseyin stipulated for the holders of these offices were quite strict. The *muftī*, for example, had to be a jurist capable of independent judgment (*mujtahid*), a rank that could hardly be claimed by any Ottoman jurist. For all officeholders, he prescribes consultative decision making and just rulings as indispensable principles of government.

The second part of *Laṭāʾif al-Afkār* is a succinct universal history and a discussion of the concept of history in general with the aim of placing the Ottoman dynasty in the context of world history. It starts with the creation of Adam and eschatological prophesies about the life of the earth. On the authority of past historians, Hüseyin implied that the life of the earth should last until 7000 years after Adam and should not extend more than 1400 years after the hegira.[270] At the time Hüseyin wrote his treatise in 935 Hegira, millenarian expectations were already on the rise. He comforted the reader that the end of days was at least four centuries away. He then described how different ancient peoples started their calendars and explained the establishment of the Muslim calendar. After providing a clear picture of creation, the earth's life, the start of history, and the calendar, he recounted the history of caliphs starting from the first human being and caliph Adam all the way to the Ottomans. He thus placed the Ottoman caliphate in a single lineage that started with Adam and continued through various dynasties. What is striking in his exposition is that, after explaining the caliphate of the Mamluks, he started the Ottoman caliphate with Selim I, who conquered Egypt and ended the Mamluk dynasty, rather than with the founder of the Ottoman dynasty. For Hüseyin, the caliphal lineage continued after the Mamluks through the caliphates of Selim I and Süleyman.[271]

A contemporary of Hüseyin was Muhammed b. Mehasin el-Ensari, who dedicated his work, *Tuḥfat al-Zamān ilā al-Malik al-Muẓaffar Sulaymān* (The Present of Time for Süleyman the Victorious Ruler), to Süleyman.[272] *Tuḥfat al-Zamān* is an advice book combining ethical topics and juristic principles of rulership, written from a distinctly Hanafi perspective but without sectarian consciousness. Ensari's principal source of inspiration appears to have been Turtushi's *Sirāj al-Mulūk*, which expounded similar juristic views on government and society. His long eulogy for Süleyman in the preface praised the sultan for saving Muslims from oppression, poverty, and heresy. In speaking of the ranks of governorship in Arab provinces he instructed the sultan that the proper hierarchy would be, in a descending order, Damascus, Aleppo, Tripoli, Hama, Safed, Homs, and Baalbek. This suggests that the work must have been written shortly after the ascension of Süleyman to the throne, around 1524, when the Ottoman government suppressed a major rebellion by the governor of Egypt, Ahmed Paşa, and secured order in the newly conquered provinces of Egypt and Syria. Ensari must have been a Hanafi jurist from Syria because the few specific remarks he made about his time all referred to this region.

Tuḥfat al-Zamān bears the stamp of late Mamluk writings on rulership.[273] Besides Birgivi's brief statement about the community's obligation to obey rulers in his *Dhukhr al-Mulūk*, this is the only other treatise that problematized the question of obeying the ruler in this period. Works that were dedicated to the sultan or the grand vizier tended to avoid the question of legitimacy altogether. However, writing from Syria, where anti-Ottoman sentiments were still high among the nobility, the author opts to establish the sultan's legitimacy in juristic terms. Ensari devoted the preface and first chapter of *Tuḥfat al-Zamān* to proving that the Ottoman rule was legitimate and that the subjects were required to pay allegiance to the ruler in accordance with the Sharia. Writing soon after the conquest of Arab lands and the suppression of major rebellions that ensued, Ensari wrote his treatise for a Syrian audience in mind, specifically the strong Hanafi establishment of the region. Ensari not only prescribed the rules of just government for the sultan to follow but also showed the responsibilities of subjects, particularly the ulema, in guiding the ruler to the path of justice. While other contemporary works were content with advising the sultan to consult the ulema, in the fourth chapter Ensari exalted the position of the ulema above that of the ruler, calling it "the ruler's adherence (*iqtidā*) to the ulema."[274] Ensari not only legitimized Ottoman rule of Syria but also reclaimed the autonomy of Syrian Hanafi jurists that they long enjoyed during the Mamluk times.

Reflecting the author's juristic perspective, *Tuḥfat al-Zamān* turns the treasury (*bayt al-māl*) and legitimate sources of revenue into principal questions of good governance. In this respect, the author appears to have preceded other Ottoman authors, such as Birgivi, Taşköprizade, and Dede Cöngi, and Fudayl Çelebi, who displayed a similar concern and wrote treatises or sections on government revenue. While Ensari made the treasury a part of political theory, the subject itself was already among the public issues dealt with by the Ottoman ulema of the period. The diversification of revenues and expenditures in the sixteenth century as well as questionable government policies regarding land regime, commerce, and taxation prompted leading jurists to provide juristic resolutions on monetary, fiscal, and economic issues.[275] The Hanafi jurists of Syria were even more sensitive on this issue as seen in the writings of Ibn Nujaym (d. 1563), whose concern Ensari seems to have reflected.[276] The Syrian bias of *Tuḥfat al-Zamān* becomes more visible on the question of non-Muslims in Muslim polity. Ensari strictly rejected the possibility of employing them in government. Given the well-established Ottoman policy of preserving local political structures after conquest, Ensari was making an appeal to the Ottoman ruler to stick with the policy of not employing non-Muslims in government and to abandon the practice of pre-Ottoman dynasties. He appears to have been so concerned about the issue that he proved the illegitimacy of employing non-Muslims on the ground of two schools of law, Hanafi and Shafi'i, although he himself and the Ottoman governing elite were mostly Hanafis.

Unlike these little known jurists whose works were imbued with literature, history, and philosophy, Dede Cöngi (d. 1567) was a high-profile jurist who wrote his treatises in a strictly juristic format. A versatile scholar who took his nickname from a popular commentary on a work of Arabic grammar, Dede Cöngi wrote on a variety of topics within the conventions of classical Islamic sciences such as *hadīth* (prophetic traditions) and *tafsīr* (Qur'anic commentary). He started his scholarly career at a relatively late age, while he was an illiterate tanner, but subsequently had a successful professional life.

After teaching in madrasas in Amasya, Iznik, Bursa, Diyarbakır, and Aleppo, he became a mufti of Kaffa, where he retired. Dede Cöngi did not aspire to high judicial positions, nor did he enjoy close relations with high-ranking statesmen.[277] He was a dedicated professor and a spiritual man who spent his retirement as an ascetic. Yet he wrote two pioneering works on government for purely scholarly purposes with no ambition to gain the favor of statesmen. For his contemporaries, he personified the good scholar for his erudition, piety, modesty, and abstinence from political engagement.

His lesser known work was a treatise on the public treasury that he composed while he was in Amasya and dedicated to Prince Mustafa.[278] In this work, he established the legitimate sources of income and their allocation to specific expenses required by the Sharia. But Dede Cöngi owed his reputation to his second treatise, for he was the first Ottoman author to write on *al-Siyāsa al-Sharʿiyya*, a political genre popularized by Ibn Taymiyya in the thirteenth century.[279] The treatise, better known as *Siyāsetnāme*, was well received throughout the Ottoman Empire as it disseminated from the Balkans to Arabic-speaking lands. It was translated into Turkish by three different authors. *al-Siyāsa al-Sharʿiyya* delineates sultanic authority in the field of criminal law, an area that was the exclusive preserve of jurists, and reconciles sultanic law (*ḳānūn*) and the Sharia. Many leading ulema among his contemporaries, including Ibn Kemal and Ebussuud, also sought to establish the Sharia basis of the sultanic laws.[280] Dede Cöngi made use of a wide range of medieval works of Hanafi jurists, including Sarakhsi (d. 1090), Marghinani (d. 1197), and Bazzazi (d. 1424). Despite being a Hanafi, he used sources from the other three major schools of law as well. Among his principal non-Hanafi sources were the Shafi'i jurist Mawardi, Maliki jurist Qarafi (d. 1285), and Hanbali jurist Ibn Qayyim (d. 1350). Dede Cöngi legitimized Ottoman criminal law and the Ottoman ruler's prerogative to pass laws by refuting contrary views from different legal schools of thought. Although Ottoman judicial bureaucracy and education were distinctly Hanafi, recently incorporated Muslim lands included dominant Hanbali, Shafi'i, and Maliki communities.[281] Unlike other fields of Sharia law, *al-siyāsa al-sharʿiyya* was an area that could not be exercised within the confines of one sect but needed to be a universal standard across the empire. Thus it had to be legitimate in the eyes of all mainstream schools of law. Yet, Dede Cöngi's preference for the Hanafi jurisprudence is unmistakable as he uses sources from other schools of law only to supplement his main sources of Hanafi law, such as Trablusi's *Muʿīn al-Ḥukkām*.[282]

In *al-Siyāsa al-Sharʿiyya*, Dede Cöngi addressed three principal issues. First, he offered a theoretical overview of the relation between the sultan's governance, including legal enactments, and the Sharia. Second, on the basis of specific examples, he discussed the domain of *al-siyāsa al-sharʿiyya* and the extent of the ruler's authority in its application. Third, he delineated the authority of judges and governors in the application of criminal law, an area that caused tension and confusion in numerous cases throughout Ottoman history. Dede Cöngi used *siyāsa* to mean both governance and law. In many cases, he simply used law (*ḳānūn*) in referring to *siyāsa*, which turned his treatise into a specific discussion of the legitimization of the Ottoman *ḳānūn* on the basis of the Sharia. He divided the *siyāsa* into two types, just (*ʿādila*) and unjust (*ẓālima*), and granted the determination of the severity of punishments necessitated to the sole prerogative of the ruler. He argued that the Sharia position is the middle course between the two extremes that he dubbed as *ifrāṭ* and *tafrīṭ*. For him, the proponents of *ifrāṭ* did not accept *siyāsa* as part of the Sharia, whereas the *tafrīṭ* party recognized any sort of *siyāsa* as legal on the basis of the Sharia.[283] He clung to two key principles in establishing the legitimacy of the *siyāsa*: change of circumstances (*taghayyur*) and social well-being (*al-maṣāliḥ al-mursala*).[284] Dede Cöngi envisioned a dynamic Sharia law and, with ample historical evidence, claimed that change in historical circumstances required adjustments (and amendments) in legal rules. This was a well-established principle of Hanafi methodology applied to the case of Ottoman law.[285] He then justified the necessity of the *siyāsa* law by referring to the Maliki concept of *al-maṣāliḥ al-mursala*, a principle that allowed adjustments to the Sharia law in favor of social well-being.[286] Its near counterpart in the Hanafi school, the *maṣlaḥa*, was widely alluded to by other leading Ottoman jurists in advocating the Ottoman law against the literal interpretations of Hanafi law in the sixteenth century.[287]

Very similar to Dede Cöngi in character and juristic views was Birgivi, whose activist juristic writings against what he considered as corruption of Islamic faith and practice inspired generations of scholars with revivalist zeal in and outside the Ottoman Empire. Among the nearly sixty works he wrote, the better-known ones fall into three broad categories of grammar, piety, and juristic polemics.[288] His short treatises on Arabic grammar were adopted as textbooks in Ottoman madrasas and conferred upon his name a rare authority that also led the audience to his works in other fields. His polemical treatises, particularly his refutation of the established view on the legitimacy of the cash foundations, brought him face to face with the most respected ulema of the time and turned him into a powerful voice of dissent and social critique. His works on piety were directed at eliminating innovations and reinstituting pristine Islam.

Takiyyüddin Mehmed b. Pir Ali (d. 1573), who later gained the epithet Birgivi for teaching in Birgi, was born into a well-known ulema family with Sufi affiliation from Balıkesir. After receiving a solid education from famed scholars, he pursued a judicial career in early life, becoming an inheritance apportioner (*ḳaṣṣām*) in Edirne in the service of a military judge, his master and patron Abdurrahman Efendi. Dissatisfied for spiritual and ethical reasons, he decided to distance himself from government and worldly pursuits, and entered the service of Sufi shaykh Abdullah Karamani of the Bayrami order.[289] Although little is known about his experience in the Sufi path, at least two of his later biographers categorized him among the Sufi shaykhs rather than the ulema, while some called him *ḳutbü'l-ʿārifīn* (the pole of knowers).[290] When his shaykh opposed ascetic ambitions and encouraged him to continue to teach and write, he became a professor in the learning establishment, never seeking promotion but devoting his life to teaching, writing, and preaching until he died. Birgivi's own spiritual journey resembles that of Ghazali, who retreated into an ascetic life and resumed teaching only after resolving his inner conflicts and attaining peace through a reconciliation of intuitive and discursive knowledge. Like many of his contemporaries, Birgivi also fell under the spell of the Ghazalian synthesis, whose influence is obvious in his works of piety.

Modern scholarship conveniently cites Ibn Taymiyya as Birgivi's main source of inspiration. But, except for his sharp language and uncompromising attitude in juristic opinions, there is no indication in his writing that suggests his reading of the Hanbali scholar.[291] Because he was a staunch Hanafi and a devout mystic with a distinctly Ghazalian cast in his writings, his works became extremely popular among mainstream learned circles and were not simply handbooks for a marginal group of religious reformers, as was the case with Kadızadelis in the seventeenth century. His epithet in the late Ottoman period was imam, a rank attributed to the most authoritative among the jurists of a given sect. His contemporary and biographer, Ali b. Bali, called him shaykh, a title that denotes his high scholarly standing, and *muḥyī al-dīn* (reviver of religion), a title usually attributed to scholars who made a marked impact on religious thought, distinguishing the false from the right.[292] Birgivi's most popular work, *al-Ṭarīqa al-Muḥammadiyya* (The Muhammedan Path), is found in more than 200 manuscript copies in Istanbul libraries alone, and was subjected to more than thirty reworkings since its compilation, in the form of translations, commentaries, and abridgements. Among the commentators of his works were such renowned scholars as Nablusi (d. 1731) and Ali al-Qari (d. 1605).[293] He was among the few ulema to emerge from the Ottoman madrasa system whose fame and influence extended across the Arabic-speaking lands of the empire as well as to India.

During his most productive years, Birgivi remained outside high scholarly circles of the Ottoman ulema, teaching in a small provincial madrasa built for him by his dear friend Ataullah Efendi (d. 1571), Selim II's tutor. He made few close friends from the leading ulema and did not attempt to gain the favor of statesmen, as he never dedicated any work to a dignitary.[294] Although he seems to have chosen to live in a small town for reasons of piety, in a letter to Ataullah Efendi, he complained about his lack of good friends or students, his inability to remove innovations and violations from public, and violence directed toward him by the local population who rose against his criticism of malpractices in the community.[295] He was a scholar of strong convictions with full confidence in his opinions and absolute certainty about what is right and wrong according to the Sharia: "Thanks to God, He enabled me to master the sciences of Arabic, Reason, and the Sharia, and conferred on me the knowledge by which I am capable of differentiating the ill from the sound, the weak from the strong and the wrong from the right. The knot of imitation in my heart was dissolved and my imitation turned into investigation and certainty of knowledge."[296] With that peace of mind and personal confidence, he preached and relentlessly criticized injustices and breaches of the Sharia he noted in Ottoman state and society.[297] In addition to his small treatises, he planned to write a comprehensive book on social critique from a Sharia perspective, aimed at eliminating iniquities in government and society:

> It occurred to me that I should write a book on the religious violations of our time: First, I would start with the violations of rulers. Then iniquities (*münkerāt*) of viziers, and jurists (*müftīn*), and professors (*müderrisīn*), and seekers of religious opinions (*müsteftīn*), and mosques, and streets, and the like. So that I could explain every one of these in detail with proof.[298]

Dhukhr al-Mulūk (Treasure of Kings) is Birgivi's only known work on government. He composed the treatise in three parts, praising the just ruler, reprimanding the unjust ruler, and advising on proper financial administration. It was written as an advice book, in a juristic language, with no criticism of government and no polemical tone. He received a request from his friend and protector Ataullah Efendi to write a book on the state's finances to which he replied positively and made certain requests to complete the project:

> If I write an Arabic treatise on the subject it should be detailed. I do not have full knowledge of the sultan's total revenues and expenses for which reports vary. I hope that God gives health to my eyes and you provide me the necessary information in some detail as requested or send me someone who knows the subject. I would also need some books such as *Badāyiʿ*, *Mabsūṭ*, commentaries on *al-Siyar al-Kabīr* and *Ādāb al-Qāḍī*, and the like.[299]

Although *Dhukhr al-Mulūk* was written on largely the same topic requested by Ataullah Efendi, it is probably not the book referred to in the above exchange. *Dhukhr al-Mulūk* is a short treatise with no specific reference to the Ottoman ruler's revenues and expenses, and it did not make use of any of the sources Birgivi felt he needed to write the treatise. Despite being a vocal critic of government, Birgivi began the treatise by endorsing the prevailing Hanafi view that it was incumbent upon all believers to obey rulers regardless of whether those rulers were just or unjust. Then he showed his distinctly

Birgivian attitude of differentiating the commendable from the reprehensible by drawing a strictly theological distinction between justice and oppression. On the authority of Maturidi (d. 944), he proclaimed that whoever calls an oppressive ruler just turns into an infidel, because considering an injustice justice is blasphemy.[300] This view was voiced more elaborately by Khayrabayti in his *al-Durra al-Gharrā*, which was translated and introduced to Selim II by Ibn Firuz.[301] Thus for Birgivi, obeying an unjust ruler did not merely entail condoning his injustice. Rather, religion made it incumbent on the subjects to distinguish justice from injustice and know the condition of their ruler, while maintaining their allegiance in order to preserve the order.

In this concise treatise, Birgivi addressed both the ruler and the ruled. After instructing the believers to obey the ruler and admonishing the ruler against committing injustice, he explained the types of revenues which he divided into three categories: gifts (*hedāyā*), treasury (*bayt al-māl*), and extortions/prohibitions (*ḥarām*). Although there is no specific reference to government practice, Birgivi aims to make Ottoman finances operate according to the Sharia law by distinguishing legitimate revenues from prohibited ones as established by the Hanafi law. Gifts, for example, could not be accepted by the ruler or the statesmen, but needed to be returned to the benefactor or to the central treasury. As for the prohibited types of income, he mentions certain tax farming practices such as those applied to fisheries in rivers and seas. For the treasury, he gave only four main categories of revenue, each allocated for specific expenses. He did not recognize any other type of income for the state other than that sanctioned by the Sharia. Unlike other leading ulema, such as Ebussuud and Ibn Kemal, who reconciled dynastic laws and administrative practices with the Sharia, Birgivi stipulated that the ruler needed to make financial administration strictly suit the Sharia code of the Hanafi jurisprudence.[302]

SUFISTIC VISIONS

Taşköprizade's short but dense treatise with a long title, *Risāla fī Bayān Asrār al-Khilāfa al-Insāniyya wa al-Salṭana al-Maʿnawiyya* (Treatise On the Mysteries of Human Beings' Caliphate and Spiritual Sultanate) recasts ethical doctrines and juristic rulings of good governance in Sufistic vocabulary.[303] Reflecting his own mystical proclivity, the treatise was based on the conviction that there is a direct correlation between the government of society and the government of self, a view that found its most elaborate exposition in the writings of Ibn Arabi.[304] Although Taşköprizade did not cite any reference in his treatise, a textual comparison shows that his two main sources of inspiration were *Iḥyā* of Ghazali and *Ẕakhīrat al-Mulūk* of Hamadani. Taşköprizade's work took its title from the sixth chapter of *Ẕakhīrat al-Mulūk*, which is *Dar Sharh-i Salṭanat-i Maʿnavī va Asrār-i Khilāfat-i*

Insānī.[305] Composed in ten chapters, *Asrār al-Khilāfa* encompasses such topics as government, ethics, and piety, each corresponding to a section in *Ẕakhīrat al-Mulūk*. Except for the first chapter, titled *Aḥkām al-Wilāya wa al-Salṭana wa al-Imāma*, the author formulates his political views in the form of "rights" (*ḥuqūq*). The remaining chapters are on the rights of the sultanate, subjects, parents, spouses, children, slaves and servants, and friends, respectively. Taşköprizade wrote the treatise for the ruler as a prescription for the attainment of the spiritual sultanate, dubbed the caliphate. The main quest of the treatise was to remind the sultan of his duties in fulfilling the rights of others. The second chapter, for example, explained the rights of the sultanate versus those of the holder of this office, the sultan. The sultanate, in this view, was conceived to be an independent office with its own requirements and principles with which the sultan, as holder of this office, had to comply. The third chapter explains the rights of subjects that the sultan had to observe. When explaining the rights of others to be observed, Taşköprizade did not simply advise the sultan to be just toward the holders of these rights but rather underscored that these rights were inalienable and must be strictly observed in juristic terms.

Unlike many other advice books of this period, *Asrār al-Khilāfa* did not tolerate any breaches of the religious code on the part of the ruler. It did not grant the ruler any prerogatives in performing religious duties and abstaining from prohibitions, and it expected him to adhere to a much higher standard of piety than his subjects. It is a tacit but subtle critique of the moral state of Ottoman rulership and a call for a return to an archetypical rulership once exercised by prophets and the rightly guided caliphs. Given the sixteenth-century peculiarities of dynastic politics, Taşköprizade seems to have prepared the treatise as a direct prescription to cure some of the ills he observed in rulership. During the reigns of Selim I and Süleyman I, Taşköprizade witnessed various measures of oppression toward the subjects, maltreatment of household servants and slaves, execution of princes by their fathers, rebellions of princes against their fathers, fierce rivalries, and infidelities among the ruling elite. In response, as part of his self-imposed moral duty, Taşköprizade instructed the ruler about the rights of others that he was expected to observe, respect, and implement in order to achieve the spiritual sultanate, the perfect state of rulership.

In educating the ruler with specific religious principles and historical illustrations, Taşköprizade did not make a single reference to the legendary kings of antiquity or medieval Islam whose deeds were commonly alluded in the mainstream of political literature. Instead, Taşköprizade presented such figures as Solomon, Moses, Joseph, and the rightly guided caliphs after the Prophet with special reverence to Ali, as models for ideal rulership. As a way of reflecting his overall view of rulership, in illustrating political views, Taşköprizade preferred only prophets and the rightly guided caliphs, not lay rulers, because the former provided authoritative and binding precedents while the latter stood only for commendable and exemplary acts of rulership.

Writing along the lines of Taşköprizade was Arifi Maruf Efendi (d. 1593), a high-profile figure in the Ottoman learning establishment. Like many of his contemporary learned men, he was a jurist by profession and a Sufi by disposition, who lived during the reigns of four sultans from Süleyman I to Mehmed III.[306] Originally from Trabzon, he worked in the service of Shah Efendi as an intern after his graduation from madrasa and received his first appointment to a small madrasa in Istanbul. He served as professor in several madrasas and then left his teaching career while he was a professor in the prestigious Muradiye madrasa of Bursa. He started his judicial service, a better-paying job with brighter prospects, with the kadıship of Izmir in 1584. After serving in Yenişehir, Amid, Damascus, and Bursa, he was appointed in 1592 as qadi of Cairo, where he died a year later.

In addition to his successful career in the Ottoman learning establishment and judiciary, Arifi left a good name in contemporary sources as a poet and a mystic. Along with many of his colleagues among the ulema he also pursued a spiritual path and entered the Bayrami order, where he completed his wayfaring and received his license (*icāzet*). His contemporaries, Beyani, Kınalızade Hasan, and Ata'i, all praised him for his mastery in mystical teachings and exceptional spiritual qualities. As a scholar and mystic, Arifi was better known in his time as the translator of Kashifi's much acclaimed biographical work on the lives of prominent Sufi saints, *Rashaḥāt ʿAyn al-Ḥayāt* (Beads of Dew from the Source of Life).[307] His contemporary, Kınalızade Hasan, praised Arifi's *Rashaḥāt* as an embellished commentary rather than a simple translation.[308] Arifi's fame as a man of wisdom and translator of *Rashaḥāt*, which he dedicated to Murad III, brought him closer to the sultan and his grand vizier. While he worked as a qadi, he also served as a counselor to Grand Vizier Koca Sinan Paşa, who served five different terms between 1580 and 1596.[309] In the words of his biographer Beyani, he was Sinan Paşa's "tutor, adviser in government, and confidante in private matters."[310] Similarly, Kınalızade Hasan portrayed Arifi as the man who guided the grand vizier in all affairs and devoted himself to public service on a permanent basis.[311] Prior to becoming Sinan Paşa's adviser in government, Arifi wrote a handbook on the vizierate in 1560, *ʿUqūd al-Jawāhir li-Ẓakhaʾir al-Akhāʾir* (Precious Necklace for Matchless Treasures), a work in Arabic that he dedicated to Vizier Semiz Ali Paşa a year before he rose to the grand vizierate.[312] Written from a markedly Sufi perspective, *ʿUqūd al-Jawāhir* is a work of exceptional quality reflecting its author's vast command of various strands of political writing. Arifi wrote the work in the mirrors for princes genre and achieved a smooth synthesis of prevailing political teachings in ethics and jurisprudence. The work was organized in three chapters, embellished with Arabic poetry, parables, proverbs, stories, Qur'anic verses, prophetic traditions, and maxims of wisdom drawn from a diverse body of sources. The three principal subjects dealt with in the work were the semantics of the term "vizier" and the juristic principles regarding the vizier, a description of the vizier's qualifications and responsibilities along with advice, and miscellaneous advice and incantations.

Unlike the two well-known jurists above who wrote from a distinctly Sufi perspective, there were a number of obscure authors of apparently Sufi background who seem to be well versed on jurisprudence as well. Among them, Hüseyin b. Abdullah el-Şirvani composed three treatises in three languages for the sole purpose of juxtaposing the Safavids against the Ottomans as their perfect other in faith and divinely guided leadership.[313] His Arabic work, *Aḥkām al-Dīniyya* (Ordinances of Religion), is replete with juristic and theological arguments, and primarily addresses the ulema.[314] *Risāle fi't-Taṣavvuf* (Treatise on Sufism), in vernacular Turkish, treats the subject matter in nonconventional esoteric ways with the aim of educating Sufis and countering the Safavid propaganda through its own idiom.[315] *al-Risāla al-ʿAdliyya al-Sulaymāniyya* (Treatise of Süleymanic Justice), on the other hand, written in Persian, is an advice book for the ruler and statesmen.[316] The explicit message in all three works is the same: The primary responsibility of a Muslim ruler is to wage war against the heretics on spiritual, discursive, and military planes. Although all three texts are dedicated to Süleyman, they are crafted to have a broader impact across the Muslim community. With its scholarly language and extensive list of quotations from authoritative works of Sunni jurisprudence and theology, *Aḥkām* has the potential to reach the global Sunni ulema network. The mirrors style of the *ʿAdliyya* and the choice of Persian as its language place it into the stream of political literature in circulation across the Persianate courts that surrounded the Safavids. *Taṣavvuf*, however, employs the idiom of Turkoman mysticism that constitued the backbone of the Safavid power and the main block of social resistance against the Ottoman rule from western Iran to the Balkans. Together, the three texts address three separate audiences to counter and refute the same threat Şirvani thought was posed by this apocalyptic heresy.

Şirvani was a staunch Sunni and a dedicated enemy of the Kizilbash, alarmed by the spread of Safavid influence among the Muslims. *Aḥkām* and *Taṣavvuf* are more about portraying the Safavid rulership as the embodiment of Kizilbash faith whereas *ʿAdliyya* offers a vision of righteous government that is destined to demolish it. *ʿAdliyya* portrays the sultan as God's chosen ruler whose primary mission was to eradicate Rafidis and the Kizilbash from the face of the earth. Şirvani composed *ʿAdliyya* in 1543 in Diyarbakır, eight years after Süleyman's eastern campaign that ended in Tabriz, and five years before his second campaign against the Safavids that ended with the conquest of Van. His references to the Melameti branch of the Halvetiyye order suggest that he must have been affiliated with one of the Sunni mystical orders present in the region.[317] The language and argumentation of the treatise are ostentatiously mystical and the author appears to be well versed in esoteric interpretation as well as Islamic occultism and eschatology. Teachings of past Sufi masters, ranging from Junayd al-Baghdadi to Hasan al-Basri, constituted the main stock of inspiration for his views. He profusely quoted from the works of Kashifi, Jami, and Isfarayini as well as the sayings and teachings of Abu Hanifa and the theological formulations of Maturidi to bolster his esoteric and idiosyncratic views with canonical statements by the highest authorities in Sufism, jurisprudence, and theology.

Another obscure author with Sufi leanings who wrote an advice book to guide the ruler with the teachings of Islamic mysticism was Mustafa b. Abdullah. Despite compiling a lengthy advice book on rulership, *Sulūk al-Mulūk* (Wayfaring of Rulers), the author left few clues about himself.[318] He completed the only extant copy of his work in 1542 and dedicated it to Süleyman while he was serving as the commander of the fortress of Çankırı. In his short introduction, the author stated that he wrote the book to be a guide in religion and the world for whoever reads it carefully and acts accordingly.[319] Unlike the usual pattern of advice books that were presented to the sultan, the writer did not preface his treatise with a panegyric for the sultan. With no manifest political agenda, *Sulūk al-Mulūk* is a pietistic work to guide statesmen to the right path, in line with the self-assumed responsibility of the ulema and spiritual guides in Ottoman political culture.

Although Dizdar did not mention any other work in his treatise, his main source of inspiration is Daye's *Mirṣād al-ʿIbād*. The two works were written in different languages but display remarkable affinity in terminology, ideas, and definitions.[320] Yet unlike that of Daye's, Dizdar's treatise does not follow a particular structure, as the work was divided into so many seemingly unrelated small chapters ranging from such topics as *futuwwa* to jihad. The first three chapters are on the caliphate, types of rulers, and justice. The final part is on advice (*mawʿiẓa*), divided into numerous sections replete with illustrative anecdotes and stories. Dizdar wrote *Sulūk al-Mulūk* one year before Şirvani's *al-ʿAdliyya al-Sulaymāniyya* in a region where the Safavid propaganda was still intense but makes no mention of the Kizilbash at all. Despite being a Sunni mystic and a fortress commander, unlike Şirvani, Dizdar looked indifferent to Safavid expansionism and proselytizing. Yet, along the lines of Şirvani, *Sulūk al-Mulūk* elaborated the intricacies of Sufism and revealed the existence of a cosmic government headed by the succor (*ghaws*). Proper rulership would be the one that combines political authority (*salṭana, khilāfa, mulk*) with that of the spiritual (*wilāya*). Dizdar reiterates the Sufi ideal of incorporating temporal power to the spiritual by subjugating the ruler to the rule of the pole unless the ruler himself was already in that position.

Languages of Political Thought

A linguistic picture of political texts written in this period reflects the inquisitive diversity and creative eclecticism that characterized Ottoman culture and polity during the age of Süleyman. Turkish, Persian, and Arabic served as principal media of expression, each with nearly equal weight. Despite the rise of Turkish as the mandarin language of the empire, there was neither a lingua franca for political writing, nor was there a sacred language for exposing political views. Besides a host of vernacular languages in use, the literary high culture of the Ottoman Empire during the sixteenth century was trilingual, a feature that Ottoman literati were proud to exploit. Arabic and Persian writings, in both prose and poetry, continued to flourish not only in parts of the empire where these languages were spoken but in Turkish-speaking regions as well. Yet, not every author was trilingual. The Arabic-speaking men of learning were conventionally the least capable of conversing in other languages and the most parochial in their grasp and reception of non-Arabic cultural expositions. Because of the universal acceptance of Arabic as a medium of Islamic disciplines, a Persian-speaking man of learning would most likely be educated in reading and writing Arabic as well, unless his experience was confined to practical training in a profession that did not require knowledge of other languages. By comparison, a Turkish-speaking learned person could most likely use both Arabic and Persian for written expression. Mastering Turkish for the native speaker of Arabic and Persian did not add much to his credentials beyond possibilities of advancement in the service of the Ottoman government. For a Turkish-speaking learned person, however, his prospects in status, prestige, and career advancement would be closely tied to the degree of his mastery of Arabic and Persian.

Ottoman authors could choose to write in one of the three languages, depending on their objectives and the relative advantage of the language of choice. By the Süleymanic age, Turkish was on a par with Arabic and Persian as a language of literature and scholarship. The use of Turkish as a written language was a challenge during the fourteenth and fifteenth centuries, when many authors felt compelled to justify their choice of Turkish. During the course of two centuries, Turkish transformed itself from a vernacular language into the primary language of cultural expression. Yet Arabic continued to be the main language of religious sciences while Persian was still attractive for artistic expression as well as historical writings and Sufi texts. Given their distinguishing features, not every language was equally suitable for a given audience, genre, idea, or purpose. Writing in Turkish, for example, gave an author the potential of reaching a broader audience within the Turkish-speaking regions of the empire. It could also be used to expose one's own cultural identity and sensibilities. Arabic offered better tools and opportunities to express juristic and theological views of rulership, especially when employed in the conventional genres of these disciplines. An Arabic text had a broader appeal to men of learning within the universal Muslim community and thus had a greater chance to reach beyond the linguistic boundaries of regional audiences. As a sacred language of primary religious texts, Arabic also implied the authority to speak for the religion. This is one reason all the juristic works on government and rulership that appeared in this period were written in Arabic. Persian lacked the universal currency of Arabic or the validity of Turkish in Ottoman learned society. But it still enjoyed an enchanting power over the imagination of Ottoman literati as a fountain of poetic beauty and a repository of wisdom literature.

Among the political works of this period, there is virtually no single text that was written solely in one language. To varying degrees, regardless of the primary language in which it was composed, each text was a joint product of the three languages. Alayi, for example, who wrote his treatise on the vizierate in Turkish, quoted Arabic couplets and aphorisms to illustrate his points and gave either Turkish or Persian translations of his citations.[321] Arabic and Persian continued to pervade texts even when they were written in plain Turkish. At the minimum, quotations from the Qur'an and prophetic traditions caused Arabic to be sprinkled throughout in Turkish texts. Most quotations of poetry were still in Persian. Persian chapter headings in Turkish works were not uncommon.[322] Although ostensibly written in one language, most texts were written with the assumption that the reader had sufficient knowledge of Arabic to understand the scriptures and adequate literary training in Persian to enjoy its poetry.

More important than the linguistic variety of political texts was the use of a specialized disciplinary or cultural language to convey political views. Whether a given author found Arabic, Persian, or Turkish more convenient for expression, each text was shaped by the use of a specific language of a given discipline or tradition, in terms of vocabulary, idioms, and the way views were formulated. There were mainly four languages that revealed modes of thinking reflected in political literature. These were juristic, sufistic, administrative, and philosophical languages. Most texts were imbued with the conventions of more than one of these languages. Identifying these languages is essential for understanding a given text and the purpose of its author. A given language shapes a text not only by the use of a specific vocabulary, but also by the specific meanings it accords to even the most common terms of mainstream political theory. Such widely used terms as *siyāsa* and *maṣlaḥa*, for example, could have diametrically different meanings in texts written in philosophical, juristic, and administrative languages. Language in this sense does not simply refer to the different meanings that words acquired in various disciplines but also to a particular mode of reasoning and argumentation. Without a strict typology, we can sort that these languages could be differentiated by certain distinguishing features: Juristic language, for example, was by definition normative and authoritative; administrative language was empirical, prescriptive, and precedential; philosophical language was idealistic, inquisitive, and analogical; and sufistic language was esoteric, speculative, symbolic, and even encryptic.

By the age of Süleyman, the full corpus of political theory expressed in Arabic and Persian languages was integrated into the mainstream of Ottoman thought. However, confining the Ottoman engagement in political ideas to textual expositions, whether through translation, commentary, or compilation would be grossly misleading. Nor can we explain the Ottoman interest in political thought as a purely humanistic curiosity for learning and exploration. As in the cases of early Arab encounters with ancient civilizations of the Near East or Mughal exposure to Indian thought, the broader Ottoman culture formed through a continuous interaction with local cultures. Writing on rulership often entailed addressing the specific legitimacy considerations of each region and community that came under the Ottoman authority. The simultaneous Ottoman expansion into old centers of Islamic learning and non-Muslim territories created a ruling elite composed of different ethnicities, confessional backgrounds, cultural tastes, and group interests that are accommodated, assimilated, and recreated in the process of forming an imperial ideology. Notions of authority, means of legitimacy, principles of government, and images of the ruler needed to be constantly reworked to reflect the changing territorial, social, and cultural configuration of the Ottoman state. Despite being founded on the fringes of a vibrant Islamicate culture, the first century of the Ottoman state formation owes very little to textual expositions of political theory. Instead, the early Ottoman literary world was filled with epics and mystical poetry. Frontier dynamics, as reflected in the *gazi* leadership and Abdalan ethos, and as manifested in the mystical orientation of early sultans, pervaded visions of rulership. The post-Timurid reconstruction involved refashioning the newborn state on the model of the tradition of Persianate statecraft conveyed through court-commissioned translation and compilation of works on rulership. With the dawn of the imperial age, initiated by Mehmed's extensive institutionalization campaign, the new Ottoman ruling elite turned more tuned to the broader streams of political thought and state traditions across the Mediterranean. The sixteenth century witnessed the rise of a broad-based discourse on rulership that promoted the very Ottoman experience, including the mystification of authority and reenvisioning the sultan as a caliph *à la* Sufi notions of cosmic ruler, as the perfect model of governance expressed through a patently Ottoman vocabulary and ideas.

CHAPTER TWO

The Caliphate Mystified

THE EARLY OTTOMAN STATE emerged at a time and place where the Abbasid order was not so distant in memory, and the subsequent Mongol order was already waning. Although western Asia Minor was well connected to the rest of the Muslim world, especially through the ulema and Sufi networks, it still was on the margins of learned Islam. Besides the neighboring emirates, early Ottoman rulers found themselves surrounded by powerful Sufi orders founded by charismatic leaders commanding over large constituencies with enchanting authority. Like any other state in the making in Asia Minor, the Ottomans too were compelled to come to terms with these emerging orders. The state-building endeavor of the Ottoman ruling elite was continuously checked, countered, or buttressed by the fraternity-building efforts of independent Sufi orders. This early configuration of Ottoman society was well reflected on ruling ideology of the time and continued to reverberate in the political discourse of subsequent centuries. With the rise of the Ottomans, as part of a broader movement in the Turko-Persianate world now largely under the Mongol rule, the post-Abbasid trajectory of intellectual articulation took a sharp turn toward Sufism through which various strands of political thought, be it juristic or philosophical, were assimilated into Sufistic imageries and recast in their figurative language. Sufis and Sufi-minded jurists revived the idea of the caliphate after the institution itself was put to end by the Mongols, and they redefined it often in opposition with each other and in defiance of the Ottoman ruling establishment who increasingly adopted the Sufistic interpretations of caliphate for its own legitimacy needs.

The Ottoman Dawla

> The great sultan, the honored and exalted shah of shahs, the source of noble attributes and morals, evidence of God in dispensing justice and equity, grantor of investitures for offices, raiser of the banners of ranks,

> the one surpassing the ultimate end of miraculous deeds, who emerges from the lightning clash of sublime stations, victorious by the divine light, whose might is proven by the hand of the Almighty, privileged for protection by the Lord of heavens, who spends his life to raise the banners of faith, the last resort of all humankind's hopes, the hero of the auspicious turn, of the world, and of religion, the lion of Islam, and the refuge of all Muslims, who knows God's command, who splits [right from wrong] by God's proof, Süleyman Paşa; the son of the greatest sultan, the most just and the most knowledgeable king, the holder of authority over the nations, raiser of the signs of virtues, embodiment of the means of happiness, Anushirvan of the age, refuge of the people of faith, extender of the pillars of peace and protection, patron of the virtuous and the enlightened, the sultan Orhan.[1]

This generous laudation for the ruler of a frontier principality, probably the earliest textual reference to Ottoman rulership, excluding a handful of documents and inscriptions, comes not from a work on statecraft but from a short treatise on the enumeration of scientific disciplines, *al-Itḥāf al-Sulaymānī fī al-ʿAḥd al-Urkhānī* (A Gift to Sülayman during the Reign of Orhan), composed by Davud-i Kayseri (d. 1350), the first professor appointed to the first madrasa built by the Ottomans in 1336.[2] The text is dedicated to Süleyman Paşa, the heir apparent to the second Ottoman ruler, Orhan (r. 1324–1362), and must have been presented before c. 1350, around when the author was reported to have died. *al-Itḥāf al-Sulaymānī* is a concise explication and synthesis of Islamic, rational, and Arabic sciences, an introductory textbook for madrasa students and the learned circle of Süleyman Paşa (d. 1357), who is eulogized as a learned commander (*ṣāḥib al-sayf wa al-ḳalam*) in the deed of the endowment founded by his father Orhan in his name in 1360.[3] The work introduces a new epistemological thinking that synthesized diverse branches of knowledge in the broader Islamic tradition, a marked characteristic of later mainstream Ottoman thought. The author himself personifies what came to be an ideal profile of an Ottoman scholar that is madrasa-based, spiritual, and versed in both rational and Islamic sciences. Davud-i Kayseri, better known as a student of Ibn Arabian mysticism and the Maragha School of astronomy at once, was part of a closely knit scholarly network between the Nile and the Oxus that pioneered the inculcation of classical Islamic learning at the Ottoman frontier and, more importantly, initiated the long-lasting learning tradition of reconciling intuitive and rational knowledge.[4]

Beyond the obvious panegyric, his depiction of Süleyman Paşa and Orhan Beg reflects Davud-i Kayseri's unified epistemology and his vision for ideal rulership, arguably the first Ottoman exposition of political self-perception. This syncretic portrayal places the fledgling Ottoman rulership within the historical continuum of Islamic dynasties through the appropriation of Seljuk regalia while accommodating newly emerging notions of rulership. It is a regal formula that conveys Perso-Islamic ideals of statecraft, Sufi visions of authority, and utopian theories of association in political philosophy. Being a *müderris* by profession, he was certainly fully competent in Islamic jurisprudence. As a mathematician from the famed Maragha school founded in 1259, he must have been aware of the observatory's director Nasir al-Din al-Tusi's canonical work on ethics that became a handbook for later political theorists of the post-Abbasid Turko-Mongolian courts across Eurasia. Finally, he was one of the foremost commentators on Ibn Arabi's works, most notably *Fuṣūṣ al-Ḥikam*, a work that became the source of endless inspiration for a wide variety of mystical explorations on a range of topics including rulership. With his strong background in philosophy and sciences, he was the first commentator that turned the Grand Master Ibn Arabi's spiritual revelations into a philosophy of mysticism.[5]

There is no question that Davud-i Kayseri's colorful image-making contains a high degree of rhetorical exhortation for his patron, as his praise for the Ottoman prince clearly outweighs that of the reigning ruler. Yet, the choice of terminology and the way the ruler is exalted reveals the author's peculiar convictions that later became more popularly shared by the learned in conceiving rulership and differentiating the Ottoman dynasty from its peers. Reflecting his Ibn Arabian conception of rulership, Davud-i Kayseri presents Süleyman Paşa as God's evidence (*āyat Allāh*) in dispensing justice and equity whose might is proven by the hand of the Almighty. Perception of authority as manifestation of God's government over His creation later constituted the foundation of designing ideal rulership among the Sufi-minded political theorists. His depiction as the chosen recipient of God's succor points to the Ottoman ruler's unique status and relationship to God, which could be maintained only exclusively on Sufi terms, a perception later propagandists of the Ottoman dynasty supplemented with ample prophecies and revelations in the service of more illustrious sultans. Possessing miraculous deeds (*manāqib*), journeying through sublime stations, and being the refuge of all Muslims and the last resort of all humankind's hopes accords the ruler the rank of spiritual perfection. In more elaborate portrayals of later Ottoman thought, Sufi-minded authors defined the perfect rulership as one that unifies both temporal and spiritual authorities, the latter being the supreme.

Davud-i Kayseri's presentation of Orhan is similar but more eclectic than that of his heir apparent. The epithet Anushirvan of the age is very typical of the mirrors literature in both Persian and Arabic varieties that commonly offered this celebrated Sassanid king, who was praised in a number of hadiths attributed to the Prophet, as the paragon of just government. Less common was his description of Orhan with reference to knowledge, happiness, virtues, and the patronage of the virtuous and the enlightened (*ʿirfān*). Here the mystical tint of Süleyman's image turns more contemplative, owing more to the philosophical tradition than Sufism. Having extensively engaged with Farabi's philosophy, Davud-i Kayseri must have been well aware of the political ideals of the philosopher, especially those attested in his *Attainment of Happiness*, *Opinions of the People of the Perfect State*, and *Virtuous City*. Farabi envisioned the ideal body politic as an association of the virtuous, under the authority of the most knowledgeable and virtuous, and for the sole goal of attaining happiness.[6] Farabian utopia was later turned into a practical philosophy of ethics and governance by Nasir al-Din Tusi, integrated into the mystical philosophy by fifteenth-century Sufi-minded ethicists such as Davvani and Kashifi, and became more pronounced to define the Ottoman state in the writings of sixteenth-century scholars such as Kınalızade and Taşköprizade.

Davud-i Kayseri's abstract vision of Ottoman rulership does not manifest any specific references to sovereignty. There is no mention of territorial space, demographic base, noble genealogy, or specific functions of the ruler. The most striking omission for any student of early Ottoman history is the ruler's characterization as a *gazi*-leader (raider for the faith). Although the appellation was in common use among Eurasian Turkic dynasties, it gained new emphasis among the western Anatolian principalities of the fourteenth century. Modern historians of Ottoman origins reached widely discrepant interpretations on the meaning and significance of *gazi* leadership. Among them, Paul Wittek considered it as a holy war ideology, an Ottoman pursuit of jihad, and attributed it a defining role on state formation.[7] Wittek's radical critics, Colin Imber and Heath Lowry, largely dissociated *gaza* from its Islamic content, equated it with the Turkish *akın* (raid), and argued that it is nothing more than an inclusive and collective entrepreneurship for looting and material gain.[8] Linda Darling argued that Ottomans rather evolved into a *gazi* state and that the notion of *gaza* increasingly converged with jihad only in the context of the fifteenth century.[9] There is no question that *gaza* was an important component of early Ottoman self-perception and state formation. But according it a pivotal role around which almost the entire early Ottoman historiography revolved tended to marginalize the broader intellectual currents, social movements, and cultural formations at force in western Anatolia. Kafadar reexamined the case by disentangling early Ottoman historiography from the hegemonic *gaza* discourse and relieved the question of *gaza* from its incompatibly strict interpretations of equating it with either Islamic holy war or plundering confederacy of nomadic Turkomans and Byzantine feudal lords. Instead, he offered cultural history as "an epistemological path" to understand *gaza* as it is manifested during the founding era of the Ottoman state in a wide variety of media from poetry to arts, without attributing it a causal role in what made the Ottomans different from their peers in rising to a world power.[10]

Yet, Davud-i Kayseri's exposition is not entirely blind to the competitive claim for *gazi* leadership. Instead, he frames Ottoman rulership in the administrative *lingua franca* of tributary and successor states of the Abbasid Empire as he presents Süleyman Paşa as the hero of the auspicious turn in leadership, and of religion and the world (*shujāʿ al-dawla wa al-dīn wa al-dunyā*). *Shujāʿ*, often accompanied with other qualifiers such as *mujāhid* or *ghāzī* (warrior in the path of God), was a heroic term that became favorable during the Buyid dynasty in the tenth century. It was one of the many chivalric titles adopted and commonly used by Anatolian Seljuks and later principalities that emphasized their service to religion and its defense.[11] Less common, and more telling for early Ottoman self-perception, however, is the use of the construct *shujāʿ al-dawla*, which seems to have gained currency only after the Seljuks. The pre-Ottoman trajectory of the term *dawla* reveals that it carries specific defining properties for the nature of authority and state formation. Since the decentralization of the Abbasid Empire in the tenth century, the newly rising dynasties sought to legitimize their reigns by resorting to pre-Islamic, mostly Iranian, imageries and by devising epithets that signify their service to the caliphate and Islam. That way, they firmly established their claim for authority within their respective territories without challenging the status and authority of the caliphate as the universal leadership over the Muslim community. The period of political fragmentation between the rise of the Buyids and the end of the Seljuks is the most innovative era, a true golden age of image-making for the tributary dynasties of the Abbasid caliphate, an undertaking that could be surpassed in vigor and creativity only by the emergence of regional empires with universalist claims in the sixteenth century. Among them was the title *shāhanshāh*, king of kings, invented by the Buyids as the secular equivalent of what the caliphate meant as a political authority during its heyday.[12] Yet the Abbasid authorities considered it as legitimate only in reference to someone on earth who is ruling temporally.[13] As attested to by a number of historians of medieval Islam, this was the time when the sultanate, as an executive power, split from the caliphate, which was confined to the spiritual and honorary authority of the Abbasid caliph's charisma.[14]

But, as far as the learned traditions of Islamic political ideals are concerned, arguably the most creative, the longest lasting, and most useful of these epithets were the ones constructed with the term *dawla*. Dozens of different constructions with *dawla* endings were devised by Buyid rulers and conferred by the Abbasid caliph, including *sayf* (sword), *ʿimād* (support), *muʿiz* (fortifier), *rukn* (pillar), and *ʿaḍuḍ* (column). In a seemingly endless stream of innovation, these constructs were invented and adopted to fit the specific legitimacy needs and visions of ruleship by later dynasties including the Ottomans. In Buyid designations, the *dawla* exclusively referred to the Abbasids, loaded with Islamic, political, and astrological references.[15] The Arabic word *dawla*, which may refer to a turn or alternation in success, office, and fortune in daily language, gradually and by implication gained a political meaning denoting to reign, supremacy, and dynasty. *Dawla* "as the divinely granted turn in power" was a familiar conception in multiple indigenous traditions of Eurasia.[16] This facilitated its easy reception by Turkish and Persian dynasties where it was reconciled with *ḳūt* in Turkish and *farr* in Persian.

Dawla acquired its distinctive meaning in political thought and historical consciousness with the Abbasid revolution.[17] For the Abbasid revolutionaries, *dawla* meant the rule of, or an age initiated by, the Abbasids, or the return of authority to its rightful owners, the progeny of the Prophet, from the Umayyads whose rule was disparaged as kingship (*mulk*). For non-Arabs, disillusioned from the Umayyad rule, the revolution stirred astrological fantasies that hailed it as an auspicious turn of rulership from the Arabs to the Persians. Despite gaining rapid currency in all strains of Abbasid intellectual and political life in reference to the reign, the dynasty, or the rule of a specific caliph, the term retained its messianic connotations, even after it came to denote the institution of state in the usage of Ottoman bureaucrats in the sixteenth century. The term never gained a juristic or theological sanction. But in political thought, imbued with philosophical explorations and ancient traditions of occultism, it symbolized an auspicious turn, an epochal initiation of a new era, and a divinely ordained rule. Ninth-century world historians from Dinawari to Tabari, who constructed world histories that recorded the Abbasid *dawla* as the current state in the glorious genealogy of universal empires, contributed to the term's gaining a specifically Abbasid coloration.[18]

Until the fall of the Abbasids in 1258, the *dawla* titles used in numerous affiliate dynasties referred to the Abbasid rule and signified their attachment to the caliphal order, more than their loyalties to individual Abbasid caliphs. Despite their independent executive authority, these dynasties emphasized their adherence to the Abbasid caliphate as the single most important source and sign of Islamic legitimacy. Among these, the Seljuks enjoyed a privileged status with their unmatched service to the maintenance of the Abbasid order and military prowess as manifested in their swift unification of much of the Abbasid realm under their authority. In 1055, when the Seljuk ruler Tuğrul Beg ended the Buyid rule in Baghdad, he was hailed by the caliph Qa'im bi-Amrillah as the ruler of the east and the west (*malik al-mashriq wa al-maghrib*) and, more importantly, designated as his partner in the leadership of the community of the faithful (*qasīm amīr al-mu'minīn*), a title the Abbasids never accorded to any other ruler before or after.[19] In 1062, Tuğrul Beg married the daughter of the Abbasid caliph by presenting himself as *khalīfat al-imām* (deputy of the leader [of the Muslim community]), therefore cunningly adopting the title of caliph without challenging the Abbasid authority.[20] Contemporary jurists, most notably Mawardi, offered ingenious legal formulae to reassert the primacy of juristic imperative on the caliphate and preserve the unified authority of the Muslim community.[21] In his *al-Aḥkām al-Sulṭaniyya* (Ordinances of Government), he resolved the problem of divided authority by framing the Seljuk sultanate as the delegation of executive authority from the

Abbasid caliph. His younger but more decorated contemporary Ghazali, in the face of growing Shiite-Ismaili threat to the Abbasid caliphate, was more occupied with the question of turning the Seljuks into champions of Sunni Islam. He composed his *Naṣīḥat al-Mulūk* in the form of a mirrors for princes that was a synopsis of practical theology with ample illustrations of proper conduct in just government, a royal version of Sunni crescendo.[22] While Mawardi's *al-Aḥkām* was confined to juristic scrutiny in Seljuk and later Ottoman milieu, Ghazali's *Naṣīḥa* turned into a textbook on righteous rulership from Bengal to Morocco until contemporary times.

Despite the jurists' painstaking efforts to offer a de jure solution to the conundrum, the Seljuk rulers, from the very beginning, were fully conscious of their de facto partnership in caliphal authority.[23] Although they initially adopted the use of the regal constructs with *dawla*, it was reduced to a mere honorific and gradually disappeared from usage. Unlike the Buyids whose loyalty was to the Abbasid rule, the Seljuks devised spectacular regalia that often surpassed those of the reigning caliph, and favored epithets that underscored their partnership with the reigning caliph, rather than adherence to the Abbasid rule. The *dawla* that represented the Abbasids came to be shared by the Seljukids. Seljuk rulers, in the main, avoided such titles as *rukn al-dawla* or *sulṭān al-dawla* with which the Buyid rulers prided themselves. The Seljuk affiliates and statesmen, however, continued to use such constructs, even more pervasively than the Buyids, to show their loyalty to the Seljuk *dawla*. Numerous inscriptions from Anatolia built under the Seljuk suzerainty by local rulers include a clause "during the reign of" (*fī dawla*) in homage to the reigning Seljuk ruler. More importantly, especially when both the Abbasid caliphate and the Great Seljuk authority weakened in the thirteenth century, Anatolian Seljuks erected a striking number of public buildings and monuments on which the epitaphs commonly inscribed the Seljuk ruler as the partner in caliphate. The Seljukids continued the Abbasid order in Anatolia by replacing their *dawla* with their own, as partner and heir apparent to the caliphal authority. Given the sheer number of lavish epigraphic representations of Seljuk regalia underlying their own turn in rulership and partnership in caliphal authority, fifteenth- and sixteenth-century Ottoman historians' glorification of the Seljuk rule as a conduit for the transmission of caliphal authority to the Ottomans may not have been a fantasy.

The waning of the Seljuk rule toward the end of the thirteenth century ignited a fierce competition among Anatolian aristocracy to inherit the Seljukid legacy. Owing to their long held bulwark service against the Crusaders and then the Mongols in protection of the realm of Islam, *shujāʿ al-dīn*, *mujāhid*, *murābit*, and *abū al-fatḥ* (champion of conquest) were among the proudest descriptive titles Seljuk rulers propagated. No question, Davud-i Kayseri and other learned men in the service of ambitious frontier principalities, having had their training in the former learning centers of the Seljuk realm, were well aware of the significance and full range of imageries and epithets for effective rulership. A foundation deed from 1324 composed in Persian, the earliest documentary reference to an Ottoman ruler, presents the benefactor Orhan as *shujā' al-dīn*. But the 1337 inscription of the Şehadet Mosque in Bursa, the earliest epithet from an Ottoman monument, composed in Arabic, blends imageries of High Islam with those of the Islamic vernacular of the frontier: "the exalted great Emir, warrior (*mujāhid*) in the path of God, sultan of the *gazis*, champion of the auspicious turn (*dawla*), and religion, and of the horizons, hero (*pehlevān*) of the age, Orhan, son of Osman."[24] The great Emir's identification with *mujāhid*, *gazi*, and *pehlevān* are similar in content and connotation. *Mujāhid* was widely used by the Seljuk rulers, an appellation of High Islamic culture that gained prominence during the Crusades. *Pehlevān*, ultimately drawn from the Persian mythology through popular epics, was more specifically used for the heroes with super powers waging war against infidels and injustices in thirteenth-century Anatolian literature. Warrior-heroes in performative frontier narratives, including the cult figures Battal Gazi, Sarı Saltuk, and Ebu Muslim, were all portrayed as *pehlevāns* commissioned for the conquest of the Rum. The idealized images of *gazi* warriors in later Ottoman accounts closely correspond to those of *pehlevāns* except the latter were endowed with superhuman powers. In popular imagination, the *gazi* designation always carried an element of chivalry and heroism, even a degree of antinomian defiance and liberty, as opposed to *müjāhid*, which implies piety, service, and conformity to the juristic norm. The inscription is crafted to display the same image of Orhan as champion of religion in the languages of literary Persian, High Islamic learning, and vernacular Islam.

The contest for *gazi* leadership manifests itself through the politics of inscriptions and blessings obtained from mystical orders at the frontier. The Aydınids, perhaps the most aggressive raiders among the frontier principalities, clearly preceded the Ottomans in the use of *gazi* title. Mehmed Beg, the founder of the Aydınid dynasty, inscribed his name on the gate of Grand Mosque of Birgi in 1312, which he erected to symbolize his conquest of the city: ". . . conquered this realm with God's succor and will, our lord the great Emir, the raider in the path of God (*ghāzī fī sabīl Allāh*) . . . hero of the auspicious turn and religion (*mubāriz al-dawla wa al-dīn*)."[25] Mehmed Beg's vigorous *gaza* campaigns and investments in Islamic learning in cities he conquered did not go unnoticed by Sufi orders. Arif Çelebi, the grandson of Rumi and the head of the Mevlevi order, publicly praised Mehmed Beg as "the sultan of *gazis*" and foretold future victories and God's succor for his progeny.[26] The title Arif Çelebi bestowed not only confirmed Mehmed Beg's leadership over his *gazi* followers but also sanctified a legitimacy claim over the broader *gazi* constituency in western Anatolia, a region characterized by porous boundaries, shifting alliances, and opportunistic loyalties.

The rulers of western Anatolia, most of whom were Seljuk vassals and later thrived under the loose Mongol suzerainty, started to craft *dawla* titles that demonstrated the *gazi* ethos. An inscription of 1329 mentions Orhan Beg of the Menteşe as *shujāʿ al-dawla.*[27] If we accept the epitaph of the Şehadet Mosque as authentic, that means Orhan of the Ottomans too identified himself with the same title.[28] Their older contemporary, the above Mehmed Beg is commemorated as *mubāriz al-dawla* on the inscription of his tomb built in 1333.[29] Some of these rulers were portrayed with more illustrious *dawla*-titles especially in dedicated manuscripts.[30] *Shujāʿ* and *mubāriz* are near synonyms for *gazi* while *jalāl* (greatness) and *falak* (heavens) convey a sense of majesty. What the *dawla* stands for, however, is hard to establish with precision. The Seljuk rulers made it clear that they were living at the time of their own *dawla*. While largely dropping the *dawla* from their titles for its traditional reference to that of the Abbasids, almost all Seljuk monuments erected by dignitaries included the phrase "during the *dawla*" (*fī dawla*), in reference to the reign of the current Seljuk ruler. Those dignitaries also continued to use *dawla* titles similar to those of Buyids, where the *dawla* always meant that of the Seljukids.

These *dawla* titles conjecturally demonstrate that each of these rulers still conceived of rulership in relation to a higher authority.[31] During the first half of the fourteenth century, with fits and starts, there were three overlaying spheres of influence over the Rum originated from the Seljuk, Mongol, and Mamluk claims of sovereignty. Although the Seljuk rule effectively ended in 1308, a series of claimants related to the dynasty, often with the support of opportunistic rulers, preserved the possibility of restoring their state throughout the fourteenth century and even beyond.[32] The Mongol rule continued in the form of a direct administration under a single governor until 1327 and thereafter as an absentee overlordship until the demise of the Ilkhanids in 1353.[33] During the time when the Ottomans were establishing their political presence under the leadership of Osman, debilitating internal struggles among the Mongol contestants diminished their influence over the Turkoman principalities at the northwestern frontier of Anatolia.[34] Yet all the Anatolian principalities remained on the Ilkhanid roster of taxation until the Mongol rule vanished. Finally, the destruction of Baghdad did not necessarily end the honorary prestige of the caliphate, which continued in Cairo under the protection of the Mamluks. For many, the Abbasid caliphate remained in effect until it faded into obscurity. Ottoman historian and qadi of Mecca, Diyarbekri (d. 1582), for example, in his universal history, gave an ubroken account of Abbasid caliphs down to al-Mustanjid Billah (r. 1455–1479).[35] The Mongols did not claim caliphal authority. The Mamluks, however, having filled in for the Seljuks as partner and protector of the caliphate, also inherited their title, *qasīm amīr al-muʾminīn.*[36]

Turkoman principalities of western Anatolia often sought the support of the Mamluks in their resistance to the direct rule of Mongols. At the same time, all these rulers who used *dawla* titles had good relationships with the Mevlevi order that openly preached loyalty to the Mongol rule and acted as a power broker, especially under the leadership of Arif Çelebi.[37] Thus their *dawla* identification may well be purposefully left anonymous due to the uncertainties of higher politics and different layers of authority at force in the Rum. However, Orhan Beg's image as *shujāʿ al-dawla* seems to have been devised as part of a deliberate claim rather than to convey a vague sense of affiliation with any of the three overarching authorities. More than a decade before the Şehadet Mosque inscription where Orhan made his *dawla*-title public, on three sets of coins he issued in 1324, 1327, and 1329, he minted the Abbasid caliph's title *al-Imām al-Mustanṣir bi-Allāh Amīr al-Muʾminīn.*[38] During the reign of Alaeddin Keykubad (r. 1220–1237), the caliph al-Mustansir's (r. 1226–1242) name was engraved on Seljuk coins, which became one of the most widely circulated currencies of the time. Against the surprising silence of historians, the few numismatists who introduced these coins to scholarship argued that Orhan may have minted them to commemorate the Abbasid caliph or simply to imitate the well-known Seljuk design in coinage.[39] Be that as it may, the mintage coincides with the death of the last Mongol governor in Anatolia whom the Ottomans long resented, which makes this coinage a blunt statement against the Mongol rule. However, given that coinage, along with Friday sermons, was the most distinctive symbol and display of sovereignty in Muslim dynasties, it is hard to imagine a rising ruler reserving this powerful instrument for commemoration.[40] The imitation thesis is certainly better rooted in historical reality as it is very common to see coins bearing the marks of others in circulation, including regalia. But designing one that displays the full title of a caliph dead for almost a century has no precedence.

So, why did Orhan associate himself with the Abbasid caliph in the same way as Alaeddin? Despite being liable to pay taxes, the Turkoman principalities of the frontier were among the least exposed to Mongol suzerainty. Remler, who classified early Ottoman mintage within the broader Seljukid–Ilkhanid coins, considered the anomaly of these coins as a declaration of independence through a gesture of loyalty to the caliphate which the Mongols had destroyed.[41] The rulers of Karesi, for example, to the west of the Ottomans, were further isolated from the Ilkhanid rule, and therefore felt confident enough to use the khan title, an exclusive mark of the Mongols, during the reigns of Yahşi Han (r. 1328–1332) and Demür Han (r. 1332–1341), both contemporaries of Orhan.[42] Such an image was even more rebellious and carries the mark of a haughty claim for universal sovereignty *à la* the Great Khan of the Mongols by defying its current bearers. Even the question of whether Orhan, perhaps to counter the Karesi claim, adopted the Abbasid caliph's title for himself, would have still stirred speculation among the politically conscious regarding the

House of Osman's intentions. Ibn Battuta, who recorded Orhan Beg in 1333 as the greatest, the richest, and the most powerful of Turkoman rulers, was impressed by his rulership style and portrayed him as an ambitious ruler with exceptional vigor and resolution: "This sultan is the greatest of Turkoman kings (*mulūk*) and the richest in wealth, lands, and military forces, and possesses nearly a hundred fortresses which he continually visits and stays a few days in each of them for inspection and putting to rights. It is said that he never stays in one place for more than a month and engaged with fighting against the infidels and besieging them."[43] Ayverdi's survey of Ottoman architecture during the reign of Orhan shows that his military campaigns were closely followed by building projects of all sorts.[44] With the Mongol power waning and emboldened by a serious of illustrious conquests, Orhan may have judged the moment opportune to declare himself as the successor to the Seljuks, therefore inheriting the *dawla* from the Abbasids. Some two decades later, when Davud-i Kayseri addressed Süleyman Paşa as *shujāʿ al-dawla* instead of the reigning ruler Orhan, the *dawla* could only refer to that of Orhan, his dynasty, or the Ottoman turn in leadership. Davud-i Kayseri's profile of Süleyman and Orhan closely resembles that of Alaeddin's public image as an illuminated ruler in the image of God. Further, Orhan maintained a close company of Babai dervishes whose mythical lore idealized Alaeddin as a perfect ruler in subservience to the founder of their mystical order, Baba Ilyas. Thus Orhan's mulling to proclaim a new beginning, a turn in leadership in the mystical cycle of providential authority in favor of the Ottomans, suits well the expectations of both learned and oral traditions.

The Contest for the Caliphate

The Ottomans or the Karesis were not alone in claiming the Seljuk legacy or supreme leadership in post-Mongol western Anatolia. Hacı Paşa (d. c. 1424), a physician and a younger contemporary of Davud-i Kayseri, who belonged to the same wider circle of learned men, designated his patron Isa Beg of Aydınids in 1380 as the *khalīfat Rasūl Allāh fī al-muʾminīn* (the caliph of the Prophet over the faithful), a title even the Seljukids never dared to identify with.[45] Hacı Paşa, who dedicated his later books to Ottoman sultans, had received his training in Egypt that started with jurisprudence under the famed Hanafi revivalist al-Baberti (d. 1384) and ended with mastering medicine at a time when debates on the caliphate and the legitimacy of the Mamluk rulers were in full bloom among the jurists.[46] Hacı Paşa's Syrian contemporary Tarsusi wrote a juristic polemic where he argued that, based on the Hanafi rulings as opposed to those of the Shafi'is, the sultanic authority of Mamluk Turkish rulers was perfectly legitimate.[47] He takes a bold step even within the Hanafi tradition and rules that the Qurayshi descent is not a condition for the caliphate. While jurists were occupied with a new formula for the legitimacy of the caliphate, Hacı Paşa must have been well aware of the status of the Abbasid caliph in Cairo whose position was largely reduced to ceremonials. This was a notable break with the eleventh-century Shafi'i resolution to the partition of caliphal authority that ruled the Seljukid authority as the delegation of Abbasid caliph's executive power.[48]

Tarsusi was writing in Damascus, where the Hanbali jurist Ibn Taymiyya had only recently redefined legitimate rulership by divorcing it from its historical and theological sanctions, such as the Qurayshi descent. Instead of ascribing to the caliphate the universal authority of the Muslim authority, a pursuit that remained broken since the end of the Umayyad Empire and further shattered by the Mongol invasions, he allowed the existence of multiple authorities by shifting the basis of legitimacy from the personal attributes of the claimant to the application of Islamic law and services prescribed by it.[49] Ibn Taymiyya's main political work gained renewed interest among the sixteenth-century Ottomans. However, as one of the most controversial jurists of his time, Ottoman scholars of the fourteenth century who typically traveled to Syria and Egypt must have been exposed to ongoing debate on the juristic legitimacy of Muslim rulership in the absence of effective caliphal authority. As part of a general trend among the post-Abbasid jurists who gradually dropped the question of the caliphate from their books on rulership, both Ibn Taymiyya and Tarsusi abstained from using the term caliph. Rising independent rulers of the Turko-Mongolian dynasties were themselves reluctant to use the term, as it could bring more trouble than prestige. The juristic notions of the caliphate or more specifically the title *khalīfat Rasūl Allāh* never gained currency among post-Abbasid rulers.

Coming from a half-educated jurist, physician Hacı Paşa's portrayal of Isa Beg as the Prophet's successor had no legal or political weight. Isa Beg's Ottoman counterparts were not interested in adopting this title, as there is no contemporary record of an Ottoman use of the title *khalīfa* in their titles from the fourteenth century.[50] When the Ottomans started using the title it was not the juristic designation as the Prophet's successor but a mystical conception of caliphate as God's viceregency (*khalīfat Allāh*) and manifestation on Earth. This *khalīfat Allāh* was qualitatively different from the one used since the early Umayyad times, which was conceived in the context of bitter succession controversies after the Rashidun caliphate collapsed. The Sunni canon instructs that the title *khalīfat Allāh* was first proposed soon after the death of the Prophet but was turned down by Abu Bakr, who preferred to be called the successor to the Prophet. Jurists and theologians developed a distaste for the term, particularly because of its anthropomorphic connotations. By discrediting this title, the jurists managed to maintain the rulership of the community within the legal imperative drawn from the Prophet's teachings. Conceiving the caliphate in relation to God meant voiding the juristic authority of its power to define and check the caliphate. The Syrian-based Umayyad military establishment with questionable credentials, who took over the leadership by force despite strong and lasting opposition, ingeniously appropriated ancient visions of divine appointment supported by fatalist tendencies spreading among the learned.[51] Despite the continuous objection of jurists and theologians, *khalīfat Allāh* was used in tandem with its juristically sanctified equivalent the commander of the faithful as two proprietary titles of the Abbasids to the very end. Such as the one inscribed on the gate of the Grand Mosque in Diyarbakır in 1124, Seljuk epigraphy commonly displays the Seljuk ruler's image as the helper of God's caliph (*muʿīn khalīfat Allāh*).[52]

The Seljuks never claimed the title *khalīfat Allāh* as it was exclusively Abbasid. Successor dynasties to the Seljuks only gradually and hesitantly adopted it. The Umayyad and Abbasid use of the term hardly received any elaboration from the learned and remained suspect for jurists and theologians. When the term reemerged in Ottoman usage it was not the royal title of the Abbasid caliphate but a new designation of ruleship as worked out by Sufis. Unlike the Umayyad and Abbasid uses of the term which were devised by imperial chanceries, the post-Seljuk *khalīfat Allāh* was itself conceived and propagated by the learned. By redefining the *khalīfat Allāh*, the Sufi-minded scholars, who were well grounded in jurisprudence and philosophy, facilitated its introduction into the mainstream. The post-Abbasid notions of *khalīfat Allāh* were grounded in an impressive spectrum of disciplines ranging from astronomy to philosophy as well as divergent orientations in Islamic praxis. Davud-i Kayseri's Ottoman Beg as God's evidence (*āyat Allāh*) shows the permeation of mystical imagination into political self-image during the Seljuk period and its reception thereafter. Najm al-Din Kubra, for example, the founder of the Kubrawiyya, which was well represented in Seljukid and later Ottoman domains, was known among his disciples as *āyat Allāh*.[53] Najm al-Din Daye and Baha Veled, two of his illustrious disciples, both settled in Konya and wrote their chief works during the reign of Alaeddin. Outshining all the other mystics of his age was Ibn Arabi whose intuitive revelations firmly established *khalīfat Allāh* as the central theme of Sufi political thought. Thirteenth-century Seljuk Asia Minor and its environs were the breeding ground for the rise of a mystical conception of the caliphate that came to dominate later political thinking in Ottoman domains if not the entire Islamic world.

The Seljuk art reveals that Alaeddin cultivated an image of cosmic rulership that was inspired by Suhrawardi's mystical philosophy of illumination that infused Platonism through the *ishrāqī* philosophy and Zoroastrian divine light through the Persian literature during the philosopher's long sojourn in Anatolia and contacts with Seljukid elite before moving to Syria.[54] The Seljuk ruler as recipient of divine light, despite its aesthetic representations in art and epigraphy, was not a decorative image but a reflection of a dramatic shift in political thought in which Suhrawardi was an early harbinger and, arguably, its first martyr. The Sufi philosopher was executed in Aleppo on charges of heresy by al-Malik al-Zahir, ordered by his celebrated father Salah al-Din al-Ayyubi in 1191 at the age of thirty-seven. Sifting through conflicting accounts of what led to this—one of the most controversial executions of Islamic history—Hossain Ziai concludes that the philosopher was condemned to death because of a perceived political conspiracy. What enraged the established ulema and Salah al-Din was the suspicion that Suhrawardi was seeking to establish the young Ayyubid prince as the ruler of age under the guidance of the illuminated philosopher.[55] To give credit to this suspicion, Suhrawardi expressed theologically troublesome views on the nature of prophethood and authority in philosophical works he dedicated to Ayyubid rivals, including the Seljukids and Artukids, to cultivate an illuminated ruler, if not to implicitly propagate himself as the ruler of the age.[56] His students are reported to have called him *Abū al-Futūḥ, Rasūl Allāh* (father of spiritual openings, the messenger of God), while he himself is recorded to have said: "without doubt I will rule the earth."[57] Suhrawardi not only mystified God's viceregency on Earth but made it attainable through knowledge and purification, turned executive power into its instrument, and claimed that at any moment there would always be a godly ruler in charge, whether manifest or concealed:

> Should it happen that in some period there be a philosopher proficient in both intuitive philosophy and discursive philosophy, he will be the ruler by right and the vicegerent of God. Should it happen that this not be the case, then rulership will belong to a philosopher proficient in intuitive philosophy but of middle ability in discursive philosophy. Should these qualities not coincide, rulership belongs to a philosopher who is proficient in philosophy but who lacks discursive philosophy. The world will never be without a philosopher proficient in intuitive philosophy. Authority on God's earth will never belong to the proficient discursive philosopher who has not become proficient in intuitive philosophy, for the world will never be without one proficient in intuitive philosophy—one more worthy than he who is only a discursive philosopher—for the vicegerency requires direct knowledge. By this authority I do not mean political power. The leader with intuitive philosophy may indeed rule openly, or he may be hidden—the one whom the multitude call the "Pole." He will have authority even if he is in the deepest obscurity.[58]

Suhrawardi's illuminationist political doctrine was predicated on his distinction between discursive (*baḥth*) and intuitive (*taʾalluh*) knowledge, the latter literally meaning "becoming a god."[59] He conceived of rulership as part of divine governance (*tadbīr-i ilāhī*) where the ruler is established by the command of God (*hākim bi-amr Allāh*) based on one's competence in intuitive knowledge as evidenced by his reception of royal light (*kharra-yi kayānī* or *farr-i īzadī*). Such rulers would be prophets, philosopher-sages, and divine kings who, as pure ones (*pākān*), will receive the light of God, which would give them power over the elemental entities (*unṣuriyyāt*). Only with competence in intuitive knowledge and reception of divine light is one designated as God's vicegerent (*khalīfat Allāh*) and the ruler of the age, who may be termed an imam or *quṭb* (pole). This authority is not an exclusive grace of God but anyone who endows oneself with wisdom would receive divine light, become the natural ruler of the world, and receive divine help in his government.[60] Through his new epistemology based on intuitive knowledge, Suhrawardi unifies distinct notions of authority envisioned in Farabi's Neoplatonism, Avicenna's peripatetic philosophy, ancient Persian ideals that were reinvented in the Shuubiiyya tradition, and Sufi cosmology elaborated since Hakim al-Tirmizi (d. 932). This powerful imagery offered new possibilities and opportunities for bitterly contesting ambitious states in the irrecoverably fragmented final stage of the Abbasid commonwealth. From Nile to Oxus, illuminationism quickly reverberated through the royal courts, madrasas, and Sufi hospices and registered a large contingent of high-profile subscribers of different sectarian proclivities. Suhrawardi's most authoritative commentator Qutb al-Din Shirazi (d. 1311), who was a student of the Maragha school like his younger contemporary Davud-i Kayseri, spent most of his professional career in Anatolia and left an indelible mark on later Ottoman thought.[61]

Suhrawardi's execution ended his illuminationist project to establish a unified authority. But Asia Minor soon turned into a theater of spiritual activism where visions of unified authority were put to the test for centuries to come. In addition to the ongoing Turkic *Völkerwanderung*, the pre-Ottoman Anatolian frontier attracted famed Sufis, jurists, and philosophers, not to count proselytizers, propagandists, adventurers, and refugees from Spain to Transoxiana. In Kafadar's depiction, this was a world of dizzying physical mobility where information, ideas, fashions, and codes were flocking in.[62] Sufis from far corners of the Islamic world, with their own convictions and orientations in life, shook and fit themselves into the already charged and diversified confessional space of Asia Minor that led to the formation of a new spiritual cosmopolitanism. Many of these Sufis were part of existing or newly forming spiritual orders, fraternities, or communities of dervishes that emerged in the increasingly divisive world of Islam with divergent notions of authority and models of social organization. Among them Yesevi, Vefai, Haydari, Kalenderi, and Melameti groups became fixtures of Anatolian spirituality. Despite the convenience of facetious enumeration of these Sufi groups, delineating social boundaries between them, identifying their distinctive marks, and tracing their origins are still the paramount questions of studies on Anatolian Sufism since they were first problematized by Fuad Köprülü a century ago. Karamustafa's relentless inquiries to chart and conceptualize Anatolian Sufism show a coral reef of devotional diversity beneath the broad categories that so long dominated the field.[63] This fertile ground soon bred its home brands of Sufi orders, such as Mevlevis and Bektaşis, that grew in tandem with the Ottoman state and expanded with their peculiar visions of authority that could not be easily reconciled with those of sovereign states. One distinctive characteristic of politically active Sufi groups was their strict communal bondage tied to the idea of *ḳuṭb*, the perfect human being who was thought to be vested by divine ordainment with absolute command over both angelic and corporal plains. *Ḳuṭb*-centered communities developed into autonomous corporate groups with broad appeal to different layers of society and negotiating power with established authorities, including the political and the learned. Each one of these communities, ranging from Yasawiyya to Kubrawiyya, envisioned a cosmological body politic, above and beyond conventional designations of authority and its boundaries. These mystical orders that populated Anatolian spiritual space had a lasting and definitive impact on Ottoman thought, dynastic self-image, and state formation.

The early Ottoman state not only was located at the geographical margins of the Islamic world but was also conceived at the uncharted frontier of revolutionary ideas in political thought. Thirteenth-century western Anatolia was the main theater where the mystical turn in political thought was empowered by a new breed of Sufi leaders and rulers seeking independence and pursuing social ideals at times at odd with those of others. This mystical turn, which found its first systematic exposition in the writings of Suhrawardi, along with the lightning spread of Sufi fraternities, evolved into a captivating intellectual current across the Abbasid commonwealth. Among many, literary masterpieces of Attar and Sa'di, spiritual explorations of Ibn Arabi, and Najm al-Din Daye's political work, all more or less composed and spread contemporaneously, turned mysticism into the most fashionable pursuit for exploring the nature of authority. These mystics conversed in the same conceptual language of Sufism that addressed and helped create the one community of letters across the deeply fragmented political space of Eurasia. The thirteenth-century mystical imprint on orientation of life, social organization, state formation, literature, arts, political thought, and even science made its mark increasingly visible on all subsequent Muslim states of Eurasia, most notably the Ottomans, Timurids, Safavids, and the Mughals.

Rulers and Dervishes

A close look into the intellectual history of mystical movements of the thirteenth century shows how Sufistic notions of authority were conceived and negotiated with the established order. Among them, Mevlevis and Babais were two politically active Sufi orders that made their mark on Anatolian and later Balkan spiritual space at around the same time.[64] These orders competed not only against the authority of rulers but also against one another.[65] Political ideas of the founders of these Sufi orders, Jalal al-Din Rumi and Baba Ilyas (d. 1240), and their dealings with reigning rulers are recorded in thrilling hagiographies in the early fourteenth century when these movements grew more powerful.

Hagiographers Elvan Çelebi, the grandson of Baba Ilyas, and Eflaki, a devout disciple of Rumi's grandson, were both contemporaries of Davud-i Kayseri. For modern historians, these texts long served as the principal repositories of inquiry for what they offer in terms of authenticatable historical data on late-Seljuk early-Ottoman Sufism. This book, however, will treat them as two carefully doctored representations of mystical political ideologies at a time when these orders were spreading faster than any reigning ruler could hope for territorial expansion. Both texts are loaded with political statements either made by the authors or attributed to founding saints of their orders, which makes these hagiographies a new genre of political writings. By depicting Alaeddin as an ideal ruler who was a friend of God's friends and submitted to the spiritual authority of their founding saints, Elvan Çelebi and Eflaki confirm what the Seljuk art and epigraphy manifested during his well-remembered reign.[66] This idealized reconciliation was verified by other contemporary evidence that shows Alaeddin inculcating an image of himself as a godly ruler while granting powerful Sufi groups privileges. The idea of an ideal ruler as friend of friends of God was emphatically maintained by Ottoman rulers from the very beginning until the reign of Mehmed II, when that image was broken but quickly rehabilitated by Bayezid II. Alaeddin was the first and, arguably, the most defining role model for the newly incorporating Ottoman rulership.

The revolt of Baba Ilyas in 1239 and his subsequent execution after wreaking irreparable havoc to the Seljuk order display two striking similarities to Suhrawardi's tragedy: Both were accused of claiming to be prophets by jurists, Kadı al-Fadl and Köre Kadı, who alarmed Salah al-Din and Ghiyath al-Din that their authority was at stake.[67] The lack of known evidence to link Baba Ilyas to Suhrawardi does not make this common accusation a coincidence but rather points to the juristic anxiety in coming to terms with a new vision of authority that was perceived to be a threat to the conventional legitimacy paradigm shaped by legal premises and administrative traditions.[68] Writing about a century later, Elvan Çelebi categorically dismisses this charge but displays no apology for the actual revolt itself except for putting the blame for sedition onto the shoulders of others.[69] He portrays his grandfather, Baba Ilyas, as a saint (*velī*) with a specific mandate from his master Dede Garkın to carry out God's command in the land of Rum to spread His message.[70] The Seljuk ruler Alaeddin, startled by the Baba's power (*ḳudret*), realizes that the saint's *dawla* was bestowed by God, turns into his servant (*ḳul*), and earns the praise of being a divinely guided ruler (*pādişāh-ı rabbānī*). He was thus initiated into the cosmic rulership of the mystic body politic.[71] The section that details the sultan's initiation refers to Baba Ilyas as the ruler of religion and the auspicious turn (*ḫudāvendān-ı dīn ü devlet*), a common title used by the Seljuk rulers, the axis of sainthood, and the center of chivalrous fraternities (*merkez-i fütüvvet*).[72] In a twisted plot, the evil-intended Ghiyath al-Din poisons his father Alaeddin and declares war against the saint by accusing him of plotting to takeover his throne. Baba Ilyas intercedes with God to cut His compassion from the land of Rum for eighty years and prophesizes that the Seljuks would be humiliated and destroyed at the hands of the Mongols who would take over the caliphate from the Abbasids.[73] One of Baba Ilyas' deputies converts Mongols to Islam and turns all the Turks and the Chinese, including Chingiz Khan, into the saint's adherents. The entire Mongol hordes turn into God's soldiers and punish the Seljuks along with the Abbasids for challenging the saint's divinely ordained authority.[74]

In confirmation of the prophecy, in the name of his brethren, Elvan Çelebi takes full credit for the demise of the Seljuks. Aided by Mongol devastations, ending the defiant Seljuk rulership and restoring the divinely ordained authority over the land of Rum is commissioned to Baba Ilyas' son, Muhlis Paşa, who was saved from the Seljuk onslaught and taken to Cairo as a child where he grew up at the palace of the ruler in Egypt. On reaching adulthood, in an obvious reenactment of the Mosaic drama of Abrahamic scriptures, Khidr, the prophet at large who is believed to have guided Moses in the Qur'an, appears to Muhlis Paşa, girds him with a sword, and ordains him with the conquest of the Rum. Muhlis Paşa bows to divine call and sets out to reconquer the Rum, where he is wholeheartedly embraced by the people of all faiths with intuitive knowledge (*ʿirfān*), including the people of the Torah and the Bible. He defeats the Seljuk sultan, temporarily resides in his palace in a symbolic display of contempt and triumph, and finally retreats to his Sufi hospice where Elvan Çelebi heard and recorded his story.[75] Muhlis Paşa saves God's community from oppressors and restores the rule of the worthy. In Elvan Çelebi's portrayal, the whole drama is not a clash between two contestants for rulership. Throughout the story both Baba Ilyas and Muhlis Paşa continuously belittle and reject temporal rulership. Elvan Çelebi frames the struggle as a rebellion of a worldly ruler to a divinely ordained authority, the *ḳuṭb*. This act of disobedience to divine command is ultimately suppressed in the way rebellious peoples who refused the call of prophets incurred divine punishment. Such a conception was in stark contrast with the way rulership is acquired, legitimized, and contested in juristic rulings.

Unlike the philosophical utopia of Suhrawardi and popular rebellion of Baba Ilyas, per Eflaki's recount, Baha Veled and Rumi's mystical ideals materialized at both spiritual and corporal planes before their deaths in peace. Eflaki's massive hagiography of the founding figures of the Mevlevis shows little modesty when it comes to illustrating their political activism and visions of rulership. *Manāqib al-ʿĀrifīn* is written with the feel of an epic and a messianic voice where romance, dreams, prophecies, miracles, and heroism are enmeshed with historical facts, juristic prescripts, theological dogmas, and esoteric symbolism in an illustrious and epoch-making narrative. It lends metahistorical significance to the catastrophic breakdown of the caliphal order and offers a new path for appeasement of existential anxieties and reconstruction of the broken order. Reminiscent of a dynastic myth-making, the grand narrative of Rumi's story starts with an auspicious marriage where the divine script unites the destinies of his grandfather, a young bachelor saint, with that of a noble princess, the daughter of the honorable ruler of Khwarazm, whose ancestry reaches the Prophet's closest companion, Abu Bakr—God's devout friend (*ṣiddīq*), the first caliph, and the originator of one of the two spiritual genealogies in Sufism. One possible impediment to the marriage, the question of *kufuw*, the expectation of parity between prospective spouses in Islamic jurisprudence, is resolved with a political statement made by the ruler's vizier who pointed that there may not be a better match for the princess than the scholar-saint whose status was superior to that of a ruler: "Kings rule over the people and scholars rule over the kings." To dispel any further doubts, by divine providence (*taḳdīr-i ilāhī*), Prophet Muhammed appears in a dream to the princess, the vizier, and the ruler simultaneously, and declares that he wedded the Princes of the world (*malīka-i jihān*) to Hüseyin Hatibi, the young bachelor.[76] This marriage not only symbolizes the birth of a new conception of authority to be personified by Rumi but also sets the precedence of a conviction that all acts of Baha Veled and his progeny would be in full compliance with the written code of Sunni Islam. In Mevlevi faith, as professed by Eflaki, miracles, visions, and intuitive explorations, which may otherwise be considered suspect by the upright, are given a juristic sanction that made their teachings particularly appealing to the learned.

Baha Veled, Rumi's father, who continuously instructs his disciples about the chosenness of his son throughout the narrative, designates him as his sole heir based on his noble ancestry and prophecies he reports. He praises the young prince-saint (*khodāvandgār*) as "a well-born king (*pādishāh-i ʿaṣlī*)" where "his friendship with God is accompanied by a noble pedigree." Baha Veled decorates Rumi with an impeccable lineage, portraying him as the progeny of such "kings of temporal and spiritual worlds" (*shāhān-i sūrī va maʿnavī*) that includes Sarakhsi (d. 1090), a descendant of the Prophet and a celebrated Hanafi jurist, Ibrahim b. Adham (d. 778?), one of the most venerated saints who abandoned his crown and wealth to join the Sufi path, Ali, and Abu Bakr.[77] Unless historically accurate, this alluring genealogy, later finessed by the masterful craftsmanship Mevlevi narrators, turned into an origination myth of the order. Rumi's Muhammedan stock makes him exceptional even among the descendants of the Prophet for being both a sharif, from Hasan's line, and a sayyid, from Husayn's line. In obvious allusion to the Prophet's tribe, which has the sole provenance in producing caliphs in juristic theory, Baha Veled often reiterates such phrases as "we Qurayshites."[78] The lineage also portrays him as the inheritor of two principal groups, the ulema and the Sufis, whose competition to represent the authority of the Prophet became more pronounced in this period. Finally, being a descendant of the first ruler of Khwarazm under the Seljuk Empire, not only accords him a blood-right to rule but also introduces him into the Seljuk aristocracy.

Throughout *Manāqib al-ʿĀrifīn,* Eflaki refers to Baha Veled as the sultan of scholars (*sulṭān al-ʿulemā*), an epithet confirmed by contemporary sources as well. This was not a eulogistic term characteristic of hagiographies where the more common honorifics would be *sulṭān al-awliyā* (king of saints) or *sulṭān al-ʿārifīn* (king of knowers of God). It is a title of stature with a claim for authority. At a time when the competition for the moral authority over religion was no less intense than the political race for rulership among the mitosistic polities of the late Abbasid period, Eflaki presents Baha Veled as having the spiritual counterpart of sovereign authority over the body politic of Sufis and scholars.[79] As the chosen one for the mission, it was no other than the Prophet who grants this position to the scholar-saint: In Balkh, 300 muftis, all jurists, see a dream simultaneously in which the Prophet, having Baha Veled on his side, commands them to call him the sultan of scholars from then on. Waking up with awe and astonishment, the muftis rush to Baha Veled to submit their loyalties and become his disciples (*murīd*).[80] The dream not only establishes the primacy of intuitive knowledge over that of discursive but also unifies the two distinct forms of piety and their adherents in one body. Eflaki's conception of ulema is comprehensive to encompass all possessors of knowledge, including both Sufis and jurists. The narrative is replete with anecdotes where mystics or scholars who disrespect Baha Veled's authority are instantly inflicted with divine punishment, including the celebrated theologian of the time Fakhr al-Din al-Razi (d. 1209). This unified authority passes onto Rumi whose arrival is foretold by the Prophet. As Baha Veled reports, Gabriel the Archangel soothes Muhammed's anxiety about the future tribulations of his community by giving him the good tidings, namely, the coming of Rumi, who resembles him most in both countenance and disposition, by showing the Prophet his figure:

> This is the form of someone from the lineage of ṣeddīq-e Akbar (Abu Bakr) who will appear at the end of time in the midst of your community and, filling the world with the lights of your secrets and truths, he will bestow beauty and elegance. Likewise, God Most High will bestow him a [firm] foot and a pen and a breath so that all the nations and those endowed with dominion (*duwal*) will become his supporters and disciples. And he will be the secret of the light which reveals the manifestation of your religion.[81]

Eflaki turns Baha Veled's emigration from Balkh to Konya into a visceral journey and an elaborate myth embedded with statements of spiritual authority, moral critique of the community of believers and their rulers, and messianic utterances that later became the founding lore of the Mevlevi order. As *sulṭān al-ʿulemā*, Baha Veled resents the scholarly establishment headed by the theologian Razi and sets out with forty of his devout muftis for the Rum, the promised land, in the same way the Prophet had to leave Mecca for Medina to distance himself from "the abuses of envious and hypocrite" disbelievers.[82] Razi, identified as the leader of philosophers, charges Baha Veled with defying their religious authority by subjugating discursive knowledge (*ʿulūm al-ẓāhir*) to intuitive knowledge (*ʿilm al-bāṭin*), and agitates the ruler that he is mobilizing masses to capture the throne. Similar to the plight of Suhrawardi, where scholars felt threatened by his unified epistemology, in the case of Baha Veled, authority is conceived to be a function of experiential knowledge. But unlike Salah al-Din of the Ayyubids, Muhammed of Kwarazmshahs was already an adherent of Baha Veled and implored the saint to stay, though not from hearth. Although the sultan vaguely acknowledges Baha Veled's rulership over two worlds, this and hereafter, he tells the saint that one of them should leave the kingdom as it would not be permissible to have two kings in one region, in obvious reference to a well-known juristic principle, and that it would be a great favor if the saint would leave the rulership of the region to the sultan.[83] This is only a more courteous way of defying the authority of the saint than what the Seljuk ruler is reported to have displayed against Baba Ilyas. And Baha Veled's response was not so different from that of Baba Ilyas:

> They call you sultan of the commanders and they call me the sultan of the religious scholars, and you are my disciple. Verily, your dominion and kingship depend on a single breath, and my kingship and dominion are also attached to a single breath. Once that breath is cut off from your carnal soul you shall not remain and your throne, good fortune, kingdom, descendants, family line, and connections shall not remain: *As though yesterday it had not flourished* (Qur'an, 10/24). They will become utterly non-existent. But when our precious breath leaves our carnal soul, our lineage and offspring, who are the Tent Pegs of the earth, will exist until the advent of the Resurrection, in accordance with: "*Every connection and family tie (koll sabab va-nasab) will be cut off except for my connection and my family.*" I will now depart. But let it be known to you that behind me will arrive the huge army of the Tatars who are the soldiers of God and scattered locusts, and are characterized by: "I created them in My rage and My anger." They will conquer the region of Khorasan and force people of Balkh to drink the bitter potion of death. They will turn the world upside-down and remove the king from his kingdom with a hundred thousand pains and sorrows. In the end you will meet your death at the hand of the sultan of Rum.[84]

Even the Abbasid caliph, despite pouring his veneration and presents to the saint, is not immune to his disdain and ominous prophecies. He declares the caliph a shame for the caliphate, worse than disbelievers, and soon to be overthrown and killed by God's soldiers, the Mongols. Baha Veled's west-bound journey leaves a trail of total wreckage behind while glorifying the Rum as the abode of a new beginning. Even the good-hearted who stay behind cannot escape this destruction of apocalyptic proportions, including his own disciples. Upon the arrival of Mongols to Balkh, the public gathers around one of Baha Veled's disciples who prays all night to intercede with God to spare Muslims, only to hear a terrifying voice responding from the heavens: "Oh disbelievers [the Mongols] kill the sinners."[85] On the road to his destination, local rulers who meet him turn into his disciples (*murīd*), plead with him to settle in their realms, and offer to relinquish their crowns under the saint's authority. The ones who accuse him of vying for the crown and plotting against him get immediately inflicted with divine punishment that results in utter humiliation and loss of their thrones.[86] While turning down each such offer by displaying a saintly disinterest in worldly rulership, in one case, he manifests the final destination of his journey: "Divine indication is to the effect that our abode shall be in the clime of Rum and our tomb is to be in the earth of the royal capital Konya."[87] Long after they settled, Rumi reveals the secret of their Rum-bound destiny to his disciples during a passionate session of revelations from the divine:

> God Most High has shown great favor to the people of Rum and through the prayer of ṣeddīq-e Akbar [Abu Bakr] they have received the most mercy in the whole Muslim community. The best of the climes is the region of Rum. However, the people of this kingdom were very ignorant and insensitive regarding the world of love toward the Possessor of Sovereignty and intense ecstatic experience (*dhowq*) of the interior. The Primary Cause of causes—His dignity is glorious and His power is exalted—undertook an act of grace and instigated a cause from the world of non-causation. Drawing us from the realm of Khorasan to the country of Rum, God gave my descendants refuge in this pure land so that we might scatter gifts from our transcendent elixir on the copper of the being of Rum's inhabitants and thus they would be entirely transformed into the philosopher's stone and become intimate with the world of divine knowledge (*ʿālam-e ʿerfān*) and familiar with the knowers of God throughout the world (*ʿārefān-e ʿālam*)."[88]

Eflaki recounts the materialization of Baha Veled's utopia of perfect rulership through a dramatic initiation ceremony in Konya where the saint finally meets with his ideal ruler and community of believers. Alaeddin invites all the scholars, knowers of God, philosophers, shaykhs, masters of chivalry [*futuwwa*], and beggars to his palace, offers his throne to Baha Veled and calls himself the saint's commander (*subaşı*) whom he greets as the rightful possessor of both outer and inner rulership (*salṭanat-i ẓāhir u bāṭin*) upon which all of the sultan's retinue and the nobles of the city turn into disciples of Baha Veled.[89] The new patron saint of the Seljuks turns this initiation into a permanent pact through his testament conveyed to Alaeddin: "As long as

I am alive . . . no person like me will appear," states Baha Veled, "wait until I pass away and you see how my son Jalal al-Din Moḥammed turns out! He will take my place and become more elevated than I."[90] On another occasion, Baha Veled, in interpreting Alaeddin's dream, declares his reign as golden and prophesizes that with every generation this will degenerate into silver, bronze, and finally in the fifth generation a total chaos will prevail and the Seljuk rule will end with the Mongol invasion. In confirmation of this prophecy long after the Seljuks were gone, Eflaki narrates a story circulating among his brethren about the downfall of their dynasty. The Seljuk ruler Rukn al-Din, who was Rumi's disciple, informs the saint that he adopted Baba Marendi, a holy man in Konya, as his new master, and that he accepted the sultan as his disciple. The enraged Rumi declares: "If the sultan has made him his father, I will take another son."[91] Rumi's authority was defied, the covenant established between Baha Veled, as the sultan of scholars, and the Seljuk ruler is broken, and Rumi pulls his protective shield from the Seljuks. Before long, Rukn al-Din himself dies a despicable death and his dynasty crumbles.

Despite speaking for two distinct and rival forms of spirituality, one formed within the learned Persianate traditions of urban high culture and the other among the primarily oral traditions of nomadic Turkoman populations, Eflaki and Elvan Çelebi both display the characteristics of the mystical turn in political thought. Being newcomers to the increasingly diversified frontier, their troubled relationship with the Seljuk dynasty and competition with established structures in society are not surprising. However, their categorical defiance of the Abbasid caliphate and endorsement of Mongol rule as divine providence reflect their expectations for a messianic new beginning with the restoration of the primordial unified authority that was thought to be partitioned. Their criticism of rulers, scholars, and mystics alike points to a perception that the unified authority of the Prophet, which was maintained by the rightly guided caliphs, was broken when these three groups distanced from each other and claimed independence within their respective spheres. However, the pursuit of unified authority among these Sufi leaders does not entail taking over the worldly kingship, which is considered a lowly position. Instead, both Eflaki and Elvan Çelebi vehemently criticize rulership, in line with the general scholarly and pietistic attitudes, repeatedly disclaim it as a goal, and profile it with abomination. In these and other hagiographies that followed, rulership is deglorified and reduced to an executive arm of saintly authority. Including the great Alaeddin of Seljuks, rulers who paid their allegiance to Baha Veled and his successors are commonly referred as their commanders (*subaşı*). However imaginary and ritualistic it may be, these Sufi leaders sought to establish in practice the divine government by subjugating temporal kingship, not by replacing it.

Thirteenth- and fourteenth-century western Anatolia was a palpitating ground with pietistic excitement, political architecturing, spiritual avantgardism, and social experimentation. The Mevlevis, having already been endowed with elite Islamic learning, turned into an urban establishment and systematically aimed to conquer traditional institutions of Islamic learning and power. Both Baha Veled and Rumi started their careers as madrasa professors. As a legacy, madrasa education as well as adjudication in Islamic jurisprudence continued to be an integral part of Mevlevi piety. Eflaki reports that Rumi instructed his disciples to prompt him even when he was in an ecstatic condition if someone came to their gate asking for a juristic opinion.[92] The ideal shaykh for the Mevlevis was the one who also acts as a jurist. Abdalan however, including the Bektaşis, opted to remain on the margins of learned Islam and its urban centers. Unlike the Mevlevis who pursued overtaking the juristic authority, Bektaşis turned more esoteric and belittled Islamic learning that was based on conveyed knowledge and discursive reasoning. That defiance also included urban Sufism that was in peace with jurisprudence. As demonstrated by Karamustafa, this Abdalan antinomianism gave birth in Anatolia to vernacular Islam expressed in the Turkish vernacular.[93]

Yet, both strains vied for supremacy over the newly forming frontier states and competed to patronize the *gazi* enterprise. The Mevlevis engaged in an ambitious campaign to expand their presence especially during the leadership of Arif Çelebi (d. 1320), who extensively traveled all of Anatolia and Ilkhanid domains to convert the rulers, statesmen, and scholars.[94] During the course of the fourteenth century, the Mevlevis mustered a number of powerful frontier rulers as their affiliates under their spiritual protectorate. In principalities with strong Mevlevi presence a new generation of çelebi-rulers emerged including Çelebi Ishak Beg of Saruhan, Çelebi Murad Arslan and Hızır Beg Çelebi of Inançs, Mehmed Çelebi of Hamids, Gazi Çelebi of Pervanes, and Çelebi-i Azam (the great çelebi) Yakub Beg of Germiyan.[95] While Mevlevi centers were sprawling in Anatolian towns, Mevlevis maintained their close alliance with the Mongols with concerted effort to bring them under their spiritual authority. When the powerful Karamanid ruler resented this policy, Arif Çelebi was reported to have replied: "We are dervishes. Our glance is turned toward the will of God. Whomever God wishes and whomever He entrusts (*tafwīz*) with His sovereignty (*mamlaka*), we are on that person's side and we want him."[96] In Eflaki's report, Sultan Veled (d. 1312), Rumi's son, called Mehmed Beg of Aydınids as his commander, praised him as the "sultan of the warriors of faith" (*sulṭān al-ghuzāt*), and blessed him with his protection. When Mehmed Bey sought spiritual assistance from Arif Çelebi for conquest, the saint informed him in a compactual statement: "know that after today this province (*vilāyat*) and several other provinces from Khodāvandgār's spiritual domain (*velāyat*) will be acquired by you."[97] In the way Eflaki revealed in 1320s, the Mevlevis thought that the Rum was already under their spiritual sway and that they could delegate the administration of its territorial space to the worthy *gazi* leaders who submit to the spiritual authority of the Mevlevi Çelebis.

But the Mevlevi order was conspicuously absent from the Ottoman domains during its first century.[98] The first Mevlevihane opened under the Ottoman rule was the one in Edirne during the reign of Murad II.[99] Instead, the Ottoman frontier was populated by the more adventurous followers of Baba Ilyas and his better known disciple Hacı Bektaş, along with a large contingent of Abdalan of the broader Melameti disposition. Outside the moral discipline of a structured urban society with imposing political establishment, institutions of Islamic learning and piety, these independence-loving mystical orders found an ideal environment at the marches where orality prevailed over literacy, spiritual piety marginalized strict norms and rituals, and symbiosis proved more rewarding than a contest for subjugation. The same was true for the Ottoman leadership. Relatively isolated from the vicissitudes of the Anatolian hinterland, the marches offered unique opportunities for mobility, coopting, and adaptation in order to expand, consolidate, and configure the nascent Ottoman state. Among many, Shaykh Edebali, Osman's father-in-law, Geyikli Baba, Barak Baba, and Abdal Musa had no less sway and popularity over the marches than the early Ottoman rulers and their celebrated *gazi* commanders.[100] Unlike the Mevlevis who sought to convert rulers in return for recognition and spiritual empowerment, the Abdalan partook in *gaza* activity alongside the Ottomans as their equals, at times even independently, but always by retaining their spiritual patronage of the newly conquered territories. The involvement of these *gazi* dervishes in the conquest and expansion of the Rum was not simply to legitimize Ottoman rulership and bestow upon them their blessings in return for favors and privileges. As manifested by Elvan Çelebi, who tied the Abdalan ethos to Baba Ilyas' visions, *gazi* dervishes were engaged in the spiritual conquest of the Rum on their own, not as servants or even patrons of worldly rulers. Abdalan hagiographies, all composed much later based on oral traditions and earlier accounts, are replete with stories of encounters, coopting, compactual agreements, and statements of denying worldly rulership as representatives of higher authority. Abdal Musa's meeting with Umur Beg of the Aydinids, another *gazi* leader that closely resemble the Ottomans, looks similar to that of Arif Çelebi's dealings with Mehmed Beg, Umur Beg's father: Upon Umur Beg's appeal for support, Abdal Musa assigns his disciple Kızıl Deli Sultan to his company, and declares that he granted the province of Rumeli to his disposal.[101]

With the fall of the Seljuk order, Sufi fraternities, particularly Mevlevis and Abdalan, rose as the building blocks of the new social order emerging in western Anatolia. With their own means of sustenance and loyal constituencies, they shared space with various political configurations while conquering the spiritual plane. While the successor states to the Seljuks were seeking symbiotic alliances with independence-loving fraternities, these Sufi groups were pursuing conversion to their spiritual body politic, albeit in loose and inclusive affiliations not necessarily expressed in strict confessional terms.

Both Eflaki and Elvan Çelebi highlight the spiritual authority of their masters across faith lines by mustering people of all faiths and sectarian affiliations, including Christians and Jews, into the community of disciples. Kafadar rightly credits this open call to people outside the boundaries of Muslim believers to the metadoxic character of newly forming communities peculiar to the frontier where traditional structures of Islamic learning and piety had less defining power and stricter expressions of normative Islam offered little appeal.[102] Yet, this relative confessional indifference was not wholly innocent as these mystical orders often behaved as uncompromising and dismissive when their sway was challenged by their devotional kins. Especially, when the epithets used by mystic masters are compared to the propagated regalia of western Anatolian rulers, the mystical embracement of diversity shows its political character. The mystics claimed their spiritual overlordship over the same territory and constituencies claimed by corporal polities. Elvan Çelebi portrays Baba Ilyas as having instituted an ecumenical power with four hundred deputies dispatched far and wide.[103] In addition to a large contingent of invisible saints in service, commanding such an impressive number of visible deputies, each having their own devotees, is a common topos in Babai-Bektaşi hagiographies. The post-Seljuk Rum was shadowed by two layers of authority: one exercised by rulers with their warriors and one exercised by Sufi leaders with their armies of dervishes where images of authority and symbols of legitimacy used by rulers and mystics were virtually identical in epithets.

The extensive use of status and authority epithets by mystics may look odd for friends of God who are expected to excel, first and foremost, by the humiliation of the self and categorical defiance of ennoblement through social hierarchy. But in the language of Sufism, these appellations referred to a higher, unified authority established in the spiritual plane as part of divine governance. Hagiographers and disciples often use these titles to glorify their masters as metaphors for distinction and authority. Yet the pervasiveness of these appellations along with propagated imageries shows that it was part of a new consciousness and understanding regarding authority beyond panegyric connotations. For those who advocated unified authority as part of divine governance, regal appellations used by rulers were metaphors for a higher form of authority. The only real rulership to designate such concepts as caliphate or sultanate was the one that formed outside the provenance of the ordinary. Thus, however comprehensive, powerful, and lofty it may be, any designation of authority constructed by human beings' will or force may be termed and can function only in the metaphorical sense. The real power to make or break always stays with God's chosen agent, beyond the reach of worldly rulers.

It is not surprising to see that Eflaki calls Hüsameddin Çelebi, Rumi's successor, as God's caliph (*khalīfa-i Ḥaq*) well before any ruler in western Anatolia could identify himself with this designation.[104] Rumi, in addition to his sobriquet Mevlana, which is a shortened form of Molla (the master teacher) of the Rum, was simply known as Hüdavendigar by his followers. As his fame spread, he came to be remembered as Mawlana Khudavandigar (Our Sovereign Master) in the broader Turko-Persianate world.[105] Similarly, Hacı Bektaş, a disciple of Baba Ilyas, whose influence arguably far surpassed that of any other mystic in the Ottoman realms, was known as Hünkar by his later followers, if not during his own time. Many from among the Abdalan of Rum commonly carried such epithets as sultan, shah, and the like. The titulature of Mevlevis and Babais is unmistakably dynastic, albeit spiritual. Each of the five sons of Baba Ilyas carried the sobriquet Paşa.[106] By contrast, Rumi himself bestowed the title Emir to his grandson Arif who continued the tradition by naming all his children with the same title.[107] It is not readily clear why Babais chose *paşa* as opposed to Mevlevi preference for *emir*, but the distinction is obvious. A further palpable difference was the Babai-Bektaşi identification with *abdal* as opposed to the Mevlevi appropriation of the title *çelebi*. By comparison, the first Ottoman named Paşa was Süleyman Paşa, a half century after Baba Ilyas' sons were named. The first Ottoman ruler who adopted the title Hüdavendigar was Murad I, almost a century later than Rumi. The use of *çelebi* as a royal title in the Ottoman dynasty must have taken place much later. It has been a truism in Ottoman historiography to refer to Mehmed I along with other sons of Bayezid I as *çelebi*.[108] The chronology of such designations in western Anatolia show that it was the rulers who adopted epithets from mystics, which indicates that, as perceived by the rising frontier rulers, the authority claim manifested by Sufi orders needed to be countered and accommodated, not to be dispensed with or disregarded.

The only epithets that seem to be the exclusive preserve of rulers were sovereign titles such as *beg* and *emir*, which are disliked by Sufis. Mystics who were called *begs* were Ahi leaders who managed to organize *futuwwa* fraternities into autonomous organizations in Anatolian towns with no political overlordship.[109] Modern historiography on the early Ottoman era commonly treats the terms *beg* and *emir* as humble emblems of royalty and signs of sovereignty with modest proportions thus equating, for example, *beg* with prince and *beglik* with principality. In the parlance of early fourteenth-century diplomatics, however, *beg* and *emir* were the highest titles of sovereignty. Gülşehri (d. after 1317), in a short hagiographic account of his master, Ahi Evran, referred to Prophet Muhammed as "the beg of Islam" (*İslāmuñ begi*).[110] As late as 1378, what appears to be an anomalous construction of regalia in the case of the Menteşe ruler Ahmed was perfectly normal for the contemporaries: "the sultan of the Persians and the Arabs, Gazi Ahmed Beg."[111] The fact that Ahmed as a *beg* was presented to be the sultan of Persians and Arabs is precisely what is intended. Here Ahmed as a sultan is a descriptive designation as part of image-making whereas Ahmed as a *beg* is a prescriptive title to claim sovereignty, not to define it. In his *beglik* anyone could be called sultan but not *beg*. Reflecting this subtle difference more plainly, Kara Hoca (d. 1397) called the Ottoman ruler of his time as Murad Beg at the end of a long list royal titles he enumerates to praise him, including such lofty designations as *melik*, *şehinşāh*, *āyetullāh*, and *şihābü'd-devle*.[112] As shown by Lütfi Paşa, as late as the mid-sixteenth century, *beg* and its verb form *beglenmek* (to become a beg) were still the principal words indicating one's becoming a sovereign ruler: "It is reported that Osman Gazi, despite earning his sovereignty (*beglenmelü old-ukda*), did not become a sovereign (*beglenmedi*) because of his respect to the Seljuks as the rulers of time (*ḥākimü'l-vaḳt*)."[113]

Following the Karesi precedent, Ottoman rulers of the late fourteenth century replaced *beg* with khan, the sovereign title of Mongol rulers, signifiying that the Ottomans now replaced the Mongols as a sovereign dynasty over Asia Minor. Much later, in the context of Ottoman–Safavid conflict of the early sixteenth century, for example, Selim I adopted shah as his preferred title of sovereignty. The titles *emir*, *beg*, *paşa*, and *çelebi* that spoke for claims of sovereignty for most rulers of western Asia Minor in the fourteenth century, including the Ottomans, gradually turned into either administrative titles for statesmen or royal titles for princes. All three titles preserved their exclusivity as they represented the ruler's executive power, therefore they still maintained their inherent relationship to sovereignty. Amid numerous descriptive titles and designations, the Ottoman rulers after the fourteenth century used only two titles, shah and khan, to the end of the empire. Given that the uses of shah as a sovereign title were mostly contingent on demanding circumstances, the one exclusive Ottoman title of sovereignty from mid-fourteenth century to the last sultan was khan. In the late fifteenth century, Aşıkpaşazade memorialized the birth of Ottoman sovereignty by narrating a story where Osman declared his independence with allusion to his khan title. Upon his conquest of Karacahisar in 1288, the locals appealed Osman, whom they called khan, to obtain the permission of the Seljuk sultan for having a qadi and a Friday congregation. But Osman replied that they have his permission instead: "I conquered this city with my own sword; what is the sultan's contribution for me to seek his permission?; my God, who gave him the sultanate, granted me the khanate!"[114]

Unlike the commonly held assumption in Ottoman studies, such terms as sultan or padishah were not among prescriptive titles of Ottoman rulers. Rhoads Murphey, in his comprehensive survey of early Ottoman titulature, does not discuss the qualitative values of titles used and considers sultan, for example, as an equivalent of khan.[115] The reason for this textbook truism is that modern scholarship does not distinguish between prescriptive titles of dynastic sovereignty and myriad other designations that describe rulership. Surviving documents are punctilious in distinguishing between descriptive designations and prescriptive titles of sovereignty to accurately convey one's status and avoid crossing the meticulously watched lines of authority.

Literary representations, however, do not always differentiate between one's proper title and image-making appellations that may at times be purposefully blurred. As in the case of Kaykavus b. Eskandar (d. 1082), even a humble ruler could be described with the once exclusive sovereign title of the Abbasids, *emīrü'l-mü'minīn* (commander of the faithful).[116] However, a clearly visible pattern reveals that a ruler's sovereign title comes after his name, which is often a single term or a phrase. No other dignitary under that ruler's realm of authority could adopt that title except for a metaphor or in descriptive sense. In Ottoman domains under the *beglik* of Osman Beg, for example, the adoption of the title *beg* by any other person means either sharing his authority or an open rebellion. In a given independent polity there may be only one *beg*, shah, or khan. A long roster of designations preceding the ruler's name often simply describes, distinguishes, and praises his rulership, and therefore are more telling as a statement of ruling ideology than entitlement. For comparison, numerous late Abbasid inscriptions end with the sovereign title "commander of the faithful" that comes after the caliph's name.[117] No other ruler seems to have used this designation as a sovereign title although it was totally acceptable to include it in the roster of descriptive regalia that precedes one's name in the case of regional rulers. Only the Seljuks, after they defeated the Buyids and became the *de facto* executive rulers of the Abbasid Empire, expressed their claim *de jure* by adapting this title to themselves as "partner of the commander of the faithful" in reflection of their shared sovereignty.

The Ottoman Dawla *Lost and Found*

As far as titles, imageries authority, and royal symbolism concerned, the early Ottomans looked more humble in comparison to autonomous dervish orders of the frontier where the same political space was overlaid by the temporal sovereignty of rulers and spiritual sway of mystics at once. The mystics, through their firmly knit fraternal organizations and unique technologies of propagation, continued to build their images of supreme authority in ever more elaborate and symbolic language of Sufism as opposed to the rulers whose imagination was limited by Islamic, Persian, and Turko-Mongolian titulature of rulership. As seen by their mystical allies, these rulers were wielders of temporal power, representing the executive power of friends of God who were destined to rule over the Rum by divine ordination. We do not see any Ottoman ruler who claimed mystical powers or unified authority. They had enough independence to use such sovereign titles as khan or shah but not caliph in the post-Abbasid mystical sense of the term. The mystics of all stripes, however, not only freely used all the royal titles but continuously redefined the concept of *khilāfa* as the Rum continued to attract Sufis from all over the Islamicate world with distinct social ideals. While the fame and sovereign authority of frontier emirates hardly extended beyond the physical boundaries of their principalities, the fraternal organization of Sufi orders recognized no geographical bounds. More significantly, Sufi leaders inculcated devotional loyalties with strong and distinguishing identities of belonging whereas frontier rulers, beyond their tribal bonds, only built constituencies by negotiation and whose loyalties were ephemeral, pragmatic, and far from according any political identity and sense of belonging. As in the case of Ibn Battuta, someone observing this most vibrant frontier of Islamicate society could only see a crowded political arena populated by little-educated, chivalrous, mostly pious *gazi* rulers whose status was not markedly above their notables and subjects. Yet the land was the seat of a startling array of high-profile Sufis, jurists, philosophers, physicians, astronomers, and poets whose fame and stand not only outshadowed temporal rulers but also extended well beyond the Rum. With defining impact on the later trajectory of Ottoman political thought, the most authoritative students of Suhrawardi and Ibn Arabi, including Sadreddin Konevi and Qutb al-Din Shirazi, perfected their career in the Rum leaving an indelible legacy of their masters on all subsequent varieties of Sufism.

The delicate balance of power between community-building charismatic Sufi leaders and state-building *gazi* rulers came to an abrubt end with the Timurid invasion of Asia Minor in 1402. The defeat not only ended the political integrity of the Ottoman state but also signified the end of their *dawla*, in the sense that their epochal license to rule was now revoked, calling into question their very worthiness to lead God's people on Earth in succession to the Abbasids and their rightful inheritors, the Seljuks. The ensuing decade-long civil war initiated a new era in Ottoman political thought and culture as to how rulership was conceived and propagated. It was geared not only toward reunifying the broken Ottoman polity but also to rehabilitating the image of the House of Osman. As noted in Chapter 1, this anxiety created a frantic quest for learning among princes and their entourage as manifested in the translation movement that produced a remarkable number of political texts in Turkish. Although the social, cultural, and intellectual dimensions of the Interregnum is yet to be duly examined, the sheer number and variety of texts indicate that the Ottoman restoration was not simply a political endeavor.

The loss of *dawla* was universally considered to be a divine sign of disapproval in the vast historical literature on the rise and fall of dynasties in both Persian and Arabic. Further exacerbated by the Timurid history writing machine that propagated an image of Timur as a divinely assisted ruler, later Ottoman historiography often treated Bayezid I with terms unfitting to an Ottoman sultan. Kastritsis's extensive analysis of the few contemporary sources that recorded the civil war shows the primacy of *dawla* in political discourse of the time.[118] The one contemporary chronicle of the civil war testifies that, at least in rhetoric, in each of the multiple encounters between princes who had the same blood-right to the Ottoman throne, negotiating parties invoked the belief that only *dawla* would determine the winner.[119] As discussed in Chapter 5, it was no accident that the two mytholigizing epics that portrayed the Ottomans, *Ḫalīlnāme* and *İskendernāme*, were penned in this period.[120] The fact that they were composed in the Turkish vernacular of the time, not the courtly language of Persian, unlike their Timurid counterparts, shows that these texts were not crafted as statements of superiority to convince the Persianate elite of Eurasia but for the local audience of western Asia to rehabilitate the shattered image of the House of Osman by proving that God's favor was not yet withdrawn. With Mehmed I's unification of former Ottoman territories in 1412, the Ottomans finally reclaimed their lost *dawla*. Soon after, in the 1430s, historian Yazıcıoğlu crafted stories proving the transfer of the *dawla* from the Abbasids to the Ottomans through the Seljuks.[121]

Despite bringing the early Ottoman state to the brink of extinction and indelibly tainting the fame of its rulers as divinely supported *gazi* warriors, the Timurid invasion turned out to be, using Schumpeter's term, a creative destruction enabling its rebuilders to transform it in ways better responding to the changing social and cultural dynamics of the Rum. During the restoration of the *dawla*, rulers and their supporters among the learned refashioned Ottoman rulership in a new language. The reinstitution of a single authority only restored the temporal sovereignty but did not necessarily establish the supremacy of Ottoman rulership over the Sufi communities who, thanks to the turmoil, grew more independent from petty rulers whose *dawla* was shattered. With the help of the Sufi-minded, it was in this context that the Ottomans started to decorate their sovereign titles with imageries of unified authority taken from Sufism, including *ḫalīfe* and *Mehdī*.[122] Abdülvasi Çelebi, a protégé of Mehmed I's vizier Bayezid Paşa and a Sufi-minded poet, portrayed the sultan as God's friend (*velī*), Mehdi (rightly-guided), and the possessor of grand *dawla* (*ulu devletlu*).[123] Abdülvasi glorified the Ottoman ruler in the poetic and symbolic language of mysticism for a community already tuned to Sufistic imageries of authority.

Abdülvasi's contemporary Hızır b. Yakub, a Sufi author with Melameti disposition, gave a clear exposition of the new mystical conception of the caliphate in reference to the ruler of his time. His *Cevāhirü'l-Meʿānī* (Essences of Meanings), composed and dedicated to an unrevealed ruler in 1406, is a commentary on God's beautiful names, well-grounded in the mystical synthesis of Ghazali, and quotes mostly from Ibn Arabi but also a host of other authorities ranging from the theologian Fakhr al-Din al-Razi to Abu Hanifa. In a formulaic tone, Hızır b. Yakub declares that rulers on earth are God's caliphs (*ḫalīfesidür*) and vicegerents (*nāʾibidür*), acting as His shadows over human beings, and therefore are entitled obedience by all. For the enactment of one's caliphate, one needs to endow with and manifest God's attributes. Otherwise, the ruler turns into the caliph of Satan.[124] Per the convention of mystic philosophers, he defined the caliphate through two well-known biblical stories detailed in the Qur'an. In the case of Adam's primordial caliphate,

Hızır b. Yakub narrates God's ordination of Adam in the same way a shaykh is designated as God's caliph, axis mundi, or perfect human being in Sufi wayfaring. Adam, after his corporal body is created, goes through a long period of trials (*çileler*) to perfect himself to manifest God's attributes. Then the author explains Adam's descent into this world as a coronation ceremony and his caliphate as a form of supreme rulership. Once he is enlivened with God's spirit, Adam is enthroned on the throne of the caliphate for which all angels are ordered to prostrate out of respect and obedience. God then appoints Gabriel as Adam's door-keeper and Michael as his treasurer in order to govern the earth (*siyāset*), requiring the loyalty of all, and the Satan features in the plot as a thief and a disloyal subject.[125]

In the second dramatized story, Solomon, after realizing that there is no stronger path to reach God other than being just, asks God for rulership. In explaining why the prophet did not ask for prophethood or knowledge, he notes that rulership (*pādişāhluḳ*) is an attribute of God whereas prophethood (*nübüvvet*) and knowledge (*ʿilm*) are human attributes, therefore below in rank to rulership.[126] Composed in vernacular Turkish, *Cevāhirü'l-Meʿānī* was certainly not a match for Timurid literary hegemony but a powerful statement against local dervish orders' political ambitions in their own language and idioms. Hızır b. Yakub's exposition of rulership in mystical symbolism by bonding it to the creation story and modeling it on Islamic prophetology became ever more recurring topos in later Sufistic visions of Ottoman caliphate.

Mehmed I not only reunified the Ottoman state but also personified the new Ottoman ruler as the wielder of unified authority. But soon after establishing himself as the sole ruler of the Ottoman Rum, the House of Osman faced another existential threat to its integrity and legitimacy, this time, using Karamustafa's term, from God's unruly friends. Bedreddin of Simavna (d. 1420), a prominent jurist and mystic who formerly served Mehmed's brother Musa Çelebi as his chief judge, openly rebelled against the new sultan that took seven years to suppress and caused an unprecedented stir in western Asia Minor and the Balkans. The exact content of his call, his leadership, and true objectives are schrouded by floating accusations of heresy that include rejection of private property. But it is certain that the rebellion mustered the support of a wide spectrum of malcontents who had been weary about the reestablishment of the central power and mobilized various fraternities and Sufi orders who resented not only the Ottoman rule but also those more powerful Sufi orders who allied with the Ottoman establishment. Perhaps what alarmed Mehmed I and his insecure establishment most was the legitimate appeal of Bedreddin's own ideas, as expressed in his writings, to the broader learned and popular constituency in the mainstream rather than the radical reform project attributed to him. Ottoman chroniclers almost unanimously report that the enigmatic shaykh was executed in 1420 as a rebel (*bāğī*), not a heretic (*zındīḳ*).[127] His own writings, which are among the most sophisticated works of Ottoman jurisprudence and Sufism, are not more questionable to the learned establishment than those of his more respected contemporaries, such as Abdurrahman Bistami. His hagiography, which seems to be compiled to rehabilitate his legacy and induct him into Ottoman memory as a *gazi* saint, almost totally disowns his revolutionary ideas and role in the rebellion.[128] Although Bedreddin and his later followers always had enough detractors at any time, by and large, he was widely respected as a jurist, a mystic, and a martyr. His most controversial work, *Wāridāt* (Occurences), is an incomprehensibly succinct and encrypted masterpiece of Ottoman Sufism, continuously reworked, doctored, translated, and commented upon by later Sufis of varying stripes. Besides the social convulsion it caused, the Bedreddin rebellion reminded the Ottoman House as well as other spiritual communities of the transformative power of Sufis and their political ideals. Subsequent rulers grew more attuned to political undertones of Sufistic ideals and, in response, charismatic shaykhs also turned wearier of the Ottoman authority.

During the relative calm of his long reign, Murad II managed to renegotiate the disrupted balance of power with the Sufi orders who, despite and perhaps thanks to the political turmoil, grew into more institutionalized fraternities. Besides home grown Sufi orders that grew in tandem with the Ottoman rule, the Rum continued to attract antinomian mystics with disruptive ideas, most notably the Hurufis whose leader, Fadl Allah, was executed in 1394 on charges of heresy.[129] This enigmatic brotherhood of messianic lettrists who turned Shiite esoterism and mystical philosophy of Ibn Arabi into an elaborate occult science of letters, signs, and numbers might have already inspired the Bedreddin movement. Despite the close scrutiny, harassment, and occasional inquision they faced from Ottoman authorities, mainstream scholars, and Sufi orders, with their exotic teachings and enchanting interpretations, Hurufis created a new spiritual excitement in the Rum and maintained a strong presence.

In response to both Bedreddinian rebellion and the new spiritual activism, Murad II sought to fetch new alliances with domiciled Sufi orders of the Rum that had maintained their mutual distance with the Ottoman establishment. Most notably, the Mevlevis, who flourished across the Ottoman borders but failed to make inroads into Ottoman territories, were now welcomed with the opening of their first Mevlevi lodge in the capital Edirne. Ottoman–Mevlevi relations had been growing more cordially along with the Ottoman expansion in western Anatolia where the order had strong presence. From Murad II's reign onward Mevlevis closely tied their prospects with that of the Ottoman House and became their staunchest allies. Similar to the Bektaşi order, as one of the few other spiritual movements whose network did not extend beyond the physical boundaries of a single dynasty, the Mevleviyye soon turned into one truly Ottoman order spreading rapidly into existing and newly added Ottoman territories. The Mevlevi alliance not only tempered the Abdalan influence but also accorded the Ottoman House the same legitimacy in urban cosmopolitan settings that their *abdal* friends once provided in the countryside. In a similar move, Murad II established close relations with the powerful Bayramiyye order centered in Ankara by meeting first with its founder Hacı Bayram Veli (d. 1430) and then granting property and tax privileges to his order.[130] Murad also made Ottoman territories more attractive to a number of Sufi orders that originated from elsewhere, such as the Zeyniyye, through offering respect and privileges, thereby tying their well-being to that of Ottoman rulership.[131]

Murad II, who grew up in the tumultuous reign of his father, was well aware of the pious appeal of frontier mystics whose social ideals and imageries of authority could swiftly turn into defiant political ideologies. He broadened his father's modest efforts to transform the Ottoman court into a learned establishment into a full-blown cultural enterprise that included attracting the learned to his entourage, commissioning composition, and translation of a wide variety of works ranging from history to literature, and building a library in Edirne.[132] He succeeded to employ or ally with some of the greatest minds of his time including the leading student of Ibn Arabi, Molla Fenari, appointed as his chief jurist, the historian and statesmen Şükrullah, the master of occult sciences Abdurrahman Bistami, and a scholar prodigy from the Timurid court, Musannifek. These and many other scholars and poets flooded the Rum with numerous works of which many turned into canons of Ottoman thought and literature. As many of these works include panegyrics glorifying the Ottoman ruler per the conventions of their respective disciplines and genres, they all worked as political texts propagating the legitimacy of the Ottoman House and creating Murad's image as a caliph and a learned ruler. The overall literary articulation of Murad's reign that fully appropriated the Islamic and Persian nomenclature of rulership, although it primarily addressed the Turkish-speaking communities of the Rum, presented the sultan as a universal ruler in the the same vocabulary as that of the Timurid court.

Among the chorus of Murad's image makers, Şeyhi (d. after 1429), who had witnessed the Timurid invasion, in his love epic *Hüsrev ü Şīrīn*, addressed Murad as *ṣāḥib-ḳırān* (lord of conjunction).[133] Bedr-i Dilşad, who translated *Qābūsnāma* and titled it with the sultan's name as *Murādnāme* (The Book of Murad), defined rulership as caliphate equal to prophethood and a manifestation of God's attribute of absolute forgiveness (*raḥmān*).[134] Mu'ini, in his *Mesnevī-i Murādiye* (Muradian Couplets), portrayed the sultan as a mystic, with a disposition of a friend of God whose character mirrors God's attributes.[135] Mahmud Şirvani (d. after 1438) and Ibn Melek (d. 1450) addressed him as God's caliph over the entire creation (*ḫalīfetullāh fi'l ʿālemīn*).[136] In his preface to *Tuḥfe-i Murādī* (Muradian Gift), Mahmud Şirvani further qualified Murad's caliphate as being the helper of God's friends (*nāṣır-ı evliyāʾullāh*) and ruler by God's proof (*ḳāʾim bi-hüccetillāh*). More, just as Muhammed was the last and the seal of prophets so were the Ottomans in the line of Islamic dynasties. Because, just as Muhammed and his followers fought against disbelievers so did the Ottomans.[137] Namely, the Ottoman House revived the prophetic mission which was believed to happen toward the end of times in Islamic eschatology.

Ankari, in *Enīsü'l-Celīs*, reminds the sultan of the same prophetic mission of fighting for the faith as "Islam is weak in the Rum," a mission that elevates rulership to the rank of prophethood. Although he does not use *ḫalīfe*, his characterization of Murad as *sulṭānü'l-İslām* (the ruler of Islam) and *āyetullāh* (God's evidence) is distinctly mystical. In allusion to the Qur'anic verse that God sent Muhammed as mercy to all creation, Ankari tells the sultan that God sent him as mercy to his people.[138] Ankari, a staunch Sunni by creed, envisions the ruler in the same fashion as the perfect human being in Sufi cosmology who, as Böwering outlined, may stand for the microcosm reflecting and mirroring the macrocosm, the point where the world of divinity touches the world of creation, the holy book revealed in the visible world, and the First Intellect.[139] Ankari describes the status of the sultan in analogy to the Qur'an's position between God and His creation. The Qur'an, as God's word, is His attribute, and thus beyond the reach of our senses but visible to humans only through letters that reflect and mirror its essence. In a similar vein, although his corporal body is visible to human beings, the divine spirit (*rūḥ-ı ḳudsī*) of the sultan to which God descends is beyond our reach. Further, he divides authority into three types: eternal without a beginning (*ezel vilāyeti*), current (*vaḳt vilāyeti*), and eternal without an end (*ebed vilāyeti*) where the sultan's knowledge (*'ilmüñ*) stands for the first, execution (*emrüñ*) for the second, and judgment (*ḥükmüñ*) for the third.[140] As such, Ankari perfectly situates the newly restored Ottoman rulership (*salṭanat*) within the Sufi cosmology as personified by Murad. While earlier rulers were simply praised for being friends of God's friends, a large contingent of Sufi-scholars in this period fully mystified rulership and diligently embroidered Murad's image as the first Ottoman caliph in the Sufistic sense, i.e. with authority on both temporal and spiritual domains.

Converging and Diverging Spheres of Authority

Murad's realignment with Sufis by extending the former Ottoman–Abdalan alliance to urban and learned orders produced a lasting pattern in rulership while facilitating the transformation of Ottoman cities into major hubs of spiritual communities. However, pleasing and appeasing Sufi orders did not necessarily change their notions of authority, but only made Sufi imageries more pronounced and more complicated. The alliance between the beneficent Ottoman ruler and his well-wisher Sufis meant that it was mutually acknowledged, thanks to the endlessly symbolic and flexible language of mysticism, that both parties have their distinct spheres of authority in temporal and spiritual realms. Yet this tacit agreement was not a covenant. The question of where lines of two spheres converge and diverge was never resolved throughout later Ottoman history. Murad II and subsequent Ottoman sultans continued to claim unified authority, conveyed mainly through their self-designation as caliph in the Sufistic sense. But so did almost all other Sufi orders for their own shaykhs. These mutually exclusive visions of authority, however, seldom clashed beyond the rhetoric unless the Sufis expressly turned them into political claims prompted by material disruptions of relationship between the Ottoman establishment and Sufi orders.

Sufi orders with Alid-piety, especially those who, inspired by Ibn Arabi's doctrines, increasingly grew more attuned to matters of temporal rulership with more practical interpretations of Sufi cosmology. Until Murad II, Ibn Arabi's influence was more or less limited to a select number of Sufi-minded scholars and his thoughts were still largely a matter of scholarly scrutiny and individual piety. But the learning revolution in the post-Timurid Rum turned Ibn Arabi's corpus from an aristocratic stock of elite spirituality into fashion items for rank and file dervishes, intellectuals, and even illiterate folks. Ibn Arabi's mysticism was already a shared spirituality between Sufis and scholars, as exemplified by Rumi, Davud-i Kayseri, and Molla Fenari who operated with the conviction that discursive and intuitive forms of knowledge stand for the same truth. With Murad II's reign, the Ottoman court joined the conversation. Ibn Arabi not only enabled the well-wishers of the Ottoman dynasty to present their rulership with the most authoritative language of Sufism but also acted as a safeguard against unbridled Sufi groups such as the Hurufis whose doctrines already contained a good dose of Ibn Arabian esoterism. Şükrullah and Eşrefoğlu Rumi, for example, whose writings are imbued with Ibn Arabian ideas, specifically highlighted the Hurufis as a major heretical threat in the land of Rum.[141] Before he raised to the status of patron saint in the sixteenth century thanks to his attributed miraculous prognostication that sanctioned the Ottoman dynasty, in the fifteenth century, his Sufi cosmology became the sacred fountain that fed newly forming visions of the Ottoman caliphate. Following Murad II's example, the Ottoman court sought to keep God's unruly friends at bay by supporting the agreeable ones, and counter esoteric political ideologies by adopting Ibn Arabi as the prime definer of Ottoman rulership.

Ahmed Bican (d. after 1465), from the Bayrami order, offered a rectified reading of Ibn Arabi to the broader reading public of the Rum through his translation of his brother Yazıcıoğlu Mehmed's commentary on *Fuṣūs al-Ḥikam*. The text was completed soon after the conquest of Constantinople in 1453 and turned into a popular read like his many other books in Turkish. Yazıcıoğlu Mehmed composed the commentary, titled *Müntehā* (Terminus), by consulting with more than twenty authoritative texts mostly on Sufism and

Qur'anic exegesis with the purpose of aligning it with the Sharia. The work gives a detailed exposition of Ibn Arabian cosmology where *ḫalīfe*, equated with, among others, the perfect human being, axis mundi, Muhammedan reality, the first intelligence, and the mother book, is the locus of the first thing that emanates from God. As reflection of God's names and attributes, the nature of *ḫalīfe* bridges the divine with all other planes, seen and unseen. *Müntehā* turns the bewildering complexity and abstractions of Ibn Arabi's cosmology into more tangible terms in his discussion and comparison of the caliphates of Adam and David. Based on his analysis of Qur'anic verses, the caliphate of David was superior to that of Adam because David was actually empowered to rule as God's caliph whereas Adam was only created with that potential but did not actually exercise it.[142] *Müntehā* not only popularized Ibn Arabi's idea of the caliphate through the medium of Turkish but also made it more acceptable by offering these ideas as confirmed by respected authorities ranging from Ghazali to Zamakhshari. At a time, when the ruler and virtually every Sufi shaykh presented themselves as caliphs in their own ways, Ahmed Bican's distinction between the caliphates of Adam and David reconciled otherwise competing claims of authority, and aimed to establish a symbiotic hierarchy between the Ottoman caliph and Sufi caliphs.

Two contemporaries of Ahmed Bican, from the same Bayrami order, Eşrefoğlu Rumi (d. circa 1470) and Akşemseddin (d. 1459), turned Ibn Arabi's teachings into a code of conduct in textbook clarity for their dervish followers. Eşrefoğlu Rumi, who later entered the Kadiri path at the direction of his Bayrami master, is better known as the author of *Müzekki'n-Nüfūs* (Purifier of Souls) in Turkish, which soon became a household item on Sufi morality throughout Ottoman domains. In response to the Qur'anic injunction of obeying those who are in charge (*ulī al-amr*), in his *Book of Sufi Path* (*Ṭarīḳatnāme*), he drew a sharp distinction between the limited temporal authority of rulers and the comprehensive authority of a designated caliph.[143] For him, although only exoteric scholars accepted temporal rulers (*begler*) as *ulī al-amr*, they need not to be disobeyed. The great shaykhs, however, accepted perfect masters (*mürşid-i kāmiller*) as *ulī al-amr*, for they are successors (*ḳāʾimmaḳām*) to the Prophet as caliph of caliphs (*ḫalīfetü'l-ḫulefā*). Temporal rulers are in charge only in the metaphoric sense (*mecāzī*) whereas perfect masters are in charge in reality. Despite his acknowledging the legitimacy of worldly rulers, Eşrefoğlu considers them as authorities "not to be disobeyed" (*anlara da ʿāṣī olmayalar*) while calling for absolute submission to caliph of caliphs which he defines as unified authority: "After the Prophet, being in charge is the right of the most noble of the world who is perfect both exoterically and esoterically (*ẓāhirde ve bāṭında*) so that he protects Muslims and apply justice with his exoteric knowledge, and train God's lovers with his esoteric knowledge."[144] Muhammed as a prophet, shaykh, pole, and ruler (*pādişāh*) at once, with orders from God, designated Ali as his successor in the capacity of shaykh and pole who, in turn, passed this mission to Hasan al-Basri from whom the Bayramiyye genealogy originates.[145]

Being a graduate of Ottoman madrasa system as a jurist, and having studied with two famed philosopher-jurists of the time, Hocazade (d. 1488) and Alaeddin Tusi (d. 1482), Eşrefoğlu easily navigates through philosophy, jurisprudence, and philosophy with full command in each discipline's specific vocabulary. By mystifying the Qur'anic concept *ulī al-amr*, namely, by equating it with the Sufistic caliphate, he appropriates the principal term on which the juristic theory of the caliphate, i.e. imamate, was founded. Jurists hardly ever used the Qur'anic depictions of Adam and David as caliphs to define the historical caliphate which they considered as succession to the Prophet, not as God's vicegerency. Rather, they equated the historical caliphate with the Qur'anic *ulī al-amr* and further elaborated it with evidence from hadith. Eşrefoğlu legitimates and calls for obedience to the Ottoman ruler per juristic rulings but nevertheless reserves the caliphate as *ulī al-amr* to the perfect human being of Sufi designation.

Akşemseddin was closer to the Ottoman court than Eşrefoğlu. The young Akşemseddin was part of the Bayrami delegation led by Hacı Bayram to meet Murad II and remained an intimate friend of the Ottoman dynasty. He encouraged Mehmed II with prophetic assurances to conquer Constantinople, delivered the first Friday sermon after the conquest, and discovered the burial site of Ayyub al-Ansari, a prominent companion of the Prophet killed during an earlier siege, who is still revered as the patron saint of Istanbul. In later Ottoman memory, Akşemseddin turned into a spiritual conqueror of Constantinople and his association with Mehmed II was idealized as a model for the association of spiritual and temporal authorities. Yet the question of who was really in charge (*ulī al-amr*) in this association or whether there was a hierarchy of authority between them would be answered differently per the convenience of either party. In *Maḳāmāt-ı Evliyā* (Stations of Saints), Akşemseddin identifies the ruler as the possessor of exoteric power (*ṣāḥib-i taṣarruf-ı ẓāhir*) whose counterpart was seven friends of God responsible for the government of seven climes by possessing esoteric power (*ṣāḥib-i taṣarruf-ı bāṭın*); he thus equates the ruler's status with that of low-ranking saints. There is, however, only one *mürşid* with absolute power over everything God created.[146] In *Kāşifü'l-Müşkilāt* (Revealer of Intricacies), in a neatly envisioned saintly hierarchy, Akşemseddin identifies individual shaykhs as caliphs of the Prophet, and the Prophet as caliph of God; therefore paying allegiance to a shaykh means obeying the Prophet and then God.

Akşemseddin's sixteenth-century hagiographer, Hüseyin Enisi, narrates that Mehmed II wished to enter the Sufi path under the shaykh's guidance, which the shaykh vehemently rejected on the grounds that this would result in neglecting the affairs of Muslims.[147] Eşrefoğlu's hagiographer, Abdullah Veliyyüddin, also narrates a similar story in which Mehmed II begs the shaykh to become his disciple but ultimately gets persuaded to return to Istanbul.[148] Both hagiographies portray the Ottoman sultan under the full spiritual command of the saint, a metaphor for the real wielder of power, in the way earlier Mevlevis and Abdalan envisioned to be the ideal arrangement. Unlike the Abdalan who denounced learned Islam altogether, similar to the Mevlevis, these Bayrami saints envisioned to have achieved this ideal by according the juristic theory of imamate a mystical interpretation where the juristic notion of authority, i.e. *ulī al-amr*, is legitimate and binding but only as a delegated power of the caliph as defined by the Sufis.

Unlike the Bayramis, who trace their origins to Ali b. Abi Talib, Sufi orders who trace their origins to Abu Bakr were relatively less touched by Ibn Arabian cosmology. As articulated by Rumi and his followers, Bakri-piety was no less political than Alid-piety but it was more accommodative of political realities historically and doctrinally. Bakri Sufis were less vocal on the question of the caliphate but not silent. One such high-profile Sufi was Musannifek, who gave two different expositions of the caliphate in two different works. In *Tuḥfa-i Maḥmūdiyya*, written in Persian for Grand Vizier Mahmud Paşa, who was reportedly a disciple of Eşrefoğlu, Musannifek conveys Persianate ideals of governance and defines the caliphate as a practical form of government. For Musannifek, based on Qur'anic examples, all rulers and governors are to be named as divine caliphs (*al-khulafā al-ilāhiyya*). When God appointed David as his caliph on Earth, He ordered him to apply justice among the people. Anyone with executive power (*nafāẕ al-ḥukm*) is a caliph of God (*khalīfat Allāh*) because the defining component of David's caliphate is his political power to rule and execute it with justice. After dividing the caliphate into three types, he defines the lesser caliphate (*al-khilāfa al-ṣughrā*) as self-governance, the greater caliphate (*al-khilāfa al-kubrā*) as ruling over others with executive power and government (*al-salṭana wa al-ḥukūma*), and the greatest caliphate (*al-khilāfa al-akbar*[*iyya*]) as the combination the kingdom of Earth (*mulk al-dunyā*) and the kingdom of religion (*mulk al-dīn*).[149]

In *Ḥall al-Rumūz* (Solving the Signs), written for Mehmed as a rectified exposition of basic tenets of Sufism, Musannifek presents a mystified version of the caliphate. After he summarized the saintly hierarchy of cosmic government, he defined the pole of the poles as caliph of God over His creation, the highest human being in rank, who is in charge of (*walī al-amr*) all "dismissals, appointments, rewards, executions, protections, removals, honorings, and shamings." This caliphate is best exemplified by Abu Bakr who ranks second to the Prophet and above Ali in God's friendship and esoteric knowledge.[150] Musannifek strives to save the mystical nature of the caliphate without alienating the ruler who was already a self-proclaimed caliph. In this cosmic scheme, Mehmed's rulership, for possessing executive power, clearly falls in the category of the greater caliphate but with the potential of evolving into the greatest caliphate, i.e. that of the pole of the poles. While presenting the greatest caliphate as a moral check on the ruler's greater caliphate, Musannifek still proposes the caliphate as a moral paradigm for someone who is already known to be a caliph.

The Ottoman dynasty in the fifteenth century did not display a marked preference for either Alid or Bakrid loyalties. But, since at least the Bedreddin revolt, along with the increased pace of centralization and institutionalization, the Ottoman policy toward Sufism clearly favored urban orders over those in the countryside. In the meantime, urban Sufism, in all its conformist and antinomian forms, came under closer scrutiny of the ulema establishment whereas the Abdalan Sufism of the countryside maintained its relative autonomy from the confessional discipline of the Ottoman state. Abdalan, or the proponents of what Karamustafa called vernacular Islam, preserved their distance from the learned establishment, including urban Sufism, by remaining firmly attached to the land of Rum over which they claimed spiritual authority and used Turkish as their principal language of expression.[151] The increasing dissociation of the Ottoman ruling elite from its original Turkoman basis turned their traditional allies among the Abdalan dervishes into spokespersons of resentment in the countryside. Among the most vocal Abdalan critics of the Ottoman dynasty's shifting social and ideological configuration was Otman Baba whose troubled relationship with Mehmed II reignited the legitimacy claims between dervishes and rulers that shaped late Seljuk and early Ottoman history. Besides Mehmed II's centralization, what aggravated the Abdalan most was his newly forming image as a universal ruler inspired by conquests that included appropriation of Roman regalia and Iranian imageries of just ruler fostered by a slew of bureaucrats well versed in the Persianate ideals of government and mushrooming urban Sufi orders that bonded with the Ottoman dynasty.

Otman Baba's resentment and critique display all the typical traits of Abdalan militancy that became a fixture of the political and spiritual scenery in the land of Rum. As champion of the truth, he severely scolds the learned (*dānişmend*), the ulema, Sufis, and shaykhs as the main culprits for corrupting the faith, oppressing the poor and the deprived, defying the spiritual authority of the pole (*ḳuṭb*), and misleading the sultan.[152] In an apocalyptic and messianic language, Küçük Abdal's hagiography of Otman Baba propagates Abdalan piety centered on Alid-loyalism, sainthood, intuitive knowledge, and poleship. Otman Baba's idea of the caliphate is not so different from, or may even be inspired by, other strains of Ottoman Sufism, including its Bakrid and urban variants. For him God's caliph is the one whose command encompasses both the heavens and the earth.[153] Through various confrontations between Otman Baba and Mehmed II, the hagiography emphatically profiles the latter as a mere embodiment of the former's executive power. The sultan is constantly reminded that all his worldly conquests are aided by Otman Baba's invisible army of *abdals* and that whenever the sultan doubts the saint's authority he is reprimanded by defeat and humiliation. Allusions to similar encounters between previous Ottoman rulers and *abdals* turn Otman Baba's hagiography into an Abdalan epic that restores the eroding lines of authority between dervishes and rulers to its original form in the land of Rum, namely, the acknowledgement of the dervish-saint as God's caliph on Earth and the sultan as his commander.

Otman Baba's idea of the caliphate is predicated entirely on sainthood (*vilāyet*) to which he ascribes a cosmological significance and considers it inseparable from prophethood (*nübüvvet*).[154] For him, Muhammed's death brought the age of the prophets to an end and started the age of saints. Thereafter, prophethood remained embedded in sainthood with the same authority once possessed by Muhammed. In that regard, just as those who opposed Muhammed turned into disbelievers those from among the Muslims who oppose the saint of the age would turn into infidels.[155] The unity of prophethood and sainthood that started with Adam, God's first caliph through whom He made Himself manifest, and continued through other prophets until it split with Abd al-Muttalib, Muhammed's grandfather, after whom prophethood passed to Muhammed and ended whereas sainthood passed to Ali and continued.[156] In the age of prophets, God manifested Himself (*maẓhar-ı Ḫüdā*) through prophethood but in the age of saints He manifests himself through sainthood.[157] Among the two levels of representing the divine, Otman Baba considers sainthood higher than prophethood and defines the former as the latter's core (*bāṭın*). This distinction inevitably yields two different notions of the caliphate: one that is predicated on prophethood and the other on sainthood.

Otman Baba despises the ulema for being the caliphs representing the exterior of prophethood (*ḫalīfe-i ẓāhirü'n-nübüvve*) whereas he presents himself as the one that stands for sainthood. Just as prophets needed angels as intermediaries between humans and God for the attainment of truth, the ulema too needed transmission of knowledge which is acquired (*kesbī*), indirect, imperfect, and limited. On the other hand, the highest point of sainthood, namely the rank of the pole of poles or the caliph of God, is a state that is, by definition, achieved when all intermediaries are removed, including the archangels, between human being and God. Besides blatantly calling himself the Truth (*ana al-Ḥaq*), a designation that cost the most famous of ecstatic Sufis, Mansur al-Hallaj of Baghdad, his life in 922, in a purposefully provocative language, Otman Baba declared that "Adam devoured God and Muhammed, and that Adam, who is God's manifestation, is me."[158] As he explains, Adam devours God in the sense that God descends into humankind's heart, and devours Muhammed to mean that Muhammed's prophethood is entrusted to sainthood after his death (*velāyet nübüvvete ısmarlanmışdur*). In line with broader Sufism, he interprets the ulema in the Prophet's saying "the ulema are the inheritors of prophets" as God's saints (*evliyā'ullāh*). Such a self-portrayal leaves no room for the sultan or the ulema to claim authority in connection to the divine or Prophet Muhammed.

Unlike Küçük Abdal's portrayal of Otman Baba as someone whose authority was ultimately acknowledged by the ulema, Sufis, and the sultan, the actual voice of the saint, as the spokesperson of Abdalan dervishes, was a fading one. As plainly stressed in the hagiography, the nemeses of the Abdalan were not so much the ulema but other Sufis who now appear to be acting in concert with the ruling establishment. Despite the growing resentment and occasional outbursts of the Abdalan, the Ottoman dynasty continued its closer alignment with the learned and urban strains of Sufism. Among the newest Sufi orders that started to take root in Ottoman urban landscape of the fifteenth century was the Nakşibendiyye that soon joined the institutional well-wishers of the Ottoman dynasty. The order started to take root in Ottoman realms soon after the Timurid invation of 1402 and became more visible on the cultural scene with the translation of the Nakşibendi classic, Muhammed Parsa's *Faṣl al-Khiṭāb* (The Decisive Speech), during the reign of Murad II.[159] Mehmed II and his entourage invited a number of prominent Nakşibendis that included the famed Abdurrahman Jami who declined but nevertheless maintained a cordial relationship with the Ottoman court.[160]

One of the order's earliest exponents, Abdullah-ı Ilahi (d. 1491) was a local figure from Simav who, after receiving his spiritual training in Samarkand from Ubaydullah Ahrar (d. 1490), returned to his hometown as a deputized shaykh for guidance. Despite being a contemporary of Otman Baba and spending most of his later life in places where Otman Baba also wandered, there is no indication of an encounter between the two. Yet, Abdullah-ı Ilahi's views on authority and rulership stand at odds with those of Otman Baba and effectively counter Abdalan Sufism's most basic tenets. His biographer Lami'i Çelebi, who penned the first biographical dictionary of Ottoman Sufis, portrayed him as a greatly revered figure at the courts of both Mehmed II and Bayezid II but as someone who piously avoided all royal favors. He wrote most of his works in simple but sophisticated Turkish which made his writings equally accessible and appealing to both urban and rural audiences. He did not write exclusively on rulership but many of his treatises convey his views on the subject, especially those that respond to contemporary issues, such as *Meslekü'ṭ-Ṭālibīn ve'l-Vāṣılīn* (The Path for Seekers and Arrivers), written in 1470, a Turkish reworking of a book he formerly wrote in Arabic and Persian.[161]

Reflecting the distinctively Nakşibendi pursuit of spiritual experience checked by Islamic jurisprudence and theology, Abdullah-ı Ilahi criticizes any form of piety that is not condoned by the Sharia in the way it is upheld by the people of tradition and community (*ehl-i sünnet ve'l-cemāʿat*).[162] Unlike the more familiar Sufi attitude of subjecting temporal rulership to that of the comprehensive authority of saints, Abdullah-ı Ilahi unequivocally stipulates that the reigning ruler must be obeyed, a view not different than the position of the mainstream Sunni ulema. He is fully aware of the fact that the mystical concept of the caliphate may easily be extended to override any claim of authority by temporal rulers. To avoid that obvious conflict, the Sufi friends of the Ottoman dynasty, from the Mevlevis to the Bayramis, were explicit in their call to their followers that the ruler in charge needed to be obeyed. In response to those who consider rulership as a distraction from God, Abdullah-ı Ilahi further considers it as a medium that brings one closer to the divine just as it did in the case of the king and Prophet Solomon.[163] He defines the supreme ruler of Islam (*pādişāh-ı islām*) as the wielder of command (*ulü'l-emr*) and imam, both juristic terms, as well as a caliph in the Sufistic sense. Yet this supreme rulership is a divine gift, not an earned position, granted only to those who possess four requirements: nobility (*ʿaṣl*), fortune (*devlet*), sound judgement, and high aspirations.[164] Abdullah-ı Ilahi's concept of the caliphate reunites the three conflicting claims of authority in the Ottoman ruler's persona as *pādişāh-ı islām*: "the sultan is the vicegerent of the Merciful (*ḫalīfe-i raḥmān*), heir to prophets (*vāris-i enbiyā*), and substitute (*ḳāʾim-maḳām-ı aṣḥāb*) to the Prophet's companions."[165] Thus spiritual, prophetic, and executive natures of the Prophet represented by the Sufis, the ulema, and the rulers respectively are now combined in Ottoman rulership. In other words, Abdullah-ı Ilahi bestows upon the secular authority of the Ottoman sultan all the principal sources of legitimacy in Islamic tradition.

Parting way from most other strands of Sufism, Abdullah-ı Ilahi's concept of the caliphate is firmly grounded in prophethood, not in sainthood. Although he maintains the usual Sufi view that the Prophet's sainthood is superior to his prophethood, in line with the Sunni theology, he draws a clear line of hierarchy between the two conditions where the highest rank of sainthood reaches only up to the lowest rank of prophethood.[166] In his Turkish works, Abdullah-ı Ilahi comfortably ascribes the caliphate to rulership as manifestation of God. Despite his full command in Ibn Arabian cosmology, he abstains from portraying a cosmic rulership of axis mundi as God's caliphate with both spiritual and temporal powers. Instead, he uses Ibn Arabi's theophanic imagination to suit the caliphate to rulership.[167] He defines the caliphate as God's shadow (*Ḥaḳḳın sāyesi ḫalīfesidür*) but in a different sense than the common connotations of the metaphor in political literature. The caliph as God's shadow (*ẓillullāh*) manifests God's image (*ẕāt ṣūreti*), acts (*fiʿilleri*), and attributes (*ṣıfatları*) at once. In this scheme, the executive power (*salṭanat*) becomes nothing but a manifestation of one of God's many attributes, such as justice, might, will, knowledge, mercy, and the like.[168] For Abdullah-ı Ilahi being God's shadow is not a metaphor but the reality itself.

Despite resorting to Ibn Arabian vocabulary, Abdullah-ı Ilahi's depiction of the ruler as caliph is exclusively confined to temporal rulership, namely, God's vicegerency on Earth, not over the entire creation as maintained by many of his contemporaries. Yet, even this equation of the caliphate with temporal rulership is firmly grounded in the Qur'anic concept of Adam's primordial caliphate which Abdullah-ı Ilahi elaborates extensively in his commentary on the rebel Shaykh Bedreddin's *Wāridāt.* In disagreement with Najm al-Din Daye, Abdullah-ı Ilahi endorses Bedreddin's view that the "trust" voluntarily undertaken by humankind from God in Adam's persona, which is the source of humankind's caliphate, is not the "knowledge of God" but "His image" (*ṣūret-i Raḥmān*). Man is His caliph because of his capacity to reflect both the divine and the created in His image: "In caliphate unite all universes (*'awālim*); Adam's body, i.e. his outer image (*al-ṣūra al-ẓāhira*), reflects the creation (*khalq*) whereas Adam's soul, i.e. his inner image (*al-ṣūra al-bāṭina*) reflects the Truth (*Ḥaq*)." Yet, humankind's capacity to reflect the divine, namely God's names and attributes, does not materialize unless he acts in accordance with them. That is why God's caliphate on Earth fully materializes only in the case of prophets.[169] For Abdullah-ı Ilahi, the caliphate is strictly a moral paradigm, not a superiority claim, in the sense that one becomes a caliph through an ontological pact that imposes one to endow oneself with godly traits (*aḫlāḳullāh*) for perfection, whether one is an ordinary person or a ruler.

A more philosophical treatment of the caliphate was offered by Ahmed-i Ilahi, who has often been thought to be the same person as the above Abdullah-ı Ilahi for being contemporaries with possibly the same Nakşibendi affiliation.[170] *Taṣavvufnāme* or *Risāle-i Ilāhī* (The Book of Sufism or The Treatise of Ilahi), a record of his responses to a series of intriguing questions on Sufism posed by first the Prophet Khidr and then Mehmed II, is a testament to the newly forming ideal relationship between rulers and saints: A learned, powerful but humble sultan inquiring about divine secrets from an equally humble but wholly enlightened saint who exposes his audience to the most intricate revelations of experiential knowledge in a way that is fully compatible with Sharia-sanctioned discursive knowledge. Unlike the Abdalan encounters with rulers, which are often memorialized with miracles, nothing spectacular happens between the two as both are portrayed to have the due recognition of the other.

Ahmed-i Ilahi does not specifically discuss questions of rulership and authority but addresses them as he explains humankind's caliphate per Ibn Arabi's cosmology and Nasafi's elaborations on the perfect human being, albeit in grossly simplified versions.[171] In the story, Ahmed-i Ilahi tells Mehmed II that knowledge (*'ilm*) and might (*ḳudret*), two attributes of God, correspond to and manifest themselves as the Prophet and the ruler respectively. In a similar vein, the Prophet reflects God's benevolence whereas the ruler reflects His sovereignty.[172] He identifies the first intellect (*aḳl-ı evvel*) as God's vicegerency (*ḫalīfetullāh*) in microcosm (*'ālem-i ṣağīr*), i.e. the individual human being. This same first intellect manifests itself as God's messenger in the macrocosm (*'ālem-i kebīr*), i.e. the universe.[173] He further equates the first intellect with the light or spirit of Muhammed and explains the hadith "God created Adam in His own image," meaning that Adam is created as reflection of the first intellect that corresponds to the spirit of Muhammed. Adam became caliph thanks to this quality which he passed to his progeny.[174] In this scheme the caliphate is not just a specific type of authority that spans over both spiritual and temporal realms but a reflection (*ṣūra*) of the One Reality that manifests itself in both microcosm and macrocosm.

Ahmed-i Ilahi's conversation with Mehmed II provides enchanting imageries in regard to the unity of being where rulership per se is limited to the manifestation of but a few attributes of the divine. In his *Pendnāme* (Book of Advice), a short mirror of princes in verse dedicated to Mehmed II, Ahmed-i Ilahi defines the sultan as God's absolute deputy (*muṭlaḳ vekīlullāh*) and the shadow of God's self (*ẓill-i ẕāt-ı Ḥaḳ*). He also adds that the only way for the ruler to reach the Truth, i.e. God, was by following the guidance of the people of the Truth, more specifically, the perfect guide (*mürşid-i kāmil*) who, in contrast to irreconcilably esoteric Sufis such as the Abdalan, is known by his unflinching devotion to the Sharia and the people of community and tradition.[175] Similar to Abdullah-ı Ilahi, Ahmed-i Ilahi does not aim to exclusively identify either spiritual or temporal authority with God's vicegerency but offers it as a condition, a divine imprint, for self-realization and, more so, as the existential code of conduct for every individual, including the ruler.

The above two encounters between a saint and a ruler, as narrated in two hagiographic accounts, show that the question of authority between the Ottoman dynasty and dervish orders who adopted the Rum as their promised homeland was far from being settled after two centuries of negotiation. In the process, rulers and saints freely adopted each other's titles, images, and means of legitimacy where spheres of authority were constantly redrawn in pursuit or response to changing claims to rule over spiritual and temporal planes. Abdullah-ı Ilahi's disciple Firdevsi-i Rumi dramatically illustrates how unified authority swings between rulers and dervishes. In 1503, in complete break with the usual Nakşibendi stand on the question, he portrayed Bayezid II as pole of the poles in a work he composed in verse and titled *Ḳutbnāme* (The Book of the Pole).[176] In content and style, the work is closer to frontier epics of warrior saints such as *Ṣalṭuḳnāme* or *Baṭṭālnāme* than royal epics in the line of his namesake's *Shāhnāma* that inspired a flurry of such accounts written for later Ottoman sultans. The fact that *Ṣalṭuḳnāme* was compiled at the behest of Bayezid's brother Djem makes the politics of literary articulation only more trivial. Although Djem was long dead by now, it still shows that endowing one's self with mystical imageries of authority was indispensable not only in addressing the Sufi constituency but also in intra-dynastic power struggle.

Although fourteenth-century Ottoman lands were predominantly populated and spiritually governed by various dervish groups of Abdalan disposition, the fifteenth century witnessed incessant waves of Sufi groups flooding into mostly urban areas where most were welcome. In the increasingly Sunni climate of Ottoman urban environments, Sufi groups with exclusively esoteric truth-claims, revolutionary ideas, low regard for normative standards of religion, and antinomian tendencies were subjected to close scrutiny by the ulema, mainstream Sufis, and the Ottoman administration. Some were outright persecuted and suppressed as in the case of Hurufis. Others, as in the case of certain Halvetis, successfully aligned themselves with the Ottoman dynasty during the reign of Bayezid II.[177] During the succession struggle following the death of Mehmed II, Halvetis played a crucial role in securing Bayezid's accession to the throne.[178] The Halveti order at large, however, never gained the full confidence of the ruling elite until well into the seventeenth century and engendered some of the most controversial figures of Ottoman Sufi establishment in the sixteenth century. Much like the thirteenth-century Seljuk cities, the rise of urban Sufism in the fifteenth century turned powerful shaykhs into power brokers in dynastic politics, which became a regular feature of Ottoman rulership until the very end.

But the main rivalry for truth claims and, therefore, the ultimate authority on Earth in God's name was between the ever increasing number of Sufi groups, most notably, between the ones that upheld the Sharia unquestionably, such as the Nakşibendis and those who instrumentalized, even denounced, normative piety such as the various antinomian groups which Vahidi, an early sixteenth-century Sufi observer, ridicules with humor. He identifies the Abdalan followers of Otman Baba, for example, with the notorious Torlaks and labels them as deviants and impostors as opposed to true *abdals*.[179] Vahidi was equally critical of the Bektaşis of his time. Although he praises Hacı Bektaş as one of God's most intimate friends, Vahidi accuses the saint's followers of exploiting his legacy and using the Bektaşi symbolism for material gain. Vahidi's main benchmark for evaluation is the Sharia. Similar to the Abdalan and Bektaşis, he charges a number of other marginal dervish groups for being deviant and corrupt. Yet, he is often careful to make a distinction between the founding figures of these orders, whom he generally praises, and current followers, whom he mocks as mere impostors, as "bandits who are marketing God's friendship."[180]

Vahidi's portrayal was not so different than the common attitude of the Ottoman ruling elite towards antinomian Sufism including the Abdalan groups and, more specifically, the Bektaşis. In the context of a growing Safavid threat, the Ottoman state pursued a two-tiered policy, "which combined active persecution with efforts to tame 'heterodox' circles under the Bektaşi umbrella as cast, or re-cast, by Balım Sultan" who was appointed by Bayezid II as the shaykh of the central Bektaşi convent in 1501.[181] Still operating within this mindset, Celalzade, Süleyman's top bureaucrat in the mid-sixteenth century, narrates the Kalender Çelebi's 1527 rebellion in his chronicle by uprooting it from its Bektaşi or even Alid and Kizilbash grounds. He vituperates Kalender Çelebi, the descendant of Hacı Bektaş and then head of the Bektaşi order, as a godless (*mülhid*) pervert who led the Kharijites into a ruthless campaign of destroying the faith and decimating the faithful. He portrays Kalender Çelebi as the polar opposite of Hacı Bektaş whom he praises as one of the greatest saints of the Rum. Celalzade not only denies Kalender Çelebi the legacy of Hacı Bektaş but also avoids charging him with the more common Safavid-Kizilbash heresy of the day. Instead he characterizes them as Kharijites, the archetypal nemesis of all branches of Alid-devotion, thus leaving no religious, historical, or moral ground to justify the rebellion.[182] Celalzade's was only one of numerous such sixteenth-century accounts where the founding figures of various dervish groups in the Rum appear as spiritual fathers of the land, patron saints of various Ottoman institutions, and friends or protectors of the Ottoman dynasty, whereas their current followers are portrayed as suspects or villains.

Firdevsi-i Rumi, one of Bayezid II's most illustrious image makers, restored the status of Hacı Bektaş as the Ottoman dynasty's spiritual founder by compiling his hagiography in tasteful literary Turkish. The hagiography was composed during the reign of Bayezid II, sometime before 1501, at a time and place shaken by unruly Kalenderi dervishes, including Otman Baba and his followers.[183] In assimilating the legacy of Hacı Bektaş into Ottoman court Sufism, the hagiography typically glorifies the saint but also fully reconciles him with mainstream Sufism, showing him in good terms with the founding figures of not only the Ottomans but also of the Ahis and the Mevlevis, the two other mystical orders that displayed strong political ambitions during the formative period of the Ottoman state in western Asia. The most striking part of the text is an elaborate coronation story where Hacı Bektaş saves Osman from the wrath of the Seljuk ruler Alaeddin and hails him as the future ruler of the Rum.[184] Among other rituals and symbolic gestures of coronation and empowerment, the saint puts his own crown on Osman's head, girds him with his own belt, and lights his torch with prayers that it will light the east and the west. He further informs the young prince that the saints of Rum have been considering others for this position but he put that on hold for seven years and reserved it for Osman. Finally, Hacı Bektaş tells Osman that he bestowed his *hünkar* title upon him. The story portrays Hacı Bektaş as the real wielder of comprehensive power over both temporal and spiritual planes, who delegates his executive power to Osman as part of divine providence. But more importantly, it neatly redraws the boundaries of authority between rulers and dervishes. By bestowing his own *hünkar* title on Osman, Hacı Bektaş relinquishes his political authority and acknowledges Osman's and his progeny's divinely ordained rulership of the temporal sphere. This reconciliatory narrative refashions the Ottoman ruler as the bearer of Hacı Bektaş's hünkar title, thus appeasing Abdalan claims of political authority by sanctifying the Ottoman rulership as one of their own.

Vahidi's contemporary Lami'i Çelebi, in his *Leṭāyifnāme* (The Book of Jests), relates a story that perfectly captures this growing rift between the Ottoman dynasty and its former dervish allies: Murad II, while on a hunting excursion, comes across a group of Torlak dervishes from among the Abdalan who stand up to him and say "our fortunate and blessed sultan, we conquered so many territories for you over which we granted you sovereignty (*beglük*) and rulership; for dervishes are well-wishers, you should give us a village from this realm, bountiful with grass and water, where *abdals* would eat and drink, enjoy the shadow of the Huma, and recite our prayers (*gülbank*)." Before finishing the story, Lami'i Çelebi inserts a satirical poem that ridicules the Abdalan that ends with the couplet: "the truth they claim to pursue; is nothing but eating, drinking and fornicating." But it was the sultan's witty reply that reminds the dervishes that such bargains were things of the past: "What you did was so foolish and wrong! While you grant me so much territories you should have kept a piece of it that you like for yourself so that you wouldn't need to ask for it later."[185]

CHAPTER THREE

The Sultan and the Sultanate

IN OTTOMAN THOUGHT, the anchor term for rulership around which the entire political discourse revolved was "sultanate" (*salṭanat*), in the sense that it refers to executive power through which sovereign authority is exercised. Yet, the sultanate itself did not stand for legitimacy or convey any specific conception of rulership except that, by definition, it meant the type of political authority wielded by a sultan. It was considered as an existential component of human association but one that needed to be explained as to how it serves its purported purpose. To define the sultanate, a long and versatile roster of designations, drawn from various traditions including Islamic disciplines, historical imageries, philosophical views, mystical visions, and administrative conventions, was used. The Ottomans did not develop or inherit an independent theory of the sultanate either. Rather, the term was qualified and conceptualized through the loaded terminology of learned and practical traditions. In response to counter claims of authority, acting on the premise that there can be no authority above the sultanate of a given sutlan, political authors consistently adopted nonpolitical designations of leadership to define the sultanate and ascribed them to rulers in a quest to qualify and establish the supremacy of rulership over other forms of authority. Thus multiple designations, such as caliph, *ṣāḥib-ḳırān*, *quṭb*, and *mahdī*, adopted from different intellectual traditions in order to envision the ruler, therefore the sultanate, in a particular way. The ever increasing numbers of such terms were not decorative titles to glorify the ruler but qualifiers to designate him in the idiom of a particular ideology, discipline, or tradition. Defining the sultanate was inherently predicated on the definition of the ruler, the sultan. The sultanate of a caliph, for example, would be different than the sultanate of a khan or a pole. The entire course of the Ottoman discourse on rulership was about qualifying the ruler, therefore the sultanate. Different conceptions of rulership then depended on the qualifiers used to designate the ruler and the way these qualifiers are defined, envisioned, compared, and propagated.

Reconciling Visions of Rulership

> No ornament is more beautiful than the ornament of greatness (*ʿizzat*), no status (*martaba*) is greater than might (*qudrat*) and effectiveness (*nafāẕ*), and no adornment is better than generosity and gratitude.[1]

This poetic expression of Jahrami captures the prevailing attitude toward rulership of the time that may have been found agreeable by most, if not all, contemporary political writers. Jahrami's exposition features three rudimentary aspects of rulership that represented a common tendency of the period: an acquiescent acknowledgment of rulership as political power, a glorifying plaudit to portray the position of ruler as the noblest rank among humankind, and an unremitting exhortation to the ruler to endow himself with noble moral traits. Albeit metaphorical, Jahrami's candid sketch was perspicacious enough to differentiate between the ordinary form of rulership, depicted as a position characterized by executive power, and the superior form, pictured as an ornament marked by generosity and gratitude. Such views that pervaded especially the prefatory sections of political treatises, in particular, turn political authority that exists by virtue of a "power to rule" into one tailored to the parameters of a virtuous regime, i.e. the sultanate qualified by virtues.

The question of whether the investiture of the less excellent (*al-mafḍūl*) was legitimate in rulership, an issue that stirred a long-lasting dispute among jurists and theologians in the medieval period, had already fallen out of favor in the political theory of the post-Abbasid era.[2] Instead, the principal question of political thought in the age of Süleyman is to turn the existing rulership into the best possible form by educating the ruler to perfect himself and his government. As commonly perceived in mainstream political theory, any ruling sultan who successfully eliminated his actual and potential rivals, and had enough coercive power to rule, was already a legitimate ruler. But what turned his "power to rule" into a virtuous regime was its design after designation. A typical approach, from this perspective, was first to recognize the sultan as ruler with such designations as caliph and *ẓill Allāh* (shadow of God), and then design the rulership by elaborating upon what these designations entailed. The utopian quest of elaborating on the personal qualifications of the perfect ruler required for the enactment of an ideal or legitimate rulership that long preoccupied medieval philosophers and jurists was almost completely abandoned in this era, replaced by a pursuit to transform the existing ruler in office into a perfect one by imposing moral requirements necessitated by how his rulership is designated. In other words, instead of speculating on how to institute the rule of philosopher-king, Ottoman intellectuals mainly occupied themselves with the question of how to make the ruler in office act as one.

With the question of legitimacy out of the way, political authors, in pursuit of perfect rulership, inquired about the nature of rulership in order to configure its parameters. At the most rudimentary level, political authority was viewed as "the sultanate," which was defined by a contemporary lexicographer as "dominion and magnificence" (*galebe ve ʿaẓamet*).[3] When modified by such qualifications as caliphate, the concept of the sultanate gained a moral and spiritual component that turned it into a higher form of rulership. With this prevailing approach, the political theory of the period was primarily moralist in its attitude, characterized by the recognition of "sheer power to rule" as the legitimate basis of rulership and the setting of moral objectives for the sultanate for the proper exercise of political power.

The Ottoman chancery was a minting house of sultanic titles, constantly inventing and re-coining existing designations in response to changing legitimacy concerns. Ottoman rulers from the very beginning accumulated a wide array of titles in tandem with their territorial expansion and new social configurations.[4] Political power and legitimacy were interdependent and any change in one required adjustment with the other. With every rebellion, dynastic dispute, natural disaster, military failure, or victory—or even building public works—sultanic legitimacy needed to be restated, rephrased, or reconfigured. Legitimacy was not a one-time justification of political power but a continuous definition of it with specific claims and statements of authority in the face of constantly changing circumstances. Nor was it a fixed motif displayed across all available media throughout the empire. The ruler needed to be legitimized in different terms in response to different political subcultures and communal conventions. For a ruler, what the Halveti Sufis considered legitimate, for example, may well be different from what jurists expected. When Selim I struck all his coins in Egypt with the khan title as opposed to the ones in Anatolia with the shah title, he aimed to propagate his image as a legitimate ruler in terms acceptable to communities that were attuned to Mamluk and Safavid claims of rulership respectively.[5] What seems to be a crowded hodgepodge of titles in official documents are all at some point adopted or invented as part of a continuous legitimizing process, picked from a royal repertoire and rearranged as demanded by the situation.

The broader Ottoman literature was no less creative in inventing or redefining an ever-increasing number of descriptive titles accorded to the sultan. A revealing example is the political uses of the pole (*quṭb*). Despite the variety of interpretations about the pole in the vast Sufi literature, a common perception was that the pole, or rather the pole of poles (*quṭb al-aqṭāb*), stationed above any other authority in the world.[6] When applied to the ruler, the pole, otherwise a strictly Sufi designation of status, often pointed to the all-encompassing authority of the Ottoman sultan by indicating that it comprised the highest mystical authority as well. An anonymous work, dedicated to the ruling sultan Süleyman, stated that the ruler (*khalīfa*) could be a pole provided that he was pious (*ṣāliḥ*).[7] In his depiction, neither caliph was the highest authority nor was political might a sufficient reason to claim authority over all other claimants. Only when complemented with spiritual perfection could one's rulership attain the rank of poleship. Seyyid Lokman (d. after 1601), the chief court historian, in commemorating Süleyman I, characterized him as "having reached to the status of poles" in his *Book of Physiognomy* written in 1588.[8] Arifi, another Sufi-minded author, used the term more specifically and referred to the same sultan as the pole of time (*quṭb al-waqt*) in the preface of this work.[9] He profiled the Ottoman sultan as having unified political might with spiritual perfection, therefore turning his sultanate into poleship. Both authors picked the concept from Sufi cosmology but none attempted to fit the Ottoman rulership to the Sufi worldview. Instead, they simply qualified the Ottoman sultanate in Sufi terms, in a way acceptable to the Sufi communities whose ideas of world leadership centered on the concept of pole. As pole, the sultan was the center of the world around whom all worldly affairs revolved. Designating the Ottoman ruler as pole converts his rulership into poleship by extending his temporal authority over the spiritual plane. "The sultan as pole" was an image certainly crafted to counter the political claims of Sufi-poles. But it was not simply a title race for the highest imaginable authority. Rather, poleship imposed its own moral requirements over the sultanate and forced the ruler to act as a pole. Thus, poleship either became a noble objective for the sultan to attain by way of his sultanate or to act accordingly if he was already designated as such.

The stock words used in political literature in relation to rulership fall into three major categories. The first category consists of a diverse body of descriptive designations and tropes, such as *sāʾis*, *rāʿī*, *zimām-dār*, and *sarvar*, which usually referred to the leadership of the ruler in his community. The second group includes royal titles referring to executive power, authority, or sovereignty, such as sultan, padishah, malik, caesar (*ḳayser*), and *ḥākim*. Other similar designations, such as shah, khan, and *ḫāḳān*, are mostly employed as royal titles when referring to the actual ruler in office as an exclusive marker of his sovereignty and rarely appear in political texts. Scribes at the chancery and court historians are more diligent in their use of these designations because of their immediate political implications at home and abroad.[10] The third group comprises designations that originated from the Qur'an and gained peculiar definitions in the broader Islamic tradition, such as *ulī al-amr*, imam, and caliph. Despite meticulously phrased official documents and punctilious political texts, these terms could be used indiscriminately in the broader literary output, which largely deprived them their descriptive values. Such titles as sultan or malik often did not entail legal, moral, or philosophical implications. Qur'anic terms, imam and caliph, on the other hand, often carried their specific juristic or Sufistic definitions. As a simple illustration to point out the difference between the two sets of designations, the term "sultan" could be used in reference to non-Muslim rulers whereas the term caliph would not ordinarily be used for such occasions.[11] Despite the unique conceptual backdrop of each term, in the hands of less punctilious authors, these terms may indiscriminately be used to simply decorate the ruler's image with the most potent vocabulary available. Partly for this vulgarization, and partly because of the pursuit of further qualifying these qualifiers, a fourth set of designations was formed.

These increasingly nebulous terms were reworked to create more specific constructs in envisioning a particular type of rulership, such as *salṭanat-i maʿnawī* (executive power in meaning), *salṭanat-i ṣūrī* (executive power in appearance), *khilāfat-i raḥmānī* (the caliphate of God's Mercy), and *imāmat-i ḥaqīqī* (the true imamate). In response to numerous such titles, designations, images, and qualifiers that plagued political discourse, Kınalızade carefully identified the ones that correspond to his vision of ideal rulership:

> Now the sovereign in meaning (*ḥākim-i maʿnī*) is the one who is distinguished by divine support and by endless divine grace so that he could manage the well-being of cities and perfect the souls of people. Philosophers call such a person absolute sovereign (*ḥākim ʿale'l-iṭlāḳ*) and his rule the art of the sovereign (*ṣınāʿat-i melik*), the moderns (*müteʾaḫḫirūn*) call him caliph and his practice caliphate, and the Shiites call him imam and his practice imamate, and Plato called him regulator of the world (*müdebbir-i ʿālem*), and Aristotle called him the civic human being (*insān-i medenī*).[12]

For Kınalızade these terms are not synonymous; each refers to a type of political authority as conceived within a particular learned tradition in its own terms. Yet all these conceptions agree on one essential quality of what he considers as ideal rulership: its distinction by divine support and grace, and the ruler's capability of perfecting the souls of people in addition to his governance. This is the same unified authority that had been advocated by Sufis and mystic philosophers since Suhrawardi. Kınalızade's main source on this subject, Tusi, had already stated that malik referred not to "someone possessing a cavalcade, a retinue or a realm" but to "one truly deserving of rulership, even though outwardly no one pays him any attention."[13] Despite employing a generic term, this definition depicts the ruler as the one who is qualified to lead by reason of his personal virtues. This shows that, even when the terms caliph and imam were used indiscriminately and equated with less loaded terms such as sultan and malik, their references to a more definite form of authority articulated in Sufistic and juristic theories may not be lost. No author, for example, seems to have endeavored to prove that such terms as caliph or imam were identical with the term sultan, shah, or malik. But many set out to prove the opposite. Lütfi Paşa and Ensari, for example, demonstrated the legitimacy of the Ottoman ruler by arguing that his very sultan title meant caliph, imam, and *ẓill Allāh*. This obfuscation of the original meanings of the terms did not conceal the appearance of two hierarchical conceptions of rulership: an ordinary one, often simply labeled as sultanate, and *mulk*, and a superior one, qualified by more specific designations, such as caliphate or imamate.

Lütfi Paşa composed his treatise on the caliphate in response to a question he was once asked as to whether it was permissible to attribute the title of caliph and imam to the sultans of the time, who lacked a Qurayshi descent, a condition stipulated by most mainstream medieval jurists and theologians.[14] Answering the question in the affirmative, he related that the ulema had stated that what was meant by sultan was caliph (*al-murād min al-sulṭān al-khalīfa*), pointing to a complete semantic overlap between the two designations.[15] Lütfi Paşa, however, was of a totally different breed among his contemporaries in his approach to rulership. By advocating a complete synonymity among all applicable titles of rulership, such as sultan, caliph, imam, *ẓill Allāh*, and the like, he strived to prove the sultan's right to claim all those titles by the very virtue of his being the sultan. Lütfi Paşa first limited the caliphate to the juristic notion of imamate, and then imamate to sultanate, that is, executive authority over which there is no other coercive power. Despite being a deeply pious person who adopted the life of an ascetic after retirement, he promoted a secular conception of the caliphate by totally dissociating it from its Qur'anic content and Sufi cosmology.

Lütfi Paşa's Sufi-minded contemporaries, however, reframed Ottoman rulership in Sufistic terms. Ebu'l-Fazl Münşi, for example, stated that rulership (*pādishāhī*) was the vicegerency of God (*khilāfat-i Khudā*), thereby equating ordinary rulership with the vicegerency of God.[16] Using similar terms, Dizdar also pointed out that sultanate denoted a caliphal vicegerency from God (*al-salṭana khilāfa ʿan Allāh*).[17] In the same vein, Ensari thought that *walāya* and sultanate together were equal to *khilāfat al-nubuwwa*.[18] The purpose of these authors, however, was in almost complete contrast to Lütfi Paşa's: They sought not to reduce these positions to the level of the sultanate but to elevate the status of the sultanate to the level of those positions. They did not uproot these concepts as Lütfi Paşa did, but instead envisioned the sultanate by replanting these titles in the field of Sufi imageries. Thus, they integrated these notions with the definition of the sultanate as qualifiers with the intention of establishing moral objectives for the ordinary sultanate. More specifically, for Ebu'l-Fazl Münşi and Dizdar, a sultanate was a caliphate only when it fulfilled the requirements expected from a caliphate.

The raison d'être *of the Sultanate*

Sixteenth-century conceptions of political authority were grounded in ontological assumptions about human nature. Proponents of even contrasting notions of rulership commonly agreed that human beings were created with an inherent need for political authority, which was considered to be a grace from God to humankind.[19] Depending on one's competence in ethical, philosophical, and Sufistic postulations regarding human beings' nature, these authors sought to identify the common human characteristics that necessitate the existence of political authority. They portrayed political authority as an indispensable component of human existence, including one's spiritual and material life. Only the presence of political authority could enable individuals to fulfill their human capacities as demanded by the creator. Political authority existed not by choice but by nature, and the guiding pursuit of political writing was to discover the type of rulership that best fits human nature. As a result, there is a strong correlation between how human nature is understood and corresponding political authority is conceived. Sufi-minded authors, for example, did not display any interest in a philosophical discussion of possibilities regarding forms of political association. Rather they focused on the potential of perfecting the existing rulership, therefore more interested in the qualitative nature of political authority than in its institutional and social configurations. The Sufis approached political authority in the same way they interpreted Islam and piety in general, where spiritual perfection prevailed over normative praxis. The attainment of perfect rulership was to be achieved in the moral and spiritual plane.

The prevailing idea in the medieval period, which pervaded the Ottoman writing on governance, was that the very existence of a political authority with executive power was more important than its form. Kınalızade, for example, well versed in medieval political and ethical philosophy, deliberately avoided discussing alternative forms of political association (*medīne*). While doing so, he opted to follow the position of Davvani rather than of Tusi, although he was extensively indebted to both authors in compiling his work on political ethics. In his template, later adopted by Kınalızade, Davvani categorized political associations as virtuous versus nonvirtuous but did not elaborate on the types of associations that fell into these categories as Tusi and Farabi before him had done.[20] Tusi, on the other hand, who combined the hitherto distinct fields of political and ethical philosophy and created the format of ethical writing that Davvani and Kınalızade followed, had extensively discussed alternative forms of political associations, virtuous and nonvirtuous, largely deriving his views from those of Farabi.[21] Both Kınalızade and Davvani agreed with Tusi and Farabi in presenting the virtuous city (*al-madīna al-fāḍila*) as the ultimate objective of political association but did not elaborate on nonvirtuous associations.

While avoiding theoretical elaborations, Kınalızade used the Davvanian model to demonstrate the distinguishing features of the Ottoman regime in comparison to its neighboring counterparts. He divided the errant city (*medīne-i dālle*) into two types: an infidel errant (*dālle-i kāfire*) and a heretical errant (*dālle-i gayri kāfire*). For the former he gave the example of northern and western neighbors of the Ottomans, such as the Europeans (*Efrenc*) and the Russians (*Rūs*), which were grouped as the people (*firaḳ*) of disbelief. He defined the latter as those who had strayed from the right path (*meẕāhib-i fāside*) and exemplified them with the case of the Safavids (*Surḫser ṭāyifesī*). He then proudly presented the Ottoman case as a virtuous association.[22] Here, Kınalızade entirely disregarded the question of how these associations were structured and, instead, categorized them per their moral quality.

Kınalızade and his main source of inspiration, Davvani, agreed with both Farabi and his close follower Tusi in their assessment of political associations based on the purpose of their inhabitants. While certainly aware of what the medieval philosophers wrote on the types of political associations, Kınalızade found Davvani's contention of defining only the virtuous association more appealing because, perhaps like Davvani himself, he thought that he was living in a virtuous city.[23] For him, political associations were to be defined by and assessed on the basis of their moral quality and objectives rather than on how they were formed. What distinguished Kınalızade from his predecessors was his selective and pragmatic use of medieval political philosophy, and his singling out of the sultanate as the only political regime worthy of mention. While the medieval philosophers discussed alternative regimes to define the virtuous association and highlight its superiority, the Ottomans mainly sought ways to turn the existing political regime into a virtuous one, displaying little concern for the alternatives.

In presenting the sultanate as the only form of government, Kınalızade's account was part of a general trend among the political writers of the time. When Kınalızade and his contemporaries referred to the need for social organization and political association, what they specifically referred to was the sultanate. For them the sultanate was not an alternative to other forms of government, but was to be identified with world order, and seen as an alternative to chaos itself. From this perspective, the existential need for political association inherent to individual human beings, and elaborated by medieval philosophers, was reduced to an existential need for rulership, which was understood as the sultanate. Thus for Ottoman authors, humanity was in need of the sultanate per se, not of some particular kind of political association. The sultanate was the only type of government by which a virtuous regime could be possible.

This universal acceptance of the sultanate as the only form of political regime among Ottoman authors of the time found its textbook exposition in Taşköprizade's *Miftāḥ al-Saʿāda*, in which he had a separate entry for the science of government (*ʿilm al-siyāsa*). Following his definition, which centered on the sultanate, he provided a list of suggested books on the subject that included those of Davvani and Tusi, the two most widely known works on the topic among Ottoman intellectuals. In this list, Taşköprizade recommended Farabi's somewhat less known work, *Mabādī Ārā Ahl al-Madīna*, in which the author elaborated on the sultanate, but did not mention his better known work, *al-Siyāsa al-Madaniyya*, in which various types of political regimes were enumerated.[24] For Taşköprizade and his contemporaries, proving the existential human need for political authority was the same as justifying the existence and legitimacy of the sultanate.

Displaying no interest in the varieties of political regimes, the main question that engaged the political authors before elaborating on rulership was to prove that the existence of a political authority in the form of the sultanate was indispensable. Three complementary propositions circulated in political literature to demonstrate this inherent human need for the sultanate. Among them, the most commonly held proposition stated that human beings were social by nature (*nevʿ-i insān medenī bi'ṭ-ṭabʿdır*), and stressed the position of a ruler in society as an arbitrator. This Aristotelian axiom, commonly adopted and elaborated upon by medieval philosophers, was already a proverb widely circulating in all forms of political writing by the time of the Ottomans. Rephrasing the view of Tusi, Kınalızade based his argument on the assumption that all human beings shared a common characteristic in their natures, which made political organization under the arbitration of a ruler indispensable for social life.[25] More specifically, human beings' need for association and for political authority was one and the same, a view widely shared by political authors of the time. Similar to his predecessors in the philosophical tradition, Kınalızade considered that the role of the ruler in society was to lead people to perfection and happiness (*tekmīl-i ḫulḳ ve lāzım-ı neyl-i saʿādet*).[26]

The second proposition highlights the diversity of human nature in explaining why the sultanate was necessary. Deriving his thoughts from Hamadani, whose ideas reflect Suhrawardian illuminationism, Taşköprizade reached the same conclusion as Kınalızade, pointing out the indispensability of the sultanate for human existence:[27]

> Know that the natures of humans, when their dispositions were created, varied in terms of different talents and various characteristics. For this reason their reception of the lights of the manifestations of Beauty differed and, because of that difference, their aims, words, practices, beliefs, attributes, and morals also differed. Thus divine wisdom necessitated the appointment of a just ruler and leader to protect the oppressed from the oppressor and apply rules, and treat people equitably, so that order may last until the end of days. And the first person appointed for that position was the father of humanity, Adam.[28]

While establishing the relationship between human nature and the need for political authority, this eloquent elaboration on the proof of rulership reveals some of the prevailing conceptions widely held at the time. First of all, Taşköprizade presented rulership as a result of diversity among human beings. Human beings were diverse not only in terms of congenital traits and talents but also in terms of acquired values and preferences. This condition made rulership indispensable in regulating the interaction among human beings whose beliefs and morals were diverse. The rest of his treatise points to a more important reason for the existence of rulership by portraying political authority as a spiritual guide for this diverse body of humankind. Second, the author conceived of human nature and rulership from an ontological standpoint, considering both as a part of creation and complementary to each other. According to this, human beings were created with an inherent need for rulership and having a ruler was a part of divine providence, making this kind of political association an existential requirement. From a historical perspective, a logical extension of this conception was that rulership and the human need for it were as old as the creation of the first human being on Earth. In this view, divine providence and human nature both require the existence of a political regime in the form of the sultanate. Third, the author stated that rulership started with prophethood, considering no difference between the two at the time of human being's creation on Earth. In this view, the first human being appeared to be the first prophet and the first ruler, pointing to the strong relationship among human nature, prophethood, and rulership. This identification of prophethood with rulership, or rather the inclusion of the latter in the former, assumed continuity between what the former prophets did and what contemporary rulers were expected to do. Thus while prophethood was conceived as a model for rulership, the rulers were put in the line of the prophets, in addition to the lineage of world rulers, and considered as inheritors of the prophetic mission.

The third proposition was the moral weakness of human beings. Enunciating this conception, Bidlisi wrote: "It is certain that the majority of human beings are weak personalities, and in regard to their dispositions (*fiṭrat*) and spirituality they are imperfect and light, and many improprieties become evident in their acts and conditions, and deeds. Furthermore, evil personalities are abundant among the people of our time."[29] Sharing this pessimistic conviction, Kınalızade also stated that the majority of people were disposed to sensuality and voluptuousness.[30] The human deficiency in creation could be compensated and complemented only by the existence of political authority. This negative side of human nature not only made rulership necessary but, according to Ensari, a grace from God as well:

> The ulema said that there is great wisdom in the existence of a ruler on Earth and its benefits for the servants of God are abundant. Because God created all the people, save the apostles and messengers, as lacking fairness (*inṣāf*) [to others] but seeking justice (*intiṣāf*) [for themselves]. Were it not for the sultan on the earth, people would have devoured each other.[31]

Ensari highlighted two main reasons that made rulership an existential requirement for humankind. First, because of the way their natures were created, people egoistically sought justice for themselves but denied it to others. Accordingly, if justice were to be instituted equitably for all, then it was rulership that could prevent encroachments among people. Second, whether humans sought it or not, rulership existed as a grace from God, as part of His divine providence. This self-justifying and counterfactual argumentation not only enhanced the legitimacy of independent rulers in the post-Abbasid era but also presented them as moral guides. Ensari's Mughal contemporary Abu-l Fazl, in support of Akbar's new vision of rulership, dramatized it as follows: "If royalty did not exist, the storm of strife would never subside, nor selfish ambition disappear. Humankind, being under the burden of lawlessness and lust, would sink into the pit of destruction, would lose its prosperity, and the whole earth become a barren waste."[32] The popular image of an ideal ruler in the age of Süleyman was one who uses his executive power for the moral perfection of the inhabitants of the political association he was leading. Such an ideal turned the sultanate into, first and foremost, a moral institution. So, as much as Sufi leaders and revivalist ulema were competing against temporal rulers to share or supersede political authority, these rulers were extending their temporal power over the moral and spiritual plains.

Kınalızade formulated this new ideal in his description of the head of the virtuous city: "Know that the administrator of the virtuous city is the righteous imam (*imām-ı ḥaḳ*) and the absolute caliph (*ḫalīfe-i muṭlaḳ*), and his governance (*ḥükūmet*) is imamate and caliphate, and its purpose is to perfect people's souls and provide means of happiness."[33] Here, Kınalızade unmistakably reconciles the juristic (imamate) and Sufistic (caliphate) notions of perfect rulership, and equates it with the philosopher-kingship of the virtuous city. But it was Taşköprizade who provided the most elaborate account of this vision:

> The great leadership (*al-riyāsa al-ʿuẓmā*) of virtuous city is one of four types: The first is the leadership of philosophy (*riyāsat al-ḥikma*), which is the leadership of the absolute ruler (*al-malik al-muṭlaq*), if available. His characteristics are three: possessing the knowledge of theoretical and practical philosophy; persuasion and vision necessary to perfect others; and the power to fight (jihad). The second is the leadership of the virtuous ones (*afāḍil*): in the absence of the absolute ruler, full governance (*al-tadbīr al-tām*) materializes with the association of three peoples who possess his three characteristics. The third is the leadership of convention (sunna): this leader knows the manners and laws of the predecessors, namely, the absolute ruler and the virtuous ones, and follows their conventions, preserves their practices, and infers from them what is commendable (*maṣāliḥ*). In the absence of the above leader, the fourth is the leadership of the people of convention. This is the institution of a group (*jamāʿa*) of people in full agreement with each other (*muttafiqat al-ārā*) to follow the predecessors and implement their wisdom in the city.[34]

The reconfiguration of rulership as moral guidance drew inspiration from that of prophethood as elaborated in the scriptures and historical accounts of prophets. These were the incapacity of humans to take the right path, and divine providence that manifested itself in the form of providing guidance via prophets. When Bidlisi declared that the position of *ẓill Allāh* was the highest rank among human beings, he was not referring to just any form of rulership, but only to the one that most resembled divine government. The purpose of political writing was to illustrate the position of rulership among humankind and advise the ruler to perform what it entailed. These conceptions of human nature led political authors of the time not only to advocate the existential necessity for a political authority but also to assert a particular type of political regime, which was the sultanate. For them the creation of human nature as social, diverse, and weak made political authority not a voluntary institution but an indispensable part of human existence and a grace from above in the form of the sultanate, at times exercised by God-sent prophets. Once the sultanate was conceived as an integral part of humankind's existence as a society and individual, then the form of political authority was irrelevant. As a result of this conception, one of the main quests in political theory was to elevate the moral quality of rulership to make it resemble God's government over creation or that of the ruler-prophets over humankind.

Rulership as Grace from God

> With divine wisdom, God entrusted one of his secrets to a bird called Huma. If Huma's shadow falls upon someone (*ʿabd*), with God's might, he becomes a sultan. How God chooses someone with His perfect favor and makes him a ruler and makes him fortunate by granting the caliphate (*khilāfa*) is known only by Him. The Prophet called him shadow of God (*ẓill Allāh*). God conferred upon him miraculous powers (*karāmāt*), glory (*ʿizz*) and honor (*sharaf*).[35]

Dizdar Mustafa, an obscure fortress commander, began his treatise on the spiritual journey of rulers by stating that the sultanate is a caliphate from God and God bestows it on whomever he wishes among his servants. The fortunate person turns into God's shadow upon receiving the Huma's shadow.[36] Dizdar's figurative description of divine providence evokes a vivid imagery that pervaded perceptions of rulership among the ruling elite. Although Huma and *ẓill Allāh* seem to have originated from the pre-Islamic Iranian and Assyrian mythologies, respectively, they were among the images most commonly alluded to in Ottoman political culture.[37] *Hümāyūn*, which meant august, fortunate, and royal in Ottoman usage, served as an official attribute of anything related to the sultan, with the implication that the sultan was the recipient of Huma's shadow.[38] Popular cosmology, poetry, and visual arts were repositories of creative Huma imageries that continuously inspired visions of rulership.[39]

If a fortress commander's usage of the Huma imagery to characterize God's grace might seem idiosyncratic, Sheikh ul Islam Ibn Kemal's report on the origins of the Ottoman dynasty shows how firmly established this belief was in the Ottoman imagination.[40] Exceptionally well versed in poetry and history, Ibn Kemal, in his chronicle of the House of Osman, narrates that a certain saint called Kumral Baba witnesses Huma casting its shadow on Osman. A man from the order of invisible saints, who unexpectedly appeares before Kumral Baba, informs him that it is the time of Osman's rise to glory, whom he characterizes as "the owner of crown and throne" (*ṣāḥib-i tāc u taḫt*). The anonymous saint further orders him to meet with Osman, then a mere tribal chief, and tells him to watch for Huma as his sign of recognition. On seeing Osman with Huma's shadow over him, exactly as foretold by the anonymous saint, Kumral Baba approaches Osman and gives him the good news from the order of invisible saints that he received his auspicious turn to rule (*baḫt ve devlet*). Both Dizdar and Ibn Kemal may have taken this story from earlier chroniclers, such as Konevi and Bidlisi, who narrated it in similar terms. But the Huma imagery itself was already in circulation in the Rum since before the inception of the Ottomans.[41] Daye, for example, a major source of inspiration for both Bidlisi and Ibn Kemal, had already presented this ancient myth in the guise of Sufi symbolism in his popular Ottoman read, *Mirṣād al-ʿIbād*.[42]

Inalcik, in his landmark article on Ottoman succession, traced the origins of this idea to the steppe traditions of Turko-Mongol states where each member of the dynasty was believed to have an equal right to succeed to the throne.[43] Because of this belief, no rule of succession took root for long in Turko-Mongol state tradition, where totemic beliefs and mythologies that shaped perceptions of rulership usually tied the origins of a dynasty to a deity or divine providence. A conspicuous prerogative of the recipient of divine dispensation to rule in Turkic steppe traditions was the possession of *ḳūt* (fortune) to which Arabic and Persian terminology of divine selection was added.[44] Especially after the decentralization of the Abbasid caliphate in the eleventh century, such concepts as *farr* (effulgence) and *ṭāliʿ* (fortune) came into wider circulation among the independent dynasties as principal means of legitimation. As alluded to in Chapter 1, the term *dawla*, which came into wide circulation with the rise of the Abbasids in the eighth century and evolved to mean "state" from the sixteenth century onwards, preserved its original meaning as "fortunate turn" until modern times, a meaning closely associated with pre-Islamic conceptions of divine grace or light.

While it was only natural for these upstart dynasties to employ means of legitimation drawn from Turkish, Mongol, or Persian cultures, the use of such imageries as divine appointment also served to compensate for their deficiencies in legitimizing their authority on the basis of juristic and theological principles. The ancient Iranian concept of *farr-i īzadī* (divine glory), for example, was integral to the Mughal ruler Akbar's popular image as a divinely chosen ruler.[45] In a similar vein, ancient imageries of legitimation and the divine connection of rulers were in full bloom with the rise of the Safavids, whose means of legitimation and claims of superiority were of crucial interest to the

Ottomans.[46] The employment of such pre-Islamic imageries of kingship by high-profile jurists and Sufis further diluted any concern about their legitimate usage by Muslim rulers. Ghazali, for example, whose writings enjoyed an almost canonical status among the Ottomans, privileged the ruler for receiving divine light: "God gave him [the king] kingship and the divine light."[47] Pointing to philosophical expositions of the idea, Ghazali notes Aristotle's statement that kings owe their greatness to divine effulgence.[48] While used by the mainstream ulema without much reservation, the imagery of divine light is at times indistinguishably fused with mystical perceptions of divine light and manifestations of God's attributes. The whole philosophy of illumination, systematized by the mystical philosopher Suhrawardi, for example, was imbued with the concept of light that emanated from God. Suhrawardi, who explicitly referred to such terms as *khvarnah* (divine glory) and divine light, was well aware of ancient imageries of divine light, and simply considered them earlier expositions of his illuminationist philosophy.[49] Thus by the time of the Ottomans, versatile and enchanting images, motifs, and metaphors denoting the divine connection of rulership were already afloat and abundant.[50]

Such imageries of providential attainment of rulership were further imbued with the grace theory of rulership, as envisioned in various strands of Islamic learned traditions, according to which God alone decides and confers kingship. The "grace theory" of rulership was enmeshed with the common Islamic idea that everything acquired by human being is God's *niʿma* (beneficence). Such a conception of grace also implied that God makes a choice in allocating His grace. Arguments used by contenders during the fierce clashes for succession that filled the political scene of this period show that, although princes firmly clung to all the necessary material means of succession, they all expected the outcome to emanate solely from divine will, at least in rhetoric. Prince Ahmed, after losing the throne to his brother Selim I, attributes his loss to God's choice:

> Since Adam, till the end of the world it has been an ancient custom for the progeny of rulers to pursue their turn in rulership. Accordingly, you pursued my father's sultanate which I sought after as well. However, in accordance with "I wish, you wish, but nothing happens except for what He wishes," God's will chose you and you attained the sultanate.[51]

Faced with the failing health of his father, Bayezid II, who was losing control of the government as a result, Prince Ahmed had already persuaded the sultan to abdicate in his favor. Under the pressure of a cohort of dignitaries who tied their prospects to Ahmed's succession, "I had no power to continue reigning," the ruling sultan reportedly stated, so "I pass the sultanate to my son Ahmed according to my own will."[52] But such an arrangement did not sound appropriate to the other two candidates, Korkud and Selim, who opposed the decision by invoking the prevailing belief in political culture that rulership was granted by God, not conferred by the ruler in office. Encountering strong resistance and tempestuous negotiations, the sultan and his dignitaries were forced to agree that there would be no heir apparent as long as Bayezid was alive, leaving the field of competition open for contenders.[53] Prince Selim further obtained a formal agreement from the sultan, who stated that "the sultan would not determine his successor during his reign but this matter shall be determined by will of God."[54] After a series of successful skirmishes and negotiations, Prince Selim, who managed to secure the support of the Janissaries, overcame Ahmed's forces and left Bayezid II no choice but to abdicate in Selim's favor. Bayezid II's dignitaries, who conspired in favor of Ahmed, consoled the defeated prince by saying that "it appeared that the matter of rulership could not be determined by an alliance between you and us but by God's will."[55] Celalzade and Bidlisi, who conveyed these reports in their chronicles, as being staunch admirers of Selim, may well have doctored or even fabricated these conversations. Yet, if these chronicles are taken as political texts, or even as propaganda media, then they speak well for the ideals of rulership and its attainment to which these authors subscribed.

The idea of divine dispensation was so prevalent in Ottoman thought that a possible rule of succession was never problematized in political writing. But there was plenty of advice for aspirants of the throne to become worthy of God's grace. Given that God's favor was by definition unconditional and unpredictable, Ottomans were especially careful to educate all princes equally, assigning them tutors to teach and instructors to train in statecraft.[56] As Mehmed II, Bayezid II, and Süleyman did, however, the reigning sultan could seek to affect the outcome of competition for succession by appointing his favorite prince to the governorship of a city that was closest to the capital to ensure his speedy takeover of the throne on the ruler's death. The sultan might also support the prince of his choice through various means without ostensibly alienating other candidates. But lessons from the cases of Bayezid II and Selim I, who succeeded against the wishes of their fathers, taught that the successor was often the disfavored prince. Even Selim II, who succeeded thanks to the direct involvement of Süleyman, was not the primary choice of his father but owed his succession to the execution of his brothers, who were accused of open rebellion against the ruling sultan.[57] In a political culture where God was believed to have the final word in attaining rulership, competition among the princes had more justification than interference by the reigning sultan in an effort to appoint his successor. As described by Bidlisi, regardless of the circumstances, persons who were born with an auspicious destiny were assured of success:

> In the world of causes (*ʿālam-i ʿilal va asbāb*), in accordance with God's wisdom, the condition of the heavens influences the outcome of good and evil, and gain and loss. One's condition changes very little

from what has been set by his star of felicity. No doubt, rulers (*ṣāḥib-i nashʾat-i khilāfat va sulṭānī*), who were born into this world under an auspicious constellation (*ṭāliʿ-i khujasta*), with their fortunate arrival, continue to rule and succeed as well as gain status and glory. Favorable fortune (*baḥt-i musāʿid*) and assistant destiny (*davlat-i muʿāżid*) are among the divine gifts (*ʿaṭiyya-i vahbī*) foretold by an auspicious constellation (*ṭāliʿ-i saʿd*). For this reason, fortunate persons (*khujasta ṭāliʿān*) always attain their sublime objectives as they wish with no effort, because of divine dispensation. Any effort they would exert to reach their objective would suit their destiny. This auspicious constellation and glorious fortune is a divine gift (*mavhibat-i ghaybī*), not an acquired prize (*ʿaṭāyā-i kasbī*).[58]

Once the sultanate was believed to be a grace from God, the ensuing logical question would be whether grace was conferred upon a specific individual predestined to rule or upon someone who deserved to be designated as such by having acquired certain qualifications and conditions. In widely-held response, the prevalent view was that no personal qualification was needed to receive God's grace. This acquiescent idea of divine appointment ended political theory's quest for a legal means of appointing a ruler and inevitably facilitated the rise of moralism in political writing. It implied that the community had no leverage in choosing the best candidate for rulership. Medieval juristic theory, constructed on the canonical premise that choosing a ruler was incumbent on the community, had centered on elaborating the conditions and qualifications for a candidate's eligibility for the office. Once the best candidate took office, there would have been less concern about educating the ruler because he was already endowed with commendable traits. But the idea of divine appointment, which took precedence in the popular imagination of the post-Abbasid period, overshadowing the juristic view, necessitated that the ruler in office needed to be instructed about good governance. As the divinely designated ruler could in theory be anyone who was chosen by God for unknown reasons, the only input left to the ruled on the question of rulership is to improve it through instruction and advice. That noble task turned the general tenor of political writing into moralism in all genres and disciplines of political thought, including juristic works.

Because most political works addressed the current ruler in office, political writers understandably paid little attention to the question of prescribing the rules of king-making. Medieval juristic and theological discourse that extensively entertained this question was only remotely echoed during the age of Süleyman. The only author who specifically wrote on the subject was Lütfi Paşa, who adopted a strictly juristic position in order to refute a theological view that put the legitimacy of the Ottoman ruler into question.[59] Others were more interested in what rulership entailed rather than what was needed to become a ruler. Nevertheless, many authors preferred to describe how rulership was attained in order to elucidate what it entailed because their views about how one becomes a ruler were indicative of what type of rulership they envisioned. When rulership was established as a grace from God, for example, then a ruler's governance was perceived to be his return of God's favor for which he needed to be educated.

Although the grace theory was prevalent, it was not the only one. There were three main views explaining the attainment of rulership: by grace (*niʿmet-i vehbī*), merit (*istiḥḳāḳ*), subjugation (*ḳahr*), or a combination of these reasons. Grace theory was by far the most widely held view while merit theory was often presented as complementary to the former to justify divine providence and make God's choice intelligible to humans. Merit theory, unlike its medieval counterpart in jurisprudence and theology that centered on one's legal qualification for the position, focused only on one's moral fitness for the office. Subjugation theory was inherently compatible with grace theory because the latter did not address the practical considerations of becoming a ruler, and by definition accepted all rulers as legitimate whether they achieved their position by merit or by force. Each of these three theories on the attainment of rulership has a strong basis in scriptures and histories making them convenient markers of legitimacy. As previously noted, rulership in the form of the sultanate was conceived to be executive authority and power to rule, and was modeled on divine government, prophethood, and sainthood, presenting the prophet-rulers as its most definitive role models. As formulated in a couplet by Celalzade, such a conception left little room for speculating about the objective qualities necessary for rulership but instead implied that the question of leadership was decided in the spiritual realm:

Indeed the sultanate is God-given
Ennobling and excellence in glory[60]

The principal proponent of grace theory was Bidlisi, who devoted a long section of his work to the question of how one becomes a ruler and examined it in a theological framework. "The greatest of God's graces (*mavāhib*) and the noblest of divine beneficences (*niʿmethā*), a virtue which Man is proud of before the heavens and angels," he stated, "is the beneficence of the vicegerency of God's mercy (*khilāfat-i raḥmānī*) and the gift of authority (*mavhibat-i iqtidār*) to oversee the affairs of people by way of divine commands and prohibitions."[61] As a proof from the Qur'an, Bidlisi mentioned the appointment of Abraham and David as leaders of the community (*imām*) whom God granted sovereignty (*mulk*).[62] These and many other Qur'anic verses present *mulk*, in the sense of rulership, as a grace from God granted to a person of His choice with no prior condition. Although there is no indication that this applies to nonprophet rulers as well, Bidlisi, like all contemporary political authors, thought that God's message in these verses extended to all kinds of authority.

Such a view on the attainment of rulership completely agrees with a well-known Qur'anic verse commonly referred to by other political authors: "Thou givest sovereignty unto whom Thou wilt, and Thou withdrawest sovereignty from whom Thou wilt."[63]

In conformity with the general Islamic view, Bidlisi considered anything that benefits man as beneficence from God and proposed divine providence as the sole reason of attaining rulership. Before characterizing rulership (*khilāfat, shāhanshāhī*) as a kind of divine beneficence (*mavhibat, ʿaṭiyya, niʿmat*), he elucidated two types of benefits: those bestowed by God (*vahbī*) and those earned by human beings (*kasbī*). Benefits such as beauty (*ḥusn u jamāl*) and success (*davlat u iqbāl*), which human beings' will and effort have no role in bringing about, are called bestowed whereas such benefits as learning arts and crafts (*ṣanʿat u ḥirfat*) and subsequently accumulating wealth through trade, which human beings' efforts (*saʿy u ghayrat*) influence, are called earned. In his view, bestowed benefits never perish as a result of external causes even if all of one's enemies unite to destroy them.[64] In full agreement with Bidlisi's view, Ibn Kemal explained the enthronement of Osman, the founder of the Ottoman dynasty, as a result of divine providence:

> When the forgiven Ertuğrul died there were two candidates to take his place and lead his noble tribe. One was his brother Dündar, a talented commander, and the other was Emir Osman, who was engaged in conquest day and night. Unavoidably, a conflict and disagreement took place between the two for some time. After divisions among the followers and companions, they finally agreed on Osman by consensus. Although it was Dündar who became the leader of his people because of his seniority in age and status, Osman gained the hearts of people by his commendable policy and moral rectitude. Sovereignty was his destined fortune (*naṣīb*). In the invisible world, when the world's property was divided among groups of rulers (*ümerā*) as well as all the poor and the rich, Osman was given that lot [sovereignty]. During the primordial assembly before creation (*bezm-i ezel*), when nobles and commoners as well as governors and subjects got drunken with the wine of *elest*, Osman was served the cup of leadership (*serverlik*). The belt of happiness was destined for his waist, and the crown of state was assigned to his head.[65]

In agreement with this prevailing tendency in this period, Kınalızade gave a new currency to grace theory. On the question of the necessary qualifications for rulership, which are nearly identical in all accounts of this period, Kınalızade chose to present them in the way revised by Davvani, not the way originally formulated by Tusi, who had said "the seeker after kingly rule (*ṭālib-i mulk*) must strive to unite seven qualities."[66] Davvani later modified this to "philosophers predicate five qualities as desirable in a prince (*pādishāh*)," a modification adopted almost verbatim by Kınalızade. However slight the difference may seem, it points to a substantial shift in the perception of how one becomes a ruler. While Tusi enumerated seven qualifications for a "candidate" to become a ruler, this view is completely lost to Davvani and Kınalızade, who present these qualifications as those recommended for the "ruler" to possess. Unlike Tusi, both Davvani and Kınalızade begin the section on "government of the realm and the manners of kings" with laudatory remarks on rulership, stating that it is God's greatest gift conferred upon man.[67]

At the other end of the spectrum was the subjugation theory whose principal exponent was Lütfi Paşa, who simply gathered carefully selected legal opinions from a variety of sources that served his conception of rulership. As such, he builds a powerful argument that gives the impression that the one and the only requirement for legitimate rulership is executive power to subjugate.[68] Lütfi Paşa was writing his treatise in the midst of destructive dynastic wars among princes, at a time when the unity of the state was more important than the moral or religious quality of the ruler. Unlike Bidlisi, for whom the sultan was no more than a passive recipient of divine favor, Lütfi Paşa portrayed a ruler profile who is in full charge of his actions with the power of making his own fate. In a formulaic statement, he stated that "if one possesses the mentioned conditions such as subjugation (*ghalaba*), domination (*qahr*), institution of religion with justice (*iqāmat al-dīn bi al-ʿadl*), commanding the good and forbidding the wrong, leadership over the public (*riyāsa al-ʿāmma*), then he becomes the sultan and deserves to be called *imām*, *khalīfa* and *wālī*."[69] With the authoritative language of jurisprudence, he repeatedly stated throughout his treatise that one becomes a ruler by procuring allegiance (*mubāyaʿa maʿah*), subjugating (*ghalaba*), subduing (*qahr*), or having the ability to exert one's power (*an yunaffidha ḥukmahu*).[70] As a jurist by profession, Bidlisi may not have objected to these practical requirements for the acquisition of rulership but what makes Lütfi Paşa different is that he never explicitly stated that any of these qualifications were granted by God without human beings' independent efforts.

Yet nowhere did Lütfi Paşa exclusively refute the grace or merit theory, and his main purpose was confined to legitimating the ruling sultan's authority as caliph and imam on juristic grounds. He was no stranger to the other two views as he also asserted in his chronicle that the sultanate was specifically granted to the Ottoman sultans, who deserved it by merit.[71] But his intention to provide a legal proof for the legitimacy of the Ottoman sultan obliged Lütfi Paşa to adopt a legal perspective that was lacking in Kınalızade or Bidlisi, who approached the subject primarily from philosophical and mystical perspectives, respectively, despite their occasional use of juristic vocabulary such as permissible (*jāʾiz*) and obligatory (*wājib*). To establish the legal basis of Ottoman rulership, allegiance by subjects and the capability of exerting control were really the two undisputable qualities of the ruling Ottoman sultan that could be drawn from the canonical juristic compendiums of the Hanafi school.[72]

The merit theory, the third principal view on rulership, did not receive any specific elaboration, despite its influence in shaping visions on Ottoman rulership. For any author who wrote on Ottoman rulership, there was no question that the reigning ruler deserved his position by merit but no one ventured to elaborate on the necessary conditions that one needed to possess in order to qualify to succeed to the throne by merit. Bidlisi, Ibn Kemal, Lütfi Paşa, Celalzade, and many others enumerated the merits of individual Ottoman sultans or the dynasty in general but did not offer them as objective requirements for rulership. Yet personal merits and virtues were among the most extensively treated subjects of political writing in this period. However, instead of promoting personal merit as a condition of legitimacy, all these authors elaborated on merit as a prescription to improve the quality of rulership without compromising the prevailing conviction that considered the sultanate as a grace from God, modeled on prophetic leadership. The question of merit was treated as a moral issue for the perfection of one's government rather than as a legal or a philosophical issue for the legitimation of one's authority. Just as the very caliphate or the poleship, the merit discourse also appeared as a moral paradigm for good governance. Enumerating the distinctive virtues of the Ottoman dynasty, for example, imposed a moral regime over the ruler in office.

Exposing his firm belief that rulership was a grace from God, Kınalızade stated that the "rulership (*salṭanat ve ḥükūmet ve pādişāhī*) is a gift from God (*ʿaṭiyye-i rabbānī ve hediyye-i ilāhī*)."[73] Despite this statement, he related an instructive story from the Ottoman experience of succession that attributed a determining role to merit in qualifying to be a ruler.[74] As told by Zati, when Zati was young, he once eulogized Prince Korkud who appointed him as his confidante (*nedīm*). In one of their excursions for entertainment at sea, he observed that Korkud treated one of his confidants despicably, making him an object of amusement. Zati then realized that Prince Korkud was not worthy of the sultanate and promptly quit his entourage, a decision that was eventually vindicated: "Indeed, his [Korkud's] star of felicity melted away and the throne of the Ottoman sultanate flew away from him."[75] Kınalızade told the story in relation to the subject of governing the people (*ehl-i medīne*) according to their merits (*istiḥḳāḳ*) and abilities (*istiʿdād*). Zati was frustrated with Korkud's behavior because he used a learned person as an object of amusement which, in his mind, made the prince unworthy for the Ottoman throne, for it showed a lack of the administrative ability required to qualify for rulership. Whether the story was authentic or not, the message Kınalızade intended to convey was that although rulership was attained only by God's grace, one needed to be qualified by merit in order to receive that grace. Kınalızade's subscription to both the grace and merit theories at the same time suggests that his conception of rulership as a grace from God was quite different from that of Bidlisi and Ibn Kemal. For Kınalızade, God granted rulership as a grace only to a worthy one thus leaving the venue open for a candidate to strive to receive that grace. Whether or not Ibn Kemal may have agreed with this notion, he does not seem to leave any leeway for such an event by explicitly stating that the individual had no role in attracting divine grace:

> The lights of leadership (*riyāset*) were illuminating his face. His words were loaded with the secrets of governance (*esrār-ı siyāset*). His nature was a mine and source of sagacity, and a manifestation and a meeting place of virtuous traits. Because it was his destined fortune to rule, rulership and governance were settled on him.[76]

A syncretic view of succession that combined the above three perceptions is illustrated by a telling story Celalzade narrates in his book of ethics about how rulership was granted:[77] God sends a letter to David by Gabriel and orders David to have it read by his sons, instructing him that only the one who could read it would succeed (*ḫilāfet*) him. No one but Solomon, the smallest son of David and the least likely, reads the letter even without opening it, and thus qualifies to inherit his father's caliphate. David then appoints Solomon as his successor and orders the scholars (ulema) of the Sons of Israel to ask questions of Solomon to test him. On Solomon's successful responses to all questions, they too decide that he deserves the caliphate. The moral of the story shows that God grants rulership without a prior qualification because He granted it to someone who seemed to be the least likely person. Nevertheless, the one who received God's grace also happened to be the most meritorious, as necessitated by God's wisdom. The crafted story lends validity to all three prevalent views on becoming a ruler: God grants rulership to Solomon as a grace who is already qualified by merit and inherits the authority to subjugate from his father. But more than Celalzade's eclecticism, the story elucidates a theological principle that made this unified view possible: With His absolute knowledge God knows who deserves rulership by merit with the potential to exert authority over others. Therefore the unconditionality of God's grace pertains to the world of causality, as perceived by humans.

Whether others were aware of this story or not, its moral may not have been objectionable to other authors on the topic, even by Lütfi Paşa, whose depiction of how Ottoman sultans attained their position in his chronicle fully condoned what Celalzade and Bidlisi advocated. One reason these authors gave different accounts in their works despite the general conformity of their ideas is that they addressed different audiences and wrote for different purposes, which may have forced them to further pronounce or tone down their convictions as demanded by the situation. Bidlisi wrote his advice book for the ruler, whose rule was already legitimate by all accounts, and his intention was to educate the ruler about the principles of good government. Yet his writing is still geared to bolster Bayezid's image both at home and abroad against his rivals. So, in order to portray Bayezid as the perfect ruler, he envisioned rulership on the model of God's government and considered it prophetic rulership.

As its exemplar, he sought to profile a ruler who was commissioned to rule in the way ruler-prophets were. According to this view, the position granted to the ruler as a grace from God was a specific kind of rulership with peculiar obligations, not any kind of political authority. Bidlisi was not concerned with proving to the ruled how a legitimate rulership was instituted, a concern that forced Lütfi Paşa to write his treatise on the Ottoman caliphate. In *Khalāṣ al-Umma*, Lütfi Paşa spoke against the skeptics of the Ottoman caliphate, and instructed the reader on the legal strictures regarding a legitimate rulership. As he recounted, the skeptics advocated a theological view of the caliphate succinctly formulated by Nasafi in his popular treatise on the Islamic creed, a view that did not grant the title caliphate to a ruler who lacked Qurayshi descent. Lütfi Paşa was forced to counterbalance that argument by remaining within the confines of Islamic disciplines, for mystical, philosophical, or cultural perceptions and imageries were useless against a theological argument. He then resorted to the mainstream views of post-Abbasid Hanafi jurisprudence and claimed that the theological formula of Nasafi had long been invalidated by leading jurists.

Lütfi Paşa composed his treatise during the height of Ottoman-Safavid conflict, accompanied by an intensive propaganda war. Ideological warfare was no less intense on the western front as the Ottomans encountered the Habsburg and Portuguese claims for universal sovereignty.[78] Around the mid-sixteenth century, when the Ottoman claims for universal rulership peaked, there seems to have been a concerted effort at the Ottoman court to revive the discourse on the caliphate through its juristic expositions, i.e. in the language of law. Mystical elaborations of the caliphate mainly addressed the broader Sufi constituency at home and the Islamicate world with little value for the global competition of universal authority. Multiple translations of political works from Mamluk jurists that would facilitate legitimating the ruler as the caliph of time testify for this endeavor. At this juncture, a certain Mahmud b. Ahmed el-Kayseri copied a comprehensive juristic treatise in Persian, *Ādāb al-Khilāfa wa Asbāb al-Ḥiṣāfa* (Manners of the Caliphate and Reasons of Good Judgement), in 1542 and presented it to Süleyman, which addressed all major questions regarding the post-Abbasid status of the caliphate.[79] It was written by a certain Ibrahim b. Muhammed in 1464 and dedicated to then reigning Shirwanshah ruler Farrukh Yasar I (r. 1462–1501), who was later killed by the Safavids in 1501. The work portrays the caliphate strictly as a historical institution and as a successorship to the Prophet, explicitly refuting the appellation *khalīfat Allāh* that became the basis of the Sufistic visions of the caliphate. Ibrahim argues that the Qurayshi descent is not a condition for the legitimacy of the caliphate and that one may legitimately become a caliph in a number of ways, including by domination (*istīlā*).[80] For comparison, Jurjani's (d. 1413) *Sharh al-Mawāqif*, the main textbook on theology in Ottoman madrasas, defined caliphate exclusively as successor to the Prophet (*khalīfat Rasūl*) and argued that Qurayshi descent was a strict condition.[81] Although out of favor, the juristic theory of the caliphate did not completely vanish in the sixteenth century, only overshadowed by more elaborate Sufistic imaginations.

The Nature of the Ruler

The perception of rulership as a grace from God, regardless of the personal merit of its recipient, did not grant the ruler the freedom to rule as he wished but instead created a contract between the ruler and God. Once rulership was conferred, then the ruler's governance became a part of God's government of His creation and the ruler was required to rule in accordance with divine will in order to maintain his rulership. Such a government, above all, depended on the moral perfection and piety of the ruler who was expected to implement justice and apply God's law on Earth. Thus reforming the ruler for moral and spiritual worthiness of God-given rulership constituted one of the central questions of political theory during the age of Süleyman. Because rulership was conceived to be an existential requirement necessitated by human nature, it had to serve a greater purpose than simply administering people's affairs. The perfect ruler is ascribed a pivotal role to straddle through temporal and spiritual realms, and mediate between the divine and the corporeal. He could perform this task only by turning himself from being a sultan to God's caliph on Earth, which required being endowed with the same qualities as the prophets or the perfect human being as envisioned by the Sufis. In envisioning this ideal ruler who could provide the necessary guidance and the means to respond to the needs of human nature, mainstream political writing of the period focused on the morality of the ruler more than the normative principles of rulership.

There were two principal approaches on the question of morality in rulership. The first was the juristic view primarily voiced by Birgivi, Lütfi Paşa, and Dede Cöngi, who preferred to express their views in a discipline that had fallen out of favor as a medium for expressing political theory in this period. By contrast, ironically, such high-profile jurists as Bidlisi, Kınalızade, Taşköprizade, or Ibn Kemal totally abandoned the juristic mode of reasoning but displayed a more mystical and philosophical approach. The juristic view, which traditionally centered on the problems of legitimacy and necessary qualifications for rulership, was concerned with moral issues only to a limited extent. By the sixteenth century, the juristic theory had become quite complacent about rulership and to a large extent had expelled moral and legal requirements for rulership from political theory, and viewed rulership only through very broad categories. In the prevailing juristic view, the ruler was usually characterized as either an oppressor (*ẓālim*) or a just (*ʿādil*) one while neither of these had any effect on the legitimacy or the design of rulership. The jurists were more concerned about the application of law than designing a morally ideal rulership because, according to an established juristic view, the ruler, especially in the post-Abbasid Hanafi strain, was not expected to morally guide the community but only to apply the law. A formulaic expression of this common juristic view is given by a certain Hacı Ilyas in a cathechistic manual he translated: "Know that the ruler does not get deposed for immoral conduct. According to Shafi'i he is deposed for immoral conduct or oppression."[82] As long as the religious law was applied, the juristic view had little to say on the design of rulership. This was one reason why many authors who were jurists by training and profession wrote their political works in genres other than jurisprudence.

According to the moralist-philosophical view by which the ruler was conceived to be a moral guide for the community, his morality became the most important aspect of rulership. Works written on rulership from this perspective focused on the personality of the ruler, inculcating the idea that the best ruler was morally the most perfect one. However, authors writing on the ethics of rulership faced a challenging practical situation. They were all aware that well-established political conventions left them little room to interfere in shaping the practice of rulership. However elaborate they might be in designing ideal rulership, they knew that there was always a greater possibility that a less worthy person might succeed to the throne. The main pursuit of moralist political theory then became how to turn the ruler in office into a worthy one.

For a political writer concerned with how to turn a rulership into a superior one by reforming the ruler, the most fundamental issue was whether the character of the ruler, or that of any human being, could be changed. In juristic political theory what mattered was a human being's actions rather than his personality. That was why juristic theory focused on a human being's actions while moral theory focused on one's personality. Moral theorists attributed greater power to one's personality in the outcome of his actions. As a result, views on the mutability of one's nature created a deep divide in political theory between Bidlisi and all other authors on rulership in the sixteenth century. At the root of this disagreement was one of the perennial questions of moral theory: whether human nature was set by birth or shaped by experience. Hızır Münşi defined character in his work on political ethics as follows:[83]

> Scholars of this science [ethics] defined character (*khulq*) as follows: character is a faculty (*malaka*) from which human acts come about naturally without thinking (*raviyyat*). Namely, character is a natural disposition (*khāsiyyat*) that enables the occurrence of ease in acts necessitated by the self, without reflection (*tafakkur*) and deliberation (*tadabbur*). If an action comes about not with ease and without thinking but with effort (*takalluf*) and thinking (*tafakkur*), then it cannot be called primordial character (*khulq-i fiṭrī*) but could be called learned behavior (*takhalluq*).[84]

This definition of character was almost identical with the one provided by Kınalızade and suits the general framework of most other writers on political ethics who did not define the term.[85] Their main goal was to endow the ruler with noble traits by changing his character for the better. Many of them were well aware of the dispute among the scholars of ethics about the mutability of disposition and felt it necessary to express their view before elaborating on the traits necessary for the ruler. Bidlisi, who stood up against the mainstream view, staunchly defended the idea that character was part of one's nature and therefore immutable: He asserted that "changing one's primordial nature (*taghyīr-i fiṭrat*) through training and effort is not possible (*maqdūr nīst*)."[86] The prevailing view in political theory, however, most explicitly voiced by Kınalızade and Hızır Münşi, was that character can change with instruction and training. As recorded by Jurjani in his encyclopedia of concepts, *Ta'rīfāt*, the majority view since medieval times among philosophers, mystics, and ethicists was that human nature was mutable.[87] For the advocates of both views, it was essential to educate and convince the ruler about the most fundamental quality of character in order to make their ethical teaching effective for him.

Hızır Münşi resorted to a very assertive language in proving that character can change. Such an approach first of all deprived the ruler of any excuse for failing to endow himself with noble traits that were deemed to be the basis of good government. Second, whether the ruler possessed a noble character or not, Hızır Münşi made him believe that his character was always prone to change for the worse or for the better. Thus he encouraged the ruler to believe that the noblest and most difficult traits, such as courage (*shacā'at*), are within the reach of human endeavor. This made moral education and guidance essential components of rulership, a noble task that Hızır Münşi and like-minded authors thought they were performing. Finally, Hızır Münşi reminded the ruler that striving to change people's characters was part of the obligations expected from rulership, first by posing as a moral role model and then by undertaking policies to improve the moral quality of subjects. Such a conception of rulership was part of the virtuous regime, highlighted as the ideal form of association by philosophers, in which the members unite for the attainment of virtues that would lead to ultimate happiness.

For Hızır Münşi, intelligent people, religious law, and words of the wise as well as eminent philosophers all agreed, without doubt, that character can change (*khulq mumkin al-taghayyur ast*). He presented his view as a summary of the accounts of Ghazali, Tusi, and Davvani, three of the most influential scholars of political ethics for Ottoman intellectuals in this period.[88] To illustrate his point he gave several cases of changing one's disposition: Among them were an ignorant (*jāhil*) person who by frequenting gatherings of scholars, tended to acquire knowledge (*'ilm*); a rebel (*'āṣī*) who gave up committing sins and repented because of listening to advice and admonition; and a cowardly and fearful person who became brave by going through battlefields and staying in places of danger and fear. Besides being examples, all these changes of disposition, namely acquisition of knowledge, being courageous, and avoiding sins, were among the most frequent admonitions directed to the ruler in political literature. Despite his firm belief in the changeability of character in principle, Hızır Münşi thought that peoples' natures (*ṭibāʿ*) and temperaments constrained their ability to change their characters.[89] Such an admission of a deeper essence in man's nature that may dictate the degree of change in character brought Hızır Münşi a bit closer to Bidlisi's position, which denied any possibility of personal edification and moral transformation.

Although his general view agreed with that of Hızır Münşi, Kınalızade was not certain about the mutability of human character and felt it necessary to discuss three principal positions on the question: First, that character was natural and thus impossible to alter in any way; second, that character consisted of two parts, one mutable and one immutable; and third, that character was not natural and therefore mutable, a view Kınalızade singled out as the right one and presented as the one held by the majority of ancient and modern philosophers:

> The majority of philosophers thought that the human soul was not naturally disposed to good or evil but capable of both and fit to move to any direction. It is possible to change all characters because no character is conditioned by nature. Then why would changing it be impossible? If it was by nature and impossible to change and convert, then the laws and regulations instituted by prophets, and the principles of education and government that scholars are united to apply, would have been absurd.[90]

What Hızır Münşi asserted to be a unanimous view of philosophers and scholars was given as the majority view by Kınalızade, in accordance with Tusi and Davvani, who, despite their convictions about the mutability of human nature, pointed to major disagreements on the subject and the difficulty of singling out the truth on the matter.[91] At the bottom of the controversy, as commonly stated, was the question of how a human being's nature was formed. No writer on political ethics in this period seems to have had any objection to the idea that all acquired habits were alterable. They also commonly believed that human nature itself was not alterable. Thus the subject of dispute was whether a human being's nature was inherently disposed to good or evil, and whether a certain kind of disposition was dictated by one's nature, which human beings had no power to change. On this point, Kınalızade looks as confounded as Tusi and Davvani by Galen's views, a respected ancient authority, who stated that human beings' nature was of three kinds: good, bad, and the one capable of both, the last constituting the majority. Despite their general conviction that character was not shaped by nature, none of them refuted Galen but were content to indicate that even if Galen's view were taken for granted, that still proved that the natures of most people were alterable. Although Kınalızade looks convinced that human nature was alterable, on empirical evidence, he agreed with Tusi and Davvani that altering every kind of nature might not be possible.[92]

The discussion of character was important because, whether they discussed the theoretical side of the subject or not, all authors writing on political ethics in this period commonly believed that a ruler needed a particular kind of character and one of the fundamental objectives of advice books was to inculcate the necessary disposition in a ruler. It was assumed that this character should be shaped by the moral ideals commonly dubbed *aḫlāḳ-ı kerīme.* Unlike the juristic approach, which emphasized right and wrong as well as obligations in terms of constrictions and commands, the moralist approach emphasized the acquisition of such a character that would lead the ruler to doing right and abstaining from wrong by nature. For these authors, such a character was necessary because first, they thought that good governance depended on the good disposition of ruler; and second, they envisioned the ruler as a moral guide for the community.

Both Kınalızade and Hızır Münşi remained within the confines of ethical philosophy. Despite their use of scriptural evidence, they argued mainly through philosophical concepts. For Kınalızade, for example, the whole relevance of ethical philosophy and religious guidance was at stake. Because accepting the mutability of human character saves ethical teachings and prophetic laws from being reduced to irrelevance. But Bidlisi thought differently. He set out to prove that, much like rulership, one's noble character (*akhlāq-i karīma*) was a grace from God. He based his argument on theological concepts of acquisition (*kasb*) and will (*irāda*). From a binary construct, he thought that human being's qualifications and possessions are either acquired or natural. In this duality one's character fell into the category of natural. Bidlisi granted human beings no power at all to alter one's character because that would mean working against the will of God.

For Bidlisi the beauty (*ḥusn*) and ugliness (*qubḥ*) of human character (*akhlāq-ı insānī*) were a preordained grace from God, because happiness (*sa'ādat*) or misery (*shakāvat*) are innate (*fiṭrī*) and congenital (*nasabī*). People have different characters because of the way they were created. He was also well aware of the perennial debate about the mutability of human beings' nature and clarified his position in his answer to the same textbook question to which Kınalızade, Hızır Münşi, and many before them responded:

> On this subject there is disagreement among the philosophers (*arbāb-i ḥikmat*) whether altering human character (*tabdīl-i akhlāq*) is practicable (*muyassar*) and possible (*maqdūr*) or whether it is fixed (*muqarrar*) and predestined (*muqaddar*), because character for the most part originates from concupiscible (*shahvat*) and irascible (*ghazāb*)

> faculties, and these corporal faculties (*quvā-yi jismānī*) are bound up with the complexion of creation (*mizāj-i unṣūr*) that was mixed with the primordial nature of human beings (*fiṭrat-i basharī*) since the beginning. Therefore nobody can alter the complexion of creation (*mizāj-i khilqat*) to another type, and natural faculties (*quvā-yi tabīʿī*) and human or animal souls (*arvāḥ-i nafsānī ve ḥayvānī*) cannot be put into a different condition (*ṭavr*).[93]

Despite sounding unyielding on this position, Bidlisi also attempted not to compromise the very reason for writing on ethics by attributing a limited role to human agency in changing one's nature. This limited change could be possible because of the structure of human nature, which potentially (*bi al-quvva*) comprises all virtues and vices. Here Bidlisi's mystical orientation came into play and he accorded only spiritual masters the capacity to change an initiate's nature. An average individual was still not given any power in changing his own nature. People who were capable of altering one's nature were dubbed spiritual doctors (*tabībān-i rūḥānī*): prophets (*anbiyā*), friends of God (*avliyā*), and righteous spiritual masters (*murshidān-i ḥaqqānī*).[94] These spiritual doctors bring the potential virtues into action while suppressing potential vices through laws (*sharʿ*), governance (*siyāsī*), and prohibitions (*māniʿa*). The ones who possess pure hearts are much more eligible than those with ugly natures.[95]

Despite the possibility of improvement through reformation under the guidance of a spiritual doctor, Bidlisi still thought that this would not change the original state of one's nature. For him, changing primordial nature (*taghyīr-i fiṭrat*) through training (*tarbiyat*) and effort (*saʿy*) was not possible (*maqdūr nīst*) unless the person was suitable by his nature (*tabʿ*) and disposition (*jibillat*). Although the manifestations (*āsār*) of one's nature could be enhanced or suppressed by training, changing or converting the fundamentals of one's nature would be beyond the capability of humans.[96] This negative view on the mutability of human character did not prevent Bidlisi from prescribing morality as the most important component of rulership:

> Good character (*akhlāq-i jibillī*) is the foundation of caliphate and world-conquering (*jihāndārī*), and in regard to the continuity of government it is similar to the parts and elements of a body. When the fortunate ones appear, their works display good habits and beautiful character, and their deeds denote their sound creation and righteous natures.[97]

Believing in the immutability of human character and writing a work of ethics may look paradoxical. But what Bidlisi aimed at was to write a moral code of behavior to follow whether one was inherently good or evil natured. He did not believe or aspire to change human nature by ethical teachings.

However, regardless of the quality of one's predisposition there was an objective morality to follow. In this regard, an evil-natured person could not change his nature but could still be moral by observing the code of behavior Bidlisi prescribed. Given that Bidlisi also believed that rulership was an exclusive grace from God without any prior condition of worthiness, he thought it equally possible for someone with moral integrity, or someone with an immoral character, to become a ruler. As he stated, a ruler who was gifted with a good nature was a great benefit for the ruled while a ruler with a weak nature was harmful to state and society.[98] Therefore, by definition, a morally perfect ruler was a guide for the community the way prophets were and deserved to be caliph, for he had the capacity to combine material and spiritual authorities. As for the rulers of a weak nature, they fall into the category of material rulers only, and are not worthy of the caliphate. To be eligible for the higher authority that extended to both spiritual and temporal realms, these rulers need to pursue a strict spiritual training to keep the vices of their nature under control and put the virtues of their creation to work. For this, they would need a spiritual doctor. Bidlisi framed moral behavior as a performative act rather than a personality change, therefore he considered perfect rulership achievable by even the weakest in moral character.

The Question of Morality

The emphasis on the moral traits of the ruler was well warranted because the main quest of political writing was to educate the sultan to turn his rulership into a virtuous one. Ethics became the mainstream of political writing because, since Farabi, the best polity was defined as *al-madīna al-fāḍila*, and numerous ethical works examined human character using the dichotomy of virtues versus vices. The ruler and the regime were evaluated according to the same criteria. Best exemplified in Farabi's works, and extensively adopted by later writers of political ethics, this construction characterized nonvirtuous regimes as *fāṣiq*, *dālla*, *jāhila*, *fāsida*, and the like, that is, according to vices that are adopted from human moral qualities. Even in juristic theory, as indicated earlier, the most common distinction between types of rulerships was primarily a moral one, between the *ẓālim* (oppressor) and the *ʿādil* (just).

In principle, the ruler was not prescribed an exclusive code of ethical conduct that was substantially different from that for the general public.[99] However, as revealed by Bidlisi, the ruler was expected to possess higher standards of morality: "Because rulers are above (*fāʾiq va mustavlī*) their subjects (*zīrdastān*) in appearance (*ṣūrat*), they should be above their followers in spirit (*maʿnī*) as well."[100] Because the ruler was envisioned to be a moral guide for the community, he was expected to reach moral perfection in noble traits (*malakāt-i karīma*). Because rulership was designed to follow the model of prophetic-rulership as a guide for the community, the ruler was, above all, envisioned to be a moral person. In addition, one of the well-established convictions about the function of rulership in society was that "people follow their rulers" (*al-nās ʿalā dīn mulūkihim*). The canonical status of this ancient maxim in political teachings further led authors to envision the ruler as a moral guide for the ruled.

To meet the expectations of a superior rulership, the kind of morality prescribed for the ruler was usually dubbed a noble character (*akhlāq-i karīma*) or divine morality (*akhlāq Allāh*).[101] The former was a general term for a morally perfect human being envisioned in the writings of ethical tradition. The latter, however, was used in a more specific sense to denote the type of morality the ruler should have as God's vicegerent on Earth. Divine morality was a code for reforming rulership on the model of divine government, which prescribed that the ruler needed to be endowed with God's moral attributes as His vicegerent on Earth and as a moral guide to the ruled. To deserve to be called *imām* (God's vicegerent), one needed to resemble Him through divine morality.

The prescription of divine morality for the ruler is more visible in the accounts of Bidlisi and Dizdar. Bidlisi stated that although a perfect manifestation (*jibillat-i maẓhar-i kāmilī*) was a result of one's primordial nature (*fiṭrat*), it is incumbent upon the ruler to endow himself with the requirement of "*takhallaqū bi akhlāq Allāh*."[102] Dizdar did not present divine morality as a requirement for rulership, but made the latter a means to attain a high moral status: "Realm (*mamlaka*) and rulership (*salṭana*) are suitable means for the attainment of commendable traits until the ruler reaches a position (*maqām*) where he is endowed with divine morality, as mentioned in the statement 'Endow yourselves with divine morality,' and is characterized by divine attributes (*ṣifāt-i rubūbiyya*)."[103] If the ruler did not follow this path, then rulership might be a means to lead the ruler to despicable traits, to the extent of claiming divinity (*rubūbiyya*), as in the case of pharaoh. In this way, Dizdar presented rulership as a medium that may lead to two opposite sets of traits, a view inspired by the two major types of regimes constructed in political philosophy as voiced by Kınalızade. After dividing regimes into virtuous and unvirtuous, Kınalızade stated that the purpose of ruling in the former case was to attain divine morality (*akhlāq Allāh*), while in the latter it was domination dictated by the concupiscent soul (*nafs-i ammāra*).[104]

When divine morality or noble character entailed such traits as generosity (*sakhā*), forgiveness (*ʿafv*), and nobleness (*karam*), they were deemed more important for rulership than other personal traits, not only because of their obvious benefits for the community but also because these traits were regarded as the most similar to God's attributes.[105] But a more or less standard description of a noble character was one that comprised the platonic cardinal virtues of wisdom (*ḥikmat*), continence (*ʿiffat*), courage (*shajāʿat*), and justice (*ʿadl*).[106] Since Ibn Miskawayh's construction of his ethical theory around these four virtues, this perception of human beings' moral character came to pervade all strands of moral teachings including political and Sufi ethics.[107] Some authors, such as Hızır Münşi and Bidlisi, built their whole theory of personal ethics on this construction and defined these traits by emphasizing their relevance to good rulership. In line with Ibn Miskawayh, they thought that these virtues comprised all other virtues and were sufficient to lead one to moral perfection. When discussing the branches of each virtue, they highlighted the traits the ruler needed most in rulership and illustrated these principles with cases from government. Despite this emphasis on the traits that the ruler needed most, the basic framework of morality was no different than the one prescribed for the common people.

Although the ruler did not have a special code of morality other than the expectation that he be an example of moral rectitude, thanks to his sovereign status, some authors granted him certain prerogatives, especially in areas that may not have affected the quality of government. These prerogatives included some special characteristics peculiar to the common images of rulership and certain common breaches of established ethical norms and religious rules. For the former, certain vices or a lack of certain virtues was considered normal for the ruler while being regarded, in principle, as reprehensible, such as majesty and splendor. Ottoman chroniclers, for example, who rarely criticized their rulers, were much more complacent about the moral condition of rulers and usually attributed the cause of their immorality to other factors.

As for the common breaches of established norms, wine-drinking had been given special attention in the advice literature. Despite strict legal prohibitions against it, drinking does not seem to have been a rare event among Ottoman rulers and the elite in general.[108] The general tendency was not to tolerate this misconduct in rulership and many authors devoted long sections to explain the prohibition of drinking by describing its harmful effects on the body and government.[109] The section on drinking alcohol in Tusi, for example, was completely omitted in Kınalızade, who followed Davvani on this matter and instead reasserted the prohibition on drinking alcohol.[110] Although Bidlisi advised the ruler to abstain from drinking, he did not use prohibitive language but showed leniency. In case the ruler could not avoid drinking alcohol, Bidlisi then advised him to drink grape wine, which he singled out as the most beneficial.[111] For Bidlisi it was not wine-drinking but drunkenness that was morally reprehensible, a view shared by Jahrami, who not only permitted wine-drinking but also provided a moral ground for such a perceived breach of the religious code: "Even if wine is prohibited by religious law," he stated, "it is considered permissible by custom."[112] Both Bidlisi and Jahrami displayed more concern about the adverse effects of wine-drinking on the body and judgment, which would hinder the ruler's ability to govern properly.[113] In this regard, they seem to follow the same concern as Nizam al-Mulk and Tusi, who, while being complacent about wine-drinking, attempted to place it in a moral framework by establishing the manners of drinking, in order to minimize its adverse effects on government and courtly life.[114]

For perfect rulership, the ruler needed to act within the moral framework drawn for government. Regardless of whether the ruler is already endowed with virtues or not, he could still achieve a higher form of rulership by simply acting as moral. There is a complete overlap between a personal quest for moral perfection and the ruler's quest for perfection in rulership. Because the morality of the ruler was deemed to be the basis of good government, the ruler's character and how to mold it became central to moralist political theory. The moral profile of an ideal ruler, however, was a matter of preference. Taşköprizade, for example, envisioned an austere ruler with the qualities of an ascetic.[115] He thought of the ruler as an inheritor of prophetic rulership and expected him to possess the same qualities as the prophets. His list of archetypical rulers included Joseph, Moses, Solomon, Muhammed, and the rightly guided caliphs who ruled the same way. There is nothing in his advice about the glory and grandeur of rulership. Instead he points to the discrepancy between the material wealth that these model rulers controlled and their personal abstention from everything that material wealth implies, such as luxury and extravagance. He did not teach the ruler rules for running the government, but moral principles to observe while ruling, such as altruism and generosity. The profile of the ruler he described stood in stark contrast to the contemporary rulership practiced in the Ottoman Empire and posed an implicit critique of Süleyman's reign. Taşköprizade did not attribute to the ruler any special privilege and only expected him to have the same moral qualities expected of anyone pursuing moral perfection. In fact all this advice that Taşköprizade directed to the sultan was set forth by Ghazali in his *Iḥyā* for any believer, denying the sultan any prerogative for moral breaches. The ruler would be subject to the same moral criteria, only with a higher standard.

The moralist writers on rulership faced a paradox when arranging prescriptions for the moral perfection of the ruler. On the one hand, they readily supplied manuals for moral training to inculcate the kind of morality they thought an ideal ruler should possess as a moral guide for the community. On the other, they were well aware of some of the common breaches of the moral code of rulership. Yet there was no institutional check on the moral misbehavior of the ruler and the only way to address it was to inculcate a sense of responsibility, and persuade the ruler about right and wrong as well as educate him to acquire a strong personality equipped with moral integrity. One of the principal instruments of persuasion was the empirical argument that immorality unavoidably leads to losing one's rulership. Because rulership was depicted to be a grace from God, His grace was presented to be contingent on one's good governance, which is in turn predicated on good morals. While no condition was necessary for the acquisition of rulership, there was a rigid set of conditions to retain it. This was one of the most persuasive ways to teach morality, well suited to the political realities of the period. The moralists' one repetitive warning to the sultan was that he receives rulership by grace but retains it only by acting moral.

Despite the instrumental use of this argument in enforcing just government, it was not merely a rhetorical device of persuasion but a sincere belief that sprang from the prevailing notions regarding cosmology imbued with theology and mythology. To illustrate this point, Celalzade, a punctiliously legal-minded statesman who spent his career in drafting numerous law codes during the reign of Süleyman, narrated a story where the non-Muslim king of Nubia teaches the last Umayyad caliph Marwan ibn Abd Allah, who had just lost his throne to the Abbasids and took refuge in Nubia, that God took back their sovereignty and bestowed it upon the Abbasids because the Umayyads committed sins.[116] Like other moralists, Celalzade knew well that, in Ottoman practice, even the least moral candidate could succeed to rulership and his rule would still be perfectly legitimate. That is why he presented morality not as a requirement for succession or legitimation, but for staying in office as a favor from God.

The Status of Rulership among Humankind

The goal of improving the moral quality of rulership was to make it suitable for the status to which it was ascribed among humankind. Because rulership was putatively considered as an existential requirement for the existence of human association, it was commonly referred to as a status, a degree, or a rank (*martaba, daraja, rutba*) of high esteem. Jili (d. 1329), for example, stated that the "highest rank among humankind is prophethood, then caliphate, then vizierate."[117] Such laudatory remarks certainly served a eulogistic function. Yet, the reasons cited for the loftiness of this position portrayed a particular type of rulership that deserved to be considered as such, and furnished the ruler with a prescription to attain that status. Excluding an author such as Lütfi Paşa, who displayed no interest in the moral quality of rulership, a common goal among the political authors in this period was to promote the status of a ruler in society from a position at the top of the political hierarchy to a status among humankind by perfecting his moral and spiritual qualifications.[118] Mehmed Neşrî (d. 1520?), for example, in the preface of his chronicle of the Ottoman dynasty, considers only scholar-rulers on the same plane as prophets:

> The noblest ranks among humankind are three: prophets (*anbiyâ*), rulers (*ümerâ*), and scholars (*'ulemâ*). Prophets are tasked with spreading the message, the ulema with scholarship and worshipping, and rulers with justice and governance. . . . If a ruler becomes a scholar of the Sharia, studies history, and learns accounts of past kings, then he unifies the three ranks in himself. Through the divine light (*envâr-ı*

> *ilâhî*) that enlightens his heart, he manifests prophethood (*nübüvvet*) and experiences (*kâşif*) the condition of prophethood (*risâlet*). Prophets spread the message but rulers execute and govern. That is why rulers are called shadow of God on Earth. They are manifestations of [God's] ordinances and governance and treasures of secrets and leadership. Prophethood and rulership (*şâhî*) are like two seals on one finger.[119]

In addressing Süleyman, the anonymous *Risāla* explicitly stated that only a particular type of rulership earns such high esteem: "If the caliph is pious (*ṣāliḥ*), then he is the one around whom the world revolves."[120] Dizdar, Taşköprizade, and Bidlisi, along similar lines, admonished the ruler against the degradation of the status of rulership caused by a failure to meet necessary qualifications. After instructing that "the realm (*mamlaka*) and the sultanate are perfect instruments for two opposite ends: the inculcation of commendable or reprehensible traits," Dizdar warned that "having reprehensible traits leads to a claim for divinity as in the case of pharaoh," a position so despicable in the Muslim tradition.[121] For Taşköprizade, if the ruler followed his whims and did not show mercy toward the people, then he turned into the vicar of Antichrist the cursed (*nāʾib al-Dajjāl al-lāʿin*) and the enemy of God and vicegerent of Satan (*khalīfat al-Shayṭān*).[122] Whether Taşköprizade considered such a ruler legitimate is not explicit in his exposition but, defying the mainstream tendency of complacency, he made no accommodation for injustice, an attitude that made him one of the most uncompromising political authors of the time.

Though not as sharp as Taşköprizade, Bidlisi also had a very low opinion of rulers who failed to meet the conditions that made them the shadow of God. For him, if the ruler did not endow himself with spiritual qualities and godly moral traits (*akhlāq-i ilāhī*), then he did not deserve to be the shadow of God. Calling such rulers sultan was as metaphorical (*istiʿāra*) as calling one piece the queen (*shāh*) in chess.[123] In this view, such a high status among humankind was earned through moral perfection combined with rulership, not simply by ascending to the top of social hierarchy. Despite the general tendency not to question the legitimacy of any ruler, the ideal for the ruler remained to be the administrator of human affairs and the moral guide of community at once. This view turned moral criticism into the basis of mainstream political discourse on rulership.

Bidlisi presented rulership in the same way Sufi masters prescribed a meticulously mapped wayfaring for the attainment of perfection: "The rank (*martaba*) of caliphate, sultanate, and the shadow of God is the most superior (*afḍal*) among the ranks of humans (*marātib-i insānī*)."[124] Bidlisi compared rulership (*salṭanat* or *mulk*) to knowledge (*ʿilm*) and wisdom (*ḥikmat*) and found rulership superior to both because the effects of rulership were more general (*aʿam*) and more comprehensive (*ashmal*).[125] He predicated his argument on two Qur'anic verses related to rulership, 4: 54 and 2: 251. In interpreting the first, he indicated that among the graces mentioned only kingdom (*mulk*) was described as "great" (*ʿaẓīm*). For the second, he pointed out that among the two graces leadership was mentioned ahead of wisdom. Thus Bidlisi sanctions the superiority of the sultanate over other forms of binding authorities among humankind on theological grounds. Here, Bidlisi breaks with the Suhrawardian paradigm that considers authority a function of knowledge. Despite being a Sufi-minded jurist, this was a statement against both Sufis and juristic arguments on the source of comprehensive authority in the Muslim community. By knowledge, the jurists meant their acquired learning as passed down from the prophet on which they considered themselves to have the interpretive monopoly as a collective body. The Sufis, however, meant God's hidden script for His creation that cannot be learned by studying but only by experience. Bidlisi was writing at a time when the authority of the Ottoman ruler was seriously challenged by mystical claims in Anatolia and the juristic establishment whose loyalties to the Ottoman sultan were not unconditional. However, Bidlisi's partisanship does not compromise his portrayal of ideal rulership as one that combines both spiritual and temporal realms. He only accords primacy to executive power over scholarly proficiency and spiritual perfection to reassert the Ottoman ruler's authority over knowledge-based claims, regardless of whether the reigning sultan met the moral and spiritual expectations for perfect rulership or not.

The like-minded Hızır Münşi stated that being a ruler was an exalted and unsurmountable rank. What made rulership most exalted for Hızır Münşi was that the order of the world depended on the existence of a ruler, as necessitated by divine wisdom: "The order of the world (*niẓām-i umūr-i ʿālam*) entirely depends on his [ruler] noble existence. The rein of the majority of human beings is tied to his firm opinion (*barāy-i razīn*). As necessitated by the absolute wisdom of the Knowing God, every multitude is tied to a single authority in order to form a community."[126] For Hızır Münşi, the ruler's status was an existential rank within the complex scheme of creation. For Lütfi Paşa, however, who seemed indifferent to the question of the ruler's moral guidance, it simply referred to one's degree of authority in social hierarchy based on executive power and capacity to dispense justice. He substantiated his view with a juristic opinion taken from a fourteenth-century legal compendium, *Tātārkhāniyya*, and stated that there was no position (*manzila*) and rank (*rutba*) above that of sultan because the benefit of his justice (*inṣāf*) was universal.[127] For him, the very executive power that created political authority was a sufficient proof of the superiority of rulership over all other ranks among humankind.

In *al-ʿAdliyya al-Sulaymāniyya*, Şirvani drew a clear hierarchical line between rulership and poleship by portraying the latter as the undisputed highest authority in the world. For most others it was the sultanate. Yet, the depiction of the sultanate as such was clearly predicated on the Sufistic notion of the perfect human being as a moral guide and, more importantly, the assumption that the ruler represented the inherited authority of the Prophet in representing God's will on Earth. In proving the supremacy of rulership, Bidlisi and Hızır Münşi argued on the basis of what this status entailed, and presented it as the closest human position to that of God's and His prophets' vis-à-vis humanity. From this perspective, the purpose of political writing was to illustrate the position of rulership among humankind and advise the ruler to perform what it entailed.

The idea that the status of ruler was the highest possible position among humankind originated from the ontological views on human nature and one's relationship with God, as elaborated in philosophy and Sufism. In this tradition, the caliphate, as an ontological status, was the highest status human beings could attain after the prophethood. In fact, even prophethood was often framed as the most perfect form of God's vicegerency, the caliphate. Thus, attaining the status of the caliphate as a human being was not the same thing as acquiring the position of caliphate among human beings, for it was a spiritual realization rather than a political acquisition. The jurists, however, and to some extent theologians, paid less attention to the spiritual component of the caliphate and were concerned more with its social and legal construction.

The depiction of the sultanate as the highest position in the world aimed to impose a moral responsibility on the ruler in office to fulfill the expectations of a proper rulership. When an author such as Alayi proclaimed that there was no better (*evlā ve eclā*) grace (*niʿmet*) than the rank (*derece*) of sultanate, he referred to the ideal rulership as he portrayed it and urged the sultan to tailor his rulership to that ideal.[128] This pursuit is more visible in the accounts of Taşköprizade, Bidlisi, and Ensari who, after reminding the ruler that he was endowed with the most exalted position in the world, elaborated on the requirements of executing and retaining this authority. The high status of this office did not necessarily confer upon the ruler the same status as prophets among humankind. Nor could the ruler elevate the status of sultanate simply by virtue of his sheer power to rule. The sultanate earns the ruler the same status as prophets only when modeled after prophetic rulership, which the Sufis equated with poleship.

CHAPTER FOUR

The Caliph and the Caliphate

Do not say, "I conquered this much land with my own sword." Indeed, the kingdom (memleket) belongs to God, then to the Prophet, and then, per God's will, to His caliph."[1]

IN 1532, SÜLEYMAN SENT a royal decree to the governor of Rumelia, Bali Bey, in response to his request for a promotion to the rank of vizier.[2] After praising him with unusually flattering language, the sultan declined the governor's request on purely administrative reasons that he had not yet earned the promotion, but nevertheless instructed him on the nature and purpose of rulership, lest he be misunderstood. The core message of the testimonial was that rulership is simply an instrument of achieving a higher reward in the afterlife; therefore it should not turn into a goal of itself. Namely, rulership should not be pursued for worldly benefits but to renounce them in favor of serving others. Instead of a promotion that would have earned him the much coveted title Pasha, the sultan granted him three spiritual rewards of which the most honoring was designating the governor as commander of the faithful (*emīrü'l-mü'minīn*), an exclusive title of caliphs until the end of the Abbasids. As discussed in Chapter 1, this was, of course, only a descriptive title as the governor's administrative title remained as Beg. Yet the juristic and historical connotations of this title cannot be lost to the Ottoman chancery. Given that Süleyman already presented himself as God's caliph, the hierarchy between the caliph and commander of the faithful is starkly obvious. For Abbasid caliphs, commander of the faithful was their sovereign title in such a way that none of the two titles could stand without the other. No Ottoman sultan seems to have used commander of the faithful as a sovereign title. Süleyman named himself as God's caliph in the sense that the caliphate was a unified authority combining both spiritual and temporal realms, where the title "commander of the faithful" pertains to the latter and therefore is applicable to those who represent the sultan's executive power.

By the time of Süleyman, common usages of the term caliph did not immediately connotate the historical caliphate as the universal political leadership of the Muslim community with the claim that it succeeded the position of the Prophet. Two contemporary dictionaries, for example, defined the caliph as great ruler (*ulū sulṭān, ulū pādişāh, sulṭān-ı aʿẓam*).[3] However, the depiction of the Ottoman ruler as a legitimate caliph and the successor to the Prophet's authority continued to be expressed in poetry, histories, and communiqués. Besides its use as mere laudation, the historical caliphate was invoked mostly to dispel doubts about the legitimacy of the Ottoman ruler or to solidify his position against challenges at home and abroad. Ottoman rulers of this period certainly considered themselves rulers in the line of prophets and caliphs. However, there was no deliberate policy to reinstate the Ottoman sultan as the universal head of the Muslim community by subjugating independent rulers in the Islamic world. Nor was there any systematic political theory to define the historical caliphate in this period. In fact, the principal term that defined the historical caliphate as the successor of the Prophet (*khalīfat Rasūl Allāh*) was rarely used. Yet the caliphate remained one of the most defining designations in use during this period. The predominant concept of the caliphate, however, was the one defined by mystics, not by jurists who considered it as God's vicegerent (*khalīfat Allāh*) that could be attained not through a contract with or subjugation of the Muslim community, but through learning, piety, morality, and spiritual perfection.

God's Government

Qualifying the sultan with such designations as *khalīfa* and *ẓill Allāh* tied rulership to God's government over His creation, which was frequently alluded to as the perfect model and an authoritative source of legitimacy for rulership. Political authors, inspired by theological doctrines regarding God's relation to the creation, inferred manifestations of God's government and compared them to temporal government in order to establish principles of ideal political authority. The most conspicuous outcome of this political reasoning was to conclude that the unity of God's government provided an absolute model for earthly rulership as a single, undivided, and comprehensive authority. This view suggested that moral objectives and true leadership could be achieved only when political authority remained unpartitioned in the form of the sultanate, modeled after God's government.

Alluding to this corollary, Alayi, for example, substantiated his view by citing Ali, a close companion of the Prophet and the fourth rightly guided caliph, who was reported to have said that rulership (*salṭanat*) does not tolerate partnership.[4] Similarly, Bidlisi supported the same view on the basis of a proof he brought from the Qur'an (21: 22), which explained the wisdom behind the oneness of God by indicating that plurality in divinity would cause disorder and conflict.[5] Although the verse does not give any indication that this monotheistic view should serve as a model for rulership, it became increasingly popular in political writings as an evidence to justify the rule of a single authority. This simple logical induction that because there is only one God then there must be only one ruler became a common trope in political literature. The analogy assumes the existence of a direct relationship between God and the ruler. Identifying the ruler (*sulṭān*) as the shadow of God (*sāya-i Ḥaq*), like all other contemporary writers on rulership, Bidlisi further made a logical statement that the shadow of God must be one as God Himself.[6] To justify the existence of rulership, Bidlisi and most of his Sufi-minded contemporaries needed no further evidence than the very government of God.

Once established as the corollary of God's government, the rule of a single person became the benchmark for rulership. To stress the principle of unity in rulership, Bidlisi wrote in a quatrain that a single oppressive ruler was better than a hundred just rulers in a realm.[7] Although he only shared his contemporaries' view, Bidlisi's own career seems to have turned him into an even more vigorous defender of this principle. An accomplished historian, before writing his work on rulership, Bidlisi was well aware of the dynastic struggles that took place for the Ottoman throne and had already witnessed two of them. In most of these struggles, the contenders disputed whether the realm could be divided among themselves. Both Prince Djem (d. 1495) and Prince Ahmed (d. 1513), for example, asked their opponents to divide the realm among themselves.[8] At the end of all these struggles, not only was there only one successor to the throne, but the concept of unigeniture had prevailed against the idea of partitioning rulership. Having constantly faced such challenges, Ottoman political writers like Bidlisi capitalized on the idea that earthly rulership should be a replica of divine government and have only one ruler.

This emphasis on the unity of sovereignty was still a serious concern even for authors living in the strictly centralized sixteenth-century Ottoman Empire because almost every struggle for dynastic succession created a breeding ground for fissiparous tendencies in rulership. Already in the late fifteenth century, Doukas (d. after 1462) observed that it had become customary to have a rebellion at every episode of succession.[9] The Ottomans always managed to neutralize this divisive potential by unflinchingly clinging to the principal of "unpartioned rulership," established as a state tradition from the very beginning. Since its inception, the Ottoman state frequently faced threats to partition the rulership. Stifling the divisive effects of their own Turkic traditions rather quickly, early Ottoman rulers consistently pursued the idea of the rule of a single person as the best feasible form of government.[10] Whether alluding to God's government provided the founders with any guidance or not in this process of state formation, the unity of sovereignty became an uncompromising canon of political theory in the sixteenth century, not only more appealing on theological grounds but also historically proven to be a more successful model in the Ottomans' own experience. The principle of a single ruler was not simply the only recipe for the institution of a virtuous regime but also served a practical political expediency of keeping the empire intact.

For authors who conceived the unity of sovereignty on the model of divine government, the bigger question was to identify the imitable qualities of God's rule for the perfection of earthly rulership. For Bidlisi and Dizdar, rulership on earth and God's rule over creation were analogous. For them rulership could be perfect only insofar as it resembled God's government, and for this reason it had to bear the same characteristics as that of God's. This conviction turned divine government into the most authoritative reference for perfect rulership. Before Bidlisi's philosophical case, his younger contemporary Tursun Beg expressed the idea in plain language in his chronicle:

> With the pen of scribes, the ruler turns the noble into a wretched, and the wretched into a noble . . . with the sword of executioners he takes lives. As such he manifests the attributes of the Necessary Existent as if he shares the sultanate with Him except that the ruler of the world is a mortal.[11]

Among the attributes of God that were invoked in reference to His rulership, Bidlisi highlighted lordship (*rubūbiyyat*) for worldly rulers to imitate. His like-minded predecessor, Davud-i Kayseri, in his commentary of Ibn Arabi's *Fuṣūṣ al-Ḥikam*, used *rubūbiyya* to characterize the governorship of Adam and subsequent poles over the creation as God's deputy.[12] In Ibn Arabi's mystical philosophy, the very act of governance (*siyāsa*), as part of his cosmological construction of government, is inherently tied to and is an extension of God's attribute of Rabb.[13] Rulers, who are endowed with proper qualities and manifest God's attribute as Rabb, for being part of God's *rubūbiyya*, are capable of ruling over His creation and enact laws that are based on divine wisdom. Although the term *rubūbiyya* does not appear in the Qur'an or hadith, the word Rabb, derived from the same root, is among the most commonly mentioned names of God in both sources. *Rubūbiyya*, the act of being a Rabb, had been widely used in mystical theology. Different from other designations referring to God's rulership, such as Malik, which implies ownership and sovereignty, Rabb implies a relational rulership between the servant and the master.[14] A sixteenth-century lexicographer, Ahteri (d. 1579), defined Rabb as possessor (*mālik*), owner (*ṣāḥib*), and master (*seyyid*), and provided its root meaning as to feed (*beslemek*), to complete (*tamām itmek*), to increase (*ziyāde eylemek*), and to accumulate (*cem eylemek*).[15] This lexicographic definition of the term alone clearly indicates that Rabb referred to a specific concept of rulership rather than a mere authority, pointing to the status of the ruler and the functions of rulership. Bidlisi's contemporary, Şeyh Mekki, defined Rabb as owner (*ṣāḥib*) and possessor (*mālik*) with the implications of subjugation (*taḥakkum*) and authority (*salṭanat*).[16] With this corollary, while referring to the unity of sovereignty, Bidlisi also pointed to a moral high ground for political authority. With *rubūbiyya*, Bidlisi argued that caring for subjects and providing guidance are indispensable for good rulership.

In tandem with his definition, Ahteri also provided an illustration for one of the derivatives of Rabb in full agreement with Bidlisi's usage of the term: "In current usage," Ahteri pointed out, "*rabbānī* refers to a knower of God (*ʿārif bi-Allāh*) who turns his knowledge into practice (*ʿilmiyle ʿāmil*)."[17] Bidlisi called these scholars with such traits as godly scholars (*ʿulemāʾ-i rabbānī*). When applied to government, one of the favorite constructs Bidlisi used to depict ideal political authority was *khilāfat-i rabbānī*, by which he stated that rulership had to be in full accordance with divine ordains.[18] He defined the true rulership, which he commonly dubbed as *khilāfat-i raḥmānī*, as endowing oneself with godly traits (*avṣāf-i rabbānī*). In framing worldly rulership in comparison to that of God's, Bidlisi further stated that what made divine government (*rubūbiyyat*) manifest was God's combination of two attributes: knowledge (*ʿilm*) and prowess (*qudrat*). For him these two were the most conspicuous attributes for the perfection of rulership on Earth. He then stated that true rulership (*khilāfat-i raḥmānī*) was an exemplar (*numūdār*) of God's authority (*iqtidār-i subḥānī*) on Earth. But true rulership, called the vicegerency of the Truth (*khilāfat-i Ḥaq*), could only take place (*ḥaqq-i khilāfat*) when the above attributes became manifest in the ruler.[19]

To further elaborate these two attributes of God, Bidlisi indicated that just rulers were manifestations of God's rulership and prowess because they had the majesty of rulership, while the prophets, the twelve imams, and the ulema were manifestations of divine knowledge because they constantly issued commands, orders, and wisdom. Thus the two attributes of God, prowess and knowledge, were at all times manifested through different human agents. In verse, Bidlisi clarified this representation: "Rulers, manifestations of the rulership of God; the wise, mirrors of the knowledge of God."[20] For him the utmost ideal and the highest rank that a ruler could attain was the representation of these two attributes of God. He stated that rulers of Islam, endowed with learning (*dānish*) and authority (*iqtidār*) as manifestations of God's knowledge (*ʿilm*) and prowess (*qudrat*), attain the highest degree of rulership.[21] Although these two attributes could be manifest in the ruler and the ulema separately, the ideal ruler for Bidlisi was one who combined them and made them manifest in himself. The idea of single unified authority had been long advocated by the Sufi orders since before Ottoman State was born as outlined in Chapter 1. What makes Bidlisi different is that he offered a pathway for the Ottoman sultan to attain it.

Likewise, Dizdar underlined two divine attributes that characterized rulers: All rulers were manifestations of God's attributes of grace (*luṭf*) and subjugation (*qahr*).[22] Like Bidlisi, he divided rulers into two kinds: rulers of the world and rulers of religion. The difference between the two types was whether they were conscious of God's manifestation or not. Worldly rulers were not aware of God's attributes of grace and supremacy that they themselves manifested, which he likened to beautiful people whose beauty only benefited others. By contrast, the rulers of religion were also manifestations of God's two attributes but were aware of this relationship. This cognitive realization enabled them to access the riches of the kingdom (*mulk*) and the treasures of the angelic realm (*malakūt*). Then they realized (*iṭṭilāʿ*), the divine secret of "who knows himself knows his God" and sat on the throne of the realm of eternity. Establishing the relation between the ruler and God as one between the one who appoints (*mustakhlif*) and the appointee (*khalīfa*), Dizdar then stated that vicegerency (*khilāfa*) does not become complete (*la tasiḥḥu*) unless the vicegerent exhibits attributes of the one he represents.[23] Among such attributes that a ruler should have were mercy (*raḥma*), compassion (*shafaqa*), clemency (*ḥilm*), nobility (*karam*), munificence (*jūd*), and dignity (*sharaf al-nafs*). To complement this representation, the ruler needed to purify himself of reprehensible qualities by abstaining from immorality (*akhlāq-i sayyiʾa*) and evil traits (*ṣifāt-i zamīma*), such as self-love (*ʿujb*), haughtiness (*kibr*), enmity (*ʿadāwa*), and disparagement.

Bidlisi and Dizdar elaborated on this divine model as a touchstone to distinguish between the two levels of rulership, one that is acquired by and limited to executive power and the one that merges it with spiritual and moral authority granted by virtue of one's knowledge and perfection. While ordinary rulers were manifestations of certain aspects of God's government, only the true rulers, endowed with godly traits, could fully manifest and consciously represent Him on Earth. According to this conception, two aspects of God's government, the unity of sovereignty and His attributes relevant to governance, appeared as two indispensable characteristics of an ideal rulership. As such, not only God's government was considered to be a binding model for good governance but also earthly rulership became part of God's overall governance over creation, whether the ruler is aware of it or not. The ruler's cognizance of it was not a mere knowledge but attaining the capacity to endow oneself with Godly attributes.

The Shadow of God on Earth

No appellative better illustrates the corollary between God's government and the sultan's rulership than "shadow of God."[24] Besides indiscriminate uses of the term as a metaphor and an honorific designation especially in literature, in political theory it was often used as a qualifier to distinguish between higher and lower levels of rulership. Unlike other titles, such as caliph, imam, and sultan, *ẓill Allāh* was rarely used individually but was mostly added to other titles as a distinctive attribute of rulership (i.e., *al-sulṭān ẓill Allāh*). For an author such as Lütfi Paşa, who was not concerned with distinguishing between superior and inferior forms of rulership, *ẓill Allāh* was only one of the titles that any ruler could claim the right to bear.[25] In his view, the very existence of rulership and the status of the ruler in relation to his subjects made him the shadow of God over his creation, regardless of the ruler's qualifications or the moral quality of his rulership. For him, being the shadow of God did not impose on rulership a moral imperative.

However, a more typical approach, voiced by such authors as Kınalızade and Taşköprizade, assessed rulership on the basis of the ruler's moral and religious qualifications and promoted *ẓill Allāh* as a rank that could be achieved only by meeting certain conditions. But the question for the ruler was not whether he was entitled to be designated as the shadow of God but to what degree his rulership conformed to such a designation. In consensus view, even in the most rudimentary form of rulership, characterized by the sheer power to rule, the ruler could still enjoy the status of being *ẓill Allāh* for resembling God's government in such traits as the unity of authority, might, and majesty. The quest then was to turn one's rulership into a mirror image, a true shadow of God, as far as humanly possible by endowing the ruler with all the godly traits applicable to earthly rulership. In this sense, *ẓill Allāh* was envisioned to be a spiritual ascention of the ruler in an endless pursuit of perfection.

Conceiving rulership as being God's shadow was largely based on a logical inference dictated by the semantic field of the metaphor itself, and interpreted mostly on the basis of mystical teachings about one's relation to God. Unlike most other titles used to qualify the sultan, the term *ẓill Allāh* does not appear in the Qur'an. The evidential basis of the term came from certain well-known prophetic traditions that were commonly quoted in political literature. The Prophet's praise of rulers as *ẓill Allāh* had certainly made it a popular designation among political writers since the earliest writings on political theory. In almost all cases, *ẓill Allāh* was used in reference to the prophetic traditions, which designated the ruler as the shadow of God. The most widely quoted tradition on the subject, circulating in different variants, was the one that portrayed the ruler as the shadow of God and advised all believers to pay him unconditional loyalty, regardless of the quality of his rulership.[26] This tradition became a staple of political reasoning to prove that any sultan was by definition *ẓill Allāh* and, thanks to this position, deserved loyalty from the ruled.

Once being the shadow of God was established as a property of the sultanate, moralist authors used *ẓill Allāh* to draw a spiritually sophisticated picture of rulership. Taşköprizade thought that a ruler could not deserve to be called *ẓill Allāh* or vicegerent of God's mercy (*al-khalīfa al- raḥmānī*) unless he met certain conditions, such as following the path of justice.[27] No less perfectionist than Taşköprizade, Bidlisi also appeared uncompromising in his depiction of *ẓill Allāh* as the highest rank in rulership, a rank reserved to such rulers whose governance resembled that of God. For him, only the kind of rulership that he dubbed *khilāfat-i raḥmānī* or *salṭanat-i ma'navī* could be considered as being the shadow of God. What earned a ruler this status was his moral and spiritual perfection: "Know that moral principles (*uṣūl-i akhlāq*) and noble traits (*malakāt-i karīma*) that are stipulated for the realization of *khilāfat-i raḥmānī* and required to deserve the designation to be the shadow of God (*ẓilliyat-i yazdānī*) are confined to four principles. . . ."[28] Those principles were none other than the four cardinal virtues of [Platonic] justice, courage, temperance, and wisdom, which he elaborated on in considerable detail.[29]

Bidlisi's and Taşköprizade's equation of *ẓill Allāh* with *khalīfat Allāh* and their depiction of both as a higher form of rulership was a commonly held view among the political writers of the period. Providing lexical proof for this conceptual overlap, Ahteri defined *ẓill Allāh* as *khalīfat Allāh*.[30] In accordance with this linguistic exposition, Dizdar offered a definition of *ẓill Allāh* in the idiom of Ibn Arabi: "this means caliph as well, because the shadow (*ẓill*) is the vicegerent of the shadow-caster (*muẓill*)."[31] Considering these conditions similar to and above that of the rudimentary sultanate, Kınalızade, in clear reference to both juristic and Sufistic notions of the caliphate, advised the ruler to become both imam and *ẓill Allāh* at the same time.[32] Both designations highlighted the bond between the ruler and God as well as the similarity between his rulership and God's governance. It was only through being *ẓill Allāh* and *khilāfat Allāh* that a simulacrum of God's governance could be established on Earth. Unlike the juristic and theological reluctance to apply the term *khalīfat Allāh* to sultan-rulers, there were no rules pertaining to the use of *ẓill Allāh*, which enabled the term to become the most widely utilized designation to impose moral imperative over the sultanate. Besides, the term *ẓill Allāh* was more easily suited to the condition of the post-Abbasid rulers because it was, in both the accepted prophetic tradition and historical experience, configured exclusively to designate the sultan-rulers. Even without the use of the term *khalīfa*, *ẓill Allāh* implied most of what *khalīfa* implied in terms of the molding of rulership after the model of God's government. Because *khilāfa* came to be used interchangeably with sultan/sultanate, the meaning of this concept became more distinctive and its qualifying significance became more telling.

Prophethood as Rulership

In broader Islamic thought, prophethood has always been an inspiration, if not a normative model, in prescribing or envisioning rulership. The perfect model for rulership that manifests God's governance on Earth was prophethood (*nubuwwa*). Such authors as Taşköprizade, Hızır Münşi, and Dizdar highlighted certain aspects of prophethood as "political," arguing that besides being a role model for all individuals, prophets had some characteristics that rulers alone should imitate. By establishing an ontological relationship as well as historical continuity between prophethood and rulership, they probed into the nature of prophethood to identify and distinguish its features that could serve as an archetype to rulership. But not all prophets were commissioned with rulership, and only those who possessed political authority were models for rulers. Ottoman-Sufistic accounts of ruler-prophets were not the same as medieval philosophical accounts of prophets as absolute guides. According to the theory of prophethood constructed by Farabi and elaborated by Avicenna, who made it the central point of his political philosophy, a prophet (*nabī*) was conceived as an indisputable ruler of his community. They identified the philosopher-ruler with the prophet and saw no distinction between political rulership and spiritual guidance of the community.[33] Davvani, however, whom the Ottomans knew better, had already modified this view, before the sixteenth-century Ottoman authors wrote on the subject, by distinguishing between prophetic-lawgiver and ruler.[34]

Along the same lines, for Sufi-minded authors, such as Ensari, *nubuwwa* and sultanate were two different missions, and the sultans inherited the prophets' mission only on matters related to rulership. A Sufi-minded Damascene author, Dimashqi (d. 1543), in his long political treatise where he profiled the ideal ruler in the personality of Selim I, hailed him as having combined all the perfect qualities of rulership as manifested by the Prophet. Quoting Ghazali, he thought that Prophet Muhammed excelled above all other prophets because of his combining prophethood (*nubuwwa*), kingdom (*mulk*), and rulership (*salṭana*) under a single authority.[35] He later expanded this treatise and dedicated it to Süleyman I with a different title.[36] A contemporary author with a similar disposition, Hamawi, who met Selim during his Egyptian campaign, later wrote a Sufistic treatise on ruleship where he reminded the sultan that the very purpose of rulership is to succeed prophets in implementing the requirements of God's lordship (*marāsim al-rubūbiyya*) and divine laws (*imḍā aḥkām al-ulūhiyya*).[37]

To explain why certain prophets were granted sovereignty (*salṭanat*), Hızır Münşi stated that "Among the prophets some were rulers (*pādishāhān*) and they conquered countries and gathered armies," and then he added, "an army without wealth cannot be gathered and wealth without an army cannot be protected."[38] Sharing a similar view, Taşköprizade explained the rulership of prophets in the case of Moses: "God combined prophethood and the sultanate for Moses after the demise of the Pharaoh. Then God ordered the army of the Israelites to attack Jericho and fight the Amalekites to free the divided country from their hands."[39] In both views, the features distinguishing these ruler-prophets from others were wealth and the army they possessed, as well as the use of these assets for conquest. Projecting the example of these and other ruler-prophets, Taşköprizade and Hızır Münşi displayed a common view among the authors of this period which held that "political power," enhanced by wealth and military might, was the single most distinguishing marker of rulership.

In agreement with Taşköprizade and Hızır Münşi, Dizdar recapitulated the views of the thirteenth-century Sufi Najm al-Din Daye, and emphasized the necessity of the ruler having coercive power to perform certain functions with which a select number of prophets were commissioned.[40] Since prophets were already designated as guides and leaders of their communities in law, morality, and spirituality, this depiction of the sultanate reduced it to the capability of exercising coercive power. To illustrate this point, Dizdar stated that "Solomon asked for sovereignty (*mulk*) [because] when the power of the sultanate and the majesty of kingdom (*shawk al-mamlaka*) unite with the power of prophethood (*nubuwwa*) it becomes more effective in destroying enemies."[41] In Dizdar's view, prophethood did not inherently entail coercive power. Therefore, a prophet who was sent by God to guide his community was not necessarily a ruler by virtue of prophethood, unless he was specifically given political authority.

Further emphasizing the political aspects of prophethood and the possession of political authority as separate from other prophetic missions, Dizdar then explained how certain prophets had multiple authorities: "The position of sultanate united with the position of *walāya* and *nubuwwa* in order to do justice among the subjects, and uphold the right of the religious path, and maintain religious ordinances (*muʿāmalāt al-sharʿiyya*), and reach to the world of certainty (*ʿālam al-yaqīn*), just as *mulk* and *khilāfa* united, in the case of David, Solomon, and Joseph, with the rank of *nubuwwa*."[42] In the first part of this statement, he portrayed sovereignty (*salṭana*), spiritual authority (*walāya*), and prophethood (*nubuwwa*) as three authoritative but separate missions that could exceptionally be combined by a select number of chosen people. In the second part, Dizdar seems to have replaced the word *salṭana* with *mulk*, and *walāya* with *khilāfa*, which may indicate that he conceived the caliphate not as a synonym of *salṭana* but of *walāya*, as a spiritual authority, in accordance with other Sufi interpretations of rulership. Although Taşköprizade's exposition is rather vague in illustrating the threefold authority that certain ruler-prophets enjoyed, it is more instructive than Dizdar's on the question of inheriting these roles:

> When Muhammed, the noblest of prophets, peace be upon him, was bestowed religion (*dīn*), power (*mulk*), and sovereignty (*salṭana*), he was the only human being who combined them. With him, God also perfected religion and ended the string of messengers (*nabiyyīn*). After him the ulema, as inheritors to messengers, followed. They found the right way and through the ulema the people found the right way. Then came the just sultans because the salvation of the world depended on them, just as the salvation of the afterlife depended on the ulema. Then followed those pious ones [Sufis] other than the ulema (*allaẕīna aṣlaḥū anfusahum*) who reformed their souls. Those who digressed from those groups are but a herd of cattle.[43]

This unambiguous depiction shows that the mission of prophets could be fully inherited through these three groups, each fulfilling a separate mission:

knowledge of religion, political authority, and spiritual guidance. Although the statement made clear that no other single person could succeed the Prophet in combining all three missions, it also elucidated that succession to the Prophet entailed knowledge, power, and piety. Despite Taşköprizade's overlooking of the question of whether these three authorities could be combined by any one individual, it does not go against the general spirit of his exposition as well as other authors' view on the subject that, ideally, these missions should be combined in the personality of one successor. The Sunni tradition was generally reluctant to recognize any historical figure as the successor of the Prophet in all his missions after the rightly guided caliphs. Taşköprizade's point may be taken as a historical observation rather than a theoretical argument on the impossibility of succeeding the last prophet in the form of a unified authority.

For Taşköprizade, prophethood still served as an authoritative source of inspiration as well as a perfect model to distinguish between material and spiritual forms of rulership. In an attempt to present role models, he first presented prophethood as a profession by highlighting prophets with executive power as rulers. This theological conviction, bolstered by an accompanying historical imagination, put ordinary rulers in the same line as the ruler-prophets, the noblest of human beings in both the prevailing theology and popular culture. From this perspective, all worldly rulers were perceived to have shared a similar task as the prophets who were granted the same sort of sovereignty to complement their prophethood. The message to ordinary rulers was then to complement their sovereignty with what was lacking in their rulership, the spiritual component of prophethood. For all prophet-rulers had perfected both their material and spiritual authorities. It was precisely because of their combination of these two authorities that they came to be designated as vicegerent of God or shadow of God on Earth. Thus what many authors envisioned by these and similar designations was rulership modeled after prophethood. As such, the ultimate goal of rulership was to combine coercive power with knowledge and spiritual perfection.

The Sultanate as Caliphate

When turned into a caliphate, a sultanate then was the type of rulership inspired by God's governance and modeled after the rulership of ruler-prophets. This perception, however, brings two questions to the fore, which some authors of the period, most notably Bidlisi, sought to answer in some detail. First, what did the caliphate mean specifically and, second, how could a sultanate turn into a caliphate? The term *khalīfa* or its seat *khilāfa*, enjoying a powerful Qur'anic sanction for being used in God's word as a praiseworthy status, assumed myriad divergent meanings in various intellectual, cultural, and political traditions in Islam. Depending on the author and the context in which they were used, a variety of meanings of the term could be observed in the eclectic political literature of the Ottomans, where in many cases these meanings, derived from different traditions, were conflated to serve the author's argument. Despite this variegation, the discourse on rulership with regard to the caliphate centered on two principal meanings of the term: individual human condition as vicegerency of God and political authority over the community, both originating from the Qur'an.[44] Unlike many other political concepts that had little or no Qur'anic sanction and were subjected to a more independent examination in political theory, the caliphate compelled authors to do the job of a Qur'anic exegete. This focus on the Qur'anic interpretation of the concept drove the historical-juristic view of the caliphate almost totally out of discussion. In political theory, invoking the caliphate as universal leadership of the Muslim community was largely confined to eulogies glorifying the Ottoman ruler as the ruler above all others or epithets of superiority, such as the caliph on the face of the earth (*ḫalīfe-i rūy-i zemīn*).

The dual conception of the caliphate as vicegerency and rulership was embedded in any use of the term in political theory that presented it as a Qur'anic designation and a superior form of sultanate. From an individual believer's perspective, the caliphate was a human condition on Earth that created a bond between the servant and Lord while opening an unlimited opportunity to reach a high status among the created by gaining proximity to the Creator. From a ruler's perspective, the caliphate was a representation of God on Earth along with a political power conferred by the highest authority. This made the caliph both subject to God and a ruler over God's community, and being a caliph referred to both a person's perfection and political rulership at the same time.

Shaping the views of the authors of this period on the definition and acquisition of the caliphate were two well-known Qur'anic verses that served as the most authoritative references. The first verse (Qur'an 2: 30), which describes the designation of human being in the person of the prophet Adam as caliphate on Earth, was mostly presented as a proof of one's distinctive nature and mission on Earth.[45] For authors, such as Bidlisi, who probed into the relationship between human being's nature and rulership, this verse proved that God created human being with the potential to act as God's vicegerent on Earth and made him responsible for doing so, thus portraying the caliphate as a high spiritual status and a moral objective for every man, the attainment of which becomes a duty. Better suiting to the self-image of Ottoman rulers in this period and more commonly used in political texts, the second verse (Qur'an 37: 26), which states Prophet David's designation as caliphate, specifically referred to David's appointment as a ruler over his community and ordered him to rule with justice.[46] During the wedding of the Grand Vizier Ibrahim Paşa, Süleyman the Lawgiver was reported to have held a debate among the leading scholars of his time as to the true meaning of the caliphate as illustrated in the case of Prophet David's depiction as such in the Qur'an.[47] For most Ottoman authors, this verse provided unquestionable proof that caliphate was rulership, turning its receiver into a ruler.

The Qur'an is explicit in its exposition that it was human being among other creatures who was chosen and who chose to be God's vicegerent on Earth, a belief that meant every individual in principle was given a choice and had the capacity to achieve this status. This vicegerency did not necessarily materialize itself as a political act but could more commonly take place through a spiritual bond between human being and God. For political authors who wrote about the caliphate of a ruler, the starting point was human being's caliphate on Earth and the ruler's status as caliph was always described within the scheme of human being's relation to God. In conceiving the caliphate of rulers, this perspective led authors such as Bidlisi and Dizdar to establish a direct corollary between the worldly rulership and God's governance, whereby the oneness of the vicegerency of God received a particular emphasis. This universalistic view supported and was itself bolstered by the vision of the historical caliphate that ideally recognized a single authority over the Muslim community. But despite the depiction of such a rulership as the similitude of God's governance, this did not change the fact that the caliphate was above all conceived of as a spiritual bond between God and man. The outcome of such a vision of the caliphate was the acceptance of a single caliph-ruler on Earth along with individual caliphs among the believers.

Because this designation was not an exclusive one and allowed both the ruler and the subject to achieve the status of God's vicegerency on Earth, it appeared to be an egalitarian one. It was this convoluted picture of the term that made it an attainable status for the Ottoman ruler and facilitated its widespread adoption while, paradoxically, allowing any subject to attain the same position, depriving the ruler of an exclusive claim to this lofty designation. Namely, attaining God's caliphate on Earth required the fulfillment of the same objective criteria for both the ruler and his subjects. This paradoxical situation made the caliphate less determinative for securing rulership and facilitated its perception as more of a moral sophistication than the exercise of actual political authority, a view that only reiterated the conception of the sultanate as the real power in rulership.

This ambiguity in conceiving of the caliphate as political authority was by no means peculiar to the Ottoman period but was enabled by interpretations given in Islamic disciplines and further complicated by historical practice. As demonstrated by Abou el-Fadl, since the earliest history of Islam, in both political theory and the experience of Muslim communities, there always remained legitimate ways for people other than the actual ruler to claim political authority.[48] Inspired by theories of the caliphate, it was quite possible for someone to claim a more comprehensive and superior authority than the ruler in office by assuming such titles as Mahdi or caliph, a kind of challenge that took place in numerous instances throughout Islamic history, including the

Ottoman era. Thus, in the face of the possibility that even powerless contenders for political authority could make a claim to the caliphate, most notably the nonconformist mystics in the Seljukid and Ottoman lands, it was categorically out of question for the Ottoman sultan not to assume this title in order to maintain his legitimate authority. In searching for the timing and reasons for the Ottoman rulers' adoption of the title caliph, one may find more clues by looking at the internal political challenges they faced and the intellectual manifestations of rulership that forced the sultans to portray themselves as caliph, rather than external challenges and the endemic competition for the universal leadership of the Muslim community.

Thus caliphate as vicegerency of God and the highest rank in the world among humankind constituted a common moral high ground that conferred authority upon those who attained it, an authority where the claims of rulers intersected with those of spiritual leaders. Some political writings that depicted the status of pole (*quṭb*, *quṭb al-aqṭāb*, or *ghaws*) as the highest authority in the world, for example, recognized rulers as sultans to the extent that their authority was limited to the government of human affairs in the visible world. They reserved the title of caliph for the pole, as the real head of all creation and the true representative of God on Earth by virtue of his spiritual perfection.[49] From this perspective, rulers of the visible world were inferior to the all-encompassing authority of the pole, whose identity was in principle secret and was known by only a select number of his agents. It was only when the pole made himself manifest and claimed his authority that this inherent conflict rose to the surface to pose a real threat against the authority of a ruler.[50] A tacit compromise, however, was that the believers of the ruler-pole conviction did not extend it into the material sphere and were content to accept that the pole was the de facto ruler of the world although the people, including the ruler, had no knowledge of it. Into the bargain, as a dynastic tradition since its inception, whether motivated by sincerity or pragmatic purposes, Ottoman rulers were especially careful to please spiritual leaders around them, allowing the members of Sufi orders to interpret the ruler's relation to their order in their own way. All Ottoman sultans, including Mehmed II, who had the least regard for Sufi leaders, constructed their public images as a friend of God's friends, which is often interpreted by the adherents of a given mystical order as the sultan's submission to the all-encompassing authority of its leader. On the other hand, this close friendship with God's friends is interpreted by the supporters of the Ottoman dynasty as the recognition of the Sultan as the highest authority by powerful Sufi leaders. In any rate, as a traditional dynastic policy, it was a wise and effective undertaking to disperse doubts surrounding one's authority.

As best illustrated in the accounts of Bidlisi, Dizdar, and Taşköprizade, caliphate was considered to be both a collective status granted to humanity and a specific position conferred on a chosen ruler. This reinterpretation of the caliphate was in line with the prevailing view in political literature that considered any form of rulership as a grace from God granted to a chosen person. On the other hand, the same authors also considered caliphate a superior rank in rulership, an exalted goal within reach of the ruler's human capacity and a noble ideal that the ruler should strive to achieve. Yet these two views were not poles apart, as they may seem. Such views on the caliphate looked confounding because, as previously noted, the caliphate had two distinct meanings as political authority and spiritual perfection as conveyed in the Qur'an. In the first view, caliphate was used as a synonym for sultanate to mean political authority, whereas in the latter, the term meant the highest degree of moral perfection that would enable the sultan to transform his sultanate into a superior form of rulership. The main purpose of the authors was to set the caliphate as a moral objective for the sultan even when they used the term simply to mean political authority. It was also a reminder that a political authority called a caliphate needed to be qualified as such to deserve this appellation.

Bidlisi, who built his whole political theory around the concept of caliphate, summarized it as an individual endeavor, a view that prevailed among his contemporaries. His starting premise was that human being became the locus of caliphate by virtue of his nature that was made of two substances: one in the angelic sphere and the other in the material sphere.[51] His superior substance was at the level of angels and his inferior substance was at the level of beasts. Human being's combination of these two substances made him unique among the creation, and it was this unity in human being that constituted the locus of caliphate. In addition, human being was created noble and, thanks to this nobility, was chosen to be God's vicegerent. This noble status of human being was due to the fact that God created human being in His own image. Human being's creation in God's image, and his relatedness to God through his spirit, created a bond between God and human being in the form of vicegerency. Probing further into human being's nature and to his potential to become a caliph of God, Bidlisi stated that human being's spirit belonged to the realm of elegance (*laṭāfat*) and nobility (*sharāfat*) whereas his or her body belonged to the realm of creation (*kavn*) and sedition (*faṣād*). The reason for human being's ennoblement with caliphate was his or her spiritual substance. Thus the attribution of rulership (*salṭanat*) and shadow of God (*ẓill-i Subḥānī*) to the material body was metaphorical. It was human being's spirit that served as the substance to accommodate these designations.[52]

Bidlisi gave a practical recipe for the attainment of caliphate by rulers: For him, *khilāfat-i raḥmānī* meant the endowment of a servant with godly (*rabbānī*) attributes and perfections (*kamālāt*), the perfection of the soul with praiseworthy faculties, giving order to the seen world, and establishing connections (*rabṭ*) between the visible world (*kishvar-i shahādat*) and the world of the unseen (*ʿālam-i rūḥānī*).[53] This individualistic view of the caliphate suggests that there is no difference between the conditions expected from a ruler or from a subject to attain the caliphate. That is to say, even a ruler already endowed with political power needed to go through the same process as an ordinary believer to be entitled to this designation for which there was no objective measure. When set as a moral objective for the ruler in political theory, the caliphate then meant the solidification of one's sovereignty with spiritual perfection as exemplified by the ruler-prophets. Only in this way, could an ordinary ruler acquire a superior status and become a guide for the community. Bidlisi's perfect rulership extends through the angelic and material spheres and mediates between the worlds of the seen and the unseen.

Prophet's Successor and God's Vicegerent

The term caliph could, in a strictly political sense, refer to two different conceptions of rulership in Ottoman political thought, or both: vicegerency of God as discussed previously, or succession to the Prophet (*khalīfat Rasūl Allāh*), that is, the historical caliphate. Although these two principal meanings may not be mutually exclusive, identifying in which sense the term was used is still crucial for understanding the kind of rulership envisioned. Political authors of the period commonly used the term imam without any reservation, and displayed little interest in the long-standing debate about whether the ruler could be designated as such.[54] Few authors specifically designated the ruler as *khalīfat Rasūl Allāh*; even when they did, their interest was limited to proving the permissibility of attributing such a title to the ruler. Given that the prevailing tendency was to use imam rather than *khalīfat Raṣūl Allāh*, when the term caliph was used alone it is more likely that it meant the ruler's vicegerency of God on Earth rather than his succession to the political authority of the Prophet. This prevalent equivocalism, demanded by the historical trajectory of the term, impelled some authors to be meticulous in their use of the term, and led them to invent constructs with more specific definitions such as *al-khilāfa al-haqīqī, al-khilāfa al-maʿnawī, al-khilāfa al-raḥmānī*, and the like.

Few authors, however, specifically used the term in the sense of succession to the prophet and instead problematized the differences among the term's principal meanings. Alayi, for example, in explaining the meaning of the well-known prophetic tradition that limited the life of the caliphate to thirty years after the Prophet's death and foretold the beginning of the reign of kings (*mülūk*) thereafter, made a distinction between the caliphate of the first four caliphs and that of the subsequent rulers, and designated the former as the perfect and true caliphate (*ḫilāfet-i kāmile* and *ḥaḳīḳiyye*).[55] He stated that attributing such titles as *ḫalīfe* and *ḫalīfe-i Resūlullāh* to rulers after the four rightly guided caliphs was permissible and did not contradict the designation of the era of the rightly guided caliphs as the true caliphate. Agreeing with Alayi's view that equates the sultanate with the caliphate, Ensari went a step further and used the term sultan in a relational construct together with God, in the way caliph was used. Thus designating the ruler as *sulṭān Allāh* on Earth, he stated that the ruler succeeded the prophetic rulership (*khilāfat-i nubuwwa*) in such functions as reforming the people (*islāḥ-i khalq*), calling the people to please God, upholding their religion, and arranging their sustenance.[56] Leadership over the affairs of Muslims was a prophetic position and the sultan succeeded the prophets by being in that position. The ruler could succeed in that mission because God made him the pivot of religious law (*madār-i aḥkām-i sharʿiyya*) and the authority over all their affairs (*marjiʿ al-anām fī jamīʿ aḥvālihim*). Without a direct reference to the last Prophet, Ensari characterized the office of ruler as a succession to the prophetic mission and held the ruler responsible for the same functions as prophets. Despite envisioning the ruler in the line of prophet-rulers, Ensari avoided using either of the two juristic terms imam or *khalīfat Rasūl Allāh*.

Whether or not Ensari's was a principled objection against attributing such titles to rulers, in spite of juristic and theological controversies, both designations were widely applied to temporal rulers in medieval political theory and practice, and less problematized in subsequent periods. The problem was usually posed as a question of titulature in juristic and theological literature and framed as whether it was permissible to attribute the title imam, in the sense of vicegerency of God, to rulers. Hidden behind the controversy over titulature, however, was the underlying concern regarding the very definition of rulership. One of the longest-lasting controversies of Islamic political thought was the question whether the caliphate was the vicegerency of God or succession to the Prophet that came to the fore during the formative period of Muslim community.[57] In contrast with the general uneasiness about designating the caliphate as God's vicegerency in early Muslim community, later generations became increasingly more receptive.[58]

By the sixteenth century, while a few doctrinal vigilantes still displayed some awareness of this medieval controversy, most saw no harm in portraying contemporary rulers as imams or caliphs of the Prophet. The juristic and theological reservations against the permissibility of designating rulers as imams relied on a set of strictly historical and juristic interpretations of scriptural evidence. Those who equated rulership with imamate, however, directly drew their evidence from the Qur'an, which suggested that the imam was not an innovation inserted into the religious creed but a perfectly legitimate title for contemporary rulers. Moreover, because it was a more comprehensive term, helped by its equivocal nature, imam by definition always implied the historical caliphate. From this perspective, the last Prophet was after all a vicegerent of God in the line of other prophet-rulers who came before him.

Since the late Abbasid period, the use of *khalīfat Rasūl Allāh* gradually disappeared from political literature in favor of imam and *khalīfat Allāh*. To point to the increasing reception of this controversial title, Rosenthal stated that "in the later Abbasid period the designation *khalīfat Allāh* for the caliph has gained wide currency . . . , in marked distinction from the insistence of earlier periods that the caliph was only the *khalīfat Rasūl Allāh*."[59] By the time Ottoman writers were contemplating how to characterize rulership in the sixteenth century, conceiving rulership as the vicegerency of God with a vaguely-implied reference to succession to the Prophet was already well established in political thought. Attempts by Alayi and Lütfi Paşa to prove the permissibility of attributing the title *khalīfat Rasūl Allāh* to the Ottoman ruler indicate that the general mood of the time was not entirely in favor of this title while no such concern was displayed about the use of imam.

When the controversy was in full bloom in medieval Islam, the ruler, whose appellation of imam was questioned, was already a universally acclaimed caliph and a successor to the Prophet in the mainstream political and juristic view. It may seem ironic that imam gained a wider currency at a time when post-Abbasid rulers' claim to the title caliph was controversial in political theory and disputable among rival dynasties. However, the use of this title seemed to have fundamentally resolved one of the enduring questions of legitimacy for the independent rulers who came to rule most of the Islamic world following the decentralization of the Abbasid Empire. The classical juristic theory of the caliphate, developed from the ninth through the eleventh centuries, had centered on the conception of the caliphate as successor to the Prophet, a theory that was still in full effect in the authoritative juristic texts by the time the Ottomans had started to identify themselves as caliphs in the fifteenth century. Best suited to the legitimacy needs of the Abbasid caliphs, the theory of a historical caliphate was hardly applicable to post-Abbasid dynastic rulers without modification, and was largely ignored in the advice literature that came to dominate the field of political writing in this period. Thus the conundrum of assuming the caliphate without meeting its requirements was bypassed with the adoption of the title imam accompanied by an indifference to the historical caliphate. Because of their affinity to post-Abbasid states, as part of a broader trend, Ottoman intellectuals inherited and adopted imam with relative ease thanks to such influential works as *Naṣīḥat al-Salāṭīn*, *Akhlāq-i Nāṣirī*, and *Mirṣād al-ʿIbād*.[60]

The Ottoman perception of the sultan as imam was related more to the design of rulership than the desire to add one more title to an ever-increasing sultanic titulature. It was not merely a matter of appellation but of designation. By shifting the source of a ruler's legitimacy from the successor of the Prophet to the vicegerency of God, political writers circumvented a rigid set of conditions established by jurists and theologians for a legitimate caliph. According to juristic and theological theories, to be a successor of the Prophet a ruler needed more than certain personal qualifications suited to the office; at least in principle, he also needed the approval of the community of believers who were given an important hand in installing a successor.[61] In the case of the vicegerency of God, however, the ruler was thought to have gained this status through his spiritual ascension and by the grace of God. Imamate was divorced from its juristic and legal foundations and accorded an ontological significance akin to the concept of the caliphate.

Once the ruler was conceived as the vicegerent of God rather than the successor of the Prophet in political literature, God Himself, more than the Prophet, became the primary model for a ruler. Most political authors referred only to God's governance as an authoritative model, and paid little attention to the governance of the Prophet and the rightly guided caliphs. Based on the examination of human nature and the search for ways to improve the quality of rulership, this approach relied on theosophical inquiry as the principal mode of political reasoning rather than the Prophet's life (*siyar*) or jurisprudence. The depiction of pre-Muhammedan prophets as vicegerents of God on Earth in the light of Qur'anic evidence made them role models for rulership. This was in contrast to the juristic theory that centers on the life of the last Prophet and his immediate successors. Thus, based on Qur'anic references, Adam and David, because of their appointment as God's vicegerents on Earth, and Solomon, who was granted rulership, came to be the most frequently alluded to as models of perfect rulership.

The common conviction that succession to the Prophet had ended with the era of the rightly guided caliphs, expressed by Taşköprizade above and others, must have accounted in part for the shift of emphasis from *khalīfat Rasūl Allāh* to imam. The latter, however, by no means displaced the former but established a more continuous lineage of rulership. By adopting the title imam, the ruler was conceived to have succeeded the ruler-prophets in their mission of being the vicegerents of God on Earth. Unlike the rigorous conditions prescribed to qualify as *khalīfat Rasūl Allāh*, assuming the position of imam was easier to support theoretically and easier to justify in historical imagination, despite the theological complications it brought up. With the title imam, the ruler could still enjoy the prestige and legitimacy conferred by the equivocal term caliph, while eschewing the obligation to meet the conditions set for *khalīfat Rasūl Allāh*. The Qur'anic designation imam was relatively free of legal injunctions. The vagueness of the term and its openness to interpretation made it more useful for political writers, for it provided the ruler and political writers with more freedom to elaborate on the nature of rulership. Besides the practical benefits of embracing such a title and the historical experience of post-Abbasid dynasties that facilitated its adoption, the purpose of most Ottoman political writers in envisioning the ruler as imam was to differentiate between the two levels of rulership. With prophet-rulers as its absolute model, the imamate served the same purpose as the caliphate in order to establish the vicegerency of God as a moral objective for the sultanate.

Rulership as Mystical Experience

When not referring to the historical caliphate, being a caliph was conceived to be a spiritual condition for the ruler and ruled alike, rather than an exclusive designation of political leadership. Such a conception deprived the ruler of being the only one to be accorded with this title. Any person could lay claim on this designation, with or without political leadership, because it was exlusively attained in the spiritual sphere. Political and Sufistic accounts of the caliphate often make no noticeable distinction between a ruler, a shaykh, or an ordinary person in attaing this status and being designated as God's caliph. When the term was used in the same sense as the sultanate, the ruler's claim and right to the title were naturally emphasized. But if the term was used as a qualifier in referring to the higher form of rulership, then the set of conditions prescribed for the ruler were no different than those set forth for the inculcation of perfect human being (*insān-i kāmil*) in Sufism. The concept of the caliphate served as the principal venue through which Sufi ideas of leadership permeated into mainstream political theory. Many leading scholars of the time who extensively elaborated on the caliphate, such as Taşköprizade and Bidlisi, both high-ranking jurists by profession, primarily reasoned on rulership within the parameters of Sufi cosmology. Sufi teachings to inculcate the perfect human being, accompanied with the prevailing moralist tendency among political writers, many of whom were affiliated with Sufi orders, provided these authors with ready-made prescriptions to apply in envisioning a superior form of rulership by educating the ruler.

Along with the flood of Sufi teachings into the mainstream of political theory, Sufi-minded authors, such as Arifi, Dizdar, and Şirvani, did not view rulership with respect to its position in a sociological hierarchy but in relation to the spiritual realm. Common to diverse currents of Sufism was the belief that friends of God (*awliyā*), in addition to their spiritual powers, were endowed with worldly powers and were organized in a hierarchical order in governing the world.[62] They were responsible for the order of the world, and for guiding human beings, though their presence was not necessarily manifest. By highlighting *walāya* as the most salient nature of prophethood, these Sufi authors conceived of the governance of the world and the inheritance of the prophetic mission as a mystical experience.

Advocating such views, Şirvani envisioned rulership as part of a cosmic government where the ultimate authority rested in the most perfect of living human beings, the pole (*ḳuṭb*), also known as the succor (*ghavs*). In the very beginning of the treatise the author elucidated the hierarchical relation between the ruler on Earth and the real wielder of cosmic sovereignty: "The truth of the succor is that he is the caliph on Earth and it is he who manages (*mudabbir*) and administers (*mutaṣarrif*) in the world. As for the rulers in appearance (*pādishāhān-i ẓāhir*), they are the recipients (*maẓhar*) and instruments (*maṣdār*) of his commands (*aḥkām*)."[63] For being the real ruler of the whole world, because of the very nature of authority that defied any corporeal constraints, the power of the pole was not delimited by any geographical or institutional constrictions, making his sovereignty absolute over all human affairs.

This vision of rulership that tied the temporal government to the universal government of the pole or the succor over God's creation was cosmic, not territorial. Thus it was qualitatively different than any other theory of rulership constructed in various strains of thought from jurisprudence to philosophy. As any typical Sufi doctrine would indicate, poleship entailed a complete union between the position and the personality of its receiver. More specifically, from such a Sufi perspective, the most comprehensive and the ultimate authority in the world was granted by God to a person who attained—or was granted by God—spiritual perfection. The most conspicuous outcome of such a depiction of rulership was that even if the ruler was believed to have combined the sultanate and caliphate, in the way he was advised to advance his sultanate to a higher level, there may still have been a pole above him, unless the ruler was also portrayed as such. Thus for this Sufi-minded author, even an ideal ruler by the contemporary standards envisioned in political literature could not enjoy the highest rank and authority among humankind for they belonged exclusively to the pole.

For the Sufi-minded, the inherent human need for authority and guidance for happiness and perfection necessitates the leadership of a perfect human being (*insān-i kāmil, quṭb*). Şirvani constructed a hierarchical structure of the friends of God in a way similar to that of the structure of actual governments of the time.[64] He divided the saintly government into eight hierarchical divisions and stated that the succor, being the pole of poles (*quṭb al-aqṭab*), was the head of that order. The treatise then defined the succor as the vicegerent of the earth (*khālīfat al-ʿarḍ*). In this hierarchy, the rest of the friends of God were like the statesmen (*umarā*) and viziers to the succor. Explaining the relation between the rulers and the saintly order, he stated that the succor and the friends of God under his command were the ones who help rulers. After clarifying the hierarchy of authority among humans, he then advised the ruler to constantly seek help from the spirits (*bāṭin*) of these friends of God. Şirvani still advocates a unified authority similar to what most other Sufi-minded authors voiced. However, he proposed this unity to take place by subjugating temporal rulership to the comprehensive authority of the pole.

According to Şirvani, although the position of pole was superior to that of a ruler, he performed the same function as an ideal ruler was expected to perform, a conception that still points to the high position of rulership among humankind. Like-minded Sufis defined the superiority of the succor through political imagery, by reducing the acting sultan to the manifestation of the pole who was depicted as the *de facto* ruler. Hamza Bâli (d. 1561), for example, who revolted against the Ottoman authority and subsequently was executed along with his followers, was recognized by his Melami followers as the pole of the time and thus superior to any authority in the world. According to the official documents, Hamza Bâli's followers recognized him as ruler along with his viziers, şeyhülislam, and other appointed officials.[65] The belief in the pole's cosmic government does not threaten the authority of the ruler so long as the succor did not make himself known when he interfered with the affairs of sultanate. Although the authority of the succor was superior and more comprehensive, the world was still divided into temporal and spiritual realms and the succor was positioned in the latter. Actual rulership on Earth became instrumental to the succor's overall sovereignty over the world as the wielder of real power. Thus presenting the succor's government as a higher authority served the same purpose as using God's government and prophethood as an example: they both provided the ruler with a source of inspiration and a binding model to mold his rulership to perfection.[66] Although silent on the question of the relation between the ruler and the pole, Dizdar exposed similar views about the position of the pole on Earth. He interpreted the Qur'anic verse regarding the appointment of Adam on Earth as caliph as a reference to the position of the pole and accordingly considered the pole as a successor to the first human being and prophet, Adam. Pointing that the terms *quṭb* and *ghaws* both refer to the same person, on the basis of evidence from the Qur'an and prophetic traditions, Dizdar portrayed the pole as the locus of God's sight (*naẓar Allāh*).[67]

Views on poleship voiced by Şirvani, Dizdar, Taşköprizade, Arifi, and Bidlisi all bear the stamp of Ibn Arabi's views on rulership.[68] Displaying the general trend that formed in the late Abbasid period, Ibn Arabi was as formal as any other jurist or theologian, such as Mawardi, Ghazali or Fakhr al-Din al-Razi, on the theory of imamate while reformulating strikingly different, but not necessarily conflicting, views in addressing different audiences. In *al-Futūḥāt al-Makkiyya*, Ibn Arabi developed a theory of rulership indicating that poleship (*quṭbiyya*) and the caliphate were identical, meaning that the real caliphate resides in the pole. According to him, the external wielders of worldly power, whether they were aware of it or not, were only his deputies (*nuwwāb*), for "the *quṭb* (pole) is the real head of the community of his epoch (*sayyid al-jamāʿa fī zamānihi*)."[69] Among others, his *Futūḥāt*, *Fuṣūṣ*, and *Tadbīrāt* were among the most widely read texts among the Ottoman ulema and Sufis alike.[70] Şirvani expounded the same conception of rulership as Ibn Arabi, only with an exclusive and emphatic language, paying no attention to the formal aspects of imamate as formulated in the juristic and theological literature.

The ideas propounded in Şirvani's *al-ʿAdliyya al-Sulaymāniyya* and the language used to phrase them were completely intelligible to the Ottomans of the Süleymanic age, regardless of their level of education or kind of affiliation. Şirvani simply alluded to the cosmic order of the invisible saints, commonly known as *rijāl al-ghayb* (men of the unseen) or *rijāl Allāh* (men of

God), and exhorted the Ottoman ruler to fit his rule to the all-encompassing government of the pole. To achieve ideal government in the world the ruler had to recognize the superior authority of the invisible saints and seek their assistance in government. Although perceptions may vary and terminology may differ, imageries regarding the invisible order of saints with supernatural powers were staples of the broader folklore in Asia Minor and the Balkans. In this regard, despite its vivid juxtapositioning of current Ottoman rulership with that of the invisible saints, there was nothing objectionable in *al-ʿAdliyya al-Sulaymāniyya* for the Ottoman ruling elite. As long as those saints were not identified and did not challenge the worldly authority of the Ottoman sultan, these perceptions constituted a shared imagery between the ruler and the ruled.

The Ottoman state itself was born into a society where Sufis and perceived saints were as powerful as worldly rulers. *Abdals*, for example, who were attributed to have a very high status in the saintly order, were very visible in early Ottoman frontier society as powerful saints.[71] From the very beginning, Ottoman rulers and their apologists were consistent in creating a popular image that the Ottoman dynasty was assisted by saints, or even associated with the invisible order of the saints. Even a top jurist in the sixteenth century, Sheikh ul Islam Ibn Kemal, perceived no oddity in believing legends that show the close association of the Ottoman dynasty with the order of invisible saints. He stated in the first volume of his history of the Ottoman dynasty that the rise of the Ottomans was not an accident of history but the materialization of what had been decided in the spiritual realm. As he reported, an anonymous saint from the order of invisible saints that govern the affairs of the world informed Kumral Baba in advance that the time of Osman's rise had arrived.[72] The anonymous saint strictly ordered Kumral Baba to join the company of Osman and never leave him during his raids because he was assured of victory and because he was the receiver of God's assistance (*muʾayyad min ʿind Allāh*). The story denoted the close association of the Ottoman dynasty with the order of invisible saints, which was manifested in actuality by the support and loyalty Sufis showed to Ottoman rulers.

Besides spreading the culture of saints among the common people as well as the ruling elite, the order of invisible saints was part of the central teaching of many of the mainstream Sufi orders in the Ottoman Empire. Although some scholars traced the origins of the idea to the very teachings of the Prophet, the first elaborate expositions about the order of saints commissioned by God to rule the material and spiritual worlds seem to have appeared in the revelations of the ascetic Sufis of the ninth and tenth centuries.[73] Ottoman men of learning, including the Sufis and the ulema, mostly received their education on the order of saints through the writings of Ibn Arabi, who gave the most detailed and striking images of the order, and from commentaries on his works. Although rarely alluding to the government of worldly rulers,

Ibn Arabi created such a cosmological imagery in which the whole creation, the material and the spiritual worlds alike, was under the rule of a strictly hierarchical order of saints, all commissioned by God, and all having specific functions and powers.

Ibn Arabi's sixteenth-century student, Yiğitbaşı Veli (d. 1505), a near contemporary of Bidlisi, wrote two separate treatises, both titled *Ṭabaḳātü'l-Evliyā* (Degrees of Saints), on the invisible saints.[74] He lived in Manisa and was the founder of the Ahmedi branch of the Halveti order, an order with strong ties to Ibn Arabi's teachings.[75] In his exposition, at the top of the order of invisible saints were the poles, who have full authority at all times concerning everything.[76] Then came the succors, who were of two kinds: The first group was endowed with full internal (*bāṭın*) and external (*ẓāhir*) authority, such as the Prophet, Abu Bakr, Umar, Uthman, Ali, and other rightly guided caliphs. The second group was only given spiritual authority, such as Hasan-ı Basri, Habib-i Acemi, Bayezid-i Bistami, and other saints. He further stated that the majority of the poles were of the second kind, lacking external authority. He stated that the very historical caliphate, the universal leadership of the Muslim community that emerged after the death of the Prophet, had begun with the poleship. Given that all Sufi orders traced their lineages to either Abu Bakr or Ali, such a belief by definition turned shaykhs into inheritors of the historical caliphate. In a radical reconstruction of the historical trajectory of authority after the Prophet, Yiğitbaşı replaced the political lineage with an exclusively spiritual one.

The perception of the pole as the ultimate authority over all creation was well-entrenched in strains of Ottoman Sufism. For the mainstream Sufi orders, the engagement with the perceived order of invisible saints was usually limited to the spiritual realm. For others, especially among groups that had a strained relationship with Ottoman rule, the universal authority of the pole was frequently associated with real personalities, posing a challenge for the Ottoman sultan. In the case of Otman Baba, for example, his hagiography presented him as God's caliph on Earth, the pole of poles, and the universal human being, whereas Mehmed II was portrayed as the wielder of the saint's executive authority.[77] Although the identification of the pole with the living head of a Sufi order was common across many diverse strands of Ottoman Sufism, it was one of the most distinguishing characteristics of the Bayrami-Melameti order.[78] It was common for the Melametis to perceive their shaykhs as poles, full manifestations of God's attributes, and appointed by God as His caliphs on Earth to oversee the affairs of this world.[79] Especially in the sixteenth century, a number of high-profile Melameti shaykhs, who were perceived to be poles by their followers, came into direct conflict with the Ottoman authority and were executed on charges of heresy.[80] In trials of these unruly shaykhs, they were not accused of claiming poleship but of using that authority to publicly prescribe heretical views of Islam.[81]

In the sixteenth century, just as the rank of caliphate was not considered an exclusive preserve of the ruler, poleship was not confined to the mystics. Along with elaborations on the pole's role in the government of the material world in a variety of Sufi writings, exceptional rulers could also have the rank of poleship attributed to them. In such a context of complex and overlapping imageries of the caliphate and poleship, Süleyman's depiction as a pole by the apologists of the dynasty did not seem to have struck contemporaries as out of the ordinary.[82] Such a depiction of course was incompatible with those that invited the sultan to recognize the authority of poles whose governance was not ostentatious. If one reason for portraying the sultan as pole was the fusion of mystic and temporal imageries of governance, another was the practical necessity of counterbalancing claims of poleship among the unruly Sufi groups.

The introduction of the idea of the pole into mainstream political theory, at least in the works under consideration that were dedicated to the ruling sultan, did not aim at challenging the authority of the ruler by establishing an alternative. Rather, with the goal of educating the ruler about the higher levels of rulership, authors referred to the position of the pole and illustrated his rulership to provide a moral check and an example for the ruler. In this way, the type of rulership that the pole exercised, and the way he attained such a position, provided a moral exemplar for the sultan. By depicting the pole as the undisputed leader of the world, Sufi writers advised the ruler to act in accordance with the religious instructions of their tradition. Unlike the sultanate, poleship was decided on purely moral grounds. One could attain that highest position on Earth only by virtue of spiritual perfection. From this perspective, the superior form of sultanate appeared to be the one that turned into a manifestation of the pole's rulership and that status could only be achieved through the ruler's spiritual perfection, therefore earning the rank of acting as the pole's executive arm.

Conceived as such, poleship appeared as a third model of inspiration in political theory besides those of God and ruler-prophets. None of these models was presented to be entirely imitable but as authoritative sources of inspiration. Illustrating poleship in this way served the same purpose as holding up divine government or prophethood as models for rulership. In mainstream Sufism, inviting the ruler to submit to the authority of an unseen pole rather than the current shaykh of the order was a crafty way of imposing a strict moral regime without antagonizing the ruler and denting his charisma. The promotion of this conception in political theory was also expedient for establishing the legitimacy of rulership for Sufi-oriented subjects, and thus served a practical cause as well. In Ottoman society, the Sufi affiliation was perhaps at its highest popularity in the history of Islam. In most, if not all, of the Sufi organizations in Ottoman lands, in one form or another, the existence and authority of a seen or unseen perfect human being was acknowledged. In many Sufi orders, there could by definition be no higher authority on Earth than the pole, whether his identity was explicit or not. Thus it was only natural that the Sufi writers exposed one of their most fundamental Sufi beliefs when they wrote on political theory. From this Sufi perspective, good rulership was one enacted with the acknowledgment of the superior authority of the pole.

The Caliphate as Unified Authority

What the conception of poleship as rulership dramatically displayed in *al-ʿAdliyya al-Sulaymāniyya* was the depiction of true rulership attained by spiritual perfection and the existence of such a superior authority regardless of the sultanate. The logical inference for the reader was then that two distinct authorities, spiritual and temporal, could exist at the same time. Although the idea of poleship was expressed only by a few, the main idea underlying this conception was by no means a marginal view among the political writers of the period. With no reference to poleship, Bidlisi, for example, portrayed two different types of rulership pertaining to temporal (*kishvar-i shahādat, mulk-i ṣūrat*) and spiritual realms (*kishvar-i maʿnī*), with distinct authorities. For Bidlisi the world is never deprived of two authorities ruling in their distinct spheres who work to perfect individuals (*takmīl-i nufūs*) in form and meaning (*ṣūrat yā maʿnī*). Because "the divine favor necessitated that among the caliphs of human beings and the sultans of the world one has to be instituted in one of these two positions of caliphate (*maqām-i khilāfat*)."[83]

> Prophets (*anbiyā*), friends of God (*avliyā*), and the men of God (*ahlullāh*) are sovereign governors (*vālī-i mustavlī*) and padishahs in the kingdom of existence (*mulk-i vucūd*). A group of rulers (*mulūk u sālāṭīn*) from among the people of the appearance (*ṣūrat*) are in charge of justice (*maʿdilat*) by way of rulership (*jihāndārī*).[84]

In this elaborate exposition Bidlisi divided the government of humankind into two distinct realms, each ruled by appropriate authorities, with particular requirements to fulfill. He also pointed out that the administration of the two realms was ordained by divine providence. When considered together with his view about the human need for rulership, it appears that humanity needed two authorities to administer each of the material and spiritual worlds. These authorities, however, were not equal to each other and the one pertaining to the spiritual realm was superior to the one belonging to the temporal realm:

> At times the external vicegerency (*khilāfat-i ṣūrī*) and exoteric rulership (*salṭanat-i ẓāhirī*) happen to be in accordance with the prophetic law (*sharīʿat-i nabavī*) and the path of the spiritual vicegerents (*āyīn-i khulafā-i maʿnavī*). Such people (*maẓharī*) could be named as both the vicegerent of God (*khilāfat-i Ḥaq*) and the commander of the faithful. And it is necessary to listen to and obey their prohibitions and commands . . . At times the viceregency in meaning (*khilāfat-i maʿnavī*)

> and true leadership (*imāmat-i ḥaqīqī*) materialize in the personality of one person. But because these do not become manifest as a temporal power (*tamshiyat-i davlat-i ṣūrī*) probably most people deny or harass that receiver of perfection (*maẓhar-i kamāl*). Dervish-like and poor-looking friends of God and the prophets have reported that although they were poor and powerless, with divine guidance and direction, they were commissioned for vicegerency of God's mercy (*khilāfat-i raḥmānī*).[85]

Here the ruler of the external realm could be the vicegerent of God only by following the real vicegerents of God, thus indicating the superiority of the latter. One form of rulership was imperfect for governing all the affairs of humans and meeting all their needs and exercising God's will in the world.

> The rulers of the realm of meanings (*salāṭīn-i kishvar-i maʿānī*): Although they were not authorized to give orders and apply prohibitions in the temporal realm (*mulk-i ṣūrat*), they attained leadership (*sarvarī*) in the realm of meaning (*ʿālam-i maʿnī*) by virtue of their endowment with human perfection (*kamālāt-i basharī*). Because they combined the perfection of knowledge and practice in themselves, they deserved to be leaders to be followed among humankind. They are called the rulers of the realm of meaning.[86]

Any one type was then by definition imperfect and ideal rulership was the one that combined these two forms:

> It is proven that vicegerency of God's mercy (*khilāfat-i raḥmānī*) consists of endowing the fortunate person himself with, to the extent humanly possible, divine (*rabbānī*) traits and perfections, and perfecting himself with praiseworthy human faculties (*malakāt-i ḥamīda-i insānī*) to give order to the temporal world (*jihat-i niẓām-i ʿālam-i jismānī*), and attaching this temporal realm (*kishvar-i shahādat*) to the spiritual world (*ʿālam-i rūḥānī*). If that receiver of perfection (*maẓhar-i kamāl*), in this passing world (*dar dār-i dunyā-i sarīʿ al-intiqāl*), possesses grandeur and majesty on a throne of leadership, then he is called the sultan in appearance and meaning at once (*sulṭān-i ṣūrat va maʿnī*) such as the rulers (*salāṭīn*), prophets (*anbiyā*), friends of God (*awliyā*), the rightly guided caliphs, and the guiding imams (*aʾimma-i hudā*).[87]

As only a few individuals were endowed with such powers, in practice, the rulers of the material and the spiritual worlds were separate and imperfect, performing only one aspect of the rulership, but nevertheless functioning as complementary to each other. As such, rulership was split into two parts, run by two authorities. When combined, the governance of the two realms was but two sides of the same rulership, which could be conducted by one ideal ruler endowed with two authorities or by two separate rulers in their respective spheres.

Bidlisi's conception is similar to that of Şirvani's in the sense that there was a spiritual realm distinct from the temporal realm, and that a separate and superior authority pertaining to the former existed regardless of the latter. To turn the sultanate from a mere executive power into one qualified with spiritual powers, Şirvani advised the ruler to submit his rulership to the authority of the pole and remained silent on the issue of whether the ruler had the capacity to combine these two authorities. Although Bidlisi might not have disagreed with him on this advice, the ideal ruler for him was the one who combined those two authorities. From this perspective, the temporal and spiritual realms or pertaining authorities appear as two aspects of the same rulership, attainable by the ruler. It was precisely this goal to which Taşköprizade fully subscribed as well:

> Know that just as the sultanate in appearance (*al-salṭana al-ṣūriyya*) requires a vizier, a deputy (*nā'ib*), a qadi and the like, similarly, the sultanate in meaning (*al-salṭana al-ma'nawiyya*) requires the knowledge of its conditions (*ma'rifat aḥwāliha*) such as the administration of realm and its protection from enemies.[88]

After drawing this parallel, Taşköprizade devoted the rest of his treatise to the explanation of what the spiritual sultanate entailed and how the ruler could achieve it. This line of reasoning in differentiating between the two types of rulership was followed by other contemporaries as well: Ebu'l-Fazl Münşi, for example, while compiling his work based on that of Najm al-Din Daye's *Mirṣād al-'Ibād* on mystical philosophy, made his account more readable and instructive for a royal reader by inserting guiding chapter headings. Telling a similar story to that of Bidlisi, the four consecutive chapters of his work flowed as follows:

> First Chapter, on the description of rulership and governance in appearence (*salṭanat va ḥukūmat-i ṣūrī*) . . . ; Second Chapter, on the description of the conditions of rulers (*mulūk va salāṭīn*) . . . ; Third Chapter, on the explanation of vicegerency in meaning (*khilāfat-i ma'navī*) and the secrets of the vicegerency of human beings, and the condition of spiritual government (*kayfiyat-i siyāsat-i rūḥānī*) . . . ; Fourth Chapter, on the wayfaring of messengers (*anbiyā*) and prophets (*rusul*) who were adorned with vicegerencies in appearance and meaning (*khilāfat-i ṣūrī va ma'navī ārasta būd-and*). . . .[89]

Although constructed differently and expressed in more elaborate terms, the concept of rulership conceived of by Bidlisi, Taşköprizade, and Ebu'l-Fazl Münşi also distinguished between its ordinary and superior forms. By temporal rulership they meant the ordinary kind referred to by others simply as the sultanate, *pādishāhī*, or *mulk*; to define the superior form of rulership they used *khilāfa* or *ẓill Allāh*. But given that these designations about rulership came to be used indiscriminately and synonymously in this period, they preferred to further qualify these terms to depict the higher form of rulership. As a result, the distinction between the terms sultan and caliph that Dizdar made, for example, was the same as the one Bidlisi made between *khilāfat-i ṣūrī* and *khilāfat-i maʿnavī*. Despite Bidlisi's omission of poleship, his distinction between temporal and spiritual rulership appears to be a reformulation of Ibn Arabi's conception of cosmic government as expounded in his *al-Futūḥāt al-Makkiyya*:

> There are those for whom authority is manifest and who hold the exterior caliphate just as by virtue of their spiritual degree they hold the interior caliphate. Such was the case of Abu Bakr, of Umar, of Uthman, and of Ali, of Hasan and of Mu'awiya b. Yazid, of Umar b. Abd al-Aziz and of Mutawakkil. Others only hold an interior caliphate and have no exteriorly-manifested authority: such is the case of Ahmed b. Harun al-Rashid al-Sabti or of Abu Yazid al-Bistami and the majority of the poles.[90]

Bali Efendi, a Halveti shaykh from Sofia and the most widely read commentator of Ibn Arabi's *Fuṣūṣ al-Ḥikam*, described the Ibn Arabian conception of the caliphate with textbook clarity in his Sufistic manual on the seven stations of mystical experience (*eṭvār-ı sebʿa*).[91] Besides his definition of the caliphate in total disregard of the juristic canon, what makes his presentation more politically charged is his justification of it by reinterpreting the early Islamic succession of authority and promoting himself as the inheritor of the highest rank, once possessed by Ali. For him the caliphate is of two types: *ṣūrī* (exoteric, in appearence) and *maʿnevī* (esoteric, in meaning) just as the Sharia has its outer (*ẓāhir*) and inner (*bāṭın*) components. The *ṣūrī* caliphate represents the outer form (*ẓāhir*) of the Sharia for the purpose of implementing justice, and therefore requires moderate disposition (*iʿtidāl-i mizāc*).[92] Abu Bakr was chosen to be the first caliph because he was the most moderate and just among the companions of the prophet. From Abu Bakr until Ali, the succession was determined on one's fitness to apply the outer Sharia, and the line of succession reflects a hierarchy of perfection in this regard. Ali was inferior in his disposition to apply the outer Sharia. This was why he was delayed in assuming the caliphate in this capacity. Yet, Ali was the recipient of the *maʿnevī* caliphate immediately after the death of the Prophet.

Bali Efendi defined the *maʿnevī* caliphate as being in charge of the inner Sharia (*bāṭın-ı şerʿin taṣarrufu*). Ali inherited this caliphate directly from the Prophet whereas Abu Bakr and other holders of the outer caliphate received it through the contract of the community. After the Prophet, all his companions continued to receive esoteric knowledge and spiritual guidance from Ali, even

Mu'awiya who later opposed Ali's succession in the outer caliphate. Being the recipient of the *maʿnevī* caliphate, Ali was axis mundi, or pole of the poles (*ḳuṭbü'l-aḳṭāb*), and the manifestation of God's greatest name (*ism-i aʿẓam*). For Bali Efendi, it was this esoteric caliphate that was transmitted from the Prophet through Ali and all other subsequent shaykhs, which, by definition makes himself as the latest on this spiritual genealogy. In the context of raging Ottoman–Safavid conflict, Bali Efendi was well aware of the repercussions and possible misunderstandings of such views. For the Sunni establishment, the broader Halveti order was already a suspicious one for its Alid-piety and a number of antinomian Sufis who incurred the hatred of Ottoman authorities. So, he adds a well-articulated disclaimer for the resemblance between the Halveti truth he conveyed and what the Shiites (*revāfiḍ*) claim that the first three caliphs usurped the authority from Ali. But he also modifies the Sunni view that accepts the line of succession among the four rightly guided caliphs as a rank of superiority.[93] For Bali, this superiority is only in their capacity of exoteric caliphate; namely, Abu Bakr, Umar, and Uthman excelled over Ali only in *ṣūrī* caliphate but were inferior in *maʿnevī* caliphate, which is itself superior to the former.

Bali Efendi was a politically tuned shaykh who wrote a number of letters to Ottoman officials urging them to take action against both Safavid Shiism that turned Alid-piety into Alid-loyalism and Sunni revivalism that questioned the legitimacy of the Ottoman establishment. At a time when legitimate political, spiritual, and epistemological authorities were openly challenged among rulers, mystics, and scholars, Bali Efendi offered a working paradigm that accords recognition to all these while reconciling the Halveti concept of caliphate with that of jurists, in a language that may sound less offensive to the Kizilbash. Bali's recognition of the first three caliphs as well as their ranking per moral superiority was in full agreement with the Sunni doctrine of the caliphate. The juristic canon did not recognize the spiritual component of the caliphate which, for them, was a contractually formed authority. The division of the caliphate into two components would still be objectionable for the doctors of both Sunni and Shiite theology but it does not directly negate either view. For Bali, all four caliphs were legitimate but only Ali had the capacity to unite both halves of the caliphate. So, in truth, Ali was the sole inheritor of the Prophet's authority in his both political and spiritual capacities.

The affinity of Sufi interpretation of Islamic history and doctrines to both Sunni and Shiite theologies was not uncommon. Founding figures of Sufism as an intellectual tradition, from Suhrawardi to Ibn Arabi were equally well received among both Sunni and Shiite worlds. The more treacherous issue Bali aimed to straighten in this treatise was the nature of authority, namely, the lines of convergence and diversion between the two types of authority represented by Sufis and worldly rulers, whether Sunni or Shiite. To this question, Bali offers a very direct answer. The Sufis, more specifically the Halvetis, represent the esoteric caliphate of Ali directly received from the Prophet and passed on to the worthy through a spiritual line. The ruler, on the other hand, represents the exoteric caliphate, founded by Abu Bakr and passed on to others who met the conditions. Ali was inherently superior to the other three caliphs except for his capacity to implement the material aspects of the Sharia but ultimately unified both halves of the caliphate with the decease of others. The immediate implication of this understanding was that regardless of who was in charge of the exoteric Sharia, that is, the ruler, there was always a higher authority who was in charge of the esoteric Sharia. But, as in the case of Ali versus Abu Bakr, this dual authority may not necessarily amount to a clash. Given that Bali and Süleyman I stood for Ali and Abu Bakr, respectively, this was, by implication, an ideal model for the coexistence of two authorities that represent the Prophet's two natures. Bali's exposition was a response to other Sufi orders as well, especially to Mevlevis, who not only traced their spiritual genealogy to Abu Bakr but also considered him superior to Ali as the first caliph of Islam who succeeded the Prophet in both his political and spiritual capacities.

This conception of the caliphate, which originated from the mystical philosophy of Ibn Arabi, found a much greater echo among Ottoman writers on rulership than the juristic or theological formulations. The distinction between material and spiritual forms of rulership characterized the political teachings of Bidlisi, Dizdar, Taşköprizade, Ebu'l-Fazl Münşi, and Şirvani while influencing a host of other authors in their perceptions of rulership. Regardless of whether these authors were affiliated with any Sufi order, they employ a distinctly Sufi language in expressing their views of political authority. More specifically, as far as their political views are concerned, in the broadest sense, they all belonged to the school of Ibn Arabi's mystic philosophy. Although Ibn Arabi and his followers had always been very influential in the Ottoman culture of learning and Sufi orders, his fame and authority on mystic teachings solidified after the conquest of Arab lands by Selim I in 1516–1517. Interpretations of his writings to extract prophecies that foretold the rise of the Ottomans turned him into a dynastic patron saint.[94] The assumed discovery of his grave by Selim I and the construction of a tomb over it established an unbreakable fraternity between Ibn Arabi and the Ottoman ruling elite.

Despite the controversies about his teachings, thanks to his immense popularity, Ibn Arabi's writings, particularly *al-Futūḥāt al-Makkiyya* and *Fuṣūṣ al-Ḥikam*, reached a wide circulation among Ottoman men of learning, including the ulema and the Sufis.[95] Besides his own writings, the works and commentaries of his immediate and distant disciples, such as Konevi, Davud-i Kayseri, Molla Fenari, Ahmed Bican, Bali Efendi, and Hamadani, also enjoyed a wide circulation among the Ottomans.[96] Ottoman authors writing on rulership during the age of Süleyman were already familiar with mystic interpretations of the caliphate and cosmic government of the saints through Ibn Arabi's own writings. But it was mostly his disciples who introduced the esoteric and complex teachings of Ibn Arabi's mystical philosophy into the mainstream of political theory and made them applicable to contemporary notions of rulership.

Equally influential in the introduction of Sufi teachings into mainstream political theory was Najm al-Din Daye, a younger contemporary of Ibn Arabi, whose works were loaded with mystical conceptions of the caliphate. Although his views were strikingly similar to those of Ibn Arabi, there is no evidence that he ever met with Ibn Arabi or read his works. In *Mirṣād al-ʿIbād*, a popular work read among Ottoman learned men in its Persian version as well as in Turkish translations, Daye equated the sultanate with the caliphate and attributed to it the same status as prophethood.[97] He divided rulers into two categories: the rulers of world (*mulūk-i dunyā*), who showed God's attributes in appearance (*ṣūrat*) without being aware of it, and the rulers of religion (*mulūk-i dīn*), who received God's attributes and manifested them.[98] Elsewhere, he characterized the two types of rulers as those of appearance (*pādishāhān-i ṣūrat*) and true rulers (*pādishāhān-i ḥaqīqī*), two designations widely used by Ottoman authors.[99]

In *Manārāt al-Sāʾirīn*, Daye established a sophisticated theory of the caliphate that displayed a close affinity with Bidlisi's views as expressed in *Qānūn-i Shāhanshāhī*.[100] Daye conceived of the caliphate with reference to the historical caliphate by referring to the well-known prophetic tradition, which prophesized the caliphate's lifespan as thirty years after the Prophet's death.[101] For him, the caliphate was part of human being's very existence. God made human being his caliph because He created him as qualified for the caliphate (*makhṣūṣ bi al-khilāfa*), combining in him both earthly (*ʿarḍī*) and angelic (*malakūtī*) attributes.[102] He defined the truth of the caliphate (*ḥaqīqat al-khilāfa*) as executive power (*taṣarruf*) in the world (*mulk*) and in the heavens (*malakūt*) as God's deputy (*bi niyābat al-ḥaq*).[103] For him, "because God owns and governs the world (*mulk*), which is the earth (*dunyā*), the exterior part (*ẓāhir*) of existence (*kavn*) and everything in it as well as the heavens (*malakūt*), which is the afterlife (*ākhira*), the inner part (*bāṭin*) of existence (*kavn*), the caliph must be endowed with tools (*ālāt*) of both the world (*mulkiyyāt*) and the heavens (*malakūtiyyāt*) in order to govern the world and the heavens as God's deputy."[104] The universe of created things (*mukavvanāt*) that the caliph was commissioned to govern consisted of two realms, the realm of spirit (*rūḥāniyyāt*) and the realm of material bodies (*jismāniyyāt*).[105] Daye then explained that caliphs are grouped into three layers (*ṭabaqāt al-khulāfā*): Members of the first group carry out the caliphate only by utilizing their corporeal capacities; the second by fully using their corporeal and some heavenly capacities as well; and the third group fully uses both corporeal and heavenly capacities. This third group consists of prophets and saints who belong to the highest status of the caliphate because they have achieved a mirror image of God in His attributes.[106]

Unlike those of Daye, Davud-i Kayseri's works were not quoted by authors who wrote on rulership during the Süleymanic age but they were among the best known texts on Ibn Arabi's mystical philosophy among Ottoman learned men. The introduction he wrote for his commentary on Ibn Arabi's *Fuṣūṣ* received particular acclaim from later Ottoman students of Sufism.[107] For making the dense and intricate formulations of *al-Futūḥāt al-Makkiyya* and *Fuṣūṣ al-Ḥikam* more legible for the Ottoman reader, both his commentaries and treatises played an important role in the dissemination of Ibn Arabi's vision of the caliphate and rulership in Ottoman realms. In his treatise *al-Tawḥīd wa al-Nubuwwa wa al-Wilāya*, he divided the Sharia into its esoteric (*bāṭin*) and exoteric (*ẓāhir*) parts, and stated that both parts had their caliphs (*khalāʾif*). All of these caliphs were subject to the authority of the caliph who had knowledge of both the esoteric and exoteric parts.[108] For Davud-i Kayseri, God made the caliphate an existential requisite because every one of His attributes needs to have a receiver in order to be manifest, just as his name Merciful (*raḥmān*) requires the existence of one who shows mercy (*rāhim*) and one who receives mercy (*marḥūm*).[109]

The very foundation of Ibn Arabi's mystical philosophy exposed in *Fuṣūṣ al-Ḥikam* as well as Davud-i Kayseri's commentary was the concept of the caliphate, a comprehensive concept that explained the creation of humanity, human being's mission on Earth, and the purpose of one's existence as well as relationship with God and the whole creation. *Fuṣūṣ al-Ḥikam* created such a powerful and vivid imagery of human being's status as God's caliph that the followers of Ibn Arabi could easily translate his mystical teachings into a political theory explaining the meaning and the nature of rulership. In commenting on the caliphate of the universal human being (*insān al-kāmil*), Davud-i Kayseri exlained that every human being had a share (*naṣīb*) from the caliphate, by which the sultan governs his realm, a father governs his family, and an individual governs himself, making every human being a caliph in his own right.[110] As for the true caliphate (*khilāfat-i ḥaqīqī*), which represents the reality of Muhammed (*ḥaqīqat-i Muḥammadī*), Davud-i Kayseri depicted it as the absolute deputyship of God, without excess or deficiency (*ziyāda* or *nuqṣān*) in manifesting all His attributes.[111] Such a caliphate, dubbed the grand caliphate (*khilāfat-i ʿuẓmā*) or great caliphate (*khilāfat-i kubrā*), that rules both the exterior (*ẓāhir*) and interior (*bāṭin*) halves of creation, never ceases to exist.[112]

In response to a more mundane problem of the caliphate, Davud-i Kayseri dealt with the question of whether the coexistence of two caliphs at the same time was permissible, a question that busied medieval jurists. Davud-i Kayseri subscribed to the minority view among jurists who ruled that one of the caliphs had to be executed because the caliphate, representing the unity of the Muslim community, does not tolerate dual leadership. But Davud-i Kayseri objected to the dual caliphate for a different reason, justifying the execution of the second caliph by alluding to the mystical interpretation of the caliphate. He first divided the caliphate into two kinds: the caliphs of the exterior (*ẓāhir*) and the caliphs of the interior (*bāṭin*), and stated that the caliph of the interior has always been appointed by God. As for the caliphate of the exterior, there could be only one directly appointed caliph because, by definition, the caliph is a full manifestation of God's attributes including his oneness. Having two exterior caliphs would imply that there were two deities to manifest.[113] A sixteenth-century commentator of *Fuṣūṣ al-Ḥikam*, Bali Efendi of the Halveti order, one of the most celebrated mystics of the age of Süleyman and a staunch supporter of official policies of the Ottoman government, explained the problem in the same way as Davud-i Kayseri.[114]

Ottoman men of learning were exposed to mystical teachings on rulership in the works of Daye and Davud-i Kayseri as a part of their overall mystical philosophy that centered on the relationship between human being and God. But it was Hamadani, in his *Ẕakhīrat al-Mulūk*, who introduced these hithertofore scattered sufistic teachings about the caliphate into a comprehensive theory of rulership. By dividing rulership into two parts, external rulership (*salṭanat-i ṣūrī*) and spiritual rulership (*salṭanat-i maʿnavī*), Hamadani devoted his work to the perfection of the latter without which the former cannot be perfected. For him, although the realm of human being's body (*mamlakat-i vujūd-i insānī*) is a microcosm (*ʿālam-i ṣaghīr*) in appearance, in reality it is a macrocosm (*jihān-i kubrā*) and just like rulership of the material world, its government requires a strict set of principles. In this macrocosm the spirit is the caliph and the heart is its seat whereas the intellect is the vizier and its seat is the brain.[115]

Thanks to the pervasive growth of political texts imbued with Sufistic ideas since the inception of the Ottoman state, sixteenth-century authors as well as the central chancery increasingly became more comfortably conversant in alluding to imageries of rulership in a distinctly Sufistic idiom. In reflection of this trend, Ibn Arghun al-Shirazi, in his preface to his commentary on Jurjani's (d. 1413) *Book on Logic*, addressed Selim I in 1512 as the holder of "*khilāfat al-ʿuẓmā wa salṭanat al-kubrā*."[116] Ebussuud, Süleyman's chief of religious hierarchy endowed with unprecedented powers, edified this Sufistic notion of the caliphate. In two letters written to Süleyman, he characterized the sultan as "caliph of the prophet" (*ḫalīfe-i resūl*) and his rulership as "greatest governance and greatest authority" (*siyāset-i ʿuẓmā ve salṭanat-ı kübrā*).[117] As the empire's top jurist who ingeniously profiled the Ottoman ruler in a way that was acceptable to the Hanafi code in his juristic writings, Ebussuud did not hesitate to portray Süleyman in the language of Sufis. In a number of sultanic law codes or inscriptions he composed he consistently portrayed Süleyman as either caliph of the prophet or the holder of the grand caliphate (*ḫilāfet-i kübrā*).[118] He knew well that calling the Ottoman sultan caliph as a "successor to the Prophet" was at best a very contentious issue in Hanafism, if not in all Sunni legal schools. So, what he meant by *ḫalīfe-i resūl* was Süleyman's vicegerency of God with the same capacity as the Prophet in the sense that it holds sway in both temporal and spiritual realms. In his letters, Süleyman's rulership as *siyāset-i ʿuẓmā ve salṭanat-ı kübrā* refers to unified authority, the kind of rulership that combines the *ṣūrī* and *maʿnevī* authorities per mystical imageries. Similarly, but more explicitly, *ḫilāfet-i kübrā* is a patently Sufistic and, more specifically, an Ibn Arabian concept. Ebussuud's status as the highest ranking jurist only accords more validity to the Sufistic conception of the caliphate.

Adding the adjectives *kubrā* or *ʿuẓmā* to royal titles in order to allude to their greatness was not a post-Abbasid invention of the Sufis. Neither was the addition of *ḥaqīqa* (in truth) to distinguish it from others qualitatively. Yet, medieval constructions were deprived of the spiritual component or the cosmological import later Sufis accorded to these signifiers. In the lexicon of medieval jurists and theologians such as Abu Ya'la (d. 1066) or Baqillani (d. 1013), *al-imāma al-kubrā/ʿuẓmā*, for example, referred to the universal authority of the Muslim community as opposed to the growing number of virtually independent regional rulers.[119] Farabi's concept of *al-malik fī al-ḥaqīqa* (the king in truth), however, was a close kin to that of the Sufis in the sense that it referred to the kind of authority embodied by the Prophet or the philosopher-king.[120] Farabi's ultimately Neoplatonist visions of rulership certainly had a deep and lasting impact on later Islamic mysticism but it was the Sufi philosophers, such as Suhrawardi and Ibn Arabi, who redefined prophethood in a new espistemology marked by the authority of discursive knowledge and accorded new meanings to such constructs. Though different from that of jurists, Farabi's conception of perfect rulership was still definable by moral and intellectual qualification, independent of the *wilāyā* and *khilāfa* that were central to Sufistic visions of rulership. Farabi's concept of the first intellect (*al-ʿaql al-awwal*), identified as the "light of Muhammed" (*nūr al-Muḥammed*) by Ibn Arabi, was further equated with the *khilāfa* of Qur'anic verses and offered to define the caliphate as the cosmic link between God and His creation.[121]

From Sultanate to the Caliphate

Using such terms as sultanate, *pādishāhī, riyāsa, khilāfa, imāma, ẓilliyya*, and others, political writers of the period threaded their concept of rulership with already well-established notions that had been refined in various traditions of learning and statecraft. The prevailing mode of political reasoning on the subject was either to project one's ideal of leadership into political theory, as in the case of Şirvani, or to appropriate refined notions of leadership from various strains of political theory and harmonize them to build one's own ideal design, as in the case of Lütfi Paşa. In either case, envisioning rulership in this period appears to have been an act of customization and reformulation. Although this approach yielded some piecemeal theories of rulership, as in the case of Arifi, it did not fetter the hands of political visionaries, such as Bidlisi, in composing genuinely designed theories of rulership. That means a particular vision of rulership could only be understood by tracing the origins of concepts and visions that are used to define one's notion of rulership.

Whether a piecemeal compilation of political principles or a coherent design of rulership, all political treatises portrayed two levels of rulership, both depending on the personality of the ruler. When authors such as Lütfi Paşa and Şirvani, who remained on the fringes of the theoretical spectrum on rulership, are excluded, it appears that political writers cast their designs of rulership in order to furnish the ruler with a manual of what true leadership entailed and admonish him about the consequences of failing to meet the expectations that came from having such an authority. The result of this quest was to establish an ideal form of rulership, which was defined through a variety of designations whose opposites were depicted as its degraded forms. This ideal rulership was formed through the moral and spiritual perfection of the ruler following the examples set by the ruler-prophets after the model of God's governance. The quality of the sultanate was judged not on the basis of how it was structured, but rather on the basis of who the ruler was in terms of his moral and spiritual qualifications. Such a conception of rulership led Hayali, for example, a master poet of his time, to portray Süleyman as a saint:

> He is governor of people and shadow of God
> Indeed, he is an absolute friend of God[122]

These Sufi-minded moralists expressed their designs of ideal rulership in one of two ways: One way was to designate rulership as caliphate, imamate, *ẓilliyya*, and the like and elaborate on what these designations entail. In this view, such designations were used to build one's conception of an ideal rulership. This was not to simply equate the sultanate with the caliphate or imamate. Rather the caliphate or any other higher designation was offered as a moral paradigm against which one's sultanate was to be judged and modeled upon. Of course, when offered as a model, each of these designations were redefined, mystified, and suited to Sufi cosmology. Another way was to further qualify the proposed model with such constructs as *imāmat-i ḥaqīqī* or *khilāfat-i raḥmānī* to address a ruler whose self-designation as imam or caliph did not reflect what these terms implied. In this depiction, the ruler is reminded that unless qualified, his imamate or caliphate is no different than the sultanate.

Without question, most political writers were equally attentive to providing rulers with principles of good governance, which would make their government beneficial for the community and be in accord with their idealistic conceptions, regardless of the moral condition of the ruler. But, as one of the most basic premises of political reasoning, it was believed without doubt that good governance rested on good character, thus the assumption that once a ruler attained moral and spiritual perfection, then his rulership would necessarily be a good one. Because of this prevailing moralist tendency, dictated by the strong Sufi background of most authors, including the bureaucrats, in political theory, the quest of inculcating an ideal ruler by imposing a strict moral regime on the model of the governance of God, poles, or ruler-prophets far outweighed the search for formulating the practical tools of good government. The moralism of the Sufi-minded was qualitatively different than that of philosophers, ethicists, or jurists whose moral regime, from which good governance emanates, was confined to making virtuous behavior dominant over vices. Sufistic moralism, however, literally meant one's endowment with godly moral traits (*akhlāq Allāh*) which would turn him into a caliph, imam, pole, succor, perfect human being, shadow of God, and vicegerent of God's mercy at once, which corresponds to the nature and status of ruler-prophets and full manifestation of God's names and attributes. This concept of rulership was a practical application of Ibn Arabi's mystification of Farabi's notion of philosopher king.

CHAPTER FIVE

The Myth of the Ottoman Caliphate

BY THE SIXTEENTH CENTURY, Ottoman mystics, scholars, and statesmen envisioned their government to be the only rightful inheritor of the historical caliphate founded by the early Muslim community in Medina. Yet, this new caliphate was substantially different than its medieval formulations that gained currency under the Abbasids. In both popular imagery and elite ideology, the once juristic and theological conceptions of the caliphate were mystified and reformulated as an existential component of divine providence, attained in the spiritual sphere and manifested in the material realm. Millennial anxieties, eschatological expectations, messianic claims, the ascendance of spiritualism across all sectors of the Ottoman establishment, and encounters with the newly rising universalist empires in Eurasia led the Ottomans to reconceptualize the caliphate through the language of Islamic mysticism in response to political exigencies and in engagement with prevailing confessional manifestations and cultural norms of authority.

God's Chosen Dynasty

> If asked, who is Sultan Süleyman? Is he the leader of time or not? Then we answer as follows: No doubt, he is the leader of time. He is the defender of the religious law. So are his deputies and governors. The wise men of time serve him. So do the sultans of the Arab, the Turk, the Kurd and the Persian. He has many cities under his control as mentioned. The definition of leader suits him. He is the deputy of the Prophet in upholding the religion. Thus it is incumbent upon the whole community to obey him.[1]

As exemplified in this passage by Lütfi Paşa, there was no doubt in the minds of political authors writing in this period about the legitimacy of the ruler in office and his relative stance among contemporary rulers. Lütfi Paşa and many others who took into consideration the Ottoman experience in formulating their conceptions of rulership advocated the uniqueness of Ottoman rulership by elaborating on the distinguishing features of the Ottoman dynasty. Lütfi Paşa's profile of ruler was a juristic exposition of Ottoman imperial self-image, done by a retired statesman turned jurist. As the title "defender of the religious law" could be claimed by any ruler, Lütfi Paşa's argument basically promoted political might as the sole legitimizing quality of the Ottoman sultan over all others. He thus depicted Süleyman as an inheritor of the historical caliphate and the Prophet's successor, as somebody whose authority extended over the entire Muslim community. Lütfi Paşa adopted this way of reasoning about the supremacy of the Ottoman sultan from the official Ottoman usage of time where defending the religion, having control over the majority of the Muslim community, and having a deputyship to the Prophet were enumerated as principal distinguishing features of Ottoman rule in royal decrees, formal letters, treaties, and dynastic histories.

Long before Lütfi Paşa wrote his work, a string of historians, including Aşıkpaşazade and Bidlisi, hinted at the unique qualities of the Ottoman dynasty as precedents for good governance. Ibn Kemal's court-sponsored chronicle of the Ottoman dynasty began with a section titled "On the superiority of the noble Ottoman sultans and the imperfectness of other rulers" that turned his historical narrative into a mirror for princes.[2] In their elaborations on the uniqueness of the Ottomans, Bidlisi and Ibn Kemal, both decorated with shining credentials in Persianate learning, were fully cognizant of the long war of words between the Ottoman and Timurid courts. Their older contemporary, Nizami Bakharzi (d. 1503), for example, narrates a story that shows the Ottomans inferior to the Timurids even during the reign of Mehmed II whose fame could hardly be matched by any of his contemporaries. According to this probably fictive but telling story, in the presence of the notables of his territories, Mehmed II asked whether there is anyone who equaled him among the rulers of the world. They replied in concert that he had no equal thanks to his residing on the seat of the caliphate, noble genealogy that goes back to the Seljuks, reaching the zenith of learning, observance of religious law, undertaking holy war, generosity towards the talented without discrimination, administering his entire realm under the jurisdiction of the administrative council, and having innumerable soldiers. To this laudation, some just people added that the Ottomans lacked a precious jewel like Abdurrahman Jami, the Timurids had a superior Chingizid lineage, and that the Timurid ruler had the authority to exercise independent reasoning on juristic questions (*ijtihād*) whereas Mehmed II only knew some philosophy.[3] Throughout the sixteenth century, Ottoman intellectuals grew more confident about their own political and cultural identities, and treated the Ottoman dynasty as both the originator and manifestation of what makes the Rum special. Court historian Talikizade added a chapter to his otherwise humdrum chronicle of a military campaign that summarized the distinguishing attributes of Ottoman rulers in twenty articles, all of which could be found elsewhere in bits and pieces.[4] From the seventeenth century onwards, long and systematic treatises were compiled as digests of imperial ideology and guiding principles of government with constitutional import.[5]

In the age of Süleyman, the spreading belief in the Ottoman dynasty's extraordinariness among the ruling elite was accompanied with a distinctive identity and a sense of superiority that pervaded the vast literary corpus and artistic expressions of the period. This was a time when poets, historians, and scholars explicitly expressed their pride in their history, dynasty, language, arts, land, society, and institutions.[6] The imperial establishment considered *Āl-i ʿOs̱mān*, the Ottoman dynasty, an indispensable part of their cultural, confessional, and political identities, which led them to attribute special qualities to this lineage, and compare its superior characteristics to other dynasties. In historical imagination of the period, the very ruling dynasty was accorded a pivotal status in the formation of what it meant to be an Ottoman. This distinctive identity was largely confined to Asia Minor and the Balkans, and extended only to the imperial establishment in provinces. It was elitist and inseparably tied to the Ottoman dynasty. This identity found its most explicit expression in the newly emerging genres in Ottoman literature, particularly biographical dictionaries and universal histories. Among them, Taşköprizade's *al-Shaqāʾiq al-Nuʿmāniyya*—the first of its kind to give brief biographies of notable Ottoman scholars and Sufi masters—included only people who belonged to the cultural and political milieu of Asia Minor and the Balkans, leaving out scholars and mystics, for example, who lived and produced in provinces where Arabic or Persian was dominant. Similarly, the first dictionary of poets by Sehi (d. 1548) applied the same criteria as Taşköprizade and surveyed only poets who composed in Turkish.[7] To be included in this cultural stratum one had to belong to one of the ruling institutions or converse in Turkish. Both works were divided into sections according to the reigns of the Ottoman sultans, pointing toward the close association of this cultural identity with the history of the Ottoman dynasty. What preceded these biographical dictionaries in their approach, and perhaps served as models, was the first generation of great Ottoman histories commissioned by Bayezid II. The histories of Bidlisi and Ibn Kemal were divided into chapters corresponding to the reigns of Ottoman sultans.[8]

Incessant political conquests, imposing architectural monuments that became the distinguishing markers of the Ottoman space from Budapest to Cairo, and a flood of widely acclaimed literary output created a sense of triumphalism that shaped the self-perception of the Ottoman elite. As displayed in the official correspondence of this period, the men of letters saw no equals in the East or the West. In royal decrees and correspondence it became customary to display the extent of Ottoman rule by enumerating dozens of distant lands now turned into administrative provinces that they knew only from the geographical literature a few decades before. To authors writing in the sixteenth century, the Ottoman experience seemed uniquely successful by all accounts, comparable to the universal empires of the ancient and medieval worlds.[9] The Ottoman ruler came to be regarded in the same category as Alexander the Great and Chingiz Khan. The Ottoman lineage, which had always suffered from a sense of inferiority compared to the Chingizid or the Qurayshi descents, now established itself as a self-promoting lineage as noble as any other.[10] Despite increasing criticism from scholars and statesmen about the malpractices in government, the Ottoman elite of the period not only took pride in their imperial expansion but in their state-building as well, particularly the military and the learning establishments.[11]

The contest for supremacy among the regional Muslim empires of the early modern period, most notably between the Ottomans and the Safavids, required stronger bonds between the literati and their patrons, and demanded that they compare and distinguish themselves from rival dynasties. Despite limited physical contact and geographical barriers, the Sa'dids of Morocco, the Mughals of India, and the Shaybanids of Central Asia also posed challenges to the supremacy of the Ottoman ruler.[12] Both the Sa'dids and the Mughals were particulary well-tuned to the Sufistic and messianic repertoire of authority, legitimacy, and supremacy.[13] The Ottomans, however, never pursued a systematic policy to establish themselves as the universal leaders of the Muslim community in the way the Abbasids did, and there was no project to revive the pre-Mongol caliphate, at least until the latter half of the nineteenth century. Yet, they claimed to be the leader of all Muslims and superior to other dynasties for waging war against the infidels and defending the realm of Islam. This was a legitimizing idea for the expansionist policies of the Ottoman state on all fronts in this period, a necessary ingredient of Ottoman policies not only against other Muslim dynasties but against the Habsburgs as well. No other Muslim dynasty could come close to the political might of the Ottoman state at the time of Süleyman. Competing against the Roman Catholic Habsburgs at the heart of Christian lands was one distinguishing mark that no other Muslim dynasty could take credit for. Contemporary Muslim dynasties could redefine their ruling ideologies within the confines of the broader framework of Islamic and indigenous traditions. In portraying Süleyman's supremacy, the Ottoman chancery, however, had to take into account the universalist ambitions and imperial imageries of Christian powers from Habsburgs to the Portuguese as well. Despite this unrivaled power, and because of the discontinuity in the universal leadership of the Muslim community, the Ottoman dynasty never enjoyed the same leadership as the Abbasids. However pragmatic the Ottomans might have been in their claims for universal leadership, they needed to respond to counterclaims that might have challenged their status and affected their policies. The Ottomans felt obliged to consistently use their distinctive qualities that were lacking in other dynasties, such as being the custodians of holy cities and defenders of the faith against the infidels and the heretics.

The increasingly competitive Eurasian space for universal supremacy turned Ottoman intellectuals well tuned to political ideas and imageries afloat across various cultural media and at points of encounters. But a more demanding motivating factor behind the constant embroidering of the imperial ideology with creative imageries was the transformation of the Ottoman social fabric with bewildering speed, continuously producing problems and questions of political nature to be addressed on the intellectual plane as well as administrative. In response, the Ottoman elite looked adamant in according their dynasty the status of a noble lineage that was chosen by God, foretold in scriptural texts, and prophesied by friends of God. One of the least likely exponents of these views was Lütfi Paşa, who stressed in both his *Tevārīḫ* and *Khalās al-Umma* that the house of Osman was commissioned by God to serve a specific purpose. For him, three members of the house of Osman were renewers (*mujaddid*) of religion, according them a unique status in the increasingly competitive space to reclaim the supreme rulership vacated by the Abbasids. Since at least Sharaf al-Din Yazdi, Timurid historians and later Aqquyunlu historians were comfortably adding this title to propagate the supremacy of their rulers.[14] Lütfi Paşa's older contemporary Ruzbihan Khunji (d. 1521) profiled the Shaybani Khan (d. 1510) as a renewer of religion.[15] The contemporary Sa'did rulers of Morocco enjoyed being fashioned as *mujaddids*, only in more emphatic terms.[16] Besides being a sign of uniqueness, the designation of the ruler as "renewer of religion" was part of the post-Abbasid and post-Mongol pursuit of bolstering dynastic legitimacy for the newly rising states in the Islamic world with universalist ambitions.[17] Lütfi Paşa based his argument on a well-known prophetic tradition that indicates the coming of a renewer of religion at the beginning of every century:[18]

> Perhaps the person sent by God does not have to be a scholar (*ʿālim*). Perhaps at times he could be a scholar, at times a caliph, at times a leader (*muqaddam*) or a ruler (*malik*) who is followed. And sometimes it happens that at one time he [the renewer] may be a caliph and *malik* and *amīr*, and God does not appoint a scholar or else to this position. It is necessary that a person's word is welcome (*maqbūl al-qawl*) and people turn to his word and refrain from what he prohibits and do what he commands, whoever the renewer is.[19]

As portrayed by Lütfi Paşa, since its rise as a political entity three centuries before his time, the house of Osman yielded a lineage that produced all three renewers sent by God: Osman I, Mehmed I, and Selim I.[20] This portrayal alone points to the uniqueness of the Ottoman dynasty among all Muslim dynasties, past and present, making it the only one that produced three renewers, establishing with certainty that it was the chosen lineage to serve God's will. Lütfi Paşa did not elaborate on the deeds of these sultans as renewers and was content with indicating that they revived the righteous religion for their respective ages. But he must certainly have been led to think as such by the ongoing Ottoman–Safavid conflict that turned the large Turkoman basis of the empire to its confessional other. As a self-recognized jurist, Lütfi Paşa must have been aware of what the term *iḥyā* (revive) specifically connotes in the context of fierce religious debates of the sixteenth century. His fellow learned men better knew the term from the title of al-Ghazali's celebrated work *Iḥyā ʿUlūm al-Dīn* a book that gained an unprecedented popularity among the Ottoman readers. Writing at the height of a growing Ismaili-Shii threat to the Caliphate, Ghazali's reconciliation of the Sunni branches of knowledge and piety and providing political legitimacy to the newly rising Turkic dynasties earned him an authoritative status among his Ottoman disciples who found themselves obliged to respond to similar questions. Taşköprizade's *Mawḍūʿāt al-ʿUlūm* (Encyclopedia of Sciences) speaks for the extent of penetration *Iḥyā al-ʿUlūm* exerted in Ottoman scholarship. *Mawḍūʿāt* was compiled under the protective shadow of *Iḥyā* and aimed to become its more systematic and expanded reinstatement. Ghazali was not only the author of the *Revivification* but also widely considered to be a scholar who actually revived religious sciences at a time of political and epistemological crisis. Lütfi Paşa's crediting the Ottoman sultans for reviving religion, more specifically, means the mission Ghazali only articulated was materialized.

But the tradition of according rulers the providential mission of renewing the religion had deeper roots and more eschatological connotations than simply decorating the sultanic regalia against competitors. As diligently unpacked by Hayrettin Yücesoy, the idea was a product of the Abbasid political technology and made its debut as a marker of political legitimacy during the reign of al-Ma'mun (r. 813–833) when boundaries between political authority and religion were violently contested and renegotiated in the context of raging civil wars, floating messianic claims, and the inquision (the Mihna). al-Ma'mun, in his quest to reclaim the religious authority denied to caliphs by the ulema, as the *corrector et reparator* of religion, furnished himself with messianic imageries as *mujaddid* and Mahdi, to restore his secularized authority to its purported original form with sway over the religious domain.[21] It is not coincidental that both Selim I and Shaybani Khan, each confronted by the same Safavid claim for a new political and religious order, were portrayed as renewers of religion. It is ironic that Lütfi Paşa considers al-Mu'tasim (r. 833–842), al-Ma'mun's brother, as the renewer of the third century of Islam despite the fact that it was al-Ma'mun's term that dominated the beginning two decades of the third century. But al-Ma'mun was better known in historical memory for his Shiite proclivities and obviously was not the right name to designate as a former *mujaddid* in the context of Ottoman campaign against the Shiites. Lütfi Paşa accuses al-Ma'mun for his Shiite and Mu'tazilite symphaties and credits al-Mu'tasim for his campaign against these heresies.[22] For Lütfi Paşa, al-Mu'tasim was a renewer of religion precisely because of his defeating Shiism in the same way Selim I was portrayed.

Lütfi Paşa borrows the very idea of renewing religion from *al-Fawā'iḥ al-Miskiyya*, which identified al-Ma'mun as the renewer of religion of the third century but made no mention of his Shiite leanings.[23] Its author Abdurrahman Bistami predicted in 1440 that Mahdi, as God's caliph, would appear soon and the world would come to an end. But the anonymous translator of the work in 1570, updated the text's historical information and prophesies. To dispel anxieties, he pushed the possible timing of the end of the world further into the future. But in the absence of Mahdi's apprearence, he added Selim to the list of renewers of religion for eliminating the Safavid heresy and conquering Egypt because of the Mamluk ruler's alliance with Shah Isma'il.[24]

When Lütfi Paşa was composing his chronicle, Selim I's image as *mujaddid* was already inscribed on the literary plane through the rapid growth of *Selīmnāme* epics, most notably by that of the Andalusian émigré Maghribi in 1517.[25] *Selīmnāme* writing capitalized on and responded to the immensely influential such epics, from *Tīmūrnāma* and *Shāhnāmā-i Ismāʿīl*, in propagating supremacy among competing rulers from Iran to India.[26] Ebu'l-Fazl Mehmed, writing about a decade after Lütfi Paşa, depicted only Selim I as one of the chosen but elaborated more on the deeds that earned him the title. In his preface to his father Bidlisi's history of the reign of Selim I, *Selīmshāhnāma*, like Lütfi Paşa, he cited the famous prophetic tradition about the coming of renewers but extracted the precise evidence about the renewership of Selim I from Qur'anic verse 21: 105–106, which indicates that only the good among His servants would inherit the land.[27] From this prognostic verse he unearthed a prophecy by calculating the numerical value of the word *ẕakara* and obtained H. 920/C.E. 1514, the year in which the Ottomans defeated the Safavids and eliminated the greatest threat in the perception of many contemporaries. As renewer of the laws of religion, Selim I was perceived to have saved the land from the heretics (the Safavids), ended seditious disorder (*fitna*), and reinstituted the right religion. For Ebu'l-Fazl Mehmed, this chronographic evidence proved that the Ottoman wars against the Safavids were not only justified on religious grounds but were also sanctioned and foretold by God.

The noble progeny of Osman that produced renewers of religion was immaculate and protected, a view voiced by many with great pride. Kınalızade praised the Ottoman lineage, for all the rulers prior to his age were pure in their belief and belonged to the people of tradition and community (*ehl-i sünnet ve'l-cemāʿat*).[28] Given that the right creed was among the most important aspects of rulership for the writers of this period, such an impeccable record in dynastic history attributed to Ottoman rulership an undisputable superiority over others who failed to produce such rightly guided lineages. Kınalızade's book of ethics was a philosophical treatise with few illustrations about the ideals of morality and social life and this was one of several places where he offered the Ottoman example as a textbook case. Lütfi Paşa, who was the opposite of Kınalızade in character and scholarly interests, was in full agreement with him here. In his chronicle, written with a blatant criticism of a long list of malpractices, he singled out the Ottoman dynasty as the most immaculate of all past dynasties:

> After the era of the rightly-guided caliphs ended, no people emerged who were worthy as the Ottoman people of crown and throne, whose creed was pure and prophetic, and who were adorned with generosity, morality, the law of past rulers and the customs of noble rulers. Each one of the other peoples that came to be rulers from among the community of Islam were accused of a defect: Some of the Umayyads were Kharijites. And even some of the Abbasids were known to be Mu'tazilites and Shiites. And the majority of the Banu Lays, the Buyids and the Fatimids were known to be Karamitas, namely heretics (*zendeḳa*) and apostates (*ilhād*).[29]

Under the shadow of a well-established tradition of glorifying the Ottoman dynasty in chronicles and poetry, few rulers ever received any kind of criticism from the Ottoman literati and historians writing about their history in this period. Even these criticisms were usually directed to the sultan's entourage, and mostly confined to administrative matters or personal excesses rather than their upholding the right religion.[30] A commonly cited criticism of misgovernance was Bayezid I's excessive drinking habits, for which his wife, the daughter of the Serbian despot, was blamed. A prevailing image of the Ottoman dynasty in this period was that all Ottoman rulers succeeded by God's grace and ruled by divine guidance as well as by merit, while they were at times misled by the malicious around them.

Accompanying the idea of immaculateness was the perception of perfection accomplished by the Ottoman dynasty. For the learned admirers of the dynasty, the Ottomans had already achieved the utmost objectives of rulership laid out in the canons of political thought and turned utopian ideals into reality. Among them, Ibn Kemal thought that rulership had reached its ultimate form with the Ottomans: "This matter of rulership (*emāret*), which consists of extending and applying the laws of leadership (*ḳavānīn-i shāhī*) and the principles of rulership among all the distinguished and common people, reached perfection in their practice."[31] In comparing the Ottomans to other Muslim dynasties, Ibn Kemal further stated that all other dynasties except the Ottomans, were unrightfully confiscating property, exacting onerous and unfair levies because they lacked sufficient resources to run their government: "If these unrightful revenues were lifted then the total sum of all their revenues combined would not even equal the market taxes (*bāc*) and tributes (*ḫarāc*) taken from non-Muslims in the Rum. Because the Rum is prosperous (*maʿmūr*) while other places are not."[32] As one of the principal maxims of political wisdom literature, there was an ontological correlation between good governance and prosperity, and the Ottoman elite were often eager to pinpoint wealth as a sign of perfection in rulership.

Ibn Kemal's declaration of the Rum as prosperous points to an ideal commonly highlighted in political literature as one of the noblest goals of rulership. The term *maʿmūr*, or its verbal noun *ʿimāra*, in political theory usually denoted a state of the utmost achievement in materializing social ideals, as a result of successful human endeavor led by political leadership.[33] It was, for example, one of the indispensable components of an ideal polity displayed in the circle of justice.[34] No less utopian than Ibn Kemal, Kınalızade confidently declared that, thanks to Süleyman, all cities in the realm of the Ottomans were virtuous cities (*medīne-i fāżıla*).[35] The perfect state of political association in the philosophical tradition since Farabi was the virtuous city upon which all subsequent philosophical-minded scholars based their political theory. A depiction as such points to an unmatched achievement that clearly distinguishes the Ottoman dynasty from all others. Before Kınalızade, however, Davvani, had already declared Aqquyunlu cities as virtuous cities as well, evidence that the Ottomans were not alone in their self-perception of having reached the end stage of perfection.[36]

Yet these portrayals of perfection did not distinguish the Ottomans enough from their Muslim counterparts. Arguably the most jealously guarded title of Ottoman rulers was also the earliest and the most modest, the *gazi* title, which was reinvented in this period in the context of renewed clashes with the rising Catholic powers of Europe against whom the battlefield extended from the Mediterranean to the Indian Ocean. The Ottomans were among the few Muslim dynasties located at the frontier of the abode of Islam in ceaseless encounters for expansion and defense but the principal power to assume the position of spreading God's word and defending the realm of Islam against the infidel. From their inception, the Ottomans always considered their *gazi* leadership a privileged position among the Muslim dynasties and displayed their *gaza* activity as a marker of their distinction. For Ibn Kemal, for being *gazis*, the Ottoman dynasty was superior to other Muslim dynasties, which earned their leadership by overcoming others. Unlike other Muslim dynasties, the Ottomans "opened the abode of war, the Rum [for conquest], killed many infidels, and consumed only the gain of their own raids and the fruit of their pikes."[37] As for the Ottoman conquests in the east and the south toward Muslim lands, in Ibn Kemal's view, they were obliged by religious law to conquer these Muslim dynasties for defensive purposes because they always posed hurdles in the way of waging *gaza* against the infidels.[38] To their credit, the Ottomans founded their state in a land that they added to the abode of Islam, without challenging the authority of any other legitimately established Muslim dynasty.

Such perceptions created an image of a dynasty that was chosen and immaculate, which materialized the ideals of mainstream political theory, and therefore proved to be irreplaceable. In explaining why the Ottoman sultans did not engage in conquering the whole world while they possessed all the means to do so, Ibn Kemal stated that no one could be found to act as a trustee in the whole realm even as a temporary deputy:

> Such a campaign would have been feasible only if somebody could have been found to replace him on the throne as his deputy, at a time when the ruler sets out, whom the notables (*ḫavāṣ*) and the commons (*ʿavām*) would obey in such a way that people would think that their rulers had not left them. It is known that, according to the well-established customs (*āyīn-i metīnleri*) and true/manifest laws (*ḳavānīn-i mübīnleri*) of the noble sultans of the house of Osman, may God perpetuate their days, whether free or slave, nobody emerged who could manage to be followed by all (*maḫdūmü'l-kül*). This ancient law (*ḳānūn-ı ḳadīm*) and the sound custom are causes of the continuity of order (*istimrār-i niẓām*) and the stability of the arrangement of the affairs of the majority (*istiḳrār-i intiẓām-i umūr-i cumhūr*). This is because of the effects of their [sultans'] good governance in strengthening and corroborating the knots of the rules of leadership and government.[39]

For Ibn Kemal the irreplaceability of the Ottoman sultan was required by the very laws and customs that distinguished the Ottoman state from others. Such a system did not allow the formation of even temporary loyalties to anyone other than the sultan himself. In agreement, Lütfi Paşa attested that "one cannot find someone who resembles the Ottoman sultan in the mentioned traits in such a way that people (*nās*) unite in agreeing that he deserves the complete rulership (*al-salṭana al-kāmila*) and caliphate in times of sedition (*fitna*)."[40] Lütfi Paşa further explained this feature of the Ottoman polity in more explicit terms:

> Certainly the majority of the people of our time are his [Süleyman I] freedmen, and his father's freedmen, and his grandfather's freedmen, and sons of their freedmen, and sons of the sons of their freedmen. It is impossible for this people (*ṭāʾifa*) to unite in paying loyalty to somebody else for no one else is given victory (*nuṣra*) except for the Ottomans because the Ottomans are immaculate in upholding the religion, in justice (*inṣāf*), and in fighting for the faith (jihad).[41]

With these exclusive arguments Kınalızade, Ibn Kemal, and Lütfi Paşa portrayed a political regime inseparable from the Ottoman dynasty, a view that other authors who pointed to the unique features of the Ottoman dynasty must have found agreeable. Despite attributing more prestigious titles such as "renewer" to certain sultans, in all these accounts of the uniqueness of the Ottoman dynasty, the emphasis is on the lineage or the house rather than individual sultans. All these attributes, whether acquired or granted by God, were thought to be the common property of the Ottoman lineage passed from one ruler to another. This conception granted the Ottoman lineage an exclusive right and privilege to rule the Ottoman state, the land of Rum, and stand supreme over all other dynasties. These authors who advocated the uniqueness of the Ottoman dynasty thought that the Ottoman lineage was not only chosen by God to rule but also that the individual members of this lineage had proven that they were worthy of such an exclusive right to rule by merit. This perception of predestination and historical triumphalism created an image that only a ruler from the House of Osman had an exclusive right and capability to rule over the people who could not possibly pay tribute to any other ruler.

Mystification of the Origins

The sixteenth-century imperial ideology and imageries of Ottoman dynasty owed a great deal to a century-long effort of myth-making that gained momentum at the turn of the fifteenth century. The Timurid invasion of Asia Minor in 1402, which shattered the early Ottoman state, was far from a passing military humiliation. Besides the long political turmoil it created, including a decade long civil war and a popular rebellion by a charismatic Sufi with impeccable juristic credentials, it was a defining moment in Ottoman self-perception and restructuring. The hubris and bravado Bayezid I displayed against his counterpart, Tamerlane, in a war of diplomatic dispatches showed that he had no regard for the cultural sophistication of the Timurid realm but perceived the clash in purely military terms.[42] In the view of contemporary literati the Timurid defeat of the Ottomans was a takeover of an upstart state by an *haute culture*. Fourteenth-century Ottomans had not yet a visible place in the annals of history, receiving only a passing mention in travel books, geographies, and histories.[43] The Timurids, however, having already inherited the glorious Chingizid legacy, were not only the most illustrious dynasty of the time but also courted the most eminent contingent of poets, artists, and scholars. From the Timurid perspective, this clash was led by the lord of conjunction against a rogue frontier prince. Later Ottoman historians in the main, despite their resentment for the catastrophe, felt compelled to acknowledge Timur's status as a universal ruler and appreciate his era as a climax in arts and learning.[44] Timur, far from being demonized as in the case of Shah Isma'il, continuously inspired Ottoman literati and statesmen as they became more exposed to the literary masterpieces of the Timurid court such as the *Ẓafarnāmā* of Sharaf al-Din Yazdi.[45]

The infamous Battle of Ankara brought the fledgling Ottoman state to its heels but, unlike the notorious Timurid practice of conquest, fell short of wholly engulfing the political space as Tamerlane quickly left without establishing his direct rule. Paradoxically, while the contesting Ottoman princes were searching for ways to consolidate their power, that very defeat sparked the process of the Ottoman state's cultural construction. Two masterpieces of early Turkish literature, Ahmedi's *İskendernāme* (The Book of Alexander) and Abdülvasi Çelebi's *Ḫalīlnāme* (The Book of Abraham), served as foundational manifestations for Ottoman self-perception and historical signification. Ahmedi (d. 1412–1413) drafted the first version of his text in the 1390s, at the height of sweeping conquests of Bayezid I, and finally completed it in the 1410s when the Ottoman order was in seemingly irrevocable disarray.[46] The work reflects both the hope of an aspiring world empire and existential anxieties of a bankrupt enterprise. *İskendernāme* was first conceived to be an epic story of Bayezid I (d. 1403) whose blitz campaign for world conquest could only be likened to that of Alexander the Great. At the end, the work turned out to be a world history, an epic story of the House of Osman, a mirror for princes, and a literary statement for cultural coming of age for the fledgling Turkish vernacular at once. Catered toward the specific needs of a nascent state in the process of being reconfigured, *İskendernāme* is an encyclopedic repository of wisdom and information on literature, sciences, history, and statecraft. As one of the most popular works for the learned, it staged the first debut of the Ottomans into the narrative scene of world history, a foundational reference the Ottomans consulted to see their distinctive marks for generations.

What turned this epic history of the world into a reference source for Ottoman identity is its final section titled "The Story of the History of the House of Osman."[47] Unlike writing a separate chronicle of early Ottoman history, integrating the story of the Ottomans into a universal trajectory of great empires accords the fledgling Ottoman state a metahistorical status at a time when they were barely noticed by their more formidable contemporaries. Ahmedi paints a refined image of the Ottoman dynasty through a historical critique of preceding states and empires that involves marking their defects and merits. The implied inference is that the Ottomans come out as the most perfect of them all, bereft of blemishes that led to the downfall of past great empires, while being endowed with qualities that made them excel. In response to the undergoing crisis of conscience that prompted statesmen and the learned to inquire what made the nascent Ottoman order fail, *İskendernāme* presents a didactic analysis of the rise and fall of past dynasties. The immediate message of the text is that the Timurids, for being oppressors, are bound to fall while the Ottomans, for upholding justice, would recover and prevail. Being gifted with an unblemished faith and a perfect record in upholding the righteous religion, the Ottomans were conferred a noble mission, a mission to rule and protect God's trust as prescribed in God's words and fulfilled by his chosen servants. From the most down-to-earth idea of *ḳānūn* to the most esoteric ideas such as reading heavenly alignment's impact on human affairs, principal themes of the *İskendernāme* were widely consumed and reprocessed as the staples of later Ottoman political and historical corpus.

Ḫalīlnāme was composed in 1412, a decade after the Battle of Ankara—the heaviest catastrophe the Ottomans faced before the empire was irrecoverably dissolved by the end of World War One. At first glance, *Ḫalīlnāme* is a didactic account of Prophet Abraham on morals and spirituality in verse. Written during the Interregnum that followed the Battle of Ankara, the very title and subject of the work reflect an existential anxiety and voice a unifying call in a politically fragmented and religiously diverse frontier society. The main narrative surprises the reader with an abrupt nesting of a brief story of the Ottomans in the midst of a flowing tale of prophetic piety and miraculous acts.[48] Just as it started, the Abrahamian epic then unassumingly continues without conceding an apology for distraction. How then can we interpret this anachronistic patching of an anecdotal snapshot of the Ottomans into a sublime story that earned a privileged mention of God in the Qur'an? The key may be the very contradiction between a timeless, sublime, and deeply symbolic prophetic tragedy and an unfolding drama of a very earthly House of Osman, whose only majestic asset had been its cut-and-dried accounts of chivalry. At this moment of crisis, the Abrahamian tragedy provides an empowering reference to signify the tumultuous afflictions the Ottomans faced and embed themselves into the divine order of things by mystifying their very existence. As such, *Ḫalīlnāme* is an act of creating a glory from a humiliation that just befell the Ottomans. The plight of the Ottomans then presents itself as the latest recurrence of its grander archetype as demanded by the cyclical laws of divine cosmology.

Yet, despite all the heart-wrenching tribulations of a prophet and soul-captivating morals of his piety, *Ḫalīlnāme* is a manifestly straightforward political statement. From the very beginning, one cannot but immediately notice that this is a political struggle between a just ruler and a vicious tyrant: between Abraham, the protagonist, and Nimrud, the villain. Besides the symbolism and similes that immediately spark meaningful corollaries between a prophet and the Ottoman sultan, the text speaks with a domesticated idiom of rulership. The section on the Ottomans, for example, starts with Abraham's being declared to become a just sultan after defeating Nimrud while the subsequent section is titled "On Abraham's becoming the sultan of Babylonia." Here, Abdülvasi Çelebi does not conceal his intention of signifying Mehmed I's succession struggle with his brother Musa with a prophetic archetype as he transitions into the Ottoman section with the line "similarly, our shah is the great sultan." Mehmed I, whom Abdülvasi Çelebi designates as Mehdi, the promised ruler of Islamic eschatology, is not only portrayed as having received

God's succor but also is exceptionalized by being included among the prophets and saints in bravery and rulership. Abdülvasi Çelebi credits him with the qualities of his namesake, Muhammed, and enumerates his most explicit qualities as faith, bravery, justice, and service to humankind—the same qualities highlighted for Abraham. Yet the text recounts Mehmed's otherwise modest victory against his brother with an explicitly political agenda and a lofty anti-Timurid claim for universal rulership. He is depicted as having surpassed all legendary rulers of antiquity in every distinctive trait that made them exceptional. The celebrity list includes Nushirevan in his justice, Alexander in his world conquest, and Feredun in his enlightenment. Solomon, who was thought to have been gifted with all these qualities, was cited to be Mehmed's true ancient simile. The Ottoman sultan is then envisaged to have appropriated the Greek, Iranian, and Abrahamic legacies of rulership that reigned supreme in popular imagination; in other words, the best known character models of medieval legitimacy that were only more illustriously highlighted by Timurid propagandists.[49] But the text goes even further with a more tangible and direct denouncement of Timurid's monopoly for universal rulership: The author extends Mehmed's glorious conquests and the political space under his rule into regions under the Timurid rule, including Samarkand, Khurasan, and Shiraz, which the Ottomans could only have imagined at the time, and never ventured to conquer afterwards. This was not an imaginative revenge or a political takeover of enemy territory but a recipe for a reconstruction of the Ottoman state through symbolic appropriation of the then most florescent centers of culture. It was no accident that subsequent Ottoman rulers, most notably Mehmed II, pursued aggressive policies to attract learned men from the east and collect works of art and literature produced in these regions.

A lingering legacy of the Timurid invasion was the Ottoman preoccupation with crafting a suitable lineage that prompted almost a century-long undertaking starting with Yazıcıoğlu's modest attempt, and finally gaining its canonized form in the sixteenth century. A series of chroniclers provided the Ottoman dynasty with a noble stock based on specific circumstances, ideological leanings, and available sources.[50] A few dozen chronicles written in plain Turkish, mostly anonymous and commonly titled *Histories of the House of Osman*, took up this noble task and popularized it among the ruling circles and the broader reading public. Most, if not all, seem to be descended from a master text, first composed by Yahşi Fakih in the early fifteenth century, continuously reworked, abridged, and expanded by the learned servants of the court, ranging from humble scribes to heads of chancery.[51] However elaborate and useful these constructions may be, they all display the pain of reconciling the Islamic, Turko-Mongolian, and Iranian notions of nobility and legitimacy, and bridge folkish legends and learned traditions. Around the turn of the sixteenth century, the art of lineage definitively unified ethnic and prophetic genealogies by firmly establishing that the Ottomans descended from an ancestry that was, at the same time, Turkic, Semitic, and Islamic. Historians of the reign of Bayezid II were markedly more attuned to the significance of noble origins. Having followed the blistering conquests and institutionalization of Mehmed II, this was, in many ways, a period similar to the Interregnum, marked by the lengthiest succession struggle that crippled the authority of the sultan and brought the Ottomans into serious conflict at many fronts, including the increasingly weary Mamluks and the Venetians, and the newly rising power of the Safavids. Apart from the crisis-bred considerations, a more sophisticated configuration of a noble lineage with a more acceptable vocabulary needed to be catered toward the self-identification of an expanding religious establishment, a learned bureaucracy, a new *devşirme* class that came to rule, and the rapidly spreading but diverse Sufi orders that crowded spiritual space.

Although Aşıkpaşazade's *Histories and Epic Deeds of the House of Osman* emerged as the master narrative of early Ottoman historical consciousness by synthesizing earlier frontier accounts and reasserting the dynastic identity on the theme of *gazi* ideals and Turkic folklore, it was his near contemporary Ruhi who ingeniously reformulated the laborious findings and fabrications of past historiography. For Ruhi (d. 1522), the Ottoman legitimacy was proven by religious law, reason, custom, and transmitted knowledge (*şerʿan ve ʿörfen ve ʿaklen ve naḳlen*), leaving no room for speculation. The linchpin of this legitimacy was a prophetic genealogy, affirming the new sensibilities brought about by the changing demographics of Ottoman power structure. Despite the general agreement of earlier chroniclers of Kayı Khan as the primordial founder of Ottoman royalty, identifying his exact kinship with prophet-rulers was a matter of choice. A number of genealogy makers tied him to Japheth, son of Noah, therefore according the Ottoman ancestry a complete visibility down to Adam. However, this line of connection stopped short of giving the Ottomans a distinguished status for the origins of all humanity was ultimately traced to one of Noah's six sons as every learned person would then have known by heart. In Ruhi's account, Oghuz Khan, Kayı's father, also appears to have a testament whereby he bequeathed the rulership exclusively to the descendants of Kayı. All other rulers descended from the line of Oghuz were therefore unrightful usurpers.[52]

It was, however, Bidlisi, the most decorated image-maker of the Ottoman dynasty, who eloquently rectified this unimpressive lineage by tying Kayı to Abrahamic kinship.[53] Bidlisi, having acknowledged the existence of other conflicting reports, identifies Kayı as Isaac's son Esau. This idea, too, was mentioned by earlier Ottoman historians, including Enveri and Ruhi. But in Bidlisi's authoritative rendering with embellished prose it was given an ontological archetype that lends a divine meaning to otherwise prosaic dynastic intrigues of the house of the Ottomans. As gathered from Qur'anic commentaries and universal histories, by divine providence, Isaac bequeaths his spiritual and temporal authority separately to his sons Jacob and Esau, respectively. Based on that primordial compact, all subsequent prophets were destined to descend from Jacob while all rulers from Esau, his less fortunate brother. Esau, having already manifested signs of leadership, turns embittered, invokes the quarrel between Abel and Cain, and moves to the east to manifest his rulership. The discord between siblings looks only natural while the rage between them becomes manifest as a sign of leadership. Bidlisi was too familiar with Bayezid I's long bickering with his brother Djem, and the tragic bloodshed among all four of his sons for a position, as Bidlisi implies, even the progeny of revered prophets could not escape. Yet the most cogent point Bidlisi insinuates is not to provide a prophetic example for dynastic competition but to endow the Ottoman ruler with an entitlement bequeathed by a prophet as he emphatically states that all the rulers among the Turks, Arabs, Persians, and Romans descended from this noble stock of Esau, that is, Kayı. This historical and religious identification perfectly undergirds the Ottoman rulers with one of the most favorite titles, "the Sultan of Romans, Arabs, and Persians."[54]

The Kayı genealogy bestowed the Ottomans with a blood right to rule and elevated them to a respectable status among the post-Chingizid dynasties that were now ruling most of what the deceased Abbasid Caliphate once ruled. The legitimacy crisis created by the Chingizid invasions turned out to be an epochal opportunity for the newly rising dynasties across the former Abbasid lands, particularly in the east of the Nile. Responses from the competing courts were twofold: first, appropriation and assimilation of the Chingizid legacy by Islamizing his noble stock and attributing his destructive conquest to divine providence and, second, construction of a dynastic genealogy tying one's own to the Abbasids, and therefore to the Prophet and his immediate successors. Unlike the contemporary witnesses who recorded the Chingizid invasions with abhorrence, subsequent chroniclers now serving at the post-Chingizid courts managed to reconcile between the newcomers and the locals by ascribing the guilt of the catastrophe to corruption, namely, to the victims. The fact that the final centuries of the Abbasid rule were already shaped under the shadow dynasties of Transoxanian origin certainly eased the tensions between invaders and subject populations. A confessional reaction against infidel domination was easily subsided by cultural affinities and facilitated the assimilation of the Mongols. Reflecting this cultural kinship, one of the earliest Ottomans who deliberated on the question, the aforementioned Ahmedi, presented the perceived Chingizid oppression as justice because of what looked like oppression to Muslims was an implementation of law that reigned supreme in Chingiz's government.

> If they oppressed, they oppressed with the law (*ḳānūn*)
> They did not paint their hands with blood
>
> If oppression results from law and control
> It is welcomed by people like justice[55]

Accrediting the Ottoman rulership with noble and Islamic origins was not a matter of dynastic bragging but an indispensable ingredient of imperial ideology for survival and countering in a fiercely competitive political and spiritual landscape of Eurasia. In the contest for more noble genealogies, the Ottomans were not only competing against surrounding Muslim rulers but also, perhaps more so, against the more powerful Sufi fraternities at home. Crafting a fictive genealogy through myth and legend encountered no objection from the Ottoman establishment. More challenging was to devise a dynastic relationship between the historical caliphate and its new claimants. For the undertaking, the decorated historians of the empire turned to mythic stories of origination. Accounts of genealogical justification in Ottoman historical writing were often accompanied by an investiture story in which the founders of the dynasty were reported to have received a right to rule from a Seljuk ruler, who in turn received it from the Abbasid Caliph. Because the Seljuk dynasty, a partner of the Abbasids in caliphate and the patron of the Ottomans, was ended by Mongol invasions, the Ottoman dynasty was purported to be the only remaining legitimate authority to rule and defend the realm of Islam. This attempt to portray the Ottomans as the heir apparent of the Abbasid caliphate was still inextricably tied to the shocking Timurid invasion and the subsequent legitimacy crisis. Counting the Timurid invasion of 1402, in this trajectory, the Ottomans were the third major dynasty defeated by the Mongols but the only one that survived.

Different variants of the foundation story narrate in concert that Ertuğrul, Osman's father, was first commissioned to defend the Abbasid realm from the Chingizid onslaught at the behest of the Seljuk ruler Alaeddin I. After the fall of the Abbasids, in recognition of Ertuğrul's dedicated and honorable service, his son Osman was designated to protect the Seljuk realm from the ongoing Mongol attacks by its last independent ruler Alaeddin II (r. 1298–1302). The story of Osman's or, in some variants, Ertuğrul's reception of royal insignia from a Seljuk ruler quickly became a refrain of Ottoman dynastic narrative, highlighted in the introduction of almost all histories as the most valuable relics even after Selim I's appropriation of a sacred treasury trove during his Egyptian campaign that included items belonging to the Prophet.[56] The story plainly elucidates the Ottomans as the rightful inheritors of the Abbasid–Seljuk realm by being formally appointed to repel Mongol attacks. But more than an inheritance right for territorial claim, the Ottoman dynasty was conceived as having reunited the divided authority over the Muslim community between the executive power of the Seljuks, the sultanate, and that of the spiritual of the Abbasids, the caliphate. The encounter with the Timurids led the subsequent Ottomans to reconstruct, if not fabricate, a historical memory that earned them the credit for being the only Muslim dynasty that resisted the two-century-long Mongol invasions.

This reconstruction of history saves the historical caliphate from disappearance and reestablishes its unbroken continuity through the Ottomans who reinstituted it to its original form. Saving the charisma of the caliphate did not simply result from an attempt to bolster the Ottoman dynasty's legitimacy considerations and expansionist ambitions, it was part of a broader quest voiced within the disoriented Muslim community, now humiliated to live under pagan rulers, who were accustomed to live with the idea of the superiority of Islam over all other faiths. Responses to the universal crisis caused by the collapse of the unifying authority of the Abbasids were versatile. Individual scholars, Sufi groups, and broken dynasties sought to accommodate the undeniable reality while looking for ways to reinstitute the social ideals of Medieval Islam. In the meantime, the very successor states of the Chingizid Empire successfully rooted themselves within the Islamic tradition and reclaimed the legitimacy apparatus of the former caliphate, with the help of a large contingent of accommodationist scholars and courtiers, while retaining their own Turko-Mongolian credentials of rulership. Dynasties that were spared from a full Mongol takeover such as the Mamluks, however, rebonded with the Abbasids in stronger terms. The Ottomans did this by reestablishing the continuity of the caliphate, attributing an eschatological significance to what befell the Muslim community by Mongol invasions. However, the political unity of the caliphate was no longer an achievable reality. In the post-Mongol world, the universal and unified authority over the Muslim community could be claimed only on the spiritual plane. The Muslim space might still be politically fragmented but it might be unified spiritually through a new cosmologically envisioned caliphate. In reflection of these considerations, Ottoman historical narratives portrayed the House of Osman as having earned the caliphate by merit and inherited it by right as part of a divinely ordained eschatological scheme.

With all the spiritual and worldly signs pointing to the predestined rise of the Ottomans, Osman was reported to have been elected at a formal meeting of an electoral assembly that involved the leaders of the Oghuz clans. In Ruhi's account, the trajectory of events that led to this occasion was inherently linked to the rise of the Mongols. For him, until the Chingizid disruption, Turkestan had been ruled by the descendants of Kayı who were forced to leave this realm and take refuge in the land of Rum under the aegis of the Seljuks. In the story, chiefs of all the existing Oghuz branches came to Osman and formed a consultative assembly (*ḳurultay*) to ask him to replace the Seljuk rule, which they thought had already effectively collapsed. They invoked the testimony of Oghuz Khan, who bequeathed leadership exclusively to the descendants of Kayı, of whom Osman was the leading figure: "Kayı Khan was the leader and khan of all the Oghuz tribes after Oghuz Khan. Therefore, per customs of the Oghuz, no other clan is fit for leadership (*ḫānlıḳ ve pādişāhlıḳ*) as long as the Kayı progeny continues."[57] Once Osman accepted the investiture, this was not the foundation of a new dynasty but a reinstitution of leadership that rightfully belonged to Kayı's tribe after a long interlude caused by the Mongols. The story thus communicates Osman's legitimacy with the diverse Turkic community of Anatolia through an idiom that would be fully understandable to these autonomous, mostly nomadic, tribes. Taken together, the two investiture stories tie the Ottomans to the Islamic and Turko-Mongolian lineages at once.

These obscure bits and pieces of stories pertaining to the origins were mystified and recast into an illustrious foundational myth in Bidlisi's mystical philosophy of history, which fully embedded the Ottomans into divine providence in his masterful account that could only be compared to the much envied narratives of Persian historiography composed under the Mongols after they converted to Islam. He, too, banks on and fully engages with the master narratives of history that turned an otherwise catastrophic Mongol interlude into an unprecedented feat of world conquest. Bidlisi praises, competes against, and gets inspired by the epoch-making histories of Juvaini and Vassaf.[58] Writing at a time that offered an apologist plenty of deeds and glorious conquests to play with, he boasts to juxtapose his work to those he labels as the historians of Chingiz Khanids, and presents his work to counter the cruelty and worldly ambitions of the Mongols with the Ottoman sultans' service to Islam. He makes this intention so obvious by titling his work *Accounts of the Ottoman Caesars*, a title the Mongols lacked, and underlines the Ottoman conquests of infidel lands.[59] In style, language, and message, earlier dynastic histories, from Yazıcızade to Aşıkpaşazade, only addressed the domestic audience of the broader western Asia Minor and the Balkans, and did not even aim to counter the virtuoso portrayals of the Aqquyunlus or the Timurids in the literary masterpieces of Persian historiography that long enchanted the Ottomans. But Bidlisi composed *Hasht Behesht* to universalize the Ottoman myth and to inscribe it on the annals of history by perfecting the same language and literary devices that were used to memorialize what he commonly referred as the Chingizids. Bidlisi refashioned the vernacular imageries created in hagiographic chronicles and frontier epics and recast the portrait of Ottoman rulers in the images of Alexander and Chingiz, anointed by prophecies.

Besides his piety and lawmaking, fifteenth-century Ottoman historiography mythologized Osman mainly by glorifying his *gazi* leadership. An anonymous Arabic chronicle written in 1451 credits Osman for advancing "from the rank of smaller rulership (*siyāsa wa al-amāra al-ṣughrā*) to the rank of great rulership (*salṭana wa al-imāma al-kubrā*)" thanks to his conquests.[60] Although the designation "great rulership" resembles those of Sufistic unified authority, it was an entirely juristic and historical reference in the sense that Osman excelled above all other rulers. This was still a very lofty claim in clear reference to the universal rulership once held by the Abbasid, but it was still confined to the temporal sphere. Aşıkpaşazade, who deliberately portrayed Ottoman rulers in the language of frontier Sufism as dervish-*gazis*, looks reserved in according them the Sufistic imageries of rulership. In reflection of his own spiritual belonging, he considered the sultans of the House of Osman as friends of God's friends whose authority was limited to the temporal sphere. Thus the Ottoman sultan as caliph in the Sufistic sense is conspicuously absent from much of the fifteenth century Ottoman vernacular historiography.

Bidlisi, however, to emphasize Islamic credentials of the Ottoman dynasty, goes beyond the investiture story and *gazi* ethos, and establishes a spiritual kinship with the pre-Mongolian caliphate. For him, the Ottomans were exalted because of a spiritual genealogy (*nasab-i maʿnavī*) that tied them to the first four caliphs and the twelve imams, the ultimate authorities and absolute role models in Sunni and Shiite branches of Islam, respectively. Bidlisi's inclusion of the twelve imams in the spiritual paternity line of the Ottoman dynasty clearly geared toward appropriating the legitimacy apparatus of the Safavids and denying them their most prized distinction. Although the Ottomans did not physically belong to the Prophet's family or earlier caliphs, Bidlisi attributes them kinship by way of a spiritual line (*ṭarīqat va ḥaqīqat*).[61] By divine will, the Ottomans find themselves unquestionably linked to the early caliphate as revealed by the auspicious sign that Caliph Uthman was the namesake of the Ottoman founder. The conquest of Rum started by Caliph Uthman, later continued by the Marwanid–Umayyad caliphs who descended from his family had remained incomplete owing to the incompetence of the latter. It was his namesake Osman who resumed this conquest that was completed by his descendants.[62] A successful undertaking of this noble mission establishes the Ottomans as God's chosen dynasty for the execution of His will and makes them the only rightful inheritor of the rightly guided caliphate. Being a jurist by profession, Bidlisi knows well the genealogy requirement for the validity of the caliphate, namely the caliphs belonging to the Quraysh tribe. He ingeniously circumvents this physical requirement and overshadows it with a spiritual genealogy he creates. Bidlisi's contemporary, Oruc Beg, makes that linkage more tangible.[63] In his account, it was Ertuğrul, Osman's father, who receives the royal insignia from Alaeddin, which included the sword of Caliph Uthman, a sword he received from the Prophet. Alaeddin had received this sword from the Abbasids residing in Egypt. In either account, the Ottoman dynasty is portrayed to be the rightful inheritor of the historical caliphate.

Bidlisi unfolds this divine scenario by mapping out the spiritual space that housed the Ottomans and identifying its specific actors that partook in the foundation of the Ottoman state. In his report, it was no other than Abu al-Najib al-Suhrawardi, for example, who was commissioned by the Abbasid caliph to bring the caliphal decree that deputized Alaeddin I who, in turn, passed this authority to Ertuğrul, Osman's father.[64] In addition to the Suhrawardiyya, which ultimately originated from the teachings of this grand master of Sufism, a number of popular offshoots spread across Eurasia, making him among the most venerated of saints among Ottoman mystics. Referring to the Mongol onslaught again, Bidlisi states that the Seljuks in Anatolia became the refuge of God's friends who fled the Chingizid oppression, including Najm al-Din Daye, Baha'eddin Muhammed, Sadreddin Konevi, al-Rumi, Shams-i Tabrizi, Sultan Veled, Husameddin al-Urmawi, and Zarkub al-Tabrizi.[65] All these figures turned out to be integral parts of Ottoman thought and spirituality in their peculiar ways. Bidlisi specifically targets the now formidable Sufi establishment by unquestionably establishing the spiritual legitimacy of the Ottomans through a roster of the most revered saints. The founders of the Ottoman dynasty thus not only served God's friends well but also received their blessing for rulership.

Bidlisi reinterprets the so-called dream story by narrating this all too well-known episode as a poetic love saga by which he reveals the little noted secrets of divine plot through his mystic gaze.[66] During one of Osman's meetings with the mystic Shaykh Edebali, from whom he had been receiving spiritual guidance, Osman sees his daughter by accident and immediately falls in love. She declines his offer for marriage on the grounds that temporal rulers are not fit to establish such a relationship with men of God and that this is not commended in the Sharia for holders of the crown to merge with those who are poor and in need, that is, the dervishes. As a test of Osman's will and worthiness, she rejects the union of spiritual and temporal authorities. For being the top jurist of his time, Bidlisi implies that the Hanafi principle of stipulating parity (*kufuw*) between prospective spouses was not met. Dismayed, he seeks the intermediacy of his then friend, the ruler of Eskişehir, whose mediation fails as the proposal is declined by Edebali and his companions. Then we see the mediator turning into a villain, devising plans to marry the girl himself, which leads to clashes between the two. Having not lost his resolution, Osman defeats his opponent and proves his already recognized chivalry and worthiness, a clear sign for this predestined marriage. In the meantime, despite the refusal, he continues to visit Edebali for his companionship. It is in one of these Sufi assemblies that he passes out for a moment following the late night prayer and wakes up being heralded with good news in his dream. A master of dream interpretation, Edebali instantly reads God's message, consents to the divine command, and agrees to have Osman marry his daughter.

Bidlisi's narrative shows more than Osman's being chosen as the founder of a world empire that would put the Ottomans on a par with others such as the Chingizids, but not above. What distinguishes Osman from other illustrious dynastic founders was his portrayal as a wayfarer of the spiritual path alongside his mundane rulership. The dense symbolism in the story better exposes itself when read through Sufi terminology. To begin with, his love affair with Malhatun may not simply be taken as an accidental attraction to a beauty but rather an attraction to the beloved from whom the power of attraction emanates. It is too reminiscent of love epics of Arabo-Persian Sufi literature in which the protagonist is captivated by a burning love that could be achieved only by annihilating the self, of which, perhaps the best known example is the story of Leyli and Majnun. At the foundation of Islamic mysticism is the love of God and the intermediaries that lead to Him, including the Prophet and the master shaykh to whom one submits. Osman's tribulations and perseverance also look too meaningful from the perspective of dervishes as suffering was ritualized in many branches of Sufism for character test and purification. In this heavily dramatized story, Malhatun represents the love of God and the marriage stands for Osman's spiritual union with God. In many such stories found in the vast hagiographical literature, the protagonist relinquishes his throne and wealth to purify himself for the attainment of God's love, of which the legendary example of Ibrahim b. Adham was a folk knowledge. Yet, in mainstream Sufism, the formal renouncement of the world is often taken as a sign of lesser saints because they simply strip themselves from distractions. A higher level of renouncement would be preserving one's worldly engagements while totally detaching oneself from them in heart. In Osman's case, he is depicted to have achieved spiritual worthiness without relinquishing worldly status, a trait often accorded to the prophets and ranked saints. Such interpretations of famed marriages from the perspective of Sufi symbolism were not uncommon Ottoman literature. In a similar story narrated by Bali Efendi, Bidlisi's younger contemporary, Prophet Abraham's marriage to Hagar is explained as the union of one's spirit (*rūḥ*) and soul (*nafs*) out of which the light of prophethood, that is, Ishmael was born.[67]

Bidlisi portrays Malhatun as someone who was trained by her master father in the mystical path as well as the Sharia, which makes her already a sophisticated female mystic, learned and even authorized for spiritual guidance. Turning Osman into a disciple of Edebali, a condition that Bidlisi perhaps deliberately keeps obscure, would lead to Osman's renouncing of his worldly titles and conceding all authority to his shaykh. Instead, Bidlisi carefully makes the spiritual authority comes to him by way of love. As such, his marriage symbolizes the perfection of his rulership by uniting temporal and spiritual plains. The dream itself also denotes Osman's spiritual worthiness. In Sufism, dreams were an integral part of spiritual training and manifestation of a disciple's status in his mystical wayfaring.[68] A disciple tells his dream, and the shaykh interprets and guides accordingly. That's how it happens in Osman's case, too. Edebali, who opposed the marriage until then, instantly notices what was revealed and condones Osman's rising status in the spiritual realm. The shaykh explains the nature of Osman's rule:

> In accordance with "whose root is firmly fixed and its branches in the havens" (Qur'an 14: 24) it is certain that the good fortune of kingship will belong to the seer of this dream. Branches of this noble root will thrive under the shadow of divine succor. All of his progeny will manifest the caliphate of religion and the world. They will become the rulers of both temporal and spiritual kingdoms.[69]

Bidlisi presents the wedding as if it were a coronation for Osman's new rulership during which a certain dervish, Tarud, approaches him with a manner that befits the king of kings and congratulates him for possessing both religious and worldly authorities as God's deputy (*kadkhudā*) over His creation. As the first act of his new rulership, Osman bestows Tarud with an estate on the condition that the dervish's promise (*vaʿd*) gets materialized, an act that pleases Huma, the legendary bird of Iranian mythology that casts its shadow only over the royals. The promise comes true, Osman bestows the dervish a Sufi convent, and the dervish further prays and promises dervishes' protection of the dynasty for perpetuity. Bidlisi's poetic and mystic language conflates the marital union with coronation as the promise the dervish made could be taken as marriage, coronation, or both. The occasion creates not only a marriage contract but also a pact with the order of dervishes. While the presence of God's manifest friends was known well and propagated, more mysterious was the miraculous succor provided by the order of invisible saints.

Bidlisi's older contemporary Konevi narrates the story of a certain dervish saint, Kumral Baba, who discovered that Osman was designated as the lord of conjunction (*ṣāḥib-qirān-i ʿālam*) by divine providence (*ʿālam-i vahbiyyat*).[70] Bidlisi and later Ibn Kemal recount the same story to confirm the pact between rulers and saints, and the union of temporal and spiritual authorities in Osman's leadership. In his narration, Kumral Baba, a *gazi* dervish with no prior knowledge of Edebali or Osman before, meets with an anonymous agent of God from the order of invisible saints who govern the affairs of the world. The saint informs the astounded Kumral: "In these days someone who is approved by our order will appear in this place. The keys for the rulership of this world and hereafter will be in his hands and his progeny's. Until the Day of Judgment, they will speak for Islam, conquer the lands of infidels, and smash idols."[71] He then strictly orders Kumral Baba to join the company of Osman as this is the greatest happiness. In Ibn Kemal's account, he orders Kumral never to leave him during his raids because he was assured of victory, and because he was supported by God's assistance (*muʾayyad min ʿind Allāh*).[72] When Kumral moves to join with Osman along with his dervishes, he miraculously sees the fabulous bird Huma laying its wings to shade over Osman, an undisputable sign that he was in fact God's chosen ruler. To reward Kumral's joining, Osman grants him an estate for his Sufi convent, and as a sign of his bestowal he gives him his sword and tankard, which may be taken as two symbols of his temporal rulership and mystic authority, *salṭanat* and *ṭarīḳat*.

Mehmed II and the Making of the Ottoman Archetype

Osman's image-making capacity was only eclipsed by Mehmed II, who turned the Ottoman ruler from a *gazi*-sultan to a pompous caesar and conqueror thanks to his conquest of Constantinople, which drastically altered the Ottoman perception of the self. Konevi, who composed his chronicle of the Ottoman dynasty in Persian at Mehmed's behest, depicted him as the absolute caliph (*khalīfa-i muṭlaq*) and "the owner of Constantin's throne, God's caliph in the East and the West" (*ṣāḥib-i taḥt-i Quntstantīn, khalīfat Allāh fī mashāriq al-ʿarḍ wa maghāribihā*).[73] But the *gazi* fabric of the Ottoman rulership was not something to dispense with at will. Since the very beginning, the Ottoman rulers enjoyed a well-propagated image for being *gazi* sultans, a title they prided themselves with to the very end. The title emphasized their distinction from other rulers who inherited their regalia along with their territories that were already brought to Islam. When chronicles of Ottoman sultans began to be compiled in the early fifteenth century, it became an oft-cited mark of Ottoman sultans that they earned this title and acquired their own territories. For Ottoman historians and chiefs of chancery who composed sultanic decrees, this title communicated their exclusive right to rule in their conquered lands. The title itself did not have much use during the medieval Islam beyond being an occasionally invoked honorific when conquests ceased and lost their legitimizing value. It became more frequently used during the renewed zeal for conquest among the newly Islamized Turkic tribes of the eleventh century as they initially found it better serving to conquer northern India instead of carving up ruling space by encountering the well-established dynasties under the aegis of the caliphate.

The *gazi* image of the Ottoman sultan was overshadowed by the new imperial imageries inculcated by Mehmed II following his conquest of Constantinople and restructuring the state into an empire. The Persianate tradition of post-Abbasid Turko-Mongolian states offered the most accessible and suitable repository of recipes and human resources for Mehmed II's empire-building project. A large contingent of bureaucrats, scholars, and Sufis, flooding into Ottoman territories since the Interregnum, quickly rose to the highest ranks in Ottoman administration.[74] Having already been trained by these Persianate scholars, Mehmed II continued his warm relations with men of learning who stayed in the east and tried to lure them with prodigious rewards. The reign of Mehmed II was the golden age of Ottoman Persian as opposed to the sudden surge of Turkish in the preceding half century. Until Süleyman, all three sultans, Mehmed II, Bayezid II, and Selim I, wrote their own poetry mostly in Persian with the pen-names Avni, Adli, and Selimi. In Osman's time, interpretation of heavenly signs was mediated primarily through wise men, the dervishes, who still acted in the same role as Turko-Mongolian shamans while being immersed in Islamic mysticism. In the case of Mehmed II, this task was taken up by professional astrologists, divinators, and prognosticators who were not necessarily friends of God.

Why did the holly alliance between the dervish orders and the Ottoman dynasty break down? Modern historians commonly point to the centralization and institutionalization of the Ottoman state or its transformation into an empire initiated with the scandalous execution of Grand Vizier Candarlı Halil Paşa, who resisted Mehmed II's dissociation of rulership from its conventional basis. But Mehmed II's swift reforms after the conquest of Constantinople suggest that he was already taken with the idea of a centralized world empire. He was not the initiator but a product of a new learned circle that dominated Ottoman political and cultural milieu, which furnished princes and sultans with the canons of ideal rulership, mostly of Persian origin. Unlike his predecessors, who received hands-on training in statecraft along with Turkoman chiefs, *gazi* leaders, and dervishes, he was educated in the palace with tutors who thought him the merits of a centralized state on the model of past great empires. In Mehmed II's ideal state there was no room for sharing authority with dervishes, commanders, and chiefs. Reconstruction of the Ottoman state after the Battle of Ankara and the ensuing Interregnum increasingly turned into an empire-building project that involved distancing the ulema, the Sufi orders, Turkoman tribes, and *gazi* bands from the power stratum and assigning them nonpolitical functions for the operation of the newly envisioned imperial establishment.

Mehmed II only exacerbated the rift between traditional dervish orders and the Ottoman dynasty that had been forming at least since the Interregnum. The alienated dervish orders increasingly turned into spokespersons of dissenting Turkoman masses as in the case of Otman Baba who openly clashed with Mehmed and defied his authority in the name of the broader Abdalan constituency of the countryside, which had wholeheartedly embraced the Ottoman dynasty during the reigns of founding sultans.[75] The inauguration of the first Mevlevi house in Edirne under the aegis of Murad II in 1427 signified the Ottoman dynasty's newly acquired taste for urban-Persianate Sufism as opposed to vernacular-Turkic dervish piety. The origins of incessant rebellions in the Anatolian countryside in the sixteenth century should be sought during the reign of Mehmed II at the latest, if not the final years of Mehmed I's reign when the Bedreddin revolt was supressed. The enchanting Safavid propaganda found easy converts among the Turkoman tribes that were already dissenting from the centralizing efforts of the Ottoman administration.[76] This confrontation was only exacerbated by the Safavid propaganda, not created by it as commonly maintained by both Ottoman chroniclers of the time and modern historians.

Mehmed II's new image building by dissociation from Osman's legacy and folk imagination of rulership was deliberate. He confiscated a number of religious endowments, mostly estates granted to dervish orders by his predecessors, with the intention of strengthening his central institutions that harbored his newly conceived political ideology.[77] He effectively broke the founding pact instituted between Osman and the dervish community that characterized the decentralized early Ottoman social order. The reaction was multilayered. A number of disillusioned advocates of the previous order, such as Aşıkpaşazade, penned the first full accounts of the Ottoman history where they idealized the *gazi* lifestyle and the modesty of earlier sultans. While avoiding confrontation with the reigning sultan directly, they voiced their criticism by scapegoating the viziers of *devşirme* origin and foreign elements, such as the Persians, that corrupted the Ottoman order. These chroniclers were accompanied by even a larger number of Abdalan hagiographers who accorded the early dervishes a founding role in the rise of the Ottoman rule and idealized, if not doctored or even fabricated, the original setup where sovereignty was split between temporal and spiritual planes. It is not a coincidence that the second half of the fifteenth century witnessed an explosive growth in hagiography writing. By defying the new spiritual regime imposed, Abdalan hagiographies, in particular, were written with a mission to record fading memories of an order in decline for its own sake and survival and reinstitute Abdalan autonomy by portraying the famed dervishes of the old regime as constitutional partners of the Ottoman enterprise. Despite their eroding power and prestige, Abdalan communities never willingly relinguished their purported monopoly in acting as the sole interlocutors between God's absolute rule and that of temporal rulers. Abdalan hagiography, in general, was a manifestation of resistance against being reduced into well-wishers of the Ottoman dynasty from their self-assumed role of dispensing political power.

Although the new imperial rulership was widely contested, a new class of learned friends and servants of the Ottoman dynasty managed to create the definitive image of an Ottoman sultan in the personality of Mehmed II. For Bidlisi, the difference in rulership between Osman and Mehmed II was analogous to the one between Adam and Muhammed, the former being the originator and the latter its perfection.[78] Bidlisi was writing at a time when reconciliation was sought under the growing threat posed by the disprivileged Turkoman base. Having already inherited a considerable opposition from the countryside, pressed with threats from two fronts, the Mamluks and the Venetians, and at the same time carefully steering the threat posed by his runaway brother, Bayezid II opted to mend relations with the Turkoman constituency and its most vocal representatives, the Abdalan dervishes. One of his first acts was to return the confiscated endowment property to their rightful grantees.[79] The long-lasting succession struggle between Bayezid and Djem forced both claimants to seek the support of former allies of the Ottoman dynasty. The composition of *Ṣalṭuḳnāme* that reglorifies *gazi* ethos at the behest of Djem, signals a rapprochement between the Ottoman family and *gazi* circles.[80]

Bidlisi was an ideal candidate to mend fences by assimilating the Abdalan legacy into the new imperial configuration: Muslim-born, Turkish-speaking, Persian-lettered, accomplished jurist, seasoned mystic, master of poetry and prose, and experienced statesman. He was also familiar in dealing with opposition and autonomous groups as he served in the tribal confederation of the Aqquyunlu dynasty, an experience that he would apply to establish peace with the Kurdish chiefs of the east on his later patron Selim's order. His monumental chronicle, *Hasht Behesht*, still spoke for the imperial project but fully incorporated the folkic lore of Ottoman historical writing. He gave a new currency to the founding stories of the dynasty narrated in the *gazi* literature with its treasure trove of legitimizing tropes, and presented them with the high language of Arabo-Persian imageries of rulership that would intimately appeal to the worldviews of the ulema, the urban Sufis, bureaucrats, and the military.

He merged the two distinct conceptions of history before the rift between imperial and *gazi* histories got materialized. The *Tevārīḫ-i Āl-i ʿOs̱mān* literature was a collective enterprise by the dismayed opponents of empire-building who advocated the purity, simplicity, and lax social order of the founding century. There is a startling corollary between the medieval attitudes toward early Islam and that of the first generation of Ottoman historians in the fifteenth century whose portrayal of Osman's reign was no less than the utopian benchmark to be imitated by subsequent sultans. Early Ottoman history writing was not simply sparked by a humanistic curiosity but prompted by a definite political and social agenda. These histories, of which the most popular ones were compiled during the reign of Bayezid II, provided the foundation and justification for the sultan's reversal of Mehmed II's policies and appeasement of the dervish orders. Titles of early histories such as *menāḳıb* (epic deeds), *düstūr* (guide), *gazavātnāme* (book of raids), and *dāstān* (epic narrative) reflect this intent. The *gazi* historians often voiced their resentment towards the empire by criticizing the institution of novel practices and invoking the Ottoman *ḳānūn* as the true configuration of state and society. Ironically, the idea of *ḳānūn* as the founding feature of the Ottoman state was not the outcome of a developed Ottoman bureaucracy in the imperial age but of the *gazi* intellectuals who clinched the idea of a fundamental law when they felt unfairly stripped of their earned privileges. Behind the idea of *ḳānūn* in Ottoman political and historical thought was not the dynastic will or the bureaucratic quest for order but the class-based claim for collective rights. These histories were not shy of detecting and shaming culprits who first breached the perceived fundamental law of the Ottomans.

Bidlisi uses Mehmed II to confirm the Ottoman myth and establish continuity through his well-conceived teleology.[81] While endorsing the *gazi* idealists' expectations of an ideal ruler, he creates a more perfect model in the personality of the Conqueror. He appeases the *gazi* historians' apprehension and pessimism by creating a positive scheme of history that shows progress and perfection since the foundation of Ottoman dynasty. He hails Mehmed II's caliphate as an infusion of the body by its soul and praises him as the final drawing of the Artist as the one who carried the banner of Islam to the highest point since the time of the rightly guided caliphs. In Mehmed II, Bidlisi finds the replica of the Prophet and manifestation of God's attributes. Among all the rulers known, Mehmed II is the one who resembles the Prophet most, not only in name and character but also in his deeds and the circumstances in which he rose to power, a characterization that rightfully earns him the title prophetic ruler (*pādishāh-i nabavī*) and turns his rule into the Prophet's vicegerency (*khilāfat-i nabavī*). On the authority of the people to whom God's secrets were open, he proves Mehmed II's uniqueness through reading esoteric signs that revolve around the mystery of the number seven, which he claims is inherently linked to the notion of the caliphate. Mehmed is the seventh ruler of the Ottoman dynasty just like Muhammed, who appeared in the seventh millennium after the creation of Adam, and an embodiment of the seven attributes of God. Just as Muhammed was the seal of Prophets so was Mehmed the seal of rulers. Further, Mehmed and Muhammed were housed by a cosmological cycle as both appeared at an auspicious conjunction when seven heavenly bodies aligned. Among other evidence drawn from the ontology of the number seven, Bidlisi draws a parallel between the creation of the seventh heaven, God's metaphoric seat (*ʿarsh-i karīm*), and Mehmed's being chosen as the seventh ruler of the Ottomans. In proof of his worthiness, Mehmed displayed a perfect character, a condition that could be bestowed only on the most worthy friends of God at the seventh stage of their spiritual ascension. Bidlisi's argumentation in proving Mehmed's designation as the foretold ruler in scriptures is strikingly similar to that of historian al-Baghdadi in portraying his patron, the Aqquyunlu ruler Uzun Hasan.[82] Reminiscent of the Ottoman chronicles' portrayal of Osman as a dervish-ruler, in Bidlisi's account, Mehmed II is portrayed as a friend of God, shown with the vocabulary of learned Sufism.

With this image of Mehmed, Bidlisi removes accidentalism from history and reconstructs historical events by placing them within the Heaven-dictated grand scheme unfolding. Among others, he recasts an otherwise scandalous incident in Mehmed's life as an auspicious event. Murad II had abdicated for retirement in favor of his son Mehmed while he was only a young teenager. He was soon forced to leave the throne by a Janissary rebellion instigated by high-ranking statesmen who doubted his ability to lead. Some chroniclers attempted to save the Ottoman ruler's broken image by claiming that he himself invited his father to the throne. But in Bidlisi's account, not only is Mehmed's image fully rehabilitated but the whole instance is also given a divine significance. For him, Murad II did not simply wish to retire but withdrew from rulership in favor of his son, on whose face he miraculously observed the signs of

God's benevolence (*raḥmat-i ilāhī*), just as David stepped down in favor of his son Solomon, who was endowed with superior qualities as a Prophet-ruler.[83] Bidlisi, posthumously recreates Mehmed II, the most disliked Ottoman ruler by Sufis of the countryside, as the most spiritually perfect of them all.

The conquest of Constantinople not only earned Mehmed II a new title, the Conqueror, but also accorded the Ottoman dynasty a renewed significance. Ahmed Bican, who pointed to Mehmed II as an ominous sign of the approaching end of time, after the conquest, hailed him as the awaited *gazi* warrior now poised to take Rome as well.[84] The epochal event stirred apocalyptic anxieties that have been on the rise since the Mongol invasions and gave a new impetus to the use of divination and prognostication through a renewed scrutiny of sacred texts, histories, and cosmological representations. Using the same material, apologists of the Ottoman dynasty turned it into an auspicious event, the fulfillment of the Prophet's prophecy and, therefore, an unmistakable sign of divine providence in favor of the Ottomans. This materialized prognosis emboldened the learned to work more comfortably toward figuring out the signs of auspicious destiny. Once an obscure but tolerated art with which only odd mystics would engage, prognostication became a legitimate part of historical analysis. Even chronograms quickly turned into an Ottoman tradition marking significant moments. The science of reading God's signs and writing one's spiritual discoveries in encrypted writings became common knowledge for any learned Ottoman.

Apparently, the Ottomans made very little use of the vast and versatile repertoire of medieval Islamic prophecies regarding Turks.[85] These prophecies fall into two broad categories: The first praises Turks for their valor, morality, loyalty, and military skills, which seem to have been crafted in the context of the Abbasid caliphate's reliance on Turkish guards. Second, the Turks are portrayed as part of a destructive force of catastrophic proportions, often associated with apocalyptic agents of evil such as Gog and Magog. With Mongol invasions, these prophecies gained a new life to specifically explain the new situation. While the newly converted Turko-Mongolian courts propagated these prophecies as fulfillment of the Prophet's good tidings, others turned them into apocalyptic warnings. But there was no consensus as to who these Turks were and what divinely foreseen function they served. Most formidable dynasties who fought against the Mongol armies were also Turkic dynasties, including the Seljuks. Further, the post-Abbasid Muslim world from Egypt to India came under the rule of dynasties of Central Asian or Caucasian origins. Ottoman prognosticators and historians look very diligent when identifying the Ottomans with the Turks of medieval prophecies. One obvious reason is the negative view of Turks as the forewarned hordes from the East. Another, more important, reason was that the Ottoman elite of the sixteenth century generally thought of themselves as the people for Rum, rather than as Turks.[86]

Endowed with the fashionable skills of prognostication, Bidlisi is unequivocal in drawing a direct continuity from Prophet Muhammed's conquests to those of Mehmed II. For Bidlisi, the conquest of Constantinople shows more than an affirmation of Mehmed II as the promised ruler prophesied by the Prophet. It also confirms the accuracy of the foundation myth and proves the prognosis and spiritual power of the early Ottomans' protector saints. Even the least learned among Ottoman literati would point to the prophecy to show the chosenness of the Ottoman dynasty albeit through the personality of Mehmed II. It has become a custom in Ottoman historiography to insert a separate chapter on the history of Constantinople from its beginnings down to their respective times. These accounts assimilated Byzantine history and established continuity in the land of Romans. This enterprise finds its most elaborate exposition in Bidlisi's interpretation, which fully integrates the city's history into the trajectory of world history centered on the Islamic accounts of prophethood and rulership.[87] This involves establishing affinities between Muslims and the Romans that came to found and rule the city by watering down the hostile images of the Roman rule that came to dominate Ottoman historical writing. The tone of his account is very different from those *gazi* narratives describing battles and victories against the infidel. On the contrary, it highlights the Byzantine rulers' belonging to the faith of Prophet Jesus. The conquest is not hailed as the destruction of an evil state but a succession event on the part of the Ottomans and their entitlement to caesarship.

Bidlisi's interpretation of the prophecy shows that numerous Muslim rulers in the past failed to take over the city as part of the divine plan that necessitated its conquest by Mehmed and that the Ottomans replaced the Romans in the land of Rum while fully inheriting its legitimacy apparatus. The Ottoman identification with the Rum becomes all the more striking when Bidlisi employs this new alignment to enliven an already fulfilled prophecy to explain the Ottoman clashes with the Aqquyunlus, a Turkic dynasty based in Iran and eastern Anatolia, during Mehmed's reign. The Constantinople prophecy was conveyed in a collection of prophetic traditions that was not considered part of the Sunni canon. But the one that foretold the eventual defeat of the Persians by the Romans came from the Qur'an and therefore was better known among the learned.[88] Bidlisi maintains that the prophecy equally applies to the Ottoman–Aqquyunlu wars by identifying them as the Romans versus the Persians. With an initial apology explaining how prognostication applies to recurring prophecies in cosmic cycles, he examines the events, dates, names, and locations of the confrontation in detail to make it fully explainable in God's words. In this reading, the Aqquyunlus not only represent the Persians but also are presented as a leftover from the earlier conflict between the Seljuks and the Ilkhanids, to which the same prophecy also applies.[89] Ironically, historians of the Aqquyunlu court where Bidlisi started his career, also invoked this metahistoric antagonism between the Romans and the Persians where they identified the Aqquyunlus with the Romans and their archenemy, the Qaraquyunlus, with the Persians.[90] Bidlisi considered Roman-Persian wars a recurrent theme of history where each time the Romans would prevail. But his allusion to Roman-Persian conflict was only a more dramatized version of something the Ottomans already knew. Ahmed Bican, whose many popular works in Turkish were replete with prophesies and apocaliyptic interpretations, stated in the mid-fifteenth century that Persians were condemned forever for disparaging the Prophet's call.[91] Ebu'l-Hayr el-Rumi, who, at the height of the Ottoman–Aqquyunlu conflict, spent years to collect stories regarding the legendary life of a frontier hero, Sarı Saltuk, presented his epic to Prince Djem in 1480 where he, or the sixteenth-century redactors of the text, identified the Persians as the main source of all evil:

> Şerif (Sarı Saltuk) said: Muslims! It is from the lands of Acem and Babil that came all wickedness and oppression and from Arab that came all the prophets. Until the apocalypse it will be from Acem that all the malicious will keep coming. They are not auspicious people. Besides, our venerable Prophet damned the East (*şarka beddua itmişdür*). This Rum is a harmonious people (*sulh taifedür*), they are loyal.[92]

This topos gained even more currency with the outbreak of Ottoman–Safavid conflict. A treatise written for Selim I at the height of Ottoman–Safavid conflict in 1513 attributed the reason behind this Qur'anic prophecy to the Prophet's cursing of the Persians. Muhammed sent letters to invite the Roman and Persian rulers. On receiving Muhammed's call, Heraclius immediately converted to Islam but remained a secret Muslim. The Prophet prays: "May God continue their kingdom until the end of times." The Persian ruler, on the other hand, tore up the letter and threw it away upon which the Prophet prays: "May God burn their kingdom and never give them back kingdom forever."[93] The secret conversion of Heraclius was common knowledge in medieval Islamic and Ottoman historiography to which Bidlisi also alludes in the context of the history of Constantinople.[94] For Bidlisi, Roman-Persian wars started at the time of the Prophet between a Muslim Roman emperor and an infidel Persian king. Although the identification of the Ottomans with the Romans only solidified the prophetic signature of their divine ordination, this historical scheme was equally useful from the Safavid perspective when stripped of the Islamic narrative. The same Bidlisi, a few years after he submitted his *Hasht Behesht*, during his self-imposed exile in Mecca, wrote letters to his Safavid contacts offering his service to Shah Isma'il by alluding to the Roman-Persian conflict to vilify his former patron: "Your majesty created tremors in the Rum, Destroyed the Caesars's palace and erected the Dome of Khosrow (*Tāq Kasrā*)."[95]

In the image of Mehmed, who deliberately parted ways with friends of God, Bidlisi reinterpreted far-fetched prophecies to create a perfect ruler who combined both executive and spiritual authorities. What facilitated his undertaking was the materialization of the Constantinople prophecy that silenced the critics of esoteric phantasies of occultists and opened the gates for a new era of prognostication by lending a degree of truth to even the most fanciful explorations. With that prestige, from Bayezid II onwards, esoterism and occultism were fully incorporated into mainstream political works. Bayezid's policy of conciliation toward disgruntled Turkoman dervishes, now captivated by the messianic call of the Safavids, entailed the making of a new imperial image that is acceptable to the reinvigorated friends of God against the Ottoman dynasty. No less conducive were a series of disasters including famines, plagues, fires, and earthquakes that led Bayezid's court to seek consolation and guidance in divinatory arts. Bayezid's new title, friend of God (*velī*), propagated a sense of security in the midst of unfolding existential anxieties.

As the Ottoman literati were acclimated to occultic forecasting, Bidlisi and his contemporaries incorporated prophecies into the mainstream of historical and political writings with enthusiasm and popularized eccentric arts of onomancy and geomancy in the service of the Ottoman dynasty. Among this new breed of political counselors skilled in elite sciences (*'ilm-i ḫavās*) was Muhammed b. Sharaf al-Din, a custodian of the pious foundations in Mecca and Medina, who presented a talismanic prayer book to Bayezid II in which he formulated specific incantations based on his interpretation of the symbolism embedded in the sultan's name. The author states the purpose of his initiative as an exploration of the secrets of the sultan's name and its correlation to God's names for the purpose of discovering specific prayers (*awfāq*, *dhikr*, and *awrād*).[96] This enigmatic Sufi presents Bayezid's name as the sultan's personal code of communication with the divine for constant protection and guidance. Bayezid, other than being the name of a venerated early Islamic mystic, had no scriptural origins or significance. Yet in Muhammed b. Sharaf al-Din's account it turns into an encrypted moral treatise to educate the sultan through what his name relates to ontologically. In his exposé, the name Bayezid suggests that the sultan is created for a purpose and destined to act in a particular way. To grow into the role for which he was created, the sultan is reminded to act in accordance with what his name imposes. So, apart from the general teachings of Islam and moral theory based on reason and experience, which the sultan is expected to follow, he needs to get acquainted with and submit to the specific instructions encrypted in his name. Muhammed b. Sharaf al-Din instructs Bayezid II that there is an existential correlation between his name and his character as well as his destiny, status, and, above all, mission on Earth.

Similar to the crafting of sultanic regalia, interpretation of proper names of sultans was an exclusive royal art in the service of dynastic legitimacy and propaganda as much as a recipe for the cultivation of an ideal ruler. The Seljuks in Anatolia were infatuated with the names of ancient Persian heroes and kings, which they adopted as sultanic titles. It was a common practice among Muslim rulers since the Abbasids to adopt a royal nickname after enthronement, such as Mu'iz al-Dawla, as in the case of the Buyids. Ottoman sultans, however, were content with unpretentious names. With the exception of a few names of Turkish origin, they preferred Arabic names often taken after prophets and venerated figures. Yet, for the apologist, these ordinary looking names were no coincidence. Name interpreters were well aware of the ontological significance attributed to names in Islamic tradition, particularly in Sufism. The Qur'anic verse telling that God taught Adam all the names to make him superior to angels was of course a folk knowledge. There is a vast Islamic literature on the meaning and implications of names. The ontological relationship between name and the named was a fashionable topic in Islamic philosophy and theology. Knowing and reciting names of God and His Prophet, for example, was an integral part of piety. Especially in Sufism, exploring the deeper meanings of God's ninety-nine beautiful names was the key to knowing God.[97] The most prized discovery of spiritual wayfaring in Sufism was God's greatest name (*al-ism al-aʿẓam*). By the time Muhammed b. Sharaf al-Din was composing his work, the grand master of Hurufism, Fadl Allah Astarabadi, was already a cult figure among the Ottomans who were infatuated with the elite science of interpreting names and numbers. Ferişteoğlu Abdülmecid (d. c. 1469) translated many of Astarabadi's works into Turkish.[98] The popularization of Hurufi texts in Turkish and widespread use of Hurufi techniques disenchanted the esoteric knowledge from the exclusive ownership of the spiritually worthy such as the Sufis, and offered it to common consumption. That made interpreting numbers and names a favorite tool to discover prophecies and decipher God's messages regarding visions of rulership.

Muhammed b. Sharaf al-Din's divinatory analysis through kledonomantic calculations of the letters of Bayezid, and their correlation to God's names and other numeric signs on which the creation rests, portrays an image of the Ottoman sultan as the true manifestation of God on Earth. The six letters of his name, for example, reflect the number of days in which God created the heavens and the earth. This manifestation, in turn, demonstrates that all in the heavens and on Earth would be pleased with the bearer of this auspicious name.[99] More specifically, four letters in his name refer to the four foundational matters of creation: Ba stands for earth, Alif for fire, Za for air, and Dal for water. For him, these four essential elements of existence from which everything is created indicate that all of God's creation (*jamīʿ al-makhlūqīn*) would benefit from his existence.[100] The letters in the Sultan's name not only reveal his character but also lay out his future as well. Ba refers to the fact that in his lifetime extraordinarily good things will happen, such as conquering new territories and turning them into abode of Islam. Alif simply stands for his close association with the divine and true faith. Ya demonstrates that his territories will remain as the abode of Islam till the end of times because it is the final letter of the alphabet. Za reflects his noble status in both this world and the hereafter. Dal signifies that, thanks to his gracefulness and through his existence, God protects the community of believers from all harm and blesses them with happiness.[101] Muhammed b. Sharaf al-Din elevates the Sultan to a chosen status because of whom God extends his bounty and protection to the community of believers.

Muhammed b. Sharaf al-Din reserved the introduction of the text to thank God for sending humankind a ruler with whom His servants would seek refuge and succor. It was a long established custom in Islamic texts that the invocatio is confined to thanking God for His beneficence and blessing. This unconventional construction of invocatio became more commonly expressed in the sixteenth century. Here the term for succor is *aghāsa* from the same root as *ghaws*, the succor as God's deputy on Earth in Sufi imagination. The author, with his self-ascribed spiritual powers, confirms his onomantic encoding with his own experience. When he arrived at the land of the Ottomans he was stricken with the realization that the ruling sultan was in fact a *ghaws* and assisted by His cardinal angels through whom God helps the common people.[102] Bayezid's being a succor is not merely a material good governance and service to humanity but a much deeper, spiritual protection in the general realm of cosmology. This is a clear reference to *ghaws*, which a number of mystical traditions purported to have existed as God's one chosen deputy over his creation, with both temporal and spiritual powers, through whom He manages the affairs of humanity and with whom believers, from ordinary subjects to rulers and from scholars to mystics, would seek mediation for their spiritual and material troubles.

Süleyman I and Designing the Ottoman Epitome

Following the trails of Bidlisi, his younger contemporary Ibn Kemal penned a short treatise to decipher the prophecies regarding perhaps the most illustrious of Ottoman military campaigns, Selim I's conquest and incorporation of the Arabic-speaking hinterland of the former caliphate. Inspired by the Constantinople prophecy, it became customary to narrate principal events, particularly military undertakings, as manifestations of divine will. The fact that the treatise is attributed to the chief jurist of the empire makes the authorship of this onomantic statement questionable. However, Ibn Kemal's interest in esoteric teachings and occultic arts was well known. He passed juristic rulings to exonerate Ibn Arabi and Ibrahim-i Gülşeni from charges of heresy and composed various treatises on the validity of teachings and arts outside the conventional Islamic disciplines. Posthumously, he was also credited with being the first chronogrammer among the Ottomans. His description of the Egyptian campaign via Qur'anic prophecies indicates that engagement with elite sciences found acceptance at the highest level of Ottoman ulema hierarchy.

Ibn Kemal's treatise is an onomastic commentary of a Qur'anic verse that became an increasingly popular quote in pro-dynastic apologia: "My servants the righteous, shall inherit the earth."[103] By examining the letters and terms of the expression, Ibn Kemal reconstructs the entire campaign in the form of a clear-cut scenario dictated by the divine. The exact date; location; the ease of the victory relative to the challenges posed; the progenitor of the dynasty that led the campaign, Osman; as well as its current ruler, Selim; and the subsequent transmission of rulership from the house of slaves (the Mamluks) to the righteous ones were all specifically foretold in the verse as Ibn Kemal reveals. A report from a seventeenth-century Moroccan traveler to Istanbul further trivializes the context that led Ibn Kemal to voice his prognostication. According to Ayyashi (d. 1679), Ibn Kemal foretold the trajectory of the campaign, not after the fact. In multiple consultative assemblies Selim I gathered before deciding to set out, Ibn Kemal stood alone in support of the sultan's decision against a host of scholars who ruled it not permissible for waging war against other Muslims without being prompted; it would be illegal.[104] Alusi (d. 1854), a celebrated nineteenth-century Qur'anic commentator from Baghdad, felt it necessary to note the story, now in popular circulation, and indicated that Selim took the verse as a good omen (*tafā'ul*). Alusi nevertheless found Ibn Kemal's prognostication a coincidence and his reasoning untrustworthy. Ottoman ulema who wrote full commentaries on the Qur'an such as Ebussuud and Bursevi did not hint at the embedded prophecy at all. Yet the verse continued to serve to reveal further prophecies in political and historical writings.

Selim I's spectacular conquests, easily aligned with prophecies, firmly established the belief that the Ottomans were the chosen dynasty of the end of times and that their military campaigns were all manifestations of divine providence. By comparison, Süleyman's policy of conquest into Europe was much less dramatic and even less meaningful in the context of Muslim eschatology. None of his conquests, Belgrade, Rhodes, or Budapest, had any direct references in Islamic sources. Yet the tradition continued to signify and mystify Ottoman conquests and turned Süleyman into a greater figure. An enigmatic court physician, Tabib Ramazan, penned two of the earliest accounts of Süleyman's reign where he revealed the signs of the sultan's divine guidance. Writing only six years after the Safavid War, his writing reflects the relatively subsided Kizilbash anxiety at the Ottoman center. Nevertheless, Süleyman's Belgrade campaign, with no noticeable provocation from the Habsburgs, startled the contemporaries who were fixated on the growing Safavid threat because of spreading confessional sympathies in Anatolia. Despite Shah Isma'il's humiliating but indecisive military defeat only a short time earlier, Tabib Ramazan feels obliged to start his *Risālā Fatḥiyya Sulaymāniyya* (The Conquest of Süleyman) with a chapter outlining the logical reasons that led Süleyman to turn his attention to the West instead of facing the Kizilbash. Of the three reasons he elaborates, the first is the sultan's submission to God's command for *gaza*, as sanctioned by scholars and the pious. In comparison, he considers Selim I's suspension of *gaza* activity as an anomaly, an exigency caused by an immediate threat. Selim I's Eastern campaign was a defensive measure. Once the Safavid strength was broken and they were no longer able to raid into the Rum, Süleyman resumes *gaza*. He thus credits Süleyman with reopening the gates of *gaza*.[105]

Tabib Ramazan, although unflinchingly harsh on his accusations of the Kizilbash, presents *gaza* as a raid specifically against the infidel, not against the heretics.[106] His contemporary Mevlana Isa "imputes to the dying Selim I an expression of regret that he died before the Kizilbash, that he did not build an *ʿimāret* for himself, and that he did not wage Holy War."[107] With theological certainty, Tabib Ramazan cites the Kizilbash among the five most harmful nations for the community of believers. Tabib Ramazan's justification of the change of conquest policy speaks for the pressure exerted by powerful sections of the Ottoman establishment toward the renewal of the *gaza* activity, which had remained dormant since the death of Mehmed II. Apart from the new Habsburg formation as the new powerhouse in eastern Europe, Ottoman raider families who were stationed in the western frontier whose economy and status depended on *gaza* as well as the Janissaries' ambivalent convictions toward the legitimacy of a war against the Kizilbash, must have weighed in this strategic decision.

Tabib Ramazan's reflections on the reasons behind avoiding further clashes with the Safavids reveal an underlying anxiety among the Ottoman policymakers. Despite all the propaganda effort, the Safavid campaign and subsequent encounters were never popular among the ruling establishment and less so among the general populace. In fact, no other military campaign until the eighteenth century when the Ottomans started to lose large provinces in the western half against the rising European powers fetched more ideological support than the anti-Safavid writings of the sixteenth century. The abundance of royal decrees, legal opinions by jurists, and polemical treatises by Sufis and the ulema alike point to a lack of public support and the need to legitimize the campaign. As shown by folk poetry, songs, epics, and hagiographies, the Ottoman ruling establishment had lost the ideological warfare against the Kizilbash from the very beginning and never overcame this deficit despite a series of military victories. The "Ottoman" name among the Turkomans has never been more blemished until the rise of nationalism in the late eighteenth century in the Balkans. Defeating the Safavids and suppressing their supporters in the countryside only created more martyrs, legends, and protest writings. Despite an unprecedented mobilization of the Ottoman Sunni establishment for the cause, waging a war against the Shiites never became a popular undertaking especially among the Turkoman tribes of the countryside or the very Ottoman military.

The first reason, according to Tabib Ramazan, is that eliminating the Kizilbash sedition would only be possible by mass killings of their supporters but such an undertaking would never be feasible because both Persia and the Ottoman realm were full of such people. Second, the Kizilbash was effectively incapacitated to attack the Rum. Invading their land would not eliminate them but only weaken the power of true believers. The third, and the most preventive, reason is that the caliph of the Rum was not responsible for eradicating oppression in the realm of the Ajam. Likewise, the caliph of the Rum had no such responsibility on the far corners of the east and the west. He was, however, directly responsible for any disorder within the Ottoman realm and its immediate vicinity. As the Christian powers across the western frontier were already posing a greater threat for Ottoman subjects Süleyman was inspired to turn his attention to the West.[108] Tabib Ramazan exalts Süleyman rather than diminish his position by alluding to the perennial conflict between the Romans and Persians and reaffirming Süleyman's identification with the former. Thus his turning attention to the lands of the Rum was only logical and demanded by his divine mission.

Tabib Ramazan's confinement of Süleyman's caliphate to the Rum and his disclaimer for Persian lands comes despite the fact that he designates Süleyman as the sultan of "the two Easts and two Wests," and more specifically "the caliph of the Rum and the Ajam."[109] For an analytical author who bases his arguments on logical premises these statements look incoherent if not outright contradictory. Yet the court physician does not appear to have seen it the way the text implies. In fact, his reasoning offers the reader an insight into how to understand one of the fundamental questions of Ottoman imperial ideology, namely, maintaining with complete harmony the claims of universal or even cosmological leadership with those of regional and communal on the same plain. Claiming these two seemingly conflicting authorities was the result of an acknowledgment of juristic realism and the pursuit of mystical idealism at once. In explaining the reasons behind Selim I's Kizilbash campaign and Süleyman I's abstention, Tabib Ramazan exclusively relies on juristic arguments, such as the physical limitations the sultan faced. Just as the prophets and rightly guided caliphs before him enjoyed the status of universal leadership and, at the same time, specifically limited their sovereignty to their domains or communities in governorship so did Süleyman.

Tabib Ramazan does not appear to be well versed in either conventional Islamic disciplines or esoteric sciences. But he appears to be well informed, probably thanks to his proximity to the ruling circle because of his profession, about the new legitimizing discourse at the Ottoman court. At the time of his writing he was in all likelihood a disillusioned physician who fell from favor and tried to regain his position by authoring hagiographic chronicles to glorify Süleyman. Although Tabib Ramazan claims to offer rational (*ʿaqlī*) evidence for Süleyman's assured victory in his *gaza* campaigns, his method resembles Hurufism except that while the Hurufis mainly use scriptures as their source material, Tabib Ramazan uses secular material through a self-justifying circular logic. Similar to Muhammed b. Sharaf al-Din, Tabib Ramazan reads the divine script through names. In all three of Süleyman's campaigns he witnessed—namely, Belgrade, Hungary, and Rhodes—he dissects these three names and interprets what each letter in these names refers to. There seemingly is no justification for these references other than what he purports. For the five letters of Hungary in Ottoman script, for example, Alif refers to Muslim's conquest of enemy territory, Nun to victory, Kaf to nobility, Ra to mass conversion of disbelievers, and Sin to the Sultan's dispensing justice and welfare in the realms of the Rum, Arab, and the Ajam after victory.[110] The coherence in attributing certain meanings to letters in different names suggests that he is relying on a preworked system of signs, which he does not reveal. For the letter Sin, for example, which is the final letter in both Rhodes and Hungary, in Ottoman script, he reveals the same outcome, namely, Süleyman's extending his rightful rulership over the lands of the Rum, the Arab, and the Ajam. Süleyman was guided to head toward certain targets whose names already reveal his conquests. In all these conquests Süleyman was assisted by God, His Prophet, and the saints.[111] What makes Tabib Ramazan's portrayal of Süleyman out of the ordinary is not the mystification of the Ottoman ruler's image through occultism but his blunt characterization of him with prophetic qualities by comparing him to Solomon, the prophet-ruler.[112] For Tabib Ramazan, each of these three conquests was unprecedented and surpassed in glory any other victory gained by past conquerors or prophets alike.

Süleyman's incessant engagement and encounters with Roman Catholic powers of Europe accorded him recognition far beyond the Ottoman borders as the protector of the universal Muslim community. He was also deeply involved in the power struggles of continental Europe as a key playmaker with self-assumed overlordship over the non-Muslim world as well, which involved inculcating an image of a universal ruler that includes legitimacy symbols of Christian empires.[113] Despite undertaking thirteen fully mobilized military campaigns on land and many no less comparable naval expeditions at high seas, Süleyman was not so much interested in conquering the world as in ordering it. His *gazi* image is far eclipsed by his incessant promulgation of edicts of law and an extensive building spree for infrastructure and public institutions. Süleyman's grand projects of canals on the Suez and Don–Volga basin, and clashes to end the Portuguese ambitions of establishing trade monopoly in the Indian Ocean, were driven by his global vision to preserve order in the old world and revive its economic blood flow against the detrimental effects of newly rising ocean-borne empires of Europe. As pointed out by Casale, Süleyman's involvement in clashes between expanding European powers and local populations extended his sphere of power as a universal ruler, but more specifically as the highest authority over the Muslim community at large, in such remote regions as Gujarat and Zanzibar.[114] Süleyman's profile as a universal ruler is extensively propagated in royal insignia, diplomatics, and artistic representations but had little impact on the way rulership is conceived in political theory. [115] Mevlana Isa, for example, looks well aware of the contest for universal rulership. He reported in his *Gazavātnāme* (Book of Raids) written in 1543 that Süleyman I openly challenged Charles V for a showdown: "Since you have claimed universal lordship (*ṣāḥib-ḳırān*), if you are a man, meet the one who is advancing towards you."[116] Yet, political authors and mystic adherents of the Ottoman dynasty were still preoccupied with the Safavid threat, now perceived to be a struggle between true faith and heresy. Thus perceptions of the Safavids and Shiism had a defining impact on the Ottoman conceptions of perfect rulership in this period.

The swift rise of the Safavids into a political power and its unstoppable expansion in the east initially aroused more curiosity than panic among the Ottomans. Despite the existence of a socially active and widely dispersed Kizilbash constituency of Anatolia and the Balkans, there is no visible anti-Shiite political or cultural campaign among the Ottoman elite prior to the sixteenth century. Excluding the Bedreddin rebellion during the Interregnum, Turkoman-based or Alevi-Bektaşi-led uprisings were often protests of resentment rather than rallies behind a revolutionary ideal. Ottoman ruling establishment delegitimized these protest movements on the basis of the general criminal law of Islam as well as the Ottoman *ḳānūn* without bringing about a sectarian reaction. In the context of Ottoman–Safavid conflict, Alevites in Anatolia and the Balkans were often referred to as Rafidis and Shiites in juristic writings and official documents. However, these juristic and theological terms pertaining to heresy were mostly confined to formal teachings of Islamic disciplines and were hardly, if ever, used in reference to actual communities that profess questionable ideas from the perspective of Sunni tradition. Although we cannot say for certain whether or to what extent Alevi-Bektaşis were perceived as Shiites before the rise of the Safavids, the Ottoman elite, in the main, seems to be indifferent to confessional identities or different manifestations of Islamic piety and creed unless they turn into ideologies of defiance.

A similar observation may be made for the Alevi-Bektaşis constituency's perception of the Ottoman authority. Despite frequent clashes, there is no indication to show that these Alevi-Bektaşis considered the Ottomans as their confessional other. An informed confessional critique of the Ottomans was hardly ever the case in rebellions of which the primary discourse revolved around oppression versus seeking justice despite the fact that grievances may be expressed through religious and messianic vocabulary. Sectarian consciousness was not prevalent among the Ottoman elite and various confessional communities prior to the sixteenth century. When the Safavid propaganda started to resonate strongly in the Anatolian countryside, the Ottomans seem to be very little educated on Shiism, and less prepared to counter this captivating call. Most of what the Ottoman ulema knew about Shiism was formal doctrines of Sunni theology taught in madrasa textbooks, such as Jurjani's *Sharh al-Mawāqif* (Commentary on the Stations), that were far from being readily applicable to define the Safavids or the Kizilbash from a sectarian angle.[117]

Sectarian consciousness was not the cause of the Ottoman–Safavid conflict but its consequence. For the Ottoman ruling elite, the rise of the Safavids was initially no more than a political threat. Aşıkpaşazade, who gave one of the earliest accounts of the rise of the Safavids in 1502, explain their gradual transformation from a Sunni Sufi order into an ambitious political movement with heretical views reminiscent of the Rafidis.[118] However, as they became more acquainted with the Safavid ideology, the conflict gained a sectarian character. Even after the political threat was effectively eliminated through a series of clashes, Ottoman relations with its eastern neighbor remained to be perceived as a sectarian conflict until the end of the empire. The Ottoman elite by the end of the sixteenth century were better informed and intensely more anti-Shiite in comparison to the beginning decade of the century. The Ottoman Sunnis only gradually identified the Safavids with the Rafidis, as recounted in theological literature, and established the continuity between the historical Shia and the Kizilbash. The reasons for this ignorance are the rise of the Safavids as a Sufi movement, the deeply symbolic language they employed in propagating their legitimacy, the very evolution of their own convictions, and the Ottomans' general indifference to confessional diversity in its domains. In this context, a flood of learned Sunni émigrés who fled Safavid invasions and took refuge in Ottoman domains played a critical role in informing the Ottoman Sunni establishment, identifying the Kizilbash with the Rafidis, and mobilizing the Ottoman authority against the Safavids.

Among them was Şirvani, an overzealous mystic and a passionate enemy of the Safavids, who skillfully integrated advanced divinatory techniques in his treatises he wrote at the height of the Kizilbash threat in late 1530s and early 1540s. He capitalized on the staples of Ottoman eschatology drawn from Qur'anic verses and Prophetic traditions, all eventually pointing to either the Roman-Persian confrontation or the historical dialectics of Sunni versus Shiite struggle. Şirvani was an irate Sunni advocate who, in his own words, fled the incessant Safavid oppression. His interest in Qur'anic and prophetic prophecies was driven by a manifest desire to prompt the Ottomans to be aware of their divinely assigned role of defending the faith against the heretics. Having experienced the overwhelming Safavid propaganda that capitalized on the messianic repertoire of Shiism and Persianate Sufism, he was well informed to counter and outdo those claims by mining the scriptures of Islam and interpreting them in favor of the Ottomans, whom he regarded as the last beacon of true faith. Based on his onomastic explorations of prophecies from the Qur'an and hadith, Şirvani sets out to prove that the Ottoman dynasty is a chosen one, destined to rule at the end of times with a specific mission.

Besides his own mystical convictions, Şirvani exploits Ibn Arabi's mystical cosmology to counter Safavid spirituality and promote that of the Ottomans.

At the time, there was a concerted effort to mobilize the Sufis of the Rum around the teachings of Ibn Arabi to defeat the Safavids at the spiritual and ideological level. That was part of the campaign to promote Ibn Arabi as a nondenominational grand master of spirituality from whose esoterism all Sufi orders could get inspired, and ideologized, in defense of the Sunni faith and its political patrons. Jurisprudence and theology fell short of providing persuasive tools to effectively counter the mystical call of Savafid Shiism. These texts were self-justifying sources with no authoritative value for a Shiite. Even the well-established Sufi orders, such as the Nakşibendiyye and Halvetiyye, were all too normative to lend any flexible arguments to counter the unfettered Safavid esoterism unless, of course, they express their doctrines in Ibn Arabian idiom or even that of the Hurufis.[119] Thus we see a gradual acceptance of Ibn Arabism as a spiritual paradigm that not only learned scholars but also mainstream Sufi orders could utilize to further mystify their messages for a wider appeal.

The Safavid challenge brought about a deep distrust among the Ottoman authorities toward the Sufis. It reminded the Ottomans of the ideological potential, social power, and popular appeal of the Sufis in turning their vision of authority into executive power. The Ottoman response was twofold: On the one hand, Sufi groups were put under increased scrutiny. Condemnation of Ibn Arabi and execution of some of his leading proponents show this reprisal. On the other hand, the Ottoman ruling elite opted to exploit Sufism to counter the Safavid propaganda. A number of leading jurists, among them most notably Bidlisi and Ibn Kemal, rushed to rehabilitate Ibn Arabi and use his teachings of endless complexity to mine concrete signs for the legitimacy of the Ottoman dynasty. Selim I, whose campaing against the Safavids involved mobilizing the Sufi corps of the realm of Sunni bent, commissioned Shaykh Mekki (d. 1520), a student of Abdurrahman Jami, to vindicate Ibn Arabi against his detractors. Shaykh Mekki composed a long treatise that refuted common charges against Ibn Arabi and explained his controversial ideas in a way fully acceptable to a Sunni mindset.[120] To use Ibn Arabi as propaganda material he had to be first reclaimed for the mainstream Sunnism, which involved the persuasion of a powerful contingent of rigid jurists and theologians of the Ottoman madrasa establishment.[121] This was achieved through the conscious efforts of high-profile jurists who not only had an authoritative voice in learning but also enjoyed the power of being placed at the top of a strictly hierarchical learning establishment with the power of promoting like-minded scholars to important positions. Their own ascent to highest positions among the ulema owed a great deal to their views of Sufism, particularly of Ibn Arabi. That also entailed the marginalization of jurists who were critical of Sufism, such as Çivizade. While sacralizing the Ottoman dynasty through esoteric techniques, much like Shaykh Mekki, Şirvani reconciled between esoteric and exoteric knowledge by establishing an epistemological unity between Sufism and normative knowledge. For him, Sufis and jurists often disagree not because they hold different views but because they use different terminology for the same truth.[122]

After validating the truth of eccentric Sufistic teachings through juristic and theological doctrines of mainstream Sunnism, Şirvani provides a prescription for spiritual perfection for the sultan and those who are set to contront the heretics which also entails the recognition of the saintly order of the world. Illustrated by anecdotes drawn from hagiographies of past mystics, *ʿAdliyya* guided the sultan to refine his devotion (*zuhd*) and piety (*taqvā*).[123] While he urged the sultan to follow the Sufi path to attain spiritual perfection as a way of achieving ideal rulership, he also informed the sultan about the real government of the world, which was the order of invisible saints, and advised him to recognize and seek help from the overarching authority of the existing head of this order, the *quṭb*, who was also the *ghavs*.[124] He ensures the sultan that he would be aided by the pole, the real wielder of power on Earth as God's deputy. As proof, he asserts that the current pole in the world was a Hanafi, while the previous poles were Shafi'is for 258 years, probably referring to the Mamluk era.[125] Besides giving the impression that the pole of the universe is at the same time an adherent of a juristic school of law, namely, still operating within the confines of the Sharia, this was a further piece of evidence that the pole was on the Ottoman side with the shift of the political leadership of the Sunni world from the Mamluks to the Ottomans. Establishing the Hanafi-Sunni identity of the pole and portraying the Ottoman rule as a manifestation of his executive power aimed at disproving the Safavid claims of spiritual superiority that not only invoked similar imageries of poleship but also that of the Mahdi. As Mahdiship was likely to create more doctrinal complications, claiming the exclusive support of the pole was the only way Safavid claims of superiority could be countered on both Sufistic and juristic grounds.

As a Sufi with Melami proclivities, Şirvani must have been fully aware of the Safavid's birth-right to claim the pole's backing. His Melami contemporary Abdurrahman el-Askeri effectively dissociates the pole from the Safavid legacy by specifying where the current pole was based. In Askeri's account, just like the epochal turns in the reception of *dawla* and the caliphate, the seat of poleship also changes across time and nations. As he reports, Prophet Muhammed passed the divine secret (*ṣırr-ı ilāhī*) to both Abu Bakr and Ali b. Abi Talib. The people of love (*erbāb-ı ʿışḳ*) followed Ali as the absolute leader of saints whereas people of thoughts (*erbāb-ı ḫavātır*), i.e. contemplative Sufis, followed Abu Bakr. With Ali, the secret of love passed from Arabs to the abode of Persians and remained there until the time of Hace Ali-i Erdebili (d. 1429). Then, Erdebili's deputy took the divine secret to the Rum where it remained till its current recipient Pir Ahmed, the sultan of the realm of meaning, pole of time, and caliph of God's mercy.[126] Erdebili was the grandson of Shaykh Safiyyuddin, the founder of the Safavid order, from whom the spiritual genealogy of Bayramis in Anatolia also emanates. Askeri thus identifies Şirvani's Hanafi-Sunni pole with Bayrami-Melami shaykhs of the Rum whom he praises as the source of honor for both the realm of Rum and the Ottoman dynasty.[127]

Into Süleyman's long reign, the difference between the current Kizilbash devotion of the Safavids and their earlier Sunni origins became increasingly clearer. But during the early years of their rise, the confessional identity of the Safavids was confounding, not only for the Ottomans but for the traditional Shiite establishment as well. The Safavid conversion to Shiism was gradual and contained elements that might be equally objectionable by Twelver Shiism as much as the Sunnis.[128] Even al-Karaki (d. 1533), the first prominent Shiite scholar of Safavid Persia and the staunchest supporter the dynasty, never accepted the Kizilbash recognition of shahs as the rightful Imams.[129] Being emanated from a Sufi order with a distinct Turkoman social base it was a familiar case for the Ottomans as they had been dealing with a series of Turkoman rebellions led by charismatic mystics. To complicate things further, at a time when the Safavids were marching toward statehood, Bayezid II was busy making amends with the Sufi orders to appease widespread resentment caused by souring relations during Mehmed II's empire-building centralization. Contemporary accounts portray Bayezid II as too complacent about the growing Safavid threat and attribute his inaction to his ailing physical and mental health. His inaction was in part dictated by his general policy of appeasement toward the Sufis and his policymakers may not have seen the new Kizilbash activism as any different from previous Turkoman uprisings. There was a stark difference between Selim I, then governor of Trebizond, the easternmost province at the time, and Bayezid II as to how they perceived the Safavids. Selim I was overly vigilant and had already engaged in a campaign to suppress the growing Safavid influence. What must have alarmed him was Shah Isma'il's image that started to shadow that of the Ottoman ruler in the East accompanied by his swift expansion. As elaborately explained by Kathryn Babayan, Isma'il's promoted image as a king, warrior (*gazi*), and a saint at once had a captivating impact on the unruly Turkoman constituency of Eurasia.[130] Selim's anti-Safavidism was as much a personal matter as a doctrinal vigilance. Bayezid II and his favorite son for the throne, Ahmed, however, looked indifferent, even wished that Selim be defeated to clear the path for Ahmed's succession. During the civil war of succession Prince Ahmed openly sought alliance with the Safavids. In fact, Ahmed's son Murad joined the ranks among the Safavids in order to mobilize the Turkoman Kizilbash against Selim.[131] When Selim succeeded, he owed his triumph to his skillful exploitation of the Safavid threat and well-propagated heroism he established as the sole defender of the Ottoman realm. Later, he furthered his image of defending the Ottoman realm into defending the realm of Islam. By the time Süleyman ascended to the throne he had already developed his own opinions about the Safavids as his support for Selim's campaign against the Safavids, both before and after his succession, was critical.

Şirvani's exposition of prophecies was indispensably tied to an eschatology triggered by the rise of the Safavids.[132] On the authority of the famed Kashifi, he relates a prophetic tradition that forewarns the community of Muslims of the appearance of a heretical group at the end of times (*āḫir zamān*) who would call themselves Sufis, morally indifferent (*mubāhiyya*) in their words and deeds, and that they are worse than polytheists and renegades.[133] Şirvani not only identifies this group as the Kizilbash but also endeavors to prove that they were the Rafidis. He never uses the term Shiite to characterize the Safavids. The general tendency among Ottoman polemicists was to avoid calling them Shiite, which might imply that they were the party of Ali. After centuries of fierce debates, at least by the tenth century, Shiism was admitted by Sunni theologians as a borderline community rather than being dismissed as heretic nonbelievers. Although Rafidis may be used as a synonym for Shia, it generally refers to what Sunni theologians call extreme Shiites, and therefore not part of the acceptable family of Muslim sects. Since the days of the first civil war between the supporters of Ali and Mu'awiya in 656 C.E. a vast literature on the characteristics and refutation of the Rafidis had formed among the Sunnis. Identifying the Kizilbash with the Rafidis enables Şirvani not only to specify who they were but also draw from a refined tradition of profiling and refutation. To show that the Kizilbash were none other than the Rafidis, perhaps the most defamed sect among the Sunnis, Şirvani provides the most comprehensive account of the Safavid convictions with a sophisticated vocabulary of Sunni theology in a markedly agitative language. In fact, the very title of the main treatise on the subject, *Ordinances of Religion*, suggests up front that confronting the Safavids was not about eliminating sedition and reestablishing order but was part of a fundamental conflict between the true faith and its distortion.

Şirvani reports that the Kizilbash worship their shah as a deity, believing that the divine nature of Ali gets reincarnated through the shahs.[134] More specifically, they believe that Shah Isma'il manifested himself in Tahmasb.[135] This is a stark reminder to the sultan, at a time when Ottoman-Safavid relations were relatively calm, that the persona of Shah Isma'il is very much alive in Kizilbash faith and that the question is not about one adventurous Turkoman mystic who was humiliated by Selim I but about the idea that accords these leaders divine status in perpetuity. For him, that makes them more harmful than Christians and Jews who attributed divinity to Jesus and Uzayr, respectively, because the Rafidis were corrupting the very religion that was revealed to rectify past deviations.[136]

Şirvani provides a long list of Safavid sins and devious practices that would provoke any pious Muslim, yet alone the Sunni-minded. However, this collection of accusations is not what distinguishes Şirvani's texts from other anti-Safavid polemics that abounded in this period. He presents them as part of the cataclysmic events of the end of times, thus according his carefully selected charges an eschatological import by diligently tying them to a foretold prophecy through a skillful use of Hurufi techniques. Unlike other heretical sects who were only deviant, the Kizilbash was deviant and deviating at the same (*dāl wa mudil*), leading Muslims astray.[137] The Ottomans, however, were their exact opposite as they continuously converted non-Muslims as manifested by the system of child levy (*devşirme*) they had long practiced. *Devşirme* had never been problematized or idealized by previous Ottoman authors and only seldom mentioned by later ones. The main attitude among the Ottoman learned was indifference mainly because of the legal problems it posed to justify this practice. Yet for Şirvani, an outsider, it became one of the defining marks of Ottoman distinction and legitimacy. This makes sense only against the backdrop of what Şirvani criticizes about the Safavids. For him, the greatest crime they commit was to force the children of Muslims to deviate from the straight path. By definition, however juristically troublesome it may be, the Ottoman practice of converting the children of non-Muslims becomes a stark evidence of their righteousness.

Once the Safavids are portrayed as such, the struggle against them would be no ordinary one. Şirvani labels the anti-Safavid campaign as *jihād-i kabīr*, the great jihad and praises the virtue of raids and battles (*faḍīlat-i ghazā va ṭarīq-i muḥāraba*).[138] He is silent, if not discouraging, on raiding for the faith against the infidels. Each time he uses the terms jihad, *ghazā*, and *muḥāraba*, he exclusively means the fight against the Kizilbash.[139] On the basis of evidence from authoritavie Sunni sources, he states that the Kizilbash are no different than polytheists (*mushrik*) and infidels (*kāfir*) in faith, but are worse in practice and intent. He further claimes that killing them is a more commendable religious obligation than killing infidels, and raiders for the faith (*mujāhidūn*) are allowed to appropriate their property and women as legitimate booty.[140] He makes no reference to specific beliefs of the contemporary Kizilbash or the Safavids; instead, in order to motivate (*taḥrīs*) the sultan to wage war against them, he mostly enumerates the age-old Sunni accusations of the Shiites, gathered from medieval works of polemical theology, about their perverted beliefs.

Labeling a war against heretics as the greatest jihad does not suit well to conventional expositions of Ottoman warfare. This is not a protection of the *dār al-Islām* (abode of Islam) or spreading God's name to *dār al-ḥarb* (abode of war). This characterization not only points to the greatness of the threat but also to its extent; a jihad that includes spiritual and ideological struggle as much as physical confrontation. In Sufi idiom *jihād-i akbar* denoted purification of one's self from temptations and striving for moral perfection. Şirvani's contemporary Abdurrahman el-Askeri clearly distinguishes between the two forms of jihad: the one based on the Sharia, and the one based on the Sufi path (*ṭarīkat*). He defines the former as a pursuit of desires and the latter as the pursuit of overcoming them. Unless one successfully completes his spiritual jihad, or the greater fight, one cannot conduct the physical one, i.e. the smaller fight, as sanctioned by the Sharia. Per the Bayrami-Melami teachings, Askeri requires spiritual training as a pre-requisite for raiding for the faith, that is, *gaza*.[141] At the time, the term *gaza* was also commonly used by the Safavids during their campaigns against the Ottomans as well as other Muslim dynasties.[142] Thanks to their Sufi origins and immersion in esoteric Shiism, the Safavid expressions of *gaza* were already deeply imbued with spiritualism. Sectarian consciousness and alternative truth-claims that dominated the ideological background of the Ottoman-Safavid conflict loaded jihad and *gaza* with more spiritual and theological content. In the language of anti-Safavid propagandists, the term *gazi*, which conventionally meant raiding for the faith against the infidels, came to signify raiding for the true faith against the heretics. Further, there had been a sudden surge in jihad literature from the reign of Bayezid II through the reign of Süleyman. But this reinvigoration of the idea of jihad had more to do with rectifying confessional corruption than spreading the name of God and expanding the realm of Islam. The defense and protection of Islam's hinterland gained primacy over the zeal of gaining infidel territories.

As in all aspects of political thought, Sufi worldview also permeated into conceptions of jihad in this period. Unlike the nature of rulership, which had been a common question for all strands of Islamic thought, jihad was largely an exclusive topic for jurists to discuss. Since the mystical turn, however, Sufis enjoyed equating their spiritual wayfaring to jihad and increasingly incorporated moral purification to jihad books that dealt with the normative rules of waging wars against the infidel. A certain Sıddıki, for example, who dedicated his work *Zād al-Jihād* (Provisions of Jihad) to Bayezid II, allocated the final one-third of the treatise to greatest jihad where he outlined moral and spiritual recipes for sultan's campaign against the vices of himself.[143] Sıddıki composed his work in the form of a mirror for princes with one major difference: In a typical mirror there is a special emphasis on the morality of the ruler where it is presented as a personal regime of discipline to inculcate virtues and cleanse vices. With Sufis, spirituality takes precedence over morality. Spiritual perfection entails command of one's good self over one's entire self. Morality was intelligence based, whereas spirituality was soul based. The ruler was already depicted by mystics as the soul of the realm, a spiritually purified ruler has a soul that rules the realm of his body. Thus, as the soul of the world, a spiritually reformed ruler is considered to be the insurance of good morality and true faith in society. Şirvani's jihad calls for a spiritual warfare against all vices including those caused by the heretics.

Şirvani evokes abhorrence of the morally upright by accusing the Kizilbash of moral decay, which calls for the greatest jihad to eliminate. For him, The Safavids, in their divine capacity, behaved indifferent to good or evil, and permitted such cardinal sins as adultery and alcohol drinking.[144] He specifically accuses the Safavid ruler of his time, Tahmasb, of incest. Furthermore, the

Safavids cruelly forced the Sunnis they came to rule over to adopt their faith and practices. Şirvani enumerates the names of famed Sunni scholars and mystics who were killed at the hands of the Safavids. But his most provocative charges were the Safavid destruction of holy shrines including the tombs of the venerated mystic Abd al-Kadir al-Jilani, better known as the *ghaws al-aʿẓam* (God's greatest succor), and the most venerated jurist for the Ottomans, Abu Hanifa. Şirvani also reports Shah Isma'il's plans to march to Mecca and Medina with the intention of demolishing the two Holy Sanctuaries and change the direction of prayers (*qibla*) from Mecca to Ardabil in Ajamistan, their homeland.[145] As such the Safavid shah was no different than Abraha who set out from Yemen to destruct Kaaba and incurred God's wrath to be perished by clay throwing birds, as recounted in the Qur'an.[146] Yet, he stipulates that the Ottomans carry out their mission by strictly staying within the confines of justice, their most distinguishing mark.[147] In order to avoid oppression and be compassionate toward his subjects, the sultan should constantly seek the advice, guidance, and assistance of the people of spiritual perfection.

Şirvani's tendentious portrayal of the Safavid movement suits the eschatological expectations of the end of times that abounded in this period. That level of upheaval necessitates the emergence of a leadership in messianic capacity in the sense that no ordinary ruler, however exceptional, would be able to eliminate. Şirvani repeatedly states that in the history of humankind no community has come to Earth worse than the Kizilbash as they display all the characteristics of former devious communities combined.[148] This depiction does not simply reflect a pious rage against perceived evil. Rather, it points to Şirvani's ideologization of the conflict by magnifying the degree and nature of disorder to suit foretold events in Sunni eschatology. The conflict of prophetic proportions could be steered only by a chosen agent of God specifically endowed with skills demanded by the mission. Şirvani describes the Ottoman sultan's confrontation with the Safavid shah with the same vocabulary God uses in the Qur'an to narrate the epic encounters between His messengers and defiers of God's call. Shah Isma'il, who turns into a rebel (*baghy*), claims divinity just as the pharaoh does, who also rebels openly against God (*ṭaghā*). God sends (*arsala*) Selim I as "the sultan of the East and the West" for the destruction of this false deity just as Moses, along with his brother Aaron, were commissioned to confront the pharaoh.[149] The word *arsala* that expresses Selim I's move is the same word that is used for God's sending His prophets in the Qur'an and the hadith literature. Designating someone as *baghī* already justifies the execution of the perpetrator according to the Islamic law. Isma'il's rebellion, however, was directly against God's authority in the same way as the pharaoh's; therefore his punishment would come directly from God. More striking is the depiction of Selim I as "the sultan of the East and West," a clear allusion to the well-known Qur'anic verse where God is glorified as "the Lord of the East and the West."[150]

This same prophetic nomenclature applies to the reigning Süleyman with more emphasis. Similar to Tabib Ramazan, Şirvani starts both *Taṣavvuf* and *Aḥkām* by thanking God for sending Süleyman to lead humankind. A typical text from this period starts with a gloria where God, Prophet Muhammed, and the rightly guided caliphs are praised. Only after the start of the main body of the text the reigning sultan may be praised. Here Şirvani bypasses the convention and devotes the entire gloria section to Süleyman: "He deputized him (*khālafahu*) as the caliph of the caliphs of Iran and Turan and sent him (*baʿatha*) as the destroyer of disbelievers."[151] Süleyman's caliphate over other caliphs of the Turko-Persianate world signifies a cosmic leadership over God's other chosen deputies, namely the mystics who were considered to be granted that status in the spiritual realm. Representatives of Shah Isma'il in Anatolia were also commonly designated as caliphs. The term for Süleyman's being sent, *baʿatha*, is again an exclusively Qur'anic word used for God's dispatching messengers to convey His word. For Şirvani, as attested by the ulema and statesmen, Süleyman was unique because he was sent over the Muslims by God to lead them to the right path, and eliminate oppression and harmful innovation: "Blessed is humanity for they were sent a helper, and people thank God for sending (*arsala*) him as bearer of good tidings."[152]

Şirvani's conjectural arguments, based on prognosis to identify prophecies and signify current circumstances, lay out a carefully crafted program of ideologizing the Ottoman–Safavid rivalry. His revelations are geared to prove that the cataclysmic events of the end of times were precisely foretold in the Qur'an or statements of the Prophet and saints. With Qur'anic and Prophetic certainty, Ottomans were identified as the restorers of true faith whose victory over the corrupters was assured.[153] In *ʿAdliyya*, he calculates the onomantic value of the Qur'anic phrase "*yarithuhā ʿibādī al-ṣāliḥūn*" as H. 951/1544 C.E., pointing to the reign of Süleyman. In addition, the phrase "*ʿibādī al-ṣāliḥūn*" has the same value as the names Muhammed and Süleyman, which is 303, with purported implication that Süleyman is sent for the same mission as Muhammed.[154] For him, the Ottoman rulership over the holy sanctuaries of Mecca, Medina, and Jerusalem proves the truth of this prophecy. He accords the Ottoman ruler the same position as the Prophet as some Qur'anic commentaries indicated that the inheritance of land by God's righteous servants implied the initial Muslim conquests under the Prophet and his companions.[155] For the hadith, "*khayr al-favāris*" he comes up with H. 916/1510 C.E., a year that signifies the beginnings of Selim I's rise to the throne, whose reign proved the Ottoman supremacy over the Safavids.[156] As dictated by divine will, Selim I restores true faith and renovates Holy sanctuaries. In other words, the sultan of the Rum undid the harm caused by the Persians.

In *Taṣavvuf*, Şirvani's math of prognostication gets less specific but more authoritative. He infers his prophecy from the opening verse of every chapter of the Qur'an save one, the *Basmala*, one of the most fundamental phrases in the Muslim tradition with which the pious start every action. In his calculation, *Basmala* and Süleyman have the same numerical value. On the authority of Ibn Arabi, he quotes a prophecy from Ali b. Abi Talib who foretold that when the letters of *Basmala* are reached in time, the Mahdi arrives. For Şirvani there was no contemporary ruler named Süleyman to possibly identify with the prophecy.[157] Despite Ali's clear indication, Şirvani did not elaborate on the Mahdi in his conjecture. Instead, following Ibn Arabi's interpretation, he pointed to the coming of a great sultan in the final days whose name would have the same letters as *Basmala*. This great sultan would be endowed with the same qualities as his namesake Prophet Solomon who was a *sāhib-ḳirān*, the lord of conjunction. To prove the prophecy, Şirvani compares Süleyman to Prophet Solomon, his archetype. Prophet Solomon's five characteristics were prophethood, sainthood, rulership of the auspicious junction, inviting infidels to true faith, and conquest of which Süleyman possessed all but prophethood.[158] After establishing the eschatological scene, Şirvani reveals the trajectory of Ottoman–Safavid confrontation, which unfolds as a reenactment of the perennial clash between the Romans and the Persians. For him, the Qur'anic verse "*ghalabat al-Rūm*" (the Romans prevailed) yields the date 929 whereas the verse "*yarithuhā ʿibādī al-ṣāliḥūn*" indicates the year 951. The former date shows the beginning of Süleyman's conquest including Belgrade and Rhodes while the latter informs that Süleyman will complete the conquest of the entire Persia (*vilāyet-i ʿAcemistān*).[159] Per God's word in the Qur'an, the Ottoman victory over the Safavids was assured.

The Seal of the Caliphate

The polyphonic messianic arena of the first half of the sixteenth century was overcrowded with self-designated Mahdis, occultists excited with a plethora of signs signaling the end of times, Sufis preoccupied with deciphering prophecies embedded in scriptures, and weary jurists who rediscovered the Sunni canons on Islamic eschatology with the hope of subsiding the millenarian excitement. The idea of Mahdi was always in the air among the urban networks of Bayrami–Melami Sufis whose pantheistic proclivities, idiosyncratic rituals, and bluntness in calling their shaykhs *quṭbs* often brought them face to face with Ottoman authorities and upright jurists. Among the many persecuted, in one of the most tragic incidents of heresy, a twenty-year-old, known as Child Shaykh, was executed on a long list of charges including his claim to be Mahdi after a juristic opinion passed by the top jurist Ibn Kemal who, ironically, happened to be one of the most Sufi-minded of Ottoman ulema.[160] A Turkoman dervish Şahkulu rebelled against the Ottoman authority in 1511 as manifestation of God, two years after a major earthquake, called little doomsday, shook Istanbul, and secured much of western Anatolia before he disappeared into obscurity.[161] Increasingly tuned to the Safavid call, restless Turkomans remained on the rise through a number of popular revolts behind charismatic dervish-leaders with Messianic appeal.

The best known of all Mahdis was none other than the one who was most disturbed by popular messianism, Süleyman. Even Lami'i Çelebi, who was renowned for his distance from the Ottoman establishment, could comfortably praise Süleyman as the Mahdi of time and the seal of the caliphate.[162] As Cornell Fleischer argued, Süleyman enjoyed his new image as Mahdi during the early decades of his rule, if not inculcated it by his own will.[163] His extensive building and restoration projects propagated the idea that he was no ordinary ruler. In Jerusalem, for example, he inscribed his name with such epithets as the Second Solomon (*thānī Sulaymān fi mulk al-ʿālam*), the possessor of the greatest imamate, and inheritor of the greatest caliphate.[164] Despite the unprecedented opulence of titles, such as *müceddid* and *ṣāḥib-ḳırān* that befits only a chosen ruler, official documents carefully avoided the theologically problematic Mahdi in sultanic regalia. But this deficit was overfilled with literary expressions of many sorts by his close circle of confidants and his admirers from the broader ruling establishment. Even Celalzade, his utterly legal-minded chief of chancery, named him Mahdi with no qualms. Süleyman's no less legally conscious grand vizier Lütfi Paşa did not see it odd to posthumously characterize Selim as the Mahdi of the end of times (*Mehdī-i āḫir zamān*). In similar fashion, Levhi in his *Cihādnāme* of 1529, Sena'i in his *Süleymānnāme* (Book of Süleyman) of 1540, and Haki in his same-titled work from 1556–1557 all depicted Süleyman as a universal sovereign with divine appointment within an apocalyptic framework.[165] Two earlier masters on esoteric knowledge, Ibn Arabi and Bistami, turned into cult authorities on prognostication. Ibn Arabi's texts served as a seemingly endless source of prophecies to confirm and further cultivate the Ottoman sultan's image as a chosen ruler.[166] Ibn Arabi's pseudo-epigraphic work *al-Shajara al-Nuʿmāniyya fī al-Dawla al-ʿUthmāniyya* (The Crimson Tree on the Ottoman Glory), among many prognoses it contained, designated the House of Osman as the final dynasty before the end of times.[167] Bistami's corpus on the science of names and letters, most notably his *Miftāḥ al-Jafr al-Jāmī* (The Key to the Comprehensive Prognostication), became the master text for profession.[168]

But even before the sixteenth century, the Mahdi appellation of Ottoman rulers was not uncommon. Every sultan since, at least, the Interregnum is called Mahdi but this messianic imagery never took a firm hold in Ottoman imperial ideology. Apocalyptic consciousness in the broader Islamic community had never ceased to exist in any generation since the death of the Prophet, as the belief in the immanency of the apocalypse had always been part of Islamic faith and piety.[169] A continuous stream of cosmological undertakings to discover the length of life on Earth was always accompanied with a more popular tradition of writings on the existing and expected signs of the end times. It is not surprising to see Mahdi claimants at any given moment, even without any ostensibly conducive factors. It is also not surprising to see that political crises, confessional confrontations, or natural disasters turned the faithful more attuned to messianic signification of unfolding events that resonated in social movements and cultural expressions. Yet in no other era of Ottoman history did messianism find such captivating appeal on both courtly circles and broad masses, each with its own varieties. The broader content of the apocalyptic and messianic literature produced by the Ottoman elite points to three factors that prompted eschatological tendencies in political thinking. First, approaching the end of the millennium on the Muslim calendar aroused widespread curiosity that not only revived medieval prophecies but also directed the learned to make use of new techniques drawn from the latest advances in astronomy and Hurufism. Second, the concomitant rise of the Safavids and Habsburgs to power turned Süleyman into the chief defender of faith against infidels and heretics at once. Third, Sufi imageries of cosmic government, more specifically the idea of pole as axis mundi and caliph as the unifier of both temporal and spiritual with superhuman attributes, made any image of Mahdi a familiar one.

The textual representations of messianism during the first half of Süleyman's reign were more direct than at any other period of Ottoman history. Mevlana Isa, a provincial qadi who was affiliated with a network of occult specialists, composed his *Gazavātnāme* (Book of Raids) in three recensions in the quaint form of a versed history between 1520 and 1543.[170] His reading of heavenly alignments and deciphering of scriptural prophecies point out that, as renewer of religion (*müceddid*) and lord of conjunction (*ṣāḥib-ḳırān*), Süleyman was either Mahdi himself or his conquering forerunner (*serʿasker*).[171] These same ideas were voiced at Süleyman's court by Haydar Remmal, a geomancer from the east, who established himself as one of the closest confidants of the sultan and caused quite a stir in palace circles including his involvement in the execution of Süleyman's grand vizier and childhood friend Ibrahim Paşa whom the geomancer accused of plotting against the sultan with the certainty of prognosticative evidence.[172]

A contemporary of Mevlana Isa and Haydar Remmal, Ibn Isa Saruhani, was not so much interested in Süleyman's messianic persona. Instead, by making use of the same authoritative sources and techniques he strived to establish the House of Osman as the final dynasty on Earth. Among others, two of his works presented prognoses regarding the future trajectory of the Ottoman dynasty: a hagiographic account of Mecdüddin Isa, his father, and a detailed future history of the Ottomans until the end of times. According to the hagiography of his father he penned after 1530s, Süleyman's tutor visits the shaykh in 1516 while the future sultan was the governor of Manisa at the request of the young prince who, in all probability, was curious about his and the Ottoman dynasty's future in the midst of widespread Turkoman uprisings. The shaykh of the Bayrami order, famed for his saintly spiritual might and the mastery of prognostication, reveals that the opening chapter of the Qur'an, known as the mother of the Book, gives a snapshot of the entire trajectory of the caliphate from Adam until the end of times.[173] In his brief, the caliphate from Adam to Muhammed is embedded in the letters of *Basmala*, the opening formula of Qur'anic chapters. *al-Ḥamd li-Allāh* refers to Muhammed's caliphate as it contains all the letters of the Prophet's name. *Rabb al-ʿālamīn* stands for the first four rightly guided caliphs after Muhammed. Then until the age of the Ottomans the caliphate remained in the letters of *al-raḥmān al-raḥīm*, and *mālik yawm al-dīn*. *Yawm al-dīn* refers to the caliphate of the last Seljuk sultan Alaeddin from whom the Ottomans inherited the caliphal authority. Finally, the saint adduces from *iyyā-ka naʿbudu* the beginning of the Ottoman turn in the caliphate. At the very moment, the saint-prognosticator reveals that the Ottoman caliphate is at the stage of *ihdinā al-ṣirāṭ al-mustaqīm* (guide us to the straight path) and it will continue until the chapter ends. The word *ihdinā* comes from the same root as Mahdi and the straight path is commonly taken for the Sunni creed. The wording and message of the verse perfectly comports contemporary visions of Ottoman rulership.

Turned more curious, Süleyman's tutor asks how long the House of Osman would rule over the world and whether he could enlighten the sultan of the Saint's revelations. In response, the shaykh shares a bit more of his foreknowledge with a strict stipulation that the tutor does not inform the Sultan with a warning that he will not be able to detail any further, for the tutor may not be able to bear the weight of these secrets. From his time all the way to the year 2028 C.E., the shaykh informs, the caliphate will remain in the hands of the Ottomans. Then with the accession of a female sultan to the throne, the subsequent lineage gets necessarily mixed, from which a ruler called Ali Veli appears during whose reign Sufis gain prominence and the shaykh's convent alongside with his tomb is rebuilt.[174]

Five years later, during the siege of Rhodes in 1521, Mecdüddin Isa received another visitor from the Ottoman court. This time, it was Bektaş Efendi, the praying leader of Süleyman, who came to him asking for his assistance for victory against the seemingly invincible Knights of Rhodes.[175] The shaykh prophesied that the fortress would not fall unless a person from among the friends of God falls martyr. The long siege finally ends with victory as soon as the said friend of God is killed by infidels, as revealed by the shaykh. Astounded by the shaykh's foresight, the sultan's imam inquires about the future of the Ottoman dynasty and the caliphate. Expecting a confirmation, he specifically asks who would be the caliph after Süleyman and whether the sultanate would ever cease to belong to the House of Osman until the end of times. The shaykh repeats his former revelations with more details and certainty. For him, as long as this religion and this rite stay on Earth, the caliphate will belong to the Ottomans. He further foretold that, in the year H. 1200/1785 C.E. an Ottoman ruler called Ali would move the capital to Aleppo and capture all of the lands of Rum, Arab, and the Ajam, and inaugurate a new era in which rulers will govern the world in consultation with shaykhs, unlike the situation during Mecdüddin's time.

In compliance with his father's testimony to write a book of revelations in Turkish, Ibn Isa composed *Rumūzü'l-Künūz* (Secrets of Treasuries) in 1557 to narrate Ottoman history for the next 2000 years.[176] It is a comprehensive collection of prognoses on the future of the Ottoman Empire in twelve chapters, each devoted to a constituent group, starting with the Ottoman family and ending with Sufi community. The text is continuously edited to reconcile prophesies with actual occurrences since its inception. The earliest manuscripts are dated from early seventeenth century and with the passage of time the text grew in popularity as an increasing number of prognoses presented are purported to be verified by actual events in later recensions. Similar to pseudo-Ibn Arabi's *al-Shajara al-Nuʿmāniyya*, it is impossible to distinguish the original text from later revisions. But, at the least, the text gives us a fin-de-siècle direction of Ottoman millenarianism and eschatological thinking. *Rumūzü'l-Künūz* does not reflect the millenarian anxieties and messianic excitement of the first half of the sixteenth century. It is not an apocalyptic statement either. Although eschatological in tone, it is not a pious interpretation of cataclysmic events that portend the end of times. Ibn Isa foresees that the perennial war between the Romans and the Persians continues. Writing just two years after the Amasya peace treaty between the Ottomans and the Safavids, the Bayrami shaykh appears much less alarmed with the Kizilbash threat than his contemporaries and avoids attributing apocalyptic significance to confessional confrontation between the Sunnis and the Rafidis. Instead, he foresees cyclical encounters between the Rum and the Ajam where each time a ruler from the Ajam takes over the Rum, a righteous ruler from the House of Osman rises and defeats the latter.[177]

The text is perfectly timed in reorientating future expectations to appease millenarian anxieties of the time. Ibn Isa not only defers the end of times by a few millennia but also tells both the ruling circles and the subjects that the Ottoman rule would continue until the rise of the Messiah. His treatment of messianism was largely therapeutic, not apocalyptic. Yet *Rumūzü'l-Künūz* is not a utopian glorification of the Ottoman order. It is a salient critique of contemporary state and society. In explaining future events, the text resembles Aşıkpaşazade's chronicle in its critique of the Ottomans for breaching the etiological pact between the dervishes and the House of Osman. Ibn Isa projects this resentment into the future and constructs a trajectory of history where the Ottomans in alliance with the dervishes rule both the material and spiritual worlds. Again, much like Aşıkpaşazade, the prognosticator adheres to the Ottoman *ḳānūn* as the foundation of proper Ottoman order. For the judicial administration, for example, Ibn Isa prognosticates that a jurist called the Great Ahmed will compile a major legal compendium. Then someone with esoteric knowledge will appear and compose a law code (*ḳānūnnāme*) based on the science of letters as a supplement to Ahmed's legal compendium. The sultan promulgates a law that would last for seven centuries during which all the judges under his authority would rule in accordance with these two references.[178]

Ibn Isa's prognosis not only reveals the triumph of the Ottoman dynasty but also, as the most distinctive mark of this final era, the ascendance of Sufism. In line with the prevalent Sufi attitudes toward the learned, Ibn Isa's prophecies are replete with ulema mischief causing corruption in government and religion as well as incurring divine punishments in the form of natural disasters. He praises the Ottomans for accommodating God's friends but also complains that they have not been treated well since the conquest of Constantinople. Pointing to a grand turn in teleological time, he reveals that until the seventh century of the Hegira calendar, friends of God (*ehlullāh*) were stationed in the realm of Ajam. When the Rafidis took over Ajam, the most prominent friends of God migrated to the Rum. Thus, until the time of his composing the treatise, friends of God in the Rum had been above those of the Ajam. However, he observes in his own time that these spiritual authorities started to migrate to the west (*garb*), the Ottoman frontier in Europe.[179] During the reign of Süleyman a number of high profile Sufis, many from the same or related order as Ibn Isa were persecuted or killed on charges of heresy and rebellion. Despite this observation, he foresees a continuous flood of God's friends in the Rum. As a result, God's friends establish their sway over the spiritual space of the Rum where they unify esoteric with exoteric knowledge and everyone turns into a knower of God (*ʿārif*).[180] This spiritual perfection of the Rum is complemented by a mass conversion to Islam along with the recognition of the Ottoman sultan, Bayezid-i Veli, as the supreme leader of all other rulers.

Despite its critical tone, Ibn Isa's future history of the Ottomans was a reflection of a growing sense of finality among the ruling elite during the age of Süleyman. Sufism, historiography, literature, occultism, and even jurisprudence all contributed in their own ways to the formation of an imperial ideology that was anchored in the idea of Ottoman rulership as perfect, unique, chosen, and the final one. It was Süleyman's tomb-keeper who recast these ideas for the consumption of the broader reading public. Ali Dede (d. 1598) was a Halveti Shaykh from Mostar who wrote his works in Szigetvár, Hungary, during the reign of Murad III (r. 1574–1595) where he came to be known as the Shaykh of the Tomb. The very fact that a prominent Halveti master served as Süleyman's tomb-keeper shows the saintly status Süleyman quickly acquired even among the most unruly of Sufi orders. Although the original pact between the Ottoman dynasty and the Abdalan was irreversibly broken by Mehmed II, a new alliance sought by Bayezid II came to full fruition during the reign of Süleyman. The Abdalan, who lost their privileged position as the protector saints of the Ottomans, never became fully incorporated into the

Ottoman establishment again. Yet, the early generation of Abdalan remained venerated as proofs of Ottoman dynasty's spiritual credentials in canonized narratives of history. In the new spiritual alliance, learned Sufism that pervaded urban life and the ruling establishment supplanted the Abdalan. Despite occasional outbursts of protests by propounders of normative piety, as in the case of Kadızadeli movement in mid-sixteenth century, the broader Sufi establishment inseparably docked to the ruling elite and became the Ottoman dynasty's chief designers of ruling ideals and spokesmen for imperial ideology.

In three of his works, Ali Dede synthesized the Ottoman conception of the caliphate that widely resonated in later Sufi thought from Sarı Abdullah Efendi (d. 1660) to Ismail Hakkı Bursevi (d. 1725). He wrote all three works in genres outside conventional Islamic disciples in Arabic despite the fact that he himself, being a Halveti Shaykh, was better versed in Persian, the language of choice among the Ottomans living in Hungary.[181] His choice of language suggests that he aimed the readership of a broader Muslim community. *al-Intiṣār li Qidwat al-Akhyār* (The Book of Victory for the Exemplary Leader of the Most Eminent), is the story of an Ottoman campaign into Caucasia under the command of Özdemiroğlu Osman Paşa (d. 1585) in 1583.[182] Unlike what the subject implies, the treatise is anything but a chronicle of events for he was neither historian nor had any intimate knowledge of the campaign. He turned the event into a verification of prophecies regarding the Ottoman dynasty and a statement of its unique attributes. Ali Dede presented the campaign as a reenactment of Alexander the Two-Horned's world conquest, a finalization of an eschatological spectacle that had remained unfinished till the coming of the Ottomans. *Muḥāḍarat al-Awāʾil wa Musāmarat al-Akhāʾir* (Conversation on the Firsts and the Lasts) is a universal account of firsts and lasts in human history modeled after Jalal al-Din Suyuti's (d. 1505) same-titled work.[183] But he must have also used Bistami's *al-Fawāʾiḥ al-Miskiyya* who added prognostication drawn from occult interpretations based on the arcane science of letters. By fully incorporating the Ottoman markers into the universal trajectory of human history, Ali Dede uses this popular genre as a showcase to display the Ottoman moment with its connections to the past and the future. *Khawātim al-Ḥikam* (The Seals of Wisdoms) is a comprehensive digest of Ottoman intellectual life in the sixteenth century, presenting the author's responses to 360 popular questions.[184] Questions on the nature of rulership show how politically tuned were Ottoman intellectuals and how eager they were to gain a deeper understanding of Sufi expositions of the caliphate. Ali Dede ties together historical, occultistic, Sufistic, and juristic interpretations and presents a coherent exposé of the Ottoman turn in rulership. He reestablishes the historical roots and ontological status of the Ottoman dynasty and identifies its unique marks through a unified epistemology in which intuition, rational science, and conveyed scriptural knowledge were reconciled. A dream by an obscure dervish, for example, could be interpreted with the help of astronomical knowledge, linguistic analysis, hadith reports, and juristic reasoning. Yet the findings and convictions of diverse literary traditions were assimilated into Sufi worldview and expressed with a distinctly mystical language. The outcome was an imperial ideology expressed in terms equally appealing to inquisitive minds of all proclivities, from jurists to astronomers.

Ali Dede's exposition testifies for his extensive knowledge of previous Ottoman writings on history, rulership, and eschatology as well as the broader oral tradition that carries gossip, conspiracies, doubts, and curiosities about the status and future of the Ottoman dynasty. He uses all the evidence he draws from his sources to prove beyond doubt that the Ottoman rule was the final one before the end of times. He characterizes the coming of the Ottomans as the seal (*khātam*) of the auspicious turn (*dawla*) in caliphate and the sultanate.[185] The finality of the Ottomans could not be expressed with more powerful words. In the minds of contemporaries, whether learned or nescient, *khātam al-duwal*, the seal of *dawlas*, immediately connotes Prophet Muhammed's Qur'anic epithet, *khātam al-Anbiyā*, the seal of prophets.[186] The seal metaphor signifies not only finality but perfection. After all the evidence he gathered in its proof, Ali Dede confirms this point by his own spiritual discovery giving the impression that such findings are not speculation based on idiosyncratic interpretation of scriptural texts. Rather, the divine constantly communicates facts about the status and future of the Ottoman dynasty to His friends. Ali Dede was writing his works during the reign of Murad III who himself thought God was in constant communication with him through dreams, which he routinely recorded and conversed about with his spiritual guide, Shaykh Şüca from the Halveti order.[187] Halveti Shaykhs were well known for their expertise in the art of interpreting dreams and visions. In 1574, a decade after Süleyman's death and the year of Murad III's enthronement, Ali Dede went for a pilgrimage where he had a vision in which he was shown 999 on the wall of the station of Prophet Abraham (*Maqām Ibrāhīm*). After consulting with the saints of Mecca, Ali Dede concluded that the triple nine points to the three qualities of the Ottomans, which are finality, perfection, and ascent (*nihāya, ghāya, taraqqī*). God sealed the *dawla* (*khatmiyyat al-duwal*) with the Ottomans and He will not grant it to any other dynasty. The Ottoman *dawla* will last until the end of times and they will continue to thrive and perfect as their end is destined to be better than their beginnings.[188]

Ali Dede derives his scriptural evidence from a number of prophetic hadiths that circulated in the politically charged climate of the late Abbasid period when both supporters and detractors of Turks sought to voice their partisanship through the Prophet's tongue. In a new twist to apocalyptic genealogies, Ali Dede identifies the Ottomans with "the descendants of Qantura" who would be the last ones to rule over the Prophet's community (*umma*). It was well known in popular legendary histories that Prophet Abraham had a son called Turk from his slave girl Qantura. The prided Ottoman title, Servant of Two Holy Sanctuaries (*khādim al-ḥaramayn al-muḥtaramayn*), is what the Prophet alluded to when he told his companions that the Turks are their friends (*aṣḥāb*).[189] Ali Dede divests the Ottoman lineage from its Turko-Mongolian origins constructed by fifteenth-century historians who strived to situate themselves within the scheme of the Chingizid turn in world domination. By the age of Süleyman, the Ottoman ruling elite already thought of eclipsing the Chingizid successor states and, with the incorporation of the Abbasid hinterland, they reincarnated pre-Mongolian legitimacy apparatus. In Ali Dede's exposition the House of Osman is portrayed to be an Abrahamic dynasty, a close kin of Arabs, and a continuation of the Abbasids in caliphate. With this new genealogy Ali Dede establishes one divinely ordained lineage for the caliphate starting from Abraham and ending with al-Mahdi, who was prophesied to come from the descendants of the Prophet Muhammed.

Ali Dede finds the good tidings for the coming of the Ottomans in the words of the Prophet, who is quoted to say that "Persia is one thrust (*naṭḥa*) or two, then there is no Persia forever." After an ingenious argumentation that exploits the odd rules of Arabic syntax, he concludes that Persia as the locus of the caliphate will end with the collapse of the Abbasids.[190] The caliphate would then move to the Rum, as foretold by the Prophet: "The Rum is the bearer of ages." For the transmission of the Caliphate, Ali Dede provides more specific historical connections than his historian predecessor Bidlisi that lends more certainty to the investiture story repeated in Ottoman chronicles. Against the common knowledge, he first establishes that the Ottoman rule was first conceived during the reign of the last Abbasid caliph al-Musta'sim with Osman's succession to the Ottoman throne. Osman becomes sultan with al-Musta'sim's authorization to whom he declares his loyalty *(bayʿa)*. Ali Dede finds both the Abbasid Caliphate and the eight dynasties that appeared under the Abbasids as deficient in the sense that the caliphate lacked sultanate, the executive power, while the affiliate dynasties lacked the caliphate while possessing executive power, the sultanate. With the execution of al-Musta'sim by the Mongols, the caliphate passes (*intaqala*) to the Ottomans and Osman combines *khilāfa* with *salṭana* to reinstitute the caliphate in its original form (*al-khilāfa al-ʿaṣliyya*).[191]

He quoted Ibn Arabi having stated in his mantic revelations that the firmly established *dawla* [that of the Ottomans] would continue until the time of Mahdi to whom they will deliver the caliphate, and become his party (*shīʿa*) and helpers. Until then the Ottomans would be protected from sedition, takeover, and sharing authority that caused the fall of the Abbasid caliphate and other dynasties before them. For divine protection, Ali Dede uses the term *ʿiṣma*, the same word used in Sunni theology for the infallibility of prophets.[192] Just as prophets were infallible so was the Ottoman dynasty in rulership. The Ottoman dynasty was a living testament for the truth of the prophecy al-Saffah (r. 749–754), the first Abbasid caliph, declared in his first sermon after the reinstitution of the caliphate to the progeny of the Prophet: "Know that the caliphate is with us, not with any outsider, until we deliver it to the awaited Mahdi and Jesus, son of Mary." It was no other than the Ottoman rulers who illuminated (*nawwara*) the Abbasid Caliphate. Ali Dede recounts how Süleyman reacted to al-Saffah's statement of carrying the banner of the caliphate until its God-sent owner arrives:

> I hear many times from Shaykh Ibn Nur al-Din, may God bless his soul and pour upon us his revelations, that this story was once mentioned in the presence of Süleyman el-Gazi, may God forgive him, and asked "if the Mahdi appears in your time would you deliver the caliphate to him without any doubt and contest?" He replied: "I see my very self contesting for the leadership of the caliphate (*riyāsat al-khilāfa*) because the last thing comes out from the hearts of true believers is the love of leadership (*ḥubb al-riyāsa*)."[193]

Birgivi, a vigilant jurist on the moral decay of his time and an undissuaded critic of Ottoman administration, mentioned the love of leadership as a moral vice in his treatise on ethics but further commented that if this pursuit is for the sake of upholding the standards of religion then it may well be considered a virtue.[194] Ali Dede does not take Süleyman's response as a sign of haughtiness and arrogance but an impressive display of his prophetic qualities similar to Joseph who had acknowledged his weakness and sought God's protection from committing sin.[195] Despite his manifest spiritual attachment to Süleyman, the tomb-keeper does not portray him as an exceptional ruler. Süleyman simply displays the exceptional qualities of the Ottoman dynasty as the seal of *dawla*. Ali Dede's appellative for Ottoman rulership in all three texts is *al-dawla al-farīda al-ʿUthmāniyya*, the precious Ottoman *dawla*, clarifying that the *dawla* belongs to the Ottomans. The *dawla* in Ali Dede's usage stands for an exclusive divine license to rule over humanity, a collective and epochal right to rule as part of divine providence. Although it is hard to pinpoint the beginnings of the construct, we know that the Ottoman rule came to be commonly labeled as *devlet-i ebed müddet* (the eternal *dawla*), which is often translated by modern historians as eternal state or eternal fortune. In the 1480s, Konevi had already declared Osman's fortune, or turn to rule, as eternal (*davlat-i ʿOs̱mānī jāvidānest*).[196] But Ottoman bureaucrats of the sixteenth century certainly attributed the term a holistic institutional import to mean the collective ruling establishment. Celalzade, for example, who often used *devlet* and *memleket* (kingdom) in tandem, when he called the grand vizier as the pole of *devlet* or the chancery as its buttress, he meant the institution of the Ottoman polity as the embodiment of the sultan's right and fortune to rule.[197] A formulaic sentence from Ali Dede's *al-Intiṣār* exposes the deep semantics of the term that formed in Ottoman thought: "The final *dawla* of Islam in the Abbasid Caliphate is the exceptional and concluding *dawla* of the Ottomans, may God protect and prolong it until the day of judgement."[198] Despite the term's popularity and myriad other meanings in daily language and written expressions, the conception of the *dawla* in the construct was fermented with mystical visions of the caliphate and seasoned with Ottoman bureaucratic traditions.

Conclusion

THE CATACLYSMIC EVENTS from the Crusades to the Mongol invasions that had just preceded the rise of the Ottomans left permanent markings on all later political and cultural formations. In political thought, the period roughly marked by the Seljuk rule was characterized by a new orientation in conceiving authority that reflects the formation of a cosmopolitan Sufi commonwealth that gradually replaced the standardizing juristic ecumenism of Muslim society. The mystical turn in political thought, as far as the learned traditions are concerned, did not necessarily push the juristic establishment outside the elite art of validating, designing, and critiquing rulership. Nor did it dismantle the juristic edifice in setting the norms of legitimacy, standards of good government, and parameters of public morality. On the contrary, juristic knowledge continued to be inextricably woven into any political argumentation that is claimed to be Islamically binding. But jurists, per se, ceased to be the sole authorities on juristic knowledge, best exemplified in the rise of a new type of juristically trained Sufis giving fatwas on legal matters, a function that had been the conventional reserve of jurists. The mystical turn was an epistemic movement that involved all branches of knowledge from theology to philosophy as well as arts and literature. Fenari's enchantment in Sufism as a jurist was no less deep than Rumi's immersion in jurisprudence as a Sufi. Mysticism, in its endlessly varying articulations, permeated into all scholarly, literary, and artistic explorations that profoundly altered the way political leadership is envisioned and manifested. The history of Ottoman political thought from its frontier origins to imperial manifestations in the age of Süleyman was at the same time a resounding story of the mystification of rulership.

The popularization of the caliphate after the demise of the historical caliphate looks paradoxical. Though it may look truistic, the void created by the collapse of the caliphate could only be filled by the caliphate itself, albeit in a different form. The overwhelming Mongol regime of Eurasia, the ongoing political fragmentation of the former Abbasid hinterland, and the rise of new social structures from Sufi orders to chivalrous fraternities turned the reunification of political leadership into a distant utopia. Yet the jurists across the

Islamicate world continued to operate and reason as if they were still living under one universal authority as they never significantly revised the theory of caliphate-based imamate in their books. Although jurists, as demanded by their very profession, responded to political change by offering their localized solutions they never abandoned the universal caliphate as the juristic imperative, however utopian it may now be seen. The caliphate was more than a mere imperial, religious, or a geopolitical order. It was the embodiment of the body politic of the Muslim community at large, a formal necessity for the rendition of a number of public services, a historical link to the ideal past, and, above all, a habitus for the community of believers. At the time of its collapse, its presence was likely to be less felt than its traumatic non-esixtence. That is why mystical notions of the caliphate started to gain prominence during the last century of the Abbasids when the institution of the caliphate became less present in both material and spiritual spheres as manifested by al-Nasir li-Din Allah's (r. 1180–1225) efforts to reorganize the *futuwwa* as the spiritual organ of the caliphate commissioned to one of the most venerated Sufi shayks of the time, Shihab al-Din Umar al-Suhrawardi (d. 1234).

Neither jurists nor temporal rulers of the post-Abbasid world seriously pursued to revive the unified imperial caliphate until the dawn of modern panislamism. Ottoman, Mughal, Moroccan, and Shaybanid claims for the historical caliphate were confined to the ideal sphere, if not to rhetoric, and never turned into a deliberate policy. Yet the caliphate continued without the caliphate thanks to mystics and rulers who adopted mystical imageries. A wide variety of Sufis, learned and unlearned, urban and rural, conformist and antinomian, commonly denied, much like the Ismailis or twelver Shiites, the ontological possibility of not having a universal supreme leader. Thus, there would always be a caliph, as God's vicegerent on earth, however that person may be named, whether pole, succor, shadow, or perfect human being. However imaginary, virtual, or even fictive this may seem to an outsider, as Hodgson rightly noted, for the followers of a given shaykh it was reality per se. The mystical notion of the caliphate became as real as the former historical caliphate as Sufism further gained ground across Eurasia and converted not only ordinary believers but the very learned, including jurists, bureaucrats and scientists, en masse. Based on the Qur'anic primordial caliphate of Adam, as exemplified by David, the Sufis not only recreated the caliphate as the new body politic of believers but also accorded it all the authority, power, privileges, and functions that were once part of the historical caliphate.

When applied to rulership, the Sufistic notion of the caliphate found a solid basis of support even from the ulema constituency thanks to its capacity to preserve the sanctity of Muslim rulership. With the collapse of the historical caliphate, a new generation of indigineous rulers as shahs, khans, and begs with largely non–Arabic-speaking constituencies were adopting means of legitimacy outside the juristic norm or even the scriptures in general. They were now truly independent, in the sense that there was no imperial universal caliphate above them. To be a khan or shah, no religious sanction was needed. In fact, these mostly Mongol and Turkic rulers emphatically promoted their profiles through secular titles and imageries of rulership, thus owing less to the traditional power structures of Islamicate society, most notably the ulema. Even after being fully assimilated into the political traditions of the caliphate, these rulers diligently maintained their titulatory autonomy to the very end. The mystification of the caliphate enabled khans and shahs to become caliphs without losing their indigenous titles of sovereignty, therefore facilitated its rapid adoption. Whether profiled as Mahdi, caliph, axis mundi or the like their sovereign titles, namely the *de jure* basis of their political authority, always remained outside the command of religion. In the case of Ottomans, excluding the initial decades when they were *begs* and their occasional, often contingent uses of shah, the one exclusive title of sovereignty they had was khan. To impose a moral regime, Sufis or jurists alike wrote political treatises to designate rulers as caliphs who were already unquestionably self-designated as khans or shahs. Each notion of secular rulership may have been prescribed a code of conduct embedded in the broader political culture or political theory. However, being a khan or shah did not readily carry a moral component in Islamic theory unless it was imposed one. For rulers, the caliphate may be negotiable but not their khan or shah title. The caliphate, when mystified and redefined, could harmoniously and symbiotically house both Islamic and non-Islamic notions of rulership. Such imageries as Huma, *dawla*, *ḳūt*, and *farr-i īzadī* are either outright non-Islamic or scriptural only through forced and esoteric interpretations. Even Mahdi, *mujaddid*, or *insān-ı kāmil* could only be verified through hadiths, not with respect to the Qur'an. But the caliphate, sanctioned by the Qur'an and historically recognized by the community of believers, squarely accords religious sanction and denies moral autonomy to its claimant.

The mystical turn converged and redirected different strains of political theory in a quest for reconstructing the unified authority that was thought to be partitioned between the executive power of rulers, the spiritual sway of Sufis, and the strictly guarded position of jurists as spokespersons for Islamic faith and praxis. Thirteenth century Sufi pursuit of this objective was neither an abstract ideal nor a mere intuitive experience. Around the time when the Ottoman state was conceived, Sufism was not only the most powerful institution in western Anatolia but also, unlike the ulema, the least dependent social network on political authorities in its economic sustenance. When the first madrasa opened in the mid-fourteenth century in Iznik, the Ottoman space was already replete with dervish orders and hospices. Although Ottoman cities remained relatively isolated for another century, Sufi orders were thriving in the rest of urban Anatolia. Even more drastic was the captivation of prominent philosophers, jurists, and artists with mysticism, giving the impression of a mass conversion among the learned. Sufism fast became the connecting tissue between different branches of learned traditions from astronomy to theology. Mathematicians, poets, artists, and political theorists with strong Sufi proclivities constituted the typical in Ottoman learned traditions. Sufism and intuitive knowledge opened new frontiers of intellectual, artistic, and scientific exploration through which juristically questionable ideas, practices, and forms of piety were introduced into the mainstream of the broader Islamic culture.

Quṭb or *ghaws*, that is, axis mundi, was a patently Sufi notion of comprehensive leadership that merged political, epistemic, and spiritual authorities. Yet, in this triad, epistemic authority presided over the political and the spiritual. All political power and authority to interpret religion emanated from one's degree of knowing God. The Sufi conception of "knowing" was qualitatively different than juristic and philosophical knowledge. However it is constructed, whether *ʿirfān*, *ʿilm-i makhdūm*, or *ʿilm-i bāṭin*, it was above and comprised what other ways and forms of knowledge entailed, whether framed as *ʿilm*, *ḥikma*, or *burhān*. A *quṭb*'s unified authority, above all, stemmed from his experiential knowledge of God that cannot be acquired by learning but only attained. This was the undivided primordial authority with which God endowed Adam, perfected in Muhammed's prophetic persona, and continued thereafter by the rightly guided caliphs and the *quṭbs* from among the friends of God. In elaborate expositions of Sufi cosmologies, the world is never deprived of the presence of a unified authority from Adam to the Messiah. Thus the thirteenth century pursuit of reunifying authority that combines, in Sufi formula, *nubuwwa*, *salṭana*, and *wilāya*, was a process of converting the unaware to acknowledge its reality and position oneself accordingly.

Although the conceptual origins of *quṭb* go back to the formative era of Islamic thought, at least to the expositions of early tenth century mystic Kattani (d. 934), the term itself was not drawn from the scriptural writings of Islam.[1] It gained its definitive and authoritative meaning in Ibn Arabi's writings and increasingly associated with the Qur'anic designation of the caliph. The Sufistic conception of the caliphate was often, if not always, predicated upon the notion of the *quṭb*, whether explicitly or implicitly. This is where the Sufistic caliphate parted ways with that of the juristic, which was predicated upon the notion of the imamate, a contractual institution of leadership that confined it to the sphere of government and law. Fourteenth-century Ottoman leadership was fully aware of the Sufistic conception of unified authority through their etiological association with the *abdals* as well as an increasing integration of Sufi-minded scholars into the courtly life and educational institutions. That turned the *abdal* network, and later the entire Sufi establishment, with all its divergent expositions, into potentially the strongest friends or the most dreaded challengers of the Ottoman dynasty. A permanent legacy of this mutually wary fellowship was the Ottoman self-designation as friends of God's friends. Through diligently crafted literary expositions, land grants, and ceremonial acts, Ottoman leadership created an image specifically catered to the expectations of Sufi orders conveying the impression that the reigning ruler was the executive hand of God's cosmic government headed by the *quṭb*. Increasingly after the double trauma caused by the Timurid invasion and the rebellion of Shaykh Bedreddin in the early fifteenth century, Sufi-minded courtiers, scholars, and artists projected the Sufistic vision of unified authority to Ottoman rulership to refashion the ruler's image in order to counter higher notions of authority developed at the Timurid court and home-grown Sufism.

Portraying the Ottoman sultan as a true caliph who combines both spiritual and temporal realms was a direct response to Sufistic claims of authority that became more comprehensive than those of worldly rulers. The notion of unified authority enabled the sultans to reclaim their impaired sovereignty by conquering the spiritual realm which was, by definition, considered to be an exclusive reserve of God's friends. However, this new comprehensive authority came with its own imperative. Namely, the caliphate as a unified rulership was conceived as a moral paradigm for the individual ruler to comply with. Morality was already considered indispensable for rulership in all strains of political thought the Ottomans inherited. Even the contractualist juristic doctrine that de-stipulated it for legitimate rulership traded off the ruler's moral condition only in return for maintaining the integrity of public morality through the application of Islamic law. Yet, the moral paradigm presented by the Sufi-minded to redefine the caliphate was materially different than what the vast and diverse ethics literature offered. It entailed the reconstruction of the caliphate as a mirror image of the divine. The caliph's vicegerency of God meant his being endowed with Godly attributes, thereby becoming part of His government of both angelic and material realms. The attainment of this cosmic status wholly depended on one's moral qualification which, by definition, involves the "rulership in appearance" (*salṭanat* or *ḫilāfet-i ṣūrī*) as its worldly manifestation. Conventional political literature, for example, enthusiastically and relentlessly advised rulers to be merciful toward the subjects to the extent that they commonly warned that oppression is the single most obvious cause of losing one's rulership. Yet it was never put forth as a condition for the attainment of rulership or its legitimation. By comparison, *ḫilāfet-i raḥmānī*, as the vicegerency of God's Mercy, could be attained only by one's duly endowing himself with that divine attribute, namely being compassionate toward God's entire creation. What Bidlisi and other sixteenth-century authors meant by the vicegerency of God's Mercy squarely corresponds to what Fenari (d. 1431), the first reported sheikh ul Islam of the Ottomans, meant by the perfect human being. Per Ibn Arabian cosmology, all existents are manifestations of God's names which are all manifested by the perfect human being. But because mercy predominates all other attribues of God, He and all He created could only be fully manifested in someone whose prime quality was mercy.[2] In all variants of political theory, the true caliphate was commonly predicated on God's beautiful names and attributes only, namely being a caliph was same as acting as

God's mercy, clemency, munificence and the like. This theophanic humanism embedded in the caliphate cut through social hierarchies and natural bounds, brought rulers to accountability, and formed the basis of the caliphate as a moral paradigm.

The mystical conception of the caliphate, although drastically different from juristic caliphate that reduced it to imamate was, paradoxically, similar to the Islamic ideal of rulership that the jurists themselves formulated but historicized and limited to the era of the first four caliphs. Sunni jurists and juristic-minded historians, in consensus, ruled that the true caliphate had ended with Ali, and continued thereafter in the form of kingship, a qualitatively denigrated form of rulership. Jurists and hadith scholars of the early Abbasid era, with obvious political sensitivities, still considered the Umayyad authority as caliphate, therefore legitimate, but nevertheless sharply delineated it from the early caliphate, which they dubbed as the rightly guided, *rāshidūn.* One of the earliest records of the designation *al-khulafā al-rāshidūn* appears in a famous hadith that came into circulation in the tenth century in which the Prophet was attributed to have instructed his community to follow the rightly guided caliphs with no specific names or timeframe mentioned.[3] The fact that the most famous of all Abbasid caliphs, Harun, who mended the relations with the community of scholars who later came to be labeled as Sunnis, adopted the title al-Rashid may suggest that the early caliphate was already perceived to be the true caliphate that the Abbasids thought to have revived.

In subsequent Sunni theory of the caliphate, the *rāshidūn* qualification referred to the early caliphs' succession to Muhammed in his full capacity except for *risāla* and *nubuwwa*, that is, the Prophet's being God's messenger and recipient of His revelation. As strict followers of the Prophet's *sunna*, they were conceived to have had full authority over all aspects of religion, more specifically on the *sunna*, with unpartitioned executive power. In Sunni canon they were the undisputed possessors of authority over both *ʿilm* and the leadership of community. Jurists measured and characterized their piety as their strict adherence and observance of the Prophet's *sunna*, ranked them as the highest among the most virtuous of the Muslim community but did not speculate about the nature of their spiritual authority. It was the Sufis, who interpreted their piety and spiritual rank, and accorded them the capacity of having succeeded the third nature of the Prophet, which they dubbed as *wilāya*, God's friendship. In Sunni Sufi orders that began to take form in the eleventh century there were two principal lineages that conducted the unified authority of Muhammed. Every Sufi order's spiritual genealogy ended with either Abu Bakr or Ali b. Abi Talib, and in some cases with both, if the founding shaykh obtained authorizations from both lineages.

With the mystical turn, the Sufistic theory of unified authority revived the idea of the true caliphate, which the jurists confined to the pre-dynastic age of Muslim rulership and ruled that it would be restored only with the coming of

Mahdi. Thus the Sufistic notion of the caliphate conflated messianic time with historical temporality and, in a way, historicized what the idea of a Mahdi represented in Islamic eschatology. That is why visions and depictions of rulers or saints as caliphs increasingly became virtually indistinguishable from what is expected of the awaited Mahdi. Thus the Mahdi myth of the end of time turned into a temporal reality in the persona of a ruler or a saint as God's caliph and renewer of religion. By dissociating the caliphate from dynastic rulership, the Sufi-minded envisioned an unbroken chain of caliphal authority through God's chosen agents, some manifest, some hidden, and therefore reestablished the continuity of the caliphate. More, the caliphate now posed itself as the only unbroken genealogy of authority from Adam to Jesus where the current ruler acts as a caliph to pass the torch unless he poses himself as the final one on the relay.

From Mehmed I onward, attributing the Mahdi title to an Ottoman sultan was not uncommon and there was no strong objection from the learned establishment. Setting the eulogistic appellations aside, the Ottoman ruler as Mahdi was less apocalyptic and more reflective of the Sufi conception of unified authority. As declared by the most authoritative Ottoman text on eschatology, Mahdi was, like prophets, first and foremost God's caliph (*khalīfat Allāh*).[4] Ottoman messianism, first conceived during the political turmoil of the Interregnum, remained a fixture of ruling ideology, decorated with more apocalyptic tones during the reign of Mehmed II, and briefly occupied the center stage of the literary showroom for the ruler's self-image during the reign of Süleyman. The broader Ottoman messianic political thought was expressed within a Sufistic framework and language. Despite the fact that the main repository of Islamic eschatology was the hadith corpus, the juristic occupation with messianism, even among the most Sufi-minded, was confined to pietistic warnings by tagging contemporary events with signs of the end of times prophesied by Muhammed. Jurists, in the main, looked remarkably comfortable with the Ottoman sultan's image as Mahdi, given that the title was often claimed more emphatically by the adversaries of the Ottomans from Timur to Shah Isma'il and a series of dissenting dervishes and shaykhs from among the *abdals* and learned Sufism. Astrologists, geomancers, letterists, imaginative poets, and myth-maker historians resorted to Sufi imageries to frame Mahdism in more palatable terms. The type of authority Mahdi was envisioned to represent was not qualitatively different than what is attributed to *quṭb* or *khalīfa*. Because of the apocalyptic connotations of Mahdi and nonscriptural origins of *quṭb*, the Sufi-minded redefined *khalīfa* to convey the content of both terms.

Very similar to the Abbasid jurists who distinguished the true caliphate with the *rāshidūn* qualification, the post-Abbasid Sufis differentiated their notion of the caliphate with such specific qualifications as *ʿaṣlī, ḥaḳīḳī, ilāhī, rabbānī, raḥmānī*, and the like. This conception of the caliphate was inherently antidynastic and, by definition, invalidated any claim for the title by independent rulers unless they are considered to be the executive arm of the wielder of unified authority. Although this vision of the caliphate freed the Sufis from the political authority of dynastic rulers and the epistemological authority of the ulema, and established them as the third group to claim the leadership of Muslim community, sovereign rulers responded by fully incorporating this Sufistic imagery into their ruling ideologies through the writings of their Sufi allies and Sufi-minded courtiers. In the pre-imperial Ottoman state, when the independent *abdal* orders were strong and enjoyed the spiritual patronage of the Ottoman enterprise, rulers were content by painting their public profiles as friends of God's friends. Bayezid II's policy of conciliation with the Sufi orders who were alienated by Mehmed II's empire-building project did not fully restore the old regime. Instead, *abdals'* saintly patronage of the Ottoman dynasty was replaced by that of learned Sufism whose visions of leadership inspired the Sufi-minded scholars and bureaucrats to profile the sultan as the true caliph.

The mystical turn in political theory not only shaped the Ottoman understanding of the caliphate as a unified authority in the image of God's government as exemplified by His prophets, rightly guided caliphs, and an unbroken chain of poles but also accorded it a unique status in the grand scheme of cosmological time and space. Among others, millenarian consciousness, widespread domestic disturbance, competition with the Habsburgs for universal sovereignty, defending the Sunni faith against Safavid Shiism, an empire-wide construction frenzy in infrastructure and grand projects, institutionalization of administration, extensive lawmaking, the rise of Turkish as a mandarin language of the ruling elite, authoring, designing, and producing what came to be specifically "Ottoman" in literature, arts, and architecture that characterized the age of Süleyman coincided with or stirred anxiety and ardor among the adherents of the dynasty to attribute a greater meaning to what the Ottomans stood for. Ottoman literati, including historians, poets, letterists, jurists, bureaucrats, and geomancers portrayed the uniqueness of their times, land, people, art, and the dynasty in their own ways, often in comparison to well-known counterparts in literary and popular culture. This was not simply a choreographed exaltation of the achievements of the House of Osman under the sponsorship of the Ottoman court. Thanks to the expanding imperial grid, an increasing number of individuals from both the center and the periphery, with different proclivities and objectives, became more attuned to public questions and related themselves to the state, society, and culture that came to be associated with what they perceived to be "Ottoman."

By the sixteenth century, the eponym Ottoman ceased to be the exclusive mark of the dynasty and came to be closely associated with the term *Rūm*. As a political and cultural identity of the ruling elite, the Ottoman (*ʿOs̱mānlī* or *ʿOs̱mānī*) came to be used interchangeably with the Roman (*Rūmī* or *Rumlū*).

The idea of Rum, as a promised land, preceded the Ottomans and was already ingrained in the self-perception of various Sufi groups, from Yesevis to Mevlevis, who migrated or took form in late Seljuk Anatolia. With the rise of the Ottomans, their exclusive association with the Rum soon turned into one of the most distinctive marks of the dynasty as reflected in their adoption of the title "sultan of the Rum" from the preceding Seljuks. In the sixteenth century, historical literature presented the Ottoman association with the Rum as their mark of uniqueness and superiority with respect to other Islamic dynasties. The Rum, in this understanding, did not simply refer to a landmass or the political legacy of the Romans. It was a cosmologically defined geography with its land, people, and unique relationship to heavenly objects that accorded its inhabitants certain characteristics, a privileged status in divine dispensation, with defining influence on the unfolding of events. For the Ottoman ruling elite, being a Rumi meant being admitted to an elite society who surpassed all other communities in virtue with their excellence in thought, character, skill, and accomplishments of various sorts, including government and rulership. Excluding the genealogical accounts, the extensive repertoire of prophecies and occultic revelations that were collected, interpreted, and reproduced to embroider the Ottoman myth hardly had any reference to Turks. Instead, from folk stories to Qur'anic commentaries, Ottoman literature was replete with references to the Rum as an abode of extraordinariness, the locus of God's dispensing His favors, and the final theater of Islamic eschatology, including messianic visions. The general tenor of Rumi messianism was to single out the Ottoman dynasty and accord the Mahdi status to reigning sultans more for their representation of the House of Osman in the Rum than their individual distinctions. It was the Ottoman dynasty that was divinely chosen and commissioned to rule at the end of times.

In the grand scheme of God's cosmic government that unfolded in historical time, the Rum represented the next *dawla* of Islam, the epochal turn of comprehensive rulership, after that of the Arabs and the Persians. At least since the time of Orhan, as reflected in his coinage and later investiture stories, the Ottomans felt a special attachment to the Abbasid caliphate. For the early Ottomans, claiming the Abbasid authority was critical for asserting their independence from the Mongols and stating supremacy over both their dynastic rivals and equally powerful Sufi orders. The reconstruction of the Ottoman state after their catastrophic encounter with Timur led learned Ottomans to rebond with the Abbasids in a quest for countering the universal sovereignty of the Chingizids. Against the Safavid threat and Turkoman uprisings with Alid sympathies, the Abbasid affiliation confirmed the Ottoman's spiritual attachment to the family of the Prophet and emphasized their championing the true faith. These considerations created a vague impression that the Abbasid *dawla* was still in effect in the sense that the Mongols only ended the Abbasid dynasty and their executive capacity to rule while the House of Osman rightfully inherited their authority to rule over the Muslim community. Reflecting a growing sense of triumphalism, Süleyman's tomb-keeper, Ali Dede, envisioned an epochal turn between the Abbasids and the Ottomans. Namely, the Mongols ended not only the Abbasid rule but also the first *dawla* of Islam represented by the Arabs and the Persians. Osman's rise to power not only meant the transfer of the caliphate to the Ottomans but also initiated the *dawla* of the Rum, which would last until the Ottomans delivered the caliphate to the awaited Messiah.

NOTES

Introduction

1. Mona Hassan, *Longing for the Lost Caliphate: A Transregional History* (Princeton, NJ: Princeton University Press, 2017), 20–64.

2. A. Azfar Moin, *The Millennial Sovereign: Sacred Kingship and Sainthood in Islam* (New York: Columbia University Press, 2012), 9.

3. This anonymous work, which may have been written in fifteenth century Mamluk domains, copied by Maḥmūd b. Muḥammed b. Ḥacī Ḫalīfe in 1561 in Balıkesir. See *Minhāj al-Mulūk li Ahl al-Sulūk* (MS SK, Şehid Ali Paşa 1557), 11b–12a.

4. Marshall G. S. Hodgson, *Rethinking World History: Essays on Europe, Islam, and World History*, ed. Edmund Burke, III (Cambridge: Cambridge University Press, 1993), 187–188.

5. İskender Pala, *Divan Şiiri Sözlüğü* (Ankara: Akçağ, 1995), 492–494.

6. For a discussion regarding the perceptions of the reign of Süleyman among the later Ottomans, see Cemal Kafadar, "The Myth of the Golden Age: Ottoman Historical Consciousness in the Post Süleymânic Era," in *Süleymân the Second and His Time*, eds. Halil Inalcik and Cemal Kafadar (Istanbul: Isis Press, 1993), 37–48.

7. Beyani and Katib Çelebi, for example, considered it a better book than those of Tusi, Davvani, and Kashifi. See Beyâni, *Tezkiretü'ş-Şuarâ*, ed. İbrahim Kutluk (Ankara: Türk Tarih Kurumu, 1997), 183; Kātib Çelebī, *Kashf al-Ẓunūn ʿan Asāmī al-Kutub wa al-Funūn*, eds. Şerafettin Yaltkaya and Rıfat Bilge (Istanbul: Maarif Matbaası, 1941–43), 1: 37.

8. Shahab Ahmed, *What is Islam: The Importance of Being Islamic* (Princeton and Oxford: Princeton University Press, 2016), 73–85.

9. Hamid Dabashi, *The World of Persian Literary Humanism* (Cambridge, Mass.: Harvard University Press, 2012).

10. ʿAlī ibn ʿAṭiyya al-Ḥamawī, *al-Naṣā'iḥ al-Muhimma li al-Mulūk wa al-A'imma*, ed. Nashwa ʿAlwānī (Dimashq: Dār al-Maktabī, 2000).

11. Aḥmed bin Muṣṭafā Ṭāşköprīzāde, *Miftāḥ al-Saʿāda wa Miṣbāḥ al-Siyāda fī Mawḍūʿāt al-ʿUlūm*, 3 vols., eds. Kāmil Kāmil Bakrī and ʿAbd al-Wahhāb Abu al-Nūr (Cairo: Dār al-Kutub al-Ḥadītha, 1968), 1: 392.

12. Ṭāşköprīzāde, *Miftāḥ al-Saʿāda*, 1: 408.

13. Mübahat S. Kütükoğlu, "Lütfi Paşa Âsafnâmesi," in *Prof. Dr. Bekir Kütükoğlu'na Armağan* (İstanbul: Edebiyat Fakültesi Basımevi, 1991), 49–99.

14. *Kitâb-u Mesâlihi'l Müslimîn ve Menâfi'i'l-Mü'minîn*, in *Osmanlı Devlet Teşkilâtına Dair Kaynaklar*, ed. Yaşar Yücel (Ankara: Türk Tarih Kurumu, 1988), 49–144.

15. For a comprehensive survey of this literature, see Marinos Sariyannis, *Ottoman Political Thought up to the Tanzimat: A Concise History* (Rethymno: Institute for Mediterranean Studies, 2015).

Chapter 1: The Discourse on Rulership

1. İhsan Fazlıoğlu, "Osmanlı Döneminde 'Bilim' Alanındaki Türkçe Telif ve Tercüme Eserlerin Türkçe Oluş Nedenleri," *Kutadgubilig* 3 (2003): 151–184.

2. Köprülüzade Mehmed Fuad, *Milli Edebiyat Cereyanının İlk Mübeşşirleri* (Istanbul: Devlet Matbaası, 1928), 12.

3. For a brief survey of translation in this period, see Mustafa, Kara, "XIV ve XV Yüzyıllarda Türk Toplumunu Besleyen Kitaplar," *İslami Araştırmalar Dergisi* 12 (1999): 130–147; Ramazan Şeşen, "Onbeşinci Yüzyılda Türkçeye Tercümeler," in *XI. Türk Tarih Kongresi* (Ankara: Türk Tarih Kurumu, 1994), 889–919.

4. For a detailed study of the author and the work, see Mehmet Şakir Yılmaz, *Sultanların Aynası Ahmed bin Hüsameddin Amâsî ve Eseri Mirâtu'l-Mülûk* (Istanbul: Büyüyen Ay Yayınları, 2016).

5. See Naṣīr al-Dīn Ṭūsī, *Akhlāq-i Nāṣirī*, ed. Mujtabā Mīnovī and ʿAlī R. Ḥaydārī (Tehran: Khvārazmi, 1982); for an English translation, see G. M. Wickens, *The Nasirean Ethics* (London: Allen & Unwin, 1964).

6. Ghazālī, *Naṣīḥat al-Mulūk*, ed. Jalāl al-Dīn Humāʾī (Tehran: Anjuman-i Āsār-i Millī, 1972). For the Arabic version, see Ghazālī, *al-Ṭibr al-Masbūq fī Naṣīḥat al-Mulūk*, ed. Muḥammed Aḥmed Damaj (Beirut: Mu'assasa ʿIzz al-Dīn, 1996). For an English translation, see Frank R. C. Bagley, *Ghazālī's Book of Counsel for Kings (Naṣīḥat al-Mulūk)* (London and New York: Oxford University Press, 1964).

7. Amāsī, *Mirʾātü'l-Mülūk* (MS SK, Esat Efendi 1890), 2a.

8. ʿAlāyī bin Muḥibbī el-Şīrāzī el-Şerīf, *Netīcetü's-Sülūk fī Terceme-i Naṣīḥatü'l-Mülūk* (MS TSMK, Bağdat 187), 1a–90b.

9. Amāsī, *Mirʾātü'l-Mülūk*, 55b–62b.

10. Amāsī, *Mirʾātü'l-Mülūk*, 52a–55b.

11. Ibid., 66b–68b.

12. Ibid., 86a–86b.

13. Enfel Doğan, "On Translations of Qabus-nama during the Old Anatolian Turkish Period," *Uluslararası Sosyal Araştırmalar Dergisi* 5 (2012): 76–85; Rıza Kurtuluş, "Keykâvus b. İskender," *TDVIA*, vol. 25 (2002), 357; Agâh S. Levend, "Ümmet Çağında Ahlâk Kitaplarımız," *TDAY Belleten* (1963): 89–115.

14. Eleazar Birnbaum, *The Book of Advice by King Kay Kāʾus ibn Iskander: The Earliest Old Ottoman Turkish Version of his Ḳābūsnāme* (Duxbury: Harvard University Printing Office, 1981), 11, 30.

15. Birnbaum, *The Book of Advice by King Kay Kāʾus ibn Iskander*, 30.

16. Doğan, *Şeyhoğlu Sadrüddin'in Kābūs-nâme Tercümesi* (Istanbul: Mavi Yayıncılık, 2011); Doğan, "Emir Süleyman Dönemi Şairlerinden Akkadıoğlu'nun Kâbusnâme Tercümesi ve Nüshaları Üzerine," *Modern Türklük Araştırmaları Dergisi* 8 (2011): 7–24; Âdem Ceyhan, *Bedr-i Dilşad'ın Murâd-Nâmesi*, 2 vols. (Istanbul: MEB, 1997).

17. Orhan Şaik Gökyay, *Keykâvus, Kabusname* (Çeviren: Mercimek Ahmed), 3rd ed. (Istanbul: Milli Eğitim Basımevi, 1974).

18. Najm al-Dīn Rāzī, *Mirṣād al-ʿIbād*, ed. Muḥammed Amīn Riyāḥī (Tehran: Bungāh-i Tarjuma va Nashr-i Kitāb, 1973). For an English translation, see Najm al-Din Razi, *The Path of God's Bondsmen from Origin to Return*, transl. Hamid Algar (North Haledon, NJ: Islamic Publications International, 2003).

19. Razi, *The Path of God's Bondsmen*, 10–12.

20. For more information on the spread and disappearance of the Kubrawiyya in the Ottoman Empire, see Reşat Öngören, *Osmanlılar'da Tasavvuf: Anadolu'da Sûfîler, Devlet ve Ulemâ (XVI. Yüzyıl)* (Istanbul: İz Yayınları, 2000), 219–220.

21. Moḥammad-Amīn Riāḥī, "Najm-al-Dīn Abū Bakr ʿAbd-Allāh," http://www.iranicaonline.org/articles/daya-najm-al-din (Accessed 1 October 2016).

22. For an analysis of Razi's Qur'anic commentary, *Baḥr al-Ḥaqāʾiq*, and its influence on Ottoman Sufism, see Mehmet Okuyan, *Necmuddîn Dâye ve Tasavvufî Tefsiri* (Istanbul: Rağbet Yayınları, 2001).

23. See Ebū'l-Fażl el-Münşī al-Şīrāzī, *Dustūr al-Salṭana* (MS BNF, Persan 135).

24. Şehabeddin Tekindağ, "İzzettin Koyunoğlu Kütüphânesinde Bulunan Türkçe Yazmalar Üzerinde Çalışmalar I," *Türkiyat Mecmuası* 16 (1971): 133–162.

25. The editor briefly discusses the possibility that the work could be a translation of *Mirṣād al-ʿIbād* and prefers to accept it as a genuine compilation. See Kemâl Yavuz, *Şeyhoğlu: Kenzü'l-Küberâ ve Mehekkü'l-Ulemâ* (Ankara: Atatürk Kültür Merkezi, 1991), 10–16. Hüseyin Ayan, who edited Şeyhoğlu's *Ḫurşīd-Nāme*, compared *Mirṣād al-ʿIbād* and *Kenzü'l-Küberā*, and concluded that the latter is an expanded translation of the former. See Şeyhoğlu Mustafa, *Ḫurşîd-nâme (Ḫurşîd ü Feraḥşâd)*, ed. Hüseyin Ayan (Erzurum: Atatürk Üniversitesi Yayınları, 1979), 16–23.

26. Kâsım b. Mahmûd Karahisârî, *İrşâdü'l-Mürîd ile'l-Murâd fî Tercemeti Mirsādü'l-ʿİbâd*, ed. Özgür Kavak (Istanbul: Klasik, 2010), 28–34.

27. Öngören, *Osmanlılar'da Tasavvuf*, 45; For his hagiographical biography, see Mahmud Cemaleddin el-Hulvî, *Lemezât-ı Hulviyye ez Lemezât-ı Ulviyye*, ed. Mehmet Serhan Tayşi (Istanbul: Marmara Üniversitesi İlahiyat Fakültesi Vakfı Yayınları, 1993), 437–439; ʿAlī bin Bālī, *al-ʿIqd al-Manẓūm fī Dhikr Afāḍil al-Rūm* (Beirut: Dār al-Kitāb al-ʿArabī, 1975), 224.

28. Şeyḫ Bālī Efendī, *Risāle der Sīret-i Pādişāhān-ı Pīşīn* (MS SK, Hekimoğlu 589); for the relationship between Kasım Çelebi and Bali Efendi, see Mecdî Mehmed Efendi, *Şakaik-i Nu'maniye ve Zeyilleri: Hadaiku'ş-Şakaik*, ed. Abdülkadir Özcan (Istanbul: Çağrı Yayınları, 1989), 521–522.

29. Abū Bakr ʿAbd Allāh ibn Shāhāwar al-Rāzī, *Manārāt al-Sā'irīn wa Maqāmāt al-Ṭā'irīn*, ed. Saʿīd ʿAbd al-Fattāḥ (Cairo: al-Hay'a al-Miṣriyya al-ʿĀmma li al-Kitāb, 1999).

30. Fritz Meir, "Stanbuler Handschriften dreirer persischer Mystiker: ʿAin al-quḍāt al-Hamadānī, Nağm ad-Dīn Kubrā, Nağm ad-Dīn Dāja," *Der Islam* 24 (1937): 1–42; Razi, *The Path of God's Bondsmen*, 14–15. Algar confirms Meir's classification of *Manārāt* as an Arabic translation of *Mirṣād* but finds it strange that it was translated back into Persian. My own comparison of the two texts shows that the two works are completely different.

31. Ḳāsım b. Seydî el-Ḥāfıẓ Anḳarî, *Enīsü'l-Celīs*, ed. Azmi Bilgin (Istanbul: İstanbul Üniversitesi Yayınları, 2008).

32. For a detailed survey of apocalyptic anxieties of the time, see Stéphane Yerasimos and Benjamin Lellouch (eds.), *Les traditions apocalyptiques au tournant de la chute de Constantinople* (Paris: L'Harmattan, 1999) and Feridun M. Emecen, *Fetih ve Kıyamet, 1453: İstanbul'un Fethi ve Kıyamet Senaryoları* (Istanbul: Timaş, 2012).

33. For a brief survey of the Selimname literature, see Mustafa Argunşah, "Türk Edebiyatında Selimnameler," *Turkish Studies* 4 (2009): 31–47.

34. Emire Cihan Muslu, "Ottoman-Mamluk Relations: Diplomacy and Perceptions," (PhD diss., Harvard University, 2007), 160.

35. For the formation of this identity, see Salih Özbaran, *Bir Osmanlı Kimliği: 14.–17. Yüzyıllarda Rûm/Rûmî Aidiyet ve İmgeleri* (Istanbul: Kitabevi, 2004); Kafadar, "A Rome of One's Own: Reflections on Cultural Geography and Identity in the Lands of Rum," *Muqarnas* 24 (2007): 7–25.

36. Mecdî, *Hadaiku'ş-Şakaik*, 184–187; Ṭāşköprīzāde, *al-Shaqā'iq al-Nuʿmāniyya* (Beirut: Dār al-Kitāb al-ʿArabī, 1975), 100–102.

37. ʿAlī b. Majdüddīn el-Şahrūdī el-Bistāmī, *Tuḥfa-i Maḥmūdiyya* (MS TSMK, Emanet Hazinesi 1342); (MS SK, Ayasofya 2885).

38. For the position of the grand vizier during the reign of Mehmed II and Mahmud Paşa's tenure, see Theoharis Stavrides, *The Sultan of Vezirs: The Life and Times of the Ottoman Grand Vezir Mahmud Pasha Angelović (1453–1474)* (Leiden: Brill, 2001), 56–70.

39. Neşe Çelik, "Menaḳıb-ı Maḥmūd Paşa" (Master's thesis, Mimar Sinan University, 1998).

40. Bistāmī, *Ḥall al-Rumūz wa Kashf al-Kunūz*, ed. Yūsuf Aḥmed. Beirut: Kitāb Nāshirūn, 2013.

41. Tim Winter, "Ibn Kemāl (d. 940/1534) on Ibn ʿArabī's Hagiology," in *Sufism and Theology*, ed. Ayman Shihadeh (Edinburgh: Edinburgh University Press, 2007), 137–157.

42. Both texts are included in a bound collection of various treatises written by the author. (MS SK, Şehid Ali Paşa 2797): *Tuḥfat al-Salaṭīn*, 73b–75b; *Tuḥfat al-Wuzarā*, ff. 66b–69a.

43. Taşköprîzâde Ahmed Efendi, *Şerhu'l-Ahlâki'l-Adudiyye*, eds. Elzem İçöz and Müstakim Arıcı (Istanbul: Türkiye Yazma Eserler Kurumu Başkanlığı, 2016).

44. Sara Nur Yıldız, "Şükrullah," *TDVIA*, vol. 39 (2010), 257–258.

45. Inalcik, "Tarihçi Şükrullâh Çelebi (1380–1460)," *Acta Orientalia* 61 (2008): 113–118. For the text, see Şükrullah b. Şihabeddîn Ahmed b. Zeyneddîn Zekî, *Behcetü't-Tevârîh*, ed. Hasan Almaz (PhD diss., Ankara University, 2004).

46. Şükrullāh b. Aḥmed, *Manhaj al-Rashād* (MS SK, Ayasofya 2112).

47. Şükrullāh b. Aḥmed, *Enīsü'l-ʿĀrifīn* (MS Manisa İl Halk Kütüphanesi 5280).

48. The authorship of the work cannot be established with certainty. The language of the text displays characteristics of fifteenth-century Turkish while the content shows similarities with Şükrullah's two other works. The sole extant copy of the work is missing a few folios in the beginning and does not contain any information about its author or the date of completion. We can attribute this text to Şükrullah only on the evidence of a short bibliographic note provided by Katib Çelebi. See Kātib Çelebī, *Kashf al-Ẓunūn*, vol. 1, 198.

49. Eşrefoğlu Rûmî, *Müzekki'n-Nüfûs*, ed. Abdullah Uçman (Istanbul: İnsan Yayınları, 1996).

50. Sinan Paşa, *Maarifnâme*, ed. İsmail H. Ertaylan (İstanbul: Edebiyat Fakültesi Basımevi, 1961), 23–26.

51. Hasibe Mazıoğlu, "Sinan Paşa," *İslâm Ansiklopedisi*, vol. 10 (1966), 666–670.

52. Tursun Bey, *Târîh-i Ebü'l-Feth*, ed. Mertol Tulum (Istanbul: Istanbul Fetih Cemiyeti, 1977), xvii.

53. Inalcik, "Tursun Beg, Historian of Mehmed the Conqueror's Time," *Wiener Zeitschrift für die Kunde des Morgenlandes* 69 (1977): 55–71.

54. Tursun Bey, *Târîh-i Ebü'l-Feth*, 24.

55. Ibid., xvi, xix.

56. Ibid., 16.

57. *Mukhtaṣar fī al-Siyāsa wa Umūr al-Ṣalṭana* (MS SK, Fatih 1921), 56a.

58. Ibid., 69a.

59. This title does not appear in the main text and was recorded as a bibliographical note on the flyleaf. The autograph copy is preserved at the palace library and the work did not seem to reach outside readership. Şemseddīn Jahramī, *Risāla Barāya Sulṭān Selīm* (MS TSMK, Revan 1614).

60. For an earlier exposition of this threefold division, see Rāghib al-Iṣfahānī, *al-Dharīʿa ilā Makārim al-Sharīʿa*, ed. Sayyid ʿAlī Mīr Lavḥī (Iṣfahān: Jāmiʿat Iṣfahān, Muʿāwanīyat al-Baḥth al-ʿIlmī, 1996), 38–43. See also Rāzī, *Mirṣād al-ʿIbād*, 432, 435, 445.

61. Jahramī, *Risāla Barāya Sulṭān Selīm*, 5a.

62. Ibid., 11b.

63. Ibid., 17a–18b.

64. Abdülkadir Özcan, "İdrîs-i Bitlisî," *TDVIA*, vol. 21 (2000), 485–488.

65. For his tribulations at the Ottoman court and flirtations with the Mamluks and the Safavids, see Vural Genç, "Acem'den Rum'a: İdris-i Bidlîsî'nin Hayatı, Tarihçiliği ve Heşt Behişt'in II. Bayezid Kısmı (1481–1512)" (PhD diss., Istanbul University, 2014), 165–243; Christopher A. Markiewicz, "The Crisis of Rule in Late Medieval Islam: A Study of Idrīs Bidlīsī (861–926/1457–1520) and Kingship at the Turn of the Sixteenth Century" (PhD diss., University of Chicago, 2015), 170–196.

66. For Bidlisi's letters to Ottoman and Safavid rulers, see Vural Genç, "İdris-i Bidlîsî'nin II. Bayezid ve I. Selim'e Mektupları," *JOS* 47 (2016): 147–208; Vural Genç, "Şah ile Sultan Arasında Bir Acem Bürokratı: İdrîs-i Bidlîsî'nin Şah İsmail'in Himayesine Girme Çabası," *JOS* 46 (2015): 43–75.

67. For Bidlisi's record as statesman, see Ebru Sönmez, *İdris-i Bidlisi: Ottoman Kurdistan and Islamic Legitimacy* (Istanbul: Libra, 2012).

68. Mustafa Şentop, *Osmanlı Yargı Sistemi ve Kazaskerlik* (Istanbul: Klasik, 2005), 41–42.

69. For a list of his works, see Mehmet Bayrakdar, *Bitlisli İdris* (Ankara: Kültür Bakanlığı Yayınları, 1991), 31–52; Markiewicz, "The Crisis of Rule in Late Medieval Islam," 410–420.

70. For his upbringing and education, see Genç, "Acem'den Rum'a," 25–36; Markiewicz, "The Crisis of Rule in Late Medieval Islam," 21–38.

71. Abdülkadir Özcan, "İdrîs-i Bitlisî."

72. Genç, "Acem'den Rum'a," 58.

73. Ibid., 401.

74. Dabashi, *The World of Persian Literary Humanism*, 81.

75. Babinger, *Osmanlı Tarih Yazarları*, 51–55.

76. For his letters to Bayezid II, see Genç, "İdris-i Bidlîsî'nin II. Bayezid ve I. Selim'e Mektupları."

77. Babinger, *Osmanlı Tarih Yazarları*, 51–55; Genç, "Acem'den Rum'a," 459–483; Markiewicz, "The Crisis of Rule in Late Medieval Islam," 275–294.

78. Genç, "Acem'den Rum'a," 307–314; Markiewicz, "The Crisis of Rule in Late Medieval Islam," 277.

79. Abdullah Bakır, "Yazıcızāde ʿAlī'nin Selçuḳ-Nāme İsimli Eserinin Edisyon Kritiği" (PhD diss., Marmara University, 2008).

80. The text is edited twice: Hasan Tavakkolî, "İdrîs Bitlîsî'nin Kanun-ı Şâhenşâhisi'nin Tenkidli Neşri ve Türkçeye Tercümesi" (PhD diss., Istanbul University, 1974); Idrīs b. Husām al-Dīn Bidlīsī, *Qānūn-i Shāhanshāhī*, ed. ʿAbd Allāh Masʿūdī Ārānī (Tehran: Markaz-i Pazhūhishī-i Mīrās-i Maktūb, 2008). For the dating and dedication of the text, see Tavakkolî, "Kanun-ı Şâhenşâhi," 27; Genç, "Acem'den Rum'a," 10–11; Markiewicz, "The Crisis of Rule in Late Medieval Islam," 366–367.

81. On Davvani's influence on Bidlisi's political thought, see Tavakkolî, "Kanun-ı Şâhenşâhi," 28–29; Genç, "Acem'den Rum'a," 367–381; Markiewicz, "The Crisis of Rule in Late Medieval Islam," 356–361.

82. Tavakkolî, *Kanun-ı Şâhenşâhi*, 15–29.

83. For comparison, see Suhrawardī, *The Philosophy of Illumination*, eds. John Walbridge and Hossein Ziai (Provo, UT: Brigham Young University Press, 1999).

84. Bidlisi may have taken this division from his teacher Davvānī. See, Harun Anay, "Celâlettin Devvânî: Hayatı, Eserleri, Ahlâk ve Siyaset Düşüncesi" (PhD diss., Istanbul University, 1994), 253.

85. Idrīs-i Bidlīsī, *Mirʾāt al-Jamāl* (MS SK, Şehid Ali Paşa 2149).

86. İdrîs-i Bidlîsî, *Selim Şah-nâme*, ed. and transl. Hicabi Kırlangıç (Ankara: Kültür Bakanlığı Yayınları, 2001).

87. Mustafa Akdağ, "Medreseli İsyanları," *İstanbul Üniversitesi İktisat Fakültesi Mecmuası* 1–4 (1949): 361–387; Karen Barkey, *Bandits and Bureaucrats: The Ottoman Route to State Centralization* (Ithaca, NY and London: Cornell University Press, 1991), 156–163.

88. For a brief treatment of the relationship between philanthropy and government in Islamicate societies, see Said A. Arjomand, "Philanthropy, the Law, and Public Policy in the Islamic World before the Modern Era," in *Philanthropy in the World's Traditions*, eds. Warren F. Ilchman et al. (Bloomington: Indiana University Press, 1998), 109–132.

89. For Turkic customs, see Rhoads Murphey, *Exploring Ottoman Sovereignty: Tradition, Image and Practice in the Ottoman Imperial Household, 1400–1800* (London and New York: Continuum, 2008), 33.

90. The illustrious career of Mahmud Paşa presents a representative case of Ottoman statesman's socially imposed patronage. Stavrides, *The Sultan of Vezirs*, 258–328.

91. For literary circles formed under the patronage of statesmen, see Halûk İpekten, *Divan Edebiyatında Edebî Muhitler* (Istanbul: Milli Eğitim Bakanlığı Yayınları, 1996).

92. On Selim I's succession wars, for a documentary study, see Çağatay Uluçay, "Yavuz Sultan Selim Nasıl Padişah Oldu," *Tarih Dergisi* 6 (1954): 53–90; 7 (1954): 117–142; 8 (1955): 185–200. For a detailed analysis, see Hakkı Erdem Çıpa, "The Centrality of the Periphery: The Rise to Power of Selīm I, 1487–1512" (PhD diss., Harvard University, 2007).

93. For a survey of succession struggles, see Mehmet Akman, *Osmanlı Devletinde Kardeş Katli* (Istanbul: Eren, 1997).

94. Şerafettin Turan, *Kanuni Süleyman Dönemi Taht Kavgaları*, 2nd ed. (Ankara: Bilgi Yayınevi, 1997).

95. For three different such cases, see Halil Inalcik, "A Case Study in Renaissance Diplomacy: the Agreement between Innocent VIII and Bayezid II on Djem Sultan," *JTS* 3 (1979): 342–368; Rıza Yıldırım, "An Ottoman Prince Wearing a Qızılbaş Tāj: The Enigmatic Career of Sultan Murad and Qızılbash Affairs in Ottoman Domestic Politics, 1510–1513," *Turcica* 43 (2011): 91–119; Turan, *Kanunî'nin Oğlu Şehzâde Bayezid Vak'ası* (Ankara: Türk Tarih Kurumu, 1961).

96. For a dated but still the most comprehensive brief study of the careers of Ottoman princes in provinces, see İsmail H. Uzunçarşılı, "Sancağa Çıkarılan Osmanlı Şehzadeleri," *TTK Belleten* 39 (1975): 659–696.

97. For Amasya, see Petra Kappert, *Die osmanischen Prinzen und ihre Residenz Amasya im 15. und 16. Jahrhundert* (Istanbul: Netherlands Historisch-Archeologisch Instituut te Istanbul, 1967).

98. For an analysis of Korkud's critical writings, see Nabil Al-Tikriti, "Şehzade Korkud (ca. 1468–1513) and the Articulation of Early 16th Century Ottoman Religious Identity" (PhD diss., University of Chicago, 2004); On Lütfi Paşa's response to the critics of the Ottoman caliphate, see Hamilton A. R. Gibb, "Luṭfī Paşa on the Ottoman Caliphate," *Oriens* 15 (1962): 287–295.

99. For relations between the Ottoman court and various Sufi orders in the sixteenth century, see Öngören, *Osmanlılar'da Tasavvuf*, 235–334.

100. An enigmatic mystic, Vahidi, recorded in 1523 a symbolic yet accurate depiction of this spiritual diversity in his critical evaluation of Sufi groups. See Karamustafa, Ahmet T. *Vāḥidī's Menāḳıb-i Hvoca-i Cihān ve Netīce-i Cān: Critical Edition and Historical Analysis* (Cambridge, Mass.: The Department of Near Eastern Languages and Civilizations, Harvard University, 1993).

101. For the political entanglements of the Halvetiyye during the reign of Bayezid II, see Hasan Karataş, "The Ottomanization of the Halveti Sufi Order: A Political Story Revisited," *Journal of the Ottoman and Turkish Studies Association* 1 (2014): 71–89.

102. For the Ottoman inquisition of antinomian or rebellious Sufis, mostly from the Halveti, Bayrami, and Melami orders, see Ahmet Yaşar Ocak, *Osmanlı Toplumunda Zındıklar ve Mülhidler (15.-17. Yüzyıllar)* (Istanbul: Tarih Vakfı Yurt Yayınları, 1998), 251–327. For Bali Efendi's letters to Ottoman officials, see Tahsin Özcan, "Sofyalı Bâlî Efendi'nin Para Vakıflarıyla İlgili Mektupları," *İslam Araştırmaları Dergisi* 3 (1999): 125–155; for Ibn Isa's eulogistic prophecies of the Ottoman dynasty, see Ayhan Özgül, "İlyas b. Îsâ-yı Saruhânî'nin "Rumûzü'l-Künûz" Adlı Eserin Transkripsiyonu ve Değerlendirilmesi" (Master's thesis, Kırıkkale University, 2004).

103. For a comprehensive analysis of the Ibn Arabi controversy within the framework of Ottoman-Islamic learned tradition, see Şükrü Özen, "Ottoman 'Ulemā' Debating Sufism: Settling the Conflict on the Ibn al-'Arabī's Legacy by Fatwās," in *El Sufismo y las Normas del Islam: Trabajos del IV Congreso Internacional de Estudios Jurídicos Islámicos, Derecho y Sufismo, Murcia, 7–10 Mayo 2003*, ed. Alfonso Carmona (Murcia: Editora Regional de Murcia, 2006), 309–341.

104. Ocak, *Osmanlı Toplumunda Zındıklar ve Mülhidler*, 230–238.

105. For Molla Lütfi's execution, see Hoca Sa'ādeddīn, *Selīmnāme* (MS TSMK, Revan 937/2), f. 72a.

106. Taşköprizade, for example, was only one of his many high-profile admirers. See Orhan Şaik Gökyay and Şükrü Özen, "Molla Lütfi," *TDVIA*, vol. 30 (2005), 255–258.

107. Kütükoğlu, "Lütfi Paşa Âsafnâmesi," p. 73.

108. Nabil Al-Tikriti, "Şehzade Korkud (ca. 1468–1513) and the Articulation of Early 16th Century Ottoman Religious Identity," 228–234.

109. Ocak treats Ottoman religious history within the framework of an orthodox Sunni center versus the heterodox periphery. See "Les réactions socio-religieuses contre l'idéologie officielle otomane et la question de Zendeqa ve İlhad (hérésie et athéisme) au XVIe siècle," *Turcica* 21–23 (1991): 71–82. Tijana Krstić puts less emphasis on particular sects but highlights the Ottoman wave of confessionalization as part of a broader early modern European phenomenon. See *Contested Conversions to Islam: Narratives of Religious Change in the Early Modern Ottoman Empire* (Stanford: Stanford University Press, 2011). Derin Terzioğlu considers Sunnitization as a longer and complicated process with multiple causes. See "How to Conceptualize Ottoman Sunnitization: A Historiographical Discussion," *Turcica* 44 (2012): 301–308.

110. Kafadar, *Between Two Worlds: The Construction of the Ottoman State* (Berkeley: University of California Press, 1995), 76.

111. Terzioğlu, "Sufis in the Age of State-Building and Confessionalization," in The Ottoman World, ed. Christine Woodhead (New York: Routledge, 2012), 86–99.

112. Abdurrahman Atçıl, "The Safavid Threat and Juristic Authority in the Ottoman Empire," *IJMES* 49 (2017): 295–314.

113. For a general overview of reactions among the learned, see Elke Eberhard, *Osmanische Polemik gegen die Safawiden im 16. Jahrhundert nach arabischen Handschriften* (Freiburg im Breisgau: Klaus Schwarz Verlag, 1970). For reactions of the Ottoman administration, see Fariba Zarinabaf-Shahr, "Qizilbash "Heresy" and Rebellion in Ottoman Anatolia during the Sixteenth Century," *Anatolia Moderna* 7 (1997): 1–15.

114. For an example of such political polemics, see Vladimir Minorsky, "Shaykh Bālī Efendi on the Safavids," *BSOAS* 20 (1957): 437–450.

115. Colin Imber, "Süleymân as Caliph of the Muslims: Ebû's-Su'ûd's Formulation of Ottoman Dynastic Ideology," in *Soliman le Magnifique et Son temps*, ed. Gilles Veinstein (Paris: La Documentation Française, 1992), 179–184; Inalcık, "Islamization of Ottoman Laws on Land and Land Tax," in *Festgabe an Josef Matuz: Osmanistik—Turkologie—Diplomatik*, eds. Christa Fragner and Klaus Schwarz (Berlin: Klaus Schwarz Verlag, 1992), 101–119.

116. Najm al-Dīn Ṭarsūsī, *Kitāb Tuḥfat al-Turk fī mā Yajib an Yu'mal fī al-Mulk*, ed. Ridwān al-Sayyid (Beirut: Dār al-Ṭalī'a li al-Ṭibā'a wa al-Nashr, 1992), 7–50.

117. Asım C. Köksal, *Fıkıh ve Siyaset: Osmanlılarda Siyâset-i Şer'iyye* (Istanbul: Klasik, 2016), 141–246.

118. See, for example, Avni İlhan, "Birgili Mehmed Efendi ve Mezhepler Tarihi ile İlgili Risalesi," *Dokuz Eğlül Üniversitesi İlahiyat Fakültesi Dergisi* 6 (1989): 173–215; Lüṭfī Pāşā, *Risāle-i Firāḳ-ı Dālle Tercümesi* (MS SK, Ayasofya 2195), ff. 110b–123a.

119. See, for example, the section on the imamate in Seyyid Şerîf Cürcânî, *Şerhu'l-Mevâkıf (Metin—Çeviri)*, transl. Ömer Türker, vol. 3 (Istanbul: Türkiye Yazma Eserler Kurumu Başkanlığı Yayınları, 2015), 666–743.

120. Celālzāde Muṣṭafā, *Mevāhibü'l-Ḫallaḳ fī Merātibi'l-Aḫlāḳ* (MS SK, Fatih 3521), 242b.

121. Kütükoğlu, "Lütfi Paşa Âsafnâmesi," pp. 73–75.

122. Ḥüseyin b. ʿAbdullāh el-Şirvānī, *al-Risāla al-ʿAdliyya al-Sulaymāniyya* (MS TSMK, Revan 1035).

123. Ebū'l-Fażl el-Münşī, *Dustūr al-Salṭana*, 3a.

124. For an analysis of the ulema mobility in and out of the Ottoman domains, see Ertuğrul Ökten, "Scholars and Mobility: A Preliminary Assessment from the Perspective of al-Shaqāyiq al-Nuʿmāniyya," *JOS* 51 (2013): 55–70.

125. Thomas D. Goodrich, *The Ottoman Turks and the New World: A Study of Tarih-i Hind-i Garbi and Sixteenth-Century Ottoman Americana* (Weisbaden: Otto Harrassowitz, 1990); Jean Louis Bacqué-Grammont, *La première histoire de France en turc ottoman: Chroniques des padichahs de France 1572* (Paris: L'Harmattan, 1997); Joseph Matuz, *L'ouvrage de Seyfī Çelebī: Historien ottoman du XVIe siècle* (Paris: Librairie A. Maisonneuve, 1968).

126. İsmail H. Uzunçarşılı, *Osmanlı Tarihi* (Ankara: Türk Tarih Kurumu, 1949), 2: 666; For the original work, see Abū al-Maḥāsin Yūsuf Ibn Taghrībirdī, *al-Nujūm al-Zāhira fī Mulūk al-Miṣr wa al-Qāhira*, ed. Muḥammed Ḥusayn Shams al-Dīn (Beirut: Dār al-Kutub al-ʿIlmiyya, 1992) for English translation, see Abū al-Maḥāsin Yūsuf Ibn Taghrībirdī, *History of Egypt 1382–1469 A.D.*, transl. William Popper (New York: AMS Press, 1976).

127. Naḥīfī, *Nehcü's-Sülūk fī Siyāseti'l-Mülūk* (Istanbul: Rıżā Efendi Maṭbaʿası, 1286/1870), 3.

128. Cornell H. Fleischer, *Bureaucrat and Intellectual in the Ottoman Empire: The Historian Mustafa Âli (1541–1600)* (Princeton: Princeton University Press, 1986.), 239–240.

129. ʿAlāyī bin Muḥibbī el-Şīrāzī el-Şerīf, *Netīcetü's-Sülūk fī Terceme-i Naṣīḥatü'l-Mülūk* (MS SK, Pertevniyal 1011), 5a–5b.

130. Tofigh Heidarzadeh, "Muhājarat ʿUlemā-i Īrān ba Imperātūrī-e ʿOs̱mānī," *Farhang* 20–21 (1975–1976): 49–94.

131. Hanna Sohrweide, "Dichter und Gelehrte aus dem Osten im osmanischen Reich (1453–1600): Ein Beitrag zur türkisch-persischen Kulturgeschichte," *Der Islam* 46 (1970): 263–302.

132. Pīr Muḥammed ʿAẓmī Efendī, *Enīsü'l-ʿĀrifīn* (MS SK, Pertevniyal 474; Lala Ismail Paşa 243).

133. Beyâni, *Tezkiretü'ş-Şuarâ*, 171.

134. Ceyhan, "Âlim ve Şair Bir Osmanlı Müderrisi: Pîr Mehmed Azmî Bey ve Eserleri," *Türk Kültürü İncelemeleri Dergisi* 1 (1999): 243–286.

135. Nev'îzâde Atâî, *Hadaiku'l-Hakaik fî Tekmileti'ş-Şakaik*, ed. Abdülkadir Özcān (Istanbul: Çağrı Yayınları, 1989), 267.

136. Firāḳī ʿAbdurraḥmān Çelebī, *Terceme-i Aḫlâḳ-ı Muḥsinī* (MS TSMK, Revan 393).

137. Beyâni, *Tezkiretü'ş-Şuarâ*, 202.

138. Latîfî, *Tezkiretü'ş-Şu'ara ve Tabsıratü'n-Nuzamâ*, ed. Rıdvan Canım (Ankara: Atatürk Kültür Merkezi Yayınları, 2000), 423; According to Mustafa Âli, Firaki marketed himself as Lami'i's pupil. See İsen, *Künhü'l-Ahbâr'ın Tezkire Kısmı*, 253.

139. Ebū'l-Fażl Meḥmed b. İdrīs el-Defterī, *Terceme-i Aḫlāḳ-ı Muḥsinī* (MS TSMK, Revan 347).

140. Atâî, *Hadaiku'l-Hakaik*, 188–190.

141. Ibid., 267, 390.

142. Tahsin Yazıcı, "Hemedânî," *TDVIA*, vol. 17 (1998), 186–188.

143. Mīr Seyyed ʿAlī Hamadānī, *Ẕakhīrat al-Mulūk*, ed. Sayyid Maḥmūd Anvārī (Tabriz: Intishārāt-i Muʾassasa-i Tārīkh va Farhang-i Iran, 1979), 39–46.

144. A textual comparison of works by Hamadani and Kayseri shows a similarity in their terminology, definitions, and views. See Hamadānī, *Ẕakhīrat al-Mulūk*, 289–334; Qayṣarī Rūmī, Muḥammed Dāvūd, *Sharh-i Fuṣūṣ al-Ḥikam*, ed. Seyyed Jalāl ad-Dīn Āshtiyānī (Tehran: Shirkat-i Intishārāt-i ʿIlmī va Farhangī, 1375), 1–286.

145. Levend, "Siyaset-nâmeler," *TDAY Belleten* (1962): 167–194.

146. Kınalı-zade Hasan Çelebi, *Tezkiretü'ş-Şuarâ*, 2 vols, ed. İbrahim Kutluk (Ankara: Türk Tarih Kurumu, 1978), 1: 394.

147. Muṣliḥuddīn Muṣṭafā Sürūrī Efendī, *Ẕaḫīretü'l-Mülūk* (MS TSMK, Revan 403; SK, Ayasofya 2858).

148. Atâî, *Hadaiku'l-Hakaik*, 32.

149. Fleischer, *Bureaucrat and Intellectual in the Ottoman Empire*, 28–29.

150. Atâî, *Hadaiku'l-Hakaik*, 23.

151. His friends, particularly Gubari, who observed a great potential in him as a mystic and scholar, criticized him for leaving higher spiritual ground for worldly gains in pursuit of positions. His biographer Kınalızade Hasan expressed that reaction as well: "While being the king of the world he turned himself into a slave." See Kınalı-zade Hasan, *Tezkiretü'ş-Şuarâ*, 458; İsen, *Künhü'l-Ahbâr'ın Tezkire Kısmı*, 229.

152. For the tutorial work of Süruri, see Kappert, *Die osmanischen Prinzen und ihre Residenz Amasya im 15. und 16. Jahrhundert*, 107–110.

153. For an incomplete list of these translations is in Istanbul libraries, see Levend, "Siyaset-nâmeler."

154. For a detailed examination of the work and its author, see Bagley *Ghazālī's Book of Counsel for Kings*, ix–lxxiv; for a discussion about the authenticity of the work, see Patricia Crone, "Did al-Ghazālī Write a Mirrors for princes? On the Authorship of *Naṣīḥat al-Mulūk*," *Jerusalem Studies in Arabic and Islam* 10 (1987): 167–191.

155. Ann K. S. Lambton, "The Theory of Kingship in the *Naṣīḥat ul-Mulūk of Gazālī*," *The Islamic Quarterly* 1 (1954): 47–55.

156. Ahmet Uğur, *Osmanlı Siyâset-nâmeleri*, (Kayseri: Kültür ve Sanat Yayınları, 1987), 85–86.

157. Atâî, *Hadaiku'l-Hakaik*, 173–174.

158. ʿĀşıḳ Çelebī, *el-Ṭibrü'l-Mesbūḳ fī Nasīḥati'l-Mülūk* (MS TSMK, Bağdat 351).

159. ʿĀşıḳ Çelebī, *Tercüme-i Ravżu'l-Aḫyār* (MS SK, Reşid Efendi 540; Laleli 1696; Meḥmed Muḥyiddīn bin Ḫaṭīb Ḳāṣım, *Rawḍ al-Akhyār al-Muntakhab min Rabīʿ al-Abrār* (MS TSMK, Emanet Hazinesi 1327).

160. For a nineteenth-century edition, see Meḥmed b. Ḳāṣım b. Yaʿḳūb el-Amāsī, *Rawḍ al-Akhyār al-Muntakhab min Rabīʿ al-Abrār* (Bulaq: Ḥusayn al-Ṭarābulusī, 1279 [1862–1863]; for a recent edition, see Ibn al-Khaṭīb Meḥmed Ḳāṣım b. Yaʿqūb el-Amāsī, *Rawḍ al-Akhyār al-Muntakhab min Rabīʿ al-Abrār*, ed. Maḥmūd Fākhūrī (Aleppo: Dār al-Qalam al-ʿArābī, 2003).

161. See introduction by the editor. Maḥmūd b. ʿUmar al-Zamakhsharī, *Rabīʿ al-Abrār wa Fuṣūṣ al-Akhbār*, 2 vols., ed. ʿAbd al-Majīd Diyāb (Cairo: al-Hay'a al-Miṣriyya al-ʿĀmma li al-Kitāb, 1992).

162. The third chapter is titled "On rulership, governorship, the vizierate, governance, justice, and forgiveness." See Amāsī, *Rawḍ al-Akhyār*, 52.

163. Mecdî, *Hadaiku'ş-Şakaik*, 399.

164. ʿĀşıḳ Çelebī, *Terceme-i Ravżu'l-Aḫyār* (MS SK, Laleli 1696), 1a–b.

165. Vuṣūlī Meḥmed Efendī, *Şems-i Hidāyet* (MS SK, Reisülküttap 772). See Sait Aykut's introduction in Muhammed b. Turtûşî, *Sirâcu'l-Mülûk: Siyaset Ahlâkı ve İlkelerine*

Dair, transl. Said Aykut (Istanbul: İnsan Yayınları, 1995), 22; Mehmed Tahir, *Osmanlı Müellifleri*, eds. A. Fikri Yavuz and İsmail Sözen, 3 vols. (Istanbul: Meral Yayınevi, 1971–5), 2: 422.

166. Mecdî, *Hadaiku'ş-Şakaik*, 311–312; İsen, *Künhü'l-Ahbâr'ın Tezkire Kısmı*, 318; Beyâni, *Tezkiretü'ş-Şuarâ*, 321–322.

167. Ṭāşköprīzāde, *Miftāḥ al-Saʿāda*, 412.

168. Aykut recorded that in Süleymaniye Library alone there are twenty-five copies of the Arabic version of *Sirāj al-Mulūk*, indicating its popularity among Ottoman readers. See Aykut's introduction in Turtûşî, *Sirâcu'l-Mulūk*, 23–24.

169. ʿĀşıḳ Çelebī, *Miʿrācü'l-ʿIyāle ve Minhācü'l-ʿAdāle* (MS SK, Şehid Ali Paşa 1556). See the introduction in İbn Teymiye, *Siyaset: es-Siyasetü'ş-şeriyye*, transl. Vecdi Akyüz (Istanbul: Dergah Yayınları, 1985), 7. For the Ottoman reception and translation of Ibn Taymiyya's *al-Siyāsa al-Sharʿiyya*, see Derin Terzioğlu, "Bir Tercüme ve Bir İntihal Vakası: Ya Da İbn Teymiyye'nin *Siyāsetü'ş-Şerʿiyye*'sini Osmanlıcaya Kim(ler), Nasıl Aktardı," *JTS* 31 (2007): 247–275.

170. On many issues, he relates views of jurists from other schools of law as well. See, for example, the question of punishing the rebels, Ibn Taymiyya, *al-Siyāsa al-Sharʿiyya fī Iṣlāḥ al-Rāʿī wa al-Raʿiyya*, ed. ʿAbd al-Bāsiṭ b. Yūsuf al-Gharīb (Dammām: Dār al-Rāwī, 2000), 117–121.

171. Lambton, *State and Government in Medieval Islam. An Introduction to the Study of Islamic Political Theory: The Jurists* (Oxford: Oxford University Press, 1981), 149.

172. For Kınalızade's criticism of excessive capital punishments, see *Aḫlāḳ-ı ʿAlāʾī*, 3: 11–14; Dede Cöngi's *al-Siyāsa al-Sharʿiyya* was in large part a treatise on the religious foundations of capital punishment. For Taşköprizade's vindication of the superiority of the *sharīʿa* over *siyāsa*, see *Miftāḥ al-Saʿāda*, 1: 404–405. For the cash foundations controversy, see Jon E. Mandaville, "Usurious Piety: The Cash Waqf Controversy in the Ottoman Empire," *IJMES* 10 (1979): 289–308. For the jurists' role in reconciling Islam and sultanic laws, see Inalcık, "Islamization of Ottoman Laws on Land and Land Tax."

173. Abdüsselâm el-Amâsî, *Tuḥfetü'l-Ümerâ ve Minḥatü'l-Vüzerâ*, ed. A. Mevhibe Coşar (Istanbul: Büyüyen Ay Yayınları, 2012).

174. İbn Fīrūz Meḥmed, *Gurretü'l-Beyżā* (MS SK, Esad Efendi, 1828). See Recep Cici, "İbn Fîrûz ve "El-Gurretü'l-Beydâ" Adlı Eseri," *Uludağ Üniversitesi İlahiyat Fakültesi Dergisi* 9 (2000): 301–306.

175. Atâî, *Hadaiku'l-Hakaik*, 529.

176. Khayrabaytī, Maḥmūd b. Ismāʿīl b. Ibrāhīm, *al-Durra al-Gharrā fī Naṣīḥat al-Salāṭīn wa al-Quḍāt wa al-Umarā* (Mecca and Riyad: Maktaba Nazār Muṣṭafā al-Bāz, 1996).

177. See Gibb, "Luṭfī Paşa on the Ottoman Caliphate;" Hulûsi Yavuz, "Sadrıâzam Lütfi Paşa ve Osmanlı Hilâfeti," *MÜİFD* 5–6 (1993): 27–54.

178. Extant copies of the work differ from each other. Levend and Cici claim that the work is an abridgement, whereas Mehmed Tahir stated that the copy he had examined was an expanded translation. See Levend, "Siyaset-nâmeler;" Cici, "İbn Fîrûz ve "El-Gurretü'l-Beydâ" Adlı Eseri;" Mehmed Tahir, *Osmanlı Müellifleri*, I: 355.

179. Abdüsselâm el-Amâsî, *Tuḥfetü'l-Ümerâ*, 144; İbn Fīrūz Meḥmed, *Gurretü'l-Beyżā*, Esad Efendi, 1828, 1b.

180. Abdüsselâm el-Amâsî, *Tuḥfetü'l-Ümerâ*, 140; İbn Fīrūz Meḥmed, *Gurretü'l-Beyżā*, Esad Efendi, 1828, 2a.

181. Abdüsselâm el-Amâsî, *Tuḥfetü'l-Ümerâ*, 145.

182. On the question of Qurayshi lineage, for example, Khayrabaytī offered a workable solution for the Mamluk ruler by ruling that if a ruler was appointed by somebody

who belonged to the Quraysh, then the Qurayshi lineage was not required for the ruler. See Khayrabaytī, *al-Durra al-Gharrā*, 118.

183. For a discussion of the work in the context of Mamluk politics, see Baki Tezcan, "Hanafism and the Turks in al-Ṭarasūsī's Gift for the Turks (1352)," *Mamluk Studies Review* 15 (2011): 67–86.

184. *Naṣīḥat al-Mulūk* (MS British Museum, OR 9728).

185. Ṭarsūsī, *Kitāb Tuḥfat al-Turk*, 19.

186. Ṭarsūsī, *Tuḥfat al-Turk*, 18.

187. Ṭarsūsī, *Tuḥfat al-Turk*, 21–22.

188. See translator's introduction in Nağm al-Dīn Ṭarsūsī, *Kitāb Tuḥfat al-Turk*, ed. and transl. Mohamed Menasri (Damascus: Institut Français de Damas, 1997), 54.

189. For some of these works, see F. Ethem Karatay, *Topkapı Sarayı Müzesi Arapça Yazmaları Kataloğu* (Istanbul: Topkapı Sarayı Müzesi, 1962), no. 6948, 6949, 6981, and 6982.

190. *Naṣīḥatnāme-i Sulṭān Murād* (MS TSMK, Revan 407).

191. For Marino di Cavalli, see Eugenio Albèri, ed., *Relazioni degli ambasciatori Veneti al senato*, vol. 11 (Cambridge: Cambridge University Press, 2012), pp. 197–230; W. Andreas, *Eine unbekannte venezianische Relazion über die Türkei (1567)* (Heidelberg: Carl Winters Universitätsbuchhandlung, 1914).

192. Abdullah Uçman, *Fatih Sultan Mehmet'e Nasihatler* (Istanbul: Tercüman 1001 Temel Eser, 1976), 12, 45. For the translator Murad Beg, see Pál Ács, "Tarjumans Mahmud and Murad: Austrian and Hungarian Renegades as Sultan's Interpreters," in *Europa und die Türken in der Renaissance: Herausgegeben von Bodo Guthmüller und Wilhelm Kühlmann* (Tübingen: Max Niemeyer Verlag, 2000), 307–316.

193. Ettore Rossi, "Parafrasi turca del de Senectute Presentata a Solimano Il Magnifico dal bailo Marino de Cavalli (1559)," *Rendiconti della R. Accademia Nazionale dei Lincei. Classe di scienze morali, storiche e filologiche*, Serie VI, 12 (1936): 680–756.

194. Birnbaum, *The Book of Advice by King Kay Kā'us ibn Iskander*, 36a–40a; Aḥmedī, *İskender-Nāme: İnceleme-Tıpkıbasım*, ed. İsmail Ünver (Ankara: Türk Dil Kurumu Yayınları, 1983), 4b.

195. Mecdî, *Hadaiku'ş-Şakaik*, 391–392.

196. Nāṣūḥī Aḳhiṣārī Nevālī, *Tercüme-i Neṣā'iḥ-i Aristaṭālīs* (MS SK, Hafid Efendi 253).

197. Nevālī, *Tercüme-i Neṣā'iḥ-i Aristaṭālīs*, 3b.

198. Mahmoud Manzalaoui, "The Pseudo-Aristotelian *Kitāb Sirr al-Asrār*: Facts and Problems," *Oriens* 23–24 (1974): 147–257. Also see, Mario Grignaschi, "L'origine et les métamorphoses du ʿSirr-al-asrâr'," *Archives d'Histoire Doctrinale et Littéraire du Moyen Âge* 43 (1976): 7–112.

199. Yuḥanna ibn al-Biṭrīq, *Kitāb al-Siyāsa fī Tadbīr al-Riyāsa (al-maʿrūf bi Sirr al-Asrār)*, in ed. ʿAbd al-Raḥmān al-Badawī, *al-ʿUṣūl al-Yūnāniyya li al-Naẓariyāt al-Siyāsiyya fī al-Islām* (Cairo: Maktabat al-Nahḍa al-Miṣriyya, 1954).

200. Grignaschi, "La diffusion du Secretum secretorum (Sirr al-asrar) dans l'Europe occidentale," *Archives d'Histoire Doctrinale et Littéraire du Moyen Âge* 47 (1980): 7–70.

201. Manzalaoui, "The Pseudo-Aristotelian *Kitāb Sirr al-Asrār*: Facts and Problems," 238–242.

202. Manzalaoui, "The Pseudo-Aristotelian *Sirr al-Asrār* and Three Oxford Thinkers of the Middle Ages," in *Arabic and Islamic Studies in Honor of Hamilton A. R. Gibb*, ed. George Makdisi (Leiden: Brill, 1965), 480–500.

203. Yuḥanna ibn al-Biṭrīq, *Kitāb al-Siyāsa fī Tadbīr al-Riyāsa*, 127–128; Nevālī, *Tercüme-i Neṣā'iḥ-i Aristaṭālīs*, 66a.

204. Nevālī, *Tercüme-i Neṣā'iḥ-i Aristaṭālīs*, 4a.

205. See, for example, Uğur, *Osmanlı Siyâset-nâmeleri*, 13–17; Levend, "Siyaset-nâmeler."

206. For the reception of the text among the Ottomans, see İbrahim Kafesoğlu, "Büyük Selçuklu Veziri Nizâmü'l-Mülk'ün Eseri Siyâsetnâme ve Türkçe Tercümesi," *Türkiyat Mecmuası* 12 (1955): 231–256.

207. Hüseyin Yılmaz, "Osmanlı Tarihçiliğinde Tanzimat Öncesi Siyaset Düşüncesi'ne Yaklaşımlar," *Türkiye Araştırmaları Literatür Dergisi* 1/2 (2003): 231–98.

208. Ṭāşköprīzāde, *Mawsūʿa Muṣṭalaḥāt Miftāḥ al-Saʿāda wa Miṣbāḥ al-Siyāda fī Mawḍūʿāt al-ʿUlūm*, eds. Rafīq al-ʿAjam and ʿAlī Daḥrūj (Beirut: Maktaba Lubnān Nāshirūn, 1998).

209. For a list of his works, see Ali Rıza Karabulut, "Taşköprü-zâde'nin Eserleri," in *Taşköprülü Zâde Ahmet Efendi (1495–1561)*, ed. A. Hulûsi Köker (Kayseri: Erciyes Üniversitesi Gevher Nesibe Tıp Tarihi Enstitüsü, 1989), 113–131.

210. Ṭāşköprīzāde, *Miftāḥ al-Saʿāda*, 3: 402.

211. Ṭāşköprīzāde, *al-Shaqāʾiq al-Nuʿmāniyya*, 225–331.

212. Behcet Gönül, "İstanbul Kütüphânelerinde al-Şaḳāʾiḳ al-Nuʿmāniya Tercüme ve Zeyilleri," *Türkiyat Mecmuası* 7–8 (1945): 137–168.

213. For the Ottoman reception of Ghazali and his works, see M. Sait Özervarlı, "Ottoman Perceptions of al-Ghazālī's works and Discussions on His Historical Role in its Late Period" in *Islam and Rationality: The Impact of al-Ghazālī*, ed. Frank Griffel (Leiden: Brill, 2015), 253–282.

214. Compare to similar works examined by Ahmet Subhi Furat, "İslâm Edebiyatında Ansiklopedik Eserler: h. IV.–IX/m. X.–XV. Asırlar," *İslâm Tetkikleri Enstitüsü Dergisi* 7 (1979): 211–231.

215. Although there is no evidence that Nevali had read *Miftāḥ al-Saʿāda*, his translation of the pseudo-Aristotelian text, *Sirr al-Asrār*, appeared after it was recommended by Taşköprizade.

216. Khiḍr b. ʿUmar al-ʿAṭūfī, *Daftar-i Kutub* (MS Budapest, Magyar Tudományos Akadémia Könyvtára Keleti Gyűjtemény, Török F. 59).

217. For a detailed analysis, see Yılmaz, "Books on Ethics and Politics: The Art of Governing the Self and Others at the Ottoman Court," Forthcoming in *Supplements to Muqarnas Series*, eds. Gülru Necipoğlu, Cemal Kafadar, Cornell Fleischer (Brill: Leiden and Boston).

218. İpekten and İsen, *Tezkirelere Göre Divan Edebiyatı İsimler Sözlüğü*, 26–27. A manuscript record indicates that he was in Konya in 1552, in the vicinity of Rumi's tomb where he copied Ibn Kemal's work *Nigāristān*. See Gustav Flügel, *Die arabischen, persischen, türkischen Handschriften der kaiserlichen und königlichen Hofbibliothek zu Wien* (New York: Olms, Hildesheim, 1977), 3: 285-6.

219. ʿAlāyī bin Muḥibbī el-Şīrāzī el-Şerīf, *Düstūrü'l-Vüzerā* (MS SK, Yazma Bağışlar 4421/3), 70.

220. Kātib Çelebī, *Kashf al-Ẓunūn*, 1: 755.

221. ʿAlāyī, *Düstūrü'l-Vüzerā*, 3.

222. Ibid., 68–71.

223. Alayi stated that he had seen both the Persian and Arabic versions of Ghazali's work and chose the latter for his translation. See, ʿAlāyī bin Muḥibbī el-Şīrāzī el-Şerīf, *Netīcetü's-Sülūk fī Terceme-i Naṣīḥatü'l-Mülūk* (MS SK, Pertevniyal 1011).

224. ʿAlāyī, *Netīcetü's-Sülūk*, 34b, 49b, 52a.

225. Kātib Çelebī, *Kashf al-Ẓunūn*, 1: 36.

226. The only known copy of the work was written in an exquisite *nesih* script with vowels and probably remained in the sultanic library. See, Muẓaffer bin ʿOs̱mān el-Bermekī Ḫıżır Münşī, *Akhlāq al-Atqiyā va Ṣifāt al-Aṣfiyā* (MS SK, Fatih 3515).

227. Ḥızır Münşī, *Akhlāq al-Atqiyā*, 7a.

228. Ibid., 7b.

229. For Celalzade's career as a bureaucrat and intellectual, see M. Şakir Yılmaz, "'Koca Nişancı' of Kanuni: Celalzade Mustafa Çelebi, Bureaucracy and "Kanun" in the Reign of Suleyman the Magnificient (1520–1566)" (PhD diss., Bilkent University, 2006); Kaya Şahin, *Empire and Power in the Reign of Süleyman: Narrating the Sixteenth-Century Ottoman World* (Cambridge: Cambridge University Press, 2013).

230. Latîfî, *Tezkiretü'ş-Şu'arâ*, 529.

231. For an analysis and facsimile edition of the text, see Petra Kappert, *Geschichte Sultan Süleymān Ḳānūnīs von 1520 bis 1557: oder Ṭabaḳāt ül-Memālik ve Derecāt ül-Mesālik* (Weisbaden: Franz Steiner Verlag, 1981). For a critical edition of the text, see Demirtaş, Funda. "Celâl-zâde Mustafa Çelebi, Tabakâtü'l-Memâlik ve Derecâtü'l-Mesâlik" (PhD diss., Erciyes University, 2009). I thank Funda Demirtaş for providing me with a copy of her dissertation.

232. Beyâni agrees with Kınalızade Ali and finds Celalzade's prose and verse just as pompous. See Beyâni, *Tezkiretü'ş-Şuarâ*, 292.

233. Celâl-zâde Mustafa, *Selim-Nâme*, eds. Ahmet Uğur and Mustafa Çuhadar (Ankara: Kültür Bakanlığı Yayınları, 1990).

234. For a brief summary of the work, see Aynî, *Türk Ahlakçıları*, 135–155.

235. For comparison, see Aynî, *Türk Ahlâkçıları*, 57–71, 135–154, 73–96.

236. Kınalı-zade Hasan, *Tezkiretüş-Şuarâ*, 664.

237. Beyâni, *Tezkiretü'ş-Şuarâ*, 182.

238. İsen, *Künh'ül-Ahbâr'ın Tezkire Kısmı*, 245–246.

239. ʿĀşıḳ Çelebi, *Meşā'ir üş-Şuʿarā*, ed. G. M. Meredith-Owens (London: Luzac, 1971), 181b–182a.

240. Ḳınalīzāde ʿAlī Çelebī. *Aḫlāḳ-ı ʿAlāʾī*. Bulak, 1833.

241. Beyâni, *Tezkiretü'ş-Şuarâ*, 183.

242. Ḳınalīzāde ʿAlī, *Aḫlāḳ-ı ʿAlāʾī*, 1: 10.

243. İsen, *Künhü'l-Ahbâr'ın Tezkire Kısmı*, 245.

244. Ḳınalīzāde ʿAlī, *Aḫlāḳ-ı ʿAlāʾī*, 1: 8.

245. Ibid., 1: 10.

246. Ibid., 1: 10.

247. In Istanbul libraries alone, there are sixty-five manuscript copies of *Aḫlāḳ-ı ʿAlāʾī*. See Hasan Aksoy, Kınalı-zade Ali Çelebi: Hayatı, İlmî ve Edebî Şahsiyeti" (BA graduation thesis, İstanbul University, 1976).

248. Kātib Çelebī, *Kashf al-Ẓunūn*, 1: 37.

249. Atâî, *Hadaiku'l-Hakaik*, 183.

250. For the edited text, see Ramazan Ekinci, "16. Asırda Yazılmış Mensur bir Nasihat-Nâme: Abdülkerim bin Mehmed'in Nesâyihü'l-Ebrâr'ı," *Turkish Studies* 7 (2012): 423–441. Abdülkerim dedicated another copy to Murad III in 1574, on the year of his coronation, during which the author also deceased. See Abdülkerim b. Meḥmed, *Neṣāyīḥü'l-Ebrār* (MS University of Michigan Library 389), 5–6.

251. These two texts are included in a collection of treatises but do not bear the name of the author. But a comparison of their content with *Neṣāyihü'l-Ebrār* almost certainly shows that all three texts were written by the same author. See (MS SK, Hamidiye 1469): *Cāmiʿü'l-Kelimāti'l-Ḥikemiyyāt fī Neṣāyiḥi'l-Mülūk ve'l-Beyyināt*, ff. 83b–94a; *Ḥükemā-i Selefden Baʿzı Neṣāyiḥi Müştemil Kelimātdur*, ff. 146b–157b; *Neṣāyīhü'l-Ebrār*, ff. 159b–166a.

252. Aḥmed ibn Muḥammed Ibn Miskawayh, *al-Ḥikma al-Khālida (Jāvidān Khirad)*, ed. ʿAbd al-Raḥmān Badawī (Tehran: Dānishgāh-i Tehrān, 1980).

253. Mehmet İpşirli, "Lutfi Paşa," *TDVIA*, vol. 27 (2003), 234–236.

254. Lüṭfī Pāşā, *Tevārīḫ-i Āl-i ʿOsmān*, ed. ʿĀlī Bey (Istanbul: Maṭbaʿa-i Āmire, 1341/1925).

255. Yaşar Yücel, *Osmanlı Devlet Teşkilâtına Dair Kaynaklar* (Ankara: Türk Tarih Kurumu, 1988), 49–144.

256. For a discussion of dating the work, see Baki Tezcan, "The Kânunnâme of Mehmed II: A Different Perspective," in *The Great Ottoman-Turkish Civilization*, ed. Kemal Çiçek, vol. 3 (Ankara: Yeni Türkiye Yayınları, 2000), 657–665.

257. For a critique of the decline thesis, see Kafadar, "The Question of Ottoman Decline," *Harvard Middle East and Islamic Review* 4 (1997–1998): 30–75.

258. For Bistami and his work, see Fleischer, "Ancient Wisdom and New Sciences: Prophecies at the Ottoman Court in the Fifteenth and Early Sixteenth Centuries," in *Falnama: the Book of Omens*, eds. Farhad Massumeh and Serpil Bağcı (London: Thames & Hudson, 2009), 231–243.

259. Ömer Yağmur, "Terceme-i Kitāb-ı Fevâ'ihü'l-Miskiyye fi'l-Fevâtihi'l-Mekkiyye" (Master's thesis, Istanbul University, 2007).

260. Lüṭfī Pāşā, *Khalāṣ al-Umma fī Maʿrifat al-Aʾimma* (MS SK, Ayasofya 2887), 17, 40–41.

261. *Risāla fīmā Lazima ʿalā al-Mulūk* (MS SK, Esat Efendi 1845).

262. *Risāla fīmā Lazima ʿalā al-Mulūk*, 7.

263. Many prominent scholars, Sufis, and poets wrote treatises to the same effect. Baki, for example, the most renowned poet of the time, was commissioned by Grand Vizier Sokollu Mehmed Paşa to translate Muḥy al-Dīn Aḥmed b. Ibrāhīm's *Mashaʿir al-Ashwāq ilā Maṣāriʿ al-ʿUshshāq*, a work on the virtues of jihad. Baki translated the work in 975/1567 with the title *Feżāʾilü'l-Cihād*. See Mehmet Çavuşoğlu, "Bâkî," *TDVIA*, vol. 4 (1991), 537–540; Bali Efendi, Baki's contemporary, also wrote a treatise on the same topic, exhorting believers to wage war against the infidels titled *Risāle fī Gazāʾil-Mücāhidīn* (MS İÜK, T 786).

264. *Risāla fīmā Lazima ʿalā al-Mulūk*, 11.

265. Bidlisi and Jahrami both admonished the ruler not to drink wine but nevertheless granted him the prerogative to drink. Bidlîsî, *Kanun-ı Şahenşahi*, 148; Jahramī, *Risāla Barāya Sulṭān Selīm*, 11a.

266. Ḥüseyin bin Ḥasan, *Laṭāʾif al-Afkār wa Kāshif al-Asrār* (MS SK, Reisülküttap 698). For a more detailed content analysis for the work, see Özgür Kavak, "Bir Osmanlı Kadısının Gözüyle Siyaset: Letâifü'l-efkâr ve kâşifü'l-esrâr Yahut Osmanlı Saltanatını Fıkıh Diliyle Temellendirmek," *MÜİFD* 42 (2012): 95–120.

267. Kātib Çelebī, *Kashf al-Ẓunūn*, 2: 1552.

268. Uzunçarşılı, *Osmanlı Tarihi*, 2: 344–345.

269. Ḥüseyin, *Laṭāʾif al-Afkār*, 2a.

270. Ibid., 9a.

271. Ibid., 55a–59a.

272. Flügel, *Arabischen, Persischen und Türkischhen Handschriften*, 3: 280.

273. Muḥammed bin Maḥāsin el-Enṣārī, *Tuḥfat al-Zamān ilā al-Malik al-Muẓaffar Sulaymān* (MS ÖNB, A. F. 357).

274. Enṣārī, *Tuḥfat al-Zamān*, 23a.

275. Inalcık, "Islamization of Ottoman Laws on Land and Land Tax."

276. Ibn Nujaym, *Rasāʾil Ibn Nujaym al-Iqtiṣādiyya*, eds. Muḥammed Aḥmed Sirāj and ʿAlī Jumʿa Muḥammed (Cairo: Dār al-Salām, 1998).

277. Ahmet Akgündüz, "Dede Cöngi," *TDVIA*, vol. 9 (1994), 76–77.

278. Petra Kappert, *Die osmanischen Prinzen und ihre Residenz Amasya im 15. und 16. Jahrhundert*, 111; for an analysis and translation of this work, see Akgündüz, *Osmanlı Kanunnâmeleri*, 4: 213–254.

279. Dede Efendī, *al-Siyāsa al-Sharʿiyya*, ed. Fuʿād ʿAbd al-Munʿim (Iskandariyya, [n.d.]).

280. Imber, *Ebu's-suʿud: The Islamic Legal Tradition* (Stanford, CA: Stanford University Press, 1997), 115–269; Inalcık, "Islamization of Ottoman Laws on Land and Land Tax."

281. For Ottoman Ḥanafism, see Guy Burak, *The Second Formation of Islamic Law: The Ḥanafī School in Early Modern Ottoman Empire* (Cambridge: Cambridge University Press, 2015).

282. Köksal, *Fıkıh ve Siyaset*, 197–200.

283. Dede Efendī, *al-Siyāsa al-Sharʿiyya*, 75–76.

284. Ibid., 84.

285. For more information on this topic, see Mehmet Erdoğan, *İslâm Hukukunda Ahkâmın Değişmesi* (Istanbul: Marmara Üniversitesi İlahiyat Fakültesi Vakfı Yayınları, 1994).

286. Dede Efendī, *al-Siyāsa al-Sharʿiyya*, 85–86.

287. *Maṣlaḥat* was a key concept by which Dede Cöngi's contemporary Sheikh ul Islam Ebussuud justified the permissibility of cash foundations. See Jon E. Mandaville, "Usurious Piety: The Cash Waqf Controversy in the Ottoman Empire."

288. For a bibliographical analysis of his works, see Nihal Atsız, *İstanbul Kütüphanelerine Göre Birgili Mehmet Efendi (929–981/1523–1573) Bibliyografyası* (Istanbul: Milli Eğitim Basımevi, 1966).

289. Atâî, *Hada'iku'l-Hakaik*, 179–181.

290. Ahmet Turan Arslan, *İmam Birgivî: Hayatı, Eserleri ve Arapça Tedrisatındaki Yeri* (Istanbul: Seha Neşriyat, 1992), 66.

291. Ibn Taymiyya's name does not appear in Birgivi's works although he quoted from the works of Ibn Qayyim, Ibn Taymiyya's most prolific student. See Emrullah Yüksel, "Mehmet Birgivî (929–981/1523–1573)," *Atatürk Üniversitesi İslami İlimler Fakültesi Dergisi* 2 (1977): 175–185.

292. ʿAlī bin Bālī, *al-ʿIqd al-Manẓūm*, 436.

293. Arslan lists some thirty-five commentaries and translations of this work. See Arslan, *İmam Birgivî*, 115–125.

294. The only possible exception to this is a political treatise attributed to Birgivi, which he dedicated to Selim II. E. Edgar Blochet, *Catalogue de la Collection de Manuscrits Orientaux, Arabes, Persans et Turcs Formée par M. Charles Schefer et Acquise par l'État* (Paris: E. Leroux, 1900), no. 1133/1.

295. Arslan, *İmam Birgivî*, 35–38.

296. Ibid., 51.

297. For Birgivi's frank criticism of malpractices in state and society, including those perpetrated by his friend Ataullah Efendi, see Arslan "İmam Birgivî'nin (929–981H/1523–1573) Bir Mektubu," *İlmi Araştırmalar* 5 (1997): 61–74.

298. Arslan, *İmam Birgivî*, 35; this line of thinking is usually expressed in the *Ḥisba* (inspection) literature, a field of Islamic law that allows believers to prevent a wrong when it is witnessed. A similar section, regarding iniquities in mosques, markets, streets, baths, and feasts is given by Ghazali in his *Kimyā-i Saʿādat*, a work Birgivi admired. See Ghazālī, *Kīmyā-i Saʿādat*, ed. Muḥammed ʿAbbāsī (Tehran: Ṭulūʿ va Zarrīn, 1361 [1982 or 1983]), 389–392.

299. Arslan, *İmam Birgivî*, 35.

300. Birgivī Meḥmed, *Dhukhr al-Mulūk*, Süleymaniye Kütüphanesi, Esad Efendi 615/8, 99b.

301. Khayrabaytī, *al-Durra al-Gharrā*, 248–251.

302. For such attempts of reconcilitation, see Inalcik, "Islamization of Ottoman Laws on Land and Land Tax."

303. Ṭāşköprīzāde, *Risāla fī Bayān Asrār al-Khilāfa al-Insāniyya wa al-Salṭana al-Maʿnawiyya* (MS SK, Carullah 2098; BDK, Veliyyuddin 3275).

304. See Ibn ʿArabī, *al-Tadbīrāt al-Ilāhiyya fī Iṣlāḥ al-Mamlaka al-Insāniyya*, ed. Ḥasan Āṣī. Beirut: Muʿassasa Baḥsūn, 1993.

305. Hamadānī, *Ẕakhīrat al-Mulūk*, 289.

306. İsen, *Künhü'l-Ahbār'ın Tezkire Kısmı*, 241–242.

307. Beyâni, *Tezkiretü'ş-Şuarâ*, 162; Atâyî, *Hadaiku'l-Hakaik*, 328.

308. Kınalı-zade Hasan Çelebi, *Tezkiretü'ş-Şuarâ*, 2: 600.

309. Atâî, *Hadaiku'l-Hakaik*, 328.

310. Beyâni, *Tezkiretü'ş-Şuarâ*, 162.

311. Kınalı-zade Hasan, *Tezkiretü'ş-Şuarâ*, 2: 600.

312. Ismāʿīl Bāshā Bābānī, *Hadiyyat al-ʿĀrifīn Asmā al-Muʾallifīn wa Āthar al-Muṣannifīn* (Istanbul: Milli Eğitim Basımevi, 1951–55), 2: 466.

313. For a more detailed discussion of Şirvani and his writings, see Yılmaz, "The Sunni Exodus from Iran and the Rise of Anti-Safavid Propaganda in the Ottoman Empire: The Messianic Call of Hüseyin b. Abdullah el-Shirvānī," in *Osmanlı'da İlim ve Fikir Dünyası: İstanbul'un Fethinden Süleymaniye Medreselerinin Kuruluşuna Kadar*, eds. Ömer Mahir Alper and Mustakim Arıcı (Istanbul: Klasik, 2015), 299–309.

314. Şirvānī, *Aḥkām al-Dīniyya* (MS SK, Reisülküttab 1207).

315. Şirvānī, *Risāle fi't-Taṣavvuf* (MS Milli Kütüphane, Cebeci 2705).

316. Şirvānī, *al-Risāla al-ʿAdliyya al-Sulaymāniyya* (MS TSMK, Revan 1035).

317. Şirvānī, *al-Risāla al-ʿAdliyya al-Sulaymāniyya*, 55a. Although the work does not seem to have caught the attention of Ottoman literati in general, it probably reached its intended audience, the sultan himself, as the only copy of the work, written in fine *taʿlīḳ* script, was preserved in the Palace library. The manuscript does not bear the name of its author and was catalogued as anonymous. However, in two other texts Şirvani explicitly refers to this treatise as his own. See *Aḥkām al-Dīniyya*, 99a; *Risāle fi't-Taṣavvuf*, 5a.

318. Dizdār Muṣṭafā b. ʿAbdullāh, *Sulūk al-Mulūk* (MS TMSK, Ahmed 1605). The autograph preserved in Topkapı Palace was written in a fine script and did not seem to have circulated beyond the personal library of the sultan.

319. Dizdār, *Sulūk al-Mulūk*, 1b.

320. Dizdar's ideas on the divine dispensation of rulership, for example, are exactly same as those of Razi's. See Dizdār, *Sulūk al-Mulūk*, 2a; Najm al-Dīn Rāzī, *Mirṣād al-ʿIbād*, 411–412. For an English translation, see Razi, *The Path of God's Bondsmen*, 395.

321. See, for example, ʿAlāyī, *Düstūrü'l-Vüzerā*, 16, 22.

322. As a typical example of such a literary style Hadidi wrote his history of the Ottoman dynasty in plain Turkish while using Persian in the section headings. See, for example, Hadîdî, *Tevârih-i Âl-i Osman (1299–1523)*, ed. Necdet Öztürk (İstanbul: Edebiyat Fakültesi Basımevi, 1991).

Chapter 2: The Caliphate Mystified

1. Dāvūd-i Ḳayserī, *al-Itḥāf al-Sulaymānī fī al-ʿAhd al-Urkhānī* (MS SK, Ali Emiri Arabi 2173), 1a–3a. The manuscript is not dated and the author's name appears only on the cover page which confounds the authorship of the work. I thank İhsan Fazlıoğlu, an expert on Davud-i Kayseri, for confirming Davud-i Kayseri's authorship of this work based on his comparison of the text to other works of the author.

2. There are a few other undated texts that briefly mention Süleyman Paşa's name in dedicatory notes. See Ahmed Ateş, "Burdur-Antalya ve Havalisi Kütüphanelerinde Bulunan Türkçe, Arapça ve Farsça Bazı Mühim Eserler," *Türk Dili ve Edebiyatı Dergisi*

2 (1948): 171–191; M. Esad Coşan, "XV. Asır Türk Yazarlarından Muslihu'd-din, Hamid-Oğulları ve Hızır Bey," *Vakıflar Dergisi*, 13 (1981): 101–112; İbrahim Artuk, "Early Ottoman Coins of Orhan Gāzī as Confirmation of His Sovereignty," in *Near Eastern Numismatics Iconography, Epigraphy and History: Studies in Honor of George C. Miles*, ed. Dickran K. Kouymjian (Beirut: American University of Beirut, 1974), 457–463.

3. Uzunçarşılı, "Orhan Gazi'nin, Vefat Eden Oğlu Süleyman Paşa İçin Tertip Ettirdiği Vakfiyenin Aslı," *TTK Belleten* 27 (1963): 437–451.

4. Fazlıoğlu, "Osmanlı Coğrafyasında İlmi Hayatın Teşekkülü ve Davud el-Kayseri," in *International Symposium on Islamic Thought in Anatolia in the XIIIth and XIVth Centuries and Davud al-Qaysari*, ed. Turan Koç (Kayseri: Büyükşehir Belediyesi, 1998), 25–43.

5. Fazlıoğlu, "Davud Kayserî," *Yaşamları ve Yapıtlarıyla Osmanlılar Ansiklopedisi*, vol. 1 (Istanbul: Yapı Kredi Yayınları, 1999), 370–371.

6. For Farabi's ideas on happiness, see Miriam Galston, "The Theoretical and Practical Dimensions of Happiness as Portrayed in the Political Treatises of al-Fārābī," in *The Political Aspects of Islamic Philosophy: Essays in Honor of Muhsin S. Mahdi*, ed. Charles E. Butterworth (Cambridge, Mass.: Harvard Middle Eastern Monographs, 1992), 95–151.

7. Paul Wittek, *The Rise of the Ottoman Empire* (London: The Royal Asiatic Society, 1938).

8. Heath W. Lowry, *The Nature of Early Ottoman Society* (Albany: State University of New York, 2003).

9. Linda T. Darling, "Reformulating the Gazi Narrative: When was the Ottoman State a Gazi State?," *Turcica* 43 (2011): 13–53.

10. Kafadar, *Between Two Worlds*, 58.

11. For the extensive use of the term by various dynasties, including the contemporaries of the Ottomans, see Clifford E. Bosworth, *The New Islamic Dynasties: A Chronological and Geneological Manual* (Edinburgh: Edinburgh University Press, 1996).

12. Wilferd Madelung, "The Assumption of the Title Shāhānshāh by the Būyids and "The Reign of the Daylam (Dawlat Al-Daylam)"," *Journal of Near Eastern Studies* 28 (1969): 84–108, 168–183.

13. Kathryn Babayan, *Mystics, Monarchs, and Messiahs: Cultural Landscapes of Early Modern Iran* (Cambridge, Mass.: Harvard Middle Eastern Monographs, 2002), 71.

14. Amir Hasan Siddiqi, *Caliphate and Sultanate in Medieval Persia* (Karachi: Jamiyat-ul-Falah Publications, 1942), 106–156.

15. Madelung, "The Assumption of the Title Shāhānshāh by the Būyids."

16. Arjomand, *The Shadow of God and the Hidden Imam* (Chicago: The University of Chicago Press, 1984), 98–99.

17. Franz Rosenthal, "Dawla," *EI*[2].

18. For Dinawari's world history, see Hayrettin Yücesoy, "Ancient Imperial Heritage and Islamic Universal Historiography: al-Dīnawarī's Secular Perspective," *Journal of Global History* 2 (2007): 135–155.

19. Casim Avcı, "Hilâfet," *TDVIA*, vol. 17 (1998), 539–546.

20. Abdülkerim Özaydın, "Büyük Selçuklularda Ünvan ve Lakaplar," in *Prof. Dr. Işın Demirkent Anısına*, ed. Abdülkerim Özaydın (Istanbul: Globus Dünya Basımevi, 2008), 421–433.

21. Abī al-Ḥasan ʿAlī b. Muḥammed al-Māwardī, *al-Aḥkām al-Sulṭāniyya wa al-Wilāyāt al-Dīniyya*, ed. Aḥmed Mubārak al-Baghdādī (Kuwait: Maktaba Dār Ibn Ḳutayba, 1989), 30–39.

22. Abū Ḥāmid Gazālī, *Naṣīḥat al-Mulūk*.

23. For Juwaini's accommodationist formulation, see Wael Hallaq, "Caliphs, Jurists and the Seljūqs in the Political Thought of Juwaynī," *The Muslim World* 74 (1984): 27–41.

24. Heath Lowry, *The Nature of the Early Ottoman State*, 35–36. My translation relies on that of Lowry but revises it to reflect a slightly different reading.

25. İsmail Hakkı Uzunçarşılıoğlu, *Kitabeler* (Istanbul: Devlet Matbaası, 1929), 109–110.

26. Shams al-Dīn Aḥmed al-Aflākī al-ʿĀrifī, *Manāqib al-ʿĀrifīn*, 2nd ed., ed. Tahsin Yazıcı, vol. 2 (Ankara: Türk Tarih Kurumu, 1976–80), 948. For English translation, see Shams al-Dīn Aḥmad-e Aflākī, *The Feats of the Knowers of God*, transl. John O'Kane (Leiden: Brill, 2002), 663.

27. Uzunçarşılıoğlu, *Kitabeler*, 155; Uzunçarşılı lists the Candarlıs among the users of this title but does not cite his source. See Uzunçarşılı, *Osmanlı Devleti Teşkilatına Medhal*, 2nd ed. (Ankara: Türk Tarih Kurumu, 1970), 134.

28. Among the scholars who accept the inscription authentic there is no agreement whether the particular title under consideration reads *shujāʿ al-dawla* or *shujāʿ al-dīn*: See Wittek, *The Rise of the Ottoman Empire*, 53; Lowry, *The Nature of the Early Ottoman State*, 36; Artuk, "Early Ottoman Coins of Orhan Gāzī as Confirmation of His Sovereignty;" Ekrem H. Ayverdi, "Orhan Gazî Devrinde Mi'mârî," *Yıllık Araştırmalar Dergisi* 1 (1957): 115–199.

29. Uzunçarşılıoğlu, *Kitabeler*, 112.

30. A Qur'anic commentary was dedicated to İshak Beg of İnançoğulları before 1361, by praising him as *jalāl al-dawla wa al-dīn*. See Ahmed Ateş, "Burdur-Antalya ve Havalisi Kütüphanelerinde Bulunan Türkçe, Arapça ve Farsça Bazı Mühim Eserler;" Dündar Beg of Hamidoğulları, Mehmed Beg's neighbor, was praised on the inscription of a public bath built in 1307 as *falak al-dawla*. See Uzunçarşılı, *Osmanlı Devleti Teşkilatına Medhal*, 134. A certain Muslihuddin dedicated his short treatise to Hızır Beg of Hamidoğulları, whom he addressed as *badr al-dawla*. See Coşan, "XV. Asır Türk Yazarlarından Muslihu'd-din, Hamid-Oğulları ve Hızır Bey."

31. Even in the case of two Orhans who displayed their names with this title on their own monuments, the general pattern since the Buyid times is still not broken. A ruler's identification of himself with his own *dawla* was not only unconventional but also looks rhetorically awkward. However, we cannot rule out the possibility that some of these western Anatolian principalities, in pursuit to register the Seljuk legacy to their name and reestablish the broken order in the land of the Rum under their leadership, self-referenced to their own turn, meaning the dynasty to which they belong rather than their individual self. Given that these Turkoman principalities considered authority to be the collective property of the ruling family rectifies the awkwardness of self-referencing in *dawla*-identification. The Moroccan traveler Ibn Battuta reports having attended during his visit in Kastamonu a reception with the dignitaries of Süleyman Paşa (*arbāb dawlatihi*), a lofty phrase that came into circulation during the Abbasid times but became more popular in later Ottoman usage. However, Ibn Battuta was a learned Arab who filtered his perceptions to a particular mindset and translated them to be intelligible for his own audience, so the term may be his own rather than the Candarlıs. See Ibn Batuta, *Riḥla Ibn Baṭūṭa: Tuḥfat al-Nuẓẓār fī Gharāʾib al-Amṣār wa ʿAjāʾib al-Asfār*, ed. Muḥammed ʿAbd al-Munʿim al-ʿAryān (Beirut: Dār al-Iḥyā al-ʿUlūm, 1987), 324.

32. A. C. S. Peacock, "Seljuq Legitimacy in Islamic History," in *Christian Lange, and Songül Mecit, Seljuqs: Politics, Society and Culture* (Edinburgh: Edinburgh University Press, 2011), 79–95.

33. Claude Cahen, *The Formation of Turkey: The Seljukid Sultanate of Rūm: Eleventh to Fourteenth Centuries*, transl. and ed. Peter M. Holt (Harlow, England: Longman, 2001), 211–236.

34. Halil İnalcık, "Osman Gazi'nin İznik (Nicea) Kuşatması ve Bafeus Savaşı," in *Söğut'ten İstanbul'a: Osmanlı Devleti'nin Kuruluşu Üzerine Tartışmalar*, eds. Oktay Özel and Mehmet Öz (Istanbul: İmge Kitabevi, 2000), 301–337.

35. Ḥusayn ibn Muḥammed Diyārbakrī, *Tārīkh al-Khamīs fī Aḥwāl Anfas Nafīs*, vol. 2 (Cairo: al-Maṭbaʿa al-Wahbīya, 1866), 385.

36. For Mamluk coins, see Elizabeth Puin, "Silver Coins of the Mamluk Sultan Qalāwūn (678–689/1279–1280) from the Mints of Cairo, Damascus, Ḥamāh, and al-Marqab," *Mamluk Studies Review* 4 (2000): 75–129.

37. Among many, Eflaki praised *Shujāʿ al-dawla* Orhan Beg of Menteşe as Arif Çelebi's disciple. It is not improbable to think that the *dawla*-titles of Mevlevi-affiliated rulers may refer to the Mongol reign. See Aflākī, *The Feats of the Knowers of God*, 595.

38. The dates printed on the coins are H. 624, 627, and 629, which squarely align with the reigns of al-Mustansir and Alaeddin, which makes them off-dated by a full century. Numismatists, in consensus, attributed this oddity to a manufacturing error, as the 627 coin bears a sign of number three, which indicates that it was minted in the third year of the ruler's accession. However, the printed dates are more likely to be intentional to reflect the historicity of the title. See İbrahim Artuk, "Early Ottoman Coins of Orhan Ghazi as Confirmation of His Sovereignty;" Atom Damalı, *History of Ottoman Coins*, vol. I (Istanbul: Nilüfer Eğitim, Kültür ve Çevre Vakfı, 2010), 108–115.

39. Cengiz Babacan, "Orhan Gazi'nin Abbasi Halifesi al-Mustansir'i Anan Gümüş Sikkeleri ve Bunların Tarih Taşıyan Üç Örneği," *Türk Nümismatik Derneği Bülteni: Sevgi Gönül Hatıra Sayısı* 96 (2005): 96–99.

40. For an analysis of early Ottoman coinage and sovereignty, see Rudi Paul Lindner, *Explorations in Ottoman Prehistory* (Ann Arbor: University of Michigan Press, 2007), 81–101.

41. Remler, Philip N., "Ottoman, Isfendiyarid, and Eretnid Coinage: A Currency Community in Fourteenth Century Anatolia," *American Numismatic Society Museum Notes* 25 (1980): 167–188, pl. 18–20.

42. Elizabeth A. Zachariadou, "The Emirate of Karasi and That of the Ottomans: Two Rival States," in *The Ottoman Emirate (1300–1389)*, ed. Elizabeth Zachariadou (Rethymnon: Crete University Press, 1993), 225–236; Ibn Battuta who visited the area in 1333 found this title noteworthy and defined it as the equivalent of sultan: Ibn Baṭūṭa, *Riḥla Ibn Baṭūṭa*, 313–314.

43. Ibn Battuta, *Travels in Asia and Africa, 1325–1354*, transl. H. A. R. Gibb (London: Routledge and K. Paul, 1957), 136: Ibn Baṭūṭa, *Riḥla Ibn Baṭūṭa*, 315–316.

44. Ayverdi, "Orhan Gazî Devrinde Mi'mârî."

45. Ḥācī Pāşā, *Shifā al-Aqsām wa Dawā al-Ālām fī Ṭibb* (MS SK, Ayasofya 3668), 1b–2a; Uzunçarşılıoğlu, *Kitabeler*, 134. I thank Sara Nur Yıldız for her generosity in sharing Hacı Paşa's text with me. For a detailed analysis of the author, his works, and impact, see Sara Nur Yıldız, "From Cairo to Ayasoluk: Hacı Paşa and the Transmission of Islamic Learning to Western Anatolia in the Late Fourteenth Century," *Journal of Islamic Studies* 25 (2014): 263–297.

46. Baberti's and Tarsusi's Hanafi advocacy look very similar. Hacı Paşa and Tarsusi may have been part of the same Hanafi circle extending from Egypt to Persia and including such high-profile jurists as Molla Fenari, Jurjani, and Bedreddin. For Baberti and Hacı Paşa, see Cemil Akpınar, "Hacı Paşa," *TDVIA*, vol. 14 (1996), 492–496.

47. Baki Tezcan, "Hanafism and the Turks in al-Ṭarasūsī's Gift for the Turks (1352)," *Mamluk Studies Review* 15 (2011): 67–86.

48. Mawardī, *al-Aḥkām al-Sulṭāniyya wa al-Wilāyāt al-Dīniyya*, 30–39.

49. Lambton, *State and Government in Medieval Islam*, 143–151.

50. Modern studies commonly point out that the Ottomans adopted the title caliph from Murad I (r. 1362–1389) onwards. The sole source of this erroneous attribution is Arnold's 1924 work on the caliphate. Arnold's sole evidence come from a compilation of chancery documents by a sixteenth-century Ottoman bureaucrat, Feridun Beg, who is now

established to have heavily edited early documents and projected sultanic titles of his time to early rulers. Sir Thomas W. Arnold, *The Caliphate* (London: Oxford University Press, 1924), 129–138; Mükrimin Halil Yinanç, "Feridun Bey Münşeatı," *Türk Tarih Encümeni Mecmuası* 14 (1924): 161–168.

51. For the origins and early Islamic uses of the term, see Patricia Crone and Martin Hinds, *God's Caliph: Religious Authority in the first Centuries of Islam* (Cambridge: Cambridge University Press, 1986), 4–23; Han Hsien Liew, "The Caliphate of Adam: Theological Politics of the Qur'ānic Term *Ḫalīfa*," *Arabica* 63 (2016): 1–29.

52. *Répertoire chronologique d'épigraphie arabe* (Cairo: l'Institut français d'archéologie orientale, 1931–), vol. 8, 117.

53. The use of the title for outstanding members of the learned hierarchy in the Shiite tradition was not common until the latter half of the twentieth century. The first known Shiite scholar with that appellation was Allama al-Hilli (d. 1325) but the title was accorded posthumously by al-Miqdad al-Suyuri (d. 1423); See Hamid Algar, "Āyatallāh," http://www.iranicaonline.org/articles/ayatallah (Accessed 1 October 2016); Mehdî Muhakkık, "Âyetullah," *TDVIA*, vol. 4 (1991), 244.

54. Susan Yalman notes that Kılıcarslan II (r. 1156–1192) designated himself as *maẓhar-i kalimat Allāh* (manifestation of God's word) on inscriptions and argues that this novelty in royal self-image is the outcome of Suhrawardi's illuminationist philosophy gaining acceptance in Seljuk courts. However, the orthography of inscriptions yields two possible readings of the critical term in the title which could be either *maẓhar* or *muẓhir*. A contextual and rhetorical examination of these inscriptions as well as other contemporary examples leads me to conclude that reading the phrase as *muẓhir kalimat Allāh* (the one who makes God's word manifest) would be more accurate. While the first reading portrays the ruler as a manifestation of the divine in the Suhrawardian sense, the latter only accords him an instrumental role in the service of making God's word manifest. See Susan Yalman, "ʿAla al-Din Kayqubad Illuminated: A Rum Seljuq Sultan as Cosmic Ruler," *Muqarnas* 29 (2012): 151–186. For the text, see Friedrich Sarre, *Konya Köşkü*, trans. Şahabeddin Uzluk (Ankara: Türk Tarih Kurumu, 1967), 85.

55. Hossein Ziai, "The Source and Nature of Authority: A Study of al-Suhrawardī's Illuminationist Political Doctrine," in *The Political Aspects of Islamic Philosophy: Essays in Honor of Muhsin S. Mahdi*, 304–344.

56. İlhan Kutluer, "Sühreverdî," *TDVIA*, vol. 38 (2010), 36–40.

57. John Walbridge, *The Leaven of the Ancients: Suhrawardī and the Heritage of the Greeks* (Albany: State University of New York Press, 2000), 205.

58. Suhrawardī, *The Philosophy of Illumination*, 3.

59. Walbridge, *The Leaven of the Ancients*, 204.

60. Ziai, "The Source and Nature of Authority."

61. İhsan Fazlıoğlu, "Osmanlı Coğrafyasında İlmi Hayatın Teşekkülü ve Davud el-Kayseri."

62. Kafadar, *Between Two Worlds*, 61.

63. See, for example, Karamustafa, "Origins of Anatolian Sufism," in *Sufism and Sufis in Ottoman Society*, ed. A. Yaşar Ocak (Ankara: Turkish Historical Society, 2005), 67–95.

64. For the origins, spiritual genealogies, and later trajectory of Vefais, to which Bektaşis belonged, see Ayfer Karakaya-Stump, "The Vefā'iyye, the Bektashiyye and Genealogies of "Heterodox Islam in Anatolia: Rethinking the Köprülü Paradigm," *Turcica* 44 (2012–2013): 279–300.

65. Judith Pfeiffer, "Mevlevi-Bektashi Rivalries and the Islamisation of the Public Space in Late Seljuk Anatolia," in *Islam and Christianity in Medieval Anatolia*, eds. A.C.S. Peacock, B. de Nicola and S. Nur Yıldız (Farnham: Ashgate, 2015): 311–327.

66. Elvan Çelebi, *Menâkıbu'l-Kudsiyye fî Menâsıbi'l-Ünsiyye*, eds. İsmail E. Erünsal and A. Yaşar Ocak (Ankara: Türk Tarih Kurumu, 1995), 31; Aflākī, *Manāqib al-ʿĀrifīn*, 30–31, 44–46.

67. For an analysis of contemporary records on Baba Ilyas, see Ocak, *XIII. Yüzyılda Anadolu'da Baba Resûl (Babaîler) İsyanı ve Anadolu'nun İslâmlaşması Tarihindeki Yeri* (Istanbul: Dergâh Yayınları, 1980) 104–106, 118–119; Claude Cahen, "Bābā Ishaq, Bābā Ilyas, Hadjdji Bektash et quelques autres," *Turcica* 1 (1969), 53–64.

68. Baba Ilyas' chief commander in the revolt, Baba Ishak, joined from Damascus where the memory of Suhrawardi must still have been fresh.

69. Elvan Çelebi, *Menâkıbu'l-Kudsiyye fî Menâsıbi'l-Ünsiyye*, 43.

70. Ibid., 18.

71. Ibid., 31.

72. Ibid., 26.

73. Ibid., 45–46.

74. Ibid., 157–158.

75. Ibid., 72–87.

76. Aflākī, *Manāqib al-ʿĀrifīn*, 8–9; Aflākī, *The Feats of the Knowers of God*, 7–8.

77. Aflākī, *Manāqib al-ʿĀrifīn*, 75; Aflākī, *The Feats of the Knowers of God*, 56–57.

78. Aflākī, *Manāqib al-ʿĀrifīn*, 366; Aflākī, *The Feats of the Knowers of God*, 253.

79. For rivalries among popular Sufis, see Resul Ay, "Sufi Shaykhs and Society in Thirteenth and Fifteenth Century Anatolia: Spiritual Influence and Rivalry," *Journal of Islamic Studies*, 24 (2013): 1–24.

80. Aflākī, *Manāqib al-ʿĀrifīn*, 10; Aflākī, *The Feats of the Knowers of God*, 9.

81. Aflākī, *Manāqib al-ʿĀrifīn*, 365; Aflākī, *The Feats of the Knowers of God*, 252–253.

82. Emigrating to the Rum with forty disciples was a common topos in hagiographies of famed Sufis coming from Central Asia. But Baha Veled is distinguished from others by having jurist-consults as his disciples rather than dervishes.

83. Aflākī, *Manāqib al-ʿĀrifīn*, 13; Aflākī, *The Feats of the Knowers of God*, 11.

84. Aflākī, *Manāqib al-ʿĀrifīn*, 12–3; Aflākī, *The Feats of the Knowers of God*, 13.

85. Aflākī, *Manāqib al-ʿĀrifīn*, 21.

86. Ibid., 22.

87. Aflākī, *Manāqib al-ʿĀrifīn*, 22; Aflākī, *The Feats of the Knowers of God*, 18.

88. Aflākī, *Manāqib al-ʿĀrifīn*, 207; Aflākī, *The Feats of the Knowers of God*, 144–145.

89. Aflākī, *Manāqib al-ʿĀrifīn*, 30; Aflākī, *The Feats of the Knowers of God*, 23.

90. Aflākī, *Manāqib al-ʿĀrifīn*, 52; Aflākī, *The Feats of the Knowers of God*, 40.

91. Aflākī, *Manāqib al-ʿĀrifīn*, 147; Aflākī, *The Feats of the Knowers of God*, 103.

92. Aflākī, *Manāqib al-ʿĀrifīn*, 324; Aflākī, *The Feats of the Knowers of God*, 225.

93. Karamustafa, "Kaygusuz Abdal: A Medieval Turkish Saint and the Formation of Vernacular Islam in Anatolia," in *Unity in Diversity: Mysticism, Messianism and the Construction of Religious Authority in Islam*, ed. Orkhan Mir-Kasimov (Leiden and Boston: Brill, 2014), 329–342.

94. Emecen, *İlk Osmanlılar ve Batı Anadolu Beylikler Dünyası* (Istanbul: Timaş, 2012), 195–213.

95. Uzunçarşılıoğlu, *Kitabeler*, 74; Ibn Battuta finds Mehmed Çelebi's use of the title noteworthy and gives its Arabic equivalent as *sayyidī* (my lord), Ibn Baṭūṭa, *Riḥla Ibn Baṭūṭa*, 296.

96. Aflākī, *The Feats of the Knowers of God*, 647.

97. Aflākī, *Manāqib al-ʿĀrifīn*, 947–948; Aflākī, *The Feats of the Knowers of God*, 663–664.

98. Ocak, "Türkiye Tarihinde Merkezi İktidar ve Mevleviler (XIII–XVIII. Yüzyıllar) Meselesine Bir Bakış," *Selçuk Üniversitesi Türkiyat Araştırmaları Dergisi* 2 (1996): 17–22.

99. N. Çiçek Akçıl, "Günümüze Ulaşmayan bir Tekke: Edirne'de Muradiye Mevlevihanesi," *Sanat Tarihi Yıllığı* 21 (2008): 1–21.

100. Ömer Lütfi Barkan, "İstilâ Devirlerinin Kolonizatör Türk Dervişleri ve Zâviyeler," *Vakıflar Dergisi* 2 (1974): 279–353.

101. Abdurrahman Güzel, *Abdal Mûsâ Velâyetnâmesi* (Ankara: Türk Tarih Kurumu, 1999), 149.

102. Kafadar, *Between Two Worlds*, 76.

103. Elvan Çelebi, *Menâkıbu'l-Kudsiyye fî Menâsıbi'l-Ünsiyye*, 141.

104. Aflākī, *Manāqib al-ʿĀrifīn*, 28.

105. Ahmed, *What Is Islam*, 21.

106. Elvan Çelebi, *Menâkıbu'l-Kudsiyye fî Menâsıbi'l-Ünsiyye*, xxii.

107. Veyis Değirmençay, "Sultan Veled," *TDVIA*, vol. 37 (2009), 521–522; Yazıcı, "ʿÂrif Çelebî," *TDVIA*, vol. 3 (1991), 363–364.

108. Despite later Mevlevi efforts to establish kinship between Mehmed and Rumi, the sourse and time of his *çelebi* title, if he ever adopted it, still remains in the dark. A contemporary source, however, written in 1398, refers to Mehmed's brother as "Çelebī Emīr Süleymān b. Bāyezīd." Mehmed, *Işk-nâme (İnceleme-Metin)*, ed. Sedit Yüksel (Ankara: Ankara Üniversitesi Basımevi, 1965). An anonymous short chronicle in Arabic from the mid-fifteenth century that was once owned by Bayezid II uses the *çelebi* title for Mehmed's brother Musa. See *Fütūḥāt-ı Sulṭān Meḥemmed* (MS SK, Ayasofya 3204), f. 7a.

109. Most notably, the one in Ankara which was ended by the Ottoman takeover in 1362, was often romantically referred to as an Ahi republic by modern historians. Eflaki recounts many Ahi leaders with *beg* titles for their sovereign-like rulership and also to belittle their spirituality as the Mevlevis had a troubled relationship with the Ahis. See Aflākī, *The Feats of the Knowers of God*, 668–669, 673.

110. Ahmet Kartal, "Kerâmât-ı Ahi Evran Mesnevîsi Üzerine Notlar," *Divan Edebiyatı Araştırmaları Dergisi* 2 (2009): 223–242.

111. Uzunçarşılıoğlu, *Kitabeler*, 157.

112. Murteza Bedir, "Osmanlı Tarihinin Kuruluş Asrında (1389'a kadar) İlmiye'ye Dair Bir Araştırma: İlk Fakihler," *Türk Hukuk Tarihi Araştırmaları* 1 (2006): 23–39; ʿAlāʾeddīn ʿAlī b. ʿÖmer b. ʿAlī el- Ḳarahisārī, *Rumūzü'l-Esrār Şerhu Künūzü'l-Envār* (MS Nuruosmaniye Kütüphanesi 1334), 1a–1b.

113. Lüṭfī Pāşā. *Tevārīḫ-i Āl-i ʿOsmān*, 5.

114. Âşıkpaşazâde, *Âşıkpaşazâde Tarihi*, ed. Necdet Öztürk (Istanbul: Bilge Kültür Sanat, 2013), 28–29.

115. Murphey, *Exploring Ottoman Sovereignty*, 77–82.

116. In the preface of his translation of Kaykavus b. Eskandar's *Qābūsnāma*, Şeyhoğlu describes Kaykavus with the title "commander of the faithful." See, Doğan, *Şeyhoğlu Sadrüddin'in Kabus-nâme Tercümesi* (Istanbul: Mavi Yayıncılık, 2011), 103.

117. *Répertoire chronologique d'épigraphie arabe*, vol. 10, 27.

118. Dimitris J. Kastritsis, *The Sons of Bayezid: Empire Building and Representation in the Ottoman Civil War of 1402–1413* (Leiden: Brill, 2007), 195–220.

119. Kastritsis, *The Tales of Sultan Mehmed, Son of Bayezid Khan* (Cambridge, Mass.: Sources of Oriental Languages and Literatures, 2007), 60–76.

120. Aḥmedī, *İskender—Nāme: İnceleme—Tıpkıbasım*, ed. İsmail Ünver (Ankara: Türk Dil Kurumu Yayınları, 1983), 65b–68a; For English translation, see Kemal Sılay, "Ahmedi's History of the Ottoman Dynasty," *JTS* 16 (1992): 129–200; Abdülvasi Çelebi,

Halilname (Ankara: T.C. Kültür Bakanlığı, 1996), 254–278. For English translation, see Kastritsis, *The Sons of Bayezid*, 221–232.

121. Bakır, "Yazıcızāde ʿAlī'nin Selçuḳ-Nāme İsimli Eserinin Edisyon Kritiği," 741–743.

122. In one encounter, Mehmed belittles his opponent as "the one whose *dawla* is broken" (*devleti sınmış kişi*), showing that contending hopefuls for political supremacy were deficient in charisma. In another occasion, Mehmed's chief negotiator is identified as his confidant a certain Sufi Bayezid, indicating the close partnership of the Sufi-minded in restoring political unification. Kastritsis, *The Tales of Sultan Mehmed*, 56–57; Kastritsis, *The Sons of Bayezid*, 83.

123. Abdülvasi Çelebi, *Halilname*, 255.

124. Bekir Direkci, "Cevāhirü'l-Meʿānī" (PhD diss., Selçuk University, 2010), 341.

125. Ibid., 329–331.

126. Ibid., 340–342.

127. Ocak, *Osmanlı Toplumunda Zındıklar ve Mülhidler*, 176.

128. Halil bin İsmâil bin Şeyh Bedrüddîn Mahmûd, *Sımavna Kadısıoğlu Şeyh Bedreddin Manâkıbı*, eds. Abdülbâki Gölpınarlı and İsmet Sungurbey (Istanbul: Eti Yayınevi, 1967).

129. Fatih Usluer, *Hurufilik: İlk Elden Kaynaklarla Doğuşundan İtibaren* (Istanbul: Kabalcı Yayınevi, 2014), 24–26.

130. Nihat Azamat, "Hacı Bayrâm-ı Velî," *TDVIA*, vol. 14 (1996): 442–447.

131. Öngören, "Zeyniyye," *TDVIA*, vol. 44 (2013), 367–371.

132. For a detailed survey of Murad's cultural accomplishments, see Azamat, "II. Murad Devri Kültür Hayatı" (PhD diss., Marmara University, 1996).

133. Faruk K. Timurtaş, *Şeyhî ve Husrev ü Şîrin'i* (Istanbul: Edebiyat Fakültesi Basımevi, 1980).

134. Ceyhan, *Bedr-i Dilşad'ın Murâd-Nâmesi*, 208–211.

135. Kemal Yavuz, *Muʿînî'nin Mesnevî-i Murâdiyye'si*, vol. 2 (Konya: Selçuk Üniversitesi Mevlana Araştırma ve Uygulama Merkezi Yayınları, 2007), 16–18.

136. Ferhat Kurban, "Şirvani Mahmud Sulṭāniye" (PhD diss., Marmara University, 1990), 2; Turgut Akarslan, "İbn-i Melek Muhammed bin Abdüllatif Bahrü'l-Hikem" (PhD diss., Gaziosmanpaşa University, 2010), 14.

137. Muhammed b. Mahmûd-ı Şirvânî, *Tuhfe-i Murâdî*, ed. Mustafa Argunşah (Ankara: Türk Dil Kurumu Yayınları, 1999), 70–71.

138. Qur'an 21:107; Anḳarî, *Enīsü'l-Celīs*, 62–65.

139. Gerhard Böwering, "Ensān-e Kāmel," http://www.iranicaonline.org/articles/ensan-e-kamel (Accessed 1 October 2016).

140. Anḳarî, *Enīsü'l-Celīs*, 57–58.

141. Abdullah Bağdemir, "Müzekki'n-Nüfūs" (PhD diss., Ankara University, 1997), 5; Şükrullāh, *Manhaj al-Rashād*, 83b.

142. Beyazit, "Ahmed Bîcan'ın "Müntehâ" İsimli Fusûs Tercümesi Işığında Tasavvuf Düşüncesi," (Master's thesis, Marmara University, 2008), 270.

143. Qur'an 4: 59.

144. Eşrefoğlu Rumî, *Tarikatnâme*, ed. Esra Keskinkılıç (Istanbul: Gelenek Yayıncılık, 2002), 1–2.

145. Eşrefoğlu Rumî, *Tarikatnâme*, 24.

146. Ali İhsan Yurd and Mustafa Kaçalın, *Akşemseddin: Hayatı ve Eserleri* (Istanbul: Marmara Üniversitesi İlahiyat Fakültesi Yayınları, 1994), 332–335.

147. Yurd and Kaçalın, *Akşemseddin: Hayatı ve Eserleri*, 136.

148. A. Necla Pekolcay and Abdullah Uçman, "Eşrefoğlu Rûmî," *TDVIA*, vol. 11 (1995), 480–482.

149. Bistāmī, *Tuḥfat al-Wuzārā* (MS SK, Ayasofya 2855), 26b–29a.

150. Bistāmī, *Ḥall al-Rumūz wa Kashf al-Kunūz*, 71–75.

151. Karamustafa, "Kaygusuz Abdal."

152. İnalcık, "Dervish and Sultan: An Analysis of the Otman Baba Vilāyetnāmesi," in *The Middle East and the Balkans under the Ottoman Empire: Essays on Economy and Society*, ed. Halil İnalcık (Bloomington: Indiana University Turkish Studies, 1993), 19–37.

153. Yunus Yalçın, "Türk Edebiyatında Velâyetnameler ve Otman Baba Velâyetnâmesi," (PhD diss., Erciyes University, 2008), 92.

154. Ibid., 78.

155. Ibid., 243, 273.

156. Ibid., 46–7.

157. Ibid., 146.

158. Ibid., 264–5, 273–3.

159. Dina Le Gall, A Culture of Sufism: Naqshbandīs in the Ottoman World, 1450–1700 (Albany, NY: SUNY Press, 2005), 18.

160. Ömer Okumuş, "Abdurrahman Câmî," *TDVIA*, vol. 7 (1993): 94–99.

161. Abdurrezzak Tek, *Nakşîliğin Osmanlı Topraklarına Gelişi: Molla Abdullah İlâhî* (Bursa: Emin Yayınları, 2012), 153.

162. Ibid., 498–9.

163. Ibid., 496.

164. Ibid., 493, 496.

165. Ibid., 497.

166. Ibid., 375.

167. Henry Corbin, *Creative Imagination in the Sūfism of Ibn ʿArabī* (London and New York: Routledge, 2008), 225–30.

168. Tek, *Nakşîliğin Osmanlı Topraklarına Gelişi*, 492–6.

169. ʿAbdullāh-i Ilāhī, *Kashf al-Wāridāt li-Ṭālib al-Kamālāt wa Ghāyat al-Darajāt*, ed. Aḥmed Farīd al-Mazīdī (Beirut: Kitāb Nāshirūn, 2013), 46; Ekrem Demirli, "Abdullah İlahi'nin Keşfü'l-Varidat Adlı Eserinin Tahkiki" (Master's thesis, Marmara University, 1995), 31.

170. For a discussion of his identity, see Mustafa Kara, "Molla İlâhî'ye Dair," *JOS* 7–8 (1988): 365–392.

171. For a comprehensive analysis of Ibn Arabi's concept of the caliphate, see Abul Ela Affifi, *The Mystical Philosophy of Muḥyid Dín-Ibnul ʿArabí* (Cambridge: The University Press, 1939), 66–101.

172. Mollâ Ahmed İlâhî, *Tasavvuf-nâme*, eds. Mücahit Kaçar and Ahmet Akdağ (Istanbul: Büyüyen Ay, 2015), 130.

173. Ibid., 122.

174. Ibid., 132.

175. Esra Kuru, "Şeyh Ahmed İlâhî ve Pend-Nâmesi," *Turkish Studies* 9 (2014): 771–784.

176. Firdevsî-i Rumî, *Kutb-Nâme*, eds. İbrahim Olgun and İsmet Parmaksızoğlu (Ankara: Türk Tarih Kurumu, 1980).

177. Hasan Karataş, "The Ottomanization of the Halveti Sufi Order: A Political Story Revisited," *Journal of the Ottoman and Turkish Studies Association* 1 (2014): 71–89.

178. John J. Curry, *The Transformation of Muslim Mystical Thought in the Ottoman Empire: The Rise of the Halveti Order, 1350–1650* (Edinburg: Edinburg University Press, 2010), 65–72.

179. Abdullah Türk, "Vâhidî'nin Kitâb-ı Hace-i Cihân ve Netîce-i Cân Adlı Eseri" (Master's Thesis, Atatürk University, 2009), 34.

180. Karamustafa, "Menâkıb-ı Hoca-i Cihân," *TDVIA*, vol. 29 (2004), 108–110.

181. Karakaya-Stump, "Subjects of the Sultan, Disciples of the Shah: Formation and Transformation of the Kizilbash/Alevi Communities in Ottoman Anatolia," (Phd diss., Harvard University, 2008), 117.

182. Kappert, *Geschichte Sultan Süleymān Ḳānūnīs von 1520 bis 1557*, *164b*–165a; Demirtaş, "Celâl-zâde Mustafa Çelebi, Tabakâtü'l-Memâlik ve Derecâtü'l-Mesâlik," 228–30.

183. Ocak, *Osmanlı İmparatorluğu'nda Marjinal Sûfîlik: Kalenderîler (XIV-XVII. Yüzyıllar)* (Ankara: Türk Tarih Kurumu, 1999), 96–101, 199–209.

184. Abdülbâki Gölpınarlı, *Manakıb-ı Hacı Bektâş-ı Velî: Vilâyet-Nâme* (Istanbul: İnkilâp Kitabevi, 1958), 73–77.

185. Lāmiʿī Çelebī, *Leṭāyifnāme* (MS İÜK, T 3814), 42.

Chapter 3: The Sultan and the Sultanate

1. Jahramī, *Risāla Barāya Sulṭān Selīm*, 13a.

2. For views on this question, see Lambton, *State and Government in Medieval Islam*, 17, 29, 74, 134; Rosenthal, *Political Thought in Medieval Islam* (Cambridge: Cambridge University Press, 1958), 32.

3. Musliḥuddīn Muṣṭafā Aḫterī, *Aḫterī-i Kebīr*, (Istanbul: Maṭbaʿa-i Āmire, 1892), 411.

4. For a survey of titles Ottoman rulers used, see Dariusz Kołodziejczyk "Khan, Caliph, Tsar and Imperator: the Multiple Identities of the Ottoman Sultan," in *Universal Empire: A Comparative Approach to Imperial Culture and Representation in Eurasian History*, eds. Peter F. Bang and Dariusz Kołodziejczyk (Cambridge: Cambridge University Press, 2012), 175–193.

5. For a survey of these coins, see Damalı, *Osmanlı Sikkeleri Tarihi*, vol. 1, 335–424.

6. For the conception of poleship among the Ottoman Sufi movements, see Ocak, "Kanûnî Sultan Süleyman Devrinde Osmanlı Resmî Düşüncesine Karşı Bir Tepki Hareketi: Oğlan Şeyh İsmail-i Mâşûkî," *Osmanlı Araştırmaları* 10 (1990): 49–58.

7. *Risāla fīmā Lazima ʿalā al-Mulūk* (MS SK, Esad Efendi 1845), 3.

8. Seyyid Lokman Çelebi, *Kıyâfetü'l—İnsâniyye fî Şema'ili'l—'Osmâniyye* (Ankara: Historical Research Foundation, Istanbul Research Center, 1987), 233.

9. ʿĀrifī Maʿrūf Efendī, *ʿUqūd al-Jawāhir li-Ẓakhāʾir al-Akhāʾir* (MS TSMK, Revan 415), 3a.

10. Inalcik, "Power Relations between Russia, the Crimea, and the Ottoman Empire as Reflected in Titulature," in *The Middle East and the Balkans under the Ottoman Empire*, 369–411.

11. For an exceptional kind of usage where the author refers to the Sassanid ruler Anushirvan's authority as *taḫt-ı ḫilāfet* (the seat of caliphate), see Celālzāde, *Mevāhibü'l-Ḫallāḳ* 185a/b.

12. This formulaic expression was first conceived by Tusi and reworked by Davvani before. See Ḳınalīzāde ʿAlī, *Aḫlāḳ-ı ʿAlāʾī*, 3: 75. This translation is a modified adaptation of a similar passage in *The Nasirean Ethics*. See Ṭūsī, *The Nasirean Ethics*, 192. For Davvani, see W. F. Thompson, transl., *The Practical Philosophy of the Muhammedan People* (London: Oriental Translation Fund of Great Britain and Ireland, 1839), 324.

13. Ṭūsī, *The Nasirean Ethics*, 192.

14. Lütfī Pāşā, *Khalāṣ al-Umma*, 3.

15. *Ibid.*, 6.

16. Ebū'l-Fażl Münşī, *Dustūr al-Salṭana*, 12b.

17. Dizdār, *Sulūk al-Mulūk*, 1b.

18. Enṣārī, *Tuḫfat al-Zamān*, 4a–4b.

19. See, for example, Taşköprîzâde, *Şerhu'l-Ahlâki'l-Adudiyye*, 220–221.

20. Thompson, *The Practical Philosophy of the Muhammedan People*, 365.

21. Ṭūsī, *The Nasirean Ethics*, 211–226; Richard Walzer, *Al-Farabi on the Perfect State: Abū Naṣr al-Fārābī's Mabādī Ārā Ahl al-Madīna al-Fāḍila* (Oxford: Clarendon Press, 1985), 229–259.

22. Ḳınalīzāde ʿAlī, *Aḫlāḳ-ı ʿAlāʾī*, 2: 105.

23. Fleischer, *Bureaucrat and Intellectual*, 291, n. 37; Ḳınalīzāde ʿAlī, *Aḫlāḳ-ı ʿAlāʾī*, 2: 105.

24. Ṭāşköprīzāde, *Miftāḥ al-Saʿāda* 1: 407–408.

25. Ḳınalīzāde ʿAlī, *Aḫlāḳ-ı ʿAlāʾī*, 1: 76.

26. Ibid., 2: 112.

27. For similar views, which ultimately go back to Plato for whom men were different by nature, see Hamadānī, *Ẕakhīrat al-Mulūk*, 225; see also ʿAbdurraḥmān al-Shaizarī, *al-Manhaj al-Maslūk fī Siyāsat al-Mulūk*, ed. ʿAlī ʿAbdullāh al-Mūsā (Zarqā, Jordan: Maktabat al-Manār, 1987), 163.

28. Ṭāşköprīzāde, *Asrār al-Khilāfa al-Insāniyya wa al-Salṭana al-Maʿnawiyya*, 112b; For similar views, see his *Şerhu'l-Ahlâki'l-Adudiyye*, 220–21

29. Tavakkolî, *Kanun-ı Şâhenşâhi*, 87.

30. Ḳınalīzāde ʿAlī, *Aḫlāḳ-ı ʿAlāʾī*, 3: 32.

31. Enṣārī, *Tuḫfat al-Zamān*, 5b.

32. Abul Fazl ʿAllami, *Ain i Akbari*, transl. H. Blochman (Calcutta: Asiatic Society of Bengal, 1873), vol. 1, ii.

33. Ḳınalīzāde, *Aḫlāḳ-ı ʿAlāʾī, 2: 112.*

34. Taşköprîzâde, *Şerhu'l-Ahlâki'l-Adudiyye*, 224–227.

35. Dizdār, *Sulūk al-Mulūk*, 2a–2b.

36. Dizdar seems to have adopted this idea of symbolizing God's grace with Huma from Najm al-Din Razi, who began the fifth chapter of his work on Sufism, *Sulūk al-Mulūk*, along similar lines. See Rāzī, *Mirṣād al-ʿIbād*, 411; for English, see Razi, *The Path of God's Bondmen*, 395.

37. For shadow of God, see Al-Azmeh, Aziz, *Muslim Kingship: Power and the Sacred in Muslim, Christian, and Pagan Polities* (London and New York: I. B. Tauris, 2001), 17.

38. For uses of Hümayun in Ottoman administration and its origins, see Mehmet Zeki Pakalın, "Hümâyun," in *Osmanlı Tarih Deyimleri ve Terimleri Sözlüğü* (Istanbul: Milli Eğitim Basımevi, 1983), 866–867.

39. For Huma symbolism in Ottoman poetry, see İskender Pala, *Ansiklopedik Dîvân Şiiri Sözlüğü*, 262; Ahmet Talât Onay, *Eski Türk Edebiyatında Mazmunlar* (Istanbul: Milli Eğitim Bakanlığı Yayınları, 1996), 276.

40. İbn Kemal, *Tevârih-i Âl-i Osman: I. Defter* (Ankara: Türk Tarih Kurumu, 1991), 88–92.

41. Meḥmed b. Ḥacī Ḫalīl el-Ḳonevī, *Tavārīkh-i Āl-i ʿOs̱mān* (MS Kayseri Raşit Efendi Eski Eserler Kütüphanesi, Raşid Efendi Eki 11243), 6b–7a; For Bidlīsī's account, see Vural Genç, "İdris-i Bitlisî, Heşt Bihişt, Osman Gazi Dönemi" (Master's thesis, Mimar Sinan University, 2007), 146–147.

42. Razi, *The Path of God's Bondsmen*, 395.

43. İnalcık, "Osmanlılar'da Saltanat Verâseti Usûlü ve Türk Hakimiyet Telâkkisiyle İlgisi," *Ankara Üniversitesi Siyasal Bilgiler Fakültesi Dergisi* 14 (1959): 69–94.

44. For a brief history of the islamicization of ancient theories of dynastic legitimation, see Arjomand, *The Shadow of God and the Hidden Imam*, 89–100.

45. For a discussion of Abul Fazl's legitimation of Akbar's rulership, see Abolala Soudavar, *The Aura of Kings: Legitimacy and Divine Sanction in Iranian Kingship* (Costa Mesa, CA: Mazda, 2003), 7; Ram P. Khosla, *Mughal Kingship and Nobility* (Delhi: Idarah-i Adabiyat-i Delli, 1976), 6–7.

46. Roger M. Savory, "The Emergence of the Modern Persian State under the Ṣafavids," *Iranshinasi: Journal of Iranian Studies* 2 (1971): 1–44. Savory further notes that the ancient Iranian notions of kingly glory, *kvarnah/khvaranah/farr*, were reinvested in the concept of *ẓill Allāh* during the time of the Safavids. See Savory, "The Safavid State and Polity," *Iranian Studies* 7 (1974): 179–212.

47. Lambton, "The Theory of Kingship in the *Naṣīḥat ul-Mulūk* of Ghazālī."

48. Bagley, *Ghazālī's Book of Counsel for Kings*, 73–74.

49. Ziai, "The Source and Nature of Authority."

50. For continuities between the ancient notions of divine dispensation and those of Islamic dynasties, see Arjomand, *The Shadow of God*, 89–100; Al-Azmeh, *Muslim Kingship*, 17–34.

51. Uluçay, "Yavuz Sultan Selim Nasıl Padişah Oldu (II)."

52. Celâl-zâde, *Selim-nâme*, 85.

53. Bidlîsî, *Selim Şah-nâme*, 91.

54. Uluçay, "Yavuz Sultan Selim Nasıl Padişah Oldu (I)."

55. Celâl-zâde, *Selim-nâme*, 93.

56. For the training and governorship of Ottoman princes in the provinces, see Petra Kappert, *Die osmanischen Prinzen und ihre Residenz Amasya im 15. und 16. Jahrhundert*; Uzunçarşılı, "Sancağa Çıkarılan Osmanlı Şehzadeleri," *TTK Belleten* 39 (1975): 559–696.

57. For an extensive treatment of the rivalry between the two princes, Bayezid and Selim, during the reign of Süleyman, see Turan, *Kanuni Süleyman Dönemi Taht Kavgaları.*

58. Tavakkolî, *Kanun-ı Şâhenşâhi*, 38.

59. See Lüṭfī Pāşā, *Khalāṣ al-Umma.*

60. Celâl-zâde, *Selim-nâme*, 89.

61. Tavakkolî, *Kanun-ı Şâhenşâhi*, 31.

62. For Abraham's designation as leader, see Qur'an 2: 124; for the grant of sovereignty to Abraham and David, see Qur'an 4: 54 and 2: 251.

63. Qur'an 3: 26, transl. Pickthall, M. M, *The Meaning of the Glorious Koran: An Explanatory Translation* (New York: New American Library, 1932).

64. Tavakkolî, *Kanun-ı Şâhenşâhi*, 29.

65. İbn Kemal, *Tevârih-i Âl-i Osman*, 65–66.

66. Ṭūsī, *Akhlāq-i Nāṣirī*, 351; Ṭūsī, *The Nasirean Ethics*, 227; Davvānī, *Akhlāq-i Jalālī*, 226; Thompson, *The Practical Philosophy of the Muhammedan People*, 382; Ḳınalīzāde ʿAlī, *Aḫlāḳ-ı ʿAlāʾī*, 2: 114.

67. See Ṭūsī, *The Nasirean Ethics* 226; Ṭūsī, *Akhlāq-i Nāṣirī*, 355; Thompson, *The Practical Philosophy of the Muhammedan People*, 377; Davvānī, *Akhlāq-i Jalālī*, 261; Ḳınalīzāde ʿAlī, *Aḫlāḳ-ı ʿAlāʾī*, 2: 112–114.

68. Lüṭfī Pāşā, *Khalāṣ al-Umma*, 13.

69. Ibid., 8.

70. Ibid., 9, 10, 17.

71. Lüṭfī Pāşā, *Tevārīḫ*, 4–7.

72. Imber, *Ebu's-suʿud*, 65–67.

73. Ḳınalīzāde ʿAlī, *Aḫlāḳ-ı ʿAlāʾī*, 2: 114.

74. Ibid., 3: 9.

75. Ibid., 3: 10.

76. İbn Kemal, *Tevârih-i Âl-i Osman*, 65–66.

77. Celālzāde, *Mevāhibü'l-Ḫallāḳ*, 219b.

78. Giancarlo Casale, "Tordesillas and the Ottoman Caliphate: Early Modern Frontiers and the Renaissance of an Ancient Islamic Institution," *Journal of Modern History* 19 (2015): 485–511.

79. Ibrāhīm b. Muḥammed, *Ādāb al-Khilāfa wa Asbāb al-Ḥiṣāfa* (MS TSMK, Revan 404).

80. Ibid., 18b–23b.

81. Cürcânî, *Şerhu'l-Mevâkıf*, 678–680.

82. Sinan Köseoğlu, "Hacı İlyas, "Hizânetü'l-Envâr" (PhD diss., Istanbul University, 2014), 139.

83. This definition is very similar to that of Tusi; see Ṭūsī, *The Nasirean Ethics*, 74; it also agrees with the more elaborate encyclopedic definition given by Jurjani. See Ali Ğurğānī, *Kitāb al-Taʿrīfāt* (The Book of Definitions), ed. Gustav Flügel (Beirut: Libraire du Liban, 1985), 106.

84. Ḫıżır Münşī, *Akhlāq al-Atqiyā*, 12a–b.

85. Ḳınalīzāde ʿAlī, *Aḫlāḳ-ı ʿAlāʾī*, 1: 53.

86. Tavakkolî, *Kanun-ı Şâhenşâhi*, 43.

87. Ğurğānī, *Kitāb al-Taʿrīfāt*, 106.

88. Ḫıżır Münşī, *Akhlāq al-Atqiyā*, 13a.

89. Ibid., 12a–b.

90. Ḳınalīzāde ʿAlī, *Aḫlāḳ-ı ʿAlāʾī*, 1: 20; see Ṭūsī, *The Nasirean Ethics* 76; Thompson, *The Practical Philosophy of the Muhammedan People*, 46–47.

91. Davvānī, *Akhlāq-i Jalālī*, 19–43; Thompson, *The Practical Philosophy of the Muhammedan People*, 12–51; Ṭūsī, *The Nasirean Ethics* 74–77; for a detailed analysis of Davvani's views on the mutability of human nature, see Harun Anay, "Celâlettin Devvânî: Hayatı, Eserleri, Ahlâk ve Siyaset Düşüncesi," 262–268.

92. Ḳınalīzāde ʿAlī, *Aḫlāḳ-ı ʿAlāʾī*, 1: 21–22.

93. Tavakkolî, *Kanun-ı Şâhenşâhi*, 41–42.

94. Ethics was usually referred to by ethical writers as spiritual medicine (*ṭibb-i rūḥānī*), which implies that that philosophers of ethics were spiritual doctors. Bidlīsī, however, does not include philosophers among the doctors of spirit.

95. Tavakkolî, *Kanun-ı Şâhenşâhi*, 41–42.

96. Ibid., 43.

97. Ibid., 39.

98. Ibid., 45.

99. Some pre-Ottoman ethical writers drew a sharp line between the ruler's morality and that of the general public. Among them was Jahiz (d. 868–869) who stated that "rulers' morality is not like the morality of people, and there is no common thing between the two." Samīḥ Rughaym, *Mawsūʿa Muṣṭalaḥāt al-ʿUlūm al-Ijtimāʿiyya wa al-Siyāsiyya fī al-Fikr al-ʿArabī wa al-Islāmī* (Beirut: Maktabat Lubnān Nāshirūn, 2000), 42.

100. Tavakkolî, *Kanun-ı Şâhenşâhi*, 91.

101. 'Alāyī, *Düstūrü'l-Vüzarā*, 32; Tavakkolî, *Kanun-ı Şâhenşâhi*, 74; Dizdār, *Sulūk al-Mulūk*, 4a; Ḳınalīzāde ʿAlī, *Aḫlāḳ-ı ʿAlāʾī*, 2: 112.

102. Tavakkolî, *Kanun-ı Şâhenşâhi*, 26, 74.

103. Dizdār, *Sulūk al-Mulūk*, 4a.

104. Ḳınalīzāde ʿAlī, *Aḫlāḳ-ı ʿAlāʾī*, 2: 112.

105. See Tavakkolî, *Kanun-ı Şâhenşâhi*, 26, 74; Dizdār, *Sulūk al-Mulūk*, 4a; Ḳınalīzāde ʿAlī, *Aḫlāḳ-ı ʿAlāʾī*, 2: 112.

106. See Tavakkolî, *Kanun-ı Şâhenşâhi*, 58–66; Jahramī 14a–14b; Celālzāde, *Mevāhibü'l-Ḫallāḳ*, 276; Ḫıżır Münşī, *Akhlāq al-Atqiyā*, 14a–20a; Ḳınalīzāde ʿAlī, *Aḫlāḳ-ı ʿAlāʾī*, 1: 53–75; Ṭāşköprīzāde, *Miftāḥ al-Saʿāda*, 1: 406.

107. Ibn Miskawayh, *The Refinement of Character* (Beirut: American University of Beirut, 1968), 15–26.

108. Ottoman chronicles are replete with stories of drinking rulers and other statesmen. See, for example, Lüṭfī Pāşā, *Tevāriḫ*, 45.

109. *Risālā fīmā Lazima ʿalā al-Mulūk*, 35–40.

110. Ḳınalīzāde ʿAlī, *Aḫlāḳ-ı ʿAlāʾī*, 1: 93, 2: 46

111. Tavakkolî, *Kanun-ı Şâhenşâhi*, 148–50.

112. Jahramī, *Risāla Barāya Suṭān Selīm*, 11b.

113. In contrast with this view, one anonymous author who addressed Süleyman, strongly reproved drinking of alchohol. *Risāla fīmā Lazima ʿalā al-Mulūk*, 35–40.

114. See Niẓām al-Mulk, *The Book of Government: or, Rules for Kings*, transl. Hubert Darke (London and Boston: Routledge and Kegan Paul, 1978) 122–123; Ṭūsī, *The Nasirean Ethics*, 176–178.

115. Ṭāşköprīzāde, *Asrār al-Khilāfa*, 90a–105a.

116. Celālzāde, *Mevāhibü'l-Ḫallāḳ*, 242b–243b.

117. Aḥmed b. Maḥmūd al-Jīlī, *Minhāj al-Wuzarā fī al-Naṣīḥa* (MS SK, Ayasofya 2907), 8a.

118. For a late fifteenth century exposition of this idea by one of the pioneers in Ottoman political writing, see Tursun Bey, *Târîh-i Ebü'l-Feth*, 13.

119. Mehmed Neşrî, *Kitâb-ı Cihan-Nümâ*, 2 vols., eds. Faik Reşit Unat and Mehmet Altan Köymen (Ankara: Türk Tarih Kurumu, 1949), 4–5.

120. *Risāla fīmā Lazima ʿalā al-Mulūk*, 3.

121. Dizdār, *Sulūk al-Mulūk*, 4a.

122. For similar views, see Bagley, *Ghazālī's Book of Counsel for Kings*, xliii; Bedr-i Dilşad, *Murâd-Nâme*, 1: 210.

123. Tavakkolî, *Kanun-ı Şâhenşâhi*, 15.

124. *Ibid.*, 99.

125. *Ibid.*, 32.

126. Ḫızır Münşī, *Akhlāq al-Atqiyā*, 33b.

127. Lüṭfī Pāşā, *Khalāṣ al-Umma*, 34.

128. ʿAlāyī, *Netīcetü's-Sülūk*, 92b.

Chapter 4: The Caliph and the Caliphate

1. Kemal Edib Kürkçüoğlu, "Kânunî'nin Bâlî Beğ'e Gönderdiği Hatt-ı Humâyûn," *Ankara Üniversitesi Dil Tarih Coğrafya Fakültesi Dergisi* 8 (1950): 225–231.

2. For a slightly different version of this decree recorded in a private collection to have been sent to Evrenos Beg by Murad I in 1386, see Mehmet İnbaşı, "Sultan I. Murad'ın Evrenos Bey'e Mektubu," *Atatürk Üniversitesi Türkiyat Araştırmaları Enstitüsü Dergisi* 17 (2001), 225–236. Although İnbaşı does not question the authenticity this document, its language certainly does not reflect the Turkish of 1386. Even if it is authentic, it must be rephrased and edited, if not doctored, at a later date. Updating the language of previously issued documents on reissuing was a common practice in Ottoman bureaucracy.

3. Aḫterī, *Aḫterī-i Kebīr*, 286; Mehmed b. Mustafâ el-Vânî, *Vankulu Lügati*, ed. Mustafa Koç, vol. 2 (Istanbul: Türkiye Yazma Eserler Kurumu Başkanlığı, 2014), 1491.

4. ʿAlāyī, *Düstūrü'l-Vüzerā*, 10.

5. Tavakkolî, *Kanun-ı Şâhenşâhi*, 139.

6. Ibid.

7. Ibid.

8. For Ahmed's proposal, see Uluçay, "Yavuz Sultan Selim Nasıl Padişah Oldu (II)."

9. Ahmet Mumcu, *Osmanlı Devletinde Siyaseten Katl* (Ankara: Ankara Üniversitesi Hukuk Fakültesi Yayınları, 1963), 193.

10. For the early history of ideas on partitioning or unifying the realm, see Cemal Kafadar, *Between Two Worlds*, 136–138.

11. Tursun Beg, *Târîh-i Ebü'l-Feth*, 15.

12. Qayṣarī, *Sharḥ Fuṣūṣ al-Ḥikam*, 405.

13. M. Erol Kılıç, "Ibnü'l-Arabî," *TDVIA*, vol. 20 (1999), 493–516.

14. ʿAbd al-Razzāq Kāshānī, *Iṣṭilāḥāt al-Ṣūfiyya*, ed. ʿAbd al-Khāliq Muḥammed (Cairo: Dār al-Maʿārif, 1984), 156–157.

15. Aḫterī, *Aḫterī-i Kebīr*, 333.

16. Şeyh Mekki Efendi, *İbn Arabi Müdafaası*, ed. Halil Baltacı (Istanbul: Gelenek Yayıncılık, 2004), 180.

17. Aḫterī, *Aḫterī-i Kebīr*, 333.

18. Tavakkolî, *Kanun-ı Şâhenşâhi*, 11.

19. Ibid., 15.

20. Ibid., 24.

21. Ibid.

22. Dizdār, *Sulūk al-Mulūk*, 6b.

23. Ibid., 5a.

24. For pre-Islamic origins of the term, see Al-Azmeh, *Muslim Kingship*, 17; Abolala Soudavar, *The Aura of Kings*, 45–47.

25. Lüṭfī Pāşā, *Khalāṣ al-Umma*, 29–34.

26. See, for example, Tavakkolî, *Kanun-ı Şâhenşâhi*, 133; Birgivī, *Dhukhr al-Mulūk*, 99a; Lüṭfī Pāşā, *Khalāṣ al-Umma*, 7; Enṣārī, *Tuḥfat al-Zamān*, 6b.

27. Ṭāşköprīzāde, *Asrār al-Khilāfa*, 116b; Razi and Hamadani, whose works were known to Ṭāşköprīzāde also opposed the recognition of an oppressor ruler as *ẓill Allāh*. See Lambton, "The Theory of Kingship in the *Naṣīḥat ul-Mulūk* of Ghazālī."

28. Tavakkolî, *Kanun-ı Şâhenşâhi*, 57.

29. Ibid., 58–71.

30. Aḫterī, *Aḫterī-i Kebīr*, 515.

31. Dizdār, *Sulūk al-Mulūk*, 2a.

32. Ḳınalīzāde ʿAlī, *Aḫlāḳ-ı ʿAlāʾī*, 2: 114.

33. For views on rulership and prophethood in political philosophy, see Rosenthal, *Political Thought in Medieval Islam*, 128, 140, 144; for a juristic exposition of such views, see Lambton, *State and Government in Medieval Islam*, 59.

34. Rosenthal, *Political Thought in Medieval Islam*, 217.

35. Muḥammed Ibn Muḥammed ibn Sulṭān al-Dimashqī, *Kitāb al-Jawāhir al-Muḍiyya fī Ayyām al-Dawla al-ʿUthmāniyya* (MS SBB, Spengler 198), 6b–7a.

36. Dimashqī, *Fatḥ al-Malik al-ʿAlīm al-Mannān ʿalā al-Malik al-Muẓaffar Sulaymān*, (MS SBB, Petermann I 64).

37. Ḥamawī, *al-Naṣāʾiḥ al-Muhimma li al-Mulūk wa al-Aʾimma*, 123.

38. Ḫıżır Münşī, *Akhlāq al-Atqiyā*, 27a.

39. Ṭaşköprīzade, *Asrār al-Khilāfa*, 92b.

40. Razi, *The Path of God's Bondsmen*, 399–400.

41. Dizdār, *Suluk al-Muluk*, 3b.

42. Ibid., 3a.

43. Ṭāşköprīzāde, *Miftāḥ al-Saʿāda*, 3: 449.

44. For the former meaning, see Qur'an 6: 165, 10: 14, 10: 73, 35: 39; for the latter meaning see Qur'an 2: 30, 38: 26.

45. See, for example, Tavakkolî, *Kanun-ı Şâhenşâhi*, 11; Dizdār, *Sulūk al-Mulūk*, 5a.

46. See, for example, Enṣārī, *Tuḥfat al-Zamān*, 8b; Bidlīsī 12; Dizdār, *Sulūk al-Mulūk*, 2b; Ebū'l-Fażl Münşī, *Dustūr al-Salṭana*, 12a; Ḳınalīzāde ʿAlī, *Aḫlāḳ-ı ʿAlāʾī*, 3:114.

47. Hasan Bey-zâde Ahmed Paşa, *Hasan Bey-zâde Târîhi: Tahlil-Kaynak Tenkidi*, 3 vols., ed. Şevki Nezihi Aykut (Ankara: Türk Tarih Kurumu, 2004), 36.

48. Khaled Abou El Fadl, *Rebellion and Violence in Islamic Law* (Cambridge: Cambridge University Press, 2001).

49. Şirvānī, *al-ʿAdliyya al-Sulaymāniyya*, 6b.

50. On the persecution of messianic movements and Sufi orders in the sixteenth century, see Ocak, "XVI. Yüzyıl Osmanlı Anadolu'sunda Mesiyanik Hareketlerin bir Tahlil Denemesi," *V. Milletlerarası Türkiye Sosyal ve İktisat Tarihi Kongresi: Tebliğler* (Istanbul: Türk Tarih Kurumu, 1990): 817–825.

51. Tavakkolî, *Kanun-ı Şâhenşâhi*, 11.

52. Ibid., 156.

53. Ibid., 13.

54. For views on the permissibility of using this designation, see Lambton, *State and Government in Medieval Islam*, 46, 48, 86–87, 142, and 186.

55. ʿAlāyī, *Neticetü's-Süluk*, 87b.

56. Enṣārī *Tuḥfat al-Zamān*, 5a.

57. See Madelung, *The Succession to Muhammad: A Study of the Early Caliphate* (Cambridge: Cambridge University Press, 1997), 78–140; Crone and Hinds, *God's Caliph*, 19–22.

58. For the Abbasid use of this title, see Farooq Omar, "Min Alqāb al-Khulafā al ʿAbbāsiyyīn: Khalīfat Allāh wa Ẓill Allāh," *Majallat al-Jāmiʿa al-Muṣtanṣiriyya* 2 (1971): 323–338.

59. Rosenthal, *Political Thought in Medieval Islam*, 37.

60. Lambton, *State and Government in Medieval Islam*, 117; Ṭūsī, *The Nasirean Ethics*, 9; Rāzī, *Mirṣād al-ʿIbād*, 59.

61. For views on investiture, see Rosenthal, *Political Thought in Medieval Islam*, 21–62.

62. One of the earliest and most authoritative accounts on saintly hierarchy forming the government of the whole universe was that of al-Hujwiri (d. 1072 or 1077): ". . . those who have power to loose and to bind (*ahl al-ḥāl wa al-ʿaqd*) and are officers to the Divine court there are three hundred, called *Akhyār,* and four, called *Awtād,* and three, called *Nuqabā,* and one, called *Quṭb* or *Ghawth.* All these know one another and cannot act save by mutual consent." See al-Hujwiri, *The Kashf al-Mahjūb*, 214.

63. Şirvānī, *al-ʿAdliyya al-Sulaymāniyya*, 6b.

64. Şirvānī, *al-ʿAdliyya al-Sulaymāniyya*, 52a–54b; Dizdār, *Sulūk al-Mulūk*, 7a.

65. Okiç, "Quelques documents inédits concernant les Hamzawites," in *Proceedings of the Twenty-Second Congress of Orientalists, Held in Istanbul, September 15th to 22nd,1951*, ed. Zeki Velidi Togan, vol. 2 (Istanbul: Osman Yalçın Matbaası, 1957), 279–286; Ocak, *Osmanlı Toplumunda Zındıklar ve Mülhidler*, 290–304.

66. Among the diverse expositions of the cosmic government of the pole there was a strong tendency to express its structure with reference to worldly government. Davud-i Kayseri, for example, in his treatise *al-Tawhīd wa al-Nubuwwa* equated the *imāmayn*, the two assistants of the pole in government, to the viziers of a sultan. See Dāvūd al-Qayṣarī, *Rasāʾil-i Qayṣarī bā Ḥavāshī-i Muḥammed Rižā Qumshāhī*, ed. Sayyed Jalā al-Dīn Ashtiyānī (Tehran: Mu'assasa-i Ḥikmat va Falsafa-i Īrān, 1381 [2002 or 2003]), 27.

67. Dizdār, *Sulūk al-Mulūk*, 7a.

68. For an overview of Ibn 'Arabi on poleship and the caliphate, see Michel Chodkiewicz, "The Esoteric Foundations of Political Legitimacy in Ibn 'Arabi," in *Muhyiddin Ibn 'Arabi: A Commemorative Volume*, eds. Stephen Histenstein and Michael Tierman (Shaftesbury, Dorset; Rockport, MA; Brisbane, Queensland: Element, 1993), 190–198.

69. Chodkiewicz, "The Esoteric Foundations."

70. For Ibn Arabi's influence in Ottoman lands, see Öngören, *Osmanlılar'da Tasavvuf*, 384–392; William C. Chittick, "The School of Ibn 'Arabī," in *History of Islamic Philosophy*, 2 vols., eds. Seyyed Hossein Nasr and Oliver Leaman (London and New York: Routledge, 1996), 510–527.

71. Like many other Sufi groups, *abdals* had a history of uneven relationships with the Ottoman authority, ranging from open rebellions to alliances in campaigns. For a brief history of *abdals* in Ottoman society with relation to other marginal Sufi groups, see Karamustafa, *God's Unruly Friends: Dervish Groups in the Islamic Later Middle Period 1200–1550* (Salt Lake City: University of Utah Press, 1994), 70–78; for an overview of *abdals*, see Mehmed Fuad Köprülü, "Abdal," *Türk Halk Edebiyatı Ansiklopedisi* (Istanbul: Türkiyat Enstitüsü Yayınları, 1935), vol. 1, 27–56; Süleyman Uludağ, "Abdal," *TDVIA*, vol. 1 (1988), 59–61.

72. İbn Kemal, *Tevârih-i Âl-i Osman*, 88–92.

73. Ahmet Ögke, "Bir Tasavvuf Terimi Olarak Ricâlü'l-Gayb–İbn Arabî'nin Görüşleri," *Tasavvuf* 5 (2001): 161–201.

74. Ahmet Ögke, *Ahmed Şemseddîn-i Marmaravî: Hayatı, Eserleri, Görüşleri* (Istanbul: İnsan Yayınları, 2001), 570–585.

75. For his life and place in Ottoman Sufism, see Ögke, *Ahmed Şemseddîn-i Marmaravî*, 36–63.

76. In his longer treatise he identifies *quṭb* as *ghaws* while in the shorter one he appears to present them as two different degrees of sainthood. See Ögke, *Ahmed Şemseddîn-i Marmaravî*, 571, 574.

77. İnalcık, "Dervish and Sultan."

78. Ocak, *Osmanlı Toplumunda Zındıklar ve Mülhidler*, 251–313; Also see Öngören, *Osmanlılar'da Tasavvuf*, 155–185; for a comprehensive treatment of the Melāmetiyye order and thought, see Abdülbaki Gölpınarlı, *Melâmilik ve Melâmiler* (İstanbul: Gri Yayın, 1992).

79. Ocak, "XVI. Yüzyıl Osmanlı Anadolusu'nda Mesiyanik Hareketlerin Bir Tahlil Denemesi."

80. Ocak, "Kanûnî Sultan Süleyman Devrinde Bir Osmanlı Heretiği: Şeyh Muhyiddîn-i Karamânî," in *Prof. Dr. Bekir Kütükoğlu'na Armağan*, 473–484; "Kanûnî Sultan Süleyman Devrinde Osmanlı Resmî Düşüncesine Karşı Bir Tepki Hareketi;" "Les réactions socio-religieuses contre l'idéologie officielle ottomane et la question de Zendeqa ve Ilhad (hérésie et athéisme) au XVIe siècle;" XV.–XVl. Yüzyıllarda Osmanlı İdeolojisi ve Buna Muhalefet Problemi," in *XI. Türk Tarih Kongresi*, 1201–1210; "XVI. ve XVII. Yüzyıllarda Bayrâmî (Hamzavî) Melâmîeri ve Osmanlı Yönetimi," *TTK Belleten* 230 (1997): 93–110.

81. For records of those trials, see the appendix in Ocak, *Osmanlı Toplumunda Zındıklar ve Mülhidler*, 354–375.

82. 'Ārifī, *'Uqūd al-Jawāhir*, 3a; for more elaborate views expounded by Arifi's contemporaries, such as Mevlana Isa, see Fleischer, "The Lawgiver as Messiah: The Making of the Imperial Image in the Reign of Suleyman," in *Soliman le Magnifique et Son temps*, 159–179; Fleischer, "Seer to the Sultan: Haydar-i Remmal and Sultan Süleyman," in *Kültür Ufukları: Talat S. Halman Armağan Kitabı*, ed. Jayne L. Warner (Syracuse: Syracuse University Press and Yapı Kredi Yayınları: Syracuse and Istanbul, 2001), 290–299.

83. Tavakkolî, *Kanun-ı Şâhenşâhi*, 23.

84. Ibid., 21.

85. Ibid., 22.

86. Ibid., 14.

87. Ibid., 13–14.

88. Ṭāşköprīzāde, *Asrār al-Khilāfa*, 89a; compare this to a similar passage in Hamadānī, *Ẕakhīrat al-Mulūk*, 295.

89. Ebū'l-Fażl Münşī, *Dustūr al-Salṭana*, 11a, 16a, 24a, 33b.

90. Michel Chodkiewicz, "The Esoteric Foundations of Political Legitimacy in Ibn ʿArabi;" Ibn ʿArabī, *al-Futūḥāt al-Makkiyya*, eds. ʿOs̱mān Yaḥyā and Ibrāhīm Madkūr, vol. 11 (Cairo: al-Hay'a al-Miṣriyya al-ʿĀmma li al-Kitāb, 1972), 274–275.

91. Bālī Efendī, *Eṭvār-ı Sebʿa* (MS SK, Hacı Mahmud 2927), 14a–16b; The authorship of this text cannot be established with certainty. On existing manuscripts, the author's name appears only on the flyleaf, not in the main text. Bostancı and Ögke, who recently edited two separate copies of the same text, attributed them to Bali Efendi and Marmaravi respectively. See Ali Haydar Bostancı, "Tasavvuf'ta Etvâr-ı Seb'a ve Sofyalı Bâlî Efendi'nin "Etvâr-ı Seb'a"sı." (Master's thesis, Marmara University, 1996); Ögke, *Ahmed Şemseddîn-i Marmaravî*, 550–570. Bostancı listed fifteen copies under Bali Efendi's name whereas Ögke listed five for Marmaravi. Bali Efendi and Marmaravi were both Halvetis whose writings are similar in language and content. However, when *Eṭvār-ı Sebʿa* is compared to other writings of each author it looks more in line with those of Bali Efendi and Marmaravi. But the question of authorship aside, the text is certainly a Halveti text written in late fifteenth or the first half of the sixteenth century.

92. This conception is clearly Aristotelian as elaborated by age, and temperance. From Ibn Miskawayh onwards, this quality is commonly prescribed as the benchmark of morality for the ruler. See Majid Khadduri, *The Islamic Conception of Justice* (Baltimore: Johns Hopkins University Press, 1984), 106–134.

93. For the Sunni canon, see Cürcânî, *Şerhu'l-Mevâkıf*, 718–734.

94. Fleischer, "Seer to the Sultan."

95. For the Ottoman reception of Ibn Arabi, see Ahmed Zildzic, "Friend and Foe: The Early Ottoman Reception of Ibn ʿArabī" (PhD diss., University of California, Berkeley, 2012); for the influence, dissemination, and reception of Ibn ʿArabī's works among Ottoman men of learning, see Kılıç, "Fusûsü'l-Hikem," *TDVIA*, vol. 13 (1996), 230–237.

96. For the spread of Ibn Arabi's teachings, see Chittick, "The School of Ibn ʿArabī."

97. Rāzī, *Mirṣād al-ʿIbād*, 411, 416; for English, see Razi, *The Path of God's Bondsmen*, 395.

98. Rāzī, *Mirṣād al-ʿIbād*, 412–413; for English, see Razi, *The Path of God's Bondsmen*, 396.

99. Rāzī, *Mirṣād al-ʿIbād*, 234; for English, see Razi, *The Path of God's Bondsmen*, 242.

100. Bidlīsī might have been aware of this work because it was translated from Arabic to Persian for Bayezid II, a sultan with whose court Bidlisi was closely associated.

101. Rāzī, *Manārāt al-Sā'irīn*, 261.

102. Ibid., 263, 267.

103. Ibid., 269.

104. Rāzī, *Manārāt al-Sā'irīn*, 270.

105. "The former was also identified as the unseen (*ghayb*), the sublime (*ʿulwiyyāt*), the afterlife (*ʿuqbā*), and heavens (*malakūt*) while the latter was also known as the visible (*shahāda*), the inferior (*sufliyyāt*), the earth (*dunyā*), and the world (*mulk*)." Rāzī, *Manārāt al-Sā'irīn*, 40.

106. Rāzī, *Manārāt al-Sā'irīn*, 271–273.

107. Mecdî, *Hadaiku'ş-Şakaik*, 27.

108. Seyyed Jalāl ad-Dīn Āshtiyānī, *Rasā'il-i Qayṣarī* (Tehran: Mu'assasa-i Pizhūhishī-i Ḥikmat va Falsafa-i Irān, 1381 [2002 or 2003]), 23–24.

109. Āshtiyānī, *Rasā'il-i Qayṣarī*, 37.

110. Qayṣarī, *Sharḥ Fuṣūṣ al-Ḥikam*, 402.

111. Ibid., 127–128, 961.

112. Ibid., 128, 402, 962.

113. Ibid., 963–964.

114. Şeyẖ Bālī Efendī, *Sharḥ Fuṣūṣ al-Ḥikam* (Istanbul: Dersa'ādet, 1309 [1891 or 1892], 306–307.

115. Hamadānī, *Ẕakhīrat al-Mulūk*, 289–295; for comparison, see a similar passage in Qayṣarī, *Sharh Fuṣūṣ al-Ḥikam*, 340.

116. Ibn Arghūn al-Shīrāzī, *Nikāt Muta'allaqa bi-sharḥ al-Maṭāli' wa Ḥawāshiyya al-Sharīfa* (MS Walters Art Museum, Ms. 591), 1b.

117. Abdülkadir Dağlar, "Şeyhülislam Ebussuud Efendi'nin Türkçe Mektubları," (Master's thesis, Ege University, 2001), 27–29.

118. Imber, *Ebu'ssu'ud*, 98–111.

119. Crone, *God's Rule*, 17.

120. Ibid., 184.

121. Affifi, *The Mystical Philosophy of Muḥyid Dín-Ibnul 'Arabí*, 66–68.

122. Duḳākīnzāde Taşlıcalı Yaḥyā, *Şāh ü Gedā* (Istanbul: Matba'a-i Tatyos Divitçiyān, 1867), 19.

Chapter 5: The Myth of the Ottoman Caliphate

1. Lüṭfī Pāşā, *Khalāṣ al-Umma*, 42.

2. İbn Kemal, *Tevârih*, 1: 16.

3. Ökten, "Jāmī (817–898/1414–1492): His Biography and Intellectual Influence in Herat" (PhD diss., University of Chicago, 2007), 155–158.

4. Christine Woodhead, *Ta'līḳī-zāde's Şehnāme-i Hümāyūn: A History of the Ottoman Campaign into Hungary 1593–94* (Berlin: Klaus Schwarz Verlag, 1983), 18–19, 112–136; for a recent analysis from the perspective of imperial ideology, see Gülru Necipoğlu, *The Age of Sinan: Architectural Culture in the Ottoman Empire* (Lodon: Reaktion, 2005), 27–35.

5. See, for example, Muḥammed ibn Abī al-Surūr al-Bakrī al-Ṣiddīqī, *al-Minaḥ al-Raḥmānīyya fī al-Dawla al-'Uthmānīyya*, ed. Laylā al-Ṣabbāgh (Damascus: Dār al-Bashā'ir, 1995).

6. Such high-profile bureaucrats and scholars as Ibn Kemal, Celalzade, and Mustafa Âli conspicuously took pride in their newly forming Ottoman identity by praising the cultural and social achievements of the Ottomans in the land of Rum. See Celālzāde, *Mevāhibü'l-Ḫallāḳ*, 6b–30a; İbn Kemal, *Tevârih*, 1: 11–59; for Muṣṭafā 'Ālī's views, see Fleischer, *Bureaucrat and Intellectual*, 253–257.

7. For a modern edition of the work, see Mustafa İsen, *Sehî Bey Tezkiresi: Heşt-Behişt* (Ankara: Akçağ Yayınları, 1998).

8. For the content and description of these works, see Franz Babinger, *Osmanlı Tarih Yazarları ve Eserleri*, transl. Coşkun Üçok (Ankara: Kültür Bakanlığı Yayınları, 1992), 51–55, 68–71; Fleischer, *Bureaucrat and Intellectual*, 235–252.

9. For Mustafa Âli's placement of the Ottoman Empire within the context of universal world history, see Fleischer, *Bureaucrat and Intellectual*, 235–252.

10. For the genealogy-consciousness of this period, see Imber, "The Ottoman Dynastic Myth," *Turcica* 19 (1987): 7–27; Barbara Flemming, "The Political Genealogies in the Sixteenth Century," *JOS* 7–8 (1988): 198–220.

11. Fleischer, "From Şehzade Korkud to Mustafa Âli: Cultural Origins of the Ottoman *Nasihatname*" (paper presented at Third International Congress on the Economic and Social History of Turkey, Princeton, 1983).

12. See, for example, A. El Moudden, "The Idea of the Caliphate between Moroccans and Ottomans: Political and Symbolical Stakes in the 16th and 17th century-Maghrib," *Studia Islamica* 82 (1995): 103–113.

13. Mercedes García-Arenal, *Messianism and Puritanical Reform: Mahdīs of the Muslim West*, transl. Martin Beagles (Leiden and Boston: Brill, 2006), 291–295; Moin, *The Millennial Sovereign*, 94–130.

14. John E. Woods, *The Aqquyunlu: Clan, Confederation, Empire*, revised and expanded ed. (Salt Lake City: University of Utah Press, 1999), 104–106; see Fleischer, *Bureaucrat and Intellectual*, 281.

15. Fleischer, "The Lawgiver as Messiah."

16. García-Arenal, *Messianism and Puritanical Reform*, 283–91.

17. For the Universalist tendencies of the sixteenth century, see Fleischer, "The Lawgiver as Messiah."

18. For the appearance, circulation, and reception of the hadith in the Abbasid era, see Ella Landau-Tasseron, "The "Cyclical Reform": A Study of the Mujaddid Tradition," *Studia Islamica* 70 (1989): 79–117.

19. Lüṭfī Pāşā, *Khalāṣ al-Umma*, 41.

20. For him, the renewers after the Prophet until the Ottoman turn were Abd al-Aziz, Mu'tasim, Muqtadir, Malikshah, and Ghazan Khan. Lüṭfī Pāşā, *Tevārīḫ*, 6–11.

21. Yücesoy, *Messianic Beliefs and Imperial Politics in Medieval Islam: The ʿAbbāsid Caliphate in the Early Ninth Century* (Columbia, SC: University of South Carolina Press, 2009), 133–140.

22. Lüṭfī Pāşā, *Tevārīḫ*, 8.

23. Yağmur, "Terceme-i Kitāb-ı Fevâ'ihü'l-Miskiyye fi'l-Fevâtihi'l-Mekkiyye," 58.

24. Ibid., 75–6.

25. Uğur, "Selīmnāme," *TDVIA*, vol. 36 (2009), 440–441.

26. Moin, *The Millennial Sovereign, 90.*

27. Bidlîsî, *Selim Şah-nâme*, 63.

28. Ḳınalīzāde ʿAlī, *Aḫlāḳ-ı ʿAlāʾī*, 2: 94.

29. Lüṭfī Pāşā, *Tevārīḫ*, 5.

30. For criticism of Bayezid I's reign, for example, see Lüṭfī Pāşā, *Tevārīḫ*, 43–47.

31. İbn Kemal, *Tevârih-i Âl-i Osman*, 7–8.

32. Ibid., 1: 21.

33. See also Aḫterī, 2: 83.

34. See ʿĀrifī, *ʿUqūd al-Jawāhir*, 6a; Ḫıżır Münşī, *Akhlāq al-Atqiyā*, 27a.

35. Ḳınalīzāde ʿAlī, *Aḫlāḳ-ı ʿAlāʾī*, 2: 105.

36. Davvānī, *Akhlāq-i Jalālī*, 252; this statement is omitted in Thompson's translation; see Thompson, *The Practical Philosophy of the Muhammedan People*, 366.

37. İbn Kemal, *Tevârih-i Âl-i Osman*, 17.

38. Ibid., 1: 25.

39. Ibid., 1: 27–28.

40. Lüṭfī Pāşā, *Khalāṣ al-Umma*, 45.

41. Ibid., 44.

42. Âşıkpaşazâde, *Âşıkpaşazâde Tarihi*, 103.

43. Ibn Battuta, *Travels in Asia and Africa*, 123–143.

44. For an overview of Ottoman perceptions of Timur, see Emecen, *İlk Osmanlılar ve Batı Anadolu Beylikler Dünyası*, 261–273.

45. For a late sixteenth-century admirer of Timur, Mustafa Âli, and his recreation of the Ottoman ruler in the image of Timur, see Fleischer, *Bureaucrat and Intellectual in the Ottoman Empire*, 283–286.

46. There is a long history of scholarly debate on the precise stages and patronage of the composition of this text. The 1389 version of the text was compiled under the auspices of either the Ottoman or their close and friendly neighbor of Germiyanid court. In either case, Ahmedi seems to have been close to both courts. The text was edited and expanded multiple times until it was eventually dedicated to the Ottoman prince Süleyman, son of Bayezid I. See Pál Fodor, "Aḥmedī's Dāsitān as a Source of Early Ottoman History," *Acta Orientalia* 38 (1984): 41–54; B. Babür Turna, "Perception of History and the Problem of Superiority in Ahmedi's Dastān-ı Tevārih-i Mülūk-ı Āl-i Osman," *Acta Orientalia* 62 (2009): 267–283; Carolinne Sawyer, "Revising Alexander: Structure and Evolution of Ahmedī's Ottoman Iskendernâme (c. 1400)," *Edebiyat: Journal of M. E. Literatures* 13 (2010): 225–243.

47. Aḥmedī, *İskender—Nāme*, 65b–68a.

48. Abdülvasi Çelebi, *Halilname*, 254–278; Kastritsis, *The Sons of Bayezid*, 221–232.

49. A. Azfar Moin, *The Millennial Sovereign*, 23–55; for the more embellished posthumous evolution of Timurid mythology, see Ron Sela, *The Legendary Biographies of Tamerlane: Islam and Heroic Apocrypha in Central Asia* (Cambridge: Cambridge University Press, 2011).

50. Imber, "The Ottoman Dynastic Myth;" Flemming, "The Political Geneologies in the Sixteenth Century."

51. Inalcık, "How to Read ʿĀshık Pasha-Zāde's History," in *Studies in Ottoman History in Honour of Professor V. L. Ménage*, eds. Colin Heywood and Colin Imber (Istanbul: The Isis Press, 1994), 139–156; V. L. Ménage, "The Menāqib of Yakhshi Faqīh," *BSOAS* 26 (1963): 50–54.

52. Rûhî, *Rûhî Târîhi*, eds. Yaşar Yücel and Halil Erdoğan Cengiz, in TTK *Belgeler* 14 (1992): 359–472, p. 370.

53. Ilker Evrim Binbaş, "Oğuz Khan Narratives," http://www.iranicaonline.org/articles/oguz-khan-narratives (Accessed 1 October 2016).

54. Seyid Ali Topal, "Celalzâde Salih Çelebi'nin Tarih-i Sultan Süleyman İsimli Eseri" (PhD diss., Ankara University, 2008), 91.

55. Aḥmedī, *İskender—Nāme: İnceleme—Tıpkıbasım*, 65b.

56. Konevi, for example, reports that either Osman or Ertuğrul recived a banner, a kettledrum, a horsehair, and a horn. See Ḳonevī, *Tavārīkh-i Āl-i ʿOs̱mān*, 5b.

57. Rûhî, *Rûhî Târîhi*, 375–378.

58. İdris-i Bitlisî, *Heşt Bihişt Osman Gazi Dönemi*, ed. Vural Genç (PhD diss., Mimar Sinan University, 2007), 31–32; Idrīs-i Bidlīsī, *Hasht Behesht* (MS Nuruosmaniye Kütüphanesi 3209), 8b.

59. Idrīs-i Bidlīsī, *Hasht Behesht*, 20a.

60. *Tawārīkh al-Salāṭīn al-ʿOs̱māniyya* (MS SK, Ayasofya 3204), 3a; (MS SK, Hasan Hüsnü Paşa 879), 10b.

61. İdris-i Bitlisî, *Heşt Bihişt Osman Gazi Dönemi*, 79; Idrīs-i Bidlīsī, *Hasht Behesht*, 20a.

62. İdris-i Bitlisî, *Heşt Bihişt Osman Gazi Dönemi*, 159–163; Idrīs-i Bidlīsī, *Hasht Behesht*, 40a–41a.

63. Selami Karaduman, "Oruç Beg Tarihi Manisa Nüshası" (Master's thesis, Uludağ University, 2010), 76.

64. İdris-i Bitlisî, *Heşt Bihişt Osman Gazi Dönemi*, 119–126; Bidlīsī, *Hasht Behesht*, 30a–32a.

65. İdris-i Bitlisî, *Heşt Bihişt Osman Gazi Dönemi*, 118–119; Bidlīsī, *Hasht Behesht*, 30a–30b.

66. İdris-i Bitlisî, *Heşt Bihişt Osman Gazi Dönemi*, 131–146; Bidlīsī, *Hasht Behesht*, 33a–37a.

67. Bālī Efendī, *Eṭvār-ı Sebʿa*, 16b; Bostancı, "Tasavvuf'ta Etvâr-ı Seb'a ve Sofyalı Bâlî Efendi'nin "Etvâr-ı Seb'a"sı," 64.

68. Kafadar, "Self and Others: The Diary of a Dervish in Seventeenth Century Istanbul and First-Person Narratives in Ottoman Literature," *Studia Islamica* 69 (1989): 121–150; see the editor's introduction in Asiye Hatun, *Rüya Mektupları*, ed. Cemal Kafadar (Istanbul: Oğlak Yayınları, 1994), 26–39.

69. İdris-i Bitlisî, *Heşt Bihişt Osman Gazi Dönemi*, 141–142; Bidlīsī, *Hasht Behesht*, 35b.

70. Ḳonevī, *Tavārīkh-i Āl-i ʿOsmān*, 6b–7a.

71. Ibid., 37a–b.

72. İbn Kemal, *Tevârih-i Âl-i Osman*, 88–92.

73. Ḳonevī, *Tavārīkh-i Āl-i ʿOsmān*, 2a, 28a.

74. Tofigh Heidarzadeh, "Patronage, Networks Migration: Turco-Persian Scholarly Exchanges in the 15th, 16th 17th Centuries," *Archives Internationales d'Histoire des Sciences* 55 (2005): 419–434.

75. İnalcık, "Dervish and Sultan."

76. David Morgan, *Medieval Persia, 1040–1797* (London: Longman, 1988), 116.

77. Inalcık, "How to Read ʿĀshık Pasha-Zāde's History."

78. He makes the same analogy between Mehmed I and Mehmed II as well, still showing that Mehmed II's rulership was the real breakthrough. İdris-i Bitlisî, *Heşt Behişt, VII. Ketîbe*, 9–10; Bidlīsī, *Hasht Behesht*, 337a–338a.

79. Inalcık, "How to Read ʿĀshık Pasha-Zāde's History."

80. Kafadar, *Between Two Worlds*, 147.

81. İdris-i Bitlisî, *Heşt Behişt, VII. Ketîbe*, 6–15; Bidlīsī, *Hasht Behesht*, 336a–341a.

82. Woods, *The Aqquyunlu*, 102.

83. İdris-i Bitlisî, *Heşt Behişt, VII. Ketîbe*, 7; Bidlīsī, *Hasht Behesht*, 336a.

84. Yazıcıoğlu Ahmed Bîcan, *Dürr-i Meknûn*, ed. Ahmet Demirtaş (Istanbul: Akademik Kitaplar, 2009); Kaya Şahin, "Constantinople and the End Time: Ottoman Conquest as a Portent of the Last Hour," *Journal of Early Modern History* 14 (2010): 317–354.

85. For a brief survey, see Şeşen, "Eski Araplara Göre Türkler," *Türkiyat Mecmuası* 15 (1969): 11–36.

86. Kafadar, "A Rome of One's Own."

87. İdris-i Bitlisî, *Heşt Behişt, VII. Ketîbe*, 56–62; Bidlīsī, *Hasht Behesht*, 366b–369b.

88. Qur'an 30: 2.

89. İdris-i Bitlisî, *Heşt Behişt, VII. Ketîbe*, 220–224; Bidlīsī, *Hasht Behesht*, 469b–471b.

90. John E. Woods, *The Aqquyunlu*, 102–103.

91. Ahmed Bîcan, *Dürr-i Meknûn*, 151.

92. Zeynep Aydoğan, "An Analysis of the Saltukname in its Fifteenth Century Context" (Master's thesis, Boğazici Univeristy, 2007), 80.

93. *Risālat al-Khilāfa wa Ādāb al-Salāṭīn* (MS İÜK, F 1228), 6a–7a. Nabil al-Tikriti attributed this treatise to Idris-i Bidlisi. See, Nabil al-Tikriti, "Idrīs-i Bidlisī's 1513 Treatise on Caliphal and Sultanic Protocols," in *New Trends in Ottoman Studies*," ed. Marinos Sariyannis (Rethymno: University of Crete, 2014), 741–756; Both Genç and Markiewicz, however, discounted it as being written by Bidlisi for there is no textual evidence other than a note on the flyleaf and, above all, it looks markedly different from Bidlisi's other writings in style, language, and content. See Genç, "Acem'den Rum'a," 10; Markiewicz, "The Crisis of Rule in Late Medieval Islam," 418–419.

94. İdris-i Bitlisî, *Heşt Behişt, VII. Ketîbe*, 59–60; Bidlīsī, *Hasht Behesht*, 368b–369b.

95. Vural Genç, "Şah ile Sultan Arasında Bir Acem Bürokratı."

96. Muḥammed b. Sharaf al-Dīn al-Madanī al-Shāfiʿī, *Hibat al-Fattāḥ* (MS SK, Ayasofya 1803) 2b–3a.

97. See, for example, a sixteenth-century interpretation of God's beautiful names: İbn İsâ Saruhânî, *Esmâ-i Hüsnâ Şerhi*, ed. Numan Külekçi (Ankara: Akçağ Yayınları, 2000).

98. See İsmail Arıkoğlu, "Feriştehoğlu'nun Cavidân-Nâme Tercümesi: ʿIşk-nâme" (PhD diss., Yüzüncü Yıl University, 2006). The work contains a chapter on *ʿism-i aʿẓam*, 238–240.

99. Muḥammed b. Sharaf al-Dīn, *Hibat al-Fattāḥ*, 18b.

100. Ibid., 20a.

101. Ibid., 3b–5a.

102. Ibid., 2a–3a.

103. Qur'an, transl. Yusuf Ali, 21:105; Feriştehoğlu Abdülmecid's *ʿIşḳnāme* contains a chapter on the interpretation of the verse with no prophecies. See, Arıkoğlu, *Feriştehoğlu'nun Cavidân-Nâme Tercümesi*, 135–138.

104. Mustafa Kılıç, "İbn Kemal'in Mısır Fethine Dair Bir Risale-i Acibesi," *Diyanet Dergisi* 26 (1990): 111–120; Ibn-i Kemāl, *Fetḥ-i Mıṣr Ḥaḳḳında Vāḳiʿ Olan Īmā ve İşāret* (MS SK, Esad Efendi 3729), 136a–138a; (MS Mevlana Müzesi 2315), 71b–72b.

105. Ṭabīb Ramażān, *Risāla Fatḥiyya Sulaymāniyya* (MS TSMK, Revan 1279), 27a.

106. Ibid., 6a–7b.

107. Flemming, "Public Opinion under Sultan Süleymân," in *Süleymân the Second and His Time*, 49–57.

108. Ṭabīb Ramażān, *al-Risāla al-Fatḥiyya al-Rādūsiyya al-Sulaymāniyya* (MS BNF, Arabic 1622), 15a; Ṭabīb Ramażān, *Risāla Fatḥiyya Sulaymāniyya*, 9b.

109. Ṭabīb Ramażān, *al-Risāla al-Fatḥiyya al-Rādūsiyya al-Sulaymāniyya*, 47a, 57b; Ṭabīb Ramażān, *Risāla Fatḥiyya Sulaymāniyya*, 34a.

110. Ṭabīb Ramażān, *Risāla Fatḥiyya Sulaymāniyya*, 36b–37b.

111. Ṭabīb Ramażān, *al-Risāla al-Fatḥiyya al-Rādūsiyya al-Sulaymāniyya*, 64a–65b.

112. Ṭabīb Ramażān, *Risāla Fatḥiyya Sulaymāniyya*, 34a.

113. Necipoğlu, "Süleyman the Magnificient and the Representation of Power in the Context of Ottoman-Habsburg-Papal Rivalry," in *Süleymân the Second and His Time*, 163–195.

114. Casale, *The Ottoman Age of Exploration* (Oxford: Oxford University Press, 2010), 29–31, 80–83, 147–149.

115. Necipoğlu, "The Dome of the Rock as Palimpsest: ʿAbd al-Malik's Grand Narrative and Sultan Süleyman's Glosses," *Muqarnas* 25 (2008): 17–105.

116. Flemming, "Public Opinion under Sultan Süleymān."

117. Cürcânî, *Şerhu'l-Mevâkıf*, 766–788.

118. Âşıkpaşazâde, *Âşıkpaşazâde Tarihi*, 330–333.

119. See, for example, Vladimir Minorsky, "Shaykh Bālī Efendi on the Safavids."

120. Shaykh Makkī, *al-Jānib al-Gharbī fī Ḥall Mushkilāt al-Shaykh Muḥyī al-Dīn ibn ʿArabī*, ed. Najīb Māyil Haravī (Tehran: Intishārāt-i Mawlā, 1985).

121. For detailed analysis of the controversy on Ibn ʿArabī, see Şükrü Özen, "Ottoman ʿUlemāʾ Debating Sufism."

122. Şirvānī, *Risāle fi't-Taṣavvuf*, 6b.

123. Şirvānī, *al-ʿAdliyya al-Sulaymāniyya*, 49b.

124. Ibid., 54a–54b.

125. Ibid., 6a.

126. İsmail E. Erünsal, *XV-XVI. Asır Bayrâmî-Melâmîliği'nin Kaynaklarından Abdurrahman el-Askerî'nin Mir'âtü'l-Işk'ı* (Ankara: Türk Tarih Kurumu, 2003), 200.

127. Ibid., 202.

128. For the early interaction of twelver Shiism and the Safavid dynasty, see Rula Jurdi Abisaab, *Converting Persia: Religion and Power in the Safavid Empire* (London and New York: I.B. Tauris, 2004), 7–30.

129. Ibid., 16.

130. Babayan, *Mystics, Monarchs, and Messiahs*, xxviii.

131. Yıldırım, "An Ottoman Prince Wearing a Qızılbaş Tāj."

132. However, even before the rise of Shah Isma'il, some Ottoman vigilantes had already perceived the Safavid movement as part of the end of times. See Ömer Faruk Teber, "Haydariyye Taifesine Yönelik Eleştiriler: "Risâle fî Hakki't-Tâifeti'l-Haydariyye" Ekseninde," *Çukurova Üniversitesi İlâhiyat Fakültesi Dergisi* 7 (2007): 157–177.

133. Şirvānī, *al-ʿAdliyya al-Sulaymāniyya*, 4a–4b.

134. Şirvānī, *Aḥkām al-Dīniyya*, 109a.

135. Ibid., 118b.

136. Ibid., 153a.

137. Şirvānī, *Risāle fi't-Taṣavvuf*, 5a–b.

138. Şirvānī, *al-ʿAdliyya al-Sulaymāniyya*, 118b.

139. Ibid., 40b–49b.

140. Ibid., 43a.

141. Erünsal, *XV-XVI. Asır Bayrâmî-Melâmîliği'nin Kaynaklarından Abdurrahman el-Askerî'nin Mir'âtü'l-Işk'ı*, 126.

142. Kafadar, *Between Two Worlds*, 93.

143. ʿAlī b. Muḥammed el-Ṣıddıḳī, *Zād al-Jihād* (MS SK, Ayasofya 1837), 49b–69b.

144. Şirvānī, *Aḥkām al-Dīniyya*, 147a; Şirvānī, *al-ʿAdliyya al-Sulaymāniyya*, 3b.

145. Şirvānī, *Aḥkām al-Dīniyya*, 141b–145a.

146. Şirvānī, *al-ʿAdliyya al-Sulaymāniyya*, 142b.

147. Ibid., 9a–40b.

148. Şirvānī, *Aḥkām al-Dīniyya*, 147a.

149. Ibid., 153b.

150. Qur'an, 70: 40.

151. Şirvānī, *Aḥkām al-Dīniyya*, 94b–96a.

152. Ibid., 95b.

153. Şirvanī, *al-ʿAdliyya al-Sulaymāniyya*, 4b.

154. Ibid., 4a–5a.

155. Ibid., 6a.

156. Ibid., 5b.

157. Şirvānī, *Risāle fi't-Taṣavvuf*, 1b.

158. Şirvanī, *al-ʿAdliyya al-Sulaymāniyya*, 2b.

159. Şirvānī, *Risāle fi't-Taṣavvuf*, 6a.

160. Ocak, "Kanûnî Sultan Süleyman Devrinde Osmanlı Resmî Düşüncesine Karşı Bir Tepki Hareketi."

161. Şehabettin Tekindağ, "Şah Kulu Baba Tekeli İsyanı," *Belgelerle Türk Tarih Dergisi* 3 (1967): 34–39; 4 (1968): 54–59.

162. Lāmiʿī Çelebi, "Şerefü'l-İnsān," ed. Sadettin Eğri (PhD diss., Gazi University, 1997), 490–491.

163. Fleischer, "Ancient Wisdom and New Sciences."

164. Necipoğlu, "The Dome of the Rock as Palimpsest."

165. Fleischer, "The Lawgiver as Messiah."

166. Zildzic, "Friend and Foe: The Early Ottoman Reception of Ibn ʿArabī," 83–119.

167. Fleischer, "Shadow of Shadows: Prophecy in Politics in 1530s İstanbul," *International Journal of Turkish Studies* 13 (2007): 51–62.

168. Fleischer, "Ancient Wisdom and New Sciences."

169. Yücesoy, *Messianic Belief and Imperial Politics in Medieval Islam*, 36–40.

170. Flemming, "*Der Ğāmiʿ Ül-Meknūnāt*: Eine Quelle ʿĀlīs aus Zeit Sultan Süleymāns," in *Studien zur Geschichte und Kultur des Vorderen Orients: Festschrift für Bertold Spuler zum Siebzigsten Geburtstag*, eds. Bertold Spuler, Hans R. Roemer and Albrecht Noth (Leiden: Brill, 1981), 79–92; Flemming, "Ṣāḥib-Ḳırān und Mahdī: Türkische Endzeiterwartungen im ersten Jahrzehnt der Regierung Süleymāns," In *Between the Danube and the Caucasus*, ed. György Kara (Budapest: Akadémiai Kiadó, 1987), 43–62.

171. Fleischer, "Mahdi and Millenium: Messianic Dimensions in the Development of Ottoman Imperial Ideology," in *The Great Ottoman-Turkish Civilization*, vol. 3, 42–54.

172. Fleischer, "Seer to the Sultan."

173. İlyâs İbn-i İsa Akhisârî Saruhânî, *Akhisarlı Şeyh Îsâ Menâkıbnâmesi*, eds. Sezai Küçük and Ramazan Uslu (Istanbul: Aşiyan Yayınları, 2003), 181–186. It is not clear who was Suleyman's tutor at the time. During his governorship in Manisa Süleyman was accompanied by his tutor, Hace Hayreddin (d. 1518). See Emecen, "Süleymân," *TDVIA*, vol. 38 (2010), 62–74; Mehmed Süreyya, *Sicill-i Osmanî*, ed. Nuri Akbayar, (Istanbul: Tarih Vakfi Yurt Yayınları, 1996), vol. 2, 661. He was served with two consecutive tutors (*lālā*) in this period: Kasım from 1513 to 1516 and Sinan Paşa from 1515 onwards.

174. İlyâs İbn-i İsa Akhisârî Saruhânî, *Akhisarlı Şeyh Îsâ Menâkıbnâmesi*, 187–188.

175. İlyâs İbn-i İsa Akhisârî Saruhânî, *Akhisarlı Şeyh Îsâ Menâkıbnâmesi*, 181–182; for Bektaş Efendi, see Mehmed Süreyya, *Sicill-i Osmanî*, vol. 2, 367.

176. Ibn ʿĪsā, *Rumūzü'l-Künūz* (MS SK, Fatih 3432). The text is dated from H. 1040/1630 C.E. For a transliteration of an undated copy of the text, see Özgül, "İlyas b. Îsâ-yı Saruhânî'nin "Rumûzü'l—Künûz" Adlı Eserin Transkripsiyonu ve Değerlendirilmesi."

177. Ibn ʿĪsā, *Rumūzü'l-Künūz*, 38a–45b.

178. Ibid., 30a–30b.

179. Ibid., 43a.

180. Ibid., 50b–51b.

181. Gábor Ágoston, "Muslim Cultural Enclaves in Hungary under Ottoman Rule," *Acta Orientalia* 45 (1991): 181–204.

182. ʿAlī Dede el-Sketvārī el-Bosnevī, *al-Intiṣār li Qidwat al-Akhyār* (MS SK, Köprülü Fazıl Ahmed Paşa 1381), 185a–199b.

183. ʿAlī Dede el-Sketvārī el-Bosnevī, *Muḥāḍarat al-Awāʾil wa Musāmarat al-Akhāʾir* (Cairo: al-Maṭbaʿa al-ʿĀmira al-Sharafiyya, 1311 [1389]).

184. ʿAlī Dede al-Mūstārī, *Khawātim al-Ḥikam*, ed. Maḥmud Naṣṣār (Cairo: Dār al-Āfāq al-ʿArabiyya, 2002).

185. ʿAlī Dede al-Mūstārī, *Khawātim al-Ḥikam*, 197.

186. Qur'an, 33: 40.

187. For Murad III's dreams and his conversations with Şeyh Şüca, see *Kitābü'l-Menāmāt: Sultan* III. *Murad'ın Rüya Mektupları*, ed. Özgen Felek (İstanbul: Tarih Vakfı Yurt Yayınları, 2014).

188. ʿAlī Dede, *al-Intiṣār li Qidwat al-Akhyār*, 199a–199b.

189. Ibid., 188a.

190. Ibid., 187b.

191. Ibid., 188a.

192. ʿAlī Dede, *Muḥāḍara*, 164.

193. ʿAlī Dede, *al-Intiṣār li Qidwat al-Akhyār*, 189b.

194. İrfan Görkaş, "Mehmed Birgivî'nin İlm-i Ahlâk'ı," *Türk Dünyası Araştırmaları* 107 (1997): 121–130.

195. ʿAlī Dede, *Muḥāḍara*, 164; Qur'an, 12: 33.

196. Ḳonevī, *Tavārīkh-i Āl-i ʿOs̱mān*, 7b.

197. Celālzāde Muṣṭafā, *Mevāhibü'l-Ḫallāḳ*, 209a–210a.

198. *"Ākhir dawlat al-Islāmiyya fī al-Khilāfa al-ʿAbbasiyya al-dawla al-farīda al-khātamiyya al-ʿUthmāniyya."* ʿAlī Dede, *al-Intiṣār li Qidwat al-Akhyār*, 189a.

Conclusion

1. Süleyman Ateş, "Kutub," *TDVIA*, vol. 26 (2002), 498–499.

2. Winter, "Ibn Kemāl (d. 940/1534) on Ibn 'Arabī's Hagiology."

3. Mustafa Fayda, "Hulefâ-yi Raşidîn," *TDVIA*, vol. 18 (1998), 324–338.

4. Yağmur, "Terceme-i Kitāb-ı Fevâ'ihü'l-Miskiyye fi'l-Fevâtihi'l-Mekkiyye," 47.

GLOSSARY

THIS GLOSSARY LISTS AND DEFINES a select group of terms and phrases used in the book to facilitate reading, and is limited to providing basic meanings pertinent to their contextual uses throughout the text. The glossary should be consulted as a first point of reference in understanding this terminology rather than a list of conclusive statements. For the same words taken from source texts in different languages, the variances in pronunciation are given, for which **T** stands for Turkish, **P** for Persian, and **A** for Arabic.

ʿ*Abd*: Slave; servant; a legally responsible person

***Abdal*, pl. *Abdalan*:** In various Sufi orders, a friend of God who belongs to a specific category of saints in the spiritual hierarchy of cosmic government; in popular perceptions of western Asia and the Balkans, a Sufi devotee with miraculous powers

***Abū al-Futūḥ*:** An honorific nickname often used in titulature literally meaning father or possessor of spiritual openings

ʿ*Acem*: Persian

***Ādāb al-Mulūk*:** Etiquette and manners of rulership

***Ādāb al-wizāra*:** Etiquette and manners of the vizierate or assisting the ruler

ʿ*Ādil*: Just and fair

ʿ*Adl*: Justice and fairness

ʿ*Aḍūd*: Column, pillar; support; often used as an honorific title for a high-ranking statesman

ʿ*Afv*: Forgiveness, mercy

***Ahi*:** Member or a leader of a spiritual fraternity or guild

***Aḥkām*:** Ordinances, commands, rules, and regulations

***Aʾimma-i hudā*:** Rightly guided leaders; the Twelve infallible imams of Shiite Islam

ʿ*Ajamistān*: A general designation for the larger realm of Persians

***Ākhir al-zamān*:** End of times

***Akhlāq*:** Ethics, morality, virtuosity, good manners

***Akhlāq-i karīma*:** Noble character, virtuous disposition and deeds

ʿ*Ālam-i ʿilal va asbāb*: The world that operates through causes and occasions

ʿ*Ālam-i maʿnī*: The realm of meaning, truth; spiritual world

ʿ*Ālam-i rūḥānī*: Spiritual world that is not bound by material confines

ʿ*Amal-i khādim*: The action and deeds of the servant

ʿ*Amal-i makhdūm*: The action of the Served [God]

***Amīr al-Muʾminīn*:** Commander of the faithful

***Andarūn*, T. *Enderūn*:** Inner section of the Ottoman palace establishment

ʿ*Ārif*, P. ʿ*Āref*: Knower of God, wise

ʿ*Aql*, T. ʿ*akıl*: Intellect, reason

ʿ*Āṣī*: Rebel

ʿ*Aṭāyā-i kasbī*: God's rewards, that is, virtues, that are contingent on one's actions and worthiness

ʿ*Aṭiyya-i vahbī*: God's rewards, that is, virtues, independent of one's actions and worthiness

ʿ*Avām*: Common people

***Āyat Allāh*, *T. āyetullāh*:** God's evidence or sign
***Baghy*:** Rebel in defiance of legitimate political authority
***Baḫt*:** Fortune
***Baḥth*:** Discursive knowledge; knowledge acquired by intuition and spiritual experience
***Bāṭin*:** Inner, internal
***Bayʿa*:** Formal allegiance of loyalty to an authority
***Bayt al-māl*:** Public treasury with specific sources of income and expenditure as specified in Islamic law
***Beg*:** Ruler; prince; governor
***Beglik*:** Principality
***Bidʿa*:** Innovation in faith or practice in Islam
***Çelebī*:** An honorific title first used by the Mevlevis and later adopted by rulers, scholars, and other Sufis in reference to one's being learned and cultural refinement.
***Ḍālle-i kāfire*:** Infidel errant
***Dār al-ḥarb*:** The abode of war
***Dār al-Islām*:** The abode of Islam
***Dawla*, pl. *duwal*:** Reign, dominion; auspicious turn; grace, benefice; state
***Defter*:** Register
***Devşirme*:** Institutionalized child levy collected from among non-Muslims subject for Ottoman military and administration
***Dunyā*:** Earth, world
***Efrenc*:** Franks, Europeans
***Ehl-i sünnet*:** Sunni Islam; people who profess adherence to the tradition of Prophet Muhammed
***Emīr*:** Ruler; prince
***Esrār-ı siyāset*:** Secrets of governance
***Faḍīla*, pl. *faḍā'il*, T. *fażīlet*:** Virtue
***Faqīh*, pl. *fuqahā*:** Jurist
***Farr*:** Effulgence
***Farr-yi īzadī*:** Divine light, divine glory
***Faṣād*:** Corruption, disorder, vice
***Fatwa*:** Juristic opinion passed on a specific question
***Fetret devri*:** Interregnum marked by a civil war in early Ottoman state 1402–14013
***Fiqh*:** Islamic jurisprudence
***Firaḳ*:** Religious groups and communities
***Fitna*:** Sedition, disorder
***Fiṭrat*:** One's disposition or nature
***Futuwwa*, T. *fütüvvet*:** Chivalrous fraternal order with specific mystical doctrines, and rituals that spread mostly in Asia Minor in the twelfth and thirteenth centuries especially in urban settings
***Ghalaba*:** Subjugation; overempowerment; victory
***Ghāzī*, pl. *ghuzāt*; T. *gazi*:** Raider for the faith
***Ghazā*, T. *Gaza*:** Raid, expedition
***Ghaws*, T. *gavs*:** God's succor, helper; the highest saint in spiritual hierarchy
***Ghaws al-aʿẓam*:** God's greatest succor
***Ḫāce*:** Instructor, teacher, man of distinction; merchant
***Hadīth*:** Prophethic traditions of Muhammed in the form of his sayings and practices as narrated by transmitters and recorded in various compendia
***Ḫaḳān*:** Great king in Turko-Mongolitan royal titulature
***Ḥaḳīḳat*:** Truth, essential reality

Ḥaḳīḳī: Truthful; rightful; concerning essential reality
Ḥākim: Ruler, sovereign
Ḥākim-i maʿnī: True ruler, ruler in meaning
Ḫalīfe-i Ḥaḳ: God's vicegerent
Hediyye-i ilahī: Divine gift
Ḥilm: Clemency
Ḥikma*, pl. *Ḥikam*, T. *Hikmet: Philosophy, wisdom
Ḥikmat-i ʿamalī: Practical philosophy
Ḥikmat al-Ishrāq: The illuminationist school of philosophy instituted by Suhrawardi in the eleventh century that rests on the conviction that true knowledge could be acquired through intuition without the intermediacy of discursive knowledge.
Hüdāvendigār: Ruler in Perso-Turkish titulature in reference to divinely ordained king
Ḥukūma*, T. *Ḥükūmet: Government; governance
Huma: A legendary bird originating from ancient Iranian mythology that casts its shadow on persons as a sign of good fortune, more specifically, as a good omen to become a king
Hümāyūn: Royal, august, fortunate
Ḫunkār: King
Hurufism: Philosophical and esoteric movement characterized by spirituality and learning based on the study of letters and names
Ḥusn: Goodness
Icāzet: License of authorization to teach or train in Islamic learning or spiritual traditions
Ifrāṭ* and *tafrīṭ: Acting in extremes; extreme situations in opposite directions in breach of set boundaries
Iftā: Juristic ruling
ʿIlm*, pl. *ʿulūm: Knowledge, science, discipline
ʿIlm al-bāṭin: Esoteric knowledge
ʿIlm al-siyāsa: The science of governance
ʿilm-i ḫavās: Elite science; occultism; esoteric knowledge
ʿIlm-i ilāhī: Divinity; divine knowledge
ʿIlm-i khādim: The knowledge of the servant
ʿIlm-i makhdūm: The knowledge of the Served [God]
Imam: Leader; ruler of Muslim community; in Shiism, one of twelve infallible guides in succession to Muhammed
Imamate: Leadership and guidance
Imāmat-i ḥaqīqī: True leadership
Inṣāf: Justice equity
Insān-ı kāmil: Perfect man, universal man
Insān-i medenī: Civic man
Inṣāf: Fairness, equity
Intiṣāf: Seeking justice for one's self
Iqtidār: Power, sovereignty
Irāda: Will
ʿIrfān*, P. *ʿerfān: Intuitive knowledge
Istiḥḳāḳ: By right or merit, deserving
ʿIzz: Glory
ʿIzzat: Greatness
Jalāl: Glory, majesty
Jamāl: Beauty
Jawr*, P. *Javr*, T. *Cevr: Oppression
Jibillat: Character, nature

Jifr: The occult science of prognostication
Jihād: Struggle
Jihād-i akbar: Greatest struggle in reference to one's spiritual tribulations in quest for perfection
Jihād-i kabīr: Great struggle, which may be physical or spiritual
Jihandārī: Rulership in reference to world-domination in Perso-Turkish royal titulature
Ḳāḍīʿasker: Military judge; one of the chief judges in Ottoman judicial establishment
Kadkhudā: Deputy, representative
Kāfir, **pl.** ***küffār***: Infidel
Kalām: Theology
Kamālāt: Perfections
Ḳānūn: Ordinance issued by the Ottoman ruler; fundamental law; customary law; institutional convention
Ḳānūn-ı ḳadīm: Ancient law, fundamental law, or an established custom in reference to binding practices, procedures, and rulings in Ottoman administration
Karam: Nobleness
Karāma: Miraculous powers; nobility
Kasb: Acquisition
Kavn: Creation, existence
Ḳayser: The title of Roman emperors adopted by Muslim rulers in Asia Minor and later by Ottomans
Keshvar-e maʿānī: Realm of meanings
Khalīfa: Literally a successor, deputy, vicegerent, representative; supreme ruler of the universal Muslim community; in Sufi orders, an authorized representative and successor to the head of the order
Khalīfat Allāh: God's vicegerent
Khalīfat Rasūl Allāh: Successor to God's Messenger, Muhammed
Khān: Heavenly ordained king in Turko-Mongolian titulature
Kharra-yi kīyānī: Royal light
Khāssa: Ruling elite
Khātam: Seal
Khātam al-Anbiyā: The seal of prophets in reference to Prophet Muhammed
Khawās: Notables
Khilāfa: Succession; vicegerency
Khilāfat al-nubuwwa: Succession to the Prophet
Khilāfat-i Ḥaq: Vicegerency of the Truth
Khilāfat-i ḥaqīqī: The real vicegerency
Khilāfat-i Khudā: Vicegerency of God
Khilāfat-i kubrā: Greatest vicegerency
Khilāfat-i raḥmānī: Vicegerency of God's mercy
Khilāfat-i ṣūrī: Vicegerency of God in appearance
Khilāfat-i ʿuẓmā: Greatest vicegerency
Khvarnah: Divine glory
Kishvar-i maʿnī: Realm of meanings; spiritual world
Kishvar-i shahādat: Visible world
Kizilbash: Red-head, in reference to various confessional communities with Ali-centered spirituality from the Balkans to Iran
Khulq: Human nature, disposition
Khulq-i fiṭrī: Natural character, innate disposition
Kūl: Slave, servant

Ḳūt: Fortune
Luṭf: Grace
Madrasa: Educational institution
Mafḍūl: Less excellent
Maʿdilat: Justice
al-Madīna al-fāḍila: Virtuous city
Maghrib: West
Mahdi*, T. *Mehdi: The awaited rightly guided savior of Muslim community expected to appear at the end of times in Islamic eschatology
Malakūt: Heavens, angelic realm
Malakūtī: Angelic
Malik: King
Mālik: Possessor, owner
Mamlaka: Realm, kingdom
Manāqib*, T. *menāḳıb: Miraculous deeds; hagiographic account
Maʿnī: Meaning, truth, essence, reality
Maʿrifat Allāh: Intimate knowledge of God
Martaba: Status
Maʿnawī*, P. *maʿnavī*, T. *maʿnevī: Concerning meanings; spiritual
Maṣāliḥ*, T. *Meṣāliḥ: Affairs, needs, services
Mashriq: East
Mavāhib: God's graces, gifts
Mavhibat-i ghaybī: Divine gift
Medīne-i ḍālle: Errant city
Meşveret: Consultation
Müderris: Instructor, teacher; professor in a madrasa
Muftī: Jurist issuing legal opinions
Muʿiz: Fortifier
Mujaddid*, T. *müceddid: Renewer of religion
Mujāhid: One who struggles; warrior
Mujtahid: Jurist independent in judgment
Mukavvanāt: Totality of all things created
Mukhtaṣar: Abridgement
Mülāzım: Assistant
Mulk: Kingship, sovereignty
Mulk-i ṣūrat: Kingship in appearance
Münkerāt: Iniquities
Murābit: Someone stationed in a *ribāt*, a frontier garrison for the defense; raider for the faith
Murīd: Disciple
Mutaṣarrif: Administrator
Nabī*, pl. *anbiyā: Prophet
Nafs-i ammāra: Concupiscent soul
Nāʾib*, pl. *nuwwāb: Deputy
Nasab-i maʿnavī: Spiritual genealogy
Nasabī: Congenital, geneological
Naṣīḥa: Advice, counsel
Naṣīḥatnāme: Book of advice
Niʿma*, T. *niʿmet: Grace, beneficence
Niʿmet-i vehbī: God's grace given without a cause

Niẓām: Order
Nubuwwa: Prophethood
Padishah: Great king
Pādishāhān-i ḥaqīqī: Great kings in truth and essential reality
Pādishāhān-i ṣūrat: Great kings in appearance
Pādishāhān-i ẓākhir: Great kings in appearance
Qahr*, T. *ḳahr: Overpowering, domination, subjugation
Qaḍā: Adjudication; judicial system
Qāḍī*, pl. *quḍāt: Judge
Qaṣīm: Partner in reference to shared authority in rulership as displayed in the specific case of the Seljuk partnership in the caliphate of the Abbasids
Qudrat*, T. *kudret: Power, might; God's attribute as almighty
Quṭb*, T. *ḳuṭb: Axis mundi; pole
Quṭb al-aqṭāb: Axis mundi; pole of the poles
Quṭb al-ʿārifīn: The pole of knowers of God
Quṭbiyya: Poleship
Rab: Lord
Rabbānī: Concerning God's lordship
Rafidi: A pejorative term used by Sunni theologians in reference to perceived heretics with loyalties to Ali, the fourth caliph of Islam, and various other strands of Shiism
Raḥmanī: Concerning God's forgiveness and compassion over His entire creation, Muslim and non-Muslim alike
Rāʿī: Shepherd; overseer
Raʿiyyet: Subjects; flock
Rasūl*, pl. *rusul: Messenger
Rijāl al-ghayb: Invisible men
Rijāl Allāh*, T. *ricālüllāh: Invisible friends of God
Risāla*, pl. *rasāʾil: Treatise
Riyāsat: Leadership
Rububiyya: God's lordship
Rūḥ: Soul, spirit
Rukn: Pillar
Rumi: An Inhabitant of the former Roman Empire in Asia Minor and the Balkans; A Turkish-speaking member of Ottoman ruling establishment
Saʿādat: Happiness
Sabīl Allāh: Path of Allah
Sahā: Generosity
Ṣāḥib-qirān: Lord of the auspicious celestial conjunction
Sāʾis: Groom; leader
Ṣāliḥ: Pious
Sarvar*, T. *server: Leader, sovereign
Salṭana: Executive power of rulership
al-Salṭana al-kāmila: Perfect rulership; having executive authority on both temporal and spiritual realms
al-Salṭana al-maʿnawiyya*, P. *salṭanat-i maʿnī: Executive power in truth and essential reality
al-Salṭana al-ṣūriyya*, P. *salṭanat-i ṣūrī: Executive power in appearance
Salṭanat-i ẓāhirī: Executive power in appearance
Sayf: Sword

Şehnāmecī: Court historian commissioned to write dynastic histories or chivalrous accounts of Ottoman rulers often in verse inspired by Ferdowsi's *Shāhnāma*.
Şehzāde: Prince
Serʿasker: Commander
Serverī*, T. *Serverlik: Leadership
Shāh*, pl. *shāhān: King
Shāhanshāh: King of kings
Shajāʿat: Courage
Sharaf: Honor
Sharīʿa*, adj. *sharʿī: Islamic law
Sharīʿat-i nabavī: Prophetic Law
Shujāʿ: Brave, warlike
Shujāʿ al-dawla: Hero of the reign or dominion
Shujāʿ al-dīn: Hero of religion
Sirr*, pl. *asrār: Secret
Siyāsat-i ʿāmma: The governance of general public
Siyāsat-i khāssa: The governance of the ruling elite
Siyāsat-i nafs: The governance of the self
al-Siyāsa al-Sharʿiyya: Governance in accordance with the prescripts of Islamic law; capital punishments in Islamic law
Siyāsetnāme: Mirror for princes; book of governance
Ṣiddīḳ: Devout friend of God
Siyar al-Mulūk: Virtuous account of kings
Siyāsa: Governance; horse-grooming
Subaşı: Commander
Sulṭān-i ṣūrat va maʿnī: Ruler in both appearance and truth
Ṣūrat: Form, appearance
Ṣūrī: In appearance
Taʾalluh: Intuitive [knowledge]; divinely inspired knowledge
Tāc: Crown
Tadbīr-i ilāhī: Divine governance
Ṭāghī: Rebel who breaches the confines of Islam in faith or practice
Tafsīr: Commentary; Qur'anic commentary
Tafwīz: Delegation of executive authority, entrust
Taghyīr-i fiṭrat: Changing one's nature
Taḫt: Throne
Ṭāʾifa: Group, faction, community, people
Taḳdīr-i ilāhī: Divine providence
Takhalluq: Learned behavior, inculcated disposition
Ṭāliʿ: Fortune
Ṭāliʿ-i khujasta: Auspicious constellation
Taqvā: Piety
Ṭarīḳat: Sufi order; institutionalized and ritualized spiritual path
Taṣarruf: Having capacity to execute power
Ṭasawwuf: Sufism
Tuḥfa: Gift
Ulema: Scholars of religious sciences
Ulī al-amr: Holder of authority, sovereign
ʿUlūm al-ẓāhir: Discursive sciences or knowledge

***Umarā*, T. *ümerā*:** Statesmen, rulers, governors
***Umma*:** Muslim community in the broadest sense
***Vezāret*:** Executive power of the ruler delegated to a vizier in Ottoman government
***Wājib*:** Religious requirement, obligatory
***Walī*, pl. *awliyā*; T. *velī*:** Friend of God
***Wālī*:** Ruler, governor
***Waqf*, T. *vakıf*:** Pious endowment
***Wilāya*:** God's friendship
***Ẓāhir*:** Outer, external
***Ẓālim*:** Oppressor
***Zandaḳa*:** Heresy
***Ẓill Allāh*:** God's shadow
***Ẓilliyat-i yazdānī*:** Being God's shadow
***Zuhd*:** Devotion to God
***Ẓulm*:** Oppression

BIBLIOGRAPHY

Primary Sources

ʿAbdülkerīm b. Meḥmed. *Nesāyiḥü'l-Ebrār*. MS SK, Hamidiye 1469, ff. 159b-166a; MS University of Michigan Library, Isl. Ms. 389.

ʿAbdullāh-i Ilāhī. *Kashf al-Wāridāt li-Ṭālib al-Kamālāt wa Ghāyat al-Darajāt*, ed. Aḥmad Farīd al-Mazīdī. Beirut: Kitāb Nāshirūn, 2013.

Abdülvasi Çelebi. *Halilname*, ed. Ayhan Güldaş. Ankara: Kültür Bakanlığı Yayınları, 1996.

Abul Fazl ʿAllami. *Ain i Akbari*, transl. H. Blochman (Calcutta: Asiatic Society of Bengal, 1873.

Aflākī, Shams al-Dīn Aḥmed. *Manāqib al-ʿĀrifīn*, 2nd ed., 2 vols, ed. Tahsin Yazıcı. Ankara: Türk Tarih Kurumu, 1976–80.

Aflākī, Shams al-Dīn Aḥmad-e. *The Feats of the Knowers of God*, transl. John O'Kane. Leiden: Brill, 2002.

Ahmed Bîcan, Yazıcıoğlu. *Dürr-i Meknûn*, ed. Ahmet Demirtaş. Istanbul: Akademik Kitaplar, 2009.

Aḥmedī. *İskender—Nāme: İnceleme—Tıpkıbasım*, ed. İsmail Ünver. Ankara: Türk Dil Kurumu Yayınları, 1983.

Aḫterī, Musliḥuddīn Muṣṭafā. *Aḫterī-i Kebīr*. Istanbul: Maṭbaʿa-i Āmire, 1310.

Akarslan, Turgut. "İbn-i Melek Muhammed bin Abdüllatif Bahrü'l-Hikem." PhD diss., Gaziosmanpaşa University, 2010.

Akgündüz, Ahmet. *Osmanlı Kanunnâmeleri ve Hukukî Tahlilleri*, 9 vols. Istanbul: Fey Vakfı Yayınları, 1990–96.

ʿAlāyī bin Muḥibbī el-Şīrāzī el-Şerīf. *Düstūrü'l-Vüzerā*. MS SK, Yazma Bağışlar 4421/3.

ʿAlāyī bin Muḥibbī el-Şīrāzī el-Şerīf. *Netīcetü's-Sülūk fī Terceme-i Naṣīḥatü'l-Mülūk*. MS SK, Pertevniyal 1011.

Albèri, Eugenio, (ed). *Relazioni degli ambasciatori Veneti al senato*, vol. 11. Cambridge: Cambridge University Press, 2012.

ʿAlī bin Bālī. *al-ʿIqd al-Manẓūm fī Dhikr Afāḍil al-Rūm*. Beirut: Dār al-Kitāb al-ʿArabī, 1975.

ʿAlī bin ʿÖmer. *Ravżatu'l-Mücāhidīn*. MS TSMK, Hazine 622.

ʿAlī Dede al-Mustarī. *Khawātim al-Ḥikam*, ed. Maḥmud Naṣṣār. Cairo: Dār al-Āfāq al-ʿArabiyya, 2002.

ʿAlī Dede el-Sketvārī el-Bosnevī. *al-Intiṣār li Qidwat al-Akhyār*. MS SK, Köprülü Fazıl Ahmed Paşa 1381, 185a-199b.

ʿAlī Dede el-Sketvārī el-Bosnevī. *Muḥāḍarat al-Awāʾil wa Musāmarat al-Akhāʾir*. Cairo: al-Maṭbaʿa al-ʿĀmira al-Sharafiyya, 1311 [1389].

Alper, Ömer Mahir. "İbn Kemâl'in Risâle fî Beyâni'l-Akl'ı." *İslam Araştırmaları Dergisi* 3 (1999): 235–269.

Amâsî, Abdüsselâm. *Tuḥfetü'l-Ümerâ ve Minḥatü'l-Vüzerâ*, ed. A. Mevhibe Coşar. Istanbul: Büyüyen Ay Yayınları, 2012.

Amāsī, Aḥmed b. Ḥüsāmeddīn. *Kitāb-ı Mirʾātü'l-Mülūk*. MS SK, Esat Efendi 1890.

Amāsī, Ibn al-Khaṭīb Meḥmed Ḳāṣım b. Yaʿqūb. *Rawḍ al-Akhyār al-Muntakhab min Rabīʿ al-Abrār*, ed. Maḥmūd Fākhūrī. Aleppo: Dār al-Qalam al-ʿArābī, 2003.

Amāsī, Meḥmed b. Ḳāṣım b. Yaʿḳūb. *Rawḍ al-Akhyār al-Muntakhab min Rabī al-Abrār*. Bulaq: Ḥusayn al-Ṭarābulusī, 1279 [1862–1863].

Anḳarî, Ḳāsım b. Seydī el-Ḥāfıẓ. *Enīsü'l-Celīs*, ed. Azmi Bilgin (Istanbul: Istanbul Üniversitesi Yayınları, 2008).

ʿĀrifī Maʿrūf Efendī. *ʿUqūd al-Jawāhir li-Ẓakhāʾir al-Akhāʾir*. MS TSMK, Revan 415.
Arıkoğlu, İsmail. "Feriştehoğlu'nun Cavidân-Nâme Tercümesi: 'Işk-nâme.'" PhD diss., Yüzüncü Yıl University, 2006.
Arslan, Ahmet Turan. "İmam Birgivî'nin (929–981H/1523–1573) Bir Mektubu." *İlmi Araştırmalar* 5 (1997): 61–74.
Āshtiyānī, Seyyed Jalāl ad-Dīn. *Rasāʾil-i Qayṣarī bā Ḥavāshī-i Muḥammed Riżā Qumshāhī*. Tehran: Muʾassasa-i Pizhūhishī-i Ḥikmat va Falsafa-i Irān, 1381 [2002 or 2003].
ʿĀşıḳ Çelebi. *Meşāʿir üş-Şuʿarā*, ed. G. M. Meredith-Owens. London: Luzac, 1971.
ʿĀşıḳ Çelebī, Pīr Meḥmed b. ʿAlī. *Miʿrācü'l-ʿIyāle ve Minhācü'l-ʿAdāle*. MS SK, Şehid Ali Paşa 1556.
ʿĀşıḳ Çelebī, Pīr Meḥmed b. ʿAlī. *Terceme-i Ravżü'l-Aḫyār el-Münteḫab min Rebīʿü'l-Ebrār*. MS SK, Reşid Efendi 540.
ʿĀşıḳ Çelebī, Pīr Meḥmed b. ʿAlī. *el-Ṭibrü'l-Mesbūḳ fī Naṣīḥati'l-Mülūk*. MS SK, Pertevniyal 1011.
Âşıkpaşazâde. *Âşıkpaşazâde Tarihi*, ed. Necdet Öztürk. Istanbul: Bilge Kültür Sanat, 2013.
Asiye Hatun. *Rüya Mektupları*, ed. Cemal Kafadar. Istanbul: Oğlak Yayınları, 1994.
Atâî, Nev'îzâde. *Hadaiku'l-Hakaik fî Tekmileti'ş-Şakaik*, ed. Abdülkadir Özcan. Istanbul: Çağrı Yayınları, 1989.
ʿAṭūfī, Khiḍr b. ʿUmar. *Daftar-i Kutub*. MS Budapest, Magyar Tudományos Akadémia Könyvtára Keleti Gyűjtemény, Török F. 59.
Avcı, Necati. *Kanunî'nin Belgrad Seferi (Tabib Ramazan)*. Eskişehir: Osman Gazi Üniversitesi Yayınları, 2000.
ʿAẓmī Efendī, Pīr Muḥammed. *Enīsü'l-ʿĀrifīn*. MS SK, Pertevniyal 474; Lala Ismail 243.
Bağdemir, Abdullah. "Müzekki'n-Nüfûs." PhD diss., Ankara University, 1997.
Bagley, F. R. C., transl. *Ghazālī's Book of Counsel for Kings (Nasīhat al-Mulūk)*. London & New York: Oxford Unviersity Press, 1964.
Bakır, Abdullah. "Yazıcızāde ʿAlī'nin Selçuḳ-Nāme İsimli Eserinin Edisyon Kritiği." PhD diss., Marmara University, 2008.
Bālī Efendī, Sofyevī. *Eṭvār-ı Sebʿa*. MS SK, Hacı Mahmud 2927.
Bālī Efendī, Sofyevī. *Risāle der Sīret-i Pādişāhān-ı Pīşīn*. MS SK, Hekimoğlu 589.
Bālī Efendī, Sofyevī. *Risāle fī Gazāi'l-Mücāhidīn*. MS İÜK, T 786.
Bālī Efendī, Sofyevī. *Sharḥ-i Fuṣūṣ al-Ḥikam*. Istanbul: Dersaʿādet, 1309 [1891 or 1892].
Başaran, Orhan. "İdrîs-i Bitlîsî'nin Heşt Bihişt'inin Hâtimesi." PhD diss., Atatürk University, 2000.
Beyâni. *Tezkiretü'ş-Şuarâ*, ed. İbrahim Kutluk. Ankara: Türk Tarih Kurumu, 1997.
Beyazit, Ayşe. "Ahmed Bîcan'ın "Müntehâ" İsimli Fusûs Tercümesi Işığında Tasavvuf Düşüncesi." MA Thesis, Marmara University, 2008.
Birgivī Meḥmed. *Dhukhr al-Mulūk*. SK, Esad Efendi 615/8.
Birnbaum, Eleazar. *The Book of Advice by King Kay Kāʾus ibn Iskander: The Earliest Old Ottoman Turkish Version of his Ḳābūsnāme*. Duxbury: Harvard University Printing Office, 1981.
Bistāmī, ʿAbdurraḥmān. *Fevāyiḥü'l-Miskiyye ve Fevātiḥü'l-Mekkiyye Tercümesi*. MS TSMK, Yeniler 282.
Bistāmī, ʿAlī b. Maḥmūd el-Şahrūdī. *Ḥall al-Rumūz wa Kashf al-Kunūz*, ed. Yūsuf Aḥmad. Beirut: Kitāb Nāshirūn, 2013.
Bistāmī, ʿAlī b. Mecdüddīn el-Şahrūdī. *Tuḥfa-i Maḥmūdiyya [Naṣīḥat al-Wuzarā]*. MS TSMK Emanet Hazinesi 1342; MS SK, Ayasofya 2885.
Bistāmī, ʿAlī b. Mecdüddīn el-Şahrūdī. *Tuḥfat al-Salāṭīn [Tuḥfat al-Mulūk]*. MS SK, Şehid Ali Paşa 2797, ff. 73b–75b; Esad Efendi 1663, ff. 333b–335b.
Bistāmī, ʿAlī b. Mecdüddīn el-Şahrūdī. *Tuḥfat al-Wuzārā*. MS SK, Ayasofya 2885.

Bostān Çelebī. *Cülūsnāme-i Sulṭān Süleymān.* MS TSMK, Revan 1283.
Bostān Çelebī. *Süleymānnāme.* MS SK, Ayasofya 3317.
Bostancı, Ali Haydar. "Tasavvuf'ta Etvâr-ı Seb'a ve Sofyalı Bâlî Efendi'nin "Etvâr-ı Seb'a"sı." Master's Thesis, Marmara University, 1996.
Celālzāde Muṣṭafā. *Mevāhibü'l-Ḫallaḳ fī Merātibi'l-Aḫlāḳ.* MS SK, Fatih 3521.
Celâl-zâde Mustafa. *Selim-Nâme,* ed. Ahmet Uğur and Mustafa Çuhadar. Ankara: Kültür Bakanlığı Yayınları, 1990.
Çelik, Neşe. "Menāḳıb-ı Maḥmūd Paşa." Master's thesis, Mimar Sinan University, 1998.
Ceyhan, Âdem. *Bedr-i Dilşad'ın Murâd-Nâmesi,* 2 vols. Istanbul: Milli Eğitim Bakanlığı Yayınları, 1997.
Cürcânî, Seyyid Şerîf. *Şerhu'l-Mevâkıf (Metin—Çeviri),* transl. Ömer Türker. Istanbul: Türkiye Yazma Eserler Kurumu Başkanlığı Yayınları, 2015.
Dağlar, Abdülkadir. "Şeyhülislam Ebussuud Efendi'nin Türkçe Mektubları." Master's thesis, Ege University, 2001.
Dalkıran, Sayın. "İbn-i Kemal'in Tılsımat Risâlesi." *Türk Dünyası Araştırmaları* 104 (1996): 195–207.
Dāvūd-i Ḳayserī. *al-Ithāf al-Sulaymānī fī al-ʿAhd al-Urkhānī.* MS SK, Ali Emiri Arabi 2173.
Dede Efendī, İbrāhīm b. Yaḥyā Khalīfa. *al-Siyāsa al-Sharʿiyya,* ed. Fuʿād ʿAbd al-Munʿim. Iskandariyya, [n.d.].
Demirli, Ekrem. "Abdullah İlahi'nin Keşfü'l-Varidat Adlı Eserinin Tahkiki." Master's Thesis, Marmara University, 1995.
Demirtaş, Funda. "Celâl-zâde Mustafa Çelebi, Tabakâtü'l-Memâlik ve Derecâtü'l-Mesâlik." PhD diss., Erciyes University, 2009.
Dimashqī, Muḥammed b. Muḥammed b. Sulṭān. *Fatḥ al-Malik al-ʿAlīm al-Mannān ʿalā al-Malik al-Muẓaffar Sulaymān.* MS SBB, Petermann I 64.
Dimashqī, Muḥammed b. Muḥammed b. Sulṭān. *Kitāb al-Jawāhir al-Muḍiyya fī Ayyām Dawlat al-ʿUthmāniyya.* MS SBB, Sprenger 198.
Direkci, Bekir. "Cevāhirü'l-Meʿānī." PhD diss., Selçuk University, 2010.
Diyārbakrī, Ḥusayn ibn Muḥammed. *Tārīkh al-Khamīs fī Aḥwāl Anfas Nafīs,* 2 vols. Cairo: al-Maṭbaʿa al-Wahbīya, 1866.
Dizdār, Muṣṭafā b. ʿAbdullāh. *Sulūk al-Mulūk.* MS TSMK, Ahmed 1605.
Doğan, Enfel. *Şeyhoğlu Sadrüddin'in Kābūs-nâme Tercümesi.* Istanbul: Mavi Yayıncılık, 2011.
Ebū'l-Fażl Meḥmed b. İdrīs el-Defterī. *Terceme-i Aḫlāḳ-ı Muḥsinī.* MS TSMK, Revan 347.
Ebū'l-Fażl Münşī al-Şīrāzī. *Dustūr al-Salṭana.* MS BNF, Persan 135.
Ekinci, Ramazan. "16. Asırda Yazılmış Mensur bir Nasihat-Nâme: Abdülkerim bin Mehmed'in Nesâyihü'l-Ebrâr'ı." *Turkish Studies* 7 (2012): 423–441.
Elvan Çelebi. *Menakıbul Kudsiyye fi Menasibil Ünsiyye,* eds. İsmail E. Erünsal and Ahmet Yaşar Ocak. Ankara: Türk Tarih Kurumu, 1995.
Enṣārī, Muḥammed bin Maḥāsin. *Tuḥfat al-Zamān ilā al-Malik al-Muẓaffar Sulaymān.* MS ÖNB, A.F 357.
Erkan, Nevzat. "Celalzade Salih ve Tarih-i Mısr-ı Cedid Adlı Eseri." Master's thesis, Marmara University, 2002.
Erünsal, İsmail E. *XV-XVI. Asır Bayrâmî-Melâmîliği'nin Kaynaklarından Abdurrahman el-Askerî'nin Mir'âtü'l-Işk'ı.* Ankara: Türk Tarih Kurumu, 2003.
Eşrefoğlu Rûmî. *Müzekki'n-Nüfûs,* ed. Abdullah Uçman. Istanbul: İnsan Yayınları, 1996.
Eşrefoğlu Rumî. *Tarikatnâme,* ed. Esra Keskinkılıç. Istanbul: Gelenek Yayıncılık, 2002.
Felek, Özgen, ed. *Kitābü'l-Menāmāt: Sultan* III. *Murad'ın Rüya Mektupları.* İstanbul: Tarih Vakfı Yurt Yayınları, 2014.
Fevrī. *Aḫlāḳ-ı Süleymānī.* MS SK, Ayasofya 2823.

Firāḳî ʿAbdurraḥmān Çelebī. *Terceme-i Aḫlāḳ-ı Muḥsinī*. MS TSMK, Revan 393.

Firdevsî-i Rumî. *Kutb-Nâme*, eds. İbrahim Olgun and İsmet Parmaksızoğlu. Ankara: Türk Tarih Kurumu, 1980.

Fütūḥāt-ı Sulṭān Meḥemmed. MS SK, Ayasofya 3204.

Genç, Vural. "Acem'den Rum'a: İdris-i Bidlîsî'nin Hayatı, Tarihçiliği ve Heşt Behişt'in II. Bayezid Kısmı (1481–1512)." PhD diss., Istanbul University, 2014.

Genç, Vural. "İdris-i Bitlisî, Heşt Bihişt, Osman Gazi Dönemi." Master's thesis, Mimar Sinan University, 2007.

Genç, Vural. "İdris-i Bidlîsî'nin II. Bayezid ve I. Selim'e Mektupları." *JOS* 47 (2016): 147–208.

Genç, Vural. "Şah ile Sultan Arasında Bir Acem Bürokratı: İdrîs-i Bidlîsî'nin Şah İsmail'in Himayesine Girme Çabası." *JOS* 46 (2015): 43–75.

Ghazālī, Abū Ḥāmid. *Kīmyā-i Saʿādat*, ed. Muḥammed ʿAbbāsī. Tehran: Ṭulūʿ va Zarrīn, 1361 [1982 or 1983].

Ghazālī, Abū Ḥāmid. *Naṣīḥat al-Mulūk*, ed. Jalāl al-Dīn Humāʾī. Tehran: Anjuman-i Āsār-i Millī, 1351/1972.

Ghazālī, Abū Ḥāmid. *al-Ṭibr al-Masbūq fī Naṣīḥat al-Mulūk*, ed. Muḥammed Aḥmad Damaj. Beirut: Muʾassasa ʿIzz al-Dīn, 1996.

Gibb, Hamilton A. R. "Luṭfī Paşa on the Ottoman Caliphate." *Oriens* 15 (1962): 287–295.

Gökyay, Orhan Şaik. *Keykâvus, Kabusname* (Çeviren: Mercimek Ahmed), 3rd ed. Istanbul: Milli Eğitim Basımevi, 1974.

Gölpınarlı, Abdülbâki. *Manakıb-ı Hacı Bektâş-ı Velî: Vilâyet-Nâme*. Istanbul: İnkilâp Kitabevi, 1958.

Ğurğānī, Ali. *Kitāb al-Taʿrīfāt* (A Book of Definitions), ed. Gustav Flügel. Beirut: Libraire du Liban, 1985.

Güzel, Abdurrahman. *Abdal Mûsâ Velâyetnâmesi*. Ankara: Türk Tarih Kurumu, 1999.

Ḥācī Pāşā. *Shifā al-Aqsām wa Dawā al-Ālām fī Ṭibb*. MS SK, Ayasofya 3668.

Hadîdî. *Tevârih-i Âl-i Osman (1299–1523)*, ed. Necdet Öztürk. İstanbul: Edebiyat Fakültesi Basımevi, 1991.

Halil bin İsmâil bin Şeyh Bedrüddîn Mahmûd. *Sımavna Kadısıoğlu Şeyh Bedreddin Manâkıbı*, eds. Abdülbâki Gölpınarlı and İsmet Sungurbey. Istanbul: Eti Yayınevi, 1967.

Hamadānī, Mīr Seyyed ʿAlī. *Ẕakhīrat al-Mulūk*, ed. S. M. Anvārī. Tabriz: Intishārāt-i Muʾassasa-i Tārīkh va Farhang-i Iran, 1979.

Ḥamawī, ʿAlī ibn ʿAṭīyya. *al-Naṣaʾiḥ al-Muhimma li al-Mulūk wa al-Aʾimma*, ed. Nashwa al-ʿAlwānī. Dimashq: Dār al-Maktabī, 2000.

Hasan Bey-zâde Ahmed Paşa. *Hasan Bey-zâde Târîhi: Tahlil-Kaynak Tenkidi*, 3 vols., ed. Şevki Nezihi Aykut. Ankara: Türk Tarih Kurumu, 2004.

Ḫızır Münşī, Muẓaffer bin ʿOs̱mān el-Bermekī. *Akhlāq al-Atqiyā va Ṣifāt al-Aṣfiyā*. MS SK, Fatih 3515; TSMK, Emanet Hazinesi 1354.

Hoca Saʿādeddīn. *Selīmnāme*. MS SK, Hekimoğlu 696; TSMK, Revan 937/2.

Hujwiri, Ali Bin Uthman. *The Kashf al-Mahjub: The Oldest Persian Treatise on Sufism*, transl. R. A. Nicholson. Lahore: Islamic Book Foundation, 1976.

Hulvî, Mahmud Cemaleddin. *Lemezât-ı Hulviyye ez Lemezât-ı Ulviyye*, ed. Mehmet Serhan Tayşi. Istanbul: Marmara Üniversitesi İlahiyat Fakültesi Vakfı Yayınları, 1993.

Ibn Abī al-Surūr, Muḥammed al-Bakrī al-Ṣiddīqī. *al-Minaḥ al-Raḥmānīyya fī al-Dawla al-ʿUthmānīyya*, ed. Laylā al-Ṣabbāgh. Damascus: Dār al-Bashāʾir, 1995.

Ibn ʿArabī. *al-Futūḥāt al-Makkiyya*, eds. ʿUthmān Yaḥyā and Ibrāhīm Madkūr. Cairo: al-Hayʾa al-Miṣrīyya al-ʿĀmma li al-Kitāb, 1972.

Ibn ʿArabī. *al-Tadbīrāt al-Ilāhiyya fī Iṣlāḥ al-Mamlaka al-Insāniyya*, ed. Ḥasan Āṣī. Beirut: Muʾassasa Baḥsūn, 1993.

Ibn Arghūn al-Shīrāzī. *Nikāt Mutaʿalliqa bi-Sharḥ al-Maṭāliʿ wa Ḥawāshiyya al-Sharīfa*. MS Walters Art Museum, Baltimore, Ms. 591.

Ibn Battuta. *Travels in Asia and Africa, 1325–1354*, transl. H. A. R. Gibb. London: Routledge and K. Paul, 1957.
Ibn Baṭūṭa. *Riḥla Ibn Baṭūṭa: Tuḥfat al-Nuẓẓār fī Gharā'ib al-Amṣār wa 'Ajā'ib al-Asfār*, ed. Muḥammed 'Abd al-Mun'im al-'Aryān. Beirut: Dār al-Iḥyā al-'Ulūm, 1987.
Ibn Fīrūz Meḥmed. *Gurretü'l-Beyżā*. MS SK, Esad Efendi 1828.
İbn İsâ Saruhânî. *Esmâ-i Hüsnâ Şerhi*, ed. Numan Külekçi. Ankara: Akçağ Yayınları, 2000.
Ibn 'Īsā Saruhānī. *Rumūzü'l-Künūz*. MS SK, Esad Efendi 1986; MS SK, Fatih 3432.
Ibn al-Ḳadrī Kemāl b. Ḥacī Ilyās. *Risāla fī Ādāb al-Mulūk ve Naṣā'iḥ al-Salāṭīn*. MS SK, Ayasofya 2841/1.
Ibn Kemāl. *Fetḥ-i Mıṣr Ḥaḳḳında Vāḳi' Olan Īmā ve İşāret*. MS SK, Esad Efendi 3729, 136a–138a; MS Mevlana Müzesi 2315, 71b-72b.
İbn Kemal. *Tevârih-i Âl-i Osman: I. Defter*. Ankara: Türk Tarih Kurumu, 1991.
Ibn Miskawayh, Aḥmed ibn Muḥammed. *al-Ḥikma al-Khālida (Jāvidān Khirad)*, ed. 'Abd al-Raḥmān Badawī. Tehran: Dānishgāh-i Tehrān, 1980.
Ibn Miskawayh, Aḥmed ibn Muḥammed. *The Refinement of Character*. Beirut: American University of Beirut, 1968.
Ibn Nujaym. *Rasā'il Ibn Nujaym al-Iqtiṣādīyya*, eds. Muḥammed Aḥmad Sirāj and 'Alī Jum'a Muḥammed. Cairo: Dār al-Salām, 1998.
Ibn Taghrībirdī, Abū al-Maḥāsin Yūsuf. *History of Egypt 1382–1469 A.D.*, transl. William Popper. New York: AMS Press, 1976.
Ibn Taghrībirdī, Abū al-Maḥāsin Yūsuf. *al-Nujūm al-Zāhira fī Mulūk al-Miṣr wa al-Qāhira*, ed. Muḥammed Ḥusayn Shams al-Dīn. Beirut: Dār al-Kutub al-'Ilmiyya, 1992.
Ibn Taymiyya. *al-Siyāsa al-Shar'iyya fī Iṣlāḥ al-Rā'ī wa al-Ra'iyya*, ed. 'Abd al-Bāsiṭ b. Yūsuf al-Gharīb. Dammām: Dār al-Rāwī, 2000.
İbn Teymiye. *Siyaset: es-Siyasetu'ş-şeriyye*, transl. Vecdi Akyüz. Istanbul: Dergah Yayınları 1985.
Ibrāhīm b. Muḥammed. *Ādāb al-Khilāfa wa Asbāb al-Ḥiṣāfa*. MS, TSMK Revan 404.
Idrīs-i Bidlīsī. *Hasht Behesht*. MS Nuruosmaniye Kütüphanesi 3209; MS SK, Esad Efendi 2197.
Idrīs-i Bidlīsī. *Mir'āt al-Jamāl*. MS SK, Şehid Ali Paşa 2149.
Idrīs-i Bidlīsī. *Risālat al-Khilāfa*. MS İÜK, F 1228.
İdrîs-i Bidlîsî. *Selim Şah-nâme*, ed. and transl. Hicabi Kırlangıç. Ankara: Kültür Bakanlığı Yayınları, 2001.
İdris-i Bitlisî. *Heşt Behişt, VII. Ketîbe: Fatih Sultan Mehmed Devri 1451–1481*, transl. M. İbrahim Yıldırım. Ankara: Türk Tarih Kurumu, 2013.
Idrīs b. Husām al-Dīn Bidlīsī. *Qānūn-i Shāhanshāhī*, ed. 'Abd Allāh Mas'ūdī Ārānī. Tehran: Markaz-i Pazhūhishī-i Mīrās-i Maktūb, 2008.
Ikhtiyar el-Hoseini. *Destour el-Vizaret*. MS BNF, Persan 768.
İlhan, Avni. "Birgili Mehmed Efendi ve Mezhepler Tarihi ile İlgili Risalesi." *Dokuz Eğlül Üniversitesi İlahiyat Fakültesi Dergisi* 6 (1989): 173–215.
İlyâs İbn-i İsa Akhisârî Saruhânî. *Akhisarlı Şeyh İsâ Menâkıbnâmesi*, eds. Sezai Küçük and Ramazan Uslu. Istanbul: Aşiyan Yayınları, 2003.
İnbaşı, Mehmet. "Sultan I. Murad'ın Evrenos Bey'e Mektubu." *Atatürk Üniversitesi Türkiyat Araştırmaları Enstitüsü Dergisi* 17 (2001), 225–236.
İsen, Mustafa, ed. *Künh'ül-Ahbâr'ın Tezkire Kısmı*. Ankara: Atatürk Kültür Merkezi Yayını, 1994.
Iṣfahānī, Rāghib. *al-Dharī'a ilā Makārim al-Sharī'a*, ed. Sayyid 'Alī Mīr Lavḥī. Iṣfahān: Jāmi'at Iṣfahān, Mu'āwanīyat al-Baḥth al-'Ilmī, 1996.
Jahramī, Şemseddīn. *Risāla Barāya Sulṭān Selīm*. MS TMSF, Revan 1614.
Jīlī, Aḥmed b. Maḥmūd. *Minhāj al-Wuzarā fī al-Naṣīḥa*. MS SK, Ayasofya 2907.
Kappert, Petra. *Geschichte Sultan Süleymān Ḳānūnīs von 1520 bis 1557: oder Ṭabaḳāt ül-Mamālik ve Derecāt ül-Mesālik*. Weisbaden: Franz Steiner Verlag, 1981.

Karaduman, Selami. "Oruç Beg Tarihi Manisa Nüshası." Master's thesis, Uludağ University, 2010.

Ḳarahisārī, ʿAlāʾeddīn ʿAlī b. ʿÖmer b. ʿAlī. *Rumūzüʾl-Esrār Şerhu Künūzüʾl-Envār.* MS, Nuruosmaniye 1334.

Karahisârî, Kâsım b. Mahmûd. *İrşâdüʾl-Mürîd ileʾl-Murâd fî Tercemeti Mirsādüʾl-ʿİbâd,* ed. Özgür Kavak (Istanbul: Klasik, 2010).

Karamustafa, Ahmet T. *Vāḥidī's Menāḳıb-i Hvoca-i Cihān ve Netīce-i Cān: Critical Edition and Historical Analysis.* Cambridge, Mass.: The Department of Near Eastern Languages and Civilizations, Harvard University, 1993.

Kartal, Ahmet. "Kerâmât-ı Ahi Evran Mesnevîsi Üzerine Notlar." *Divan Edebiyatı Araştırmaları Dergisi* 2 (2009): 223–242.

Kāshānī, ʿAbd al-Razzāq. *Iṣṭilāhāt al-Ṣūfiyya,* ed. ʿAbd al-Khāliq Muḥammed. Cairo: Dār al-Maʿārif, 1984.

Kāshifī, Ḥusayn Vāʿiẓ. *Futuvvat-nāma-i Sulṭānī,* ed. Muḥammed Jaʿfar Maḥjūb. Tehran: Bunyād-i Farhang-i Īrān, 1971.

Kastritsis, J. Dimitris. *The Tales of Sultan Mehmed, Son of Bayezid Khan [Aḥvāl-i Sulṭān Meḥemmed bin Bāyezīd Ḫān].* Cambridge, Mass.: Sources of Oriental Languages and Literatures, 2007.

Kātib Çelebī. *Kashf al-Ẓunūn an Asāmī al-Kutub wa al-Funūn,* eds. Şerefettin Yaltkaya and Rifat Bilge. Istanbul: Maarif Matbaası, 1941–43.

Kemāleddīn Meḥmed Efendī. *Mevżūʿātüʾl-ʿUlūm.* Istanbul: Dersaʿādet, 1313/1895.

Khayrabaytī, Maḥmūd b. Ismāʿīl b. Ibrāhīm. *al-Durra al-Gharrā fī Naṣīḥat al-Salāṭīn wa al-Quḍāt wa al-Umarā.* Mecca and Riyāḍ: Maktaba Nazār Muṣṭafā al-Bāz, 1996.

Ḳınalīzāde ʿAlī Çelebī. *Aḫlāḳ-ı ʿAlāʾī.* Bulak, 1833.

Kınalı-zade Hasan Çelebi. *Tezkiretüʾş-Şuarâ,* 2 vols, ed. İbrahim Kutluk. Ankara: Türk Tarih Kurumu, 1978.

Ḳonevī, Meḥmed b. Ḥācī Ḫalīl. *Tavārīkh-i Āl-i ʿOs̱mān.* MS, Kayseri Raşit Efendi Eski Eserler Kütüphanesi, Raşid Efendi Eki 11243.

Köseoğlu, Sinan. "Hacı İlyas, "Hizânetüʾl-Envâr." PhD diss., Istanbul University, 2014.

Küçük, Sezai and Muslu, Ramazan. *Şeyh İsâ Menâkıbnâmesi.* Sakarya: Aşiyan Yayınları, 2003.

Kurban, Ferhat. "Şirvani Mahmud Sulṭāniye." PhD diss., Marmara University, 1990.

Kürkçüoğlu, Kemal Edib. "Kânunî'nin Bâlî Beğ'e Gönderdiği Hatt-ı Humâyûn." *Ankara Üniversitesi Dil Tarih Coğrafya Fakültesi Dergisi* 8 (1950): 225–231.

Kuru, Esra. "Şeyh Ahmed İlâhî ve Pend-Nâmesi." *Turkish Studies* 9 (2014): 771–784.

Kütükoğlu, Mübahat S. "Lütfi Paşa Âsafnâmesi." In *Prof. Dr. Bekir Kütükoğlu'na Armağan,* (pp., 49–99). İstanbul: Edebiyat Fakültesi Basımevi, 1991.

Lāmiʿī Çelebī. *Leṭāyifnāme.* MS İÜK, T 3814.

Lāmiʿī Çelebi. "Şerefüʾl-İnsān," ed. Sadettin Eğri. PhD diss., Gazi University, 1997.

Latîfî. *Tezkiretüʾş-Şʾuara ve Tabsıratüʾn-Nuzamâ,* ed. Rıdvan Canım. Ankara: Atatürk Kültür Merkezi Yayınları, 2000.

Lüṭfī Pāşā. *Khalāṣ al-Umma fī Maʿrifat al-Aʾimma.* MS SK, Ayasofya 2877, 2876.

Lüṭfī Pāşā. *Risāle-i Firāḳ-ı Dālle Tercümesi.* MS SK, Ayasofya 2195, ff. 110b–123a.

Lüṭfī Pāşā. *Tevārīḫ-i Āl-i ʿOs̱mān,* ed. Āli Bey. Istanbul: Matbaʿa-i Āmire, 1341/1925.

Makkī, Shaykh. *al-Jānib al-Gharbī fī Ḥall Mushkilāt al-Shaykh Muḥyī al-Dīn ibn ʿArabī,* ed. Najīb Māyil Haravī. Tehran: Intisharāt-i Mawlā, 1985.

Matuz, Joseph. *L'ouvrage de Seyfī Çelebī: historien ottoman du XVIe siècle.* Paris: Librairie A. Maisonneuve, 1968.

Māwardī, Abī al-Ḥasan ʿAlī b. Muḥammed. *al-Aḥkām al-Sulṭāniyya wa al-Wilāyāt al-Dīniyya,* ed. Aḥmed Mubārak al-Baghdādī (Kuwait: Maktaba Dār Ibn Ḳutayba, 1989).

Mecdî Mehmed Efendi. *Hadaikuʾş-Şakaik,* ed. Abdülkadir Özcan. Istanbul: Çağrı Yayınları, 1989.

Mehmed. *Işk-nâme (İnceleme-Metin)*, ed. Sedit Yüksel. Ankara: Ankara Üniversitesi Basımevi, 1965.

Mekki Efendi, Şeyh. *İbn Arabi Müdafaası*, ed. Halil Baltacı. Istanbul: Gelenek Yayıncılık, 2004.

Ménage, V. L. "The Menāqib of Yakhshi Faqīh." *BSOAS* 26 (1963): 50–54.

Minhāj al-Mulūk li Ahl al-Sulūk. MS SK, Şehid Ali Paşa 1557.

Minorsky, Vladimir. "Shaykh Bālī Efendi on the Safavids." *BSOAS* 20 (1957): 437–450.

Mollâ Ahmed İlâhî. *Tasavvuf-nâme*, eds. Mücahit Kaçar and Ahmet Akdağ. Istanbul: Büyüyen Ay, 2015.

Muḥammed b. Sharaf al-Dīn al-Madanī al-Shāfiʿī. *Hibat al-Fattāḥ*. MS SK, Ayasofya 1803.

Muhammed b. Turtûşî. *Sirâcu'l-Mülûk: Siyaset Ahlâkı ve İlkelerine Dair*, transl. Said Aykut. Istanbul: İnsan Yayınları, 1995.

Mukhtaṣar fī al-Siyāsa wa Umūr al-Ṣalṭana, MS SK, Fatih 1921.

Münşī Çelebī. *Neṣāyiḥ*. MS SK, Hacı Mahmud 1933.

Naḥīfī. *Nehcü's-Sülūk fī Siyāseti'l-Mülūk*. Istanbul: Rıżā Efendi Maṭbaʿası, 1286/1870.

Naṣīḥatnāme-i Sulṭān Murād. MS TSMK, Revan 407.

Neşrî, Mehmed. *Kitâb-ı Cihan-Nümâ*, 2 vols, eds. Faik Reşit Unat and Mehmet Altan Köymen. Ankara: Türk Tarih Kurumu, 1949.

Nevālī, Naṣūḥ. *Aḫlāḳ-ı Muḥsinī Tercümesi*. MS SK, Hüsrev Paşa 288.

Nevālī, Naṣūḥ. *Tercüme-i Neṣāʾiḥ-i Arisṭaṭālīs*. MS SK, Hafid Efendi 253.

Ögke, Ahmet. *Ahmed Şemseddîn-i Marmaravî: Hayatı, Eserleri, Görüşleri*. Istanbul: İnsan Yayınları, 2001.

Özgül, Ayhan. "İlyas b. Îsâ-yı Saruhânî'nin "Rumûzü'l—Künûz" Adlı Eserin Transkripsiyonu ve Değerlendirilmesi." Master's thesis, Kırıkkale University, 2004.

Pickthall, M. M. *The Meaning of the Glorious Koran: An Explanatory Translation*. New York: New American Library, 1932.

Qayṣarī Rūmī, Muḥammed Dāvūd. *Sharh Fuṣūṣ al-Ḥikam*, ed. Seyyed Jalāl ad-Dīn Āshtiyānī. Tehran: Shirkat-i Intishārāt-i ʿIlmī va Farhangī, 1375.

Rāzī, Abū Bakr ʿAbd Allāh. *Manārāt al-Sāʾirīn wa Maqāmāt al-Ṭāʾirīn*, ed. Saʿīd ʿAbd al-Fattāḥ. Cairo: al-Hayʾa al-Miṣriyya al-ʿĀmma li al-Kuttāb, 1999.

Rāzī, Najm al-Dīn. *Mirṣād al-ʿIbād*, ed. Muḥammed Amīn Riyāḥī. Tehran: Bungāh-i Tarjuma va Nashr-i Kitāb, 1973.

Razi, Najm al-Din. *The Path of God's Bondsmen from Origin to Return*, transl. Hamid Algar. North Haledon, NJ: Islamic Publications International, 1982.

Risāla fīmā Lazima ʿalā al-Mulūk. MS SK, Esat Efendi 1845.

Risālat al-Khilāfa wa Ādāb al-Salāṭīn. MS İÜK, F 1228.

Rossi, Ettore. "Parafrasi turca del de Senectute Presentata a Solimano il Magnifico dal bailo Marino de Cavalli (1559)." *Rendiconti della R. Accademia Nazionale dei Lincei. Classe di scienze morali, storiche e filologiche*, Serie VI, 12 (1936): 680–756.

Rûhî. *Rûhî Târîhi*, eds. Yaşar Yücel and Halil Erdoğan Cengiz. TTK *Belgeler* 14 (1992): 359–472.

Şeyhoğlu Mustafa. *Ḫurşîd-nâme (Ḫurşîd ü Ferahşâd)*, ed. Hüseyin Ayan. Erzurum: Atatürk Üniversitesi Yayınları, 1979.

Şeyhoğlu Mustafa. *Kenzü'l-Küberâ ve Mehekkü'l-Ulemâ*, ed. Kemâl Yavuz. Ankara: Türk Tarih Kurumu, 1991.

Seyyid Lokman Çelebi. *Kıyafetü'l—İnsâniyye fî Şema'ili'l—ʿOsmāniyye*. Ankara: Historical Research Foundation, 1987.

Ṣıddıḳī, ʿAlī b. Muḥammed. *Zād al-Jiḥād*. MS SK, Ayasofya 1837.

Sılay, Kemal. "Ahmedi's History of the Ottoman Dynasty." *JTS* 16 (1992): 129–200.

Sinan Paşa, Yusuf. *Maarifnâme*, ed. İsmail H. Ertaylan. İstanbul: Edebiyat Fakültesi Basımevi, 1961.

Şirvānī, Ḥüseyin b. ʿAbdullāh. *Aḥkām al-Dīniyya*. MS SK, Reisülküttab 1207.

Şirvānī, Ḥüseyin b. ʿAbdullāh. *al-Risāla al-ʿAdliyya al-Sulaymāniyya*. MS TSMK, Revan 1035.
Şirvānī, Ḥüseyin b. ʿAbdullāh. *Risāle fi't-Taṣavvuf*. MS Milli Kütüphane, Cebeci 2705.
Şirvânî, Muhammed b. Mahmûd *Tuhfe-i Murâdî*, ed. Mustafa Argunşah. Ankara: Türk Dil Kurumu Yayınları, 1999.
Suhrawardī. *The Philosophy of Illumination*, ed. and transl. John Walbridge and Hossein Ziai. Provo, Utah: Brigham Young University Press, 1999.
Şükrullāh b. Aḥmed el-Amāsī. *Enīsü'l-ʿĀrifīn*. MS Manisa İl Halk Kütüphanesi 5280.
Şükrullāh b. Aḥmed el-Amāsī. *Manhaj al-Rashād*. MS SK, Ayasofya 2112; SK, Kadızade Mehmed 302.
Şükrullah b. Şihâbeddîn Ahmed b. Zeyneddîn Zekî. *Behcetü't-Tevârîḫ*, ed. Hasan Almaz. PhD diss., Ankara University, 2004.
Sürūrī, Muṣliḥuddīn Muṣṭafā. *Zaḫīretü'l-Mülūk*. MS SK, Ayasofya 2858.
Ṭabīb Ramażān. *al-Risāla al-Fatḥiyya al-Rādūsiyya al-Sulaymāniyya*. MS BNF, Arabic 1622.
Ṭabīb Ramażān. *Risāla Fatḥiyya Sulaymāniyya*. MS TSMK, Revan 1279.
Ṭarsūsī, Nağm al-Dīn. *Kitāb Tuḥfat al-Turk*, ed. and transl. Mohamed Menasri. Damascus: Institut Français de Damas, 1997.
Ṭarsūsī, Najm al-Dīn. *Kitāb Tuḥfat al-Turk fī mā Yajib an Yuʿmal fī al-Mulk*, ed. Ridwān al-Sayyid. Beirut: Dār al-Ṭalīʿa li al-Ṭibāʿa wa al-Nashr, 1992.
Ṭarsūsī, Najm al-Dīn. *Naṣīḥat al-Mulūk*. MS British Museum, OR 9728.
Taşköprîzâde Ahmed Efendi. *Şerhu'l-Ahlâki'l-Adudiyye*, eds. Elzem İçöz and Mustakim Arıcı Istanbul: Türkiye Yazma Eserler Kurumu Başkanlığı, 2016.
Ṭāşköprīzāde, Aḥmed b. Muṣṭafā. *Mawsūʿa Muṣṭalaḥāt Miftāḥ al-Saʿāda wa Miṣbāḥ al-Siyāda fī Mawḍūʿāt al-ʿUlūm*, eds. Rafīq al-ʿAjam and ʿAlī Daḥrūj. Beirut: Maktaba Lubnān Nāshirūn, 1998.
Ṭāşköprīzāde, Aḥmed b. Muṣṭafā. *Miftāḥ al-Saʿāda wa Miṣbāḥ al-Siyāda fī Mawḍūʿāt al-ʿUlūm*, 3 vols., eds. Kāmil Kāmil Bakrī and ʿAbd al-Wahhāb Abū al-Nūr. Cairo; Dār al-Kutub al-Ḥadītha, 1968.
Ṭāşköprīzāde, Aḥmed bin Muṣṭafā. *Risāla fī Bayān Asrār al-Khilāfa al-Insāniyya wa al-Salṭana al-Maʿnawiyya*. MS SK, Carullah 2098; MS BDK, Veliyyüddin 3275.
Ṭāşköprīzāde, Aḥmed bin Muṣṭafā. *Risāla fī Faḍīla Makārim al-Akhlāq*. MS SK, Carullah 2098.
Ṭāşköprīzāde, Aḥmed bin Muṣṭafā. *al-Shaqāʾiq al-Nuʿmāniyya*. Beirut: Dār al-Kitāb al-ʿArabī, 1975.
Tavakkolî, Hasan. "İdrîs Bitlîsî'nin Kanun-ı Şâhenşâhisi'nin Tenkidli Neşri ve Türkçeye Tercümesi." PhD diss., İstanbul University, 1974.
Teber, Ömer Faruk. "Haydariyye Taifesine Yönelik Eleştiriler: "Risâle fî Hakki't-Tâifeti'l-Haydariyye" Ekseninde." *Çukurova Üniversitesi İlâhiyat Fakültesi Dergisi* 7 (2007): 157–177.
Tek, Abdurrezzak. *Nakşîliğin Osmanlı Topraklarına Gelişi: Molla Abdullah İlâhî*. Bursa: Emin Yayınları, 2012.
Thompson, W. F., transl. *The Practical Philosophy of the Muhammedan People*. London: Oriental Translation Fund of Great Britain and Ireland, 1839.
Timurtaş Faruk K. *Şeyhî ve Husrev ü Şîrin'i*. Istanbul: Edebiyat Fakültesi Basımevi, 1980.
Topal, Seyid Ali. "Celalzâde Salih Çelebi'nin Tarih-i Sultan Süleyman İsimli Eseri." PhD diss., Ankara University, 2008.
Tursun Bey. *Târîh-i Ebü'l-Feth*, ed. Mertol Tulum. Istanbul: Istanbul Fetih Cemiyeti, 1977.
Ṭūsī, Naṣīr al-Dīn. *Akhlāq-i Nāṣirī*, eds. Mujtabā Mīnovī and ʿAlī R. Ḥaydārī. Tehran: Khvārazmi, 1360/1982.
Ṭūsī, Naṣīr ad-Dīn. *The Nasirean Ethics*, transl. G. M. Wickens. London: George Allen & Unwin LTD, 1964.

Türk, Abdullah. "Vâhidî'nin Kitâb-ı Hace-i Cihân ve Netîce-i Cân Adlı Eseri." Master's Thesis, Atatürk University, 2009.

Uçman, Abdullah. *Fatih Sultan Mehmet'e Nasihatler.* Istanbul: Tercüman 1001 Temel Eser, 1976.

Uzunçarşılıoğlu, İsmail H. *Kitabeler.* Istanbul: Devlet Matbaası, 1929.

Vânî, Mehmed b. Mustafâ. *Vankulu Lügati*, 2 vols, ed. Mustafa Koç. Istanbul: Türkiye Yazma Eserler Kurumu Başkanlığı, 2014.

Vuṣūlī Meḥmed Efendī. *Şems-i Hidāyet.* MS SK, Reisülküttap 772.

Walzer, Richard. *Al-Farabi on the Perfect State: Abū Naṣr al-Fārābī's Mabādī Ārā Ahl al-Madīna al-Fāḍila.* Oxford: Clarendon Press, 1985.

Woodhead, Christine. *Ta'līḳī-zāde's Şehnāme-i Hümāyūn: A History of the Ottoman Campaign into Hungary 1593–94.* Berlin: Klaus Schwarz Verlag, 1983.

Yağmur, Ömer. "Terceme-i Kitāb-ı Fevâ'ihü'l-Miskiyye fi'l-Fevâtihi'l-Mekkiyye." MA thesis, Istanbul University, 2007.

Yalçın, Yunus. "Türk Edebiyatında Velâyetnameler ve Otman Baba Velâyetnâmesi." PhD diss., Erciyes University, 2008.

Yavuz, Kemal. *Mu'înî'nin Mesnevî-i Murâdiyye'si*, 2 vols. Konya: Selçuk Üniversitesi Mevlana Araştırma ve Uygulama Merkezi Yayınları, 2007.

Yılmaz, Mehmet Şakir. *Sultanların Aynası: Ahmed bin Hüsameddin Amâsî ve Eseri Mirâtu'l-Mülûk.* Istanbul: Büyüyen Ay Yayınları, 2016.

Yücel, Yaşar, ed. *Osmanlı Devlet Teşkilâtına Dair Kaynaklar.* Ankara: Türk Tarih Kurumu, 1988.

Yuḥanna ibn al-Biṭrīq. *Kitāb al-Siyāsa fī Tadbīr al-Riyāsa (al-ma'rūf bi Sirr al-Asrār).* In 'Abd al-Raḥmān al-Badawī (ed.), *al-'Uṣūl al-Yūnāniyya li al-Naẓariyāt al-Siyāsiyya fī al-Islām.* Cairo: Maktabat al-Nahḍa al-Miṣriyya, 1954.

Yurd, Ali İhsan and Kaçalın, Mustafa, eds. *Akşemseddin: Hayatı ve Eserleri.* Istanbul: Marmara Üniversitesi İlahiyat Fakültesi Yayınları, 1994.

Zamakhsharī, Maḥmūd b. 'Umar. *Rabī' al-Abrār wa Fuṣūṣ al-Akhbār*, 2 vols, ed. 'Abd al-Majīd Diyāb. Cairo: al-Hay'a al-Miṣriyya al-'Āmma li al-Kitāb, 1992.

SECONDARY SOURCES

Abisaab, Rula Jurdi. *Converting Persia: Religion and Power in the Safavid Empire.* London and New York: I.B. Tauris, 2004.

Abou El Fadl, Khaled. *Rebellion and Violence in Islamic Law.* Cambridge: Cambridge University Press, 2001.

Affifi, Abul Ela. *The Mystical Philosophy of Muḥyid Dín-Ibnul 'Arabí.* Cambridge University Press, 1939.

Ágoston, Gábor. "Muslim Cultural Enclaves in Hungary under Ottoman Rule." *Acta Orientalia* 45 (1991): 181–204.

Ahmed, Shahab. *What is Islam: The Importance of Being Islamic.* Princeton and Oxford: Princeton University Press, 2016.

Akçıl, N. Çiçek. "Günümüze Ulaşmayan Bir Tekke: Edirne'de Muradiye Mevlevihanesi." *Sanat Tarihi Yıllığı* 21 (2008): 1–21.

Akdağ, Mustafa. "Medreseli İsyanları." *İstanbul Üniversitesi İktisat Fakültesi Mecmuası* 1–4 (1949): 361–387.

Akgündüz, Ahmet. "Dede Cöngi." *TDVIA*, vol. 9 (1994), 96–97.

Akman, Mehmet. *Osmanlı Devletinde Kardeş Katli.* Istanbul: Eren, 1997.

Akpınar, Cemil. "Hacı Paşa." *TDVIA*, vol. 14 (1996), 492–496.

Aksoy, Hasan. "Kınalı-zade Ali Çelebi: Hayatı, İlmî ve Edebî Şahsiyeti." BA graduation thesis, İstanbul University, 1976.

Al-Azmeh, Aziz. *Muslim Kingship: Power and the Sacral in Muslim, Christian, and Pagan Polities*. London and Newyork: I. B. Tauris, 2001.

Algar, Hamid. "Āyatallāh." http://www.iranicaonline.org/articles/ayatallah, (Accessed 1 October 2016).

Al-Tikriti, Nabil. "Idrīs-i Bidlisī's 1513 Treatise on Caliphal and Sultanic Protocols." In Marinos Sariyannis (ed.), *New Trends in Ottoman Studies* (pp. 741–756). Rethymno: University of Crete, 2014.

Al-Tikriti, Nabil. "Şehzade Korkud (CA. 1468–1513) and the Articulation of Early 16th Century Ottoman Religious Identity." PhD diss., University of Chicago, 2004.

Anay, Harun. *Celâlettin Devvânî: Hayatı, Eserleri, Ahlâk ve Siyaset Düşüncesi*. PhD diss., Istanbul University, 1994.

Andreas, W. *Eine unbekannte venezianische Relazion über die Türkei (1567)*. Heidelberg: Carl Winters Universitätsbuchhandlung, 1914.

Argunşah, Mustafa. "Türk Edebiyatında Selimnameler." *Turkish Studies* 4 (2009): 31–47.

Arjomand, Said A. "Philanthropy, the Law, and Public Policy in the Islamic World before the Modern Era." In Warren F. Ilchman, et al. (eds.), *Philanthropy in the World's Traditions* (pp. 109–132). Bloomington: Indiana University Press, 1998.

Arjomand, Said A. *The Shadow of God and the Hidden Imam*. Chicago: University of Chicago Press, 1984.

Arslan, Ahmet Turan. *İmam Birgivî: Hayatı, Eserleri ve Arapça Tedrisatındaki Yeri*. Istanbul: Seha Neşriyat, 1992.

Artuk, İbrahim. "Early Ottoman Coins of Orhan Gāzī as Confirmation of His Sovereignty." In Dickran K. Kouymjian (ed.), *Near Eastern Numismatics Iconography, Epigraphy and History: Studies in Honor of George C. Miles* (pp. 457–463). Beirut: American University of Beirut, 1974.

Atçıl, Abdurrahman. "The Safavid Threat and Juristic Authority in the Ottoman Empire." *IJMES* 49 (2017): 295–314.

Ateş, Ahmed. "Burdur-Antalya ve Havalisi Kütüphanelerinde Bulunan Türkçe, Arapça ve Farsça Bazı Mühim Eserler." *Türk Dili ve Edebiyatı Dergisi* 2 (1948): 171–191.

Ateş, Süleyman. "Kutub." *TDVIA*, vol. 26 (2002), 498–499.

Atsız, Nihal. *İstanbul Kütüphanelerine Göre Birgili Mehmet Efendi (929–981/1523–1573) Bibliyoğrafyası*. Istanbul: Milli Eğitim Basımevi, 1966.

Avcı, Casim. "Hilâfet." *TDVIA*, vol. 17 (1998), 539–546.

Aydoğan, Zeynep. "An Analysis of the Saltukname in Its Fifteenth Century Context." Master's thesis, Boğazici University, 2007.

Aynî, Mehmet Ali. *Türk Ahlakçıları*. İstanbul: Kitabevi, 1992.

Ayverdi, Ekrem H. "Orhan Gazî Devrinde Mi'mârî." *Yıllık Araştırmalar Dergisi* 1 (1957): 115–199.

Azamat, Nihat. "Alaeddîn Erdebîlî." *TDVIA*, vol. 11 (1995): 279.

Azamat, Nihat. "Hacı Bayrâm-ı Velî." *TDVIA*, vol. 14 (1996): 442–447.

Azamat, Nihat. "II. Murad Devri Kültür Hayatı." PhD diss., Marmara University, 1996.

Babacan, Cengiz. "Orhan Gazi'nin Abbasi Halifesi al-Mustansir'i Anan Gümüş Sikkeleri ve Bunların Tarih Taşıyan Üç Örneği." *Türk Nümismatik Derneği Bülteni: Sevgi Gönül Hatıra Sayısı* 96 (2005): 96–99.

Babayan, Kathryn. *Mystics, Monarchs, and Messiahs: Cultural Landscapes of Early Modern Iran*. Cambridge, Mass.: Harvard Middle Eastern Monographs, 2002.

Babinger, Franz. *Osmanlı Tarih Yazarları ve Eserleri*, transl. Coşkun Üçok. Ankara: Kültür Bakanlığı Yayınları, 1992.

Barkan, Ömer Lütfi. "İstilâ Devirlerinin Kolonizatör Türk Dervişleri ve Zâviyeler." *Vakıflar Dergisi* 2 (1974): 279–353.

Barkey, Karen. *Bandits and Bureaucrats: The Ottoman Route to State Centralization*. Ithaca, NY and London: Cornell University Press, 1991.

Bayrakdar, Mehmet. *Bitlisli İdris*. Ankara: Kültür Bakanlığı Yayınları, 1991.

Bedir, Murteza. "Osmanlı Tarihinin Kuruluş Asrında (1389'a kadar) İlmiye'ye Dair Bir Araştırma: İlk Fakihler." *Türk Hukuk Tarihi Araştırmaları* 1 (2006): 23–39.

Binbaş, Ilker Evrim. "Oğuz Khan Narratives." http://www.iranicaonline.org/articles/oguz-khan-narratives, (Accessed on October 1, 2016).

Blochet, Edgar. *Catalogue de la collection de manuscrits orientaux, arabes, persans et turcs formée par M. Charles Schefer et acquise par l'État*. Paris: E. Leroux, 1900.

Bosworth, Clifford E. *The New Islamic Dynasties: A Chronological and Geneological Manual*. Edinburgh: Edinburgh University Press, 1996.

Böwering, Gerhard. "Ensān-e Kāmel." http://www.iranicaonline.org/articles/ensan-e-kamel, (Accessed 1 October 2016).

Burak, Guy. *The Second Formation of Islamic Law: The Ḥanafī School in Early Modern Ottoman Empire*. Cambridge: Cambridge University Press, 2015.

Cahen, Claude. "Bābā Ishaq, Bābā Ilyas, Hadjdji Bektash et quelques autres." *Turcica* 1 (1969): 53–64.

Cahen, Claude. *The Formation of Turkey: The Seljukid Sultanate of Rūm: Eleventh to Fourteenth Centuries*, transl. and ed. P. M. Holt. Harlow, UK: Longman, 2001.

Casale, Giancarlo. *The Ottoman Age of Exploration*. Oxford: Oxford University Press, 2010.

Casale, Giancarlo. "Tordesillas and the Ottoman Caliphate: Early Modern Frontiers and the Renaissance of an Ancient Islamic Institution." *Journal of Modern History* 19 (2015): 485–511.

Çavuşoğlu, Mehmet. "Bâkî." *TDVIA*, vol. 4 (1991), 537–540.

Ceyhan, Âdem. "Âlim ve Şair Bir Osmanlı Müderrisi: Pîr Mehmed Azmî Bey ve Eserleri." *Türk Kültürü İncelemeleri Dergisi* 1 (1999): 243–286.

Chittick, William C. "The School of Ibn 'Arabī." In Seyyed H. Nasr and Oliver Leaman (eds.), *History of Islamic Philosophy*, 2 vols. (pp. 510–527). London and New York: Routlege, 1996.

Chodkiewicz, Michel. "The Esoteric Foundations of Political Legitimacy in Ibn 'Arabi." In Stephen Histenstein and Michael Tierman (eds.), *Muhyiddin Ibn 'Arabi: A Commemorative Volume* (pp. 190–198). Shaftesbury, Dorset; Rockport, MA; Brisbane, Queensland: Element, 1993.

Cici, Recep. "İbn Fîrûz ve "El-Gurretü'l-Beydâ" Adlı Eseri." *Uludağ Üniversitesi İlahiyat Fakültesi Dergisi* 9 (2000): 301–306.

Çıpa, Hakkı Erdem. "The Centrality of the Periphery: The Rise to Power of Selīm I, 1487–1512." PhD diss., Harvard University, 2007.

Corbin, Henry. *Creative Imagination in the Sūfism of Ibn 'Arabī*. London and New York: Routledge, 2008.

Coşan, M. Esad. "XV. Asır Türk Yazarlarından Muslihu'd-din, Hamid-Oğulları ve Hızır Bey." *Vakıflar Dergisi* 13 (1981): 101–112.

Crone, Patricia. "Did al-Ghazālī Write a Mirror for Princes?: On the Authorship of *Naṣīḥat al-Mulūk*." *Jerusalem Studies in Arabic and Islam* 10 (1987): 167–191.

Crone, Patricia. *God's Rule—Government and Islam: Six Centuries of Medieval Islamic Political Thought*. New York: Columbia University Press, 2004.

Crone, Patricia and Hinds, Martin. *God's Caliph: Religious Authority in the first Centuries of Islam*. Cambridge: Cambridge University Press, 1986.

Curry, John J. *The Transformation of Muslim Mystical Thought in the Ottoman Empire: The Rise of the Halveti Order, 1350–1650*. Edinburg: Edinburg University Press, 2010.

Dabashi, Hamid. *The World of Persian Literary Humanism*. Cambridge, Mass.: Harvard University Press, 2012.

Damalı, Atom. *History of Ottoman Coins*, Vols. I–IV. Istanbul: Nilüfer Eğitim, Kültür ve Çevre Vakfı, 2010.

Darling, Linda T. "Reformulating the Gazi Narrative: When was the Ottoman State a Gazi State?" *Turcica* 43 (2011): 13–53.

Değirmençay, Veyis. "Sultan Veled." *TDVIA*, vol. 37 (2009), 521–522.

Doğan, Enfel. "Emir Süleyman Dönemi Şairlerinden Akkadıoğlu'nun Kâbusnâme Tercümesi ve Nüshaları Üzerine." *Modern Türklük Araştırmaları Dergisi* 8 (2011): 7–24.

Doğan, Enfel. "On Translations of Qabus-nama during the Old Anatolian Turkish Period." *Uluslararası Sosyal Araştırmalar Dergisi* 5 (2012): 76–85.

Eberhard, Elke. *Osmanische Polemik gegen die Safawiden im 16. Jahrhundert nach arabischen Handschriften*. Freiburg im Breisgau: Klaus Schwarz Verlag, 1970.

El Moudden, A. "The Idea of the Caliphate between Moroccans and Ottomans: Political and Smbolical Stakes in the 16th and 17th century-Maghrib." *Studia Islamica* 82 (1995): 103–113.

Emecen, Feridun M. *Fetih ve Kıyamet, 1453: İstanbul'un Fethi ve Kıyamet Senaryoları*. Istanbul: Timaş, 2012.

Emecen, Feridun M. *İlk Osmanlılar ve Batı Anadolu Beylikler Dünyası*. İstanbul: Timaş, 2012.

Emecen, Feridun M. "Süleymân." *TDVIA*, vol. 38 (2010), 62–74.

Erdoğan, Mehmet. *İslâm Hukukunda Ahkâmın Değişmesi*. Istanbul: Marmara Üniversitesi İlahiyat Fakültesi Vakfı Yayınları, 1994.

Fayda, Mustafa. "Hulefâ-yi Raşidîn." *TDVIA*, vol. 18 (1998), 324–338.

Fazlıoğlu, İhsan. "Davud Kayserî." In *Yaşamları ve Yapıtlarıyla Osmanlılar Ansiklopedisi*, Vol. 1 (pp. 370–371). Istanbul: Yapı Kredi Yayınları, 1999.

Fazlıoğlu, İhsan. "Osmanlı Coğrafyasında İlmi Hayatın Teşekkülü ve Davud el-Kayseri." In Turan Koç (ed.), *International Symposium on Islamic Thought in Anatolia in the XIIIth and XIVth Centuries and Davud al-Qaysari* (pp. 25–43). Kayseri: Büyükşehir Belediyesi, 1998.

Fazlıoğlu, İhsan. "Osmanlı Döneminde 'Bilim' Alanındaki Türkçe Telif ve Tercüme Eserlerin Türkçe Oluş Nedenleri ve Bu Eserlerin Dil Bilincinin Oluşmasındaki Yeri ve Önemi." *Kutadgubilig* 3 (2003): 151–184.

Fleischer, Cornell H. "Ancient Wisdom and New Sciences: Prophecies at the Ottoman Court in the Fifteenth and Early Sixteenth Centuries." In Farhad Massumeh and Serpil Bağcı (eds.), *Falnama: the Book of Omens* (pp. 231–243). London: Thames & Hudson, 2009.

Fleischer, Cornell H. *Bureaucrat and Intellectual in the Ottoman Empire: The Historian Mustafa Âli (1541–1600)*. Princeton: Princeton University Press, 1986.

Fleischer, Cornell H. "The Lawgiver as Messiah: The Making of the Imperial Image in the Reign of Suleyman." In Gilles Veinstein (ed.), *Soliman le Magnifique et Son temps* (pp. 159–179). Paris: La Documentation Française, 1992.

Fleischer, Cornell H. "Mahdi and Millenium: Messianic Dimensions in the Development of Ottoman Imperial Ideology." In *The Great Ottoman-Turkish Civilization*, vol. 3, ed. Kemal Çiçek (pp. 42–54). Ankara: Yeni Türkiye, 2000.

Fleischer, Cornell H. "Seer to the Sultan: Haydar-i Remmal and Sultan Süleyman." In Jayne L. Warner (ed.), *Kültür Ufukları: Talat S. Halman Armağan Kitabı* (pp. 290–299). Syracuse University Press and Yapı Kredi Yayınları: Syracuse and Istanbul, 2001.

Fleischer, Cornell H. "Shadow of Shadows: Prophecy in Politics in 1530s İstanbul." *International Journal of Turkish Studies* 13 (2007): 51–62.

Flemming, Barbara. "Der Ǧāmiʿ Ül-Meknūnāt: Eine Quelle ʿĀlīs aus Zeit Sultan Süleymāns." In Bertold Spuler, Hans R. Roemer and Albrecht Noth (eds.), *Studien zur Geschichte und Kultur des Vorderen Orients: Festschrift für Bertold Spuler zum Siebzigsten Geburtstag* (pp. 79–92). Leiden: E. J. Brill, 1981.

Flemming, Barbara. "The Political Geneologies in the Sixteenth Century." *JOS* 7–8 (1988): 198–220.

Flemming, Barbara. "Public Opinion under Sultan Süleymân." In Halil İnalcık and Cemal Kafadar (eds.), *Süleymân the Second and His Time* (pp. 49–57). Istanbul: Isis Press, 1993.

Flemming, Barbara. "Ṣāḥib-Ḳırān und Mahdī: Türkische Endzeiterwartungen im ersten Jahrzehnt der Regierung Süleymāns." In György Kara (ed.), *Between the Danube and the Caucasus* (pp. 43–62). Budapest: Akadémiai Kiadó, 1987.

Flügel, Gustav. *Die arabischen, persischen, türkischen Handschriften der kaiserlichen und königlichen Hofbibliothek zu Wien*. New York: Olms, Hildesheim, 1977.

Fodor, Pál. Aḥmedī's Dāsitān as a Source of Early Ottoman History." *Acta Orientalia* 38 (1984): 41–54.

Furat, Ahmet Subhi. "İslâm Edebiyatında Ansiklopedik Eserler: h. IV.–IX/m. X.–XV. Asırlar." *İslâm Tetkikleri Enstitüsü Dergisi* 7 (1979): 211–231.

Galston, Miriam. "The Theoretical and Practical Dimensions of Happiness as Portrayed in the Political Treatises of al-Fārābī." In Charles E. Butterworth (ed.), *The Political Aspects of Islamic Philosophy: Essays in Honor of Muhsin S. Mahdi* (pp. 95–151). Cambridge, Mass.: Harvard Middle Eastern Monographs, 1992.

García-Arenal, Mercedes. *Messianism and Puritanical Reform: Mahdīs of the Muslim West*, transl. Martin Beagles. Leiden and Boston: Brill, 2006.

Gökyay, Orhan Şaik and Özen, Şükrü. "Molla Lütfi." *TDVIA*, vol. 30 (2005): 255–258.

Gölpınarlı, Abdülbâki. *Melâmilik ve Melâmîler*. Istanbul: Devlet Matbaası, 1931.

Gölpınarlı, Abdülbâki. *Sımavna Kadısıoğlu Şeyh Bedreddin*. Istanbul: Eti Yayınevi, 1966.

Gönül, Behcet. "İstanbul Kütüphânelerinde al-Şaḳā'iḳ al-Nu'māniya Tercüme ve Zeyilleri." *Türkiyat Mecmuası* 7–8 (1945): 137–168.

Goodrich, Thomas D. *The Ottoman Turks and the New World: A Study of Tarih-i Hind-i Garbi and Sixteenth-Century Ottoman Americana*. Weisbaden: Otto Harrassowitz, 1990.

Görkaş, İrfan. "Mehmed Birgivî'nin İlm-i Ahlâk'ı." *Türk Dünyası Araştırmaları* 107 (1997): 121–130.

Grignaschi, Mario. "La diffusion du Secretum secretorum (Sirr al-asrar) dans l'Europe occidentale." *Archives d'Histoire Doctrinale et Littéraire du Moyen Âge* 47 (1980): 7–70.

Grignaschi, Mario. "L'origine et les métamorphoses du 'Sirr-al-asrâr'." *Archives d'Histoire Doctrinale et Littéraire du Moyen Âge* 43 (1976): 7–112.

Hallaq, Wael. "Caliphs, Jurists and the Seljūqs in the Political Thought of Juwaynī." *The Muslim World* 74 (1984): 27–41.

Hassan, Mona. *Longing for the Lost Caliphate: A Transregional History*. Princeton, NJ: Princeton University Press, 2017.

Heidarzadeh, Tofigh. "Muhājarat 'Ulemā-i Īrān ba Imperātūrī-e 'Oṣmānī." *Farhang* 20-21 (1975-1976): 49–94.

Heidarzadeh, Tofigh. "Patronage, Networks Migration: Turco-Persian Scholarly Exchanges in the 15th, 16th 17th Centuries." *Archives Internationales d'Histoire des Sciences* 55 (2005): 419–434.

Hodgson, Marshal G. S. *Rethinking World History: Essays on Europe, Islam, and World History*, ed. E. Burke III. Cambridge: Cambridge University Press, 1993.

Imber, Colin. *Ebu'ssu'ud: The Islamic Legal Tradition*. Stanford, CA: Stanford University Press, 1997.

Imber, Colin. "The Ottoman Dynastic Myth." *Turcica* 19 (1987): 7–27.

Imber, Colin. "Süleymân as Caliph of the Muslims: Ebû's-Su'ûd's Formulation of Ottoman Dynastic Ideology." In Gilles Veinstein (ed.), *Soliman le Magnifique et Son temps* (pp. 179–184). Paris: La Documentation Française, 1992.

Inalcik, Halil. "A Case Study in Renaissance Diplomacy: The Agreement between Innocent VIII and Bayezid II on Djem Sultan." *JTS* 3 (1979): 342–368.

İnalcık, Halil. "Dervish and Sultan: An Analysis of the Otman Baba Vilāyetnāmesi." In Halil Inalcik (ed.), *The Middle East and the Balkans under the Ottoman Empire: Essays on Economy and Society* (pp. 19–37). Bloomington: Indiana University Turkish Studies, 1993.

Inalcık, Halil. "How to Read 'Āshık Pasha-Zāde's History." In Colin Heywood and Colin Imber (eds.), *Studies in Ottoman History in Honour of Professor V. L. Ménage* (pp. 139–156). Istanbul: Isis Press, 1994,

Inalcik, Halil. "Islamization of Ottoman Laws on Land and Land Tax." In Christa Fragner and Klaus Schwarz (eds.), *Festgabe an Josef Matuz: Osmanistik—Turkologie—Diplomatik* (pp. 101–119). Berlin: Klaus Schwarz Verlag, 1992.

İnalcık, Halil. "Osman Gazi'nin İznik (Nicea) Kuşatması ve Bafeus Savaşı." In Oktay Özel and Mehmet Öz (eds.), *Söğüt'ten İstanbul'a: Osmanlı Devleti'nin Kuruluşu Üzerine Tartışmalar* (pp. 301–337). Istanbul: İmge Kitabevi, 2000.

İnalcık, Halil. "Osmanlılar'da Saltanat Verâseti Usûlü ve Türk Hakimiyet Telâkkisiyle İlgisi." *Ankara Üniversitesi Siyasal Bilgiler Fakültesi Dergisi* 14 (1959): 69–94.

Inalcik, Halil. "Power Relations between Russia, the Crimea, and the Ottoman Empire as Reflected in Titulature." In Halil Inalcik (ed.), *The Middle East and the Balkans under the Ottoman Empire: Essays on Economy and Society* (pp. 369–411). Bloomington: Indiana University Turkish Studies, 1993.

Inalcik, Halil. "Tarihçi Şükrullâh Çelebi (1380–1460)." *Acta Orientalia* 61 (2008): 113–118.

Inalcik, Halil. "Tursun Beg, Historian of Mehmed the Conqueror's Time." *Wiener Zeitschrift fur die kunde des Morgenlandes* 69 (1977): 55–71.

İpekten, Halûk. *Divan Edebiyatında Edebî Muhitler*. Istanbul: Milli Eğitim Bakanlığı Yayınları, 1996.

İpekten, Halûk, et al. *Tezkirelere Göre Divan Edebiyatı İsimler Sözlüğü*. Ankara: Kültür ve Turizm Bakanlığı Yayınları, 1988.

İpşirli, Mehmet. "Lutfi Paşa." *TDVIA*, vol. 27 (2003), 234–236.

Kafadar, Cemal. *Between Two Worlds: The Construction of the Ottoman State*. Berkeley: University of California Press, 1995.

Kafadar, Cemal. "The Myth of the Golden Age: Ottoman Historical Consciousness in the Post Suleymânic Era." In Halil İnalcık and Cemal Kafadar (eds.), *Süleymân the Second and His Time* (pp. 37–49). Istanbul: Isis Press, 1993.

Kafadar, Cemal. "The Question of Ottoman Decline." *Harvard Middle Eastern and Islamic Review* 4 (1997–98): 30–75.

Kafadar, Cemal. "A Rome of One's Own: Reflections on Cultural Geography and Identity in the Lands of Rum." *Muqarnas* 24 (2007): 7–25.

Kafadar, Cemal. "Self and Others: The Diary of a Dervish in Seventeenth Century Istanbul and First-Person Narratives in Ottoman Literature." *Studia Islamica* 69 (1989): 121–150.

Kafesoğlu, İbrahim. "Büyük Selçuklu Veziri Nizâmü'l-Mülk'ün Eseri Siyâsetnâme ve Türkçe Tercümesi." *Türkiyat Mecmuası* 12 (1955): 231–256.

Kappert, Petra. *Die osmanischen Prinzen und ihre Residenz Amasya im 15. und 16. Jahrhundert*. Istanbul: Nederlands Historisch-Archeologisch Instituut te Istanbul, 1967.

Kara, Mustafa. "Molla İlâhî'ye Dair." *JOS* 7–8 (1988): 365–392.

Karabulut, Ali Rıza. "Taşköprü-zâde'nin Eserleri." In A. Hulûsi Köker (ed.), *Taşköprülü Zâde Ahmet Efendi (1495–1561)* (pp. 113–131). Kayseri: Erciyes Üniversitesi Gevher Nesibe Tıp Tarihi Enstitüsü, 1989.

Karakaya-Stump, Ayfer. "Subjects of the Sultan, Disciples of the Shah: Formation and Transformation of the Kizilbash/Alevi Communities in Ottoman Anatolia." PhD diss., Harvard University, 2008.

Karakaya-Stump, Ayfer. "The Vefā'iyye, the Bektashiyye and Geneologies of "Heterodox" Islam in Anatolia: Rethinking the Köprülü Paradigm." *Turcica* 44 (2012–2013): 279–300.

Karamustafa, Ahmet T. *God's Unruly Friends: Dervish Groups in the Islamic Later Middle Period 1200–1550*. Salt Lake City: University of Utah Press, 1994.

Karamustafa, Ahmet T. "Kaygusuz Abdal: A Medieval Turkish Saint and the Formation of Vernacular Islam in Anatolia." In Orkhan Mir-Kasimov (ed.), *Unity in Diversity: Mysticism, Messianism and the Construction of Religious Authority in Islam* (pp. 329–342). Leiden and Boston: Brill, 2014.

Karamustafa, Ahmet T. "Menâkıb-ı Hoca-i Cihân." *TDVIA*, vol. 29 (2004), 108–110.

Karamustafa, Ahmet T. "Origins of Anatolian Sufism." In Ahmet Yaşar Ocak (ed.), *Sufism and Sufis in Ottoman Society* (pp. 67–95). Ankara: Turkish Historical Society, 2005.

Karataş, Hasan. "The Ottomanization of the Halveti Sufi Order: A Political Story Revisited." *Journal of the Ottoman and Turkish Studies Association* 1 (2014): 71–89.

Karatay, F. Ethem. *Topkapı Sarayı Müzesi Arapça Yazmaları Kataloğu*. Istanbul: Topkapı Sarayı Müzesi, 1962.

Kastritsis J., Dimitris. *The Sons of Bayezid: Empire Building and Representation in the Ottoman Civil War of 1402–1413*. Leiden: Brill, 2007.

Kavak, Özgür. "Bir Osmanlı Kadısının Gözüyle Siyaset: Letâifü'l-efkâr ve kâşifü'l-esrâr Yahut Osmanlı Saltanatını Fıkıh Diliyle Temellendirmek." *MÜİFD* 42 (2012): 95–120.

Khadduri, Majid. *The Islamic Conception of Justice*. Baltimore: Johns Hopkins University Press, 1984.

Kılıç, M. Erol. "Fusûsü'l-Hikem." *TDVIA*, vol. 13 (1996), 230–237.

Kılıç, M. Erol. "Ibnü'l-Arabî." *TDVIA*, vol. 20 (1999), 493–516.

Kılıç, Mustafa. "İbn-i Kemal'in Mısır Fethine Dair Bir Risale-i Acibesi." *Diyanet Dergisi* 26 (1990): 111–120.

Köksal, Asım C. *Fıkıh ve Siyaset: Osmanlılarda Siyâset-i Şer'iyye*. Istanbul: Klasik, 2016.

Kołodziejczyk, Dariusz. "Khan, Caliph, Tsar and Imperator: the Multiple Identities of the Ottoman Sultan." In Peter F. Bang and Dariusz Kołodziejczyk (eds.), *Universal Empire: A Comparative Approach to Imperial Culture and Representation in Eurasian History*, (pp. 175–193). Cambridge: Cambridge University Press, 2012.

Köprülü, Mehmed Fuad. "Abdal." *Türk Halk Edebiyatı Ansiklopedisi*. Istanbul: Türkiyat Enstitüsü Yayınları, 1935, vol. 1, 27–56.

Köprülüzade, Mehmed Fuad. *Milli Edebiyat Cereyanının İlk Mübeşşirleri*. Istanbul: Devlet Matbaası, 1928.

Krstić, Tijana. *Contested Conversions to Islam: Narratives of Religious Change in the Early Modern Ottoman Empire*. Stanford, CA: Stanford University Press, 2011.

Kutluer, İlhan. "Sühreverdî." *TDVIA*, vol. 38 (2010), 36–40.

Kurtuluş, Rıza. "Keykâvus b. İskender." *TDVIA*, vol. 25 (2002), 357.

Labib, Subhi. "The Era of Suleyman the Magnificient: Crisis of Orientation." *IJMES* 10 (1979): 435–451.

Lambton, Ann K. S. *State and Government in Medieval Islam. An Introduction to the Study of Islamic Political Theory: The Jurists*. Oxford: Oxford University Press, 1981.

Lambton, Ann K. S. "The Theory of Kingship in the *Naṣīḥat ul-Mulūk* of Ghazālī." *The Islamic Quarterly* 1 (1954): 47–55.

Landau-Tasseron, Ella. "The "Cyclical Reform": A Study of the Mujaddid Tradition." *Studia Islamica* 70 (1989): 79–117.

Le Gall, Dina. *A Culture of Sufism: Naqshbandīs in the Ottoman World, 1450–1700*. Albany, NY: SUNY Press, 2005.

Levend, Agâh S. "Siyaset-nâmeler." *TDAY Belleten* (1962): 167–194.

Levend, Agâh S. "Ümmet Çağında Ahlâk Kitaplarımız." *TDAY Belleten* (1963): 89–115.

Liew, Han Hsien. "The Caliphate of Adam: Theological Politics of the Qur'ānic Term *Ḫalīfa*." *Arabica* 63 (2016): 1–29.

Lindner, Rudi Paul. *Explorations in Ottoman Prehistory*. Ann Arbor: University of Michigan Press, 2007.

Lowry, Heath W. *The Nature of the Early Ottoman Society*. Albany: State University of New York Press, 2003.

Madelung, Wilferd. "The Assumption of the Title Shāhānshāh by the Būyids and "The Reign of the Daylam (Dawlat al-Daylam)." *Journal of Near Eastern Studies* 28 (1969): 84–108, 168–183.

Madelung, Wilferd. *The Succession to Muhammad: A Study of the Early Caliphate*. Cambridge: Cambridge University Press, 1997.

Mandaville, Jon E. "Usurious Piety: The Cash Waqf Controversy in the Ottoman Empire." *IJMES* 10 (1979): 289–308.

Manzalaoui, Mahmoud. "The Pseudo-Aristotelian *Kitāb Sirr al-Asrār*; Facts and Problems." *Oriens* 23–24 (1974): 147–257.

Manzalaoui, Mahmoud. "The Pseudo-Aristotelian *Sirr al-Asrār* and Three Oxford Thinkers of the Middle Ages." In George Makdisi (ed.), *Arabic and Islamic Studies in Honor of Hamilton A. R. Gibb* (pp. 480–500). Leiden: Brill, 1965.

Manzalaoui, Mahmoud. *Secretum Secretorum: Nine English Versions*. Oxford: Oxford University Press, 1977.

Markiewicz, Christopher A. "The Crisis of Rule in Late Medieval Islam: A Study of Idrīs Bidlīsī (861–926/1457–1520) and Kingship at the Turn of the Sixteenth Century." PhD diss., University of Chicago, 2015.

Mazıoğlu, Hasibe. "Sinan Paşa." *İslâm Ansiklopedisi*, vol. 10 (1966): 666-670.

Mehmed Süreyya. *Sicill-i Osmanî*, ed. Nuri Akbayar, 6 vols. Istanbul: Tarih Vakfı Yurt Yayınları, 1996.

Mehmed Tahir. *Osmanlı Müellifleri*, eds. A. Fikri Yavuz and İsmail Sözen, 3 vols. Istanbul: Meral Yayınevi, 1971–5.

Meier, Fritz. "Stambuler Handschriften dreier persicher Mystiker: 'Ain al-quḍāt al-Hamadānī, Nağm ad-dīn al-Kubrā, Nağm ad-dīn ad-Dāja." *Der Islam* 24 (1937): 1–42.

Moin, A. Azfar. *The Millennial Sovereign: Sacred Kingship and Sainthood in Islam*. New York: Columbia University Press, 2012.

Morgan, David. *Medieval Persia, 1040–1797*. London: Longman, 1988.

Muhakkık, Mehdî. "Âyetullah." *TDVIA*, vol. 4 (1991), 244.

Mumcu, Ahmet. *Osmanlı Devletinde Siyaseten Katl*. Ankara: Ankara Üniversitesi Hukuk Fakültesi Yayınları, 1963.

Murphey, Rhoads. *Exploring Ottoman Sovereignty: Tradition, Image and Practice in the Ottoman Imperial Household, 1400–1800*. London and New York: Continuum, 2008.

Muslu, Emire Cihan. "Ottoman-Mamluk Relations: Diplomacy and Perceptions." PhD diss., Harvard University, 2007.

Necipoğlu, Gülru. *The Age of Sinan: Architectural Culture in the Ottoman Empire*. London: Reaktion, 2005.

Necipoğlu, Gülru. "The Dome of the Rock as Palimpsest: ʿAbd al-Malik's Grand Narrative and Sultan Süleyman's Glosses." *Muqarnas* 25 (2008): 17–105.

Necipoğlu, Gülru. "Süleyman the Magnificient and the Representation of Power in the Context of Ottoman-Habsburg-Papal Rivalry." In Halil İnalcık and Cemal Kafadar (eds.), *Süleymân the Second and His Time* (pp. 163–195). Istanbul: Isis Press, 1993.

Ocak, A. Yaşar. *XIII. Yüzyılda Anadolu'da Baba Resûl (Babaîler) İsyanı ve Anadolu'nun İslâmlaşması Tarihindeki Yeri*. Istanbul: Dergâh Yayınları, 1980.

Ocak, A. Yaşar. "XV.–XVI. Yüzyıllarda Osmanlı İdeolojisi ve Buna Muhalefet Problemi." In *XI. Türk Tarih Kongresi* (pp. 1201–1210). Ankara: Türk Tarih Kurumu, 1994.

Ocak, A. Yaşar. "XVI. Yüzyıl Osmanlı Anadolusu'nda Mesiyanik Hareketlerin Bir Tahlil Denemesi." In *V. Milletlerarası Türkiye Sosyal ve İktisat Tarihi Kongresi (Tebliğler)* (pp. 817–825). Ankara: Türk Tarih Kurumu, 1990.

Ocak, A. Yaşar. "Kanûnî Sultan Süleyman Devrinde Bir Osmanlı Heretiği: Şeyh Muhyiddîn-i Karamânî." In *Prof. Dr. Bekir Kütükoğlu'na Armağan* (pp. 473–484). İstanbul: Edebiyat Fakültesi Basımevi, 1991.

Ocak, A. Yaşar. "Kanûnî Sultan Süleyman Devrinde Osmanlı Resmî Düşüncesine Karşı Bir Tepki Hareketi: Oğlan Şeyh İsmail-i Mâşûkî." *Osmanlı Araştırmaları* 10 (1990): 49–58.

Ocak, A. Yaşar. *Osmanlı İmparatorluğu'nda Marjinal Sûfîlik: Kalenderîler (XIV-XVII. Yüzyıllar)*. Ankara: Türk Tarih Kurumu, 1999.

Ocak, A. Yaşar. *Osmanlı Toplumunda Zındıklar ve Mülhidler (15.-17. Yüzyıllar)*. Istanbul: Tarih Vakfı Yurt Yayınları, 1998.

Ocak, A. Yaşar. "Les réactions socio-religieuses contre l'idéologie officielle otomane et la question de Zendeqa ve İlhad (hérésie et athéisme) au XVIe siècle." *Turcica* 21–23 (1991): 71–82.

Ocak, A. Yaşar. "Türkiye Tarihinde Merkezi İktidar ve Mevleviler (XIII–XVIII. Yüzyıllar) Meselesine Bir Bakış." *Selçuk Üniversitesi Türkiyat Araştırmaları Dergisi* 2 (1996): 17–22.

Ögke, Ahmet. "Bir Tasavvuf Terimi Olarak Ricâlü'l-Gayb–İbn Arabî'nin Görüşleri." *Tasavvuf* 5 (2001): 161–201.

Okiç, Tayyib. "Quelques documents inédits concernant les Hamzawites." In Zeki Velidi Togan (ed.), *Proceedings of the Twenty-Second Congress of Orientalists, Held in Istanbul, September 15th to 22nd, 1951*, Vol. 2 (pp. 279–286). Istanbul: Osman Yalçın Matbaası, 1957.

Ökten, Ertuğrul. "Scholars and Mobility: A Preliminary Assessment from the Perespective of al-Shaqāyiq al-Nuʿmāniyya." *JOS* 51 (2013): 55–70.

Ökten, Ertuğrul İ. "Jāmī (817–898/1414–1492): His Biography and Intellectual Influence in Herat." PhD diss., University of Chicago, 2007.

Okumuş, Ömer. "Abdurrahman Câmî." *TDVIA*, vol. 7 (1993), 94–99.

Omar, Farooq. "Min Alqāb al-Khulafā al ʿAbbāsiyyīn: Khalīfat Allāh wa Ẓill Allāh." *Majallat al-Jāmiʿa al-Mustanṣiriyya* 2 (1971): 323–338

Onay, Ahmet Talât. *Eski Türk Edebiyatında Mazmunlar*. Istanbul: Milli Eğitim Bakanlığı Yayınları, 1996.

Öngören, Reşat. *Osmanlılar'da Tasavvuf: Anadolu'da Sûfîler, Devlet ve Ulemâ (XVI. Yüzyıl)*. Istanbul: İz Yayınları, 2000.

Öngören, Reşat. "Zeyniyye." *TDVIA*, vol. 44 (2013), 367–371.

Özaydın, Abdülkerim. "Büyük Selçuklularda Ünvan ve Lakaplar." In Abdülkerim Özaydın (ed.), *Prof. Dr. Işın Demirkent Anısına* (pp. 421–433). Istanbul: Globus Dünya Basımevi, 2008.

Özbaran, Salih. *Bir Osmanlı Kimliği: 14.-17. Yüzyıllarda Rûm/Rûmî Aidiyet ve İmgeleri*. Istanbul: Kitabevi, 2004.

Özcan, Abdülkadir. "İdrîs-i Bitlisî." *TDVIA*, vol. 21 (2000), 485–488.

Özcan, Tahsin. "Sofyalı Bâlî Efendi'nin Para Vakıflarıyla İlgili Mektupları." *İslam Araştırmaları Dergisi* 3 (1999): 125–155.

Özen, Şükrü. "Ottoman ʿUlemāʾ Debating Sufism: Settling the Conflict on the Ibn al-ʿArabī's Legacy by Fatwās." In Alfonso Carmona (ed.), *El Sufismo y las Normas del Islam: Trabajos del IV Congreso Internacional de Estudios Jurídicos Islámicos, Derecho y Sufismo, Murcia, 7–10 Mayo 2003* (pp. 309–341). Murcia: Editora Regional de Murcia, 2006.

Özervarlı, M. Sait. "Ottoman Perceptions of al-Ghazālī's Works and Discussions on His Historical Role in its Late Period." In Frank Griffel (ed.), *Islam and Rationality: The Impact of al-Ghazālī* (pp. 253–282). Leiden: Brill, 2015.

Pakalın, Mehmet Zeki. *Osmanlı Tarih Deyimleri ve Terimleri Sözlüğü*. Istanbul: Milli Eğitim Basımevi, 1983.

Pala, İskender. *Ansiklopedik Dîvân Şiiri Sözlüğü*. Ankara: Akçağ Basım Yayım Pazarlama, 1995.

Peacock, A. C. S. "Seljuq Legitimacy in Islamic History." In Christian Lange and Songül Mecit (eds.), *Seljuqs: Politics, Society and Culture* (pp. 79–95). Edinburgh: Edinburgh University Press, 2011.

Pekolcay, A. Necla and Uçman, Abdullah. "Eşrefoğlu Rûmî." *TDVIA*, vol. 11 (1995), 480–482.

Pfeiffer, Judith. "Mevlevi-Bektashi Rivalries and the Islamisation of the Public Space in Late Seljuk Anatolia." In A. C. S. Peacock, B. de Nicola, and S. Nur Yıldız (eds.), *Islam and Christianity in Medieval Anatolia* (pp. 311–327). Farnham, UK: Ashgate, 2015.

Puin, Elizabeth. "Silver Coins of the Mamluk Sultan Qalāwūn (678–689/1279–1280) from the Mints of Cairo, Damascus, Ḥamāh, and al-Marqab." *Mamluk Studies Review* 4 (2000): 75–129.

Remler, Philip N. "Ottoman, Isfendiyarid, and Eretnid Coinage: A Currency Community in Fourteenth Century Anatolia." *American Numismatic Society Museum Notes* 25 (1980): 167–188, pl. 18–20.

Répertoire chronologique d'épigraphie arabe, Vols. 8–10. Cairo: l'Institut français d'archéologie orientale, 1931–.

Riāḥī, Moḥammad-Amīn. "Najm-al-Dīn Abū Bakr ʿAbd-Allāh." http://www.iranicaonline.org/articles/daya-najm-al-din, *(Accessed 1 October 2016).*

Rosenthal, Franz. "Dawla." *EI²*

Rosenthal, Erwin I. J. *Political Thought in Medieval Islam*. Cambridge: Cambridge University Press, 1958.

Rughaym, Samīḥ. *Mawsūʿa Muṣṭalaḥāt al-ʿUlūm al-Ijtimāʿiyya wa al-Siyāsiyya fī al-Fikr al-ʿArabī wa al-Islamī*. Beirut: Maktabat Lubnān Nāshirūn, 2000.

Şahin, Kaya. "Constantinople and the End Time: Ottoman Conquest as a Portent of the Last Hour." *Journal of Early Modern History* 14 (2010): 317–354.

Şahin, Kaya. *Empire and Power in the Reign of Süleyman: Narrating the Sixteenth-Century Ottoman World*. Cambridge: Cambridge University Press, 2013.

Sariyannis, Marinos. *Ottoman Political Thought up to the Tanzimat: A Concise History*. Rethymno: Institute for Mediterranean Studies, 2015.

Sarre, Friedrich. *Konya Köşkü*, trans. Şahabeddin Uzluk. Ankara: Türk Tarih Kurumu, 1967.

Savory, Roger M. "The Emergence of the Modern Persian State under the Ṣafavids." *Iranshinasi: Journal of Iranian Studies* 2 (1971): 1–44.

Savory, Roger M. "The Safavid State and Polity." *Iranian Studies* 7 (1974): 179–212.

Sawyer, Carolinne. "Revising Alexander: Structure and Evolution of Ahmedî's Ottoman Iskendernâme (c. 1400)." *Edebiyat: Journal of M.E. Literatures* 13 (2010): 225–243.

Schmidt, Jan. *Pure Water for Thirsty Muslims: A Study of Muṣṭafā ʿĀlī of Gallipoli's Künhü'l-Aḫbār*. Leiden: Het Oosters Instituut, 1991.

Sela, Ron. *The Legendary Biographies of Tamerlane: Islam and Heroic Apocrypha in Central Asia*. Cambridge: Cambridge University Press, 2011.

Şentop, Mustafa. *Osmanlı Yargı Sistemi ve Kazaskerlik*. Istanbul: Klasik Yayınları, 2005.

Şeşen, Ramazan. "Eski Araplara Göre Türkler." *Türkiyat Mecmuası* 15 (1969): 11–36.

Şeşen, Ramazan. "Onbeşinci Yüzyılda Türkçeye Tercümeler." In *XI. Türk Tarih Kongresi*, (pp. 889–919). Ankara: Türk Tarih Kurumu, 1994.

Siddiqi, Amir Hasan. *Caliphate and Sultanate in Medieval Persia*. Karachi: Jamiyat-ul-Falah Publications, 1942.

Sohrweide, Hanna. "Dichter und Gelehrte aus dem Osten im osmanischen Reich (1453–1600): Ein Beitrag zur türkisch-persischen Kulturgeschichte." *Der Islam* 46 (1970): 262–302.

Sönmez, Ebru. *İdris-i Bidlisi: Ottoman Kurdistan and Islamic Legitimacy*. Istanbul: Libra, 2012.

Soudavar, Abolala. *The Aura of Kings: Legitimacy and Divine Sanction in Iranian Kingship.* Costa Mesa, CA: Mazda, 2003.

Stavrides, Theoharis. *The Sultan of Vezirs: The Life and Times of the Ottoman Grand Vezir Mahmud Pasha Angelović (1453–1474).* Leiden: Brill, 2001.

Subrahmanyam, Sanjay. "Connected Histories: Notes towards a Reconfiguration of Early Modern Eurasia." *Modern Asian Studies* 31/3 (1997): 735–762.

Tekindağ, M. C. Şehabeddin. "İzzettin Koyunoğlu Kütüphânesinde Bulunan Türkçe Yazmalar Üzerinde Çalışmalar I." *Türkiyat Mecmuası* 16 (1971): 133–162.

Terzioğlu, Derin. "Bir Tercüme ve Bir İntihal Vakası: Ya da İbn Teymiyye'nin *Siyāsetü'ş-Şer'iyye'*sini Osmanlıcaya Kim(ler), Nasıl Aktardı." *JTS* 31 (2007): 247–275.

Terzioğlu, Derin. "How to Conceptualize Ottoman Sunnitization: A Historiographical Discussion." *Turcica* 44 (2012): 301–308.

Terzioğlu, Derin. "Sufis in the Age of State-Building and Confessionalization." In Christine Woodhead (ed.), *The Ottoman World* (pp. 86–99). New York: Routledge, 2012.

Tezcan, Baki. "Hanafism and the Turks in al-Ṭarasūsī's Gift for the Turks (1352)." *Mamluk Studies Review* 15 (2011): 67–86.

Tezcan, Baki. "The Kânunnâme of Mehmed II: A Different Perspective." In Kemal Çiçek (ed.), *The Great Ottoman-Turkish Civilization*, vol. 3 (pp. , 657–665). Ankara: Yeni Türkiye Yayınları, 2000.

Turan, Şerafettin. *Kanuni Süleyman Dönemi Taht Kavgaları*, 2nd ed. Ankara: Bilgi Yayınevi, 1997.

Turan, Şerafettin. *Kanunî'nin Oğlu Şehzâde Bayezid Vak'ası.* Ankara: Türk Tarih Kurumu, 1961.

Turna, B. Babür. "Perception of History and the Problem of Superiority in Ahmedi's Dastān-ı Tevārih-i Mülūk-ı Āl-i Osman." *Acta Orientalia* 62 (2009): 267–283.

Uğur, Ahmet. *Osmanlı Siyâset-nâmeleri.* Kayseri: Kültür ve Sanat Yayınları, 1987.

Uğur, Ahmet. "Selīmnāme." *TDVIA*, vol. 36 (2009), 440–441.

Uluçay, Çağatay. "Yavuz Sultan Selim Nasıl Padişah Oldu." *Tarih Dergisi* 6 (1954): 53–90; 7 (1954): 117–142: 8 (1955): 185–200.

Uludağ, Süleyman. "Abdal." *TDVIA*, vol. 1 (1988), 59–61.

Usluer, Fatih. *Hurufilik: İlk Elden Kaynaklarla Doğuşundan İtibaren.* Istanbul: Kabalcı Yayınevi, 2014.

Uzunçarşılı, İsmail H. "Orhan Gazi'nin, Vefat Eden Oğlu Süleyman Paşa İçin Tertip Ettirdiği Vakfiyenin Aslı." *TTK Belleten* 27 (1963): 437–451.

Uzunçarşılı, İsmail H. *Osmanlı Devleti Teşkilatına Medhal*, 2nd ed. Ankara: Türk Tarih Kurumu, 1970.

Uzunçarşılı, İsmail H. *Osmanlı Tarihi*, vols. 1–3. Ankara: Türk Tarih Kurumu, 1949.

Uzunçarşılı, İsmail H. "Sancağa Çıkarılan Osmanlı Şehzadeleri." *TTK Belleten* 39 (1975): 559–696.

Walbridge, John. *The Leaven of the Ancients: Suhrawardī and the Heritage of the Greeks.* Albany: State University of New York Press, 2000.

Winter, Tim. "Ibn Kemāl (d. 940/1534) on Ibn 'Arabī's Hagiology." In Ayman Shihadeh (ed.), *Sufism and Theology* (pp. 137–157). Edinburgh: Edinburgh University Press, 2007.

Wittek, Paul. *The Rise of the Ottoman Empire.* London: The Royal Asiatic Society, 1938.

Woods, John E. *The Aqquyunlu: Clan, Confederation, Empire*, revised and expanded ed. Salt Lake City: University of Utah Press, 1999.

Yalman, Susan. "'Ala al-Din Kayqubad Illuminated: A Rum Seljuq Sultan as Cosmic Ruler." *Muqarnas* 29 (2012): 151–186

Yavuz, Hulûsi. "Sadrıâzam Lütfi Paşa ve Osmanlı Hilâfeti." *MÜİFD* 5–6 (1993): 27–54.

Yazıcı, Tahsin. "'Ârif Çelebî." *TDVIA*, vol. 3 (1991), 363–364.

Yazıcı, Tahsin. "Hemedânî." *TDVIA*, vol. 17 (1998), 186–188.

Yerasimos, Stéphane and Benjamin Lellouch, eds. *Les Traditions Apocalyptiques au Tournant de la Chute de Constantinople*. Paris: Harmattan, 1999.

Yıldırım, Rıza. "An Ottoman Prince Wearing a Qizilbash Tāj: The Enigmatic Career of Sultan Murad and Qizilbash Affairs in Ottoman Domestic Politics, 1510–1513." *Turcica* 43 (2011): 91–119.

Yıldız, Sara Nur. "From Cairo to Ayasoluk: Hacı Paşa and the Transmission of Islamic Learning to Western Anatolia in the Late Fourteenth Century." *Journal of Islamic Studies* 25 (2014): 263–297.

Yıldız, Sara Nur. "Şükrullah." *TDVIA*, vol. 39 (2010), 257–258.

Yılmaz, Hüseyin. "Books on Ethics and Politics: The Art of Governing the Self and Others at the Ottoman Court." Forthcoming in *Supplements to Muqarnas Series* , ed. Gülru Necipoğlu, Cemal Kafadar, and Cornell Fleischer (Brill: Leiden and Boston).

Yılmaz, Hüseyin. "Osmanlı Tarihçiliğinde Tanzimat Öncesi Siyaset Düşüncesi'ne Yaklaşımlar." *Türkiye Araştırmaları Literatür Dergisi* 1/2 (2003): 231–98.

Yılmaz, Hüseyin. "The Sunni Exodus from Iran and the Rise of Anti-Safavid Propaganda in the Ottoman Empire: The Messianic Call of Hüseyin b. Abdullah el-Shirvānī." In Ömer Mahir Alper and Mustakim Arıcı (eds.), *Osmanlı'da İlim ve Fikir Dünyası: İstanbul'un Fethinden Süleymaniye Medreselerinin Kuruluşuna Kadar* (pp. 299–309). Istanbul: Klasik, 2015.

Yılmaz, M. Şakir. ""Koca Nişancı" of Kanuni: Celalzade Mustafa Çelebi, Bureaucracy and "Kanun" in the Reign of Suleyman the Magnificient (1520–1566)." PhD diss., Bilkent University, 2006.

Yinanç, Mükrimin Halil. "Feridun Bey Münşeatı." *Türk Tarih Encümeni Mecmuası* 14 (1924): 161–168.

Yücesoy, Hayrettin. "Ancient Imperial Heritage and Islamic Universal Historiography: al-Dīnawarī's Secular Perspective." *Journal of Global History* 2 (2007): 135–155.

Yücesoy, Hayrettin. *Messianic Beliefs and Imperial Politics in Medieval Islam: The ʿAbbāsid Caliphate in the Early Ninth Century*. Columbia, SC: University of South Carolina Press, 2009.

Yüksel, Emrullah. "Mehmet Birgivî (929–981/1523–1573)." *Atatürk Üniversitesi İslami İlimler Fakültesi Dergisi* 2 (1977): 175–185.

Zachariadou, Elizabeth A. "The Emirate of Karasi and That of the Ottomans: Two Rival States." In E. Zachariadou (ed.), *The Ottoman Emirate (1300–1389)* (pp. 225–236). Rethymnon: Crete University Press, 1993.

Zarinabaf-Shahr, Fariba. "Qizilbash "Heresy" and Rebellion in Ottoman Anatolia during the Sixteenth Century." *Anatolia Moderna* 7 (1997): 1–15.

Ziai, Hossein. "The Source and Nature of Authority: A Study of al-Suhrawardī's Illuminationist Political Doctrine." In Charles E. Butterworth (ed.), *The Political Aspects of Islamic Philosophy: Essays in Honor of Muhsin S. Mahdi* (pp. 304–344). Harvard Middle Eastern Monographs. Cambridge, Mass.: Harvard University Press, 1992.

Zildzic, Ahmed. "Friend and Foe: The Early Ottoman Reception of Ibn ʿArabī." PhD diss., University of California, Berkeley, 2012.

INDEX

Aaron (biblical figure), 264
Abbasid Empire, 87, 108, 109, 114, 116, 177, 197–198, 223, 225, 233, 236–237, 246, 249–250, 273, 278, 282, 283; *dawla* in, 101–103, 105, 107, 127, 275–276, 285; decentralization of, 101, 157, 198; decline of, 1, 103, 111, 235, 274, 277; ecumenism of, 18; historical caliphate embodied by, 1, 105–106, 218, 274, 285; mystical turn in, 69, 112, 125; Ottoman Empire contrasted with, 221–222; Seljuks and, 119, 125, 126, 234; Shiites in, 103, 225; territorial expansion of, 54; tributary dynasties of, 101
Abdalan (Abdals), 96, 123, 129–130, 131, 136–137, 138, 140, 142–144, 203, 244, 280, 283–284; hagiographies of, 121, 243; learned Islam vs., 120, 135; Mehmed II's troubles with, 33, 136, 271–272; on Ottoman frontier, 121, 136, 141, 242; titulature of, 123
Abdal Musa, 121
Abd al-Muttalib, 137
Abdülkerim bin Mehmed, 75–76
Abdullah-ı Ilahi, 138–140, 141
Abdullah Karamani, 87
Abdullah Veliyyüddin, 134–135
Abdülvasi Çelebi, 127, 229–231
Abdurrahman Bistami, 66, 80, 129, 130
Abdurrahman Efendi, 86
Abdurrahman Jami, 42, 56, 58, 93, 138, 219, 258
Abel, 233
Abou el-Fadl, Khaled, 193
Abraham, 161, 230, 231, 239, 273, 274
Abu al-Lays, 81
Abu Bakr, 108, 115, 116, 118, 135, 155, 157, 204, 209, 211, 259, 282
Abu Hanifa, 93, 264
Abu-l Fazl, 155
Abu'l-Muhsin, 56
Abu Ya'la, 215
Abu Yazid al-Bistami, 209
Accounts of the Ottoman Caesars (Bidlisi), 236
Ādāb al-Khilāfa wa Asbāb al-Ḥiṣāfa (Ibrahim bin Muhammed), 166
Ādāb al-Mulūk (Kemal bin Hacı Ilyas), 24
Adam, 17, 83, 153, 184, 199, 232, 245, 250; Muhammed contrasted with, 243; as primordial caliph, 127–128, 133, 134, 137, 139–141, 192, 202, 269, 278, 280, 283
advice literature, 8, 52, 63–65, 78, 81, 83, 141, 165, 175, 198
Ahi Evran, 123
Ahis, 143
Aḥkām al-Dīniyya (Şirvani), 92, 265
al-Aḥkām al-Sulṭāniyya (Mawardi), 102–103
Aḫlāḳ-ı ʿAlāʾī (Kınalızade Ali), 6, 45, 72, 73, 74–75
Aḫlāḳnāme (*Maʿārifnāme*; *Naṣīḥatnāme*; Sinan Paşa), 35–36
akhlāq Allāh, 10, 174, 217
Ahmad bin Harun al-Rashid al-Sabti, 209
Ahmed, Shahab, 7
Ahmed (Ottoman prince), 59, 158–159, 183, 260
Ahmed Bican, 132–133, 211, 246, 248
Ahmedi, 63, 229, 233
Ahmed-i Ilahi, 140–141
Ahmedis (Halvetis), 204
Ahmed Paşa, 83
Ahteri, 184–185
Ajam, 41, 248, 254–255, 270–271
Ajamistan, 264, 266
Akbar (Mughal ruler), 157, 312n45
Akhlāq al-ʿAḍudiyya (al-Iji), 34
Akhlāq al-Atqiyā va Ṣifāt al-Aṣfiyā (Hızır Münşi), 70
Akhlāq-i Jālālī (Davvani), 74
Akhlāq-i Muḥsinī (Kashifi), 56–57, 63, 72, 74
Akhlāq-i Nāṣirī (Tusi), 25, 26, 27, 28, 36, 74
Akkadıoğlu, 29

A NOTE ON THE TYPE

THIS BOOK has been composed in Miller, a Scotch Roman typeface designed by Matthew Carter and first released by Font Bureau in 1997. It resembles Monticello, the typeface developed for The Papers of Thomas Jefferson in the 1940s by C. H. Griffith and P. J. Conkwright and reinterpreted in digital form by Carter in 2003.

Pleasant Jefferson ("P. J.") Conkwright (1905–1986) was Typographer at Princeton University Press from 1939 to 1970. He was an acclaimed book designer and AIGA Medalist.

The ornament used throughout this book was designed by Pierre Simon Fournier (1712–1768) and was a favorite of Conkwright's, used in his design of the *Princeton University Library Chronicle.*

CPSIA information can be obtained
at www.ICGtesting.com
Printed in the USA
JSHW021226301019
2158JS00001B/1

9 780691 197135